THE
KITE BUILDING &
KITE FLYING HANDBOOK
WITH 42 KITE PLANS

THE
KITE BUILDING &
KITE FLYING HANDBOOK
WITH 42 KITE PLANS

BY JACK WILEY

TAB BOOKS Inc.
BLUE RIDGE SUMMIT, PA. 17214

FIRST EDITION

FIRST PRINTING

Copyright © 1984 by TAB BOOKS Inc.

Printed in the United States of America

Reproduction or publication of the content in any manner, without express permission of the publisher, is prohibited. No liability is assumed with respect to the use of the information herein.

Library of Congress Cataloging in Publication Data

Wiley, Jack.
 The kite building & kite flying handbook, with 42 kite plans.

Includes index.
 1. Kites. I. Title. II. Title: Kite building and kite flying handbook, with 42 kite plans.
 TL759.W55   1984   629.133′32   83-18168
 ISBN 0-8306-1669-1 (pbk.)

Contents

Introduction — vii

1 Kite Facts — 1
Origin and Spread—Early Kites—Modern Kites—Types of Kites

2 How Kites Fly — 13
Basic Aerodynamics—Wind—Kite Design Variables—Design Methods

3 Manufactured Kites — 25

4 Tools, Work Areas, and Materials — 31
Tools—Safety Equipment—Workbenches—Work Areas—Materials

5 Basic Construction Techniques — 59
Kite Sticks and Frames—Kite Covering Materials—Bridle Attachments—Kite Tails—Other Useful Skills and Techniques

6 Flat and Bowed Kites — 81
Basic Two-Stick Flat Kite—Basic Two-Stick Bow Kite—Styrofoam Bow Kite—Three-Stick Kite with Converging Longitudinals—Three-Stick Kite with Parallel Longitudinals—Three-Stick Kite with Crossing Longitudinals—Two-Stick Square Kite—Two-Stick Diamond Kite—Three-Stick Hexagonal Kite—Basic Three-Stick Kite—Rectangular Kite—Arch-Top Kite—Five-Point Star Kite—Six-Point Star Kite—Eight-Point Star Kite—Octagonal Kite—Double Basic Kite—Double Square Kite—Double Diamond Kite—Four-Circle Kite—Triple-Deck Kite—Bird Kite—Dragon, Serpent, or Snake Kite—Centipede or Caterpillar Kite—Other Figure Kites

7 Cellular Kites 219
Basic Box Kite—Box Kite with Side Wings—Single-Unit Tetrahedron Kite—Four-Unit Tetrahedron Kite—Other Box Kites

8 Semirigid and Nonrigid Kites 245
Delta Wing Kite—Sled Kite—Nonrigid Kite

9 Decorating Kites 257
Basic Planning—Methods for Decorating Kites—Developing Designs

10 Flying Kites 267
Basic Flying Techniques—Ideas for Kite Flying—Contests—Clubs and Organizations

Appendix   Kite Stores 271

Index 275

Introduction

Building and flying kites has long been a popular hobby and pastime, dating back to ancient China. Today it is enjoying a popularity that is essentially worldwide.

I was first introduced to kite building and kite flying as a small child when my grandfather made kites from wooden sticks, string, paper, and rag tails. Then came the fun of flying, thrilling to the magic of a kite staying aloft by the power of the wind.

At a young age, I started making kites of my own. Early on, I learned that some performed better than others, and as time went on I began to learn some of the principles of kite design. From basic two-stick kites, I advanced to more elaborate constructions.

Over the years, I have never lost the fascination of designing, building, and flying kites. Quite the contrary, my interest and enthusiasm has grown.

Many interesting manufactured kites are now available, some at low prices, and most people begin, usually as children, with one of these kites. They provide an easy introduction to the world of kite flying.

For many people, kite flying never goes beyond using ready-made or manufactured kites. This, of course, can be an interesting recreational activity in itself, but I feel that the real excitement of kites is to go beyond this stage to designing, building, and flying your own kites.

There has long been a need for a handbook that focuses on the how-to aspects of kite building and flying. This book is an attempt to meet this need.

All of the kite plans shown are for kites that are flown on string from the ground. While kites that carry small payloads (such as message-drop kites) are included, man-carrying kites (such as those pulled by land vehicles and boats) are beyond the scope of this book.

An important feature of this book is the complete plans and instructions for making a variety of kites. Some of these are very old and proven designs; others are more recent innovations. Some are easy to make, some are more difficult. The selection was made to provide different types and designs of kites for all levels of interest and building skills. No prior knowledge of kite building or kite flying is presumed.

You may soon want to design and construct your own original kite designs. The information and projects included in this book will provide you with a solid background for doing this, because information has been included on the aerodynamics of kite flying and how to design kites.

While some people who design and build kites have little or no interest in flying them, most also enjoy taking their kites to the air. If you prefer to buy manufactured or custom-made kites and concentrate on flying, this book includes complete information for flying all types of kites.

Kite flying is a competitive sport as well as a recreational activity, and games and contests are, therefore, also covered.

Closely related to kite building is kite decorating. Painting and decorating kites can become an art form, and a chapter has been devoted to decorating kites.

This book focuses on kite building and kite flying as a hobby, but the information should also be helpful to those who want to go into a kite-related business, such as custom building kites to sell or establishing kite stores, which are not popular in many parts of the United States and other countries.

It might seem that all possible kites have been designed and constructed, but this does not appear to be the case. Major new designs have appeared in recent years, and others are almost certain to follow. Kites, like sailboats, never seem to run out of potential. Both are very old endeavors, yet hundreds of years and thousands of minds applied to the task have not exploited all of the possibilities. Even more, the amateur has a chance for a piece of the action with kites. Unlike space travel, for example, the amateur with limited funds can design and invent new kite forms. Even more, he can construct them and try them out, all on a limited budget.

This book gives you the information you need to do it yourself. It is a how-to book. By that I mean that it is intended as more than just something to be read. This book gives the information that is required for doing it yourself, but most of the learning will come from actually building and flying the kites. This book will guide the way, but keep in mind that you must not only read this book, you must also get involved with actual kite building and/or kite flying.

While much of the material in this book comes from my own kite building and flying experiences, many other people along the way shared their ideas and techniques with me. Thus, it is impossible to acknowledge all the help given for the compilation of this book. To the many people who freely shared their ideas and experiences, I would like to extend a sincere thanks.

Chapter 1

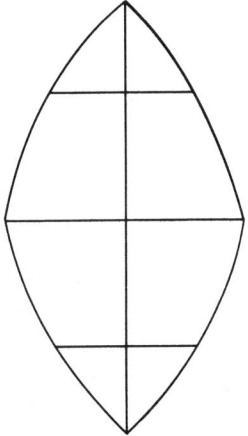

Kite Facts

A kite is a heavier-than-air device that is flown on the end of a string, line, or rope and is kept aloft by forces created by wind pressure.

Although traditional kits featured a framework of sticks of wood, bamboo, or other materials, some modern kits have no framework at all. These kites are known as *flexible kites*. One example is a parachute-like device that is flown on the end of a string.

Balloons or inflatable devices that are flown on the end of a string, only qualify as kites if they are heavier than air.

A word must be said about size and purpose. Most of us have seen, if not in person then on television at least, man-lifting kites that are towed by a land vehicle or boat. Although I believe these are kites in the real sense of the word, they will be mentioned here only from a historical perspective. This book details how to make and fly small kites, with you on the ground, holding the kite string, and the kite in the air. As far as payloads go, our concern will be only with very small ones, such as message-drop kites.

It is difficult to define exactly what is meant by small kites. There is a natural temptation to make kites a little bigger, and a little bigger, and then a little bigger yet. The kite construction detailed in this book are limited to kites on string that can be flown by one person, although records for size of kites flown by more than one person are discussed.

ORIGIN AND SPREAD

Since references to kites appear at the beginning of written history, we can assume that the kite was invented long before this. At the beginning of written history, kites were known in a number of parts of the world, perhaps from a single source that spread through commerce among the early peoples.

In China, there are a number of ancient legends and stories about the origin of the kite, and it is perhaps for this reason that credit for the invention of the kite is so often given to China. Bamboo was native to ancient China and silk was produced from about 2600 B.C. Kite frames could have been constructed from bamboo and the kite covers and string from silk. Many historians seem to think that the availability of materials is evidence that the kite was invented in China, but it should be kept in mind that many other parts of the world also had materials with which kites could have been constructed.

The idea of a single source for the invention of the kite can also be debated. Many things could have suggested the idea of the kite. The wind would tend to lift any lightweight material with a large surface area. Why not attach a line to it and keep it aloft? A banner attached to a piece of string, for example, could have suggested the idea of the kite. Perhaps the kite was discovered or invented in several parts of the world independently.

Paper was used in China by about 200 B.C. When paper became common, the popularity of kit making probably spread, as paper provided a suitable covering material that was more readily available than silk had been.

It seems likely that early Chinese kites were flat kites of rectangular shapes, but dragon-, bird-, centipede-, and figure-shaped kites are mentioned frequently in the early literature and remain popular kite forms in China today.

Some historians believe that the kite was known in Egypt sometime before 400 B.C., perhaps having been invented or discovered either independently or before those of China. There are also records indicating that a device that may have been a kite was known in Greece by 400 B.C., but, again, it is difficult to determine if the devices described were indeed kits.

Many sources state that the kite spread from China to Korea, but there are a number of Korean legends that purport that the kite originated in Korea. These stories place the origin about 500 A.D. or later, but the kite was almost certainly known much earlier than this in China, perhaps over 1000 years earlier.

The kite was probably introduced to Japan from China and became very popular in Japan at an early date. This popularity continues today, and the kite is as strongly associated with Japan as it is with China.

The popularity of the kite spread south and west as kite flying was taken up in the Malayan area. Although the date of this event is unknown, some authorities believe that it was about 2000 years ago.

There is evidence that the kite reached Arabian countries from China in the ninth century. Other than a few scattered references to devices that might have been kites or kite-like objects, however, there is little mention of kites in Europe until about the fourteenth century. European kites did not enjoy much popularity until the sixteenth and seventeenth centuries, when sailors returning from the Orient, Malaysia, and Polynesia brought home kites. By the middle of the seventeenth century, the kite was accepted as a toy for children in many parts of Europe.

The kite was not known in ancient America. It was introduced to America for the first time by European settlers.

EARLY KITES

Much of the early development and uses of kites is obscure. Early Chinese legends tell of kites being used for religious, mystical, festival, recreational, sport, man-lifting, and signaling purposes and as a dropping device, but it is difficult to separate fact from fiction. The same situation applies to the early history and development of kites in other parts of the world.

Up until about the eighteenth century, most, if not all, kites were of flat design or an arched or bowed variation of the flat design. Although the development of this design is a matter for conjecture, it became the basic standard for hundreds of years of kite making in many parts of the world. Even early Chinese and Japanese centipede and similar kites appear to have been primarily a series of flat kites attached together by strings. There is no clear evidence that tube or wind sock kites were known to ancient kite builders.

The shapes of ancient kites, within the basic flat design, varied widely. Design appears to have been largely a matter of trial and error. Early kite designers and builders took their inspiration from birds, butterflies, and other things in nature, including living things that could not fly like fish and humans. Rectangular shapes were first used, but even these were often decorated with pictures of birds, fish, insects, human, or other forms. Later the kites themselves took on, in flattened form, the shapes of these figures.

While kites may have originated from a single common source, as some historians claim, the designs that carried on into modern times became quite distinctive in many parts of the world. China became known for its dragon-, bird-, and centipede-shaped kites. These same designs were also used in Korea and Japan, but these countries also added their own designs. A hummingbird like became popular in Malaysia. Distinctive bird-shaped kites become popular in Polynesia.

Early kites were made from a variety of available materials. In China, Japan, and Korea, bamboo and wood were used for making kite sticks. Silk was used to make string and sometimes as a covering material. Paper was widely used as a covering material.

In the Pacific, especially in Polynesia, grasses, especially reeds, and leaves were often used for constructing kites. In some cases, a kite consisted of little more than a large lightweight leaf with a frame of reed or other material added. Some kites featured covering materials woven from grasses. These kites took on not only simple oval and triangular shapes, but also the shapes of birds and other living creatures.

Early kites were reportedly used for a variety of purposes. While it is a matter of conjecture as to whether early kites were used to lift people, it seems probable that they were used as signaling and dropping devices.

There is good evidence that the sport of kite fighting, where the basic object was to cut the string of the opponent's kite, was practiced early in the development of the kite.

Kites have long been used for fishing in many parts of the world.

Designing and decorating kites became an art form at an early stage of their development, especially in China, Korea, and Japan. There are still some practicing kite artists in these countries today, with the skills being passed on from generation to generation from hundreds of years ago.

MODERN KITES

Although kites were used in Europe as early as the fourteenth century, they remained largely novelty devices and toys. By the eighteenth century, many people took an interest in kites for use in scientific experimentation and for the development of flying machines. Although countries long familiar with kites seemed content to retain the kite simply for the art and amusement of flying them, the Western world seemed determined to improve kites and find new functions for them.

In England, Alexander Wilson began to use kites for scientific experimentation in the late 1740s. He is reported to have flown a series of kites in a train. Paper kites were arranged one above another on the same line. On the first attempt, he used half a dozen paper kites that were from 4 to 7 feet in height. These were launched in train and worked well. He later used kite trains to carry aloft thermometers for atmospherical experiments.

Perhaps the most famous kite experiment took place in America, in June, 1752, when Benjamin Franklin flew a kite in a thunderstorm and gave proof that lightning is electrical. Benjamin Franklin was a scientist and knew the dangers involved in such an experiment. He cautioned other experimenters that extreme care must be taken to keep the string dry. He suggested that the person holding the string stand within a door or window or under some other cover.

Other experimenters attempted to repeat and improve upon Franklin's experiments. De Romas of France even claimed to have had the idea for the electrical experiment first. He did not, however, actually carry out the experiment until June 7, 1753. Some experimenters used kites to carry animals aloft for electrical experiments.

In spite of the large numbers of experiments that were carried out during the eighteenth century, no major design improvements in kites themselves seem to have taken place during this period. In 1762, Peter van Musschenbroek, a Dutch physicist, who had made a number of electrical experiments using kites, published a brief mathematical description of how kites fly, but the main interest in using kites for experimental purposes during the eighteenth century was to lure electricity from the clouds. While Alexander Wilson had sent thermometers aloft in 1749, not much use appears to have been made of kites for meteorological purposes until the nineteenth century.

British explorer Sir William Parry, during his second voyage to the Arctic in 1822, did experimental work with Reverend George Fisher to measure variation in the atmospheric temperature with changes in height above sea level in a cold area, using a paper kite to carry aloft a thermometer. They were exhilarated when they managed to raise the kite to an altitude of about 400 feet, but the thermometer showed the same 24 degrees below zero as at ground level.

In 1835, the Franklin Kite Club was formed in Philadelphia for the purpose of performing electrical experiments. This was probably the first attempt at organizing a club for this purpose. They constructed kites with cane reed frames and muslin and silk covers, some with 20 square feet of surface area. They flew these on copper wire that rolled from a large reel mounted on insulating glass supports. They often sent up a number of kites on a single string.

The Franklin Kite Club also engaged in recreational kite flying, to the extent of importing some decorative kites from China. They used a kite to draw a sled over ice, and on at least one occasion, they used a kite to carry a kitten aloft in a basket. It was then dropped safely to the ground by parachute. It seems that the practice of carrying animals aloft with kites was not new.

J. P. Espy, a famous meteorologist of the time, was a member of the Franklin Kite Club. He used kites to study columnar clouds. In 1841, he published a book describing his experiments called *The Philosophy of Storms*. J. P. Espy's studies on cloud formations in storms, vertical air currents, and the use of weather maps were a major contribution to the science of predicting the weather. The kite was a major tool for carrying out these studies.

In 1847, W. R. Birt did experimental work with a hexagonal kite at the Kew Observatory, in England. The kite was flown by three lines, which was reported to give it great lifting power. The purpose seems to have been to develop the kite for carrying meteorological instruments aloft, although it is not known if he ever did this. His main contribution to kite design was the use of three lines for flying a kite. It is not known, however, if he was actually the first person to do this.

A number of investigators, including Cleveland Abbe and Charles du Hauvel, experimented with instrument-carrying kites in 1860s and 1870s. In 1887, E. D. Archibald, a British meteorologist, carried this work a step forward when he substituted steel wire for string. The steel wire had less weight and greater strength than string and allowed more weight to be carried aloft. He also developed a diamond-shaped kite that used a tail. The frame was constructed from bamboo, and silk was used as a covering material. The kites were flown in tandem to carry anemometers and other instruments aloft to altitudes of up to 1,500 feet.

By 1896, the U.S. Weather Bureau was using kites to carry meteorological instruments aloft at 17 stations in various parts of the country. The use of kites continued until the 1930s, when they were largely replaced by weather balloons and airplanes. The U.S. Weather Bureau used both Eddy kites and modified Hargrave kites (these designs are detailed later in this chapter).

Kites were also used for meteorological purposes in a number of other countries, including England, France, India, and Egypt. The use of kites for meteorological purposes also served to improve their design.

Design

Although credit for the invention of a number of kite designs, such as the box kite, is usually given to people in the Western world, there is also some evidence that some of these designs may have first developed in Asia or the Pacific. A number of factors, including stability, maneuverability, efficiency, and drag are important in kite design, as detailed in Chapter 2. Most early kites were, with or without an arch or bow. Even the so-called flat designs actually were not perfectly flat, as the covering material formed pockets and billows or the frames arched naturally, in flight, from the force of

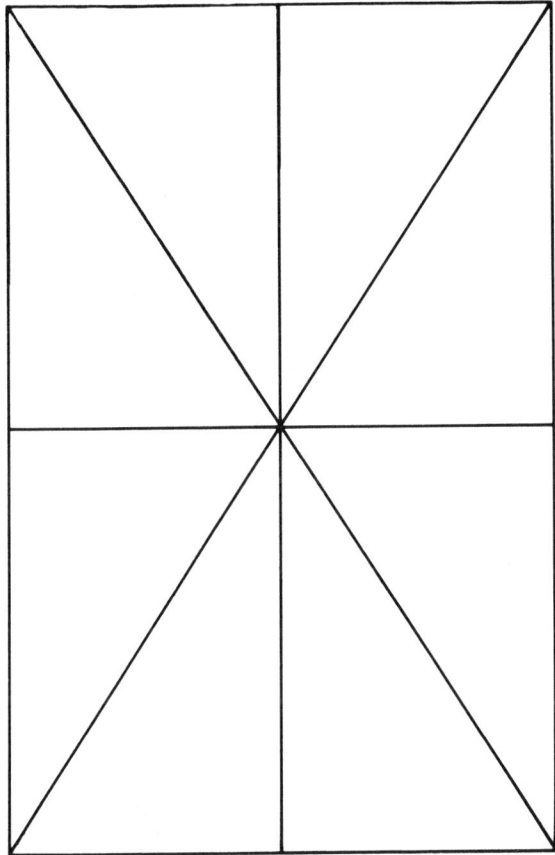

Fig. 1-1. Rectangular kite shape.

the wind. Most of the relatively flat kites, however, required some form of a tail to give them stability.

A number of shapes for flat kites became popular early in their development, including rectangular shapes (Fig. 1-1) and square shapes (Fig. 1-2), both popular for early fighting kites; leaf shapes (Fig. 1-3), such as were used for fishing kites in Indonesia and the west Pacific; and figure kites (Fig. 1-4), which were popular in many parts of the world. The figure kites took on many outline shapes, including animals, birds, humans, fish, and butterflies.

William A. Eddy, a New Jersey photographer and kite designer, is usually given credit for developing the bow kite in 1891. The basic shape of his design is shown in Fig. 1-5. This design provided stability without the use of a tail.

Eddy also used kites to carry cameras aloft to take photographs. Although he was not the first (E.D. Archibald had done this in 1887, and Arthur Batut, of France, had followed in 1888), he did much to improve the techniques.

Eddy also experimented with perforated covers to improve the stability of kites, an idea that he got from a Chinese kitemaker who was in the United States.

Perhaps an even greater kite inventor of the same period was Lawrence Hargrave, who was born in England, in 1850. When he was 16 years old, he emigrated to Australia. Hargrave studied engineering and became deeply involved in the study of aerodynamics and the problems of manned flight.

Hargrave made extensive use of kites in his experiments. He is generally given credit for developing not only the basic box kite (Fig. 1-6), but also a number of cellular kites. These inventions had an almost immediate affect, not only on kite development, but also on the development of manned flight. The Wright brothers later used a variation of Hargrave's basic box kite for their first airplanes.

The range of Hargrave's experimental designs was extensive. His cellular kites employed many

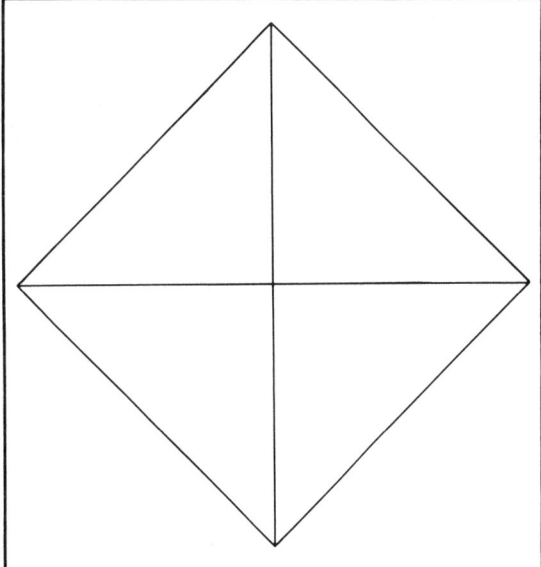

Fig. 1-2. Square kite shape.

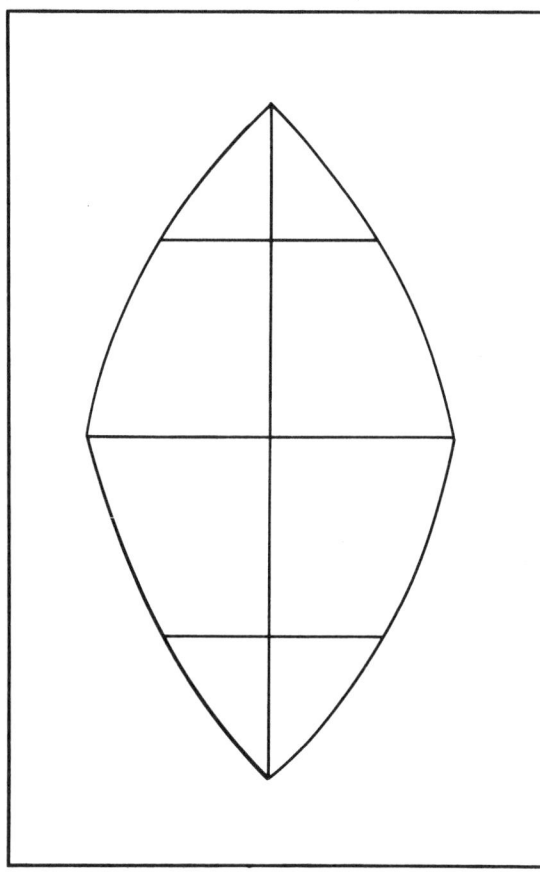

Fig. 1-3. Leaf-shaped kite.

shapes and arrangements, using both rectangular and round cells in various kite designs. He also experimented with dihedral kites. In some of his designs, he used cambered airfoils (slightly curved surfaces) to give his kites more lift. Hargrave also tried to develop soaring kites, with at least some success. The U.S. Weather Bureau made extensive use of Hargrave's kite designs, especially a modified version of his basic box kite, to gather meteorological data.

In 1896, Charles H. Lamson invented a multiplane folding kite. About the same time, H. H. Clayton developed a successful keel kite.

Alexander Graham Bell also did extensive experimenting with kites. In fact, during the period from about 1898 to 1908, he devoted much of his effort to kites and the development of the airplane. He introduced the use of tetrahedrons (Fig. 1-7) to kite design, including designs that featured as many as 4,000 cells.

For a time after the invention of the airplane, kite designing efforts seemed to decline, although the kite continued to be used for both old and new purposes. In recent years, kite flying has enjoyed new popularity as a recreational activity and sport. Part of this resurgence in interest has been brought about by new kite designs and materials for constructing them.

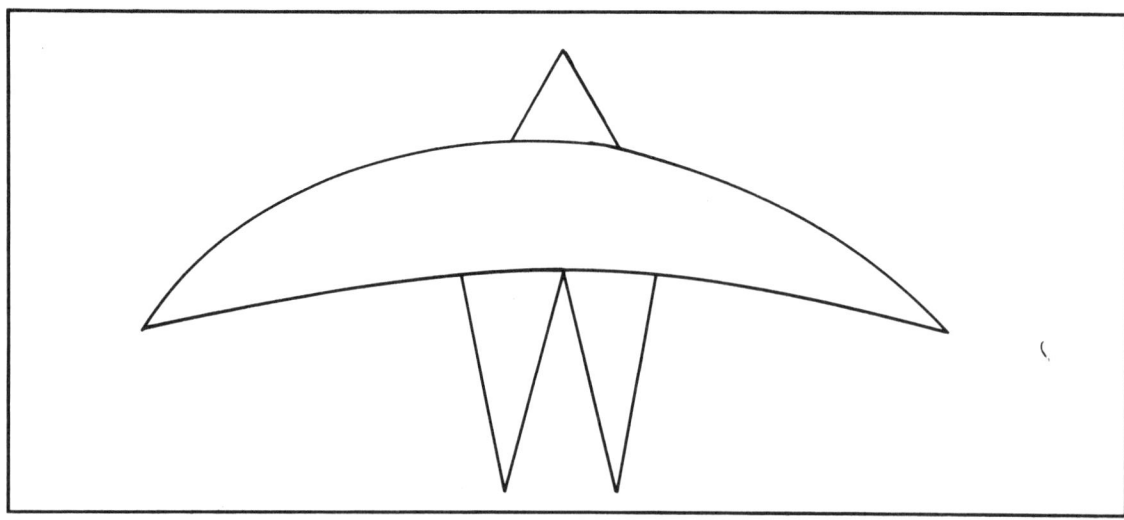

Fig. 1-4. Bird-shaped kite.

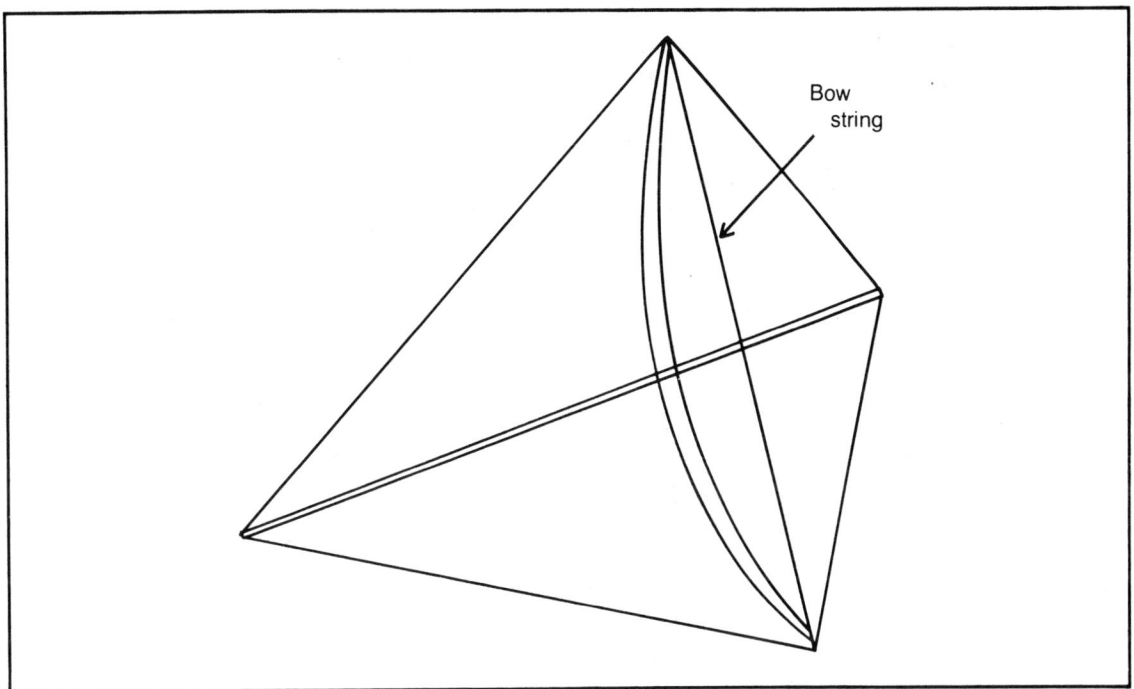

Fig. 1-5. A bow kite.

Uses

It had long been a goal of kite designers and builders to make man-lifting kites. Ancient Chinese legends tell of this having once been done in China. Marco Polo made references to having seen man-lifting kites on his famed journey there. Thus, it seems likely that, if not in ancient times, China was able to construct man-lifting kites by the time of Marco Polo's travels.

A number of claims have been made for the

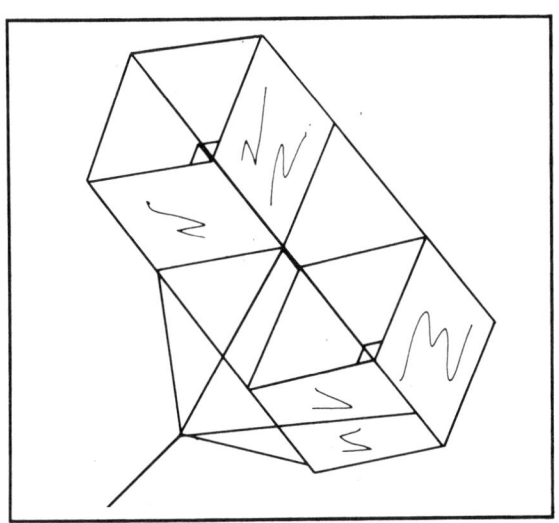

Fig. 1-6. A basic box kite.

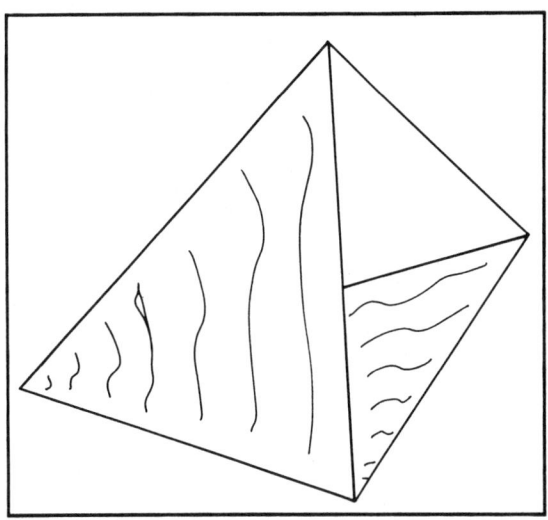

Fig. 1-7. A tetrahedron cell.

7

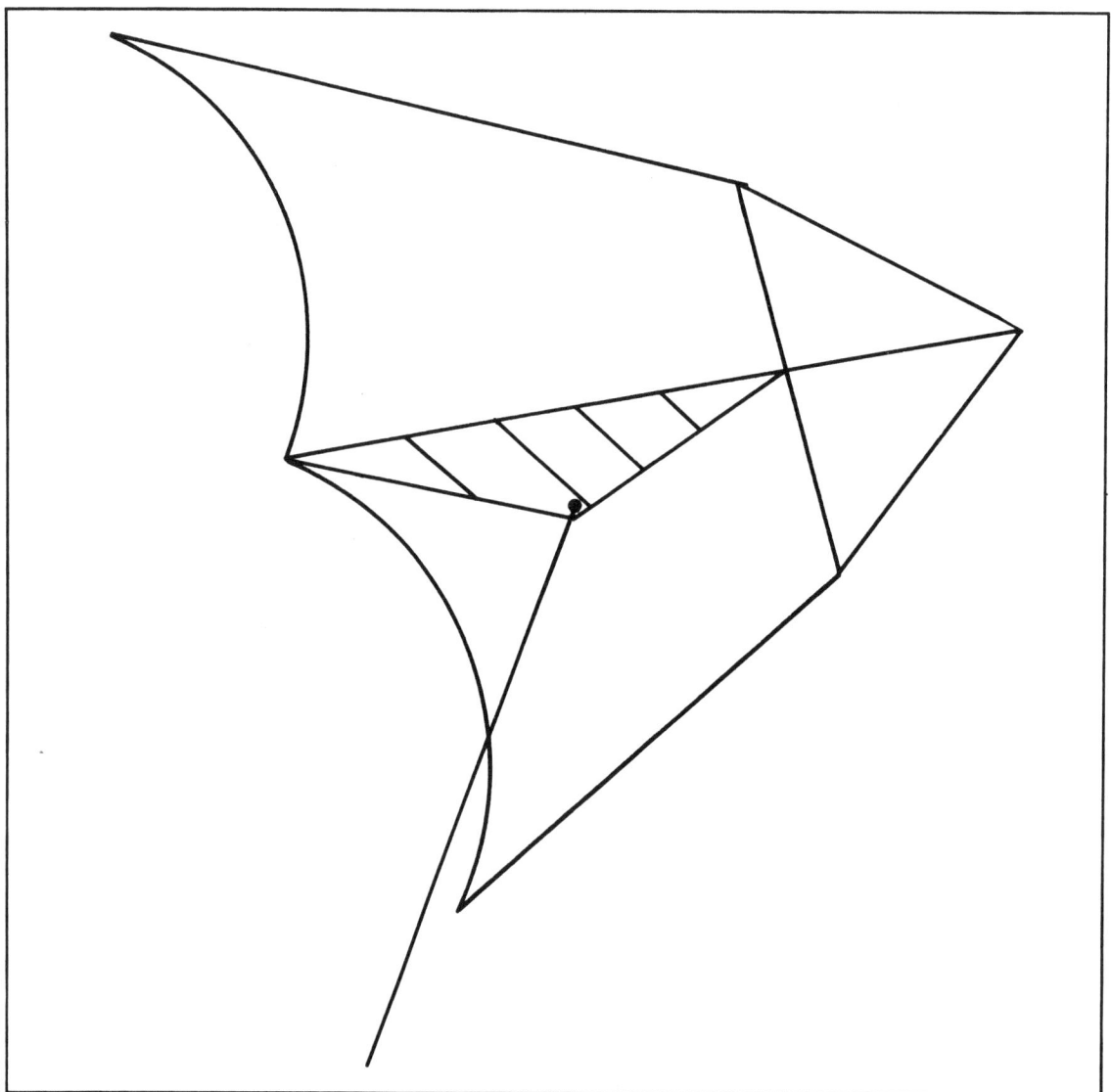

Fig. 1-8. A delta wing kite with a keel.

first man-lifting kite in the West. In England, George Pocock reportedly carried his daughter aloft by kite in 1825 or 1826. A number of other claims followed. Extremely interesting is the claim by Le Bris to have carried a man aloft by a bird-form kite glider that was pulled along by a cord attached to a horse drawn carriage.

A number of successful attempts to lift a man in a basket or on a platform suspended in some way below one or more kites were reported in the later part of the nineteenth century, including claims by Maillot in 1885, Captain Baden-Powell of Scotland, in 1894, and Lieutenant H.D. Wise of the United States, in 1896.

In 1897, Charles H. Lamson, of the United States, made an ascent holding on to an "aerocurve" kite of his design that was pulled along by men running on the ground.

Man-lifting kites became more common from this point on. Especially spectacular were the use of kite designs by S.F. Cody and Alexander Graham Bell for man-lifting purposes.

Kites were used for a number of military purposes. Man-lifting kites were used as observation posts. A variety of kites were used as targets. Attempts were also made to use kites for dropping explosives, towing torpedoes to targets, and so on.

Kites have also been used for number of nonmilitary purposes. These include traction devices for pulling boats on water, sleds on ice, and even carriages on land, and for carrying telephone wires and a variety of other things aloft, including cameras for taking photographs.

A number of more recent developments have helped to revive the popularity of kite building and kite flying. One of these is the *parawing*, which was first introduced by Dr. Francis Rogallo, in 1943. This design is often called *delta wing*. While the D-shaped wing design uses spars, the wings themselves are flexible. When used as a kite, this design often employs a *keel*, as shown in Fig. 1-8.

The *sled kite* followed Rogallo's design. It was invented by W. M. Allison of Dayton, Ohio, in 1950, and improved upon by Frank Scott, also of Dayton, Ohio. The sled kite has longitudinal sticks, but no frames to give it lateral support, (Fig. 1-9).

In 1953, Domina Jalbert developed the *parafoil,* which consists of a cloth structure without a frame, as shown in Fig. 1-10. It gets its shape by being inflated by the wind. This is an improved version of a *parachute kite,* which has been in use for a number of years.

These semirigid and nonrigid kites have added a new dimension to kite designing, building, and flying. New, lightweight and strong construction materials have also added appeal to kites.

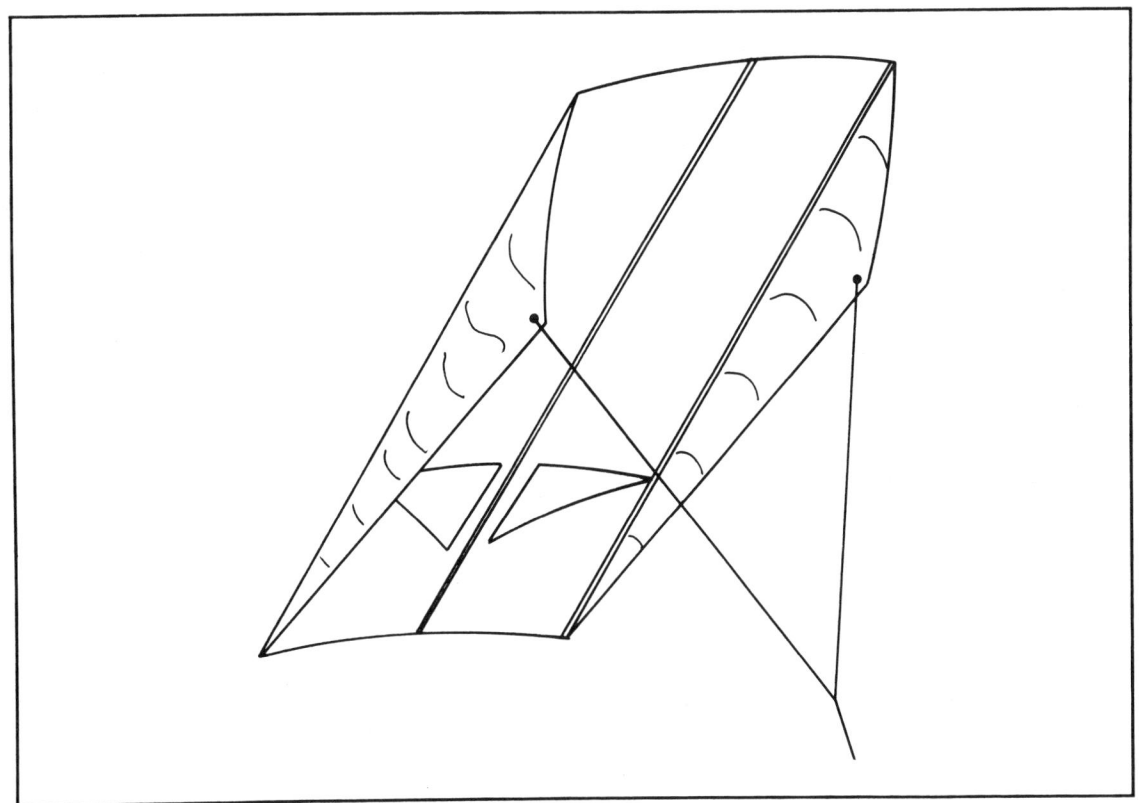

Fig. 1-9. Sled kite.

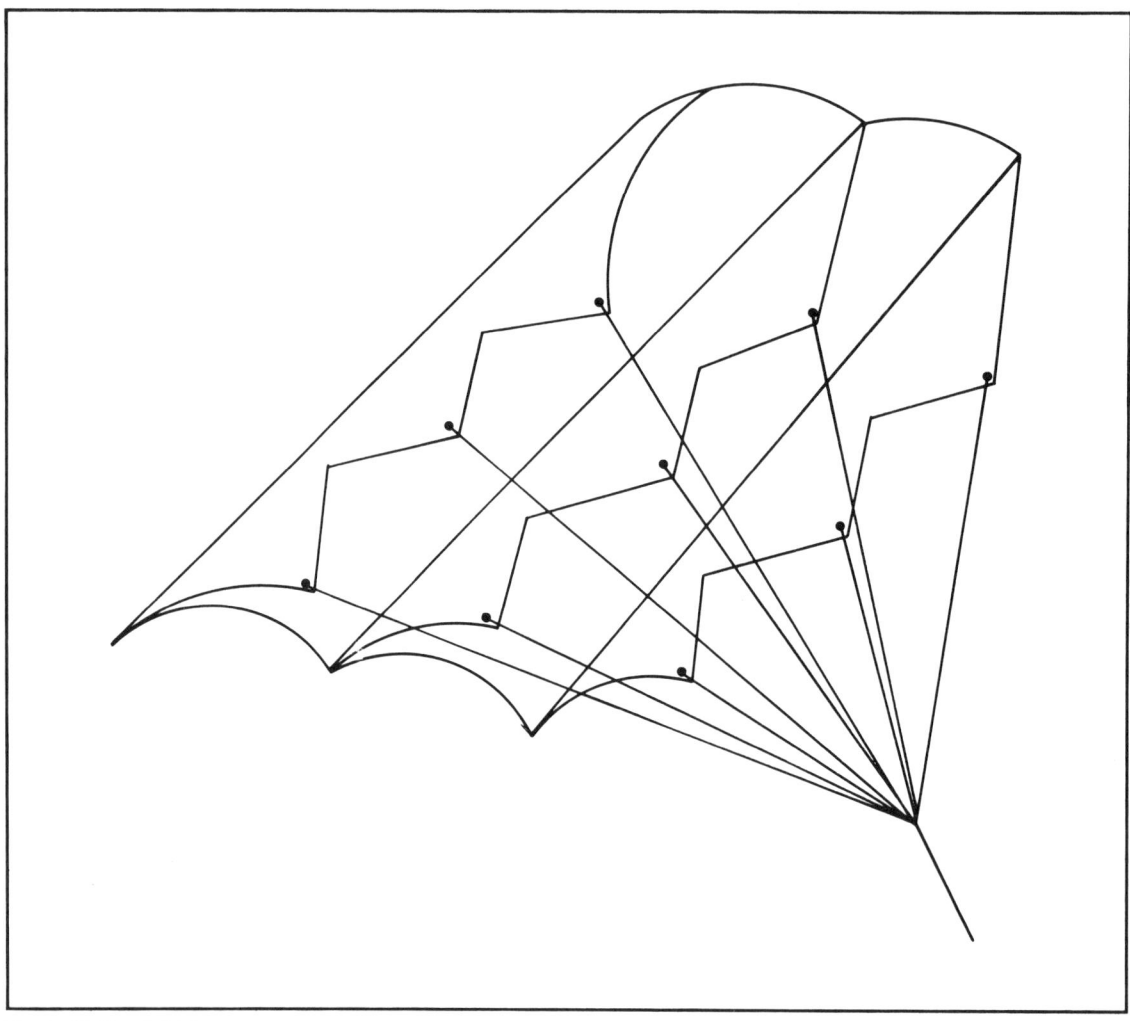

Fig. 1-10. Parafoil kite.

TYPES OF KITES

Kites come in many shapes and forms, but most belong to one of three basic types or are of some combination of these: flat kites (with or without bows), box or cellular kites, and semirigid and nonrigid kites.

Flat Kites

Flat kites consist of a flat framework with a cover of paper, cloth, plastic sheeting, or other material. This appears to be the most ancient form of kite, yet it remains popular. Flat kites usually require a tail to give them stability. Stability can also be achieved on some flat kites by adding a keel, such as is shown in Fig. 1-11. Flat kites can also be given stability by adding an arch or bow to them. This allows them to be flown without tails or keels. Although the idea of using a piece of string to bow a kite (Fig. 1-5) is generally credited to William Eddy, many earlier kites had achieved this effect by the force of the wind bending the wings as the kite was flown or by using slightly curved sticks. This allowed these kites to be flown without tails.

A primary attraction of flat kites is the many possible outline shapes that can be used, including geometric figures, insects, people, birds, and

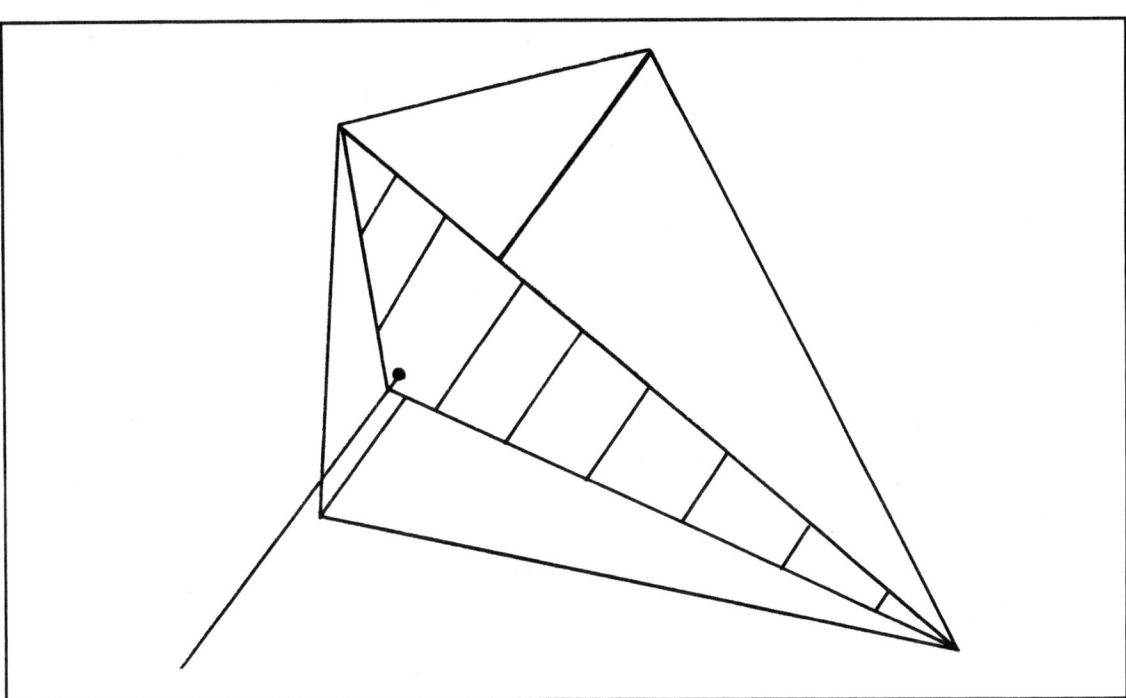

Fig. 1-11. Flat kite with keel.

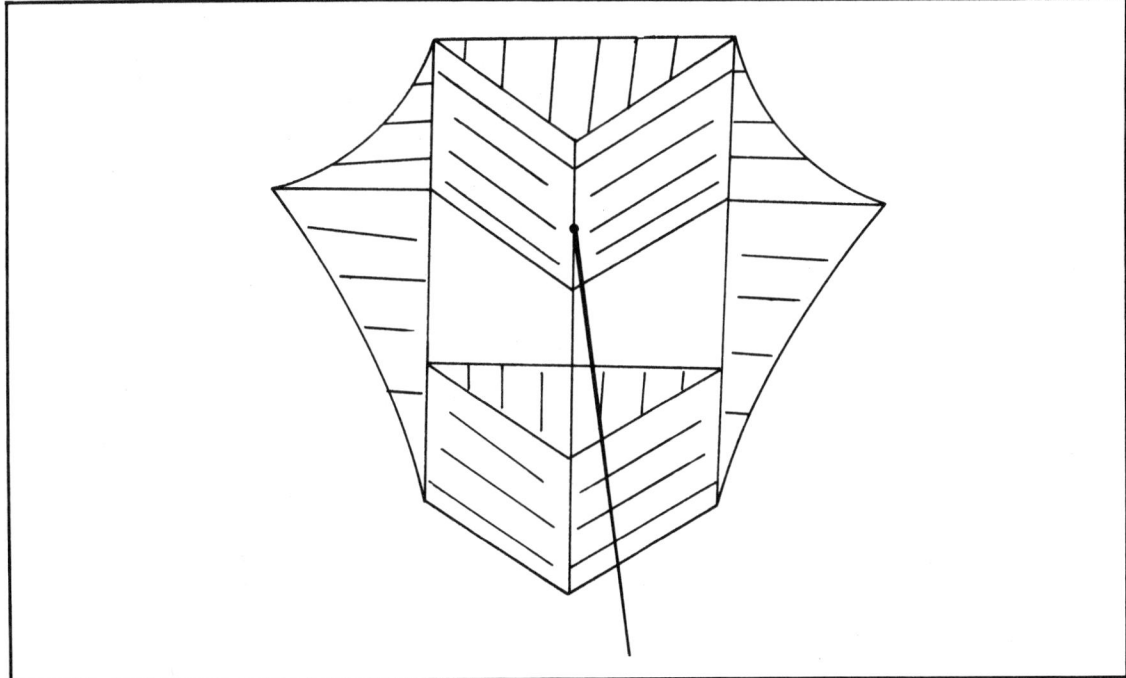

Fig. 1-12. Triangular box kite with side wings.

abstract shapes. Flat kites also make excellent surfaces for making designs and pictures.

Box or Cellular Kites

Box or cellular kites are three-dimensional. In general, they allow greater lift and stability than is generally possible with flat kites. Box or cellular kites (Fig. 1-12) can be constructed in many different shapes and sizes, with or without winged surfaces, keels, and so on.

Semirigid and Nonrigid Kites

Semirigid and nonrigid kites were developed mainly in the United States, starting in the 1940s. The main types are the parawing or delta wing, the sled, the parachute, and the parafoil. These designs have added an exciting new dimension to kite building and flying.

Other Types

Some kite designs cannot be neatly classified as flat, box, or semi- or nonrigid. *Balloon kites*, for example, are basically air-filled kites with the air used to give the kite shape and form. In use, they often take on characteristics of one or more categories of kites. Small kites made of folded paper often take on characteristics of both rigid and semirigid kites. *Rotary kites*, essentially propellers or wind spinners, do not fit in any of these categories. There are also kites rigged like sailing ships, and others shaped like gliders and airplanes, that are difficult to place in specific categories.

Chapter 2

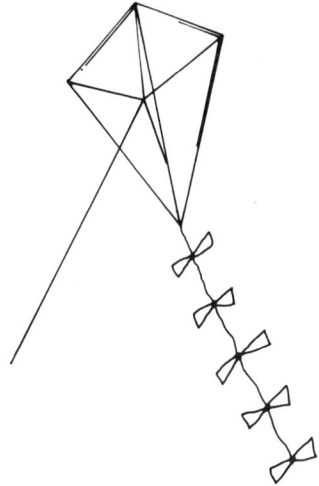

How Kites Fly

A basic understanding of how kites fly and the basic principles of their design will provide a foundation for designing, building, and flying kites.

There are two fundamental concerns to designing kites: functional and aesthetic. Both are important, but only the functional concerns, based on the laws of aerodynamics, determine if and how well a kite will fly or perform. In fact, attempts to make kites more aesthetically appealing often reduce performance. A figure kite, for example, may perform less well than a simple geometric shape, and a painted design on the covering of the kite may add weight and reduce performance.

The flying performance of a kite depends not only on its design, construction, and rigging, but also on the conditions under which it is flown (wind, temperature, and so on) and the skill and technique by which it is flown.

BASIC AERODYNAMICS

For our purposes, we will consider kites to be by definition heavier-than-air devices (they weigh more than does the volume of air that they displace). Kites are thus *aerodynes*. In order to stay aloft on the end of the string, a kite must overcome the force of gravity. The force of the wind is used to accomplish this.

Lift

Lift is the component of the total aerodynamic force acting on a flying kite perpendicular to the relative wind and normally exerted in an upward direction, opposing the pull of gravity.

Air is a colorless, odorless, tasteless, gaseous mixture that is approximately 78 percent nitrogen and 21 percent oxygen. The remaining 1 percent consists of argon, carbon dioxide, neon, helium, and other gases. The atmosphere enveloping the earth consists of air mixed with varying amounts of moisture, low-altitude pollutants, and particulate matter.

Air is made up of particles that are constantly in motion and that resist the passage of any object through it. This can be demonstrated by trying to rapidly move an object with a large surface area through the air. Air resistance can be felt as we try to ride a bicycle at high speeds; most of the energy applied to the pedals is used in an attempt to overcome air resistance.

Air resistance makes kite flying possible. Since the air resists passing through the kite, the kite, when anchored or towed along on the end of a string and angled properly, is provided lift by the force of the wind. This is brought about by the downward deflection of the air, which resists passing through the kite and takes the path of least resistance, as shown in Fig. 2-1.

It is important to note that kites frequently fly in one place, with little or no forward motion. It is the wind (moving air particles) and not the kite that is doing the moving. The effect is the same. If the wind is 10 m.p.h., the effect is essentially the same as towing the kite along at 10 m.p.h. on a calm day. If the wind is 5 m.p.h. and the kite is towed at 5 m.p.h. in a direction into the wind, the effect is essentially the same as flying the kite in a 10 m.p.h. wind or towing the kite along at 10 m.p.h. on a calm day.

It's the *relative wind* that is important in kite flying. We will assume that, unless otherwise stated, the kite is flying on a fixed length of string anchored on the ground, as would be the case when you are holding the string on the ground without moving your position, letting string out, or taking string in. In this case, the relative wind is the same as the actual wind. The relative wind is how the kite "sees" the wind.

This concept is extremely important to the aerodynamics of kite flying. If a bicycle rider moves along at, say, 10 m.p.h. on a windless day, he feels the relative wind. It is essentially the same thing as being motionless, say, on a stationary exercise bicycle and facing a 10 m.p.h. wind.

The fact that the kite remains relative station-

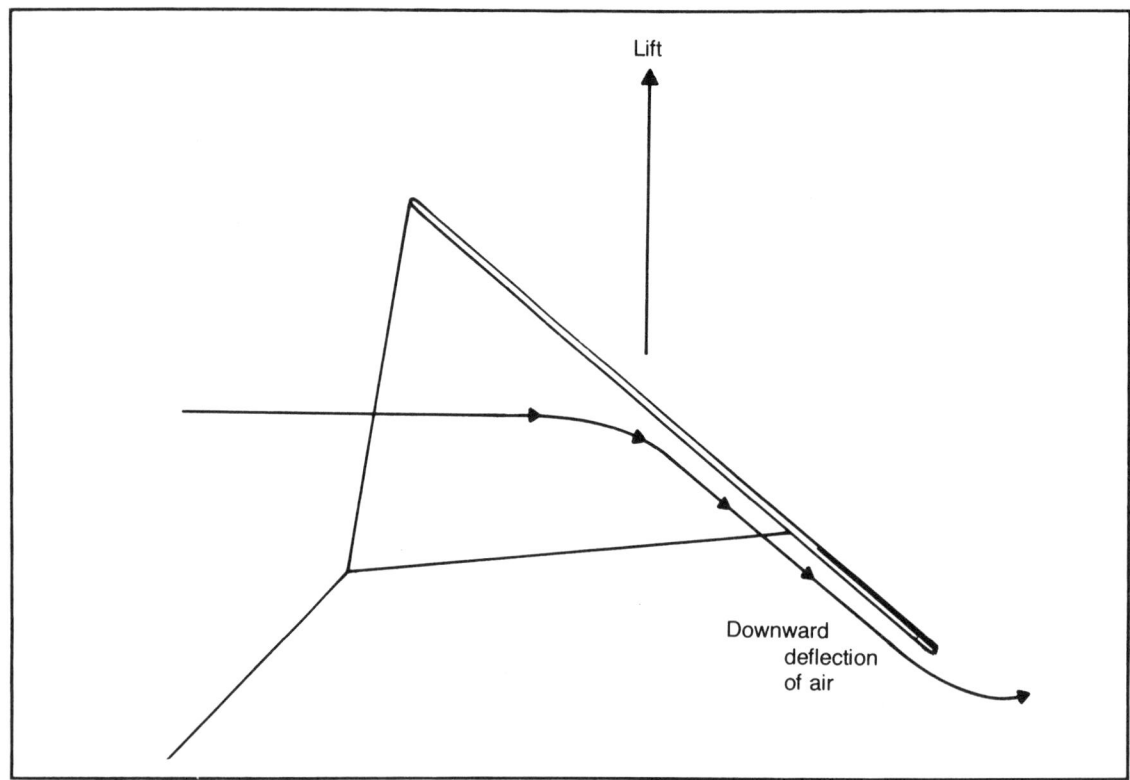

Fig. 2-1. Kite lift is provided by the downward deflection of air.

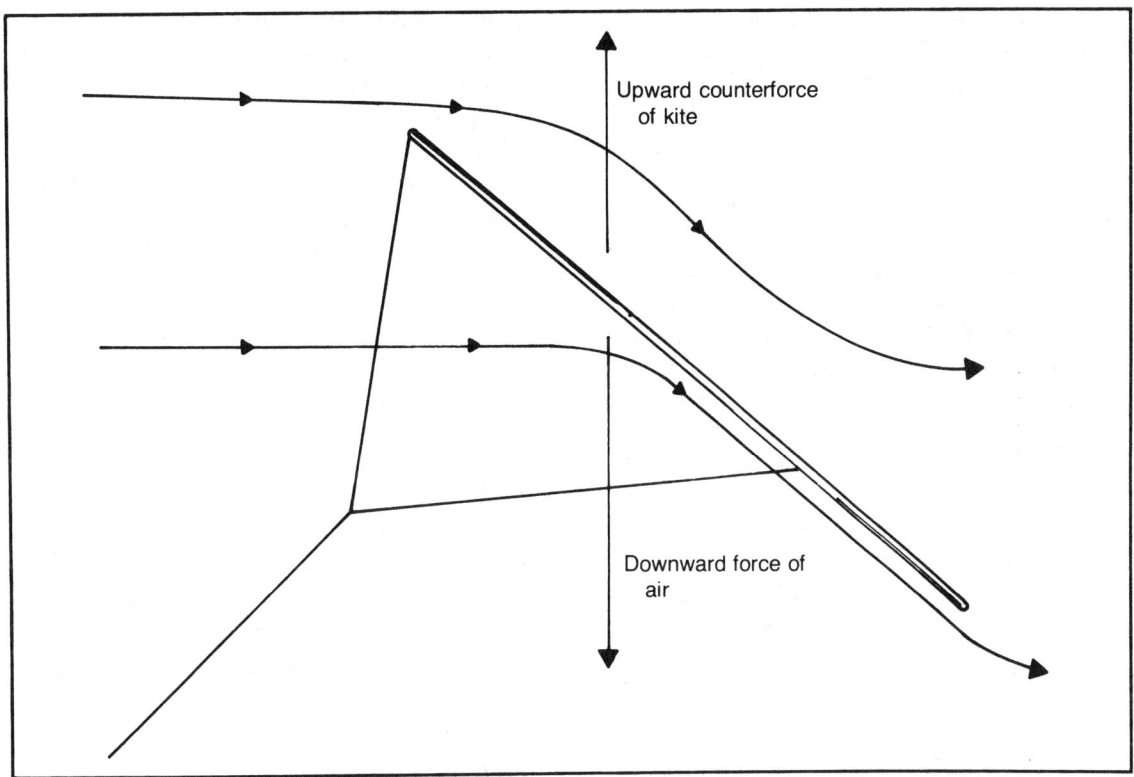

Fig. 2-2. Kite receives upward force from the downward force of air.

ary while the air moves simplifies the problem of understanding kite flight. Everything becomes much more complicated when the object, a sailboat for example, is also moving. Because the sailboat has motion in a certain direction, the relative wind (the wind that effects the sailboat) can be quite different than the actual wind.

In the case of the kite, it's the kite that stays still. The air rushes against the kite.

It is helpful to consider the kite as an inclined plane. Assume that the kite illustrated in Fig. 2-2 is aloft and is "flying" in one spot. The wind is a constant 10 m.p.h. The kite weighs 6 ounces and is heavier than air (it weighs more than the volume of air it displaces). The kite stays aloft by shoving the air down with its bottom surface and pulling the air down with its surface after it has passed over the forward edge of the top of the kite. The kite makes the air go down. In exerting this downward force upon the air, the kite receives an upward counter-force. The principle involved is known as *Newton's law of action and reaction:* for every action there is an opposite and equal reaction.

Air is actually quite heavy. A cubic yard of air weighs about 2 pounds at sea level. As the kite pushes air downward, it gets an equally hefty upward reaction.

This keeps the kite up. If the kite pushes the air down, the air must push the kite up. The kite is thus an inclined plane, an air deflector.

Bernoulli's theorem says that at the same time as air passes below a wing, air also passes above it, but since the air on the topside moves a longer distance over the curved surface of the wing, it moves faster and reduces the pressure above the wing. The air below the wing moves more slowly, which increases the air pressure below the wing. This principle was discovered by Daniel Bernoulli, a Swiss mathematician, in 1738.

In the case of the kite, it is then the change in

the relative pressures above and below the kite that causes the kite to lift (Figure 2-3). This probably explains in part, if not entirely, how kites actually fly. It is somewhat puzzling why air streamers, when placed on the topside of typical flat or bowed kites, remain so motionless.

Now, back to our 6 ounce kite that is staying aloft in one place in a 10 m.p.h. wind. For this condition to exist, the downward force upon the air would be 6 ounces, the same as the upward force upon the kite. The kite is in a state of equilibrium. The sum of all acting forces is zero.

If the downward force upon the air becomes more than 6 ounces, the upward force upon the kite also becomes more than 6 ounces and the kite moves upward or climbs.

By the same token, if the downward force upon the air becomes less than 6 ounces, the upward force upon the kite also becomes less than 6 ounces and the kite drops downward or sinks.

This is a very basic and practical way of viewing how a kite remains aloft, climbs, and sinks. It also is useful for designing kites, as detailed later in this chapter.

Our discussion so far assumed that the wind was a movement of air more or less parallel to the earth's surface. In actual practice, however, this is not always the case. For example, there are updrafts of air, especially near mountains, that would serve to lift a kite. In most kite flying this probably plays only a minor role. The strength of the wind and changes in the wind strength and/or direction are extremely important.

Angle of Attack

Kites are usually flown at an inclined angle, as shown in Fig. 2-4. Perhaps it is more correct to say that most kites must be at an inclined angle to fly. If, once aloft, a kite performs like an airplane or a

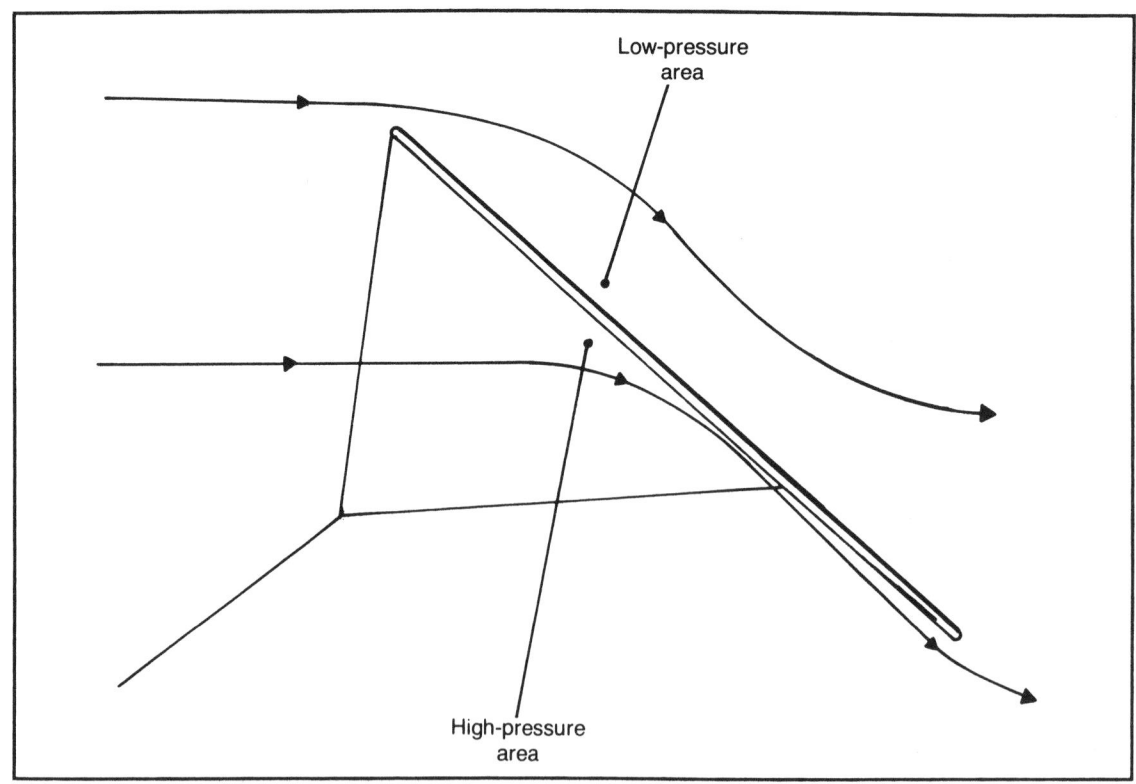

Fig. 2-3. According to Bernoulli's law, it's the change in relative pressures above and below the kite that causes it to lift.

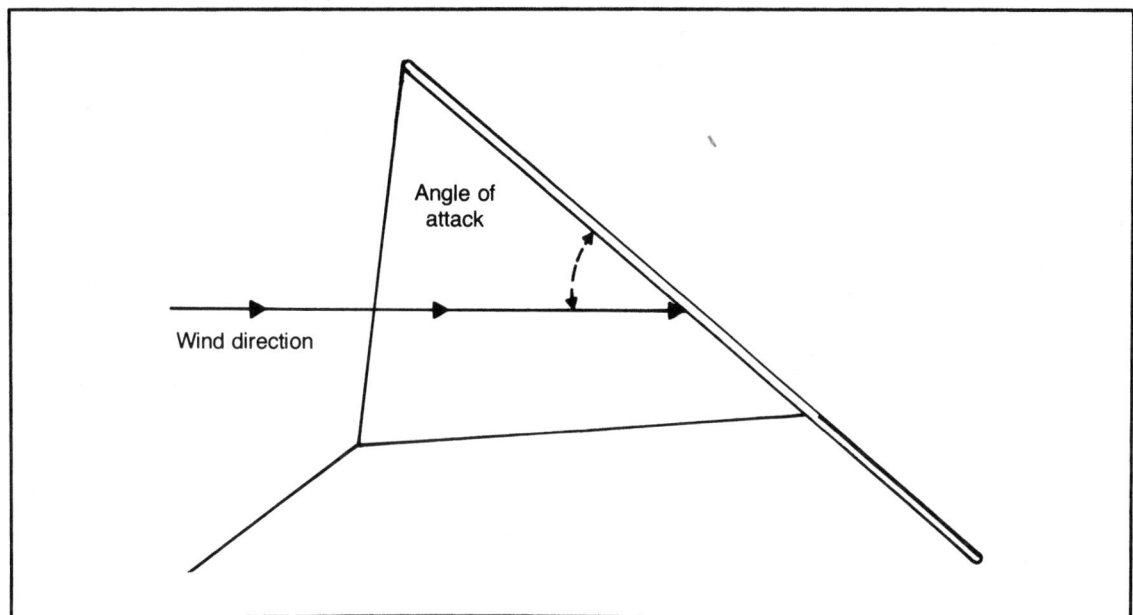

Fig. 2-4. Angle of attack.

glider with slack in the kite string, it is essentially an airplane or glider that used the kite principle to carry it aloft.

The kite is flown at an inclined angle so that as the air (by the force of the wind) passes it, the air meets the kite at an angle and is forced downward. The angle by which it is inclined in relation to the direction the air is moving toward it is the *angle of attack*, as shown in Fig. 2-4.

In kite design and flying, the angle of attack is an extremely important consideration. Kites, by nature of their design, do not all use the same angle of attack for their best performance. For a specific kite, the same angle of attack might not be best for all wind conditions.

On many kites, the flying angle can also be changed by making adjustments in the *bridle* (Fig. 2-5), by adding or reducing tail, or by making other similar adjustments.

Since a kite is anchored to the ground by a string, it moves from the ground to the highest point of the flight in an arc, assuming that the anchor position is not changed and the length of the string remains constant. If the string remains perfectly straight from the point where it is anchored to the kite, the arc that the kite moves through depends on the length of the kite string. In this case, the angle of attack becomes less as the kite reaches greater heights. This assumes that the kite remains at a constant angle in relation to the kite string. In actual practice, the weight of the kite string may cause the string to curve downward as it leads up to the kite. The angle of the kite in relation to the string may change, but the change in the angle of attack, as described above, applies at least in a general way to many kites.

Balance and Stability

To this point in our discussion, we have assumed that the kite has perfect balance and stability. The kite does not change it's angle of attack by rocking forward and backwards or twist or move from side to side. It does not stall or dive. In actual practice, however, most kites do not have perfect balance and stability. This is perhaps fortunate, as a perfectly balanced and stable kite flying only in a perfect arc at the end of the kite string wouldn't be much fun to fly. The thrill of a dragon kite, for example, would largely be lost if it didn't go through a lot of antics.

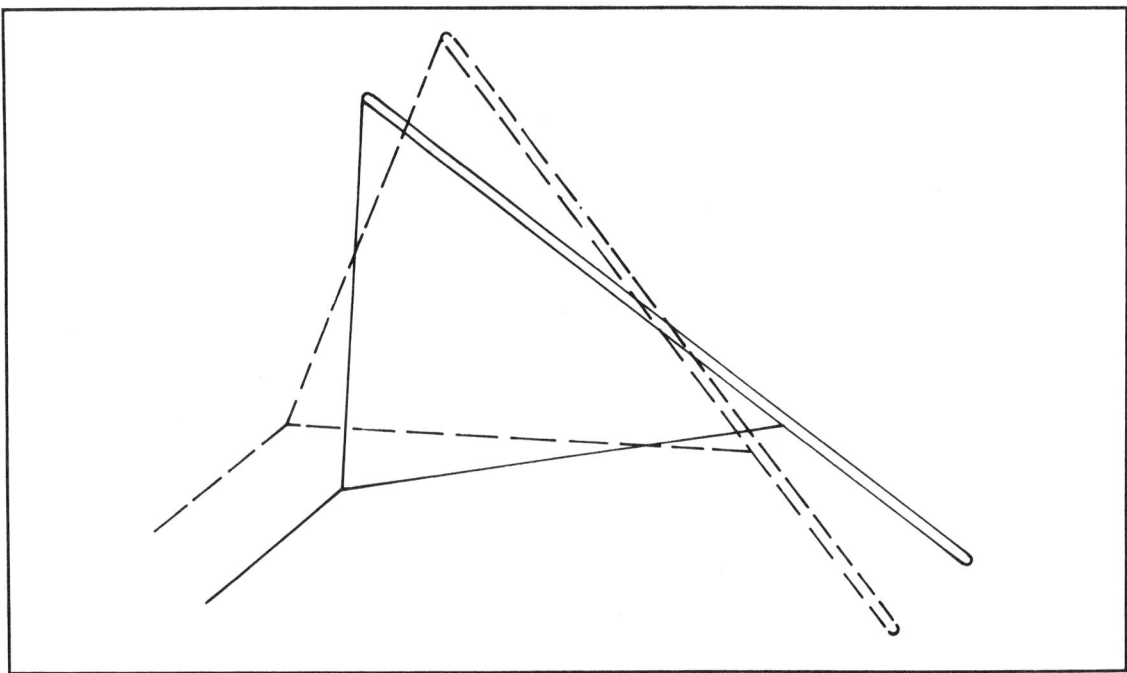

Fig. 2-5. Flying angle changed by making adjustments in bridle.

Still, in most cases a high degree of balance and stability is desirable for most kites. Balance and stability depend to a considerable extent on the design and construction of the kite. Some designs are inherently more stable than others. Balance and stability often also depend on the attachment and adjustment of the bridle strings.

Flat kites often require tails to give them adequate stability. The lift of a kite is affected not only by the weight of the kite, but also by *drag*, which is the resistance of the air to the forward and backward motion of the kite. Notice that drag is in the directions that the kite moves, not the direction of the wind. The tail of a flat kite acts not only as a weight for balancing and stabilizing, but also, and perhaps most importantly, as a drag. The increased drag brought about by the tail as used on many flat kites does limit the maximum altitude that can be reached with any given length of string to less than that of many kites without tails, but this is generally a required sacrifice to give the flat kite adequate stability. Essentially all kite designs involve compromises.

Flat kites can often be bowed to give them adequate stability without having to use a tail. The performance of many flat kites can be improved in this manner.

The addition of one or more keels is another method that can be used to give a kite greater stability. This method can be used on many kite designs, including flat and bowed kites, sled kites, and delta wing kites.

The flexibility of the cover material on many kites adds stability. The covering materials on many flat kites, for example, yield in the air pressure when they are flown, often forming curved surfaces.

The flexibility of the kite sticks or frames also add stability. Many flat kites are actually bowed kites when flown because the outer edges bow back from the pressure of the wind. This explains why some so-called flat kites are able to perform so well without tails.

Box kites and other cellular kites often have better balance and greater stability than is typical of flat or bowed kites. There are a number of reasons

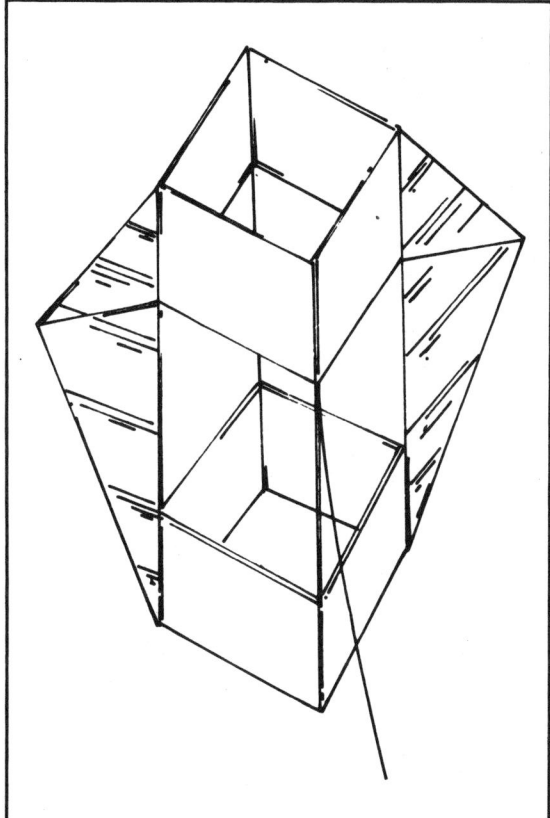

Fig. 2-6. Side wings improve stability of box kite.

WIND

The wind is an extremely important variable in kite flying. A *calm* exists when wind is blowing at less than 1 m.p.h. Under this condition, smoke rises vertically or very nearly so. *Light air* is a wind of from 1 to 3 m.p.h. Under this condition, the direction of the wind can be detected by smoke, but not by an ordinary wind vane.

A *light breeze* is wind from 4 to 7 m.p.h. Under this condition, leaves rustle, ordinary wind vanes show the direction the wind is blowing, and the wind can be felt on your face. A *gentle breeze* is from 8 to 12 m.p.h. Under this condition, light flags are extended and leaves are in constant motion. A *moderate breeze* is wind from 13 to 18 m.p.h. Under this condition, small tree branches are in motion and loose paper and dust are raised. A *fresh breeze* is wind from 19 to 24 m.p.h. Under this condition, many small trees begin to sway. A *strong breeze* is wind from 25 to 31 m.p.h. Under this condition,

for this. Sections of the covering material are often perpendicular to the main inclined planes of the kite when it is aloft, serving in effect as keels or rudders. These kites typically have greater surface areas than do flat kites.

Balance and stability is often improved on box kites and other cellular kites by adding side wings, such as shown in Fig. 2-6. Keels are used on some box kites. Shaped wing surfaces, such as shown in Fig. 2-7, have also been tried, but whether or not this significantly improves balance and stability is debatable.

Some of the modern semirigid and nonrigid kites of delta wing, sled, and parafoil designs have extremely good balance and stability. These designs were made possible by talented designers and inventors and the use of wind tunnels, computers, and modern synthetic materials.

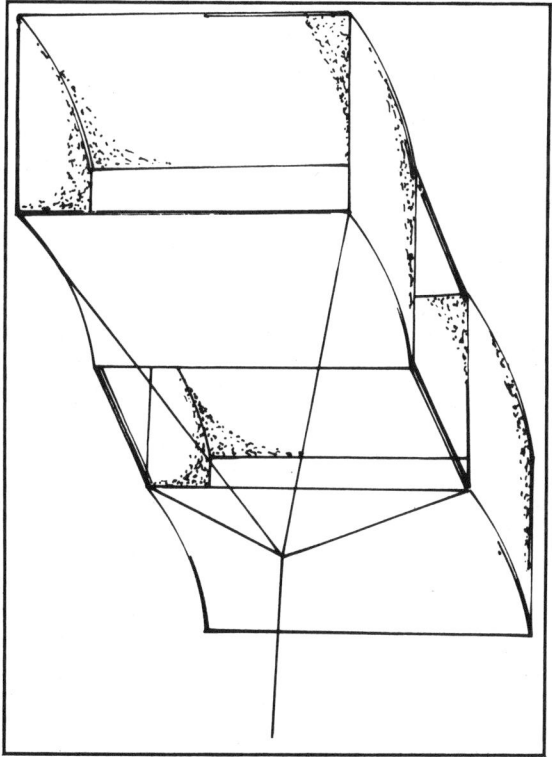

Fig. 2-7. Shape-wing surfaces used on kite.

large tree branches are frequently in motion and umbrellas are frequently turned wrong side out. Of course, winds can get even stronger, but this is generally the full range under which kites are typically flown.

Some winds have a relatively constant direction over a period of time; others are variable. Wind that appears in gusts, for example, can make kite flying more difficult.

Like sailboats, kite performance varies with wind conditions. Some kites fly well in light airs and poorly in strong winds, and vice versa.

KITE DESIGN VARIABLES

The wind is an important variable in kite designing, construction, and flying. There are many possibilities. You can wait for favorable wind conditions, or you can design and construct kites for specific wind conditions. On a day when there is a light breeze, you can then use a kite that is specifically designed and constructed for these conditions. When there is a moderate breeze, you will use another kite that is suitable for these conditions. The light-breeze kite would probably be of lighter construction and might well break if you attempted to fly it in a moderate breeze. The moderate-breeze kite would probably be of much heavier construction, and it might not get off the ground on a light breeze day.

Kite design involves working with a lot of variables. We will now take a look at some others.

Shape and Form

A kite must have some shape and form. This may be a variation of some standard kite shape or form, or it might be an original shape or form conceived in your imagination. This might be a flat or form conceived in your imagination. This might be a flat or bowed design, a box or other cellular design, or a semirigid or nonrigid design. The possibilities are almost without limit, at least until you begin to take flying performance into consideration. When flying performance becomes important, kite aerodynamics must then be considered.

Construction

Once you have a basic kite shape and form in mind, the next step is to construct the kite. There are a number of considerations here. You will need to design the sticks and frame for the kite. The kite must have adequate strength, but at the same time it is generally necessary to keep the weight to an absolute minimum if the kite is to perform well. (You may want to skip the frame and design a flexible kite.)

Once you have a basic frame for the kite, you will then need to decide on a covering material. Again, you will be faced with the problem of adequate strength with a minimum of weight.

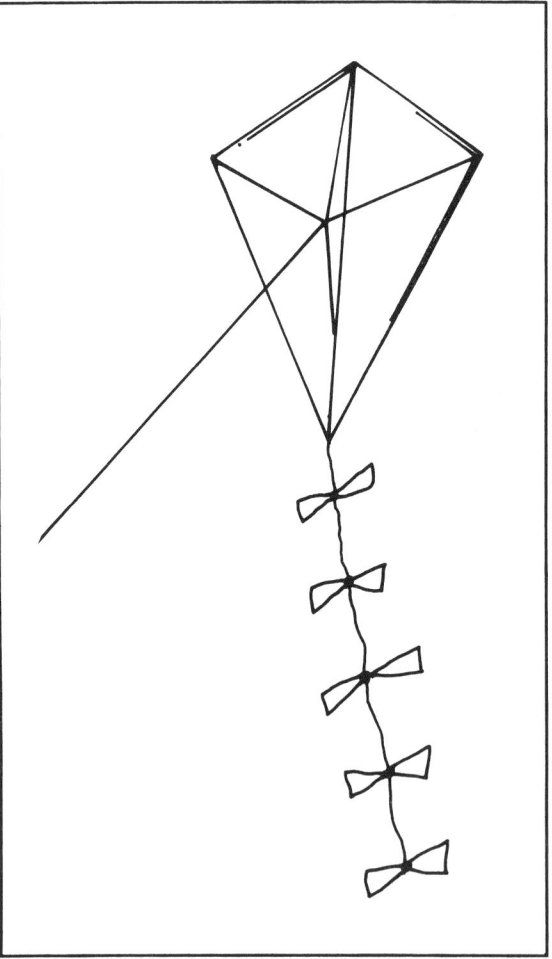

Fig. 2-8. Kite tail made of cloth strips tied at intervals to string.

Tails and Drogues

A tail does two basic things: it gives extra drag and it adds extra weight to the tail section of the kite. Both can add stability. A tail can often be the solution for a kite that uncontrollably loops and spins. The tail can increase stability by keeping the kite facing in the right direction and preventing the kite from twisting.

Tails are of various constructions, including strips of cloth tied at intervals to a length of string (Fig. 2-8) and long strips of cloth, plastic, or crepe paper (Fig. 2-9). In some cases, a single tail will be adequate; other kites require two or more tails (Fig. 2-10).

A *drogue* is basically a wind cup, as shown in Fig. 2-11. A drogue serves essentially the same purpose as a tail and in many cases can be more efficient than a tail. A drogue catches air in a manner similar to the way a sea anchor catches water.

Bowing

Bowing is another important design possibility. Bowing can increase the self-righting tendency of a kite, thus increasing the stability. When the kite turns, the wind has a favorable angle to turn the kite back, as shown in Fig. 2-12. This principle can be used for designing kites for modifying designs that turn out to be poor performers.

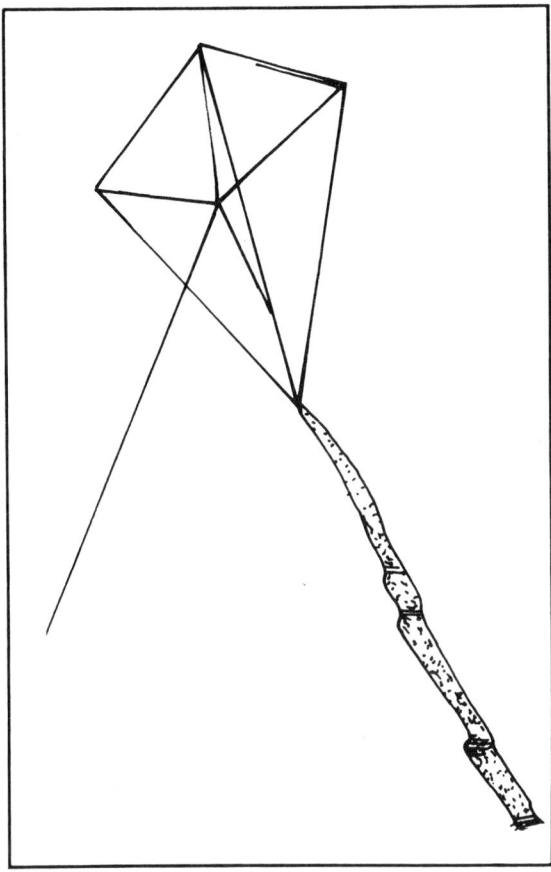

Fig. 2-9. Kite tail made from long strip of cloth.

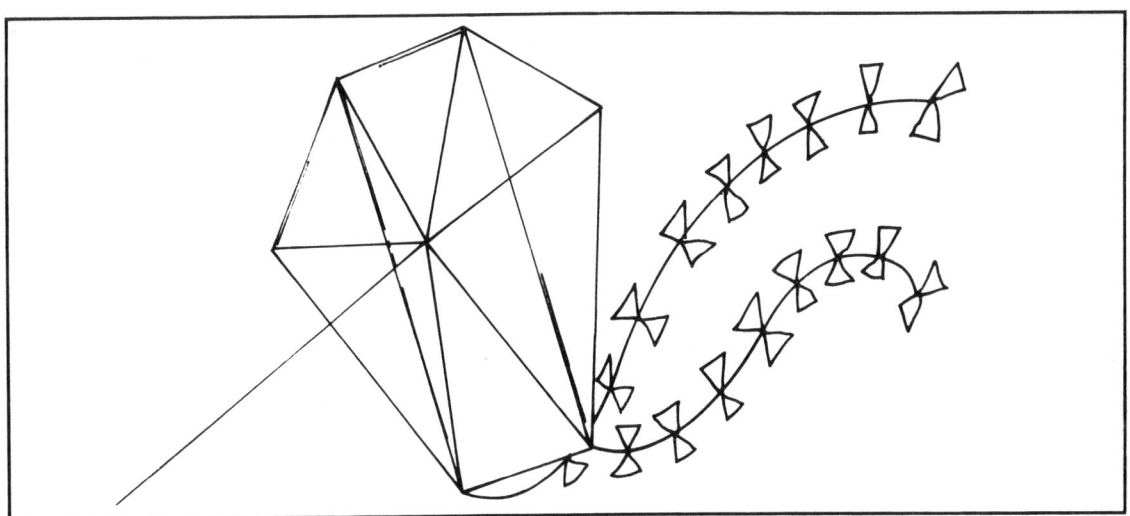

Fig. 2-10. Kite with two tails.

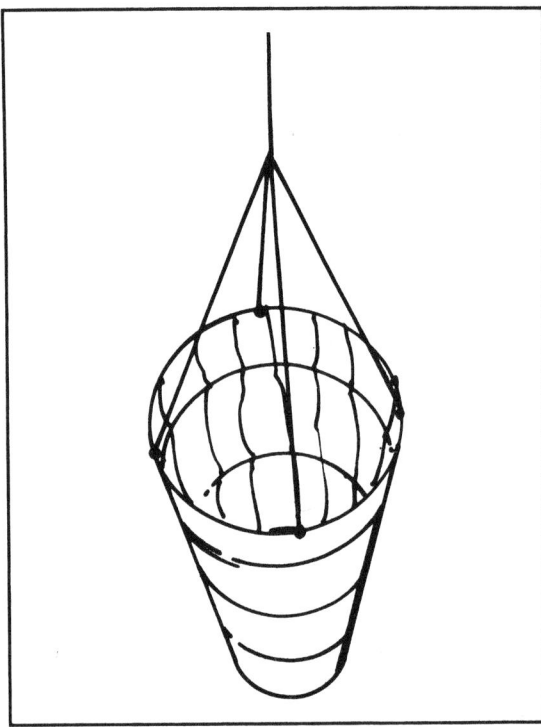

Fig. 2-11. A drogue.

Bowing can be a smooth curve, an angle at the center of the kite, or angles elsewhere (Fig. 2-13). The bowing can be slight or exaggerated, as shown in Fig. 2-14, or anything in between. An exaggerated bow does tend to reduce the size of the lift surface.

Venting

Venting is basically the addition of holes or openings in the covering material of the kite, such as shown in Fig. 2-15. Some box kites, such as shown in Fig. 2-16, have more vented area than covering area.

Venting allows air to pass through the kite and escape. When properly done, venting can add stability to some kite designs.

Other Design Variables

You may also want to experiment with a number of other design variables, such as rudders, airfoil-shaped surfaces, and tapering. Much can be learned about kite design from flying kites, as detailed in Chapter 10, both individually and in trains.

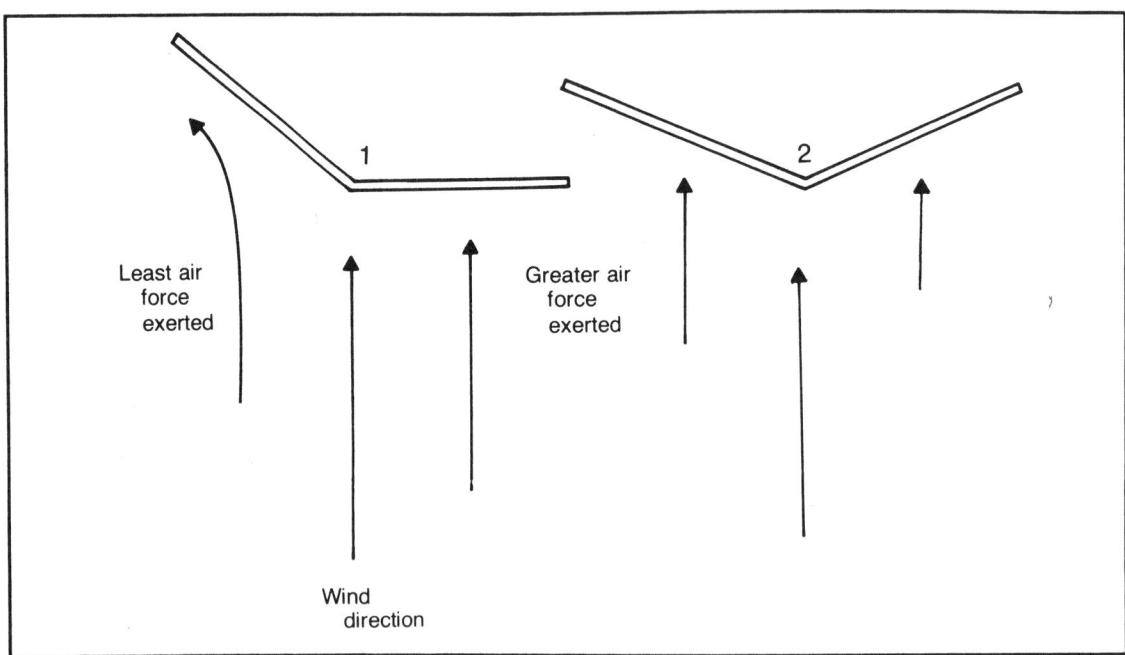

Fig. 2-12. Bowing gives kites self-righting effect.

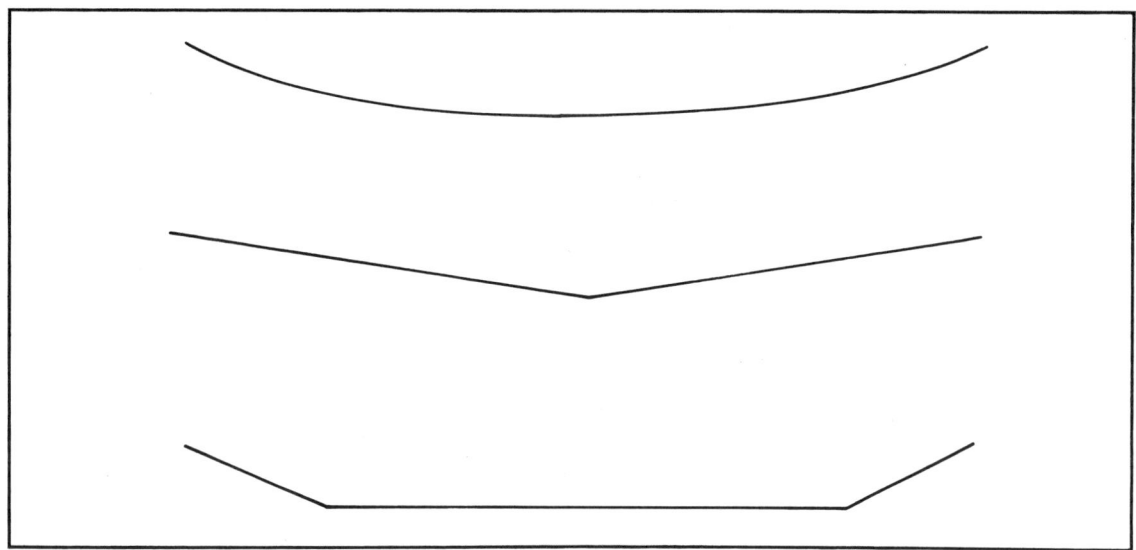

Fig. 2-13. Bowing can be smooth curve or an angle at the center of the kite or angles elsewhere.

DESIGN METHODS

There are many methods for designing kites. Kites can, for example, be designed in the imagination, on paper, or by trial and error. You make a modification on an existing kite, then you try it out. If it doesn't work, you try something else, and so on. Some kite designers are engineers and apply wind tunnels, computers, and modern materials to their kite designing. Other people take a more "backyard" approach.

There is no one way of designing kites. Amateurs on very limited budgets have made important contributions to kite design.

A growing number of kite artists design and construct kites as art objects rather than as flying objects. Kites can be nice to look at hanging from a

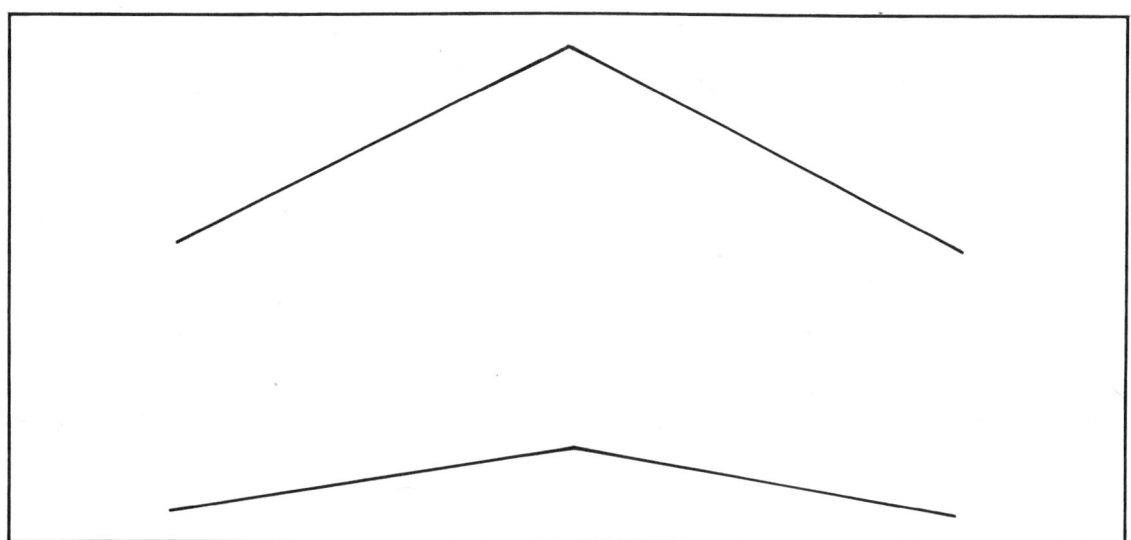

Fig. 2-14. Bowing can be slight or exaggerated.

23

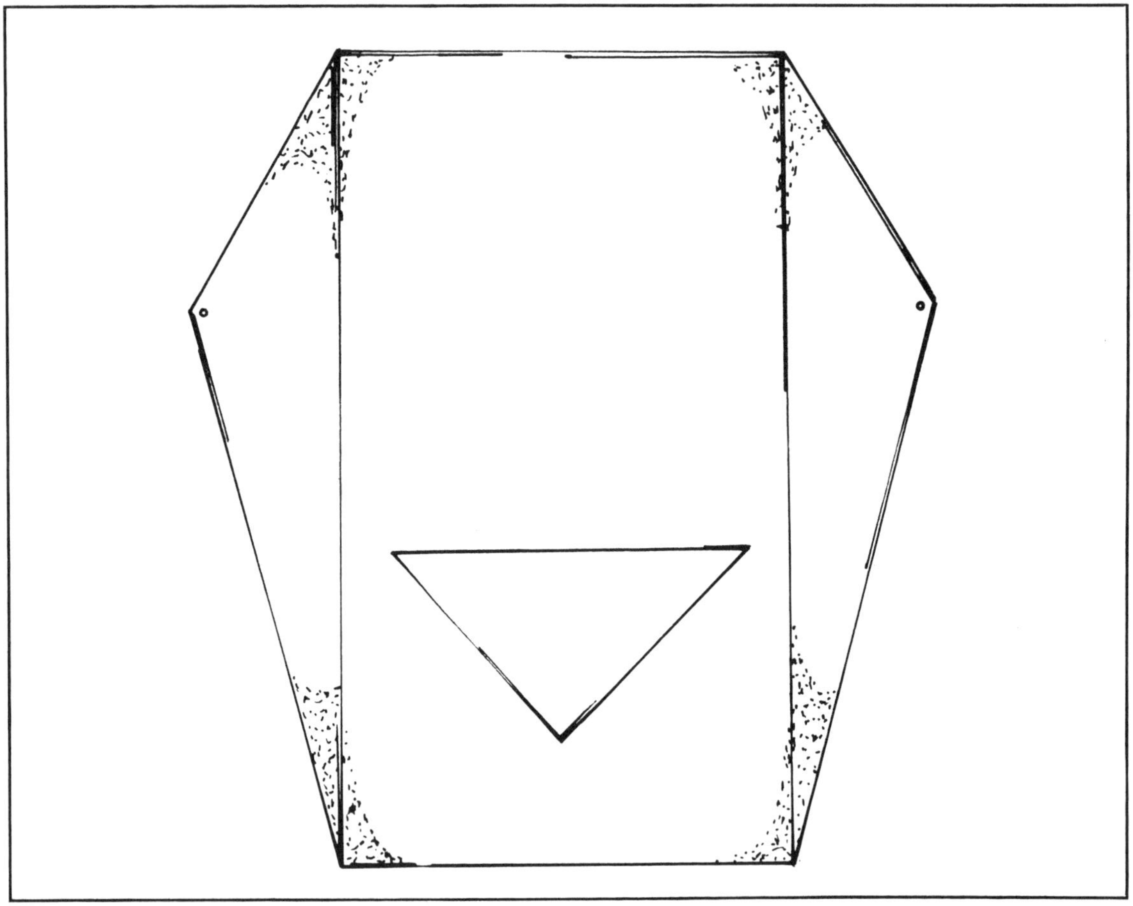

Fig. 2-15. Opening in kite covering material used as a vent.

ceiling as well as flying on the end of a kite string.

Even in flying kites there is a range of design emphasis from an all-out flying design, where how it looks is of no concern, to beautiful figure kites that barely manage to stay aloft. This does not mean, however, that a beautiful kite cannot be a good performer, too. Many kites are a blend of performance and beauty.

An important attraction to kite designing is that you are free to do it the way you want to. If a kite design doesn't work out well, generally not much is lost, and you can always try again.

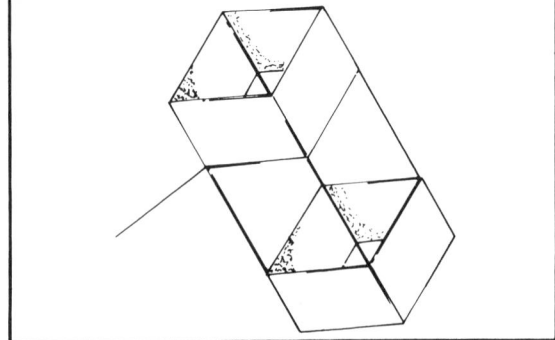

Fig. 2-16. A box kite with large vented areas.

Chapter 3

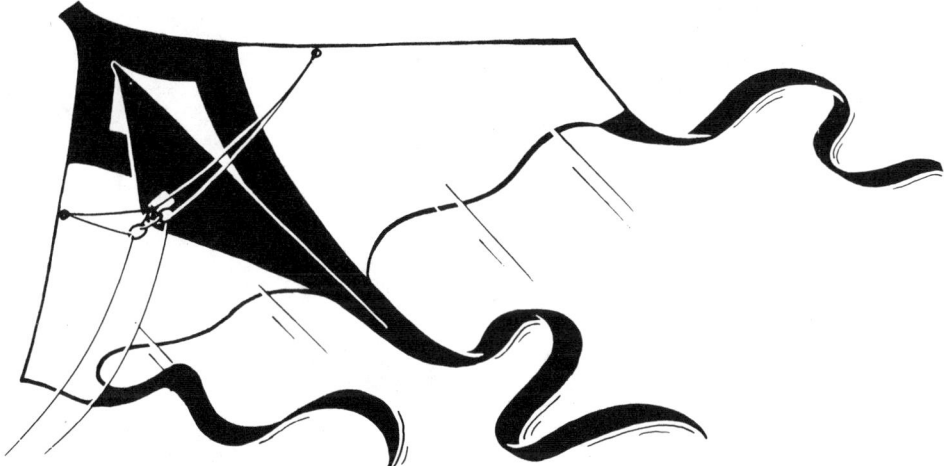

Manufactured Kites

A large variety of both imported and domestic manufactured kites is available in the United States today. These kites come in a wide range of prices. The least expensive are usually made in large numbers. The most expensive are usually custom-made kites or those made in very small numbers. Don't let the prices fool you. Many inexpensively manufactured kites are excellent performers.

Domestic kite manufacturers include the Airplane Kite Company; Gayla Industries; Hi-Flier Manufacturing Company; Sky-Way Products, Inc.; Spectra Star Kites; Squadron Kites; and Striegel Manufacturing Company. Many imported kites are also available, and practically every type of kite imaginable is available in manufactured form.

Many variety stores, hobby shops, department stores, drug stores, supermarkets, toy stores, and other stores carry kites. There are also stores in some parts of the United States that specialize in kites (see Appendix).

Gayla Industries, Inc., P.O. Box 10800, Houston, Texas, 77292, offers many interesting designs, including the Stuntmaster (Fig. 3-1) and the Astro Rover (Fig. 3-2).

Kites made by the Airplane Kite Company, 1705 West Alameda, Roswell, New Mexico, 88201, include the Spitfire (Fig. 3-3), an airplane kite in shape, design, and performance. It has a red polyethylene cover and is aerodynamically balanced. The Challenger (Fig. 3-4) is a delta wing kite. It has a 39-inch wing span and is available in a variety of colors. The Sky Hook (Fig. 3-5) is a soaring keel kite. The Space Ship Earth (Fig. 3-6) is a wind-formed kite with twin streamers. The Triumph (Fig. 3-7) is a giant box kite with three cells forward and three cells rearward. The Skyscraper (Fig. 3-8) is a square-section box kite.

While manufactured kites vary in complexity, most come in easy-to-assemble form. In most cases, it's only a matter of minutes to take a kite from its package to the air.

A variety of kite accessories are also manufactured, including kite strings, reels, shuttle systems, kite string climbers, and parachute drops.

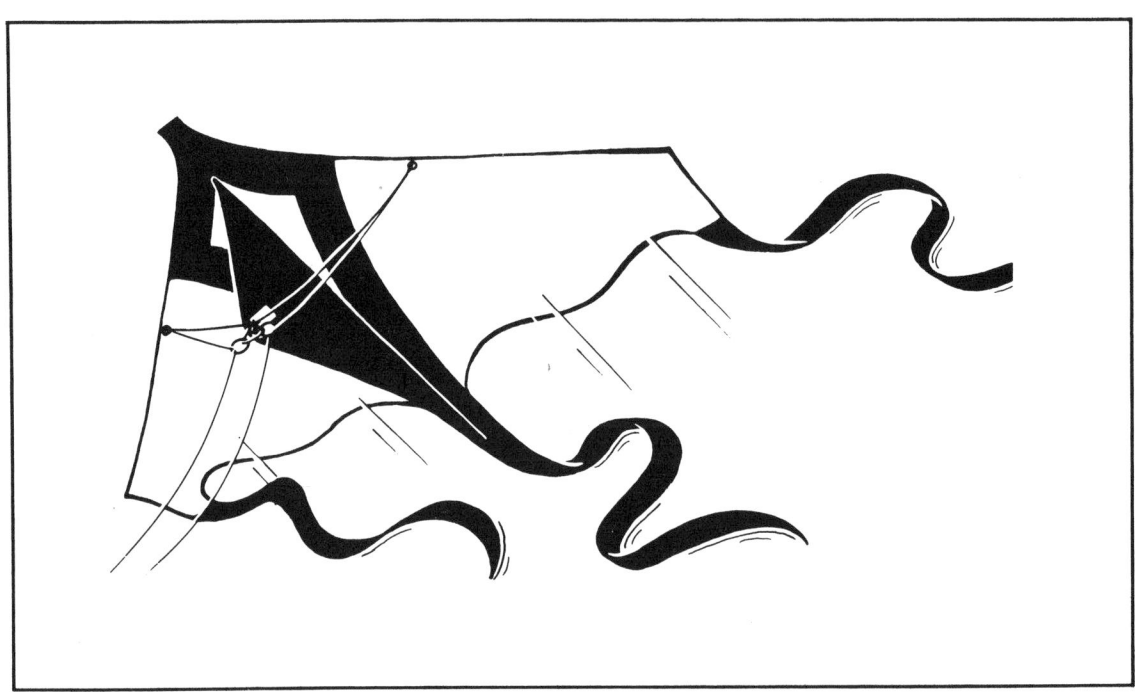
Fig. 3-1. The Stuntmaster kite (courtesy, Gayla Industries, Inc.).

Fig. 3-2. The Astro Rover kite (courtesy, Gayla Industries, Inc.).

Fig. 3-3. The Spitfire kite (courtesy, Airplane Kite Company).

Fig. 3-4. The Challenger kite (courtesy, Airplane Kite Company).

Fig. 3-5. The Sky Hook kite (courtesy, Airplane Kite Company).

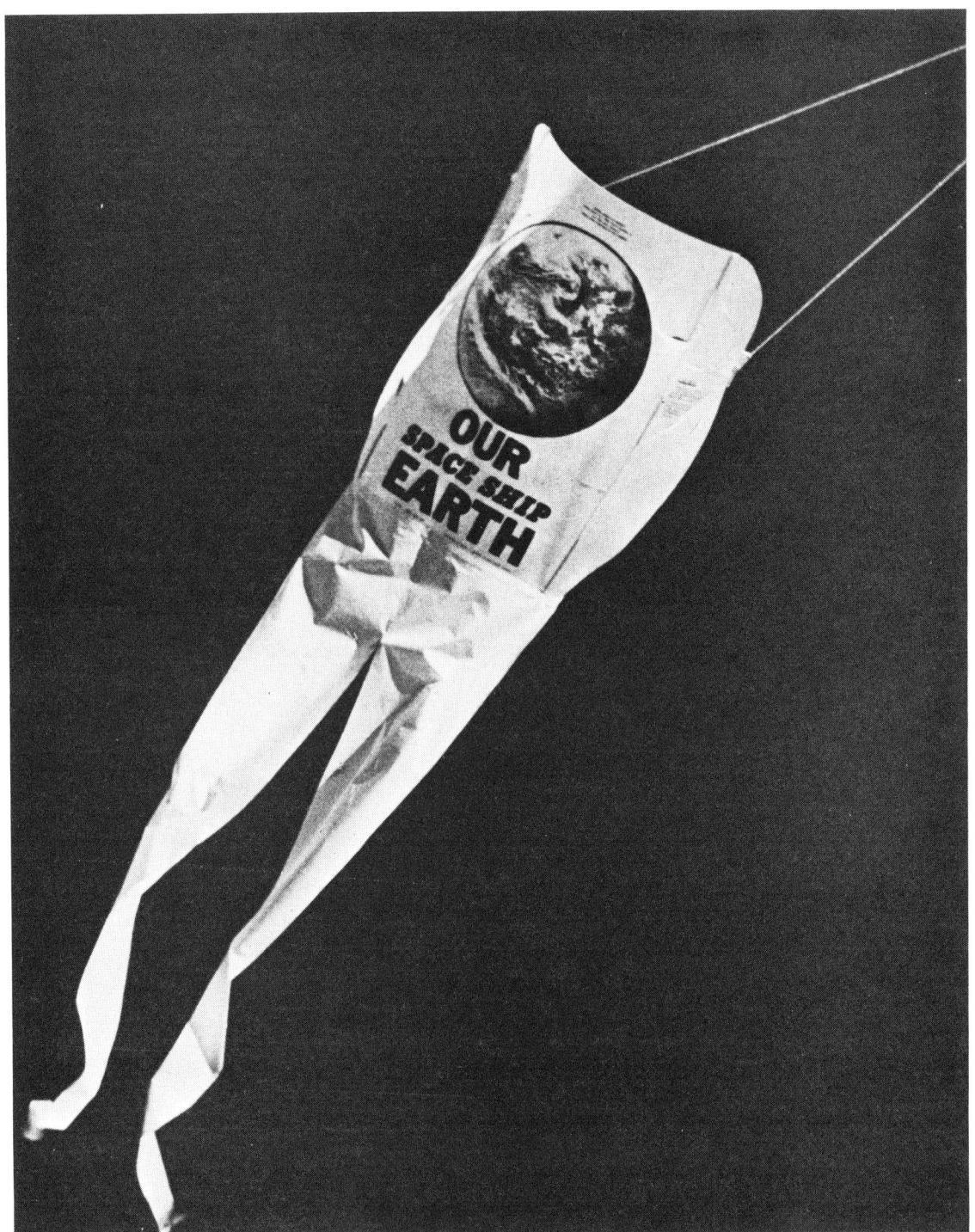

Fig. 3-6. The Space Ship Earth kite (courtesy, Airplane Kite Company).

Fig. 3-7. The Triumph is a giant box kite (courtesy, Airplane Kite Company).

Fig. 3-8. The Skyscraper, a square-section box kite (courtesy Airplane Kite Company).

These items can add greatly to the fun of kite flying. While many stores carry some of these items, you will find practically everything available at some of the larger kite stores (see Appendix).

When flying manufactured kites or using manufactured kite accessories, follow the manufacturer's directions. Instructions for rigging the kites and attaching bridles and tails must be followed. Most manufacturers have thoroughly tested their products and give valuable directions for their use.

Generally the more you pay, the better the kite you get, but I have found that many inexpensive manufactured kites, even some costing under a couple of dollars, are excellent performers. Some of the inexpensive kites use space age materials and are not only light in weight, but also durable.

Chapter 4

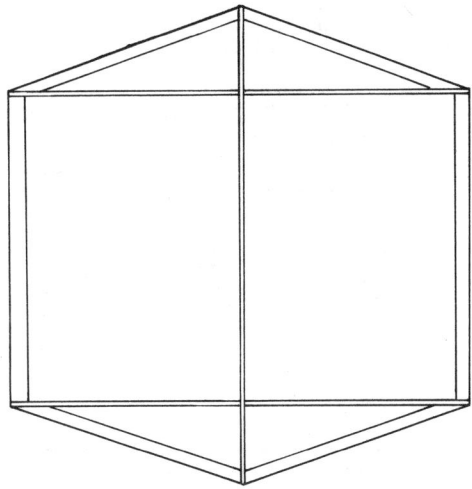

Tools, Work Areas, and Materials

Only a few tools, a minimal work area, and readily available, inexpensive materials are required to get started in kite building. As you gain experience, however, you will probably want more and better tools, a better work station, and more elaborate and expensive materials. Inadequate tools, work areas, and materials can limit your ability to make interesting and functional kites, so you should try to have the best setup possible, within the limits of your budget and interest.

If you are just starting out and have never constructed a kite before, you will probably want to keep expenses to an absolute minimum. You will want to take advantage of what you already have: a workshop in your garage or basement, for example. If you have previously built model airplanes or other related things, you probably already have many of the tools and materials on hand that you will need for making kites. Start with what you already have and then add to this as a need develops. This assumes that you already have a basic set of tools, a place to work, and some materials. If not, the essential items for getting started are detailed below.

Tools required for intermediate and advanced work, up to the custom-kite-making-as-a-business level are also listed. A variety of work stations for various levels of interest and skills are covered. Materials described begin with common items and progress upward to exotic, space-age fabrics.

TOOLS

A variety of tools are useful for kite construction work. As a general rule, quality tools are more expensive to purchase, but these are often the most economical in the long run, because cheap tools are easily broken or damaged under normal use.

Knives

Three basic knives are suitable for kite construction work: fixed blades, removable blades, and folding blades (Fig. 4-1).

Knives with fixed blades are available in a variety of shapes, sizes, and qualities. The handle can be of wood, plastic, metal, or other material, which is securely attached to the blade, often by

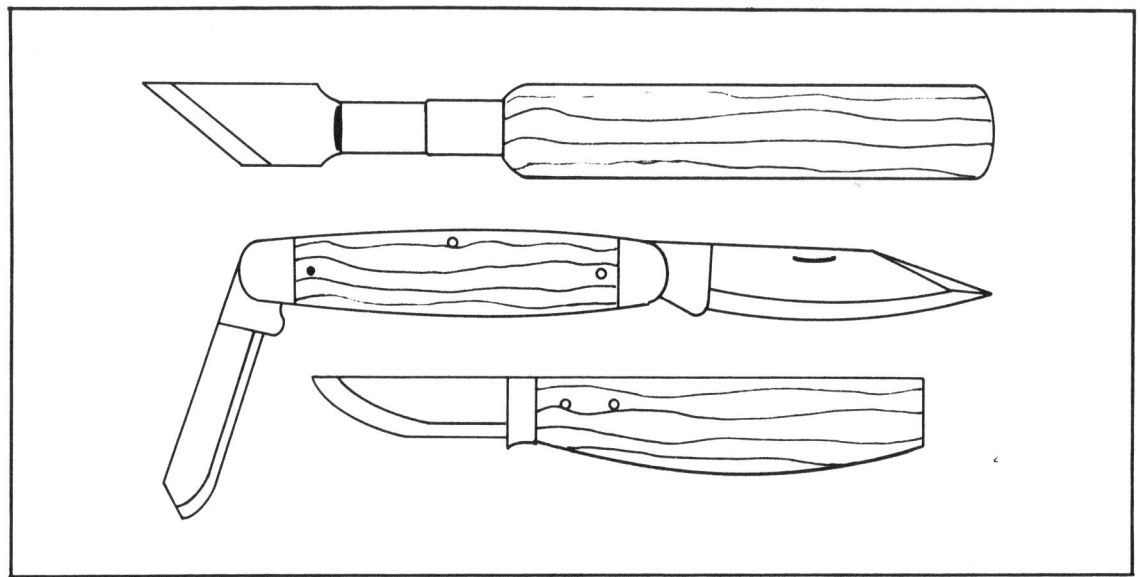

Fig. 4-1. A knife with removable blade, top; folding blades, center; and fixed, bottom.

means of rivets, in a fixed position. Carbon steel blades are best for kite construction work, although those of stainless steel are sometimes used. Carbon steel does rust unless it is lightly oiled or otherwise protected, but it holds its edge longer.

While many utility knives with fixed blades can be used for kite construction work, those designed especially for modeling and woodcarving wood are especially desirable. Some of the available shapes are shown in Fig. 4-2.

Fixed-blade knives are generally the safest type to use. If properly constructed, there is little danger of the blade coming loose or folding up, which could cut your fingers. When selecting a

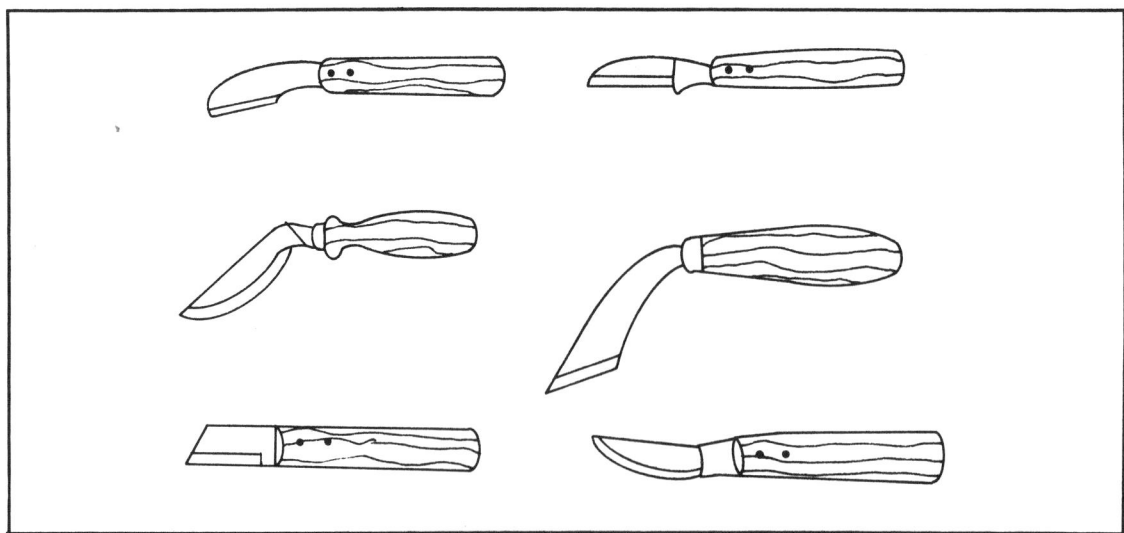

Fig. 4-2. Knives designed for modeling and woodcarving.

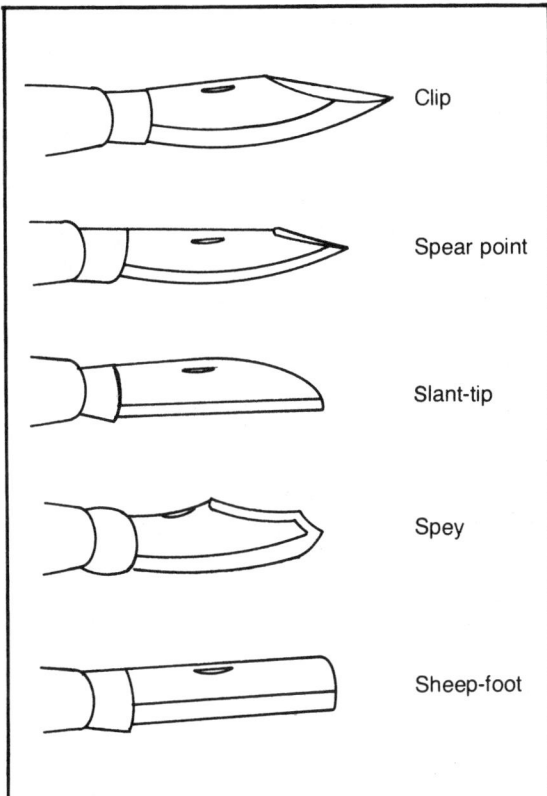

Fig. 4-3. Useful pocketknife blades.

with many blades will have some of them off-center and will be wider and heavier, making it more awkward to use.

Pocketknives are available in a variety of sizes, with those in the medium size range being most useful for general kite construction work.

While pocketknives are easy to store and carry, they do present the possible danger of snapping shut while they are being used and cutting fingers. For shop use, I prefer to use fixed-blade knives. Pocketknives, however, are useful for taking along with you when flying kites for cutting string, kite repair work, and so on.

A removable blade knife is also suitable for kite construction. They offer the advantage of using

fixed-blade knife, make certain that it feels comfortable in the hand. The quality of the steel used in the blade should be such that it will hold a fine cutting edge.

Fixed-blade knives do have some disadvantages, too. The blade of the knife can't be folded out of the way for carrying in your pocket. Also, you can't use more than one blade with the same handle.

Pocketknives or clasp knives have blades that can be folded back into the handle for carrying and storage. Pocketknives are available with one or more blades and are easy to carry. Pocketknives are available in a variety of shapes, designs, and sizes. Useful blades include the clip, spear point, slant-tip, spey, and sheep-foot, as shown in Fig. 4-3. Pocketknives with one or more of these blade types can be used for kite construction work. As a general rule, a pocketknife with one or two blades is preferable to a model with many blades, as a knife

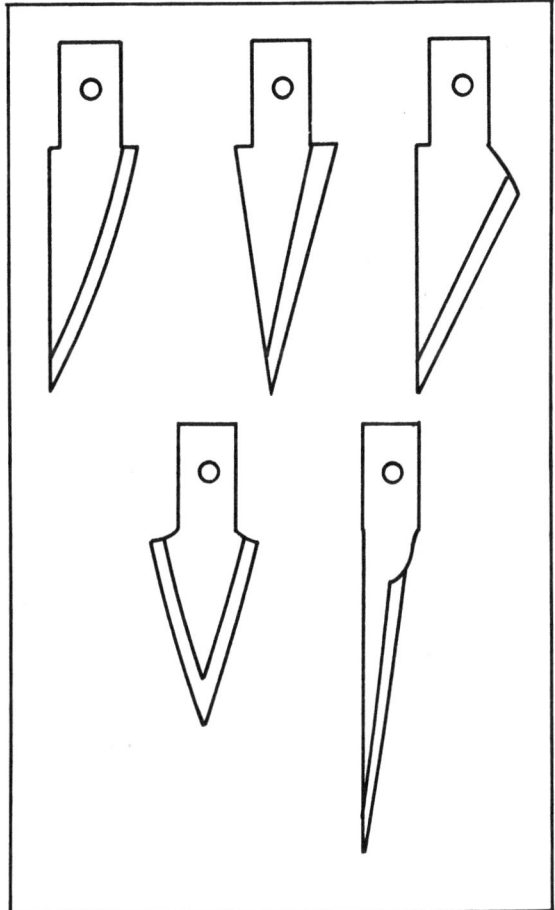

Fig. 4-4. Removable blades.

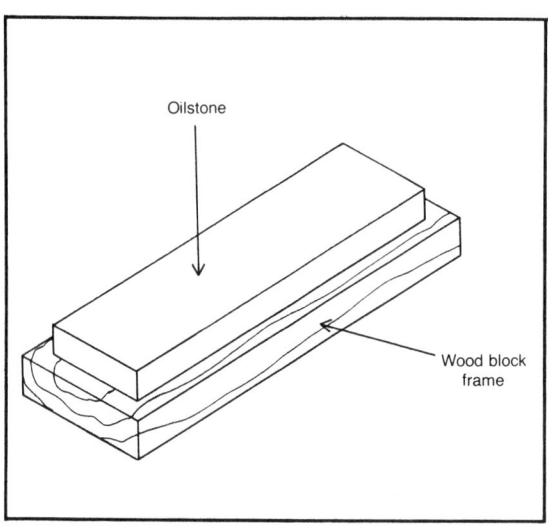

Fig. 4-5. Oilstone.

type of knife can be very useful for kite construction work, especially when working with soft woods and other easy-to-cut materials.

Regardless of the knives selected, you will want to keep them sharp. To do this, you will need an oilstone (Fig. 4-5). A number of suitable oilstones are on the market, both natural and manufactured. Especially good are the Washita and Arkansas stones, both natural stones. It's a good idea to have a slab of each, because each has different honing characteristics. The coarser Washita oilstone can be used first, followed by the finer Arkansas oilstone. You can obtain these two stones together, with the Washita on one side and the Arkansas on the other. A number of other oilstones, with similar cutting characteristics are available.

Small slabs of oilstone about 6 inches long and 1½ to 2 inches in width will suffice for most knife-sharpening work.

You will also need a smooth leather stropping pad, the same as used for razors. A piece of smooth, genuine leather will also work. This can be tacked to a block of wood to make it more convenient to use, as shown in Fig. 4-6.

a single handle for a variety of blade shapes and sizes. Make certain that the blades can be securely attached to the handles so they will not come loose while you are using them. Removable blade knives are often sold in sets with a variety of blade shapes and sizes, such as those shown in Fig. 4-4. This

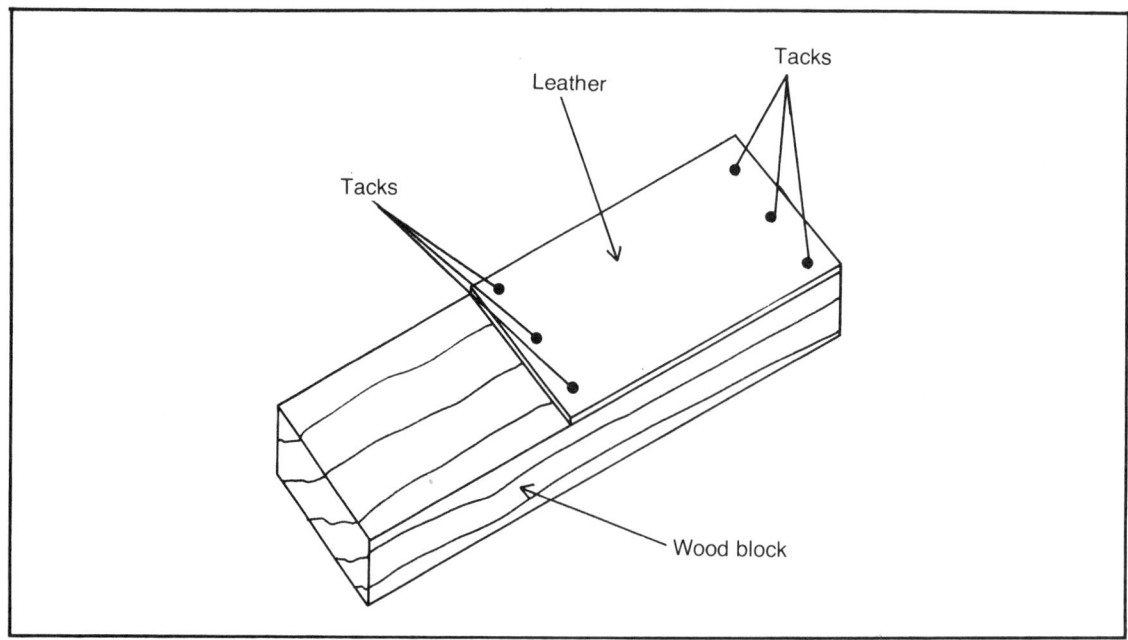

Fig. 4-6. Leather strop tacked to wood block.

A variety of other tools can also be used for sharpening knives, including grinding wheels and electric knife sharpeners, but it is easy to keep knife blades sharp and functional with an oilstone and strop alone.

Safety Razor Blades and Razor Knives

Razor blades are extremely useful, but if you use one, make certain it is a safety blade with a metal guard over one edge.

Special knives with razor-type blades are available for hobby and modeling work. Some of the knives with removable blades feature razor-type blades. These will often serve in place of safety razor blades, although I find uses for both.

Razor blades and razor knives are useful for cutting soft woods and a variety of other materials used in kite construction. They are especially useful for cutting balsa wood.

Chisels

Chisels are useful for some kite construction jobs. I find the Japanese style carving chisels to be handy for a variety of kite construction tasks. These chisels, when properly sharpened, have razor sharp cutting edges that are ideal for notching kite sticks and other similar tasks. When working on wood spars for very large kites, larger wood chisels, such as those designed for carpenter or woodcarving work are useful.

Like knives, chisel blades require frequent sharpening. Oilstones and strops, as detailed above, can be used to maintain keen cutting edges.

Saws

A variety of saws are useful for kite construction work. Extremely useful is a *coping saw* (also called *scroll* saw), as shown in Fig. 4-7. It features a handle that is attached to a U-shaped frame, and a removable blade fastened in the frame. Many coping saws allow the blade to turn to various angles. Blades, which have ripsaw-type teeth, are available with various numbers of teeth per inch. A blade with 15 or 16 points to the inch is satisfactory for general kite construction work.

Although not essential for most kite construction work, a power jigsaw or scroll saw can be very useful (Fig. 4-8). This type of saw can be used for the same types of cutting jobs as a hand coping saw, but generally with greater speed and accuracy. A power jigsaw can be very useful for anyone who decides to go into custom kite making on a business basis.

Cutting large wood stock into small spars for kite construction work presents special problems. While small ripsaws can be used, cutting accuracy can be a problem. Small, circular, bench power saws designed for hobby work can be useful here.

Larger circular bench saws can be used similarly, except that these generally have wider blades and take out a larger *kerf* (area of wood removed by blade) when sawing. This results in more waste wood when cutting small spars.

Circular saws permit a variety of cutting operations, including cross-cutting, ripping, squaring, mitering, grooving, rabbeting, and beveling. Some of these cutting tasks are useful in kite construction work.

Saber saws (Fig. 4-9) are sometimes useful in kite construction work. A saber saw can be used to do cutting tasks similar to those done with a power jigsaw or scroll saw, but generally with less accuracy. Saber saws do have the advantage of greater portability, however.

I find hacksaws to be useful for a variety of tasks. They are available with traditional frames with handsaw-type or pistol grips, (Fig. 4-10) or with file-type handles. The file-type can be used in areas where a regular hacksaw will not fit. Three

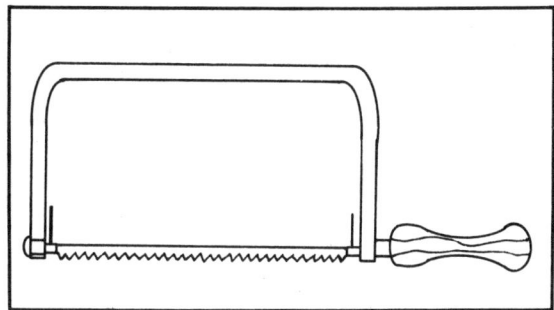

Fig. 4-7. Coping saw.

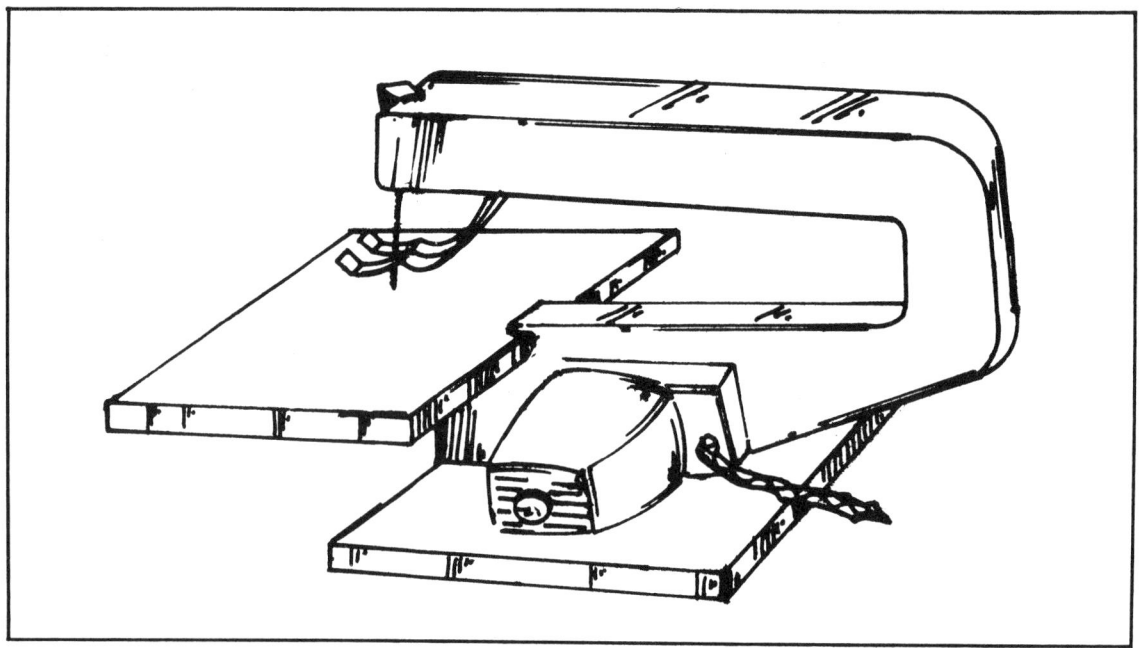

Fig. 4-8. Power jig or scroll saw.

basic teeth sets are available: alternate, raker, and wave. Blades come with various numbers of teeth per inch. The choice depends on what metal or other material is to be cut. The blades are made from several materials, the most expensive being hard tungsten. This works well for cutting hard metals. For most kite construction work, less expensive blades, such as those of molybdenum, will suffice. Although the hacksaw is primarily a metal cutting saw, it can also be used to cut many other materials, including wood and a variety of hard plastics.

A variety of other hand and power saws can also be used for kite construction work, including compass, keyhole, backsaw, and power bandsaw. Keep in mind, however, that kite construction generally involves working with small spars, so large hand and power tools are often awkward, if they can be used at all. Small tools designed especially for hobby and craft work are generally more suitable for kite construction work.

Scissors and Shears

Scissors are used for a varity of cutting tasks in kite construction work, especially for cutting paper, thin cardboard, fabric, plastic covering materials, thread, and string. Scissors are available in a variety of sizes, designs, and qualities. Scissors of at least medium quality are recommended for kite construction work, as those of low quality dull quickly and are difficult to sharpen properly. Size is a matter of personal preference.

A good pair of scissors will last a long time when properly used and cared for. Cutting metals, wires, and similar hard materials will quickly ruin

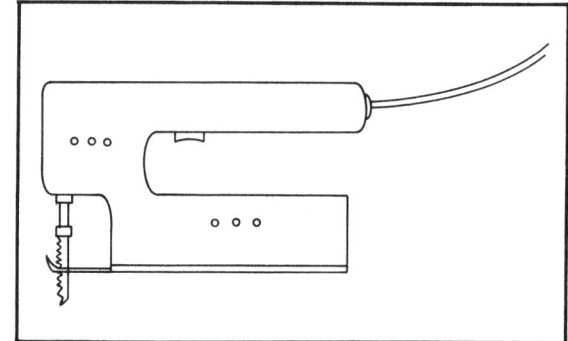

Fig. 4-9. Saber saw.

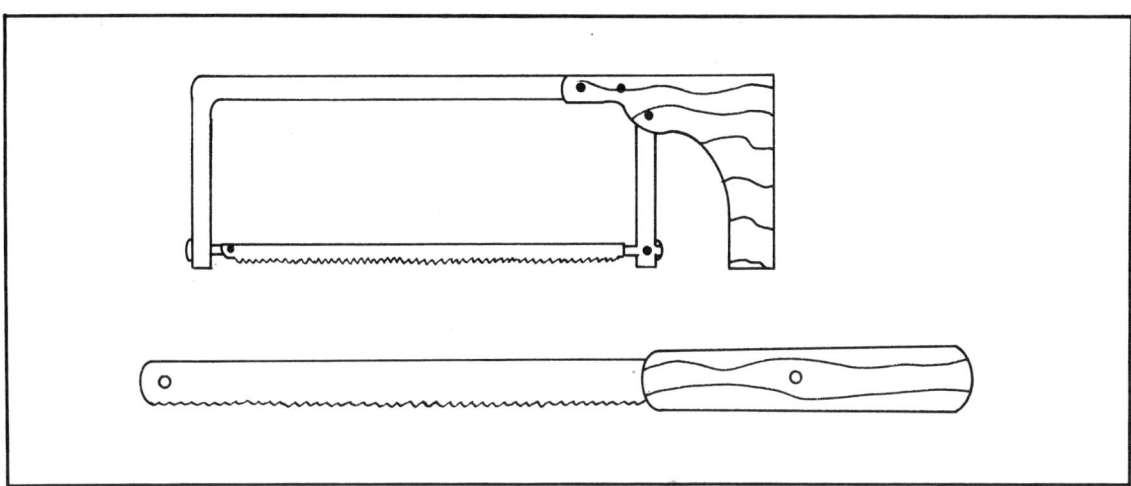

Fig. 4-10. Hacksaw with traditional frame, top; and with file-type handle, bottom.

most scissors. There are other tools better suited for these cutting tasks.

Even when used properly, scissors eventually become dull. These can be taken to commercial shops for sharpening if you don't have the tools and know-how for doing this work yourself.

Scissors should be kept clean and dry. If you get glue on the cutting blades, for example, as sometimes happens, clean this off before the glue has a chance to set.

A variety of shears or snips are available for cutting metals. Since various metals, especially soft metals, are sometimes used in kite construction, metal shears, especially small sizes, can be useful. The basic design is often called a *tinsnip*. Another type of shears, called *duckbill* or *aviation*

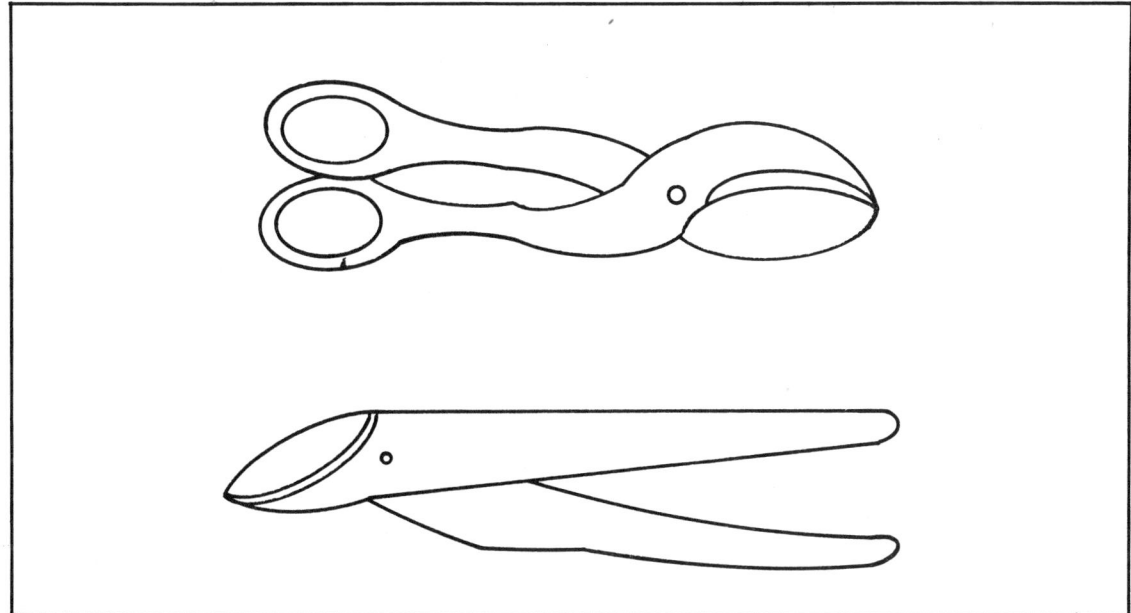

Fig. 4-11. Tinsnips, top; and duckbill or aviation snips, bottom.

snips (Fig. 4-11), are useful cutting curved patterns in metal. Special aviation snips are available for cutting left and others for cutting right. Combination aviation snips that can cut either way are also available.

As a general rule, small size metal shears are most useful for kite construction work, because you will generally be cutting thin pieces of aluminum, brass, copper, and other soft metals and alloys.

When properly cared for and used, metal shears will last a long time. Avoid cutting wire and nails, as this can quickly ruin the shears.

Metal shears eventually become dull. Take them to a commercial shop for sharpening if you don't have the tools and know-how.

Metal shears should be kept clean and dry. Apply a small amount of oil to the pivot pin from time to time.

Pliers

Various pliers are used for gripping and holding small items, cutting, stripping, and crimping. There are over a hundred different types and sizes of pliers being manufactured, and it is important to select pliers carefully for maximum usefulness for kite construction work.

Slip-Joint Pliers. These pliers (Fig. 4-12) are "regular" pliers. The jaws can be positioned for grasping small or large objects, and many slip-joint

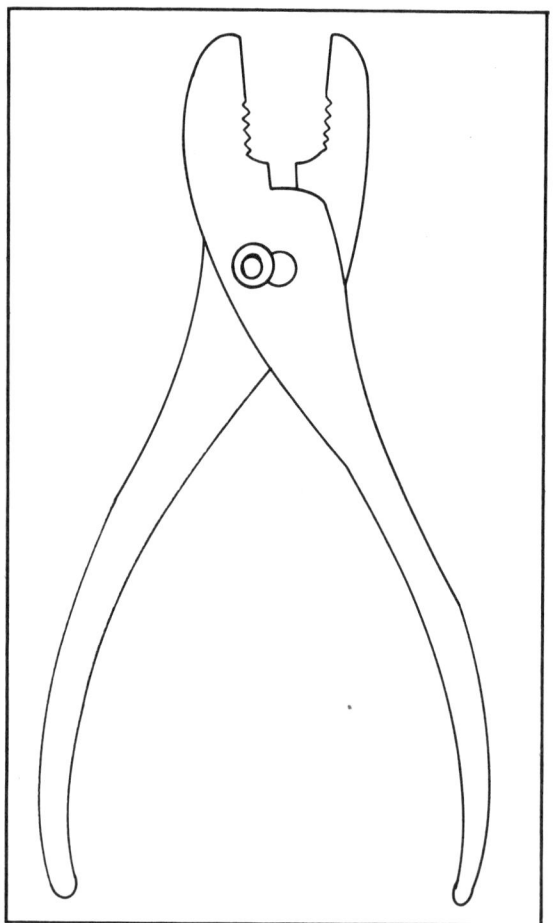

Fig. 4-12. Slip-joint pliers.

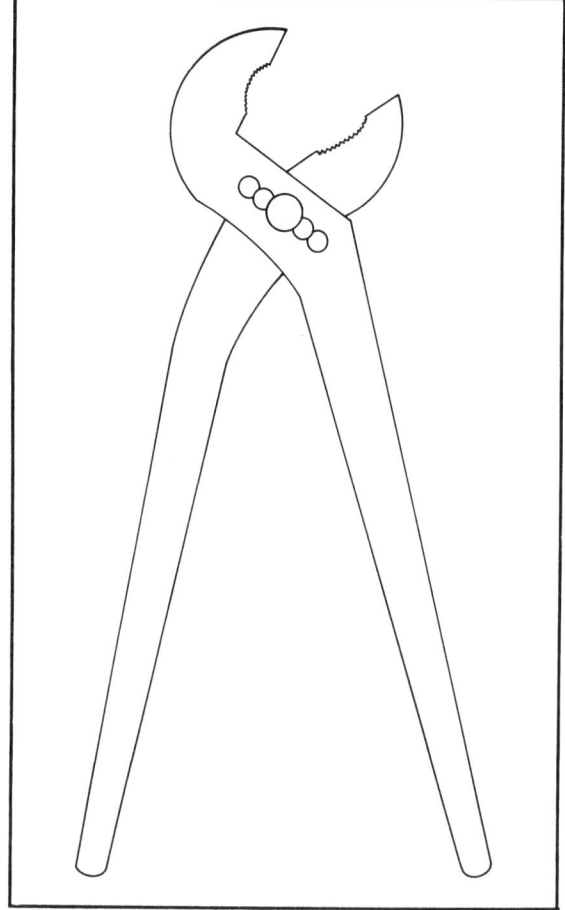

Fig. 4-13. Utility pliers.

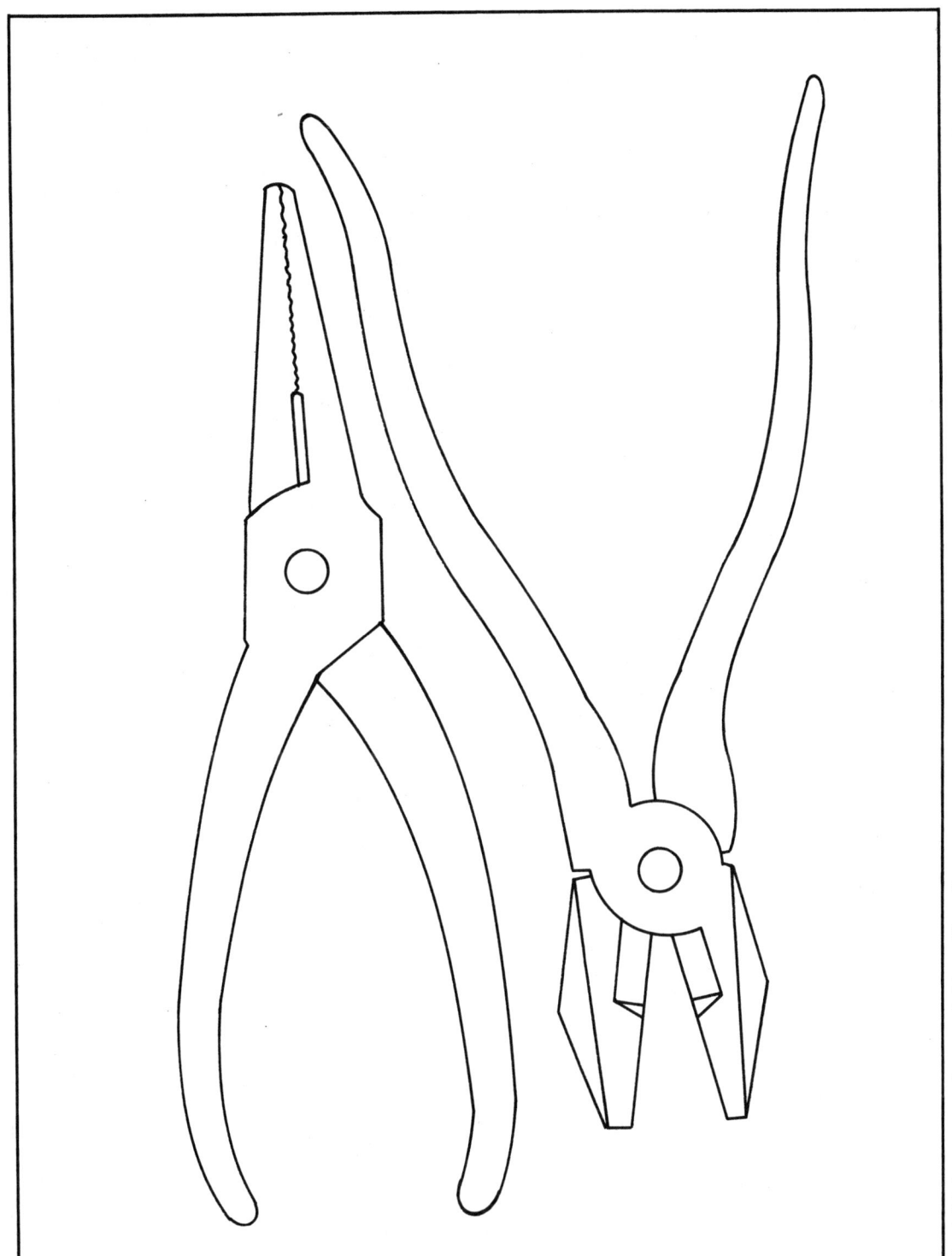

Fig. 4-14. Long-nose pliers, and side-cutting pliers.

39

pliers feature a wire cutter at the base of the jaws. These are suitable for cutting soft nails and easy-to-cut wires. Slip-joint pliers, with or without wire cutters, are available in lengths from about 5 inches to 10 inches with various shapes of jaws.

Utility Pliers. Utility pliers (Fig. 4-13) have wide capacities and can be adjusted to a number of different positions by means of multiposition slip-joints or tongue-and-groove adjustment. They come with handles in various lengths. The longer handles provide greater leverage for gripping and holding objects.

Long-nose Pliers. Long-nose pliers (Fig. 4-14) come in a variety of configurations. Designs with and without side cutters are available. Long-nose pliers are used for holding and moving small objects and doing a variety of other intricate tasks frequently required in kite construction. You will probably want to have several shapes and sizes of these in your tool collection.

Side-cutting Pliers. Side-cutting pliers (Fig. 4-14) are useful for holding, bending, and cutting thin materials. They are available in various lengths, with the small sizes especially useful for kite work.

Locking Pliers. Locking pliers (Fig. 4-15) can be clamped on an object, and they will stay in place. These are available in various sizes. Follow the manufacturer's instructions for adjusting the particular brand.

Diagonal-cutting pliers. Diagonal-cutting pliers (Fig. 4-16) come in various sizes and designs for light and heavy-duty cutting. These are for cutting only and should not be used for gripping and

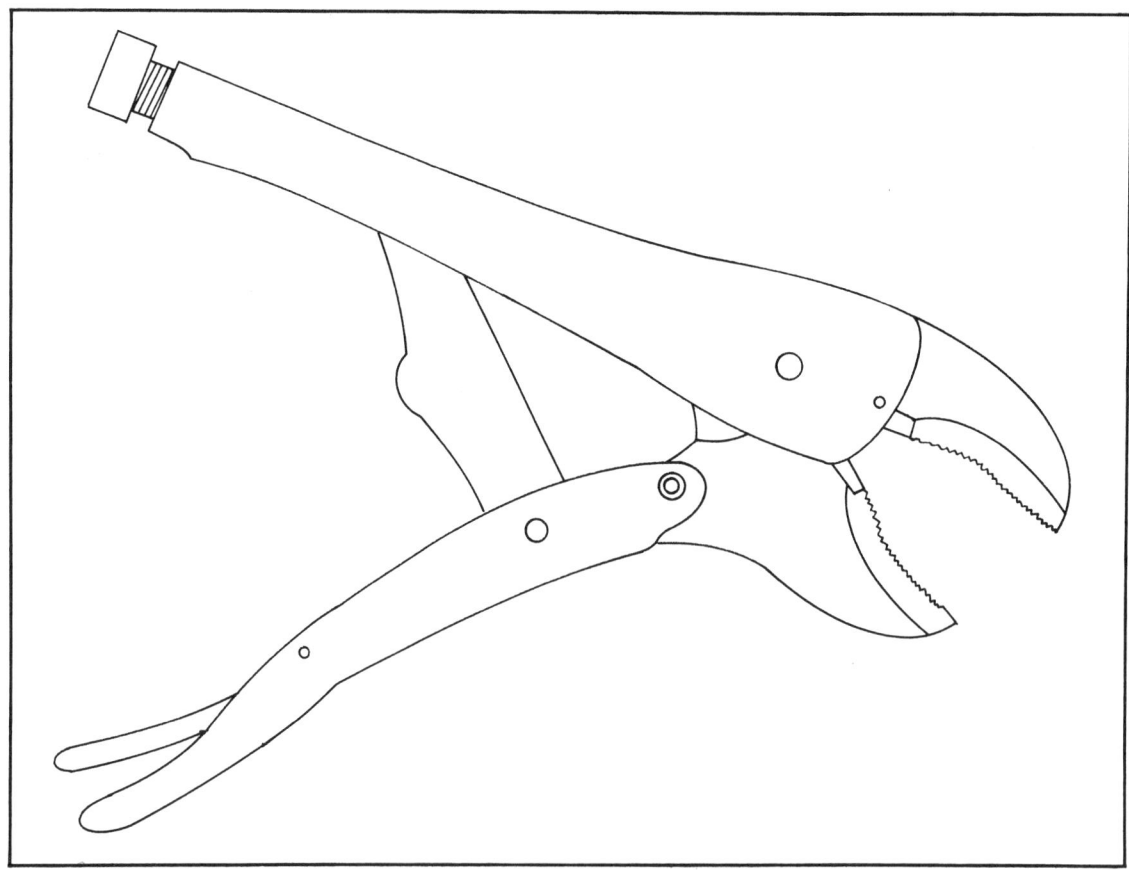

Fig. 4-15. Locking pliers.

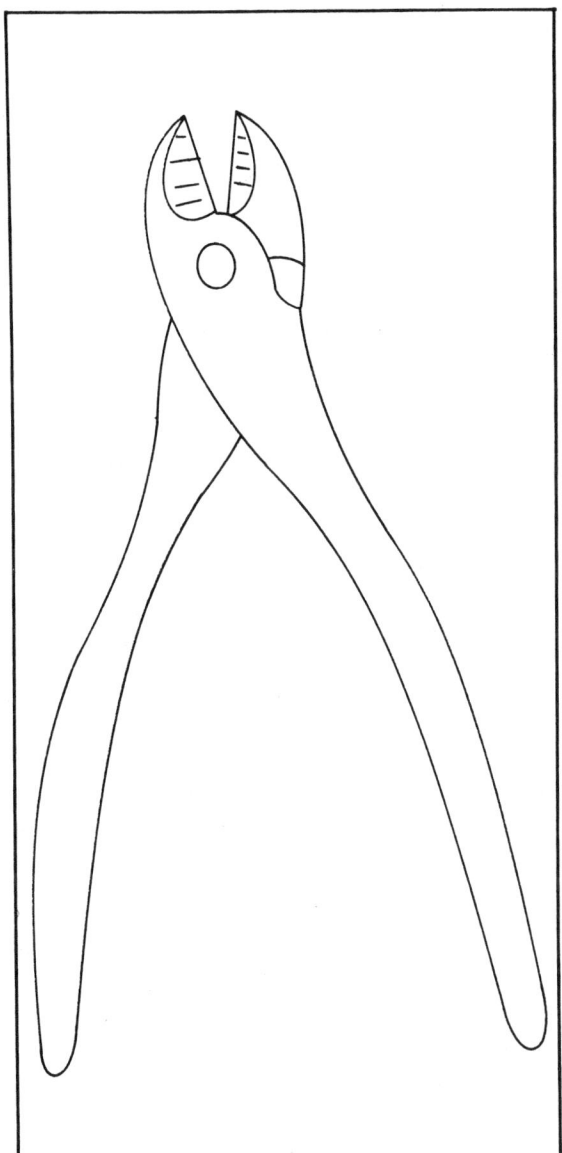

Fig. 4-16. Diagonal-cutting pliers.

Clamps

A variety of useful clamps are available for holding parts together for gluing and a variety of other tasks. A common and extremely useful type is the C clamp (Fig. 4-18). These come in a variety of sizes; small, light-duty clamps are the most useful for kite construction work. You will probably want to have a number of these in your tool collection.

Paper clips and even clothespins can come in handy for holding small parts together while gluing. Other types of clamps, especially small clamps designed for model building, will also be handy.

Hammers

A variety of types and sizes of hammers are available, with each intended for a specific range of uses. Using them for other purposes can damage the hammers or the materials you are working on and may present safety hazards.

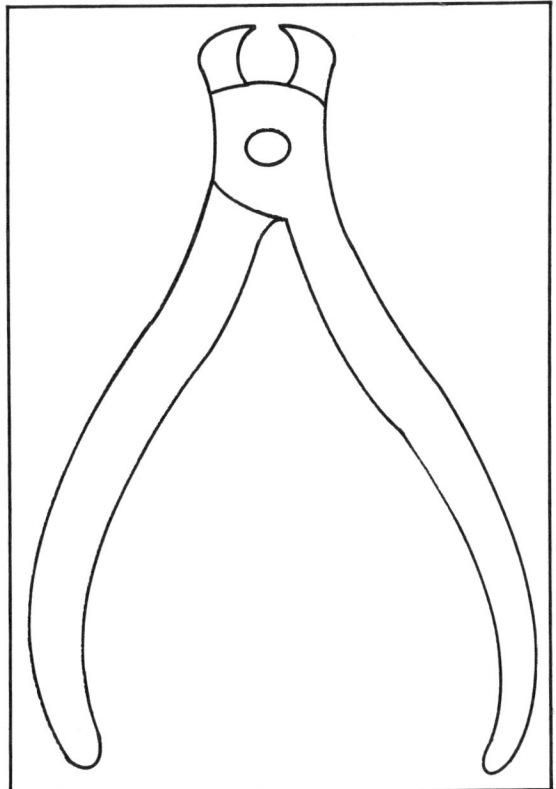

Fig. 4-17. End-cutting pliers.

holding objects. Diagonal-cutting pliers are extremely useful in kite construction work for cutting wires, small nails, and so on.

End-Cutting Pliers. End-cutting pliers (Fig. 4-17), often called nippers, are available in various designs and sizes. They have a good mechanical advantage. Small sizes are generally most useful for kite construction work.

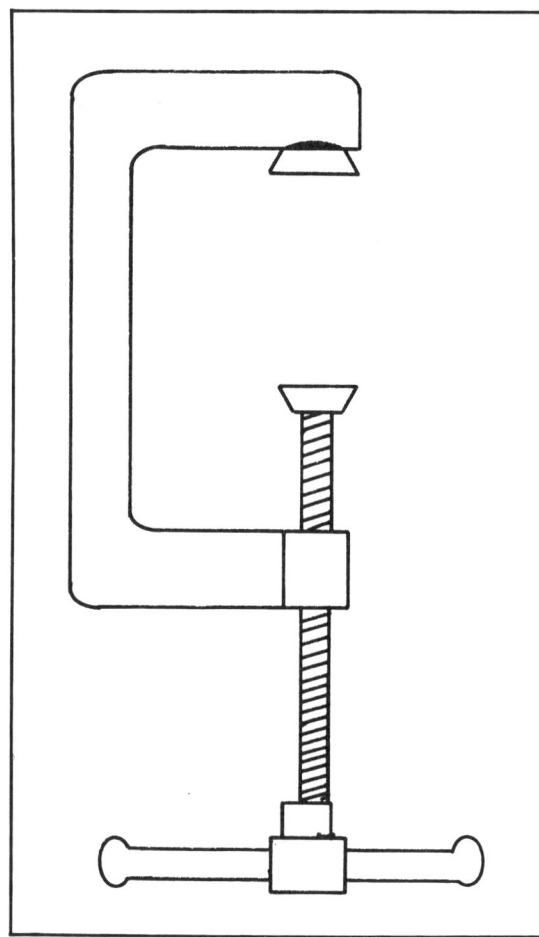

Fig. 4-18. C-clamp.

Claw Hammers. Claw hammers (Fig. 4-19) are frequently called *nail* or *carpenter's* hammer. Their purpose is to drive and pull out nails. They are available with either straight or curved claws. The nail-driving face of the hammer might be flat, slightly rounded, or even convex. The plain flat face is recommended as a general-purpose hammer. Some hammers have a wooden handle attached to a steel head; others, a one-piece steel handle and head and a rubber or plastic grip. Fiberglass handles are used on some manufactured hammers. Although claw hammers come in a variety of weights, a lightweight model is generally most useful for kite construction work.

Ball Peen Hammers. Ball peen hammers (Fig. 4-19) are available with wood, steel, and fiberglass handles. The ball peen end can be used for striking in areas where the face will not fit. They are designed for striking punches and cold chisels, shaping and straightening metal, and riveting work. They come in a variety of weights; lightweight models are the most useful for kite construction.

Mallets. Mallets (Fig. 4-19) are hammers with soft materials for heads. They are used in situations where a steel hammer would cause damage, as when striking wood and plastic objects. The faces of mallets are made from a variety of materials, including wood, plastic, rawhide, and rubber.

Tack Hammers. Tack hammers are designed especially for driving tacks. These are sometimes useful for kite construction work.

Hole Making Tools

A portable electric drill will make most hand braces and drills unnecessary for kite construction work. This is provided, of course, that you have a source of electricity or a cordless electric drill. Tools for making holes by hand are useful at times, and some people make considerable use of them.

Braces and Auger Bits. A carpenter's brace with an auger bit is a traditional method for drilling holes by hand. A separate auger bit is required for each hole size. These are generally not useful for kite construction work.

Twist and Push Drills. Twist drills, which have a hand crank and either a handle or a breast plate, and push drills, which rotate when pushed downward, can be used for drilling holes in wood, plastic, and, to a certain extent, metals. These can be useful in situations where an electric drill or electricity is not available. Small models of these drills intended for hobby and craft work are useful for kite construction.

Portable Electric Drills. A portable electric drill (Fig. 4-20) is an important and useful tool for kite construction work. There are many jobs that call for making small holes in wood, metal, plastic, and other materials. A ¼-inch drill with about 2,000 r.p.m. is satisfactory for most kite construction. Some drills have a single constant speed, and on others the speed is variable and can be adjusted.

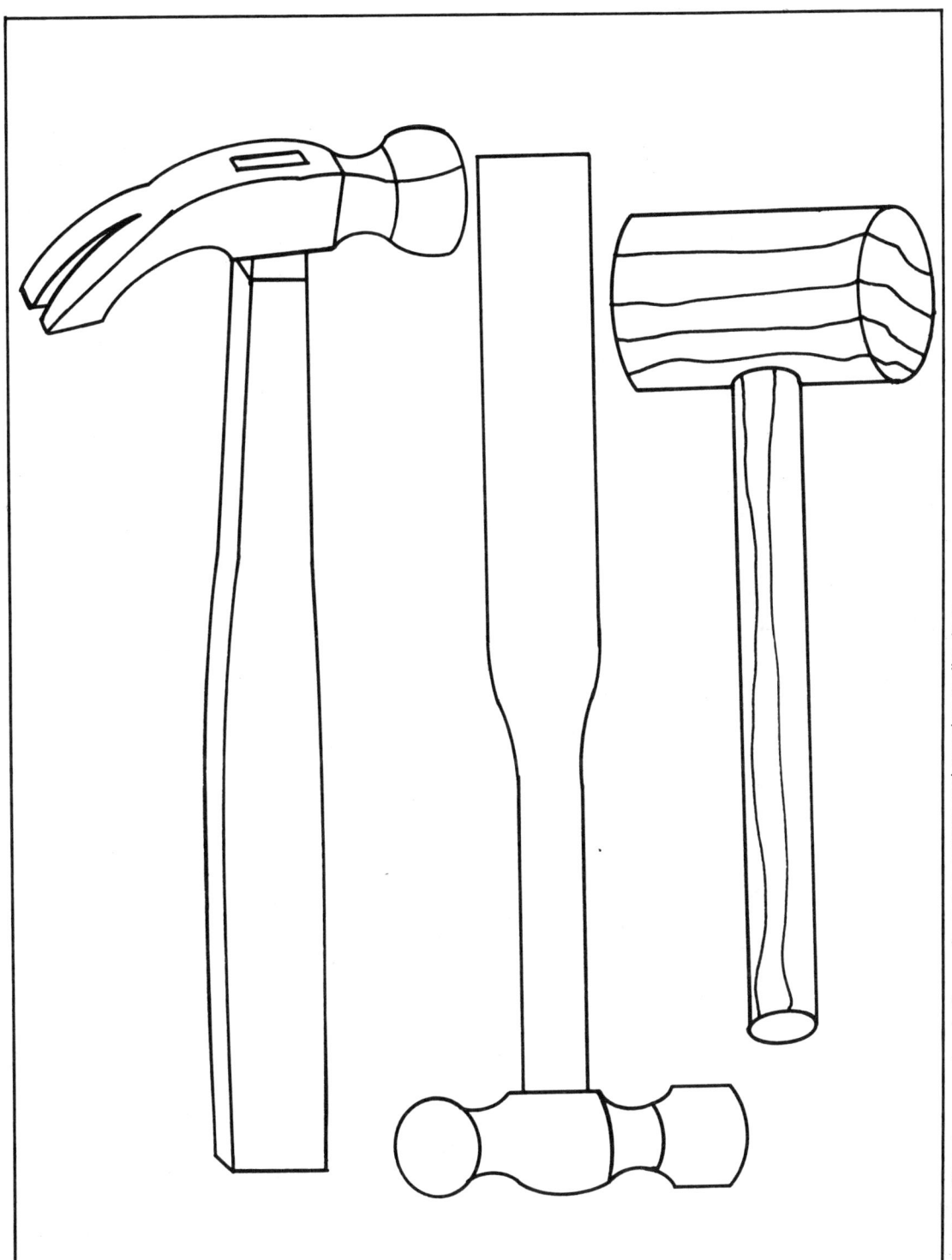

Fig. 4-19. Claw hammer, top; ball peen hammer, center; and wooden mallet, bottom.

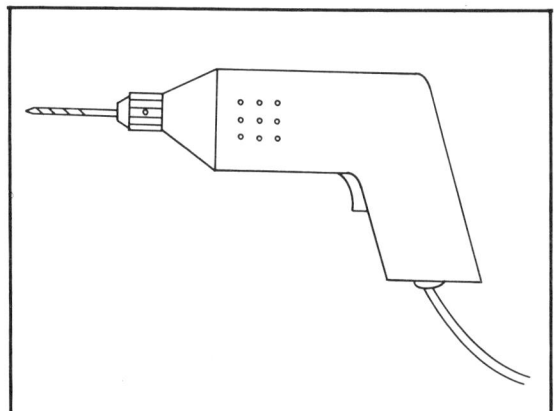

Fig. 4-20. Portable electric drill.

Some drills allow you to reverse the turning direction.

Cordless electric drills are also available. These have a battery pack located in the handle or in a separate case. Rechargable nickel-cadmium batteries are often used. These drills are useful when you are working without a source of electric power.

Regardless of the type of portable electric drill, you will need a selection of standard bits for wood and metal. Small sizes are especially useful. Grinding and sanding attachments can also be used with portable electric drills.

Drill Presses. A drill press, which allows more accurate drilling than a hand-held power drill, is useful for advanced kite construction. Many types and sizes are available. Small drill presses are available that allow you to use your standard, hand-held, portable electric drills. Small drill presses designed especially for model building are ideal for kite construction work. A variety of attachments for drill presses that make carving, shaping, sanding, and a variety of other jobs possible, are also available.

Screwdrivers

The screwdriver is a basic tool designed for driving and removing screws. A screwdriver can also make a handy pry bar for removing lids from paint cans. Since jobs tend to ruin good screwdrivers by rounding the corners of the tips and distorting their shapes, only old screwdrivers no longer suitable for driving and removing screws should be used as pry bars.

Most screws have an ordinary slotted head. Screws are made in gauge sizes, and each size has a specific slot width and depth. The tip of a standard screwdriver should fit the slot closely. Screwdrivers come with tips designed to fit specific screw-gauge sizes. Ideally, a different size screwdriver is used for each screw gauge, but it is usually possible to use a screwdriver for a screw of one gauge smaller or larger than the screwdriver was designed.

Small screwdrivers are generally most suitable for kite construction work. Even if you don't use screws as fasteners for kite constructions, you will probably find them useful for adjusting and repairing tools and related uses.

A standard screwdriver for slotted heads (Fig. 4-21) should have a straight end on the tip. If the

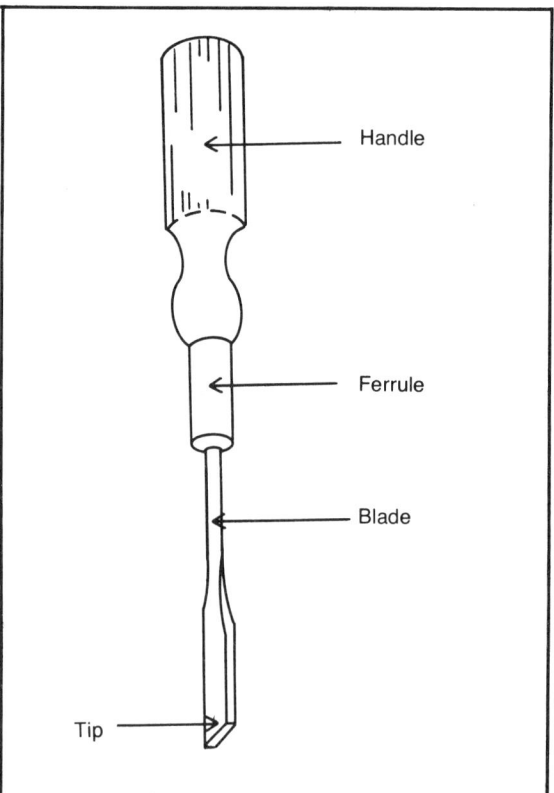

Fig. 4-21. Screwdriver.

corners are rounded, even slightly, the tip will slip out of the screw slot.

There are also screwdrivers designed for screws with recessed heads. While there are a variety of screwheads of this type in use, the *Phillips head* with a cross-slot is the most common. As with standard screwdrivers, always use a Phillips screwdriver that is the correct size for the screw. Small sizes are generally all that will be required for kite construction work.

Regardless of the type, screwdrivers come in various lengths. Greater leverage can be applied to a screw with a long screwdriver, but this is generally not required for kite construction work, except perhaps for repairing tools.

Handles should feel comfortable and provide a good grip. Handles are often fluted for this purpose. Plastic, wood, and metal handles are all satisfactory.

The price variation in screwdrivers is due to a great extent to the quality and treatment of the steel used for the shank. The shank must withstand considerable twisting force and must not crumble or break.

Combination screwdrivers with interchangeable blades are also available. These allow a variety of blades to be used with a single handle.

Screwdrivers are also available with spring-jaw screw holders. These allow one-hand action for starting screws in tight or awkward places. The screws are generally started into pilot holes in this manner and then tightened down with a regular screwdriver. Magnetized screwdrivers that will hold screws for starting are also available. These will only work on magnetic metals, however.

Planes, Drawknives, and Spokeshaves

Planes (Fig. 4-22), drawknives, and spokeshaves (Fig. 4-23), especially in small sizes designed especially for hobby and craft work, are useful tools for kite construction work. A small plane, for example, can be used to plane and smooth the edges of kite spars. Drawknives and spokeshaves can be used to round the corners of kite spars. I have found the small planes, drawknives, and spokeshaves that come with modeling tool kits to be especially handy for kite construction work.

Files, Rasps, and Surfacing Tools

Files, rasps, and surfacing tools are frequently used in kite construction work. Files have teeth that are formed by long grooves that set at an angle across the faces of the tools. There is a *tang* (Fig. 4-24) at one end that fits into the handle, which is usually made of wood or plastic. Files come in a variety of shapes, including rectangular, square, triangular, half-round, and round (Fig. 4-25). Files are made with various degrees of coarseness, determined by the number of teeth per square inch of scraping surface. The more teeth per square inch, the smoother the scraping surface. Files are available in various lengths. The smaller sizes are most suitable for typical kite construction work. You will probably also want a selection of shapes.

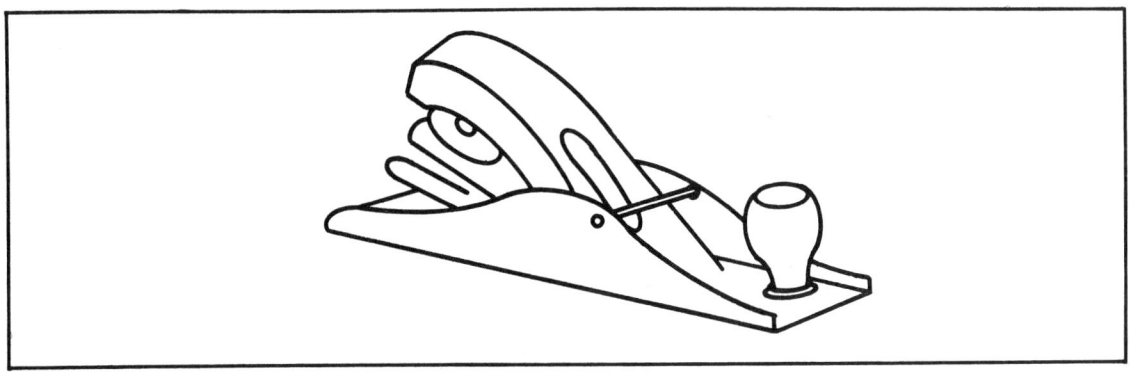

Fig. 4-22. Plane.

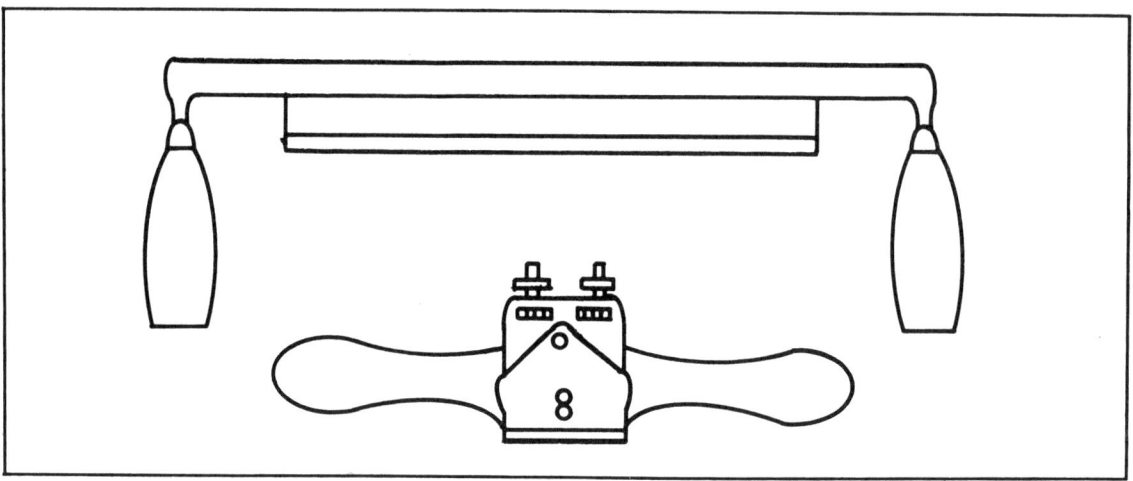

Fig. 4-23. Drawknife, top; and spokeshave, bottom.

Rasps have individual teeth that are arranged in staggered rows. They are generally used for rougher work than are files. Like files, rasps have a tang at one end that fits into a handle of wood or plastic. Rasps come in a variety of shapes, including rectangular, square, triangular, half-round, and round. They are made with various degrees of coarseness, determined by the number of teeth per square inch of scraping surface. The more teeth per square inch, the smoother the scraping surface. For example, for rough shaping of soft woods, a medium-cut rasp with 36 teeth per square inch can be used. For rough shaping of hard woods, a coarse-cut rasp with 26 teeth per square inch might

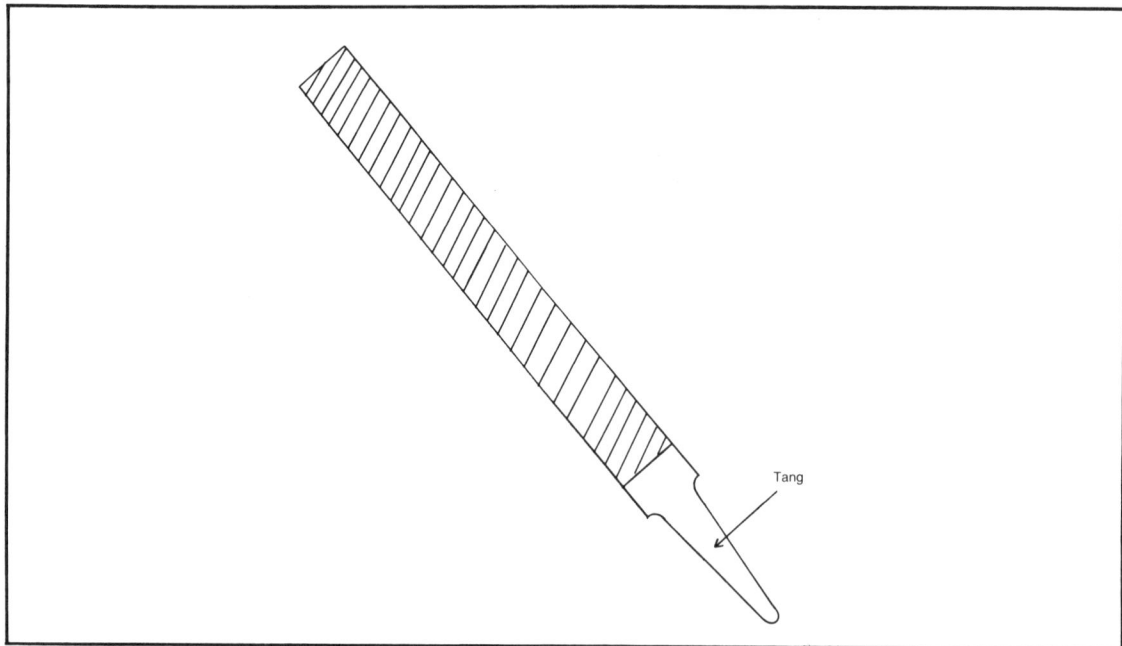

Fig. 4-24. File.

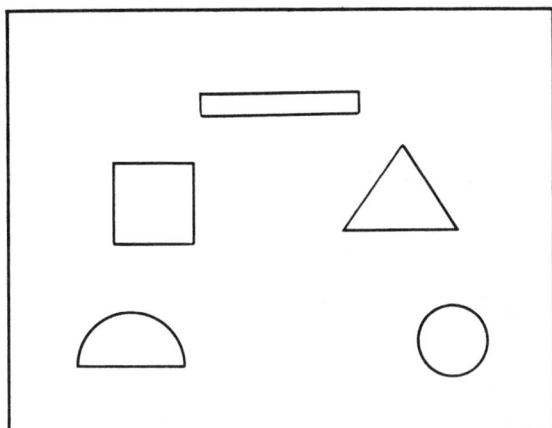

Fig. 4-25. File shapes.

be used. A smooth-cut rasp with 60 teeth per square inch can be used for finishing work.

For each particular kite construction job, you will need to select a rasp that has both the desired shape and required coarseness to accomplish the task. Rasps come in various lengths and sizes, with the shorter lengths and smaller sizes generally being most suitable for kite construction work.

Metal files are also useful for kite construction work. Like wood files, these are available in many shapes and sizes. A flat rectangular, square, triangular, and round file will serve to get you started. Other shapes and sizes can be added as a need develops. Special brushes and file cards are available for removing the metal filings that tend to clog the file teeth when you use them. Metal files can also be used for filing hard plastic materials.

Surfacing tools, also called *forming* tools, are essentially modern versions of traditional rasps, with improved scraping and cutting action due to cutting blades on the teeth and holes all the way through the blades that allow waste wood or plastic to pass through. Surfacing tools are available in a variety of shapes and sizes, including file-types (Fig. 4-26) and plane-types (Fig. 4-27).

Surfacing tools are ideal for shaping wood and soft and hard plastic materials. Considerable wood can be taken off quickly with them. The cutting action is generally superior to that of traditional files and rasps. Surfacing tools are also ideal for shaping soft, rigid plastic foam materials, such as styrofoam, which is being used in the construction of many modern kites. Surfacing tools can also be used on hard plastics such as fiberglass. They are available with both flat and rounded blades (Fig. 4-28) in a variety of sizes.

Surfacing tools are easy to use. For many jobs, I prefer to use them rather than traditional files and rasps. The small sizes and shapes designed for modeling and craft work are especially useful.

Abrasive Papers and Sanding Tools

Abrasive papers are frequently called "sandpaper," although materials other than sand are most commonly used as the abrasive on the papers. Abrasive papers are strong papers that have abrasive materials glued to them.

Abrasive papers are graded: the larger the number, the finer the grit. Most sanding starts with coarser grits (smaller grade numbers) and gradually works down to finer grits (larger grade numbers). Selection of abrasive papers will depend on the material to be sanded and the particular job at hand. Most sandpaper is now sold with, in addition to any grade or grit numbers, designations of coarse, medium-coarse, medium, medium-fine, fine, or very fine. This helps to avoid confusion when purchasing abrasive papers.

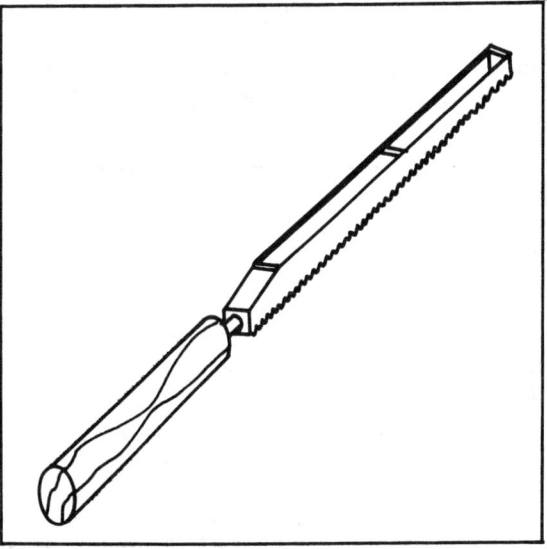

Fig. 4-26. File-type surfacing tool.

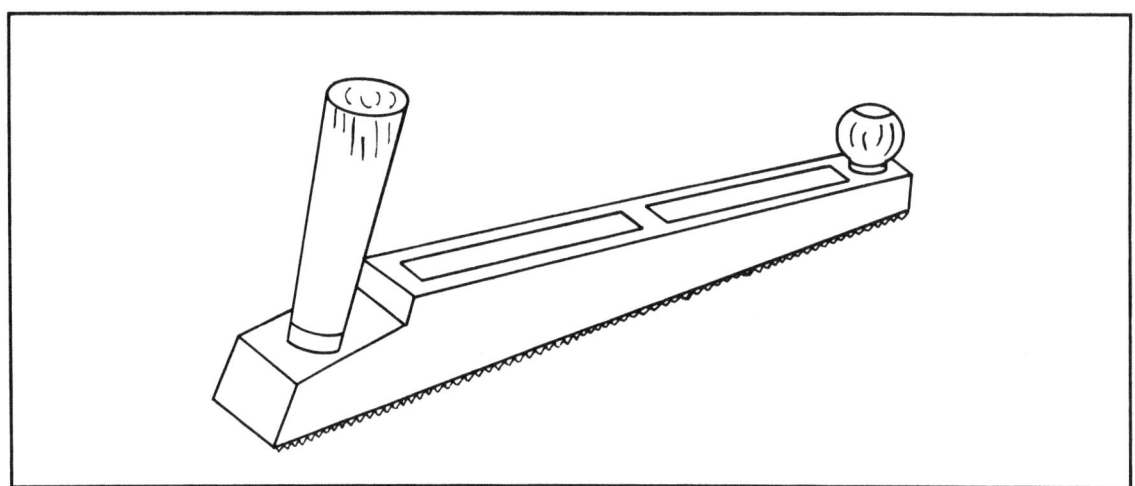

Fig. 4-27. Plane-type surfacing tool.

The common abrasives used for making abrasive papers include flint, which is made of soft sandstone; garnet, which is a hard, reddish-brown mineral; and aluminum oxide and silicon carbide, which are man-made materials. As a general rule, flint abrasive paper is the cheapest, but it does not last long. Garnet and aluminum oxide papers are more expensive, but they last longer and are often the most economical when this is taken into consideration. Silicon carbide is usually the most expensive, but works best for sanding hard abrasive materials, such as fiberglass.

Abrasive papers are sold in both small and large sheets. Large sheets can be cut or torn into smaller pieces that are the right size for hand or block sanding. Abrasive papers can be purchased in packages of assorted grades or grits. These often contain the grades or grits that will be useful for kite construction work.

Sandpaper can be held by hand or a sanding block can be used. The choice depends on the particular job at hand. For maintaining a flat surface, a sanding block is generally recommended. Either a small block of wood can be used (Fig. 4-29) or a manufactured sanding block that has provisions for clamping the paper to the block (Fig. 4-30). Small sanding blocks designed for modeling work are especially handy for kite construction.

Small power sanders designed especially for model work can also be useful for kite construction work. There are three basic types: a pad sander, a disk sander and a belt sander.

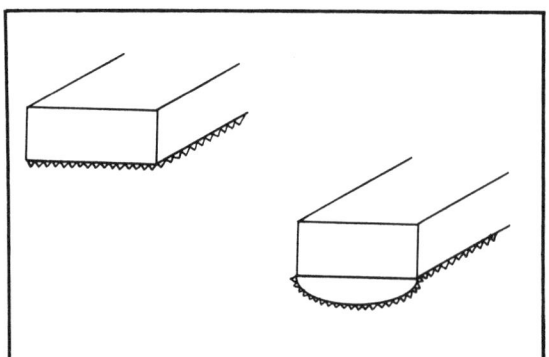

Fig. 4-28. Surfacing tools are available with flat and rounded blades.

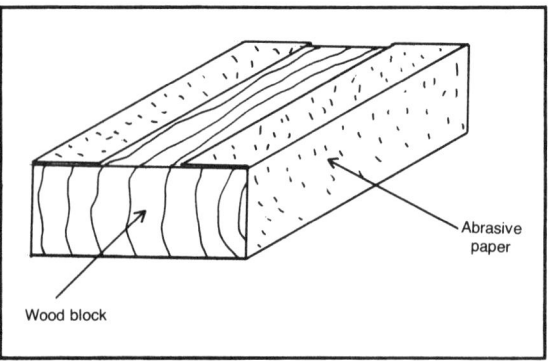

Fig. 4-29. Wood block used for sanding.

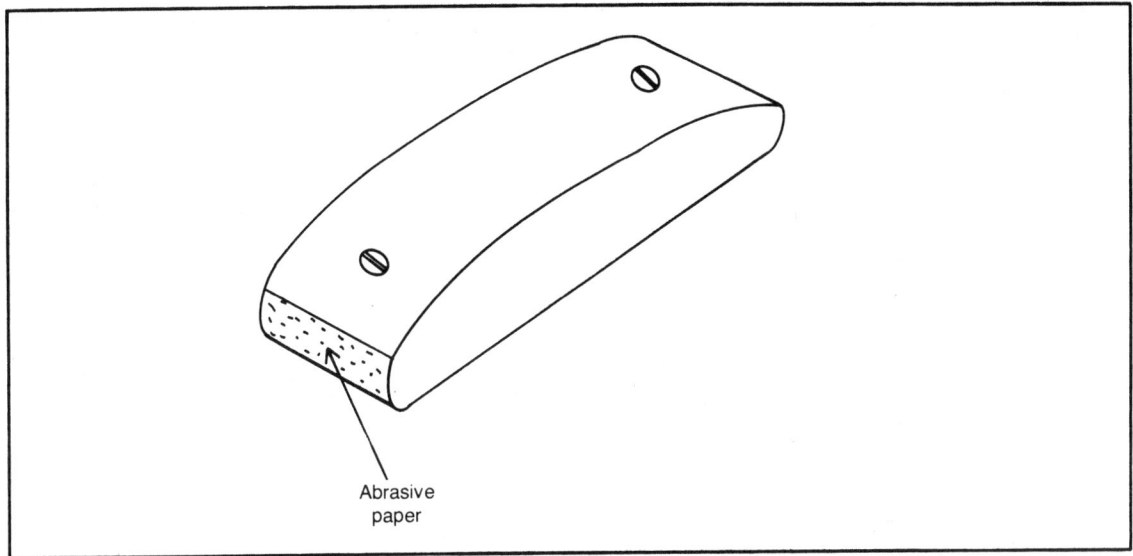

Fig. 4-30. Manufactured sanding block.

Pad sanders are made with orbital, straight line, and combination orbital and straight line actions. They are designed for finishing and light-duty work. In kite construction work, they can be used for smoothing spars and other similar jobs.

Disk sanders have abrasive paper mounted to a rotary disk. These can be attached to hobby rotary tools and portable electric drills. Disk sanders are also available with direct attachment to motors, such as those that attach to scroll saw motors, and with flexible shaft attachments. Disk sanders designed especially for modeling work can be useful for kite building.

Belt sanders, which have a belt of abrasive paper traveling over two drums, are generally not suitable for most kite construction work.

While power sanders can be helpful, they are not essential for making most types of small kites.

Measuring and Marking Tools

Tools for measuring and marking accurately are important for quality kite construction work. Two measuring systems are still in use: American standard and the metric system. The United States is presently in the process of converting to the metric system. Each system can be converted to the other (for example, 1 inch equals 2.540 cen-

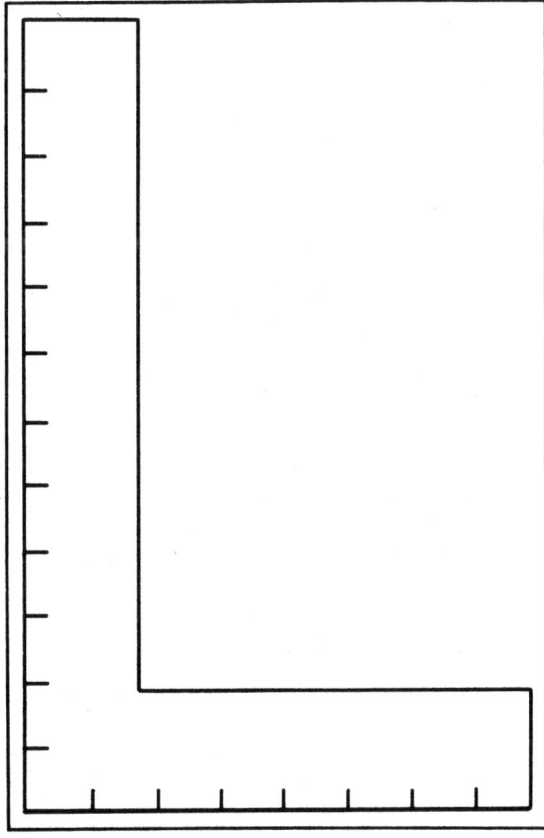

Fig. 4-31. Square.

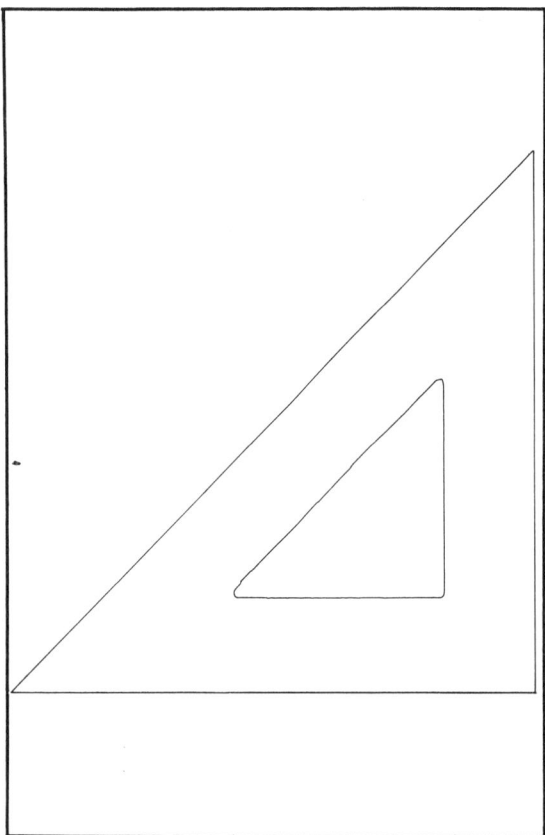

Fig. 4-32. Right-angle triangle.

A variety of drawing and drafting tools, such as drawing boards or tables, T-squares, triangles, protractors, compasses, French curves, and templates, can be useful for laying out patterns on paper and other materials.

A number of devices can be used for marking, including pencils, awls and scribers, pens, crayons, and chalk. The choice depends on the material you are marking. Pencils can be used for marking patterns on wood, paper, and a variety of other materials.

Vises

At least one vise is almost essential for kite construction work. To try to get along without one can greatly reduce the quality of kite construction work. A small vise of either the clamp-on variety (Fig. 4-33) or bench-mounted-type can be used. These vises are generally considered to be metal working vises, but you can clamp all kinds of materials in them.

You don't need a very big vise for constructing small kites, but I suggest a quality vise. The small

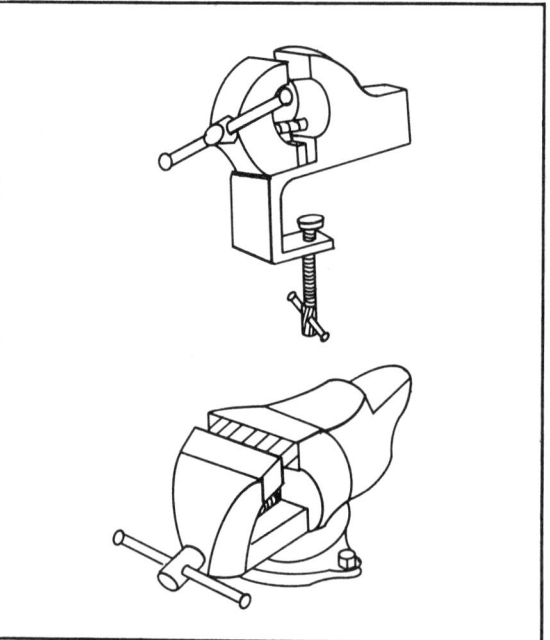

Fig. 4-33. Clamp-on vise, top; and bench-mounted vise, bottom.

timeters), but doing so can be confusing. If you are only familiar with one system, you will probably want to work mainly with it and have your measuring tools in that system. The American standard system is used in this book. A conversion chart or wheel or electronic calculator can be used to convert from one system to the other.

Many types and sizes of rules and tapes are available. For kite construction work, I suggest at least a 1-foot ruler and a yard stick. Steel rulers and straightedges are useful cutting guides for razor blades and knives. A zigzag folding rule or a metal tape rule is useful for measuring longer lengths.

Squares, such as *try squares* (Fig. 4-31), are useful for laying out lines on the materials you are working with. Right-angle triangles, such as those used for drawing and drafting work (Fig. 4-32) can be used similarly.

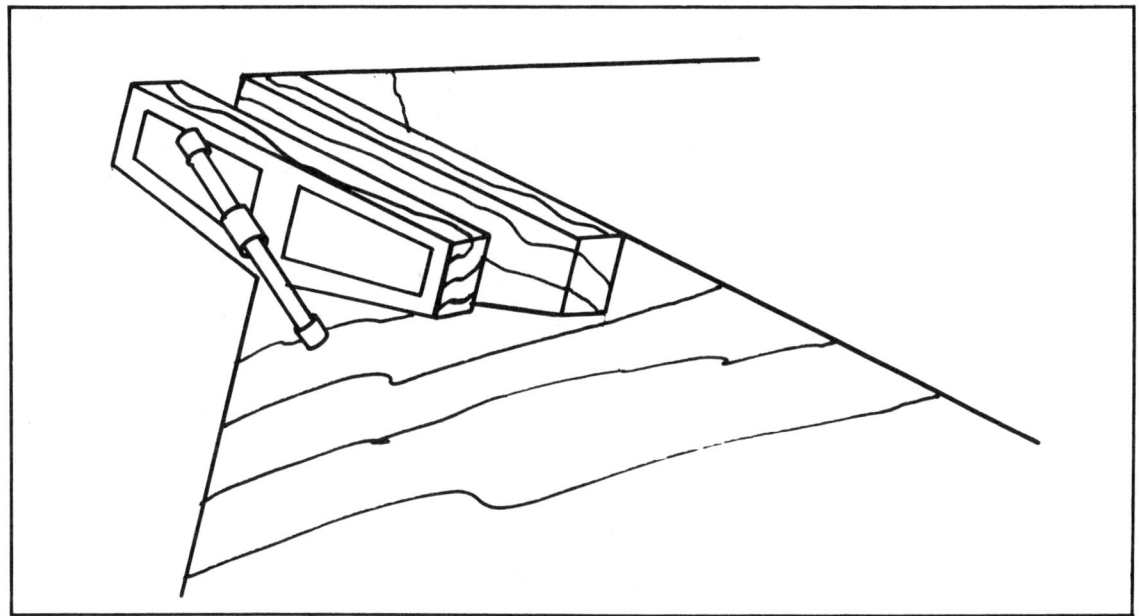

Fig. 4-34. Woodworking bench vise.

models designed for modeling and craft work are ideal, although larger vises can also be used.

A woodworking bench vise (Fig. 4-34) or a work stand with a built-in vise, especially a small hobby unit, can also be useful for kite construction work. The work stands are discussed later in this chapter.

Rotary Hobby Tools

Miniature rotary grinding tools (Fig. 4-35), such as those made by Dremel, Foredom, and Casco, can be useful for some kite construction jobs. These tools have attachments for grinding, drilling, carving, brushing, cutting, sanding, and a variety of other jobs. Some typical attachments are

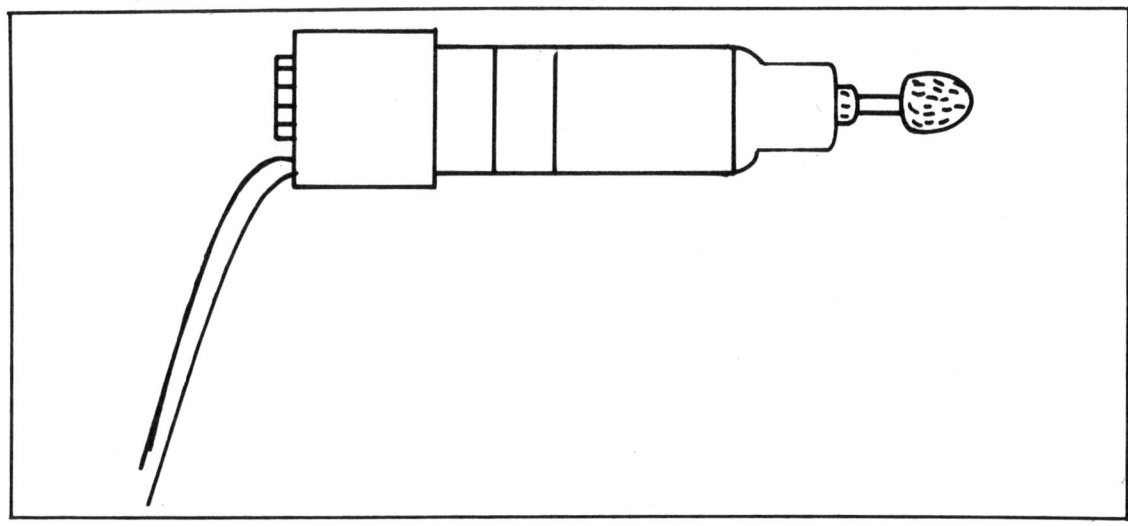

Fig. 4-35. Rotary grinding tool.

Fig. 4-36. Attachments for rotary hobby tool.

shown in Fig. 4-36. Rotary hobby tools rate high with many kite builders. A single tool with appropriate attachments can do a variety of jobs that are typically encountered in kite construction.

Rotary tool attachments can also be used on a flexible shaft that attaches to a fixed motor. Dremel, for example, makes a flexible shaft attachment that connects to their scroll saws. These can be used in a manner similar to the portable hand tools.

Soldering Tools

Soldering can add new dimensions to kite building. Soldering irons can be used for joining a variety of metals to make fittings for kites. They can also be used to seal and join a variety of synthetic fabrics.

There are two basic types of soldering irons: pencil (Fig. 4-37) and gun (Fig. 4-38). The pencil-types generally take some time to heat up, but they provide a constant heat after that. The gun-type heat up almost at once. Both types can be used for kite construction work. I find the pencil-type to be more useful.

You can also do soldering with a torch. This, however, is not generally very practical for kite construction work.

Regardless of the method you use for providing heat, you will need solder and resin or acid for joining metals together. Solders come in various mixtures of tin and lead or other metals. The choice depends on the particular metals you intend to join. Solder is available with the resin or acid as a core material, or you can purchase solder without a resin or acid core and purchase the required resin or acid separately, and apply it to the metal with a brush applicator. Solder is generally sold with directions for using it, what metals can be joined with it, and so on.

It will take some practice to learn to solder (see Chapter 5), but this can be worthwhile, especially for advanced kite construction work.

Other Tools

The tools discussed so far are the most important ones for kite construction work, but there are many other tools that you may find useful.

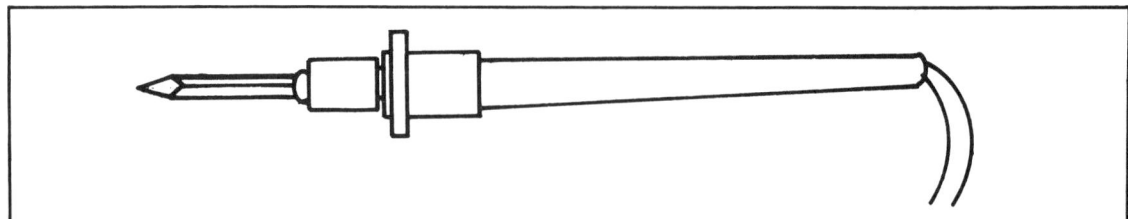

Fig. 4-37. Pencil-type soldering tool.

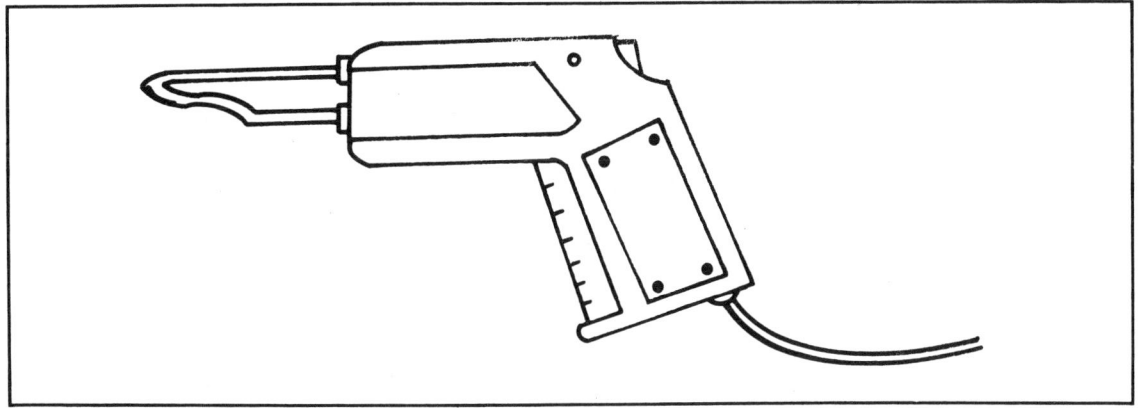

Fig. 4-38. Gun-type soldering tool.

A round-hole paper punch (Fig. 4-39) is handy for making neat holes to pass strings through paper kites. While other tools, such as an ice pick or awl, can be used for the same work, a paper punch does the job better. Paper punches can be purchased wherever stationery and office supplies are sold.

Tweezers are useful for handling small parts and pulling string through loops and other tight places.

Although a rotary hobby tool, described above, can be used for grinding and wire brushing operations, I find a larger bench-mounted power grinder to also be useful, especially for sharpening tools used for kite construction work. I like a grinding wheel on one end and a wire brush on the other. The wire brush is useful for cleaning metal parts.

You will also need brushes and various other tools for painting and decorating kites (see Chapter 9).

While small kites are not generally bolted together, although this is certainly a possibility, wrenches are frequently required for adjusting and repairing tools. Wrenches are available in a variety of types, including box, end, and adjustable configurations. If you do intend to use small bolts as fasteners on kites, you will need small wrenches that fit these.

As you go along in kite construction, you will

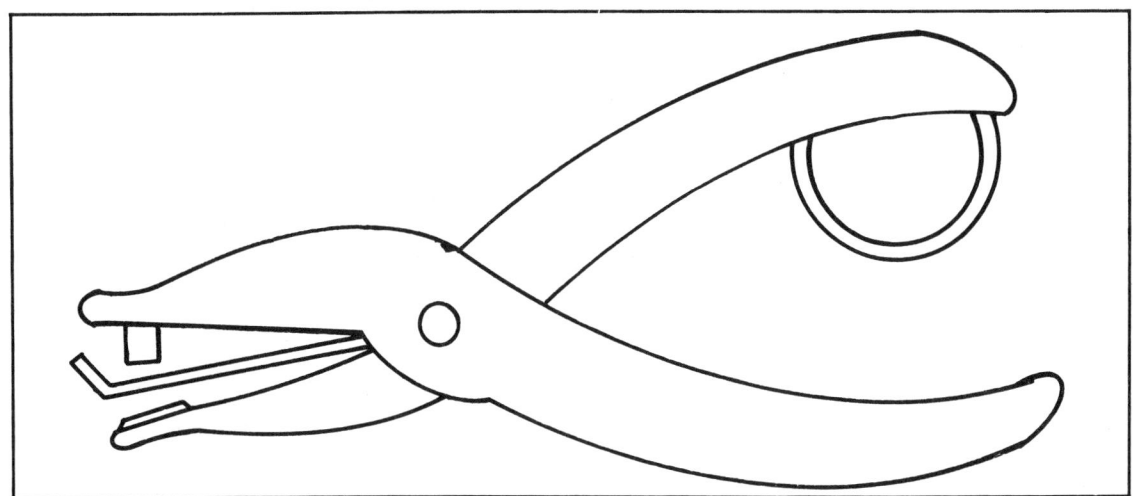

Fig. 4-39. Paper punch.

probably find that you need other tools. These can be added to your tool collection when a need develops. Kite construction tool collections have a way of growing as your interest and involvement in this hobby increase.

SAFETY EQUIPMENT

Compared to many construction hobbies, kite construction is reasonably safe. You will, however, be working with tools with sharp blades, paints and glues that may have toxic fumes or vapors, and so on. You will need all required safety guards and other equipment required for the safe use of power tools. For grinding and sanding, especially with power tools, you will need safety goggles made of tough plastic materials. Many models will fit over eyeglasses. They are quite inexpensive compared to the degree of protection they provide. You will also need a disposable dust mask. These should not be used for toxic vapors or fumes, however. For protection from toxic vapors or fumes, you will need a respirator designed especially to provide protection from the particular vapors or fumes. A plastic face shield can be worn whenever you are doing grinding work.

WORKBENCHES

It is often said that you can use the kitchen table as a workbench for a hobby like constructing kites. Well, perhaps, but I see a number of problems with this. First, kitchen tables are generally not sturdy enough to be considered "real" workbenches. Second, you can easily damage the kitchen table, especially if you use a saw or power tools. Third, you will usually have to share the table with other things (like eating). And, kitchen tables usually are not appropriately located for kite construction work. If you do sanding, for example, will the sawdust you generate get mixed in with food?

It is much better to have a "real" workbench for kite construction work. If you already have a workbench that you have been using for general woodworking, modeling work, or other uses, you can probably also use this for your kite construction work. It is generally much better to share a workbench than to share a kitchen table.

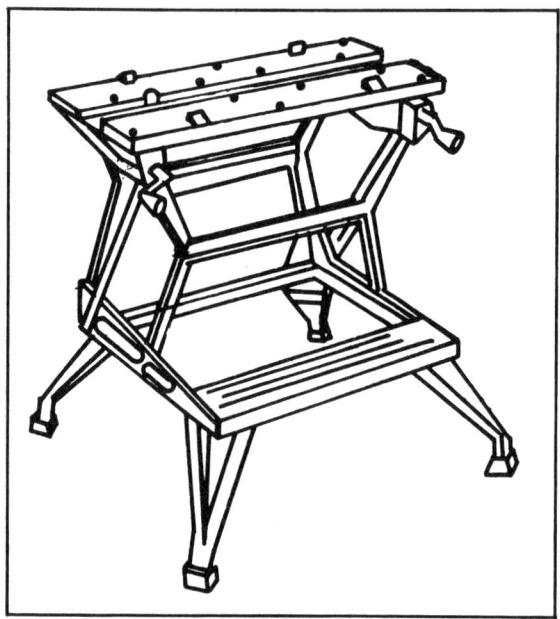

Fig. 4-40. Portable shop bench with built-in vise and clamping arrangement.

You can also purchase or build workbenches to suit your particular needs. Here are some important considerations:

● A workbench should be sturdy. If you already have a workbench that is not sturdy enough, add braces or reinforcements to improve it.

● A workbench should be at a convenient working height. This can be either for sitting or standing, depending on how you like to work.

● A workbench should have a top of adequate size for the work you intend to do. For general kite construction work, a top that is 2 by 3 feet is about the minimum practical size. A larger working area is usually better.

● Space and storage areas for tools, materials, and supplies is an important consideration.

I find a small portable shop bench of the type shown in Fig. 4-40 to be a useful addition to a permanent workbench but not a substitute for it. The unit shown has a built-in vise and clamping arrangement that I find extremely useful. The model shown has its own stand, but others are available for use on workbenches. These are especially designed for hobby and craft work.

WORK AREAS

A work area should provide protection from the weather (although this can be outdoors if the weather is good), yet allow you to do jobs such as sanding, painting, and sawing. Garages, basements, and hobby or recreation rooms are typical suitable locations. Here are some important considerations:

- The area should allow for messy work, such as sanding, sawing, and painting, Rooms in your house that contain rugs and furniture generally aren't suitable.
- The area should have good ventilation. If you plan to do much painting, you might want to consider adding an exhaust fan.
- Good lighting is important. It is difficult to do quality kite construction work if you can't see what you are doing. The lighting can be natural, artificial, or a combination of the two.
- The area should be used exclusively for kite construction or shared with other compatible activities.

MATERIALS

A variety of materials, from traditional wood, bamboo, paper, and cotton string to modern space-age synthetics, are used in modern kite construction.

Wood

Regardless of whether you use softwood or hardwood, you will need the wood cut to sticks of the desired size. You can cut you own from larger stock, as detailed in Chapter 5, or you can purchase sticks precut to various sizes. Dowels, which come in various diameters, are readily available and suitable for many kite constructions. Square and other rectangular shapes in small sizes suitable for kite sticks are also readily available.

Wood, along with bamboo is a traditional material for making kite sticks. As a general rule, you will want to use the lightest and strongest woods available, but because the heavier woods are also frequently the strongest woods, compromises will have to be made. The best compromises to make will depend on the particular kite you are making.

Balsa wood is a lightweight wood. Balsa (*Ochroma pyramidale*) is a fast-growing tree of tropical America. Most balsa wood comes from Ecuador. Balsa is botanically a hardwood, but physically it is very soft, in fact, one of the softest and lightest of all commercial woods. The approximate weight per cubic foot of air-seasoned balsa is 8 pounds. The heartwood is usually pale brown, sometimes slightly tinged with red. The sapwood varies from white to pale gray, and it has a uniform texture.

While balsa wood is widely used in model-making, it has only limited usefulness for use as kite sticks because it lacks strength. When used as kite sticks, it tends to snap from stresses placed on the kite by the wind and other factors. Balsa wood is often adequate, however, for miniature kites, as detailed in later chapters.

Balsa wood is readily available from hobby stores precut to sticks of various dimensions. This is a very convenient way to purchase balsa for kite construction. You can also purchase balsa in larger dimensions and ripsaw it into the desired stick sizes.

If you want to cut balsa with a knife, a razor-type blade is usually required. A razor blade can also be used.

Sheets of balsa, available from hobby stores, are sometimes used as covering material for miniature and small kites, as detailed later in this chapter.

Both softwoods (coniferous trees) and hardwoods (deciduous tress) can be used as kite sticks and framing. The choice depends on the particular kite being constructed. For some kites, the extra strength of the hardwoods would not compensate for the extra weight; for other types and or sizes of kites, it would.

White pine (*Pinus strobus*) is grown in the United States from Maine to northern Georgia and in Lake States. The botanical classification is softwood. The approximate weight per cubic foot of air-seasoned white pine is 25 pounds. It is a finely textured wood with a yellow-white color and is an excellent wood for kite sticks on many types and sizes of kites. It's an easy wood with which to work and is fairly inexpensive and widely available in the United States. Of all the domestic pine woods, white pine is probably the most suitable for use as kite sticks.

Ponderosa pine (*Pinus ponderosa*) grows in California, Oregon, Washington, Idaho, Montana, the southern Rockies, South Dakota, and Wyoming. It is considered to be the most important pine tree of the western United States. The botanical classification is softwood. The approximate weight per cubic foot of air-seasoned ponderosa pine is 28 pounds. The color of the wood is a light yellowish white. Ponderosa pine has a straight and uniform grain, which makes it ideal for kite sticks. It's also an easy wood to work with, is readily available, and fairly inexpensive.

Sugar pine (*Pinus lambertiana*) grows in California and southwestern Oregon. The botanical classification is softwood. The approximate weight per cubic foot of air-seasoned sugar pine is 25 pounds. It has a straight and uniform grain, making it ideal for kite sticks. It's also an easy wood to work with and is readily available and fairly inexpensive.

Spruce is a name applied to any of the various coniferous evergreen trees of the genus *Picea*. The three main kinds are eastern spruce, Engelmann spruce, and Sitka spruce. All are lightweight woods that are botanically classified as softwoods. The approximate weight per cubic foot of air-seasoned spruce is 28 pounds.

Spruce, especially Sitka spruce, has long been a favorite wood for kite sticks. It is a strong wood that is easily worked. It is readily available and reasonably priced, although generally more expensive than pine woods.

Douglas fir (*Pseudotsuga menziesii*) grows from the Pacific Coast to the Rockies, and from central British Columbia to Mexico. It is botanically a softwood. The approximate weight per cubic foot of air-seasoned Douglas fir is 31 pounds. The color varies from pale to medium red-brown. It is a moderately dense wood with a straight, close grain and is one of the strongest of the botanical softwoods. Douglas fir is suitable for kite sticks, although it does have considerable tendency to split and check. Douglas fir is readily available and fairly inexpensive.

Other fir woods, including Western fir and white fir, can also be used for making kite spars.

There are hundreds of other softwoods that can and have been successfully used for making kite sticks and frames. In many cases, you will be able to use whatever softwoods you happen to have on hand or can be obtained in the area where you live. Keep in mind, however, that some will work better than others.

For some kites, hardwoods can be used for making the sticks. One popular choice is ash (any of various trees of the genus *Fraxinus*). Ash grows in many parts of the United States, and is often readily available and inexpensive. The approximate weight per cubic foot of air-seasoned ash is 45 pounds. It is a heavy, hard, and strong wood with a straight grain.

Another popular hardwood is oak (*Quercus*). Oak grows in North America, Europe, and northern Asia. The approximate weight per cubic foot of air-seasoned oak is 43 pounds. Oak is a hard, strong wood with great lasting qualities. The two types most readily available in the United States are red oak and white oak. Oak is generally fairly expensive.

Many other hardwoods can also be used for making kite sticks. You may want to do some experimenting with locally available types.

Bamboo

Bamboo is another traditional material for making kite sticks, especially in China and Japan. Bamboo is also used extensively for modern kites and is readily available in the United States. One possibility is to obtain lengths of bamboo pole (the stems of bamboo) and then to cut these into narrow strips for kite sticks, as detailed in Chapter 5. Another possibility is to purchase the bamboo already cut into narrow strips. (A bamboo window shade can provide a quantity of suitable strips of bamboo.)

Other Materials

There is a strong trend toward using various

plastics for kite sticks. A variety of rigid plastic rods and tubings give the necessary combination of light weight and strength needed. Fiberglass rod, for example, is extremely strong, yet flexible. While the fabrication of fiberglass kite sticks from resin and glass fibers is quite involved, prefabricated fiberglass rods can be purchased. One excellent source is old fiberglass fishing rods, which turn up frequently at flea markets and junk stores.

Various lightweight metal alloys, such as aluminum, can also be used for kite sticks. For large kites, this becomes quite practical.

Other possibilities for making kite sticks and frames are explored in later chapters.

Covering Materials

A variety of materials can be used for covering kites. Paper is the most traditional material, and it remains a popular choice today. Many kinds of paper can be used, including newspapers, tissue paper, craft paper, and rice paper. Strong, lightweight papers that do not permit air to pass through them are ideal.

Cloth materials are becoming increasingly popular for use as kite covering materials. Silk has long been popular, and ordinary muslin is sometimes used for larger kites. Lightweight nylon is suitable for even small kites. It's available in weights of 1 ounce or less per square yard. Various nylon materials fabricated for sailboat spinnakers make an excellent kite covering material.

Various plastic materials are rapidly replacing paper as the favorite kite covering material. Polyethylene plastic, which is the type that many garbage and garment bags are made from, is a popular choice. It is readily obtainable. Polyethylene sheet plastic is available in various thicknesses and colors.

Various other plastic materials of the space age, such as Mylar, are becoming increasing popular for use as kite covering materials. Mylar is strong and lightweight. It is presently quite expensive, but is often worth the price when you need a covering material that is extremely lightweight and strong.

The choice of a covering material for a particular kite depends on the particular design, the size of the kite, and other factors. For some of the designs detailed in this book, a choice of covering materials will give satisfactory results. In other cases, a certain type of covering material will be essential. Also, you may want to experiment with new materials as they come on the market.

String and Thread

String or line is used not only for flying kites (see Chapter 10), but also for framing kites, binding sticks and frame pieces together, and making bridles. String and line made from natural materials is rapidly being replaced by synthetic materials. Polyester and twisted nylon string are both popular. Polyester has the advantage of having less stretch and being easier to tie. Nylon monofilament line, such as the type sold as fishing line, is another possibility, although it can be difficult to tie.

Thread can be used as string for small kites. Even small-gauge polyester and nylon thread can have a high breaking strength. I can't break the #16 polyester thread I use for hand sewing for example. Thread can be used like string for binding kite sticks together, and it is also useful for sewing covering fabrics.

Glues

A variety of modern glues are ideal for general kite construction. White hobby glues can be used for joining a variety of porous materials, including heavier grades of paper. Rubber and various plastic cements can be used for lighter papers. A variety of plastic cements formulated for model building are ideal for many kite construction jobs. Epoxy glues are ideal for making strong wood joints. Quick drying epoxy glues are now sold for hobby use that give excellent results. Plastic materials may require special glues, as detailed in later chapters.

Other Materials

There are many other materials useful for kite constructions. A variety of tapes including cellulose adhesive tape, strapping tape, and plastic tape can be used for joining materials, reinforcement, or decoration.

Fasteners can be used for joining kite parts—pins, small wire brads and nails, screws, and bolts.

Small wire is useful for a variety of jobs. A variety of metals and plastics can be used for making kite fittings. For example, a section of plastic tubing can be used for joining two wooden dowels that will just fit inside the tubing. Thin sheets of aluminum, brass, and copper are useful for fabricating small metal fittings.

Rigid plastic foam materials, especially styrofoam, are being used increasingly for kite construction. Thin sheets can be used as a covering material on some kites. Kites can also be formed from sheets of styrofoam without the use of kite sticks. In this case, the styrofoam acts as both the frame and the covering material.

For decorating kites, you may need paints, dyes, and other materials, as detailed in Chapter 9.

Chapter 5

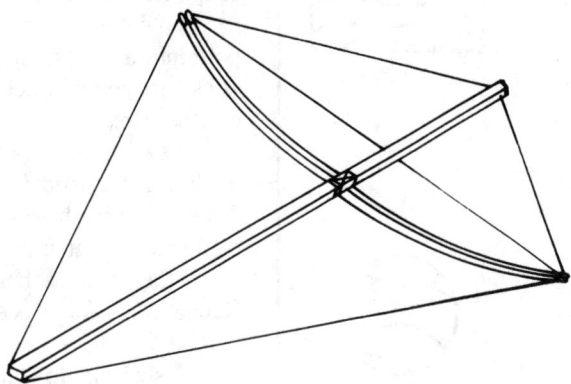

Basic Construction Techniques

If you intend to build your own kites, this chapter is extremely important. Once you master the basic skills and techniques of kite making, the construction of a variety of interesting kites, such as those detailed in Chapters 6, 7, and 8 will be relatively easy. These same techniques can also be used for constructing original kite designs.

KITE STICKS AND FRAMES

A kite's frame members are often called *sticks* or *spars*. We will use the term stick to refer to long slender frame members, regardless of whether they are wood, bamboo, metal, plastic, or some other material.

An important part of many kite constructions is assembling the individual sticks into frames. Various methods are used for joining sticks. Many frames also require various reinforcements.

Wood

A variety of woods can be used for kite sticks (see Chapter 4). Kite sticks can be one of a variety of cross section shapes, including square, rectangular, triangular, and round (Fig. 5-1). You can purchase sticks preshaped in a variety of woods (see Chapter 4). You can also cut square and rectangular shapes from larger wood stock. A variety of saws can be used for doing this. To make accurate and straight cuts, a circular table power saw with a guide can be used. The sawing can also be done with hand saws, but straight and accurate cutting can be difficult. A knife can be used to cut balsa and other soft woods into strips by using either a metal straightedge as a guide (Fig. 5-2) or a special knife guide designed for this purpose (Fig. 5-3).

After cutting the wood into sticks with the correct cross sections, sanding may be required to smooth the edges. Use a sanding block to maintain an even surface.

The sticks are next cut to the required lengths for a particular kite construction. Mark the pattern lines for the cuts on the wood with a sharp pencil. For accurate square cuts, use a square for making the pattern line (Fig. 5-4). A knife can be used to cut balsa and other soft woods, or a saw can be used for both soft and hard woods. The wood can be fastened in a vise for sawing.

For many kites, the sticks will require notches in the ends for string or connections to other sticks. Some typical notch patterns are shown in Fig. 5-5.

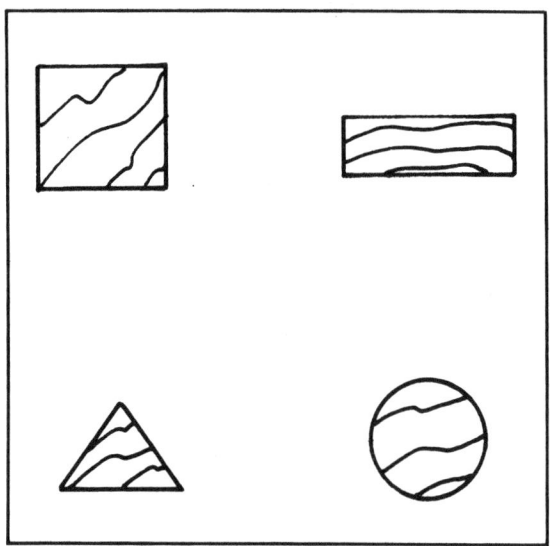

Fig. 5-1. Cross sectional shapes of wood kite sticks.

Mark the pattern lines on the wood with a sharp pencil. These can be cut in balsa and other soft woods with a knife, or a coping saw, power jigsaw, or scroll saw can be used for both soft and hard woods.

Bamboo

Bamboo makes an excellent framing material for kites and was probably used for the first kites. Bamboo can be purchased precut into narrow strips or slats. These can also be taken from the roll-up type of bamboo shades, or you can cut your own strips from bamboo poles.

To cut a bamboo pole into sticks, first cut the pole into a length slightly longer than the longest stick that you will need. A hacksaw can be used to cut the bamboo.

Next, split the pole in half. A knife with a sharp blade can be used for this, as shown in Fig. 5-6. Take half of the bamboo and use a knife with a sharp blade to split it into strips of the desired width, using the same technique used to halve the pole. Repeat the same procedure on the other half of the pole.

A sharp knife is next used to smooth the bamboo strips and shape them as desired. The knuckles should be trimmed slightly. This must be done carefully, however. The basic idea is to make the

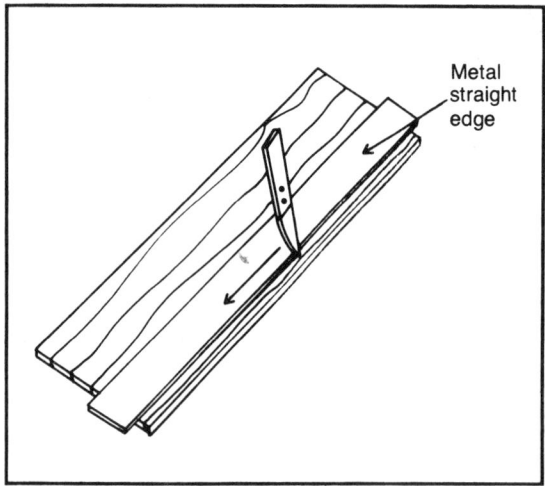

Fig. 5-2. Using metal straight edge as guide for knife for cutting wood into strips.

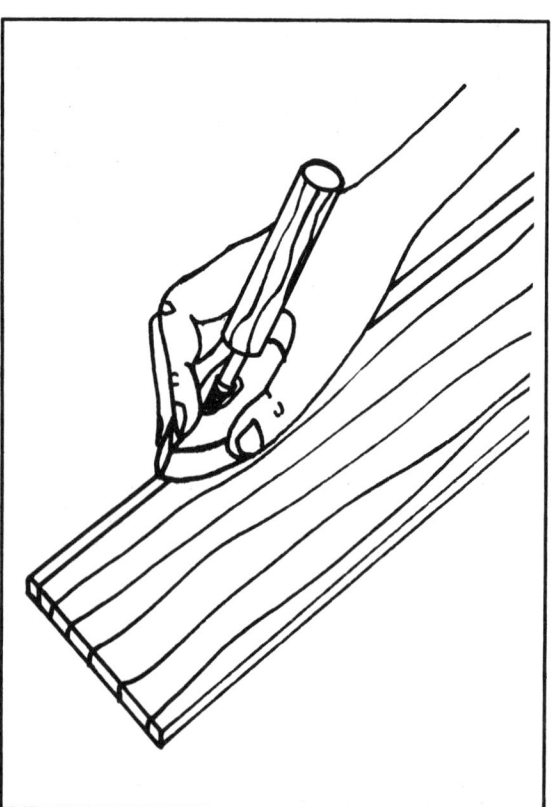

Fig. 5-3. Knife guide used for cutting wood into strips.

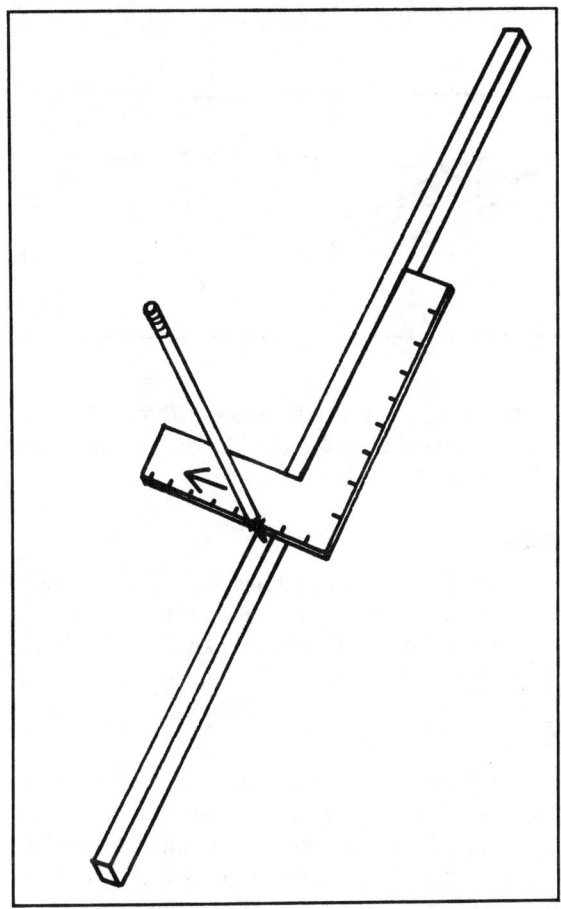

Fig. 5-4. Square is used as guide for making square-cut pattern lines.

stick as neat as possible without creating a weak area at the knuckle.

In some cases, further shaping will be required. The sticks may require taper near the ends or even a variety of thicknesses in the same stick. Most kite constructions, however, require basically straight sticks of uniform thicknesses along the entire length. Regardless of the cross section of the sticks, they can be sanded smooth using a sanding block. In some cases, the sticks are rounded. To round a stick, first use a sharp knife to round off the corners. Then even up the cuts and sand smooth with a sanding block.

Many kite constructions require notches in the ends of the sticks. A coping saw or power jig or scroll saw can be used. Mark the pattern line on the bamboo; then fasten the bamboo in a vise to saw.

Bamboo can easily be formed to desired curves by heating it. This can be done by moving it through a candle flame, as shown in Fig. 5-7. Before doing this, mark the desired curve on a piece of cardboard. Use this as a guide for shaping the bamboo. Then move the bamboo through the candle flame and bend it to the desired curve, using the pattern on the cardboard as a guide. When heating bamboo, take care not to hold the bamboo in one position too long, as this can deform the bamboo or even burn it. Overheating bamboo tends to make it brittle.

For most kite constructions, the bamboo is underbent so that it will have spring tension. For

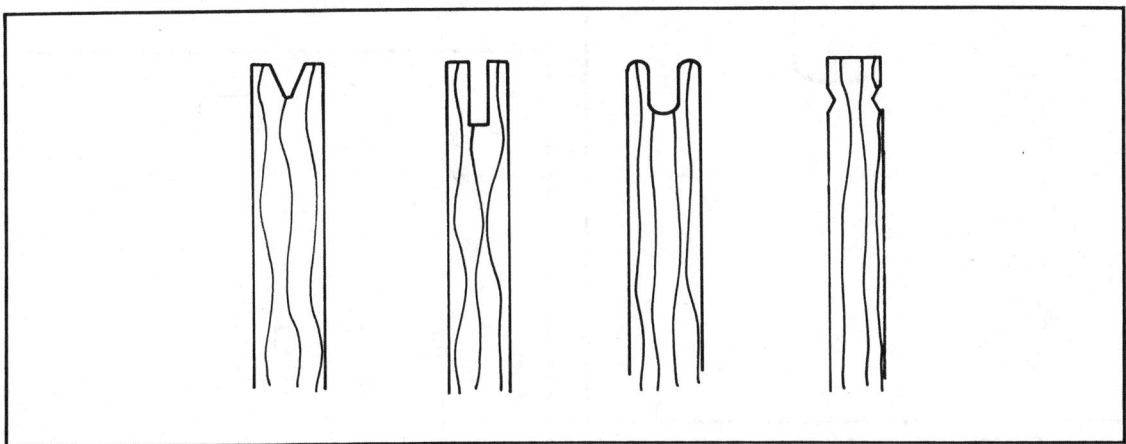

Fig. 5-5. Notches in ends of kite sticks.

61

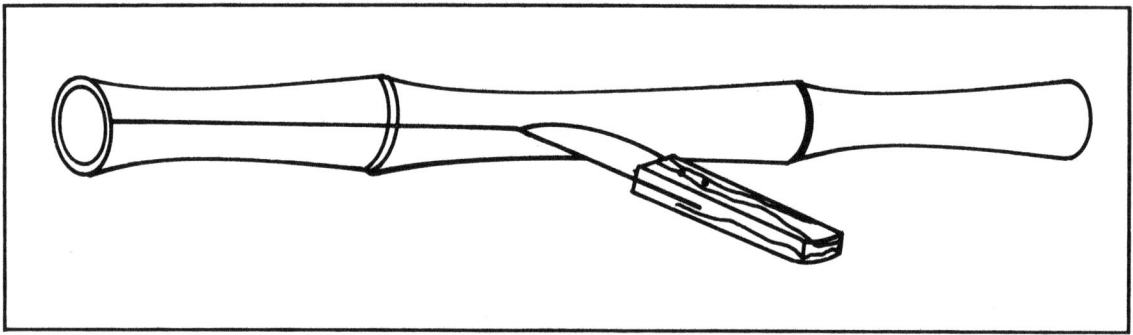

Fig. 5-6. Knife is used to split bamboo pole.

example, to form a circle, the circle is underbent. When the ends of the bamboo are joined together, the circle will be under spring tension, resulting in a stronger frame. Small sticks can sometimes be formed into circles without heating. Heating can then be used to remove any irregularities in the circle.

In some cases, small diameter bamboo poles are used for kite sticks, without cutting them into strips. This gives a round stick with considerable strength. Bamboo poles can be heat-formed in the same manner as strips.

Rattan

Rattan is also used for making curved or bowed kite sticks. Diameters of from about ⅛ inch to ¼ inch in diameter are useful for kite sticks. Rattan can be heat-formed in the same manner as bamboo.

Metal

Lightweight metals and alloys, especially thin-walled aluminum tubing, are being used increasingly for kite sticks. Aluminum rods and tubing are available in various sizes and lengths from hobby shops and hardware stores. Aluminum is also available in various other cross sectional shapes, including square, rectangular, triangular, I beam, and L shape (Fig. 5-8).

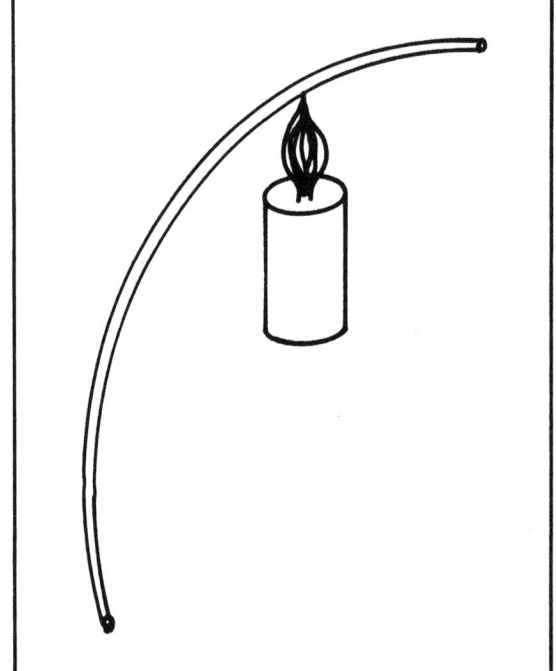

Fig. 5-7. Bamboo strip is moved through a candle flame for heat forming.

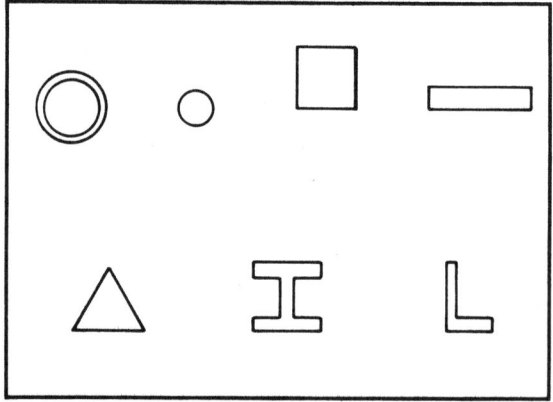

Fig. 5-8. Cross sectional shapes of aluminum.

All cross sections of aluminum can be cut with a hacksaw or other metal-cutting saw. A tube cutter can be used to cut aluminum tubing.

Aluminum can be bent to form curved kite sticks. Aluminum rod and square and rectangular cross sections can be bent by hand or over various forms, such as around a metal drum for a circle shape. Aluminum tubing can be bent similarly, except that there is considerable danger of deforming the walls of the tubing. This can be largely avoided by using a tube bender. Inexpensive tube benders are available for small diameter tubing at hobby and hardware stores.

Other metals and alloys besides aluminum can also be used for kite spars, especially those that are very light in weight.

Plastic

A variety of plastic materials can be used for kite sticks. For example, plastic straws can be used for making miniature kites. A variety of plastic rods and tubes, as well as other cross sectional shapes, have the necessary combination of strength, rigidity, and light weight for use as kite frames and sticks. Flexible and semirigid plastics show much promise for kites that require semirigid forms.

Fiberglass rod is being used increasingly as a kite framing material. Compared to its weight, fiberglass is a strong, flexible, and resilient material. Fiberglass is a combination of glass fiber reinforcing material and a resin, usually polyester or epoxy, that is used to form a hard composite material that has great strength. The physical properties of fiberglass depend on the type and amount of glass fiber reinforcing material, the type and quality of resin, the fabrication method, and other factors. Not all fiberglass is created equally.

Fiberglass is available in preshaped rod forms of various diameters that are suitable for making kite frames. Old fiberglass fishing rods, which are often available from junk and thrift stores, are another possibility.

Various nonglass reinforcing materials, including acrylic and carbon fibers, are now being used with plastic resins to form fiberglasslike materials. Carbon fiber reinforced plastic forms a material that has a greater strength-to-weight ratio than does fiberglass. This material, while presently very expensive, shows great promise for making lightweight kites that are extremely strong.

A great variety of plastic materials are available for kite sticks, and these have different properties that effect cutting, filing, sanding, and working. (Since fiberglass is an exciting material for kite construction, this material is treated in detail below). The properties of many other plastic materials that can be used for kite sticks and frames varies greatly, but many can be cut with hacksaws or other metal-cutting saws. Many can be filed with metal files. It will take some experimentation to determine what tools and techniques work best for a particular plastic. Some plastics in hardened form can be heat-formed; others can't. Some plastics are available in preshaped forms, such as rings, that are suitable for certain kite constructions. Plastic ring frames can also be cut from plastic bottles and other plastic objects.

Fiberglass has considerable potential for use as kite sticks and frames. For our purposes here, we will assume that you will be using preshaped fiberglass rods or other preshaped lengths of fiberglass to make kite sticks and frames. Fiberglassing (chemically forming fiberglass from liquid resin and fiberglass reinforcing materials) will be considered later in this chapter for the purpose of bonding fiberglass sticks and frames together, but the assumption is that you will be using preformed, cured, or hard fiberglass stock for the stick and frame pieces. (You could, however, make your own sticks and frame pieces from liquid resin and reinforcing materials, thus allowing you to vary thicknesses for strength where it is required while keeping weight to an absolute minimum.)

When working with cured fiberglass, certain health and safety precautions should be observed. Anyone who has sanded fiberglass without skin protection knows that fiberglass sanding dust makes your skin itch. This fine dust is also raised when sawing, filing, and grinding cured fiberglass. This dust can cause not only skin problems, but also eye and respiratory problems.

Protective clothing can be worn to keep the

fiberglass dust from your skin. If, despite all precautions, some sanding dust does get on the skin, this usually isn't much of a problem. A cold shower followed by application of hand lotion will often help to relieve itching. If skin rash or other unusual reactions develop, a physician should be consulted.

A properly fitted dust mask and eye goggles can be worn to give respiratory and eye protection. These precautions are extremely important.

Wearing proper protective clothing for working with cured fiberglass may be uncomfortable, especially in hot weather, but this slight discomfort and inconvenience is a necessary and important sacrifice for the protection of your health.

Frequent operations that will be required on cured fiberglass members include drilling, sawing, filing, and sanding. It is generally easy to drill small holes in fiberglass. Although a hand drill can be used, a portable electric drill or drill press will make the work much easier. Metal twist bits can be used, but you must have a different size for each hole size you intend to drill. Before drilling, carefully mark the desired location for the hole. A center punch or other sharp-pointed object is used to make a small indentation or *pilot mark* for centering the point of the bit. Center the point of the bit in a small indentation or pilot mark. Angle the drill as desired and drill the hole through the fiberglass.

There are many situations where you will want to saw fiberglass. For example, fiberglass rods for kite sticks will probably require cutting. The sawing can be done with a hacksaw or a coping saw with a fine-tooth cutting blade. When making critical cuts, leave little extra and then use a file, as detailed below, to take it to final size.

Notches (Fig. 5-9) can be cut in the ends of fiberglass frame pieces with a hacksaw or a coping saw with a fine-toothed cutting blade.

Metal files can be used for filing fiberglass. Filing can be used to round the ends of frame pieces, and to shape and make grooves and notches. As a general rule, pressure is applied to the file on the forward stroke only. Lift the file off of the work when drawing it back. If the file notches become

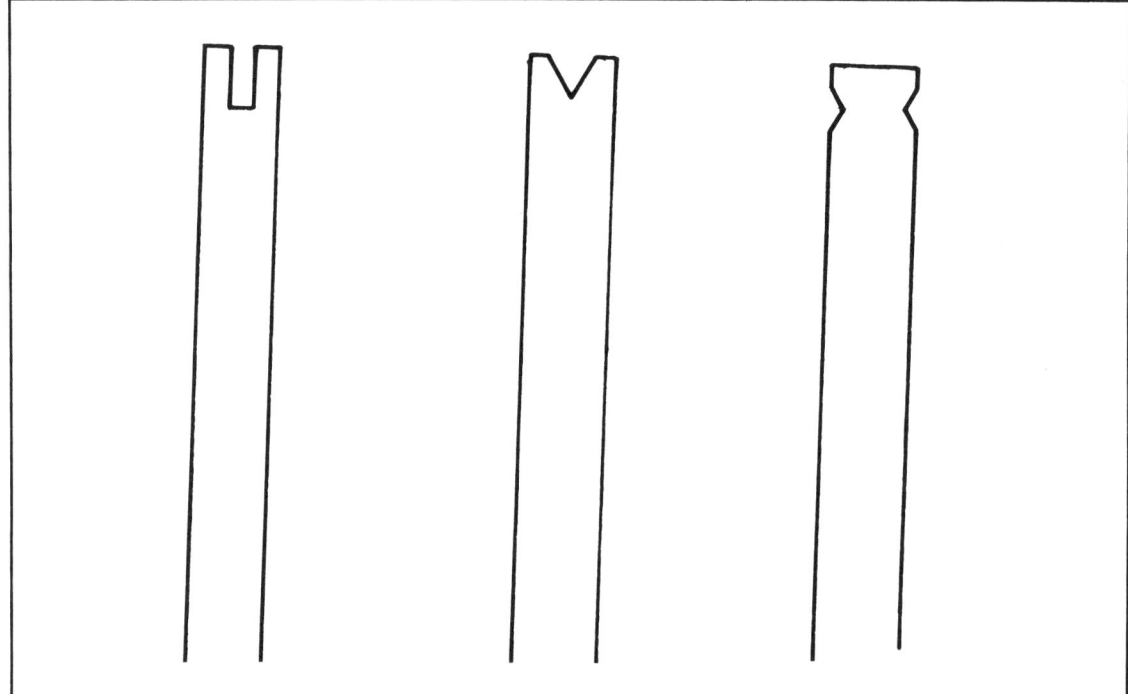

Fig. 5-9. Notches in fiberglass frame pieces.

clogged with fiberglass, a file brush or solvent can be used to clean them.

A variety of small surfacing tools can also be used for shaping fiberglass. These are used similarly to files. (see Chapter 4).

Aluminum oxide or silicon carbide sandpaper can also be used for sanding fiberglass. The general principle in sanding fiberglass is to start with the coarsest grit required for the particular job and then progressively work down to finer grits. The sandpaper can be held by hand or you can use a sanding block. A small block of wood, with or without a foam rubber pad, can be used with the sandpaper folded around the block. The sandpaper is held in place around the block while the sanding is being done. Special blocks or flexible holders that have a clamping arrangement for holding the paper in place can be used. Block sanding allows the removal of high spots without affecting adjacent low areas.

Sanding and grinding attachments can be used in rotary hobby tools for power sanding and grinding fiberglass.

Joining Sticks and Frame Members

Kite sticks and frame members are frequently joined by binding or lashing them together with string or thread, often in combination with glue, especially when wooden or bamboo members are joined. A typical binding or lashing for joining two cross sticks is shown in Fig. 5-10. If the joint is to also be glued, first apply glue, as detailed below, then tightly lash the two sticks together and tie with square knot (Fig. 5-11). Glue can also be applied to the lashings.

An alternative to using thread or string bindings is to use strapping tape or other suitable tape. The joints can be with or without glue, as desired. Strapping tape alone often provides satisfactory joints, especially for small kites.

Wooden and bamboo sticks can be joined together end-to-end by splicing, as shown in Fig. 5-12. These joints are often first glued, then lashed together with string or thread, as shown in Fig. 5-13. Tie with square knot. Glue can also be applied to the lashings to further reinforce the joint.

Kite sticks and frame members can also be joined by gluing, either alone or in combination with mechanical fastening. The choice of glue will depend on the materials being joined. In some cases, several types of glue will give satisfactory results. White resin-emulsion glue can be used for joining wood, bamboo, and a variety of other porous materials. Follow the manufacturer's directions for

Fig. 5-10. Two sticks lashed together.

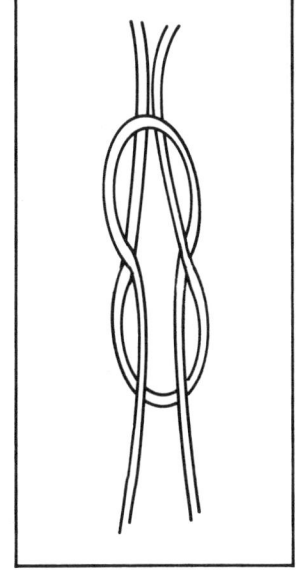

Fig. 5-11. A square knot.

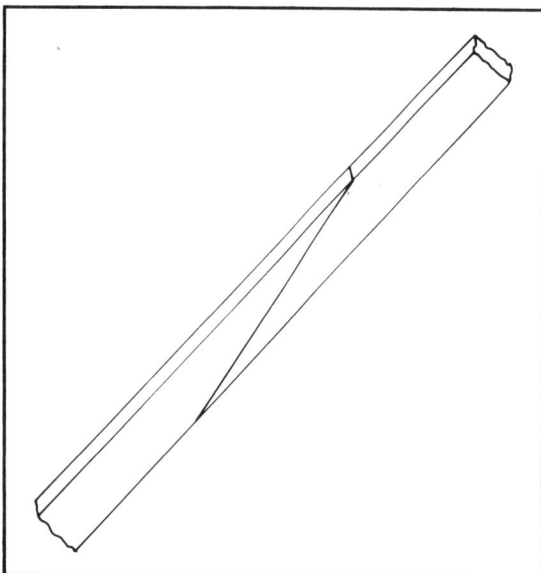

Fig. 5-12. Splice.

using the particular brand. In many cases, a thin coat of glue is applied to each surface. The joint is then clamped together until the glue has dried.

Epoxy glue gives good results on both porous and nonporous materials. Epoxy *cures* rather than dries. It usually comes in two parts, which must be mixed together before use. Mix only what you need for a particular job, because once the two parts have been mixed together, the mixture will cure even in a sealed container. The newer, quick-drying epoxy glues are especially suitable for kite construction work. Epoxy glues do present certain safety hazards if improperly handled or used. Follow the manufacturer's directions for the safe use of the particular product. In general, avoid skin contact, and avoid breathing fumes or vapors. Use only in a well-ventilated area. If skin rash or any other unusual reactions develop, consult a physician.

A variety of acetate cements and plastic cements, such as those formulated for modeling and hobby work, can also be used for joining kite sticks. Follow manufacturer's directions carefully when using these products.

A number of new "super" glues that are rapid setting and anaerobic are now on the market. These glues often advertise that a single drop will provide tons of holding power. I haven't had very good results with these glues. Some joints have popped apart when little or no loads were applied, but you may have better results with these than I have had. As a general rule, the glue is applied to one side of the joint and the parts are pressed together. Be careful when using these glues, as they will also glue your fingers together or glue you to whatever you are working on.

Sticks can also be joined with nails, bolts, screws, and other similar mechanical fasteners. Care must be taken, however, so that holes made in the sticks do not form a weak area that is likely to snap when the kite is flown. It is perhaps for this reason that these types of mechanical fasteners are not often used in the construction of small kites.

Various fittings can also be used as connecting links for joining parts. A variety of molded plastic fittings, such as those shown in Fig. 5-14, are avail-

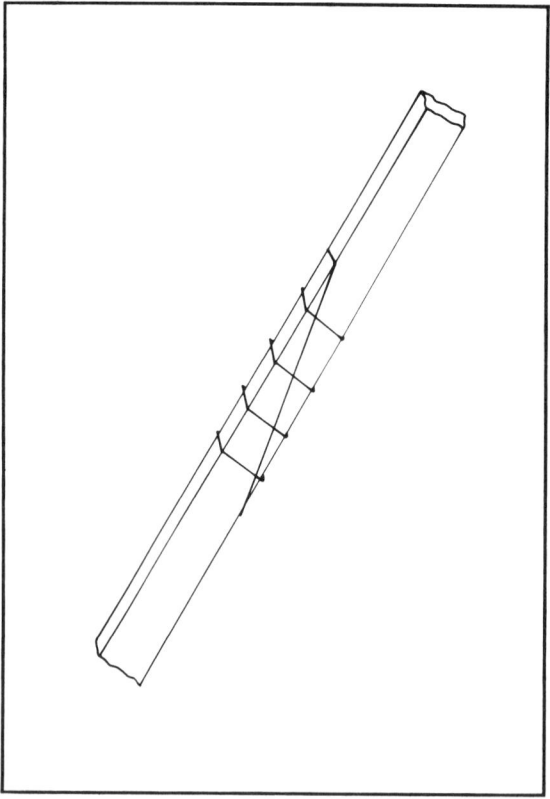

Fig. 5-13. Splice joint is lashed together.

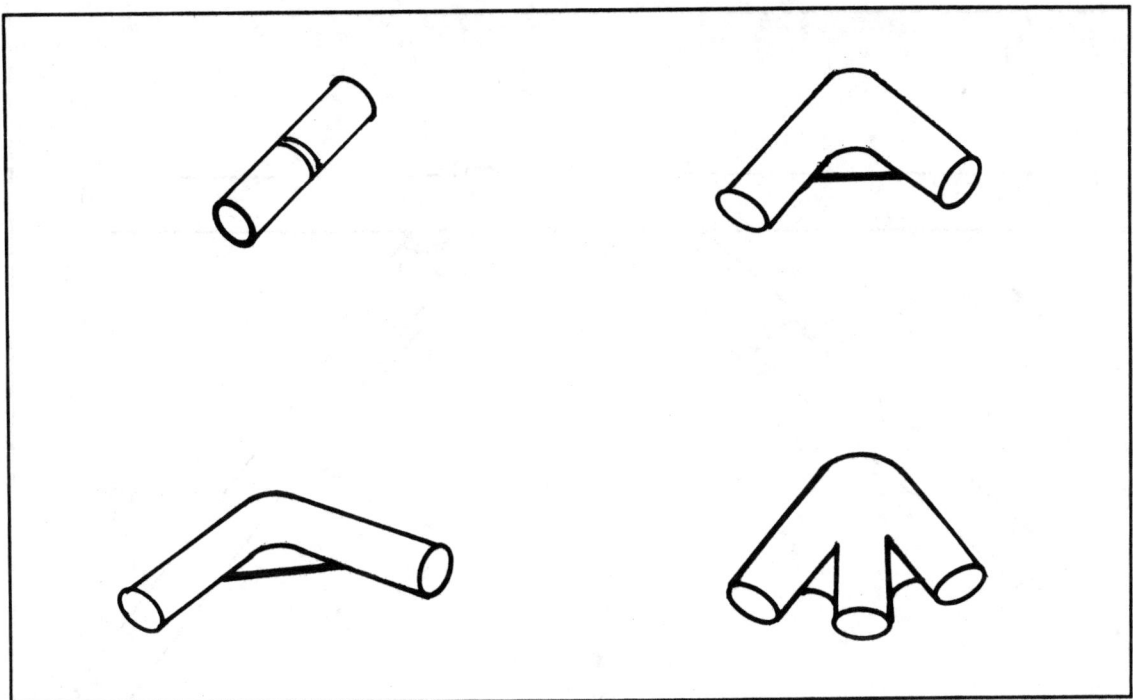

Fig. 5-14. Molded plastic fittings.

able from hobby supply stores. These provide a convenient way to join round kite sticks into a variety of kite frame patterns. If the sticks fit tightly in the fittings or are held by tension, glue may not be necessary. In some cases, you will also want to glue the sticks into the fittings.

Plastic tubing can also be used to make connections. For example, rigid plastic tubing can be used for joining two round sticks end-to-end, as shown in Fig. 5-15. Flexible tubing, such as a clear polyethylene, can be used for a variety of connections, such as those shown in Fig. 5-16.

Aluminum and other lightweight metal and alloy tubing can be used for making a variety of connecting fittings, such as those illustrated in Fig. 5-17. You can also fabricate a number of useful fittings from thin sheets of aluminum or other metals and alloys, as shown in Fig. 5-18.

Kite frame joints are sometimes reinforced by using *gussets*, such as triangular wooden inserts (Fig. 5-19) and metal angle braces (Fig. 5-20). A variety of suitable lightweight plastic and metal reinforcing members that are suitable for kite construction are available from hobby stores.

Another useful method for joining kite sticks is fiberglassing. A lightweight fiberglass cloth tape (make certain that it is intended for fiberglass

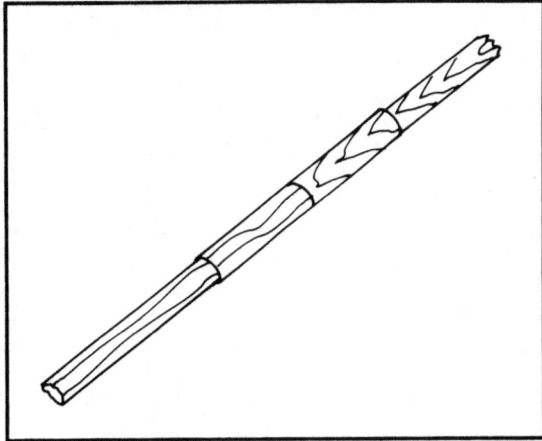

Fig. 5-15. Rigid plastic tubing used to join two sticks end-to-end.

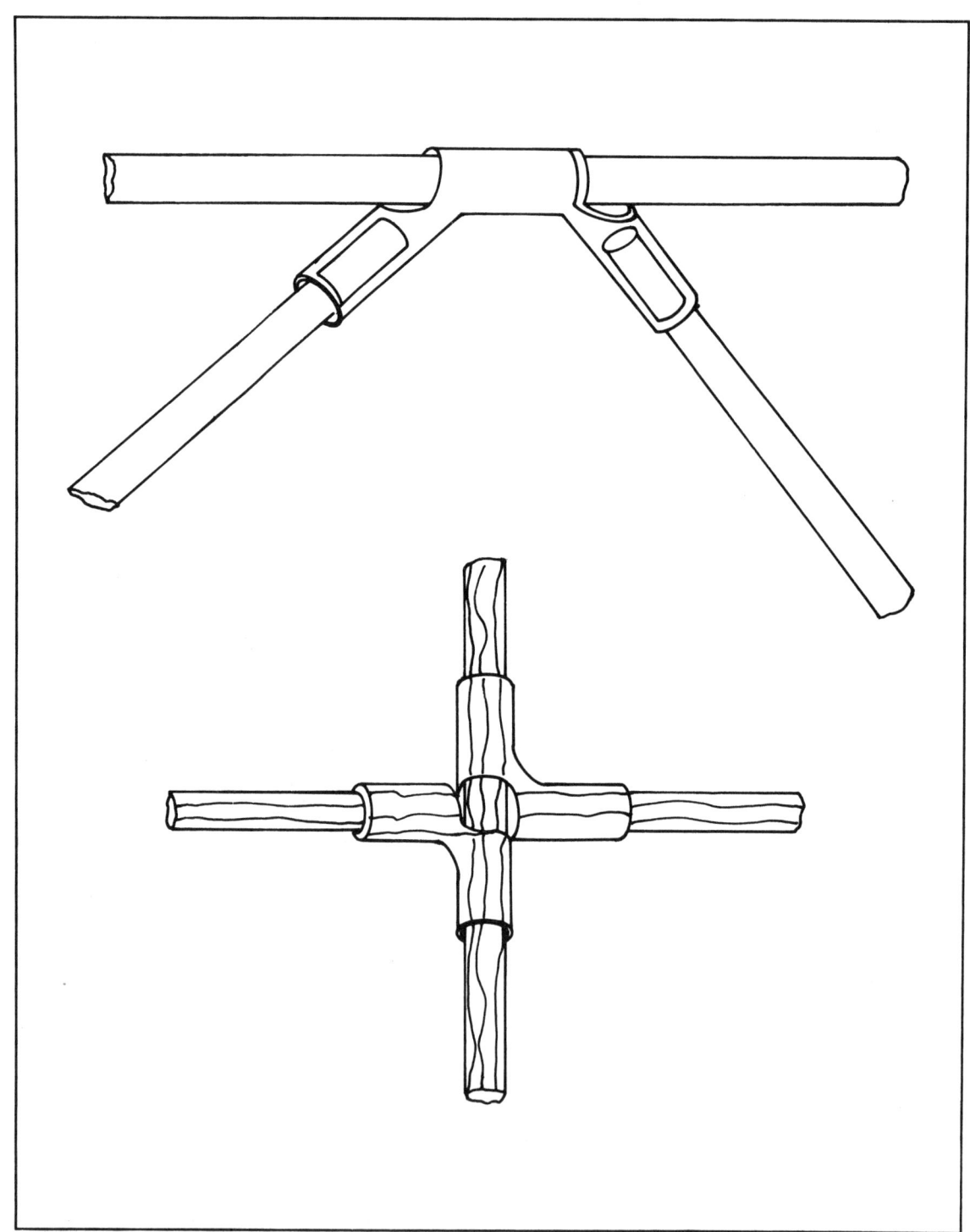

Fig. 5-16. Flexible plastic tubing used to form kite frame fittings.

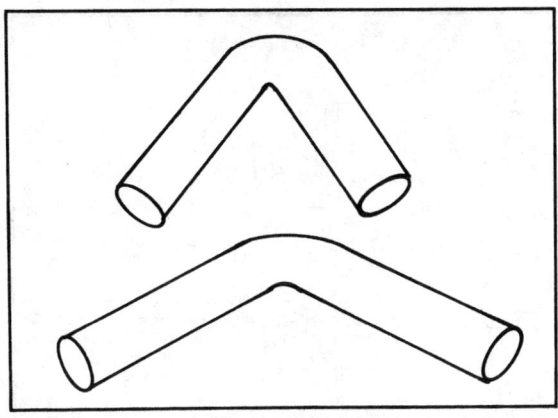

Fig. 5-17. Aluminum tubing used to form kite frame fittings.

lay-up work) is saturated with epoxy resin (with hardener added) and wrapped around the sticks to be joined. A cross-joint is shown in Fig. 5-21 and a T-joint in Fig. 5-22. Use a rapid-curing epoxy resin. Follow the manufacturer's directions for the safe use of the particular epoxy used. In general, this will mean avoiding skin and eye contact and avoiding inhaling fumes or vapors.

A typical application involves shaping and cleaning the sticks to be joined, which can be wood, bamboo, rattan, aluminum, fiberglass, or a variety of other materials. The fiberglass cloth tape is cut to suitable sizes. The epoxy resin is then mixed with the hardener according to the manufacturer's

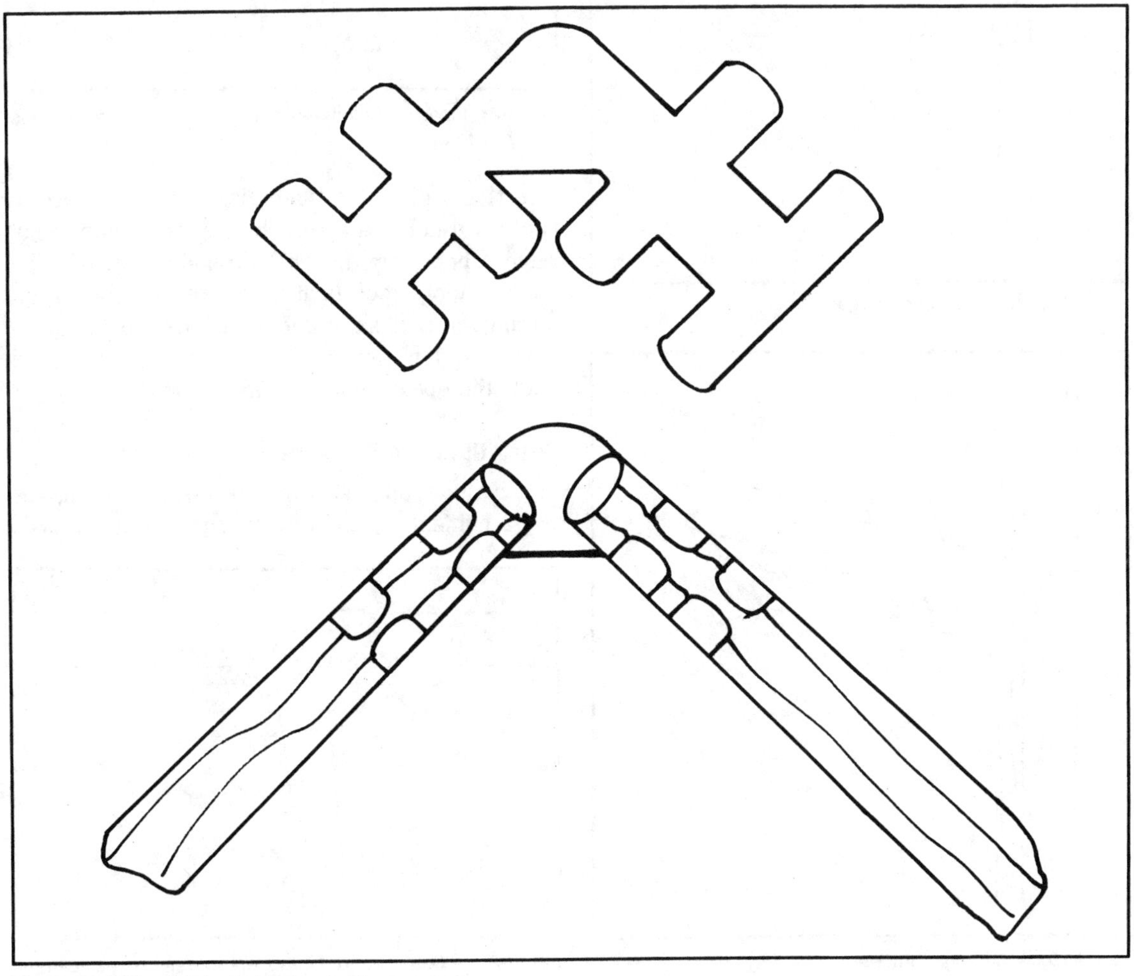

Fig. 5-18. Fitting fabricated from aluminum.

69

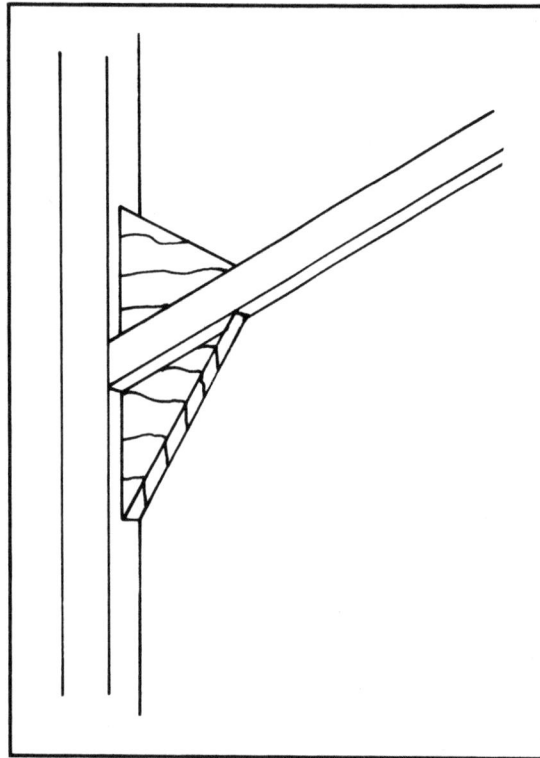

Fig. 5-19. Wooden triangular gussets.

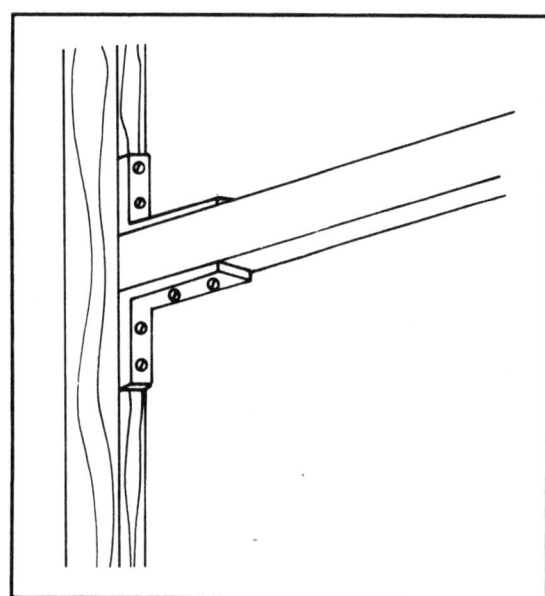

Fig. 5-20. Metal angle braces.

Fig. 5-21. Fiberglass cloth and epoxy resin used to form cross joint of kite sticks.

directions. Place the fiberglass cloth on a piece of cardboard and, using a brush, saturate it with epoxy resin. Then wrap the cloth around the parts to be joined. Apply additional pieces of fiberglass reinforcing material saturated with epoxy resin, as required. Clamp or prop the sticks in position and allow the epoxy resin to cure.

String Guys and Guidelines

String is often attached to kite sticks for use as guys, guidelines, and for other purposes. A basic

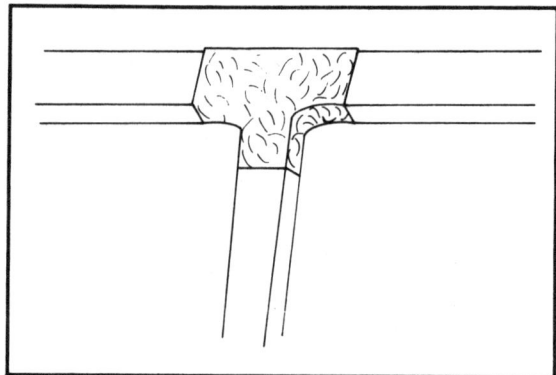

Fig. 5-22. Fiberglass cloth and epoxy resin used to form T-joint of kite sticks.

two-stick kite, for example, has a string guideline around it that passes through notches in the ends of the sticks, as shown in Fig. 5-23. The string serves as a frame for the covering material, as detailed later in this chapter, and also as *guys* for bracing the kite sticks and holding them in a cross position. The string is typically routed through the notches in the kite sticks, and the ends of the string are joined together with a square knot. The notches, especially of wooden sticks and bamboo sticks, are frequently reinforced by *string lashings,* as shown in Fig. 5-24. The lashing is first wound around the stick, usually both above and below the guideline, and then tied with a square knot.

String guys are frequently used to bow kites, as shown in Fig. 5-25. This serves not only to bow the kite, but also to put the bowed kite stick under tension. The string is usually first wound to a notch

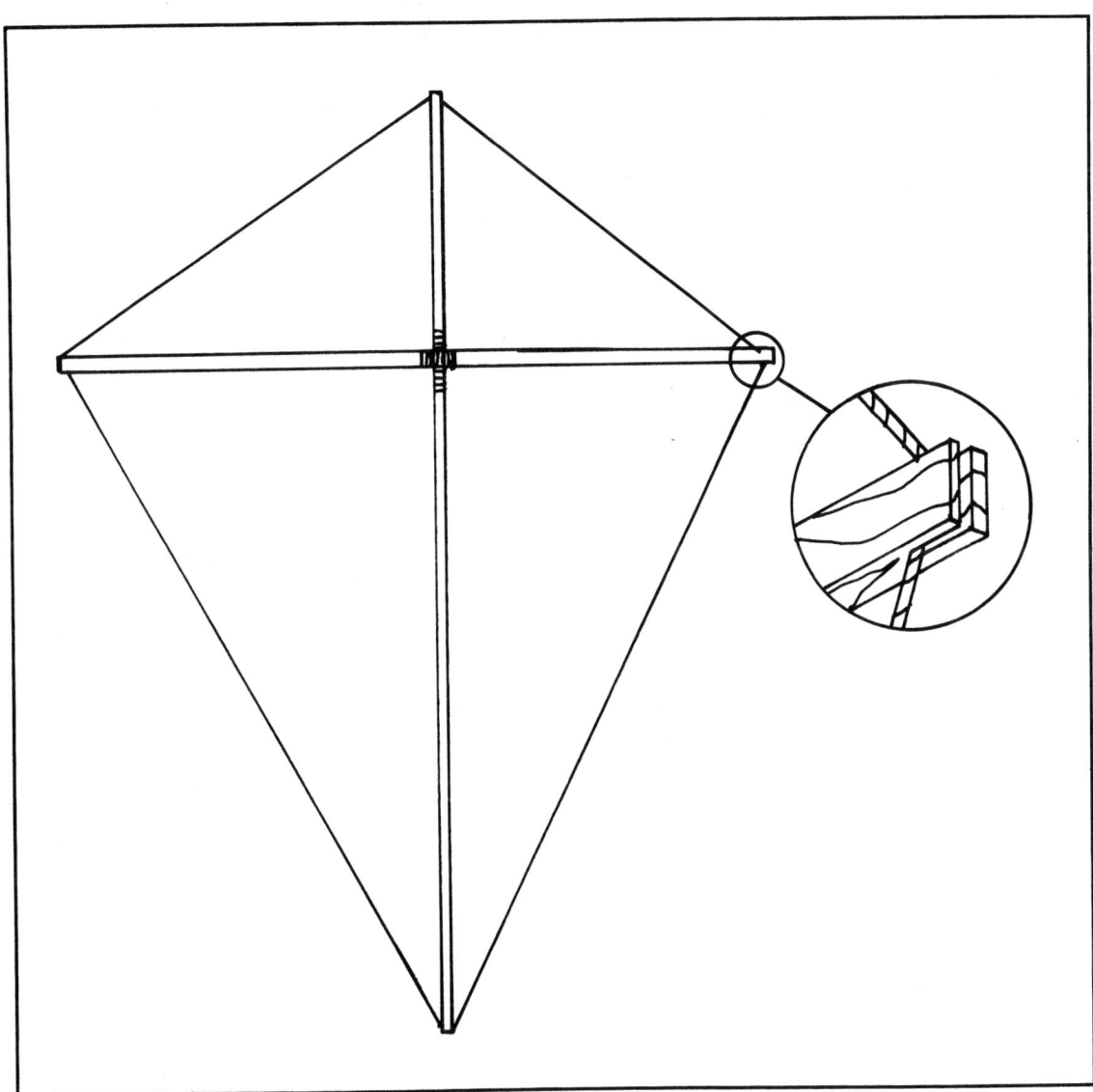

Fig. 5-23. Guideline string passes through notches on ends of kite sticks.

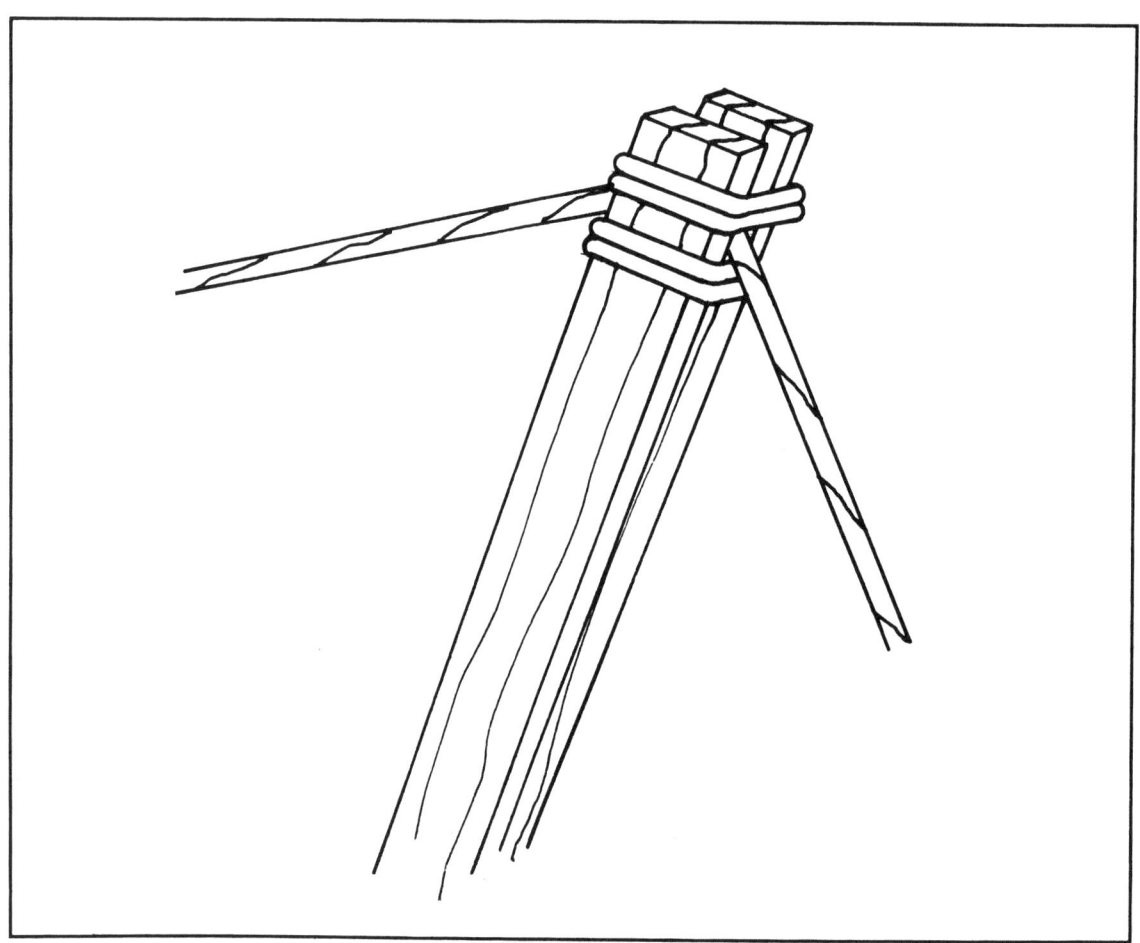

Fig. 5-24. Notch in wood stick reinforced by string lashing.

in one end of the stick and tied, usually with a square knot. The stick is then bowed by hand pressure and the guy string is wound and tied to the desired tension to a notch on the other end of the stick.

KITE COVERING MATERIALS

A variety of covering materials can be used for kites. The choice will depend on the particular kite, what is available, and other factors. For some kites, the choice of covering material is critical; for others you will have a choice of two or more different materials.

Silk was probably the earliest material used for kite coverings, and it is still sometimes used today. Paper was also used as a covering material for early kites and over the long history of kites, has been the most widely used covering material. Modern synthetic materials and plastic films are rapidly becoming the most popular kite covering materials.

An important aspect of kite covering materials is their attachment to the kite frames and guideline strings. Methods for doing this with various materials are covered below.

Paper

Paper has a long tradition as a kite covering material in many parts of the world, and it remains popular today. When my grandfather first made kites for me, he covered them with whatever paper happened to be around the house, including newspaper, craft paper, and wrapping paper.

A wide range of papers, in fact, can be used as kite covering materials. One of the lightest papers is tissue paper. It does tend to tear rather easily but has adequate tear strength for many smaller kites.

Newspaper is another possibility. It is readily available but has a low tear strength in relation to its weight, which tends to limit its usefulness. It should be pointed out, however, that many kites have been covered with newspaper and successfully flown, and it is likely that this will continue.

Many specialty papers, such as rice paper, can be used for covering kites. Art and craft stores often have a variety of lightweight papers that you might want to consider for use as kite covering materials.

Papers suitable for kite covering materials range in weight from quite light, like tissue paper, up to heavy, such as thin cardboard. Not all papers, however, are suitable for all kites. The choice will depend on the particular kite design, the size of the kite, how it will be decorated, and so on.

Papers can be joined together and to kite frames by a number of adhesives, including white resin-emulsion glue, rubber cement, and a variety of adhesive tapes. Many different techniques can be used for decorating paper (see Chapter 9), which is one of the reasons for the popularity of paper as a kite covering material.

Many papers allow little or no air to pass

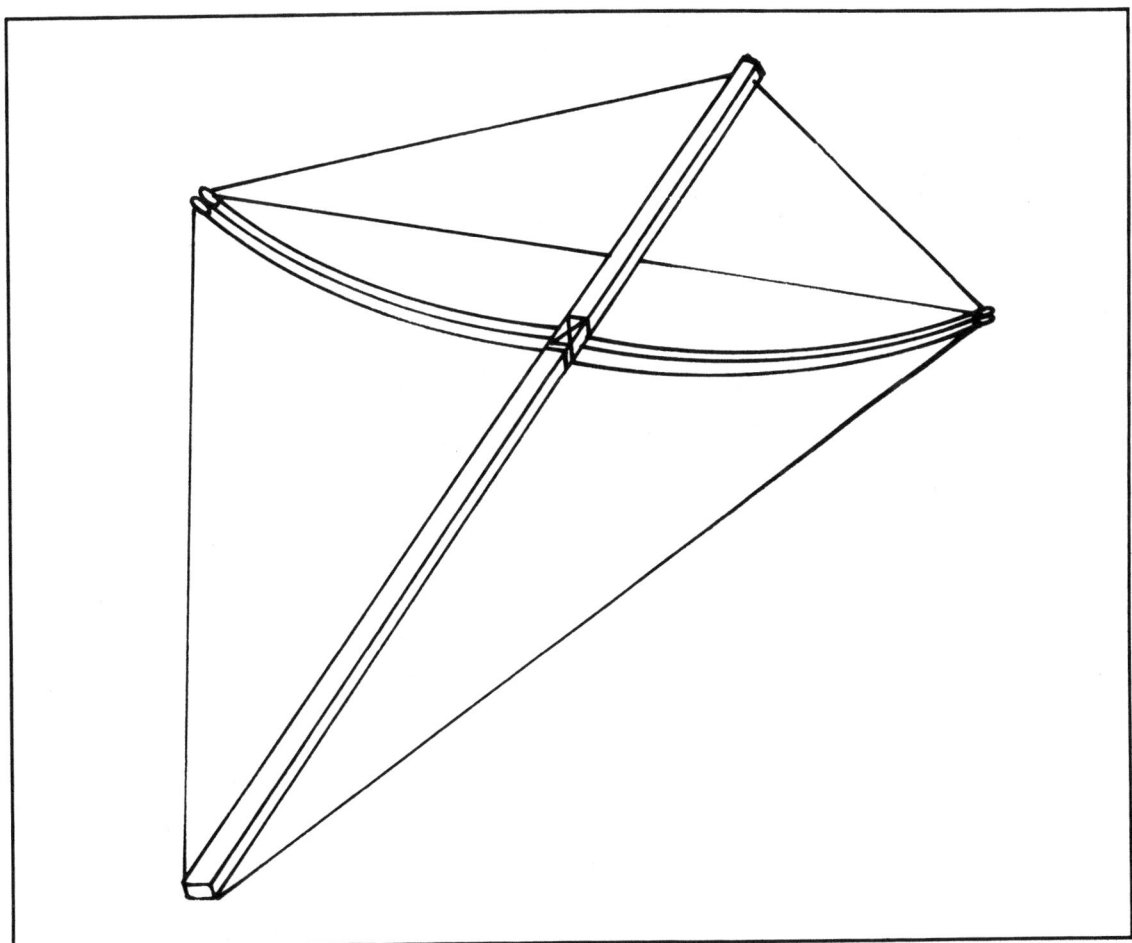

Fig. 5-25. Guy string used to bow kite.

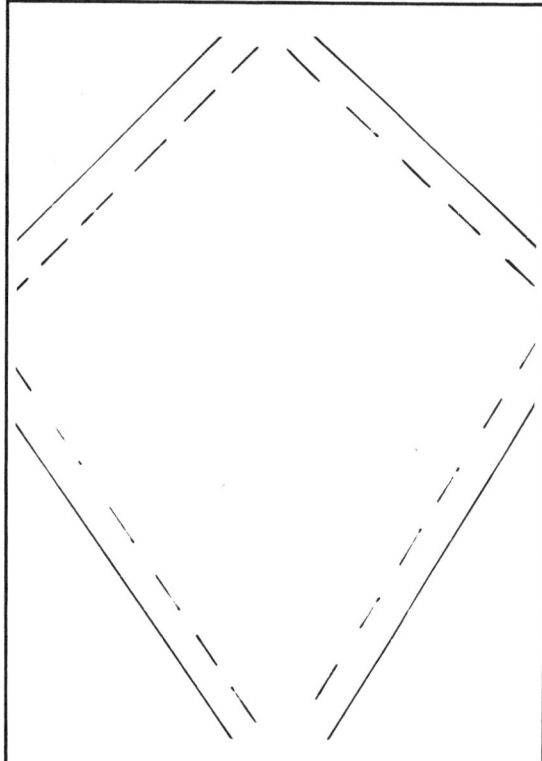

Fig. 5-26. Sample pattern for paper covering material.

through them. For most kite constructions, it is an advantage to have a covering material that does not allow air to pass through it.

As a general rule, the pattern is first marked on the paper, as shown in Fig. 5-26. Flaps are typically used for forming sleeves for guideline strings (Fig. 5-27) and for joining ends of paper together (Fig. 5-28). Scissors are used for cutting the paper to the desired pattern.

In some cases, the paper will be painted or otherwise decorated (see Chapter 9) before gluing or taping to kite frames and/or to form sleeves for guideline strings. In other cases, no decorating will be done, or the decorating will be done after the paper has been installed on the kite frame. When gluing, follow the manufacturer's directions for the particular glue used. In some cases, the glue will be applied to one surface only; in other cases, the glue will be applied to both surfaces. The parts are then pressed together.

Paper can be reinforced in areas of high stress by gluing a piece of paper to the covering material. Adhesive tape can similarly be used. Gummed binder hole rings are handy for reinforcing areas where strings pass through the paper.

Silk and Cotton

Silk and various cotton fabrics of reasonably dense construction (so that little air will pass through the material) have long been popular kite covering materials. Silk and suitable cotton fabrics range in weight from light to medium. The materials can be joined by sewing, fabric glue, and various adhesive tapes. Decorating techniques include printing and dyeing, as detailed in Chapter 9. Silk and cotton fabrics usually have from medium to high tear strength, making them suitable for many medium- to large-size kites, but, these materials are rapidly being replaced by modern synthetic materials.

To cover a kite with silk or cotton material, first mark the desired pattern on the material. The pattern can be marked with chalk or dressmaker's tracing paper. Use scissors to cut the material to the pattern.

Sleeves can be formed, ends of the material joined together, or two pieces of material joined by hand or machine sewing. If a sewing machine is used, a zig-zag stitch usually gives the strongest joints, although straight stitching patterns can also be used.

Modern Synthetic Fabrics

A variety of lightweight synthetic fabrics of nylon, polyester, and materials such as those designed for sails make excellent kite covering materials. These materials typically have tear strengths ranging from medium to high. A full range of weights, from light to heavy, are available. The lightest weights are generally the most suitable for kite construction. These materials come in a rainbow of colors and can be joined by sewing or taping. These fabrics generally have low porosity, or even zero porosity, making them ideal for most kite constructions.

The patterns are typically first marked on the fabric with chalk, transfer paper, or other means. Scissors are used to cut the fabric to the pattern.

The material can be sewn by hand or machine, as desired. Polyester thread works well for most synthetic fabrics. If a sewing machine is used, a zig-zag stitch will generally give the strongest joint, although straight stitching patterns will usually also give satisfactory results.

Plastic Films

Plastic films are extremely popular kite-covering materials. One reason for their popularity is their wide availability in the form of plastic leaf and trash can bags. A variety of plastic films, including polyethylene and polyurethane, can be used. These typically have low to medium tear strength and are available in weights from light to heavy. Most are nonporous, making them ideal for covering many types of kites.

Polyethylene, as well as a number of other similar plastic films, can be joined by heat-sealing or by adhesive tapes, such as transparent cellulose adhesive tape. Heat-sealing tools, such as those

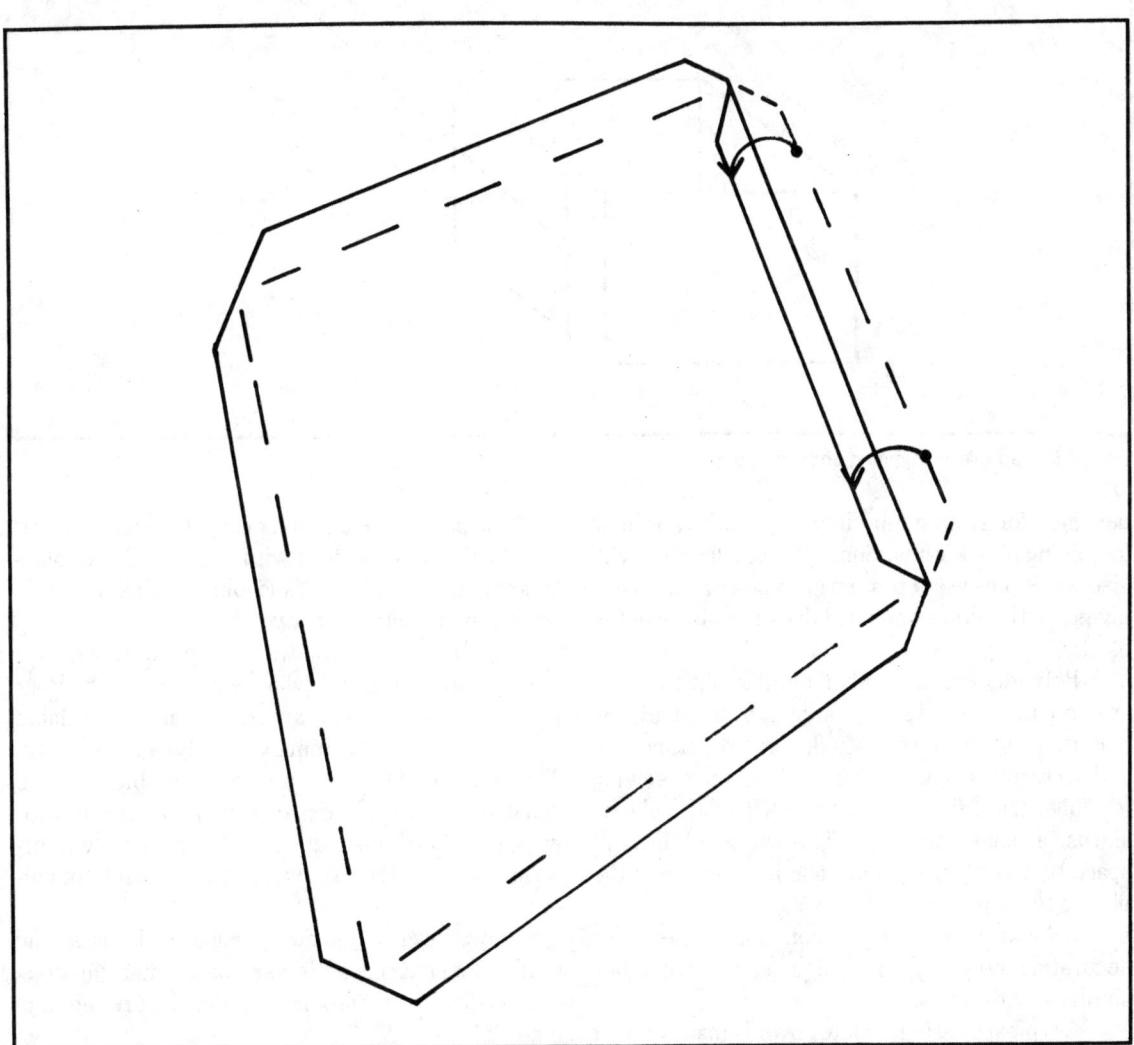

Fig. 5-27. Flap used for forming sleeve in paper cover for guideline string.

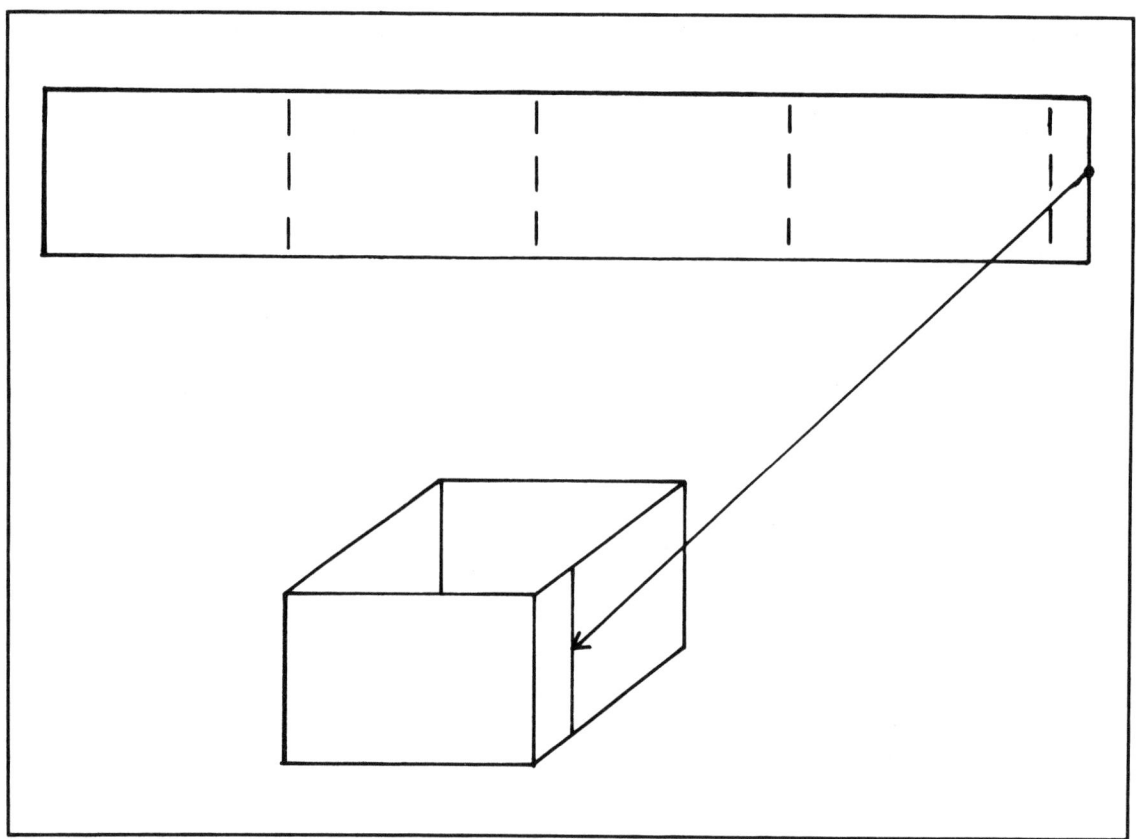

Fig. 5-28. Flap used for joining ends of paper.

designed for sealing food in plastic bags, are ideal for joining plastic films. Some plastic adhesives will also work, but use a test strip to be certain that it gives a satisfactory bond and does not dissolve the plastic.

Polyethylene and other similar plastic films are too thin to be sewn, although some plastic materials, such as thin vinyl, can sometimes be satisfactorily sewn. If this is done on a sewing machine, try it first with a test strip of the plastic and use a long stitch length. This will result in more space between needle holes and less chance of the plastic tearing under stress.

Solvent-based marking pens can be used for decorating polyethylene and a number of other similar plastic films.

A typical plastic-film kite cover is made by first marking the pattern on the plastic. A solvent-based marking pen can be used on many plastics. Then cut the plastic to the pattern with scissors. Make plastic joints to form sleeves and join ends, using one of the methods detailed above.

A plastic film that works especially well for kite construction is Mylar, which is a Du Pont product. It has a high tear strength and is available in a range of weights from extremely light to heavy. The lightweights are the most suitable for kite constructions. The extremely high strength-to-weight ratio of this material allows for very lightweight kites. Mylar is available in a variety of colors.

Mylar can be joined by using Mylar tape and other adhesive tapes. Solvent-based marking pens can be used for marking on and decorating this material.

Another new material being used for covering

kites is Tyvek, also a Du Pont product. Tyvek is a spun-bonded olefin that has an extremely high tear strength in relation to its weight. It can be glued with rubber cement as well as some other glues. If you are uncertain if a particular glue will work, try gluing a test strip first. The material can also be sewn, and it can be cut with scissors.

Some plastic materials can be joined by using small grommets. Special tools are available for punching the holes for these and setting the grommets. Grommets are also useful for reinforcing the areas where bridle, bow, and other strings pass through the material.

BRIDLE ATTACHMENTS

Bridle strings typically attach to kite sticks, in some cases first passing through holes in the kite covering material, or to the kite covering material, especially on kites that have keels. When bridle strings pass through covering material, the material is frequently reinforced by tape, gummed binder rings, grommets, or other means. Kite sticks are sometimes notched slightly in the area where bridle strings are attached to keep the string from sliding. Square knots are often used to tie the string to the sticks. (Additional information about bridles is included in later chapters.)

KITE TAILS

A variety of tails are used on kites (see Chapters 4 and 6). Plastic and fabric tails are sometimes extensions of the covering material or extension strips that are glued, taped, sewn, or tied to the kite covering material, the frame, or to both. In some cases, the tails have string attachments to the kites.

OTHER USEFUL SKILLS AND TECHNIQUES

A variety of other skills and techniques are useful for kite construction work, including working with styrofoam and other rigid-plastic foam materials, constructing heads and other forms for use on kites, applying model airplane construction techniques to kite constructions, and using soldering techniques.

Rigid Plastic Foam Materials

Styrofoam (polystyrene expanded approximately 40 times) and other lightweight rigid-plastic foam materials are being used increasingly for kite constructions. Styrofoam has the combination of both light and adequate strength and is, therefore, suitable for both the framework and covering material. Styrofoam can also be used as a covering material for some framed kites.

Styrofoam can be purchased at craft and hobby stores in sheet and block form. Pieces of styrofoam from packing cartons can sometimes also be used, although this material tends to be heavier than the styrofoam sold in craft and hobby stores.

Styrofoam can be cut with a sharp knife or razor blade. The pattern lines are usually first marked on the styrofoam with a solvent-based marking pen or scratched into the surface with a pencil or other sharp, pointed object. The styrofoam is then placed over a block of wood for cutting with a knife or razor blade.

Styrofoam can also be cut with a coping saw or a jig or scroll saw. A hot wire cutter can also be used. This melts the styrofoam and produces a smooth cut.

Styrofoam can be filed. A small surfacing tool (see Chapter 4) works well for this. It can also be sanded, but not to extreme smoothness because of its cellular makeup. It is easily drilled with standard metal bits.

A number of adhesives, including epoxy, can be used for joining pieces of styrofoam together and for joining it to other materials. However, some adhesives dissolve styrofoam and are thus unsuitable. If in doubt, try the cement on a test strip of styrofoam to see if it gives satisfactory results.

A variety of paints, including poster tempera, latex, and a number of other water-based paints, can be used for painting and decorating styrofoam. If in doubt as to whether or not a certain paint will work, try it first on a test strip of styrofoam.

Working with styrofoam is generally quite easy, and this material has many possible uses for kite constructions. Styrofoam is also useful for constructing lightweight heads and other figures for use on kites, as detailed below.

While styrofoam seems to be the most readily available of the lightweight rigid-plastic foam materials, polyurethane and other types of lightweight rigid-plastic foams can also be used. The techniques for working with these are usually the same as for styrofoam.

Making Heads and Other Figures for Kites

Some kites, such as bird kites, use lightweight, three-dimensional shaped heads and other figures. One way to construct these is to carve them from styrofoam. These can then be painted. An alternate method is to make them from lightweight papier-mâché. When this method is used, hollow out the inside of the head to keep the weight to a minimum.

Model Airplane Techniques

Model airplane construction techniques using balsa ribs and frames and balsa sticks, such as shown in Fig. 5-29, can be used for constructing miniature kites, airplane kites, bird kites, and others. In general, the parts are cut from balsa wood, then with glue. The parts are frequently held in position by pins or clamps until the glue sets. Tissue or thin plastic films are frequently used as covering materials.

Soldering

Soldering has many possibilities for advanced kite construction work. Soldering is a method of joining metals that uses a filler metal that is called *solder*. Soldering is different from welding in that in soldering the metals being joined are not actually melted. For soldering, the melting point of the solder must be lower than that of the metal parts being joined.

To solder properly, a few basic rules should be followed:

● The metal surfaces to be soldered must be clean.

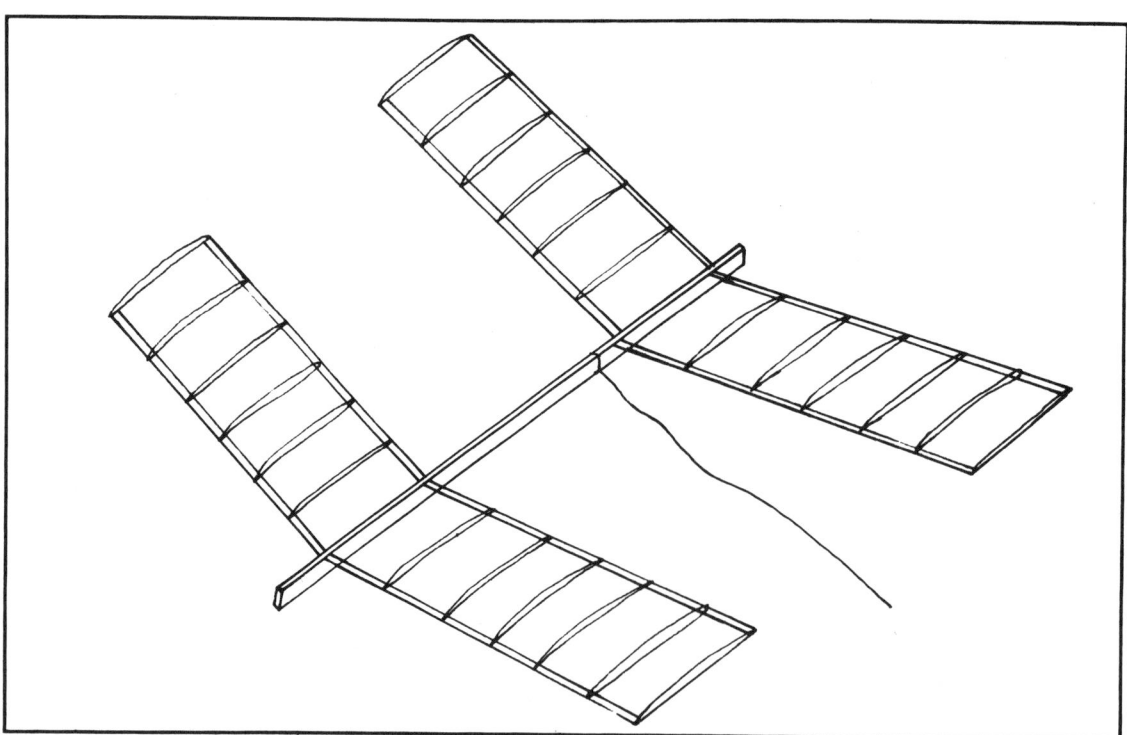

Fig. 5-29. Model airplane construction techniques can be applied to some kite constructions.

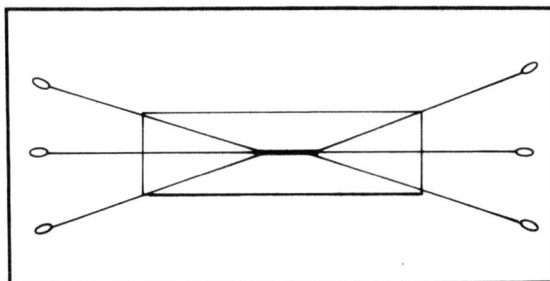

Fig. 5-30. Wire kite struts with soldered joints.

- A flux must be used that will prevent oxidation and help the flow of the solder.
- Enough heat must be used to melt the solder.
- A solder that is suitable for the particular soldering job must be used.

For metals such as tin plate, brass, and copper, a solder made from tin and lead is usually used. For general soldering of this type, a 50-50 or half tin and half lead solder that melts at about 414° Fahrenheit can be used. In most cases, a solder that has at least a 40 percent tin content should be used. Solder is sold in three basic forms: bar, solid wire, and flux-core. The flux-core solder, which is a hollow wire filled with flux, is generally the most convenient to use. To solder aluminum, you will need a special solder and flux.

The soldering flux is used to remove oxide films that prevent solder from adhering from the metal surfaces. The flux also lowers the surface tension of molten solder so that it can flow and penetrate properly. The two basic types of flux are rosin-base and acid or corrosive flux. For most kite construction work, the noncorrosive rosin-base flux is most suitable. In addition to flux-core solder, flux is also available in liquid and paste forms that can be brushed on before soldering.

Three types of heating devices can be used for soldering: a soldering iron, a soldering gun (both of which have copper tips), or a torch, such as a propane torch. A soldering iron is convenient for most kite construction soldering.

The general procedure for soldering is to clean the surfaces to be soldered with abrasive cloth or steel wool. The parts should fit closely together. If possible, clamp the parts together. The tip of the soldering iron should be clean. Heat the soldering iron and coat the copper tip with a thin layer of solder. Wipe off excess with a damp cloth. Apply the correct flux or use a flux-core solder. Heat the metal and apply solder so that it flows into the joint.

Soldering can be used to join wire to form struts and fittings for kites, such as shown in Fig. 5-30, for fabricating metal fittings, and a variety of other jobs.

Chapter 6

Flat and Bowed Kites

Most of the kites detailed in this chapter are fairly easy to construct, and some attempt has been made to place them in the approximate order of ascending difficulty. I do suggest, however, that the beginner who is building his or her first kite start with the basic two-stick flat kite described first in this chapter. After that, any kite that catches your fancy is a good choice for a second construction project.

BASIC TWO-STICK FLAT KITE

The basic two-stick kite (Fig. 6-1) has an outline shape of four sides and two equal angles that are opposite each other. Two sides of equal length meet at each of the opposite unequal angles. Each pair of sides are of different lengths.

Frame

Two sticks are required for the frame (Fig. 6-2). Sticks of pine, spruce, or similar wood that are ¼ by ⅜ inch in cross-section and 30 inches and 36 inches long are recommended. The sticks can vary

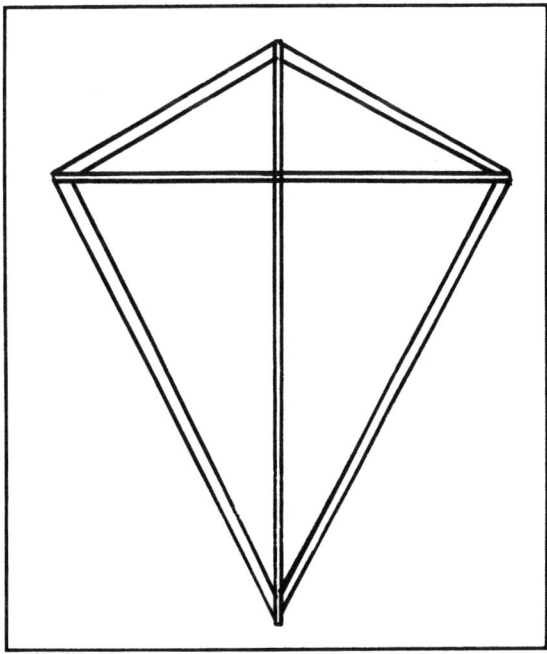

Fig. 6-1. Basic two-stick flat kite.

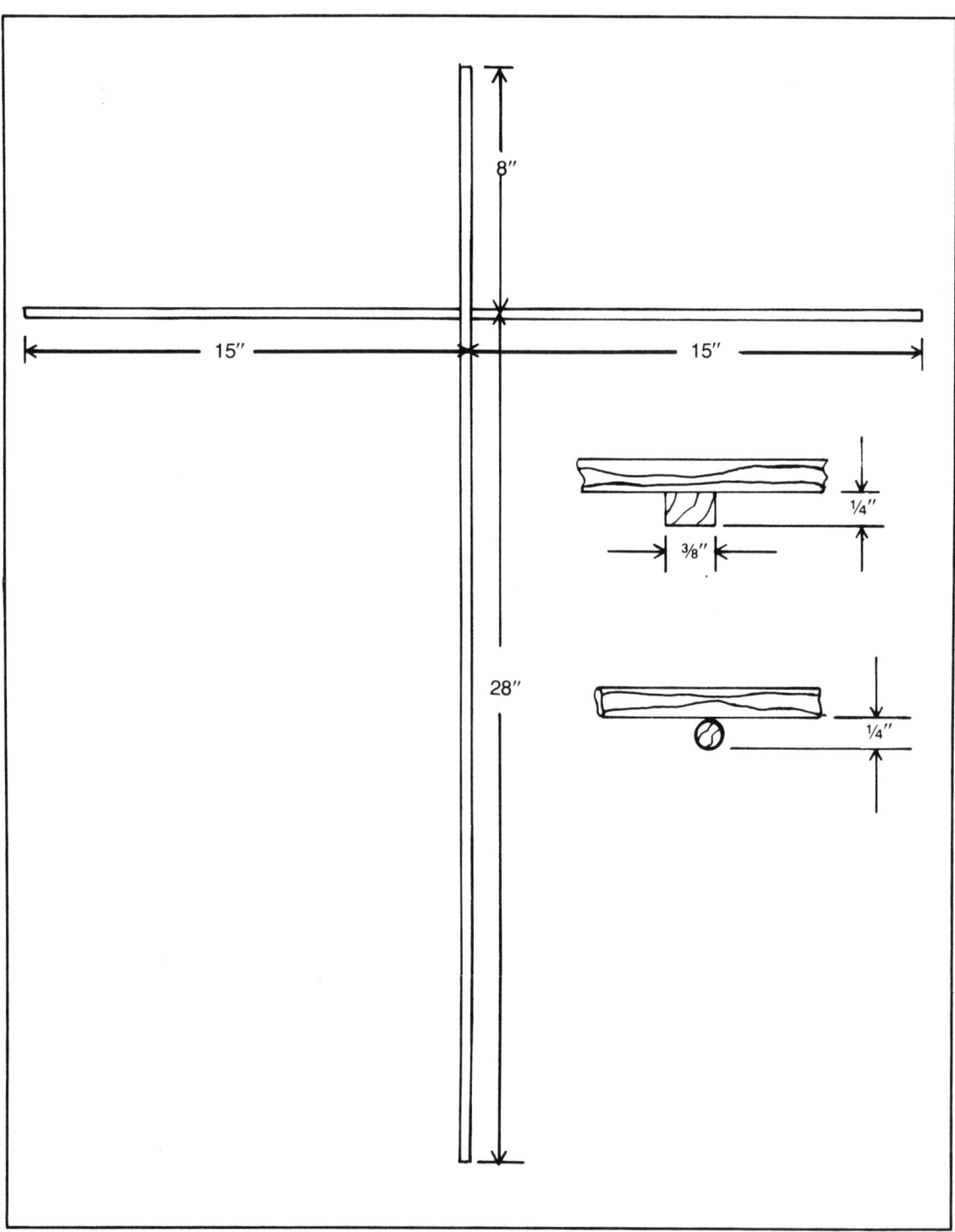

Fig. 6-2. Pattern for sticks for basic two-stick flat kite.

somewhat from the cross-sectional dimensions and still give satisfactory results. Wooden dowels that are ¼ inch in diameter can also be used. Sticks of fiberglass, bamboo, and aluminum tubing are also satisfactory, but for a first construction, I suggest that you use wood.

You can make the kite larger or smaller than the dimensions shown, as long as you keep the proportions approximately the same. For a first construction, I suggest that you use the dimensions shown; then, if you are so inclined, you can experiment with other dimensions.

Notch the ends of the sticks as shown in Fig. 6-3. Then measure and mark the intersection on the two sticks. The cross stick should also balance at the center point. If it doesn't, sand or file the stick until balance is achieved.

Glue and bind the two sticks together with a string lashing, as shown in Fig. 6-4. Tie the ends of the string with a square knot. Apply glue to the string lashing.

Install the guideline string in the notches around the ends of the sticks, as shown in Fig. 6-5. Stretch the string tight and tie the ends together with a square knot. Then add lashings around the sticks on each side of the guideline strings where they pass through the notches, as shown in Fig. 6-6. Tie the ends of the lashings with square knots. This completes the basic frame.

Covering Material

Craft-type paper or other suitable paper (see Chapter 4) is used to cover the kite. Mark the pattern shown in Fig. 6-7 on the paper. The kite frame can be used as a pattern by placing it on the paper, as shown in Fig. 6-8. Notice that the frame is positioned so that the side where the cross stick passes below the longitudinal stick is against the paper. Next, cut the paper to the pattern.

Fold and glue the hems in the paper where it crosses over the ends of the sticks, as shown in Fig. 6-9. Then position the frame over the covering material, as shown in Fig. 6-10. Fold the sleeves over the guideline strings and glue the flaps to the main sections of the covering material, as shown in Fig. 6-11.

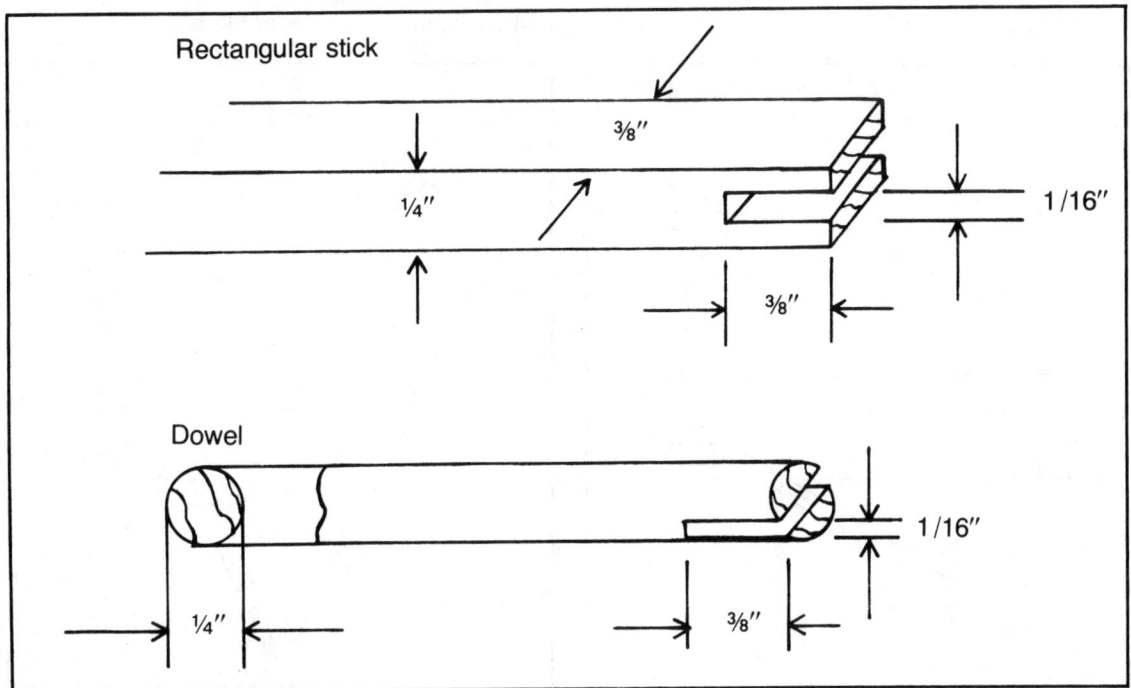

Fig. 6-3. Notches are made in ends of sticks.

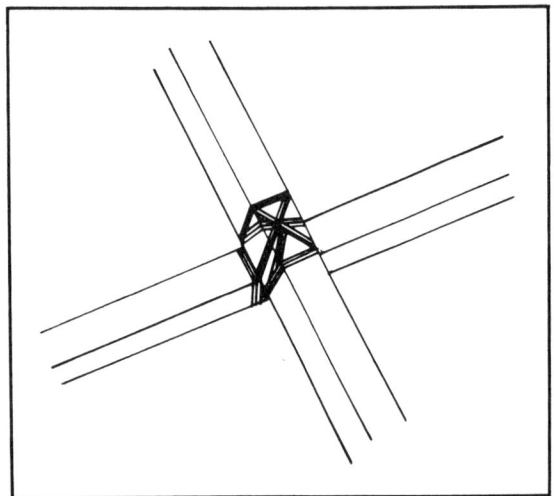

Fig. 6-4. Sticks are joined with glue and string lashing.

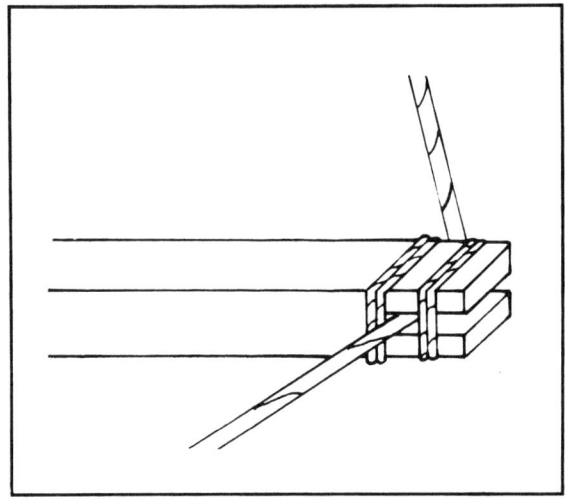

Fig. 6-6. Lashings are used on both sides of guideline string.

If desired, the kite can be painted, as detailed in Chapter 9. An alternative is to use colored paper.

The basic two-stick flat kite can also be covered with plastic film or lightweight fabric material, as detailed in Chapter 5. The seams in the plastic film can be heat-sealed, glued, or taped. Fabric is usually sewn.

Bridle

The bridle strings (Fig. 6-12) are tied with square knots to the ends of the sticks with the string passing through the notches. Use a small plastic curtain rod ring as a bridle ring, and tie the four bridle strings to the ring. To fly the kite, attach the kite string or line to the bridle ring.

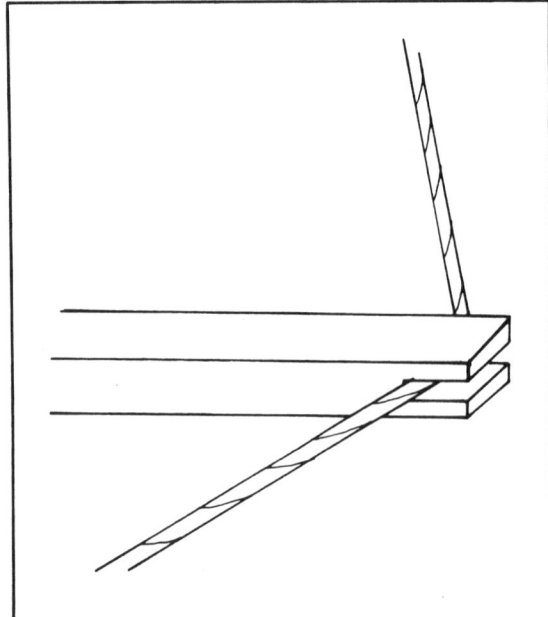

Fig. 6-5. Guideline string passes through notches.

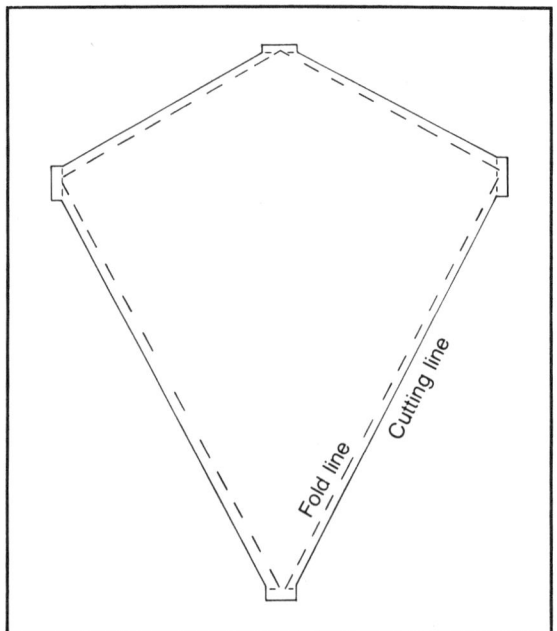

Fig. 6-7. Pattern for covering material.

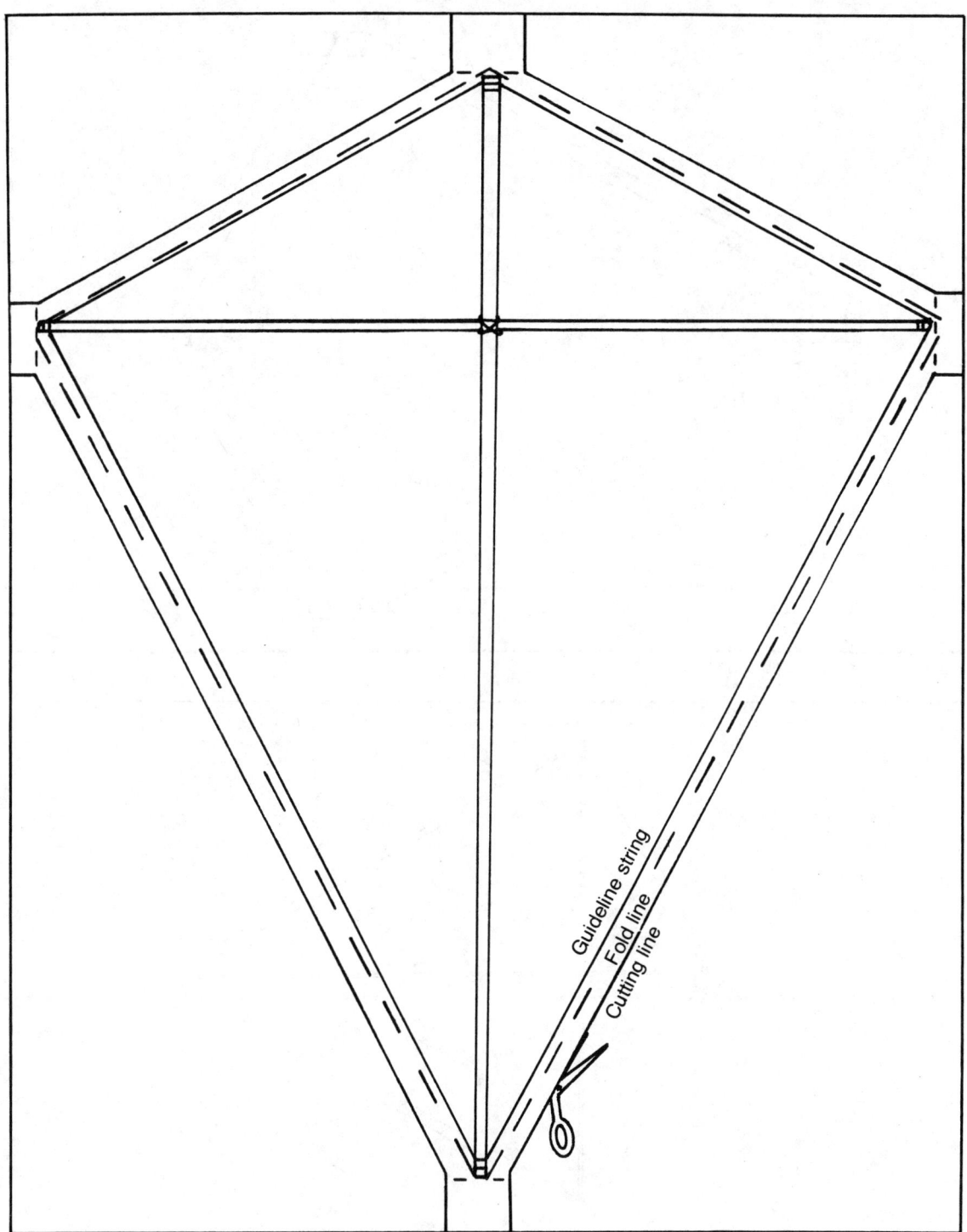

Fig. 6-8. Kite frame positioned over covering material for use as pattern.

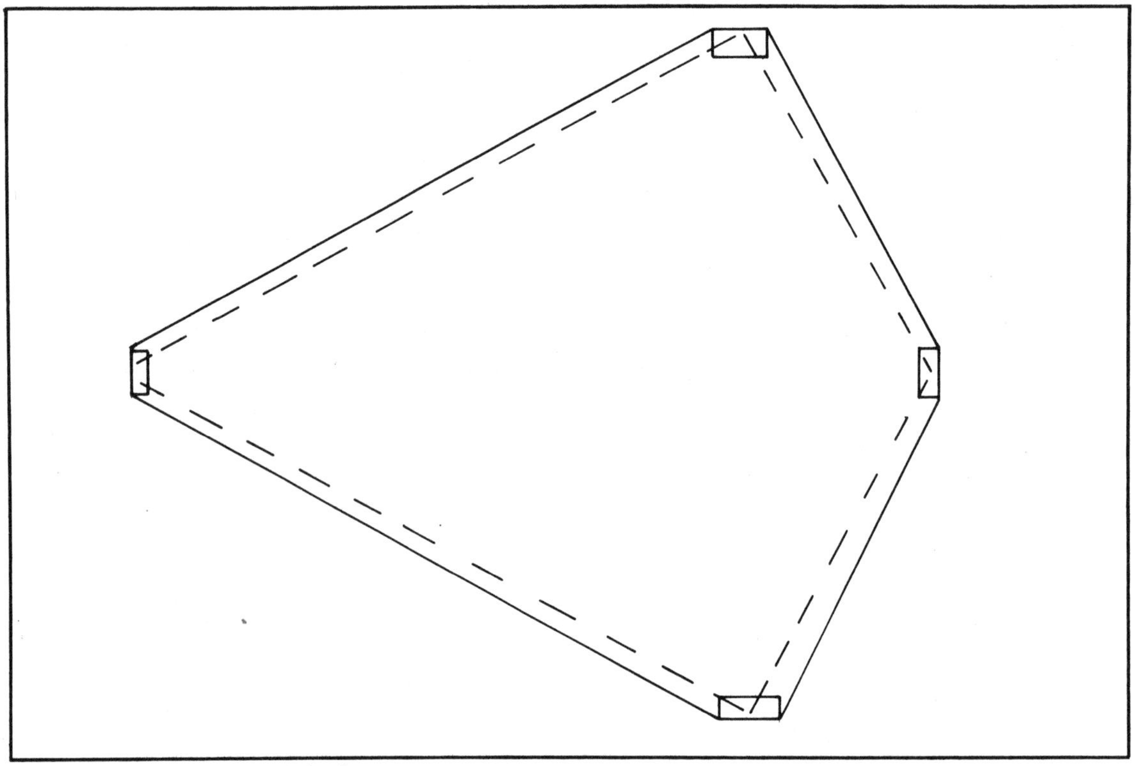

Fig. 6-9. Hems are folded and glued.

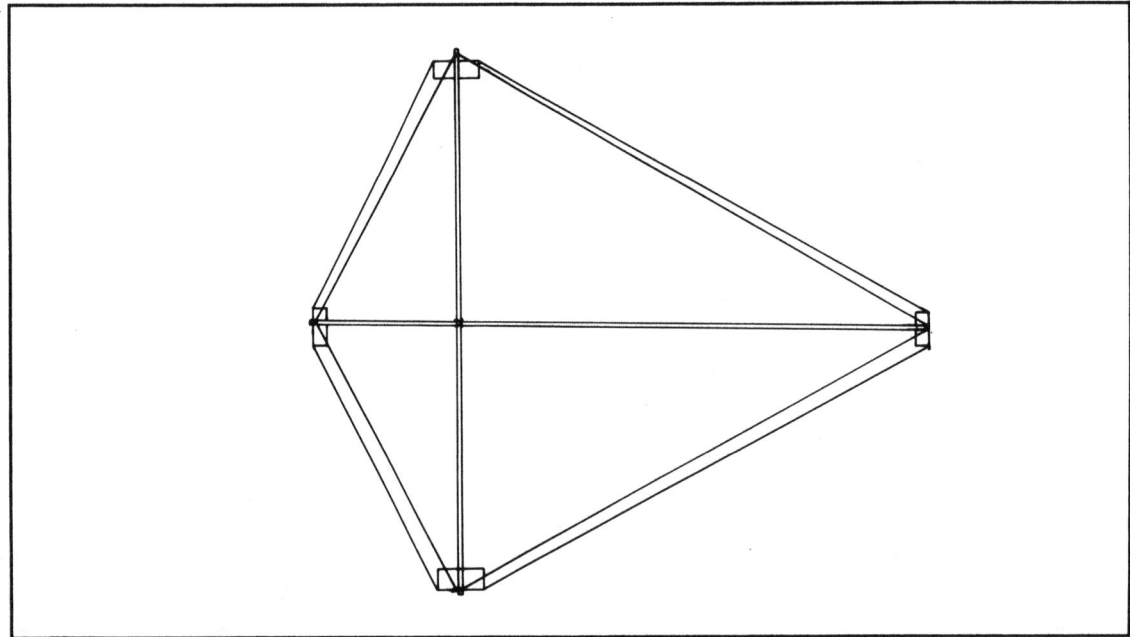

Fig. 6-10. Frame is positioned over covering material.

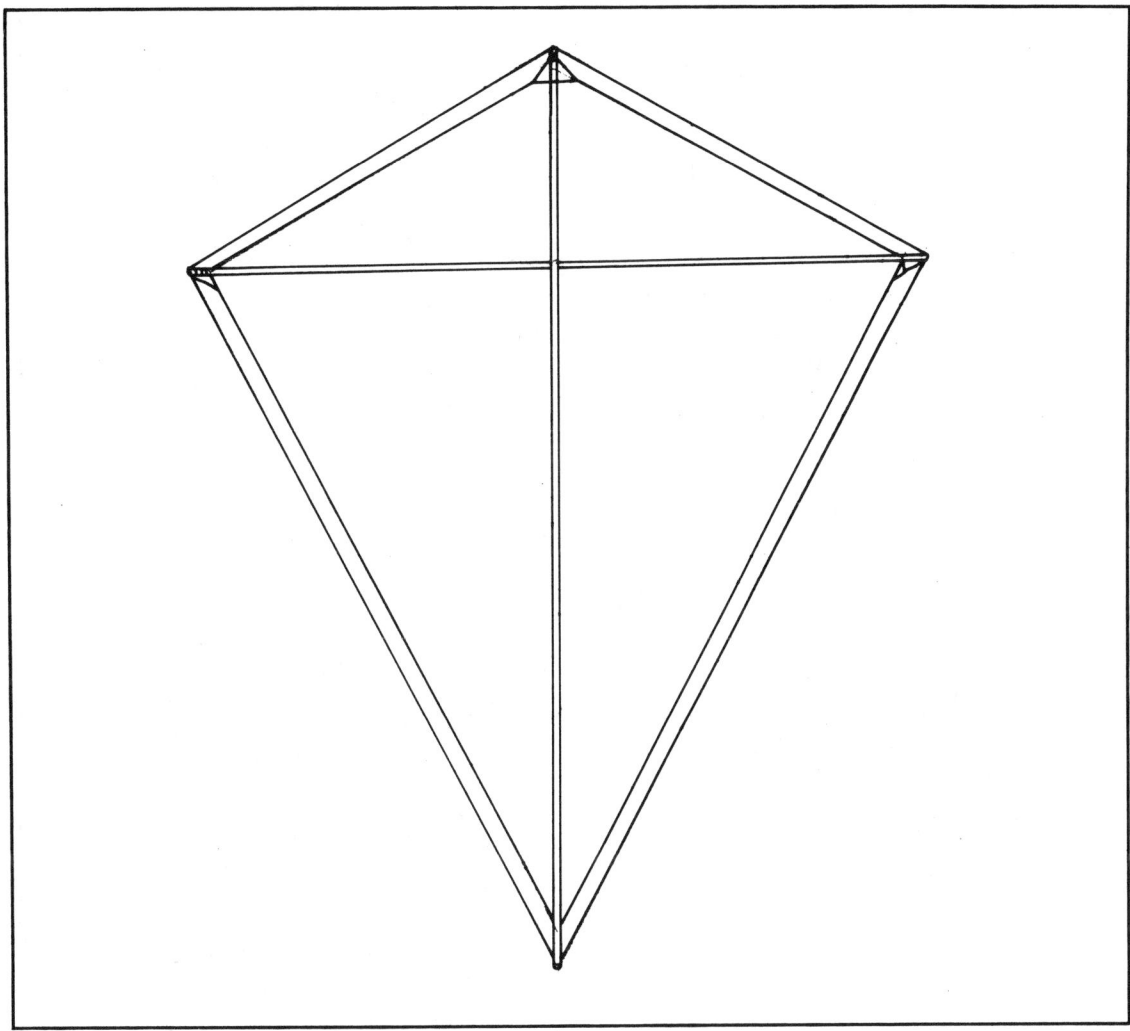

Fig. 6-11. Flaps are folded over guideline strings and glued to form sleeves.

Tail

A variety of tails can be used on this kite. The length and weight of the tail required will depend on the wind conditions when the kite is flown. A basic tail can be made from a strip of cloth approximately 6 feet long, as shown in Fig. 6-12. Tie short strips of cloth to this at approximately 6-inch intervals, as shown. Use string to tie the tail to the kite.

Tails can also be formed by tying short lengths of cloth to string or by using a long strip of fabric or plastic.

As a general rule, if the kite loops or spins, it needs more tail. Use the minimum amount of tail required to give the kite good stability.

Variations

A number of interesting variations of the basic two-stick flat kite are possible. By keeping the proportions approximately the same, the kite can be made very large: a 5-foot-long cross stick and a 6-foot-long longitudinal stick. By using balsa for the sticks, the kite can be constructed in miniature: a longitudinal stick of 1-foot or less in length. The large kites would probably be covered with fabric or

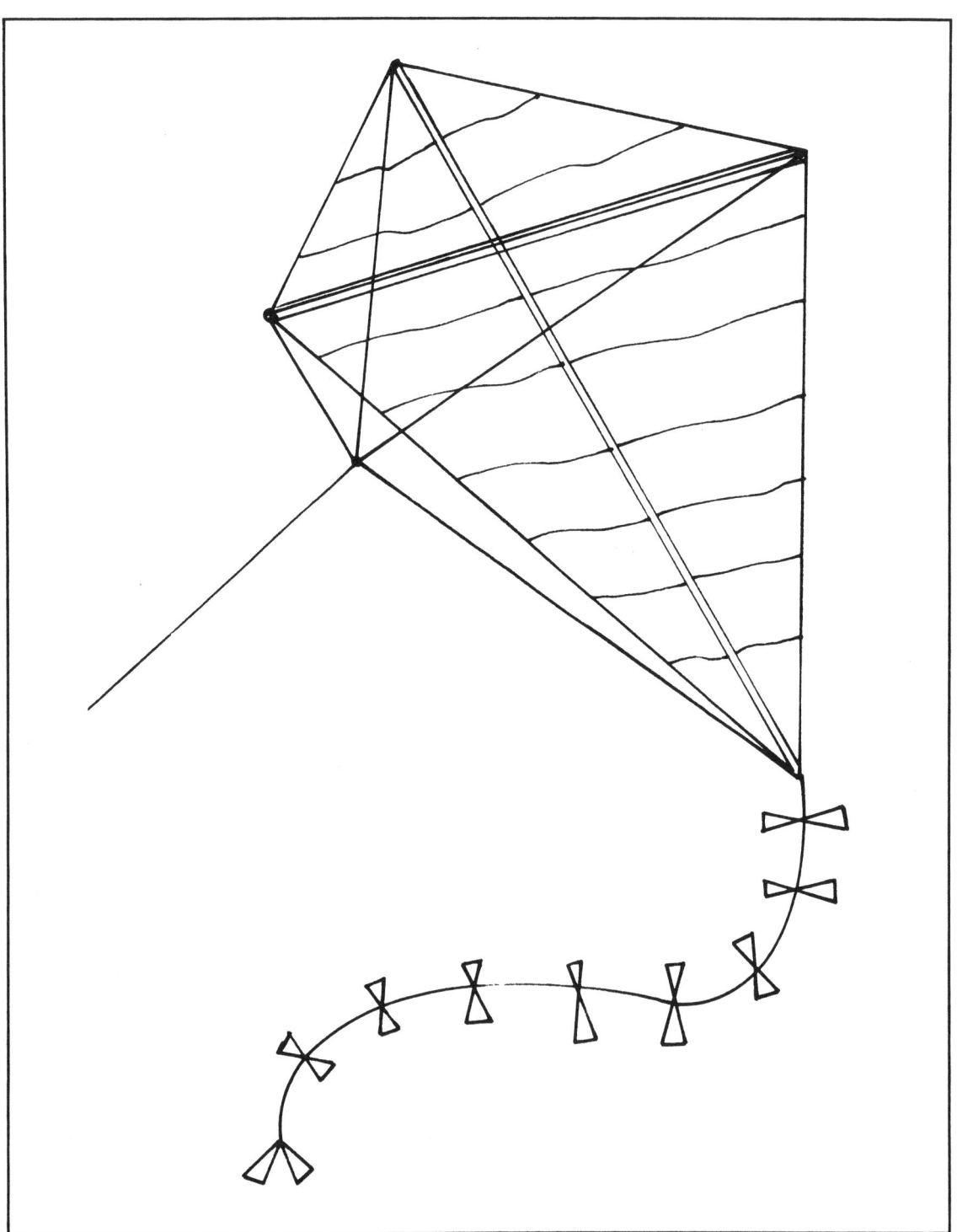

Fig. 6-12. Attachment of bridle strings and tail.

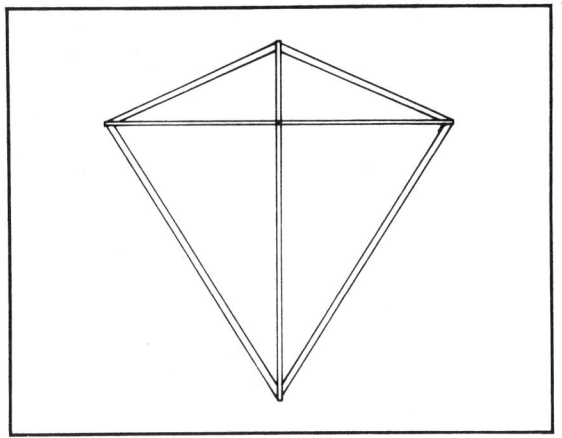

Fig. 6-13. Basic two-stick bow kite.

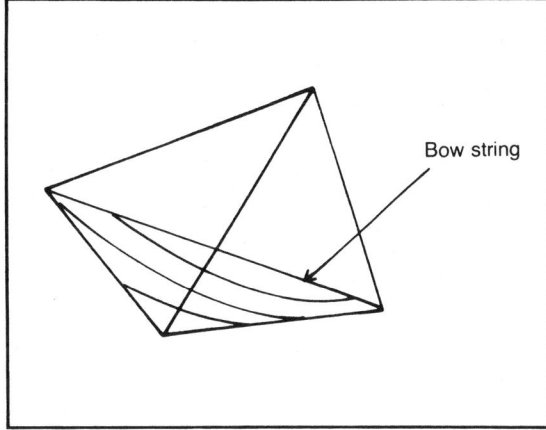

Fig. 6-14. The kite is bowed.

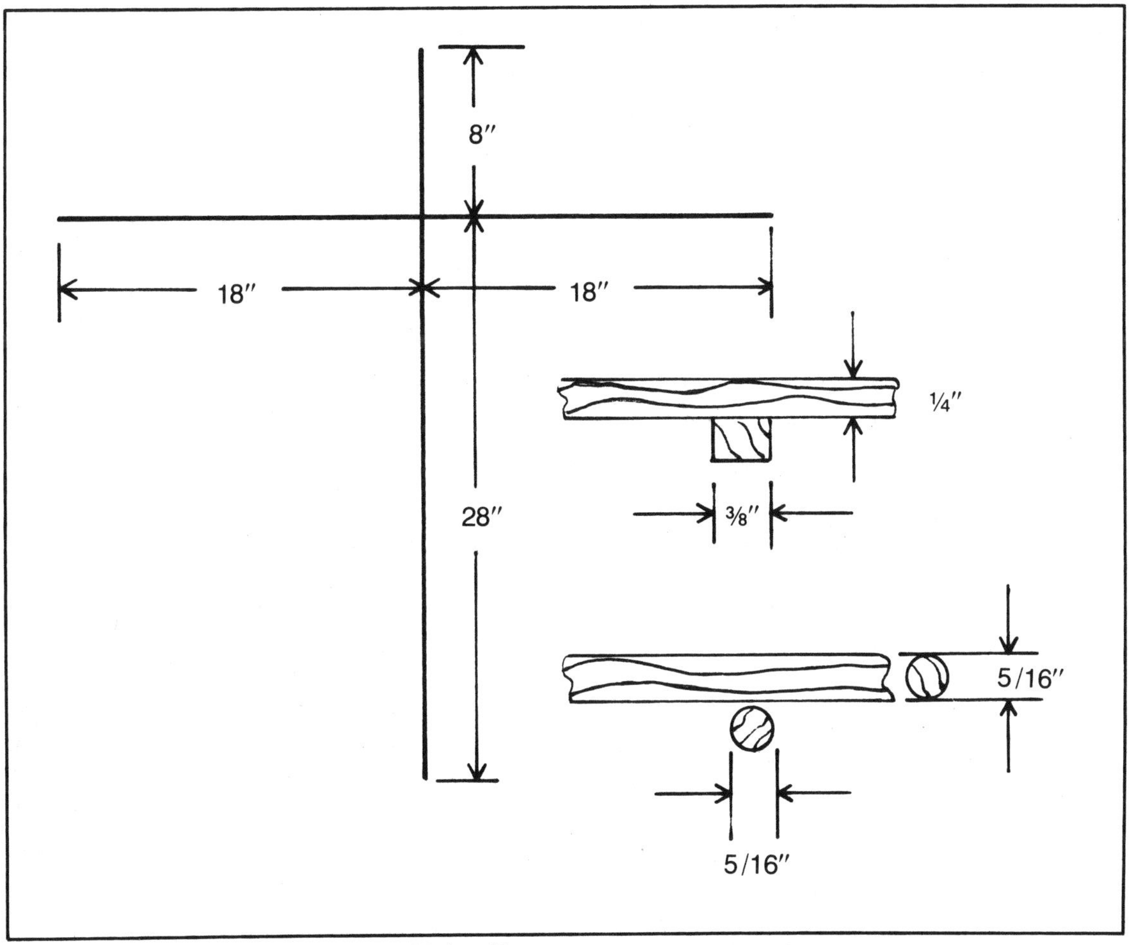

Fig. 6-15. Pattern for sticks for basic two-stick bow kite.

plastic material. A very thin tissue paper or plastic film can be used for covering small kites.

One problem with an extremely large two-stick flat kite is that a large tail is usually required to give it adequate stability. For this reason, if you want to make a large two-stick kite, the bowed model, detailed next, is recommended.

You may also want to experiment with length to breadth proportions and/or placement of the cross stick on the longitudinal stick.

BASIC TWO-STICK BOW KITE

The basic two-stick bow kite (Fig. 6-13) is sometimes called an *Eddy kite* because it was invented by William Eddy. Unlike the basic two-stick flat kite, this kite will fly without a tail. This is possible because of the wider beam and the bow (Fig. 6-14).

Frame

Two sticks are required for the frame (Fig. 6-15). Sticks of pine, spruce, or similar wood that is ¼-inch by ⅜-inch in cross section and each measuring 36 inches in length are recommended. The sticks can vary somewhat from the cross-sectional dimensions and still give satisfactory re-

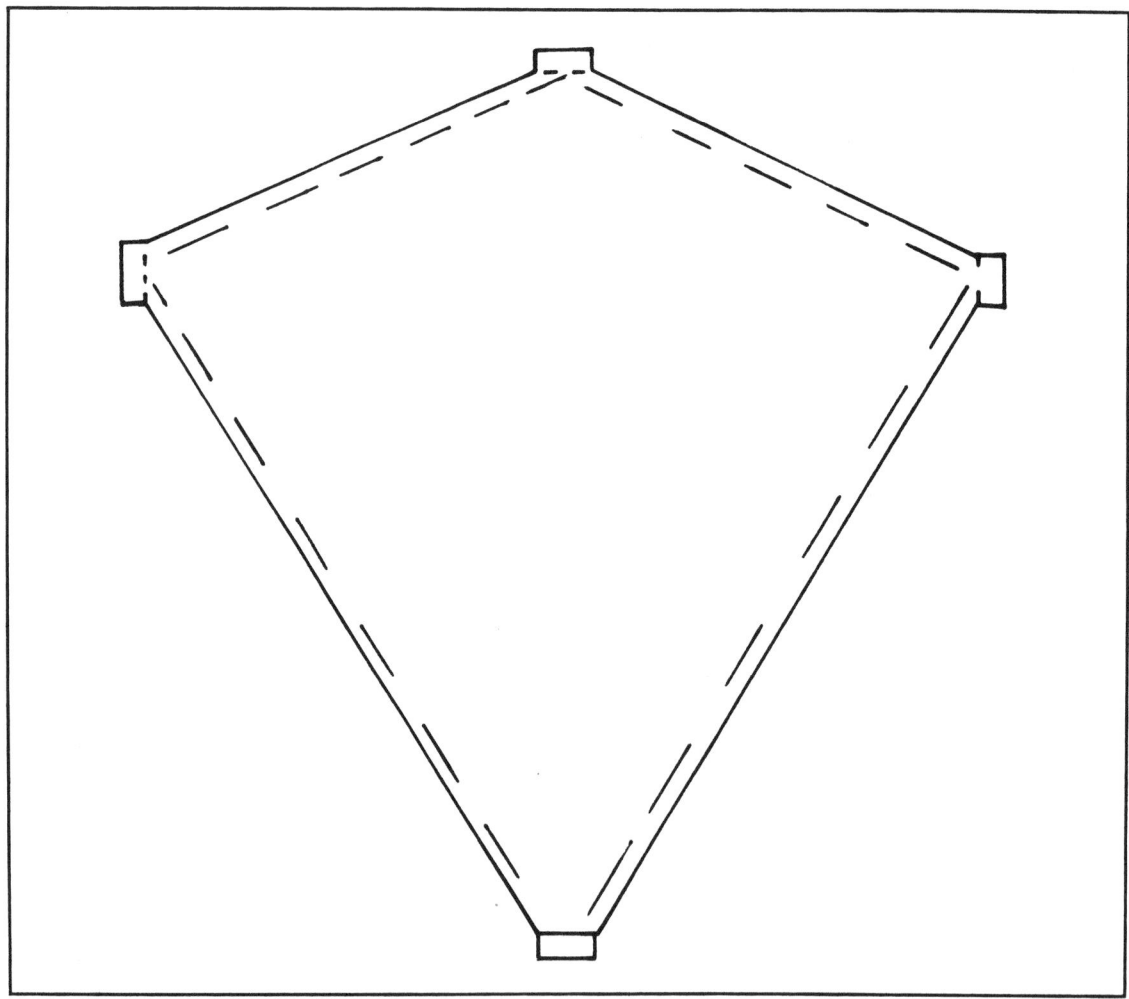

Fig. 6-16. Pattern for covering material.

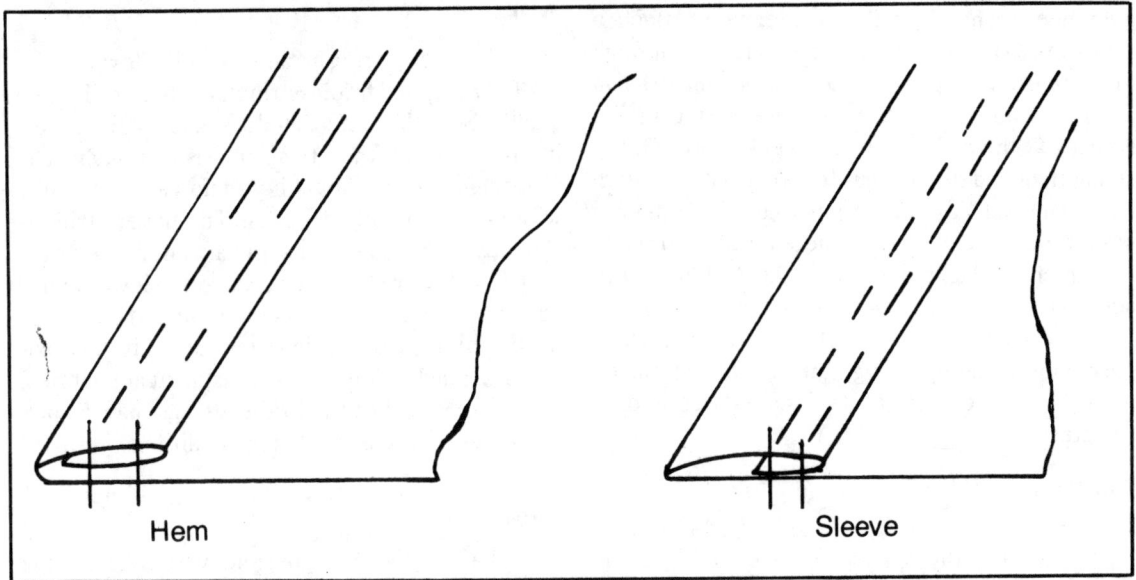

Fig. 6-17. Sewing hems and sleeves in cloth fabric covering material.

sults. Wooden dowels of 5/16-inch diameter can also be used. Sticks of fiberglass, bamboo, and aluminum tubing are alternatives, but for a first construction, I suggest that you use wood. You can experiment with other sticks later. You can make the kite larger or smaller than the dimensions shown, if you keep the proportions approximately the same, but I suggest that you use the dimensions shown. You can experiment with other dimensions later.

The ends of the sticks are notched, as shown in Fig. 6-3. Measure and mark the intersection on the two sticks. The cross stick should balance at the center point and form an even bow when bent by its ends. If not, correct the stick by sanding and filing, as required.

Glue and bind the two sticks together with a string lashing. Tie the ends of the string with a square knot, and apply glue to the string lashing.

If a sewn fabric cover is to be used, the guideline string is usually installed later, after the cover material has been sewn. If a paper or plastic film covering material is to be used, install and guideline string in the notches around the ends of the sticks. Stretch the string tight and tie the ends together with a square knot. Add lashings around the sticks on each side of the guideline string where it passes through the notches. Tie the ends of the lashings with square knots.

Covering Material

While paper covering materials can be used, a cloth or plastic material generally works better, as these stretch sufficiently to allow the kite to bow. For our purposes here, we will detail a cloth fabric cover. Methods for making covers of other materials are detailed in Chapter 5.

Mark the pattern shown in Fig. 6-16 on the fabric. The kite frame can be used as a pattern by placing a temporary guideline string around it through the notches and placing the frame on the cloth fabric, as shown in Fig. 6-8. The frame should be positioned so that the side where the cross stick passes below the longitudinal stick is against the cloth fabric. Use scissors to cut the fabric to the pattern.

Sew the hems and sleeves in the material. This is usually best done with a sewing machine, but if desired, the sewing can be done by hand. The hems and sleeves are usually folded under again before sewing, as shown in Fig. 6-17.

After the cover has been sewn, pass the

guideline string through the sleeves. Attach a safety pin to the end of the string to feed it through the sleeves. Then position the covering material on the frame and insert the guideline string in the notches at the ends of the kite sticks. Stretch the string tight and tie the ends together with a square knot. Then add lashings around the sticks on each side of the guideline string where it passes through the notches. Tie the ends of the lashings with square knots.

Construct the paper or plastic cover similarly, except join paper by gluing. Join plastic material by gluing, heat-sealing, or taping, as detailed in Chapter 5.

Bow String

Tie the bow string to one end of the cross stick, passing it through the notch in the end of the stick. Bow the kite until it has a 4-inch bow (Fig. 6-18). Then tie the bow string to the other end of the cross stick. Notice that the longitudinal stick is inside the bow.

Bridle

The bridle string arrangement is shown in Fig. 6-19. The upper bridle string attaches to the two sticks where they join. A hole is made in the covering material for the string to pass through. The covering material should be reinforced in this area with tape or by other means. The upper string is about 24 inches long to its attachment at the bridle ring. The lower string attaches to the lower end of the longitudinal stick, passing through the notch in the end of the stick. This string should be approximately 36 inches long to its attachment at the bridle ring. The length of the bridle strings may require adjustment for specific flying conditions.

Variations

There are many possible variations to the basic two-stick bow kite. The design can be made smaller and larger by keeping the proportions approximately the same. This design is suitable for large sizes with a longitudinal length of 6 feet or

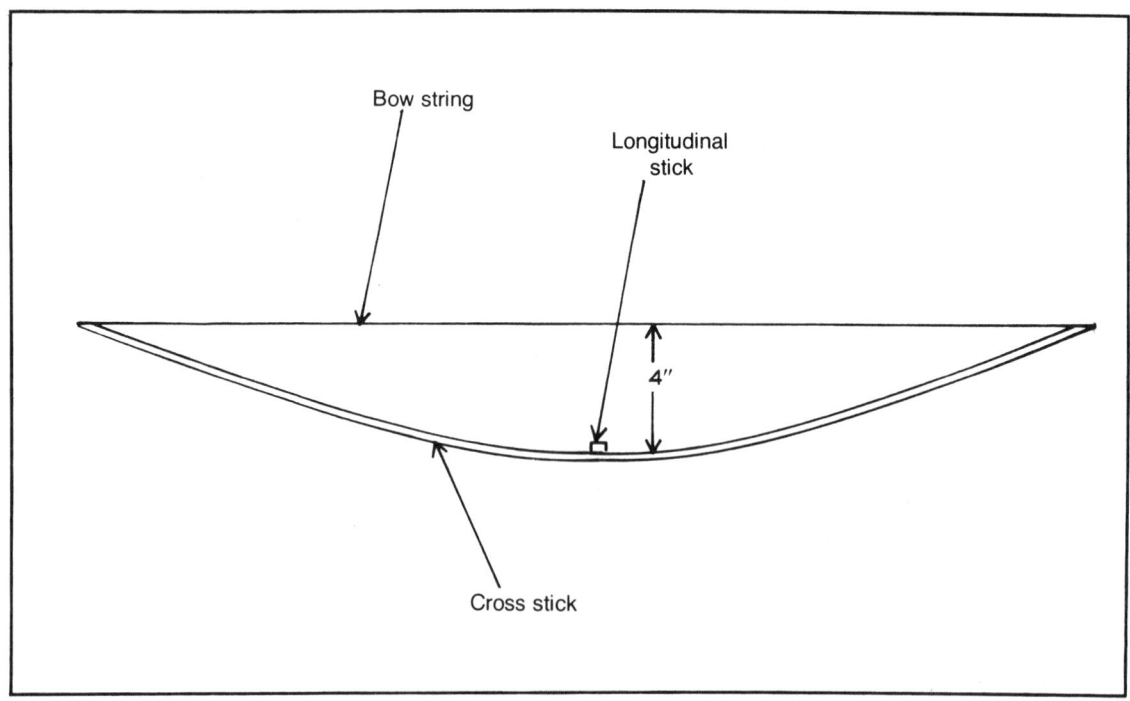

Fig. 6-18. Bow string.

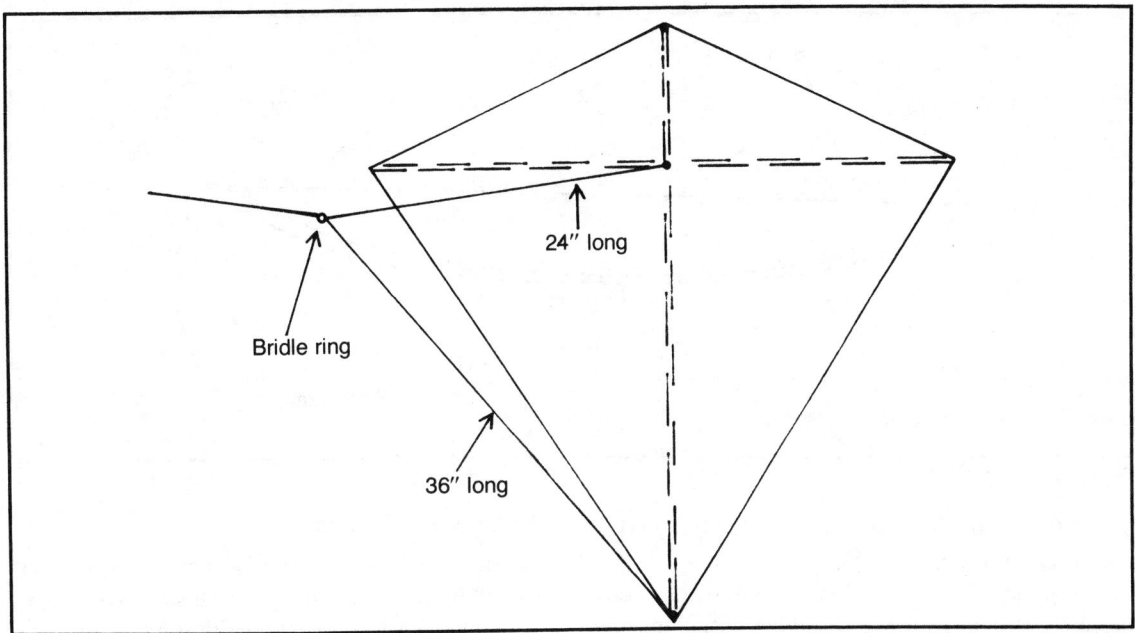

Fig. 6-19. Bridle string attachment.

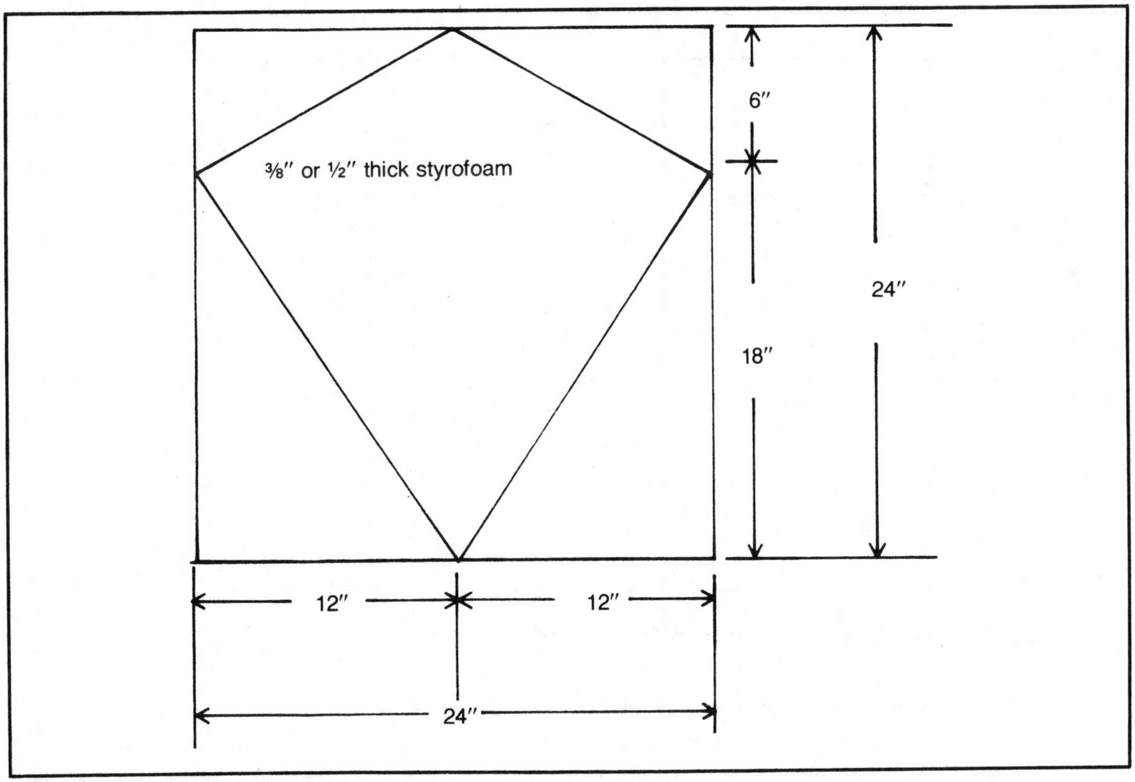

Fig. 6-20. Pattern for styrofoam kite.

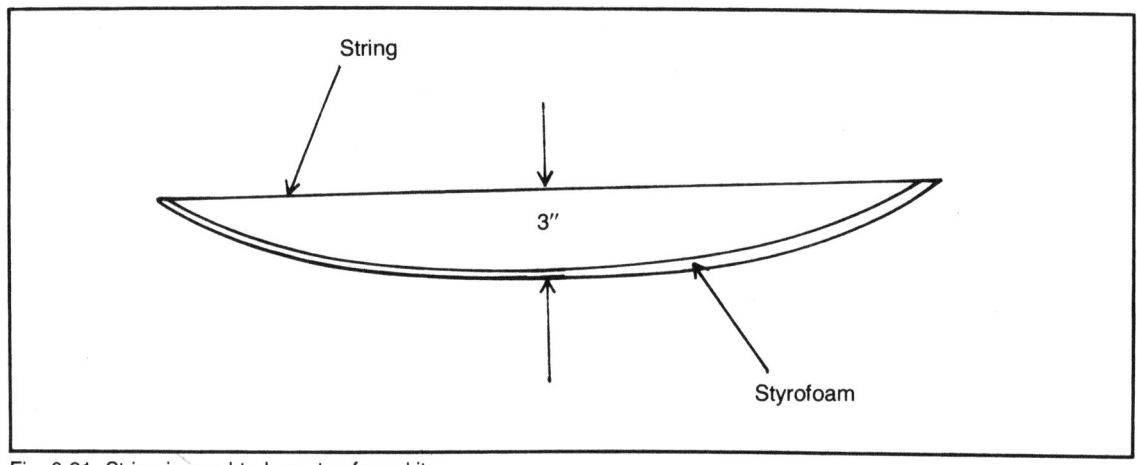

Fig. 6-21. String is used to bow styrofoam kite.

more. It has the advantage over the flat kite in that no tail is required.

You may also want to experiment by changing the proportional length of the two sticks and the placement of the cross joint.

STYROFOAM BOW KITE

An interesting bow kite can also be constructed from styrofoam, with the styrofoam serving as both the frame and covering material.

A version cut from a single piece of ½-inch

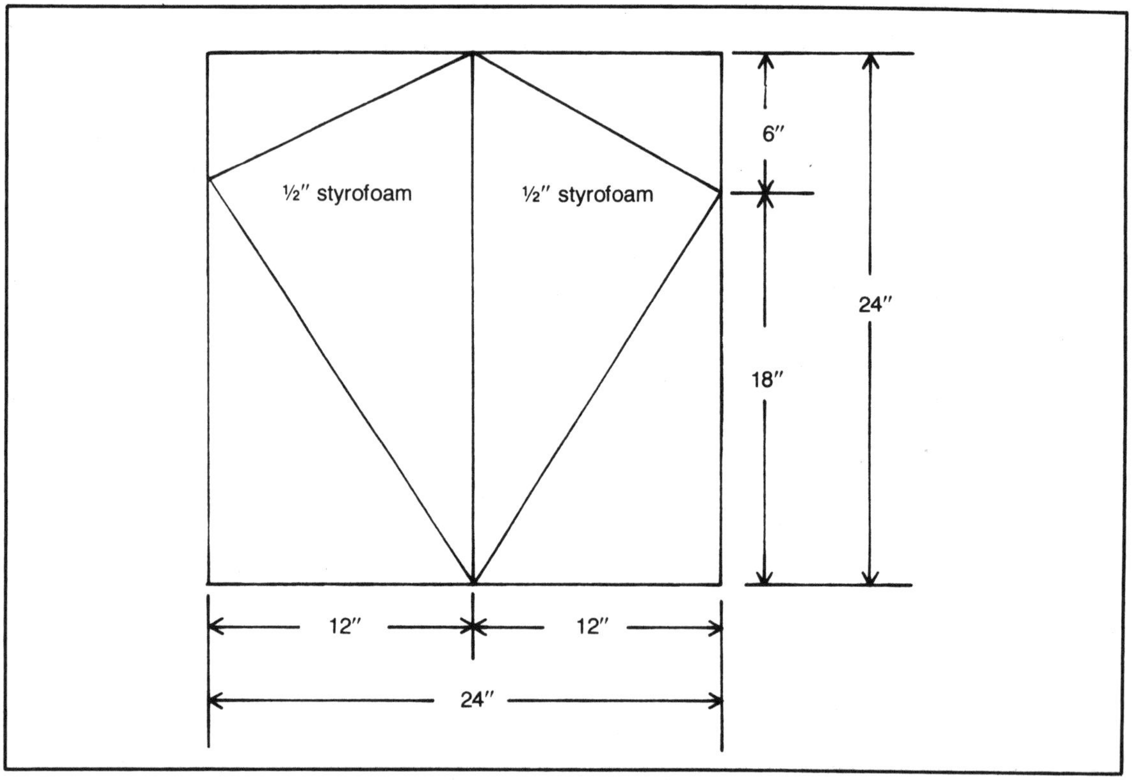

Fig. 6-22. Pattern for two-section styrofoam kite.

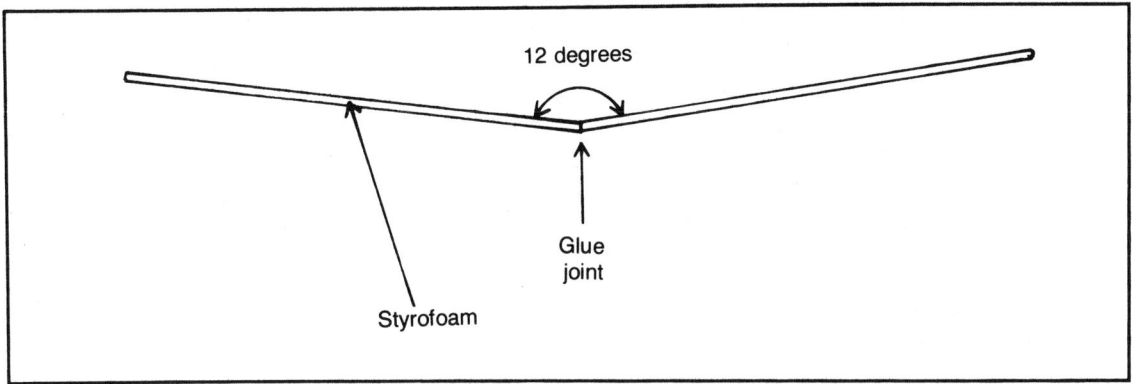

Fig. 6-23. The two sections are joined at 12-degree angle.

styrofoam is shown in Fig. 6-20. This kite is bowed with a piece of string, as shown in Fig. 6-21. The bow string passes through holes in the styrofoam, which should be reinforced with tape.

The second version is made in two sections, as shown in Fig. 6-22. One section is cut at a 12-degree angle along the centerline. The two sections are then glued together to form a 12-degree angle at

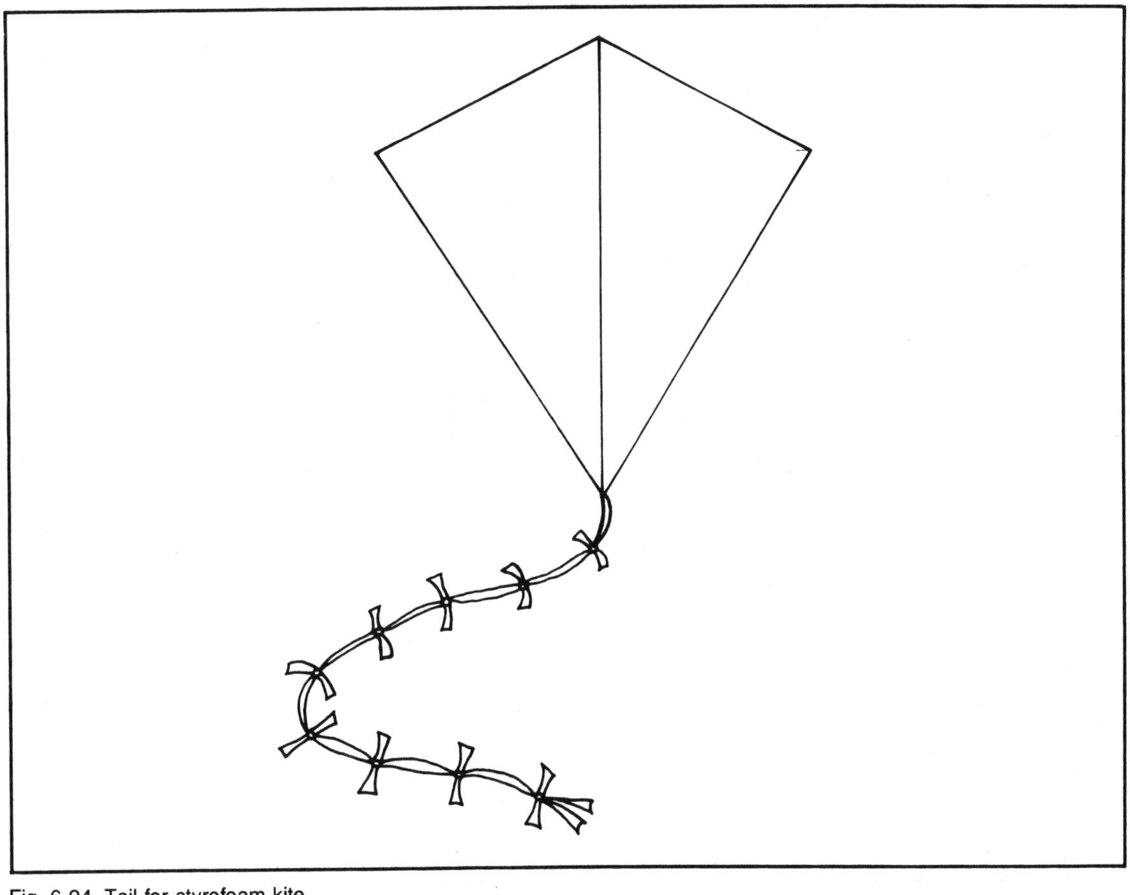

Fig. 6-24. Tail for styrofoam kite.

the centerline, as shown in Fig. 6-23.

Bridle strings are attached through holes made in the styrofoam and reinforced with tape. A tail is usually required to give these kites stability, as shown in Fig. 6-24.

You may also want to experiment with various other sizes and shapes of this basic styrofoam kite design, such as round, square, and figure forms.

THREE-STICK KITE WITH CONVERGING LONGITUDINALS

The three-stick kite with converging longitudinals is shown in Fig. 6-25. This kite can be used with or without a bow, as desired. The performance is generally improved by the simple addition of a bow string.

Frame

Three sticks, all 36 inches long, are required for the frame (Fig. 6-26). The sticks can be ¼-inch diameter round wooden dowels or have a rectangular cross section of ¼ inch by ⅜ inch. The sticks can vary somewhat from these dimensions and still give satisfactory results. For light airs, you might want

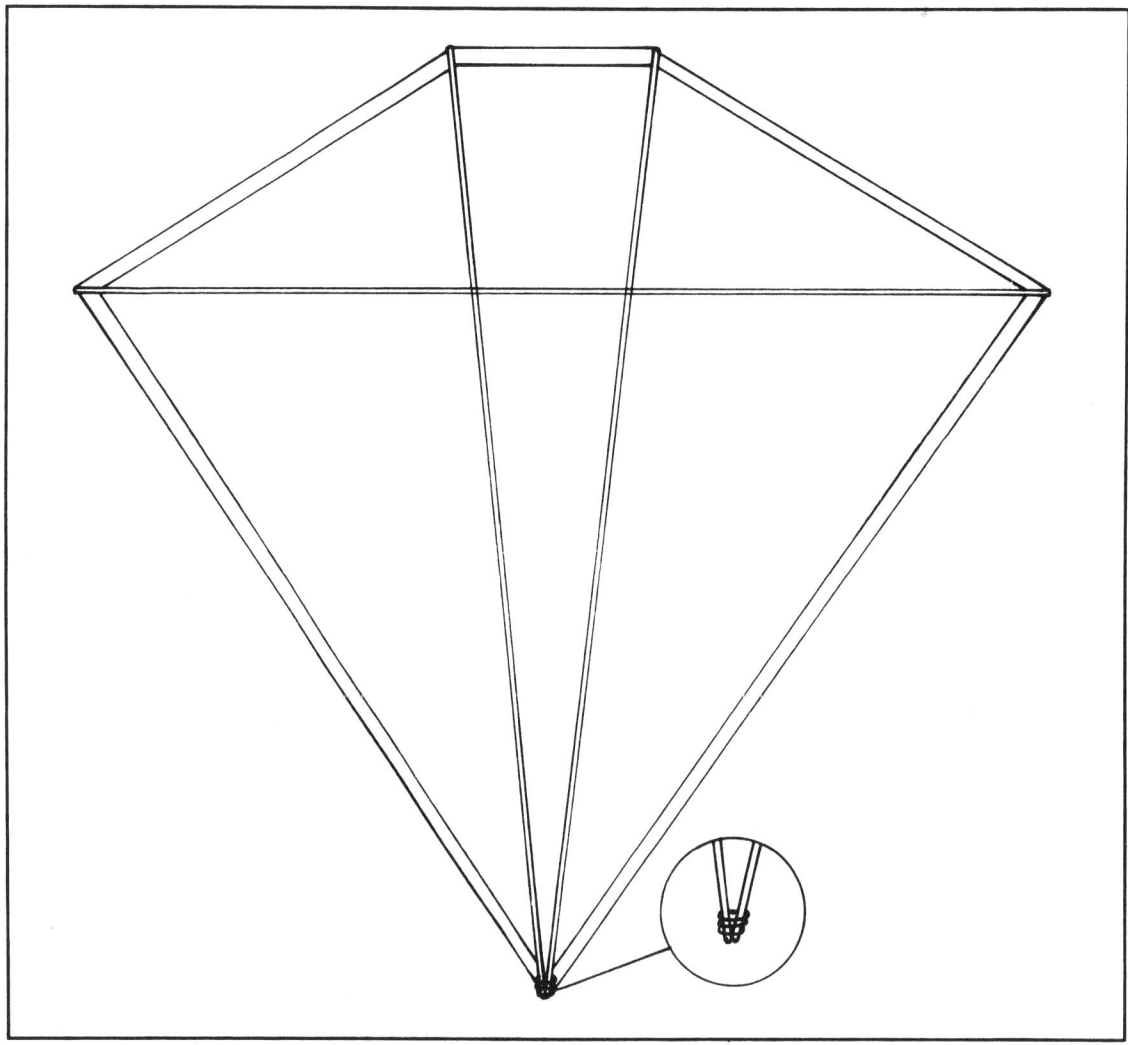

Fig. 6-25. Three-stick kite with converging longitudinals. Detail shows how longitudinals are glued and lashed together.

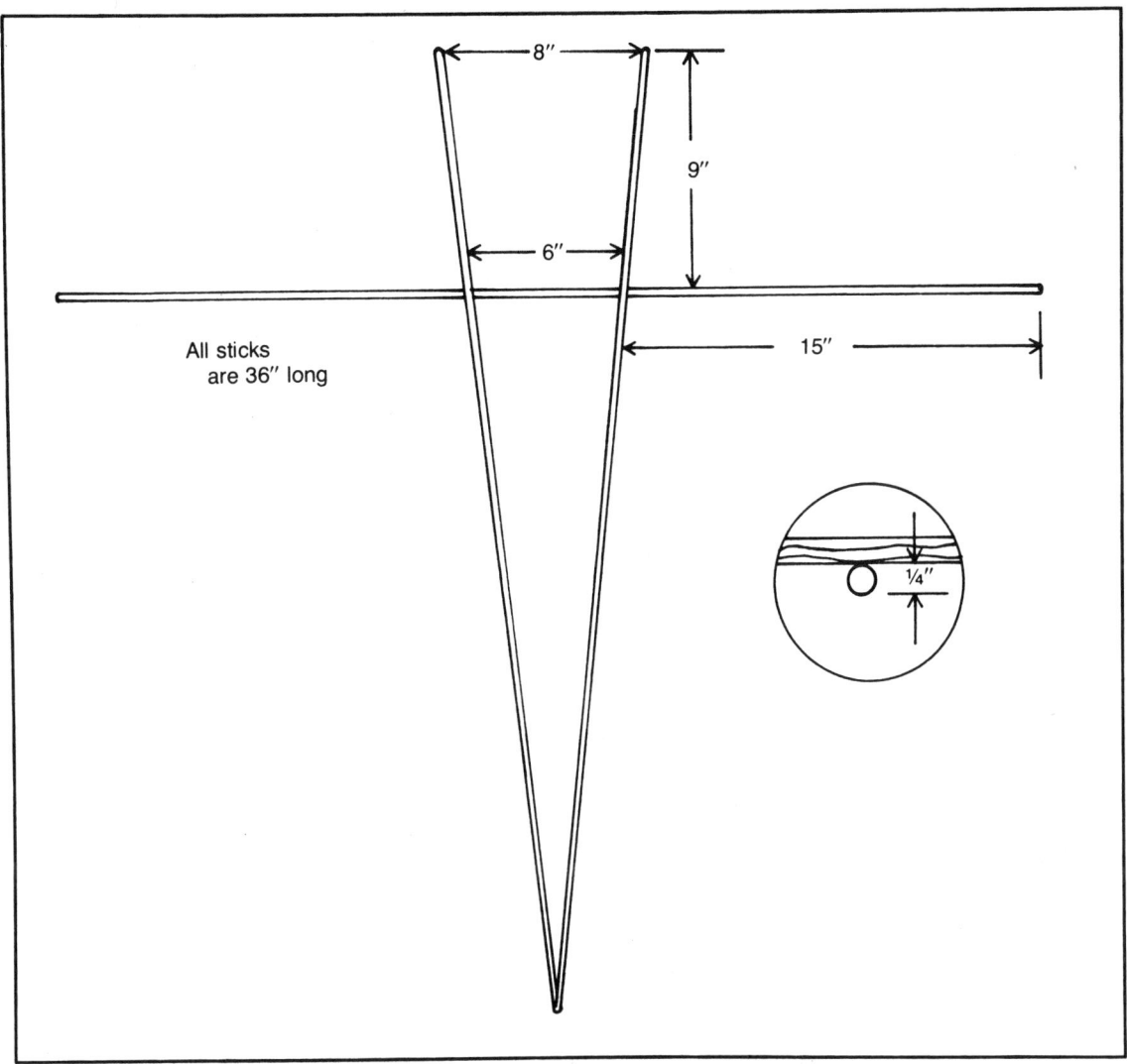

Fig. 6-26. Pattern for sticks for three-stick kite with converging longitudinals.

to use smaller sticks. For flying in strong winds, you might want to use heavier sticks. Fiberglass, bamboo, and aluminum sticks are other possibilities.

For descriptive purposes, we'll assume that you are using ¼-inch round wooden for the sticks, but construction with the rectangular sticks is similar.

The ends of the sticks are notched by making a saw cut to a depth of ⅜ inch in the end of each stick (Fig. 6-3). It is important to make certain that the notches line up at the ends of each stick.

Measure and mark the intersections on each stick, as shown in Fig. 6-26. The two longitudinal sticks are glued and lashed with string to the cross stick, as shown in Fig. 6-27. Tie the ends of the string with square knots. Glue and tie the two longitudinals together. Insert a piece of metal or plastic that will just fit in the notches (Fig. 6-28) to keep the notches lined up until the glue sets.

Install the guideline string in the notches at the ends of the sticks around the kite frame (Fig. 6-29).

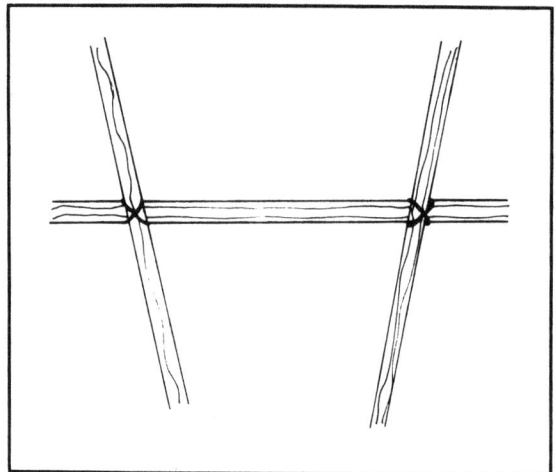

Fig. 6-27. Longitudinal sticks are glued and lashed to cross stick.

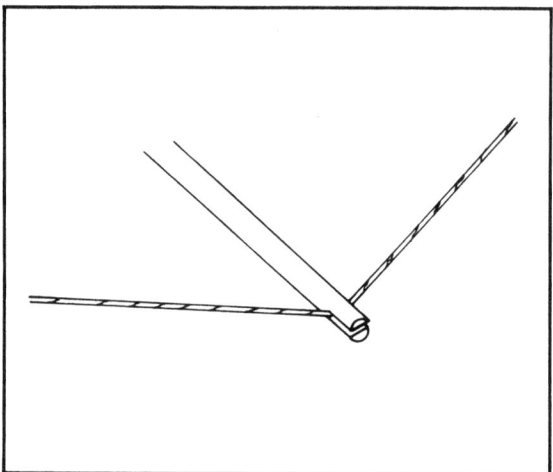

Fig. 6-29. The guideline string passes through notches in ends of sticks.

Stretch the string tight and tie the ends together with a square knot. If a sewn fabric covering material is to be used, you will probably want to wait until the cover has been sewn before installing the guideline string so that it can be inserted in the sleeves first. After installing the guideline string, add lashings around the sticks on each side of the guideline string where it passes through the notches in the sticks (Fig. 6-30). Tie the ends of the lashing strings together with square knots.

Covering Material

Paper, plastic, or cloth can be used for covering the kite, as desired. Mark the pattern shown in Fig. 6-31. The kite frame, with either the permanent or a temporary guideline string in place, can be placed over the covering material as a pattern. The frame should be positioned so that the side where the cross stick passes below the longitudinal sticks is against the covering material. This positions the cross stick correctly for bowing.

Cut the covering material to the pattern with scissors. Methods for joining covering material to form hems and sleeves depends on the particular covering material used (see Chapter 5).

Regardless of the covering material used, in-

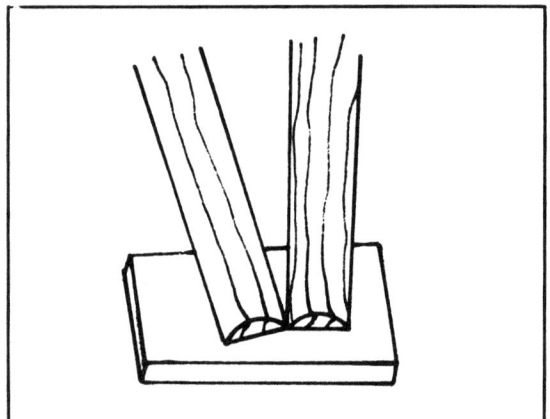

Fig. 6-28. Insert in notches keeps sticks in position until the glue sets.

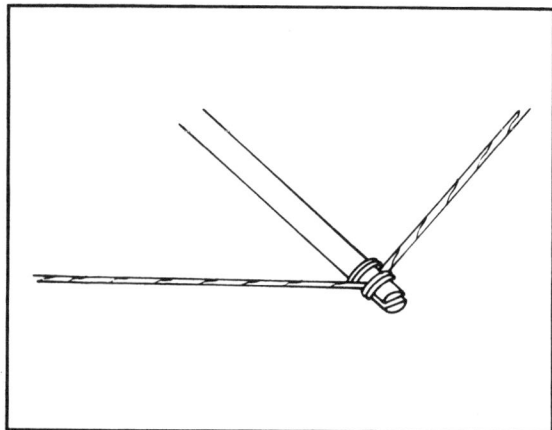

Fig. 6-30. Lashings are placed around stick on both sides of guideline.

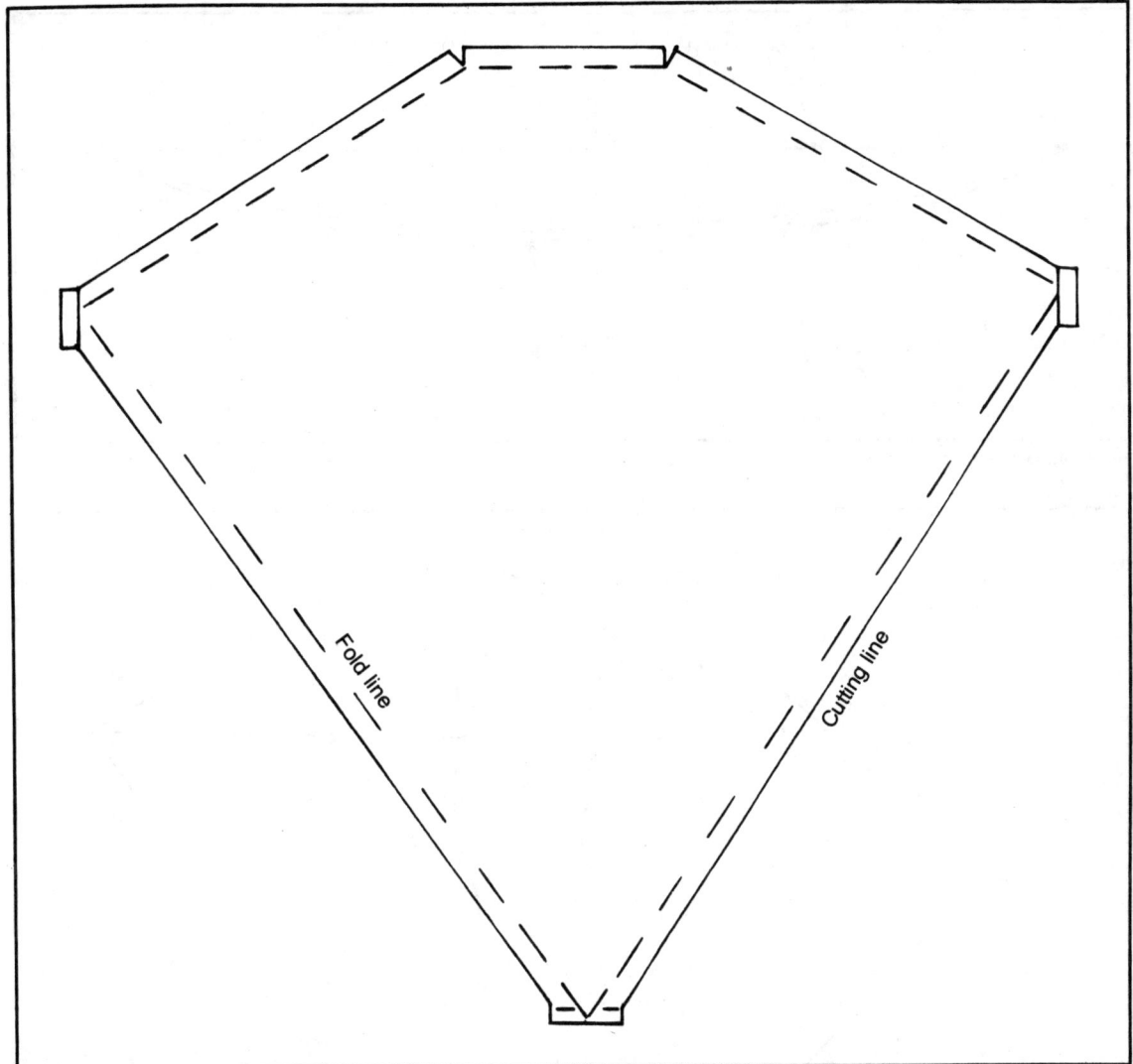

Fig. 6-31. Pattern for covering material.

stall it to the kite frame with the guideline string passing through sleeves in the covering material.

Bow String

Tie the bow string to one end of the cross stick, passing it through the notch in the end of the stick. Bow the kite until it has a 4-inch bow, as shown in Fig. 6-32. Then tie the bow string to the other end of the cross stick, passing it through the notch in the end of the stick. Notice that the two longitudinal sticks are inside the bow.

Bridle

A three-string bridle is usually used, as shown in Fig. 6-33. The strings are passed through the notches and tied around the ends of the sticks. Use a small plastic curtain rod ring as a bridle ring, and tie the bridle strings to the bridle ring. The length of the bridle strings can be adjusted for particular wind conditions. The kite string or line is attached to the bridle ring for flying.

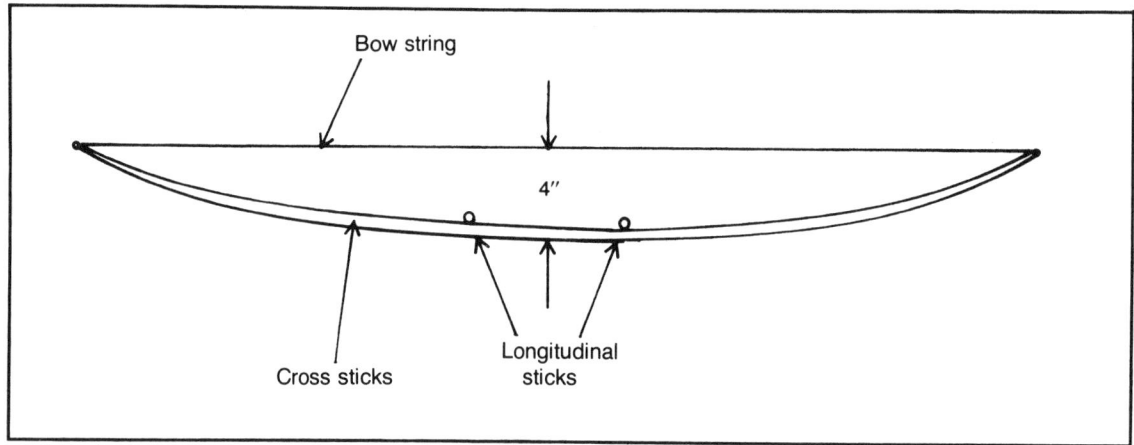

Fig. 6-32. Bow string.

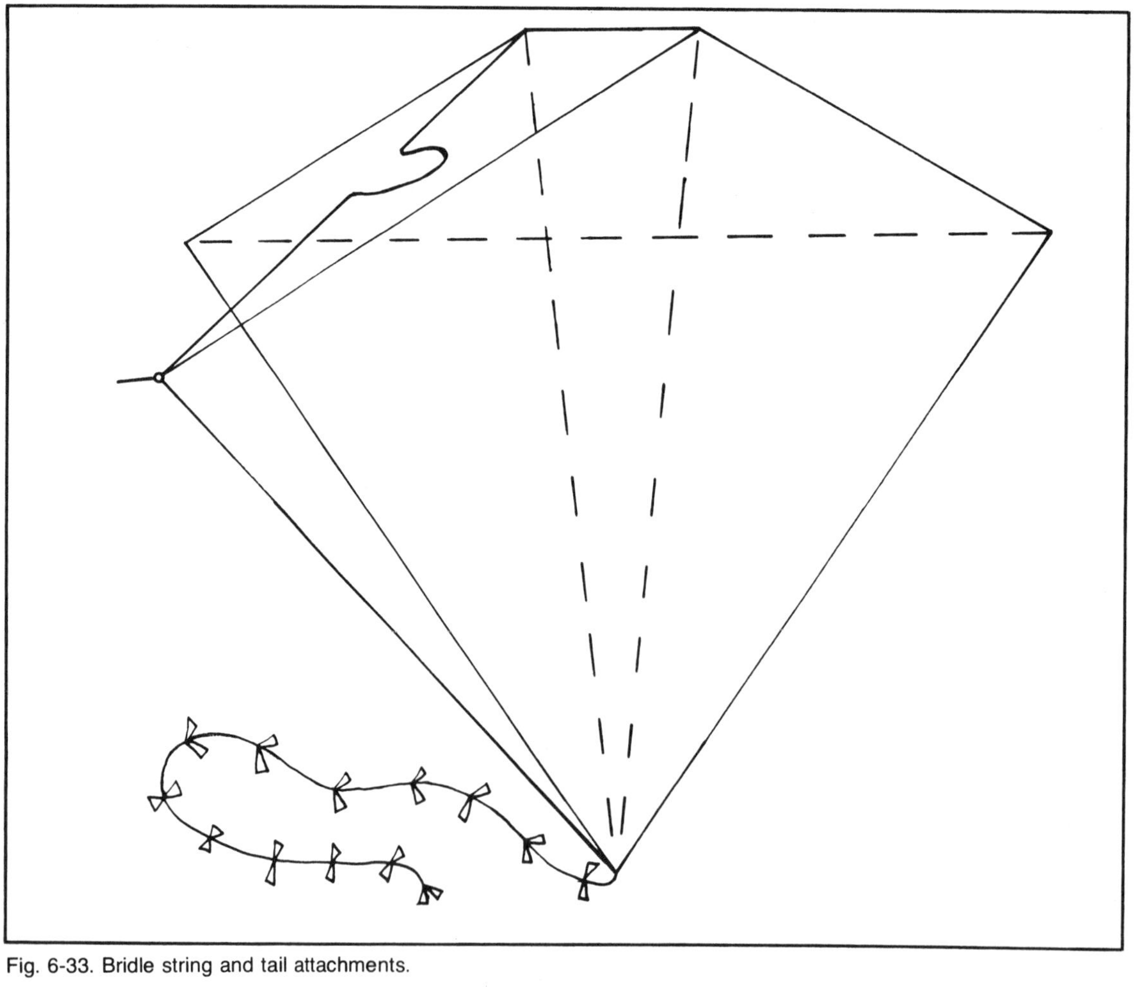

Fig. 6-33. Bridle string and tail attachments.

Tail

The three-stick kite with converging longitudinals will often fly without a tail. For some flying conditions, however, a tail may be required. The length and weight of the tail required will depend on the wind conditions when the kite is flown. A single tail attached to the bottom end of the kite frame where the two longitudinal sticks join is usually used.

Try the kite first without a tail. If the kite loops or spins, add a tail. Use the minimum amount of tail required to give the kite good stability.

Variations

The three-stick kite with converging longitudinals can be made in a variety of sizes from 1 foot or less in length and width of 6 feet or more in length and width, keeping the proportions the same. The smaller sizes require smaller sticks and lightweight covering materials; the larger sizes require larger sticks and heavier covering materials. You may also want to experiment by changing the proportions of the kite.

The three-stick kite with converging longitudinals can be flown without a bow if a tail is used, but I have found the performance to be considerably improved by the simple addition of the bow string.

THREE-STICK KITE WITH PARALLEL LONGITUDINALS

The three-stick kite with parallel longitudinals is shown in Fig. 6-34. This kite can be used with or without a bow, as desired. The performance is generally improved by the simple addition of a bow string, and this often eliminates the need for tails.

Frame

Three sticks 36 inches in length are required for the frame, as shown in Fig. 6-35. Wooden sticks with a rectangular cross section of ¼-inch diameter round wooden dowels can be used. The sticks can vary somewhat from these dimensions and still give satisfactory results. For use in light air, sticks with smaller cross sections might be adequate. For use in very strong winds, sticks with larger cross sections may be required to give adequate strength to the kite frame. Sticks of fiberglass, bamboo, and aluminum are other possibilities.

We'll assume that you will be using wooden sticks of either rectangular or round cross sections.

The ends of the sticks are notched by making a saw cut to a depth of ⅜ inch in the end of each stick. It is important to make the notches at each end of a stick in the same plane.

Measure and mark the intersections on each stick, as shown in Fig. 6-35. The two longitudinal sticks are glued and lashed with string to the cross stick, as shown in Fig. 6-36. Tie the ends of the strings together with square knots. All of the notches at the ends of the sticks should be parallel to the plane surface of the kite.

The guideline string is installed in the notches at the ends of all the sticks (Fig. 6-37). Stretch the string tight and tie the ends together with a square knot. If a sewn fabric covering material is to be used, you will probably want to wait until the cover has been sewn before installing the guideline string so that it can be inserted in the sleeves first. After the guideline string has been installed, add lashings around the sticks on each side of the guideline string where it passes through the notches in the

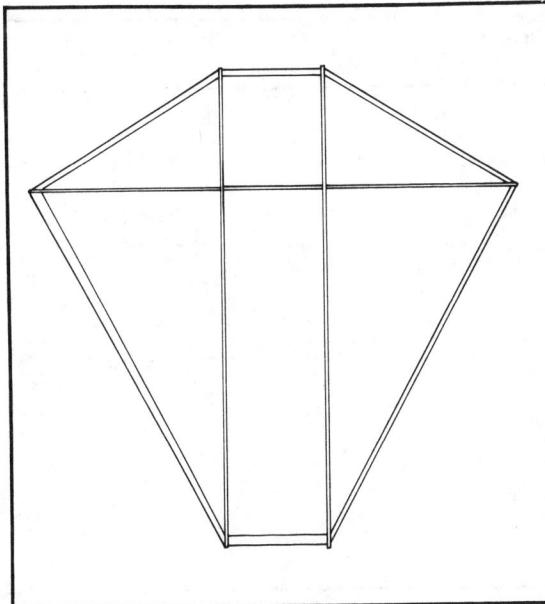

Fig. 6-34. Three-stick kite with parallel longitudinal sticks.

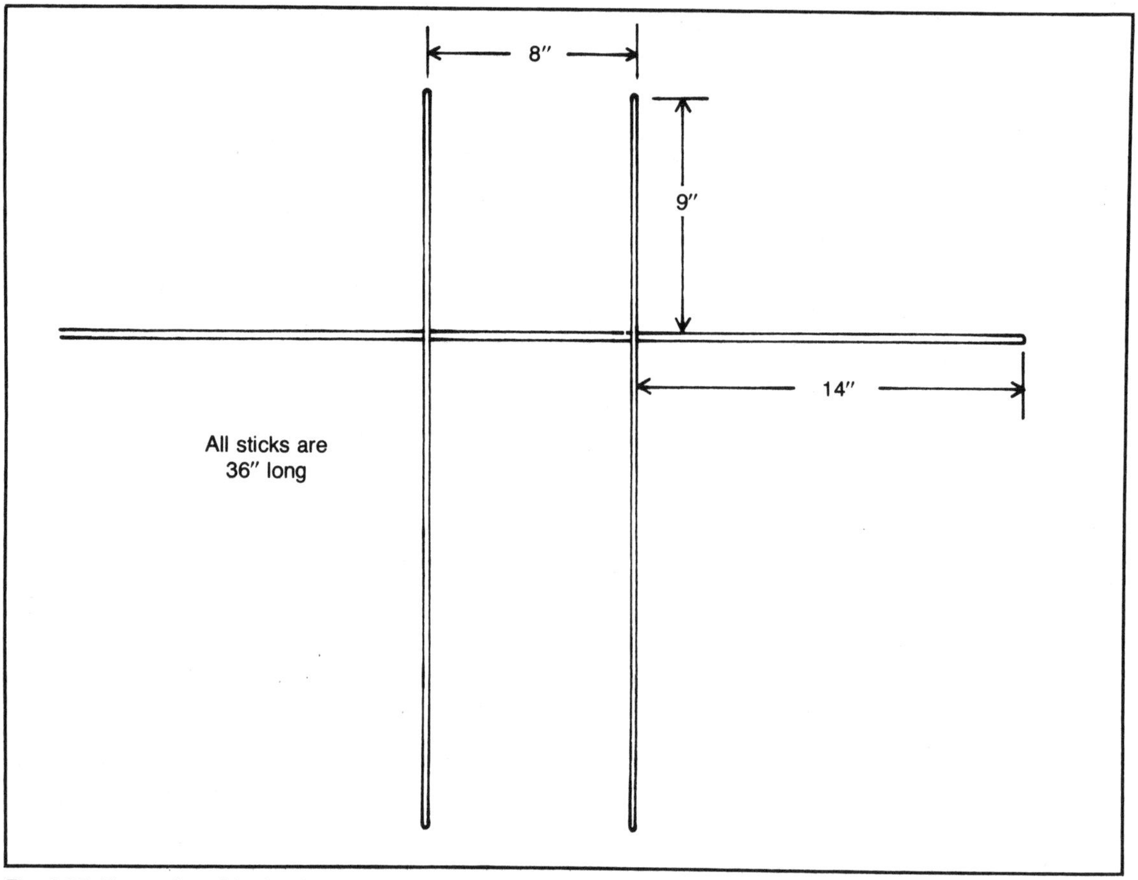

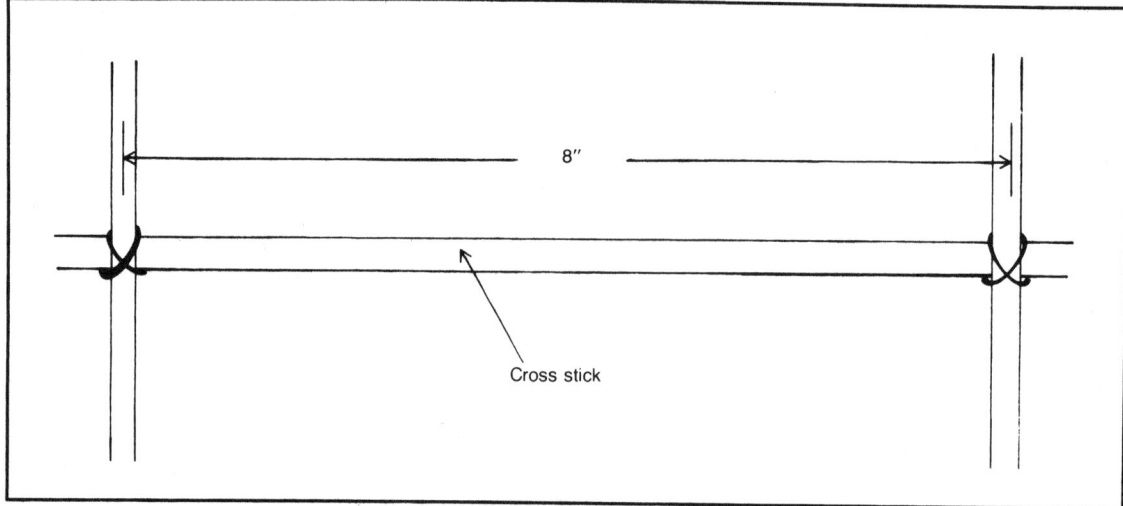

Fig. 6-35. Pattern for sticks for three-stick kite with parallel longitudinals.

Fig. 6-36. Longitudinal sticks are glued and lashed with string to cross stick.

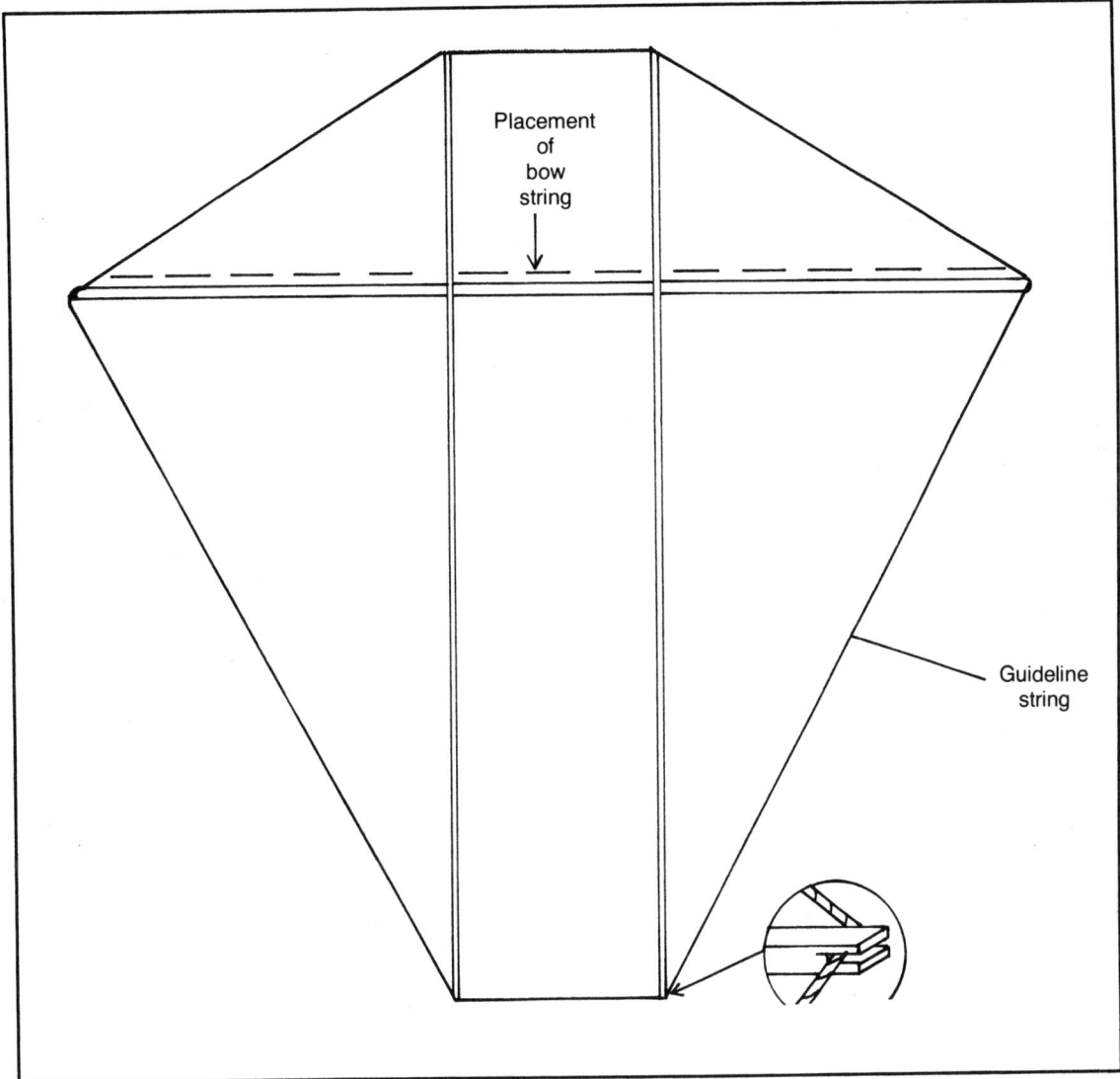

Fig. 6-37. The guideline string is installed in notches around frame sticks.

sticks. Tie the ends of each lashing string together with a square knot.

Covering Material

Paper, plastic, or cloth can be used for covering the kite. Mark the pattern shown in Fig. 6-38 on the covering material. The kite frame, with either the permanent or a temporary guideline string in place, can be placed over the covering material as a pattern. The frame should be positioned so that the side where the cross stick passes below the longitudinal sticks is against the covering material. This positions the cross stick correctly for bowing.

Cut the covering material to the pattern with scissors. Methods for joining covering material to form hems and sleeves depends on the particular covering material used (see Chapter 5). Regardless of the covering material used, install it to the kite frame with the guideline string passing through sleeves in the covering material.

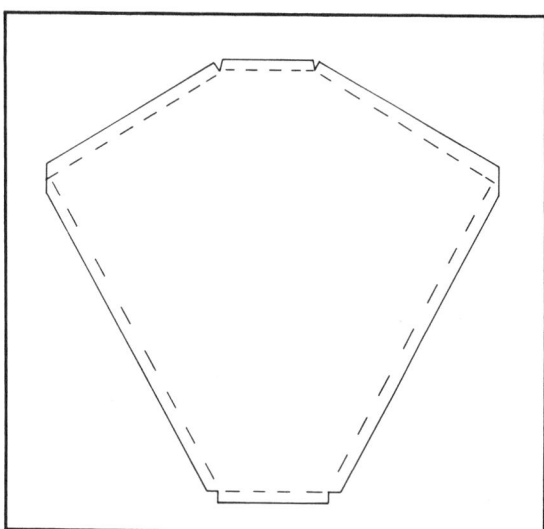

Fig. 6-38. Pattern for covering material.

Bow String

The performance of this kite is usually improved by adding a bow string. Tie the bow string to one end of the cross stick, passing it through the notch in the end of the stick. Bow the kite until it has a 4-inch bow, as shown in Fig. 6-39. Then tie the bow string to the other end of the cross stick.

Notice that the two longitudinal sticks are inside the bow.

Bridle

A four-string bridle is usually used, as shown in Fig. 6-40. The strings are passed through the notches and tied around the ends of the sticks. Use a small plastic curtain-rod ring as a bridle ring. While a loop knot can also be used, the ring makes adjustment of the bridle strings easier. Tie the bridle strings to the bridle ring. The length of the bridle strings can be adjusted for particular flying conditions. To fly the kite, attach the kite string or line to the bridle ring.

Tails

The three-stick kite with parallel longitudinal sticks will often fly without a tail if the kite is properly bowed. If the kite is flown without a bow or with a bow in some flying conditions, a tail may be required. Two tails are usually used, as shown in Fig. 6-40. These are attached to the aft ends of the longitudinal sticks. The length and weight of the tails required will depend on the wind conditions and other factors.

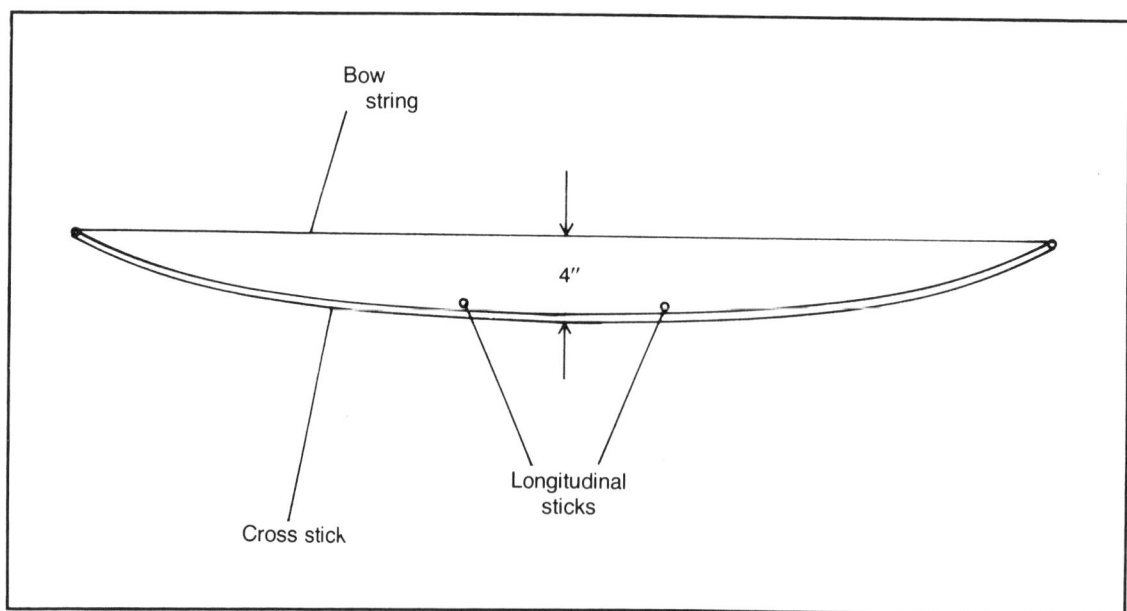

Fig. 6-39. Bow string.

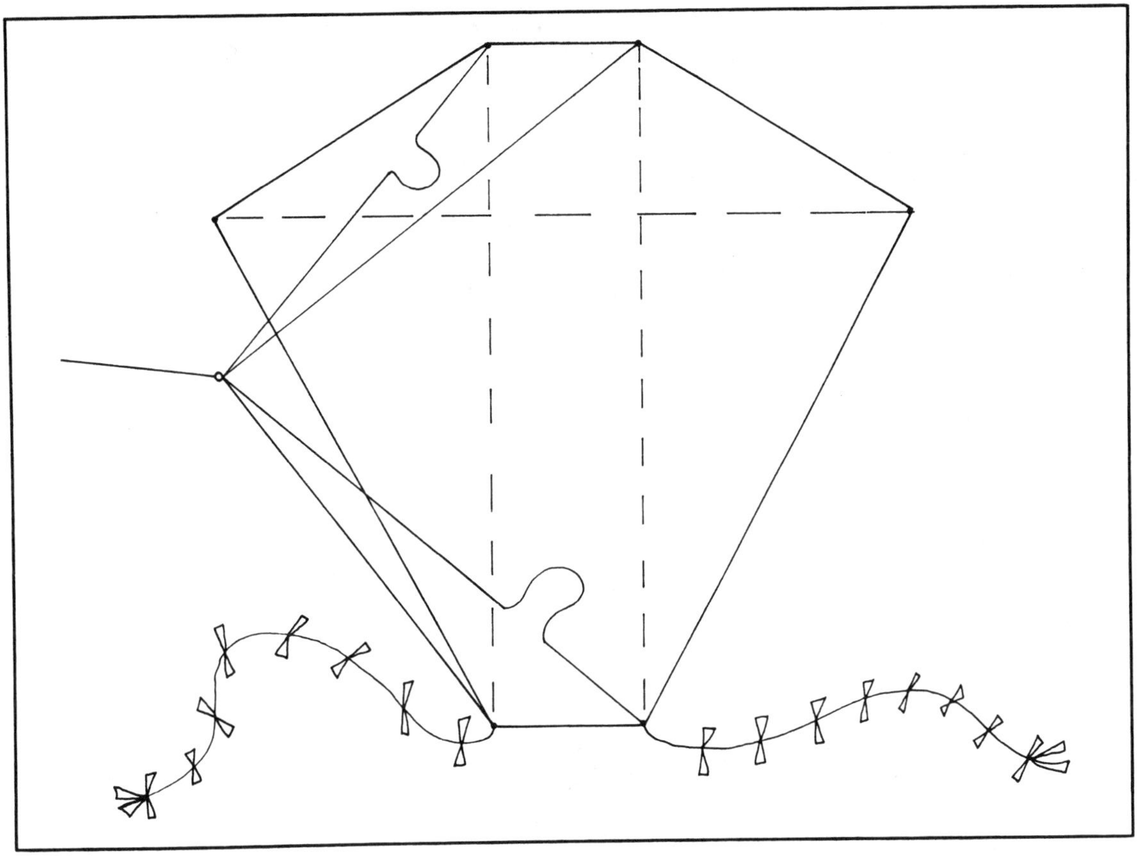

Fig. 6-40. Bridle string and tail attachments.

Construction of tails is detailed in Chapter 5. The length and weight of the tails can be adjusted for the particular wind condition when the kite is flown. Try the kite first without a tail. If the kite loops or spins uncontrollably, add tails. Use the minimum amount required to give the kite good stability.

Variations

The three-stick kite with parallel longitudinals can be made in a variety of sizes from 1 foot or less in length and breadth to 6 feet or more in length and breadth by keeping the proportions the same. The smaller sizes require smaller sticks and lightweight covering materials; the larger sizes require larger sticks and heavier covering materials. You may also want to experiment by changing the proportions of the kite, such as the width between the two lon-

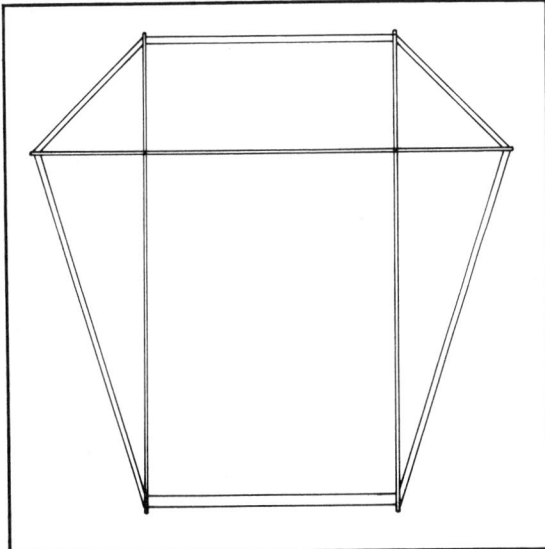

Fig. 6-41. Variation of width between parallel longitudinal sticks.

105

gitudinal parallel sticks (Fig. 6-41) and/or the distance from the top of the kite to the cross stick.

The three-stick kite with parallel longitudinals can be flown without a bow string. I have found the performance to be considerably improved by the simple addition of a bow string, and I recommend this even if you intend to use tails.

THREE-STICK KITE WITH CROSSING LONGITUDINALS

The three-stick kite with crossing longitudinals is shown in Fig. 6-42. Although this kite can be flown without a bow string if tails are used, the performance is usually improved by the simple addition of a bow string, and this often gives good performance without tails being required.

Frame

Three sticks (two are 36 inches and one 30 inches long) are required for the same frame, as shown in Fig. 6-43. Wooden sticks with a rectangular cross section of ¼ inch by ⅜ inch or round wooden dowels of ¼-inch diameter can be used. The sticks can vary somewhat from these dimensions and still give satisfactory results. If the kite is to be used only in light airs, you may want to reduce the cross sectional size of the sticks. If the kite is to

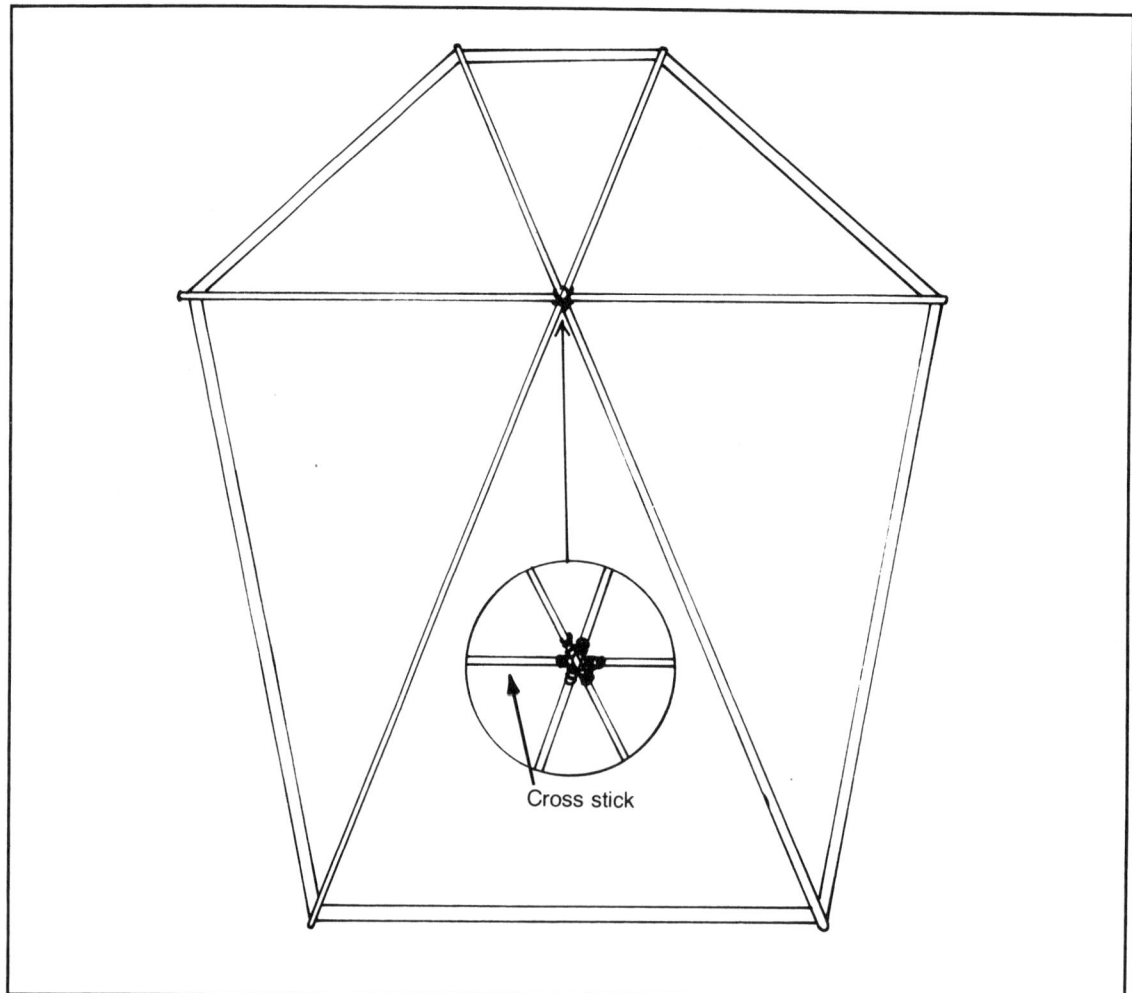

Fig. 6-42. Three-stick kite with crossing longitudinals.

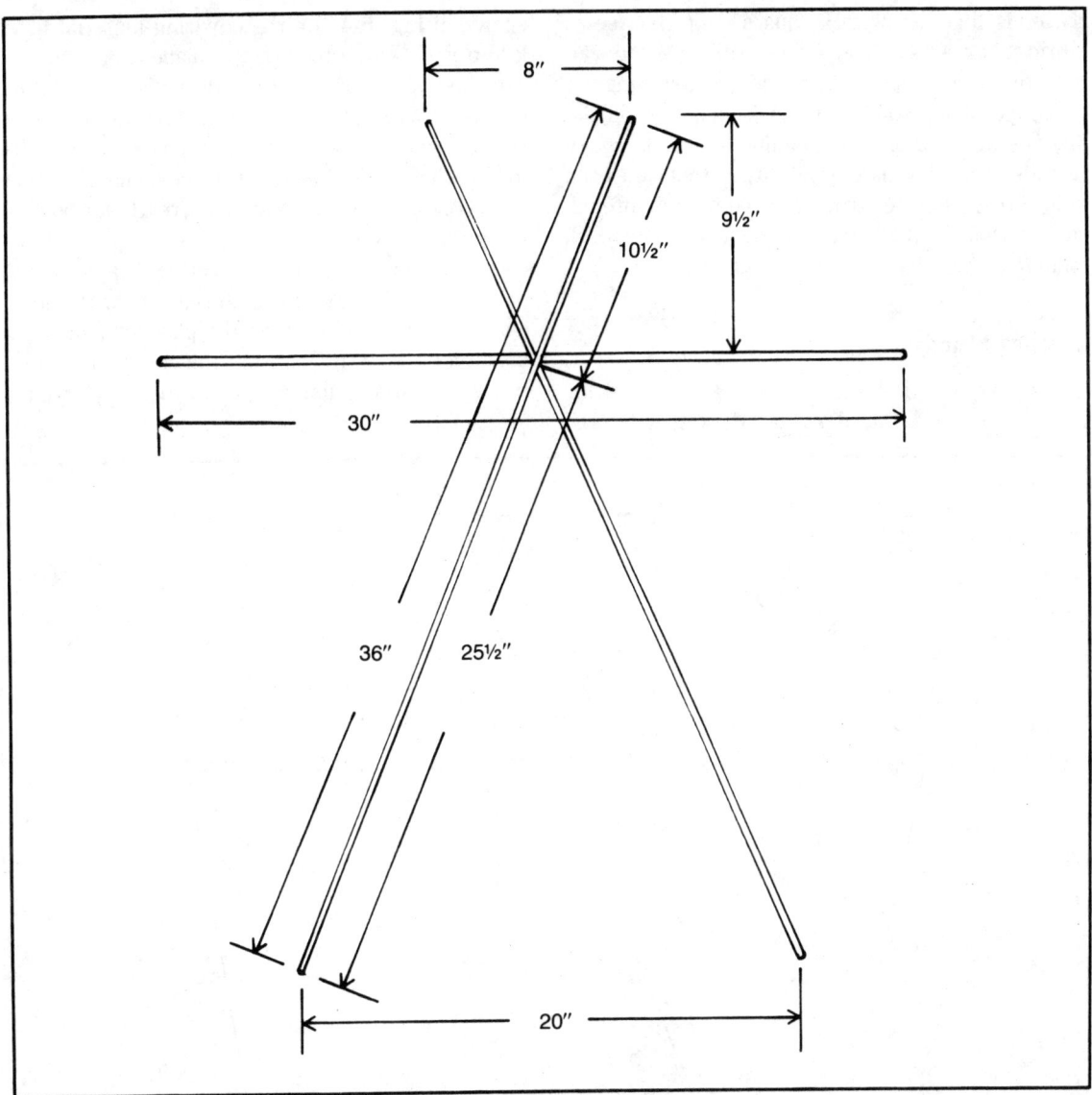

Fig. 6-43. Pattern for sticks for three-stick kite with crossing longitudinals.

be used in very strong winds, you may want to increase the cross sectional size of the sticks. Fiberglass, bamboo, and aluminum are other possibilities.

We'll assume you'll be using wooden sticks of either rectangular or round cross sectional shape.

The ends are notched by making a saw cut to a depth of ⅜ inch in each end of the stick. Make the notches on both ends of a stick in the same plane.

Measure and mark the intersections on each stick, as shown in Fig. 6-43. Glue and lash all three sticks together in a single joint. Tie the ends of the lashing string together with a square knot. All of the notches at the ends of the sticks should be parallel to the plane surface of the kite.

The guideline string is installed in the notches at the ends of the sticks around the kite frame, as shown in Fig. 6-44. Stretch the string tight and tie the ends together with a square knot. If a sewn fabric cover is used, you will probably want to wait until the cover has been sewn before installing the guideline string so that it can be inserted in the sleeves first. After the guideline string has been installed, and lashings around the sticks on each side of the guideline string where it passes through the notches in the sticks. Tie the ends of each lashing string together with a square knot.

Covering Material

Paper, plastic film, or cloth can be used for covering the kite, as desired. Mark the pattern shown in Fig. 6-45 on the covering material. The kite frame, with either the permanent or a temporary guideline string in place, can be placed over the covering material as a pattern. Position it so that the side where the cross stick passes below the longitudinal sticks is against the covering material. This positions the cross stick correctly for bowing the kite.

Use scissors to cut the covering material to the pattern. Join the covering material to form the hems and sleeves, depending on the particular material used (see Chapter 5). Install the cover to the kite frame with the guideline string passing through sleeves.

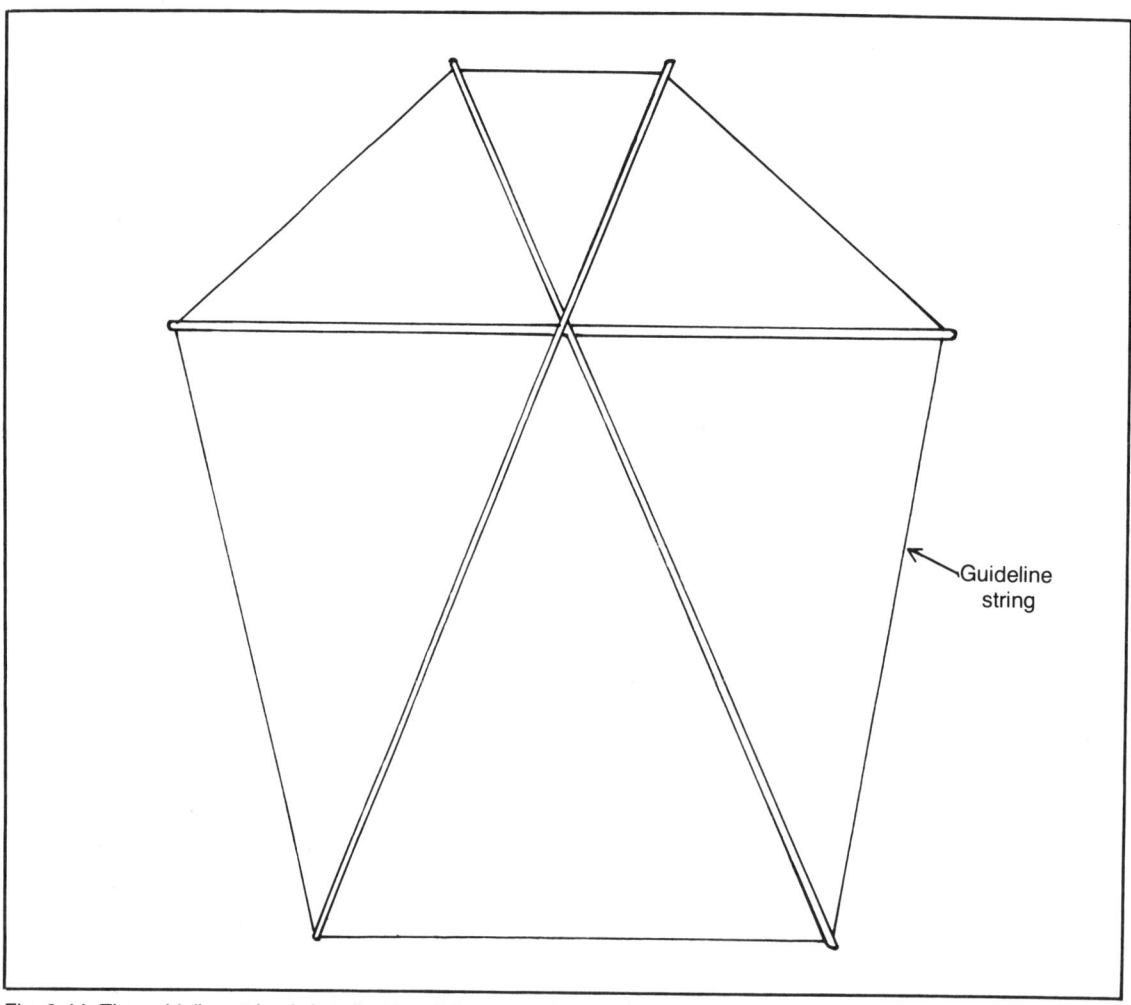

Fig. 6-44. The guideline string is installed in notches around frame sticks.

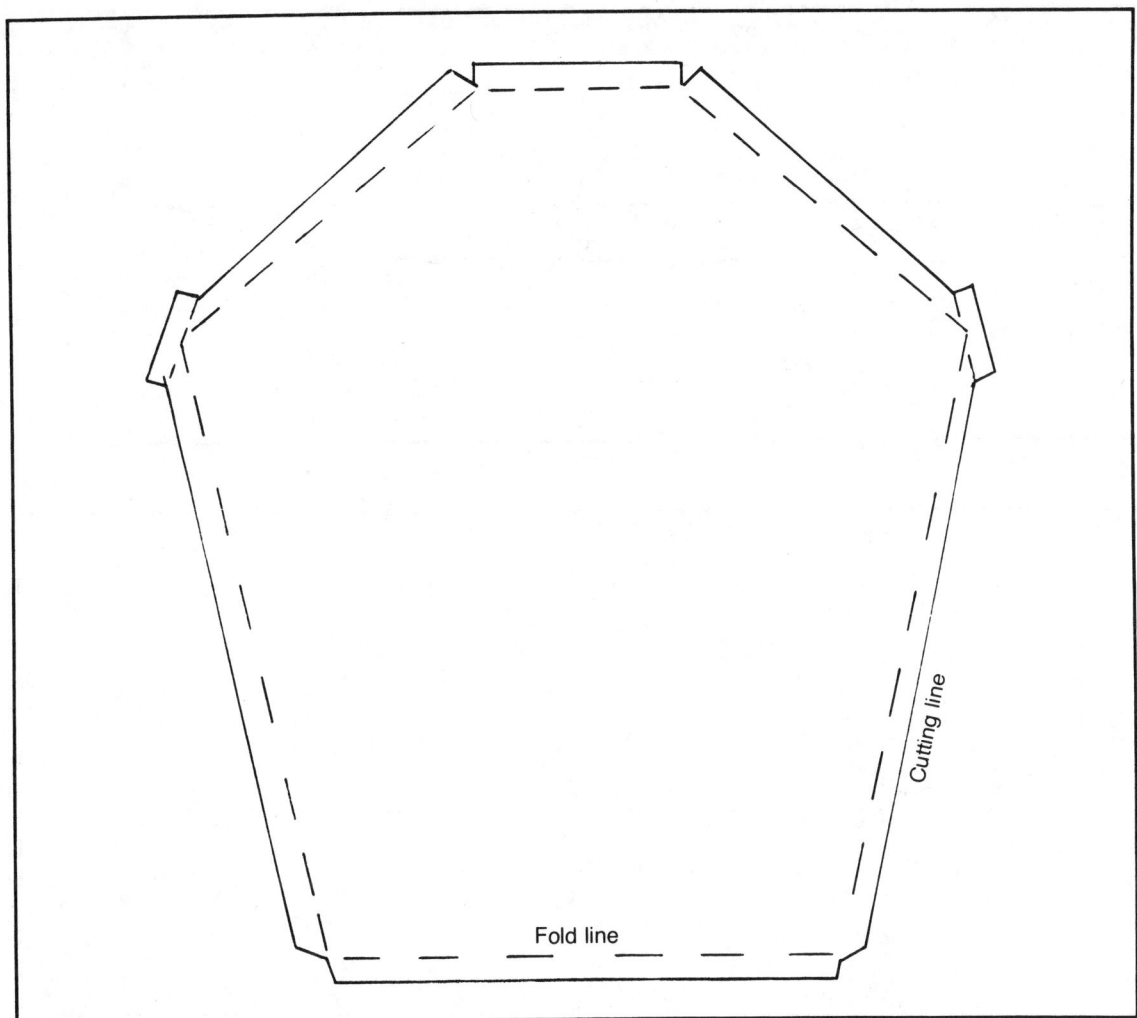

Fig. 6-45. Pattern for covering material.

Bow String

The performance of this kite is usually improved by the addition of a bow string. Tie the bow string to one end of the cross stick, passing it through the notch in the end of the stick. Bow the kite until it has a 3½-inch bow, as shown in Fig. 6-46. Then tie the bow string to the other end of the cross stick. The two longitudinal sticks are inside the bow, one above the other one.

Bridle

A four-string bridle is usually used, as shown in Fig. 6-47. The strings are passed through the notches and tied around the ends of the sticks. Use a small plastic curtain rod ring as a bridle ring. Although a loop knot can also be used, the ring makes adjustment of the bridle strings easier. Tie the bridle strings to the bridle ring. The length of the bridle strings can be adjusted for particular flying conditions. The kite string or line is attached to the bridle ring for flying the kite.

Tails

The three-stick kite with crossing longitudinal

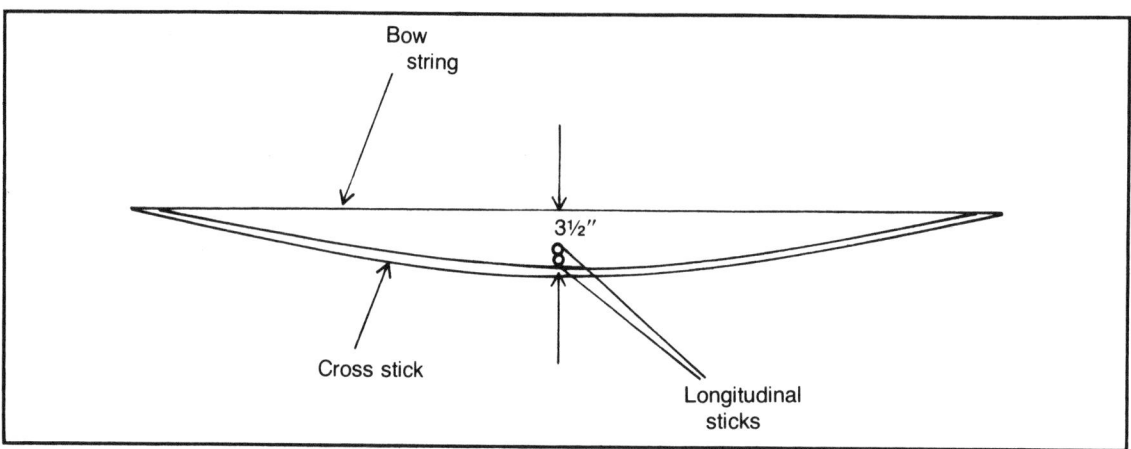

Fig. 6-46. Bow string.

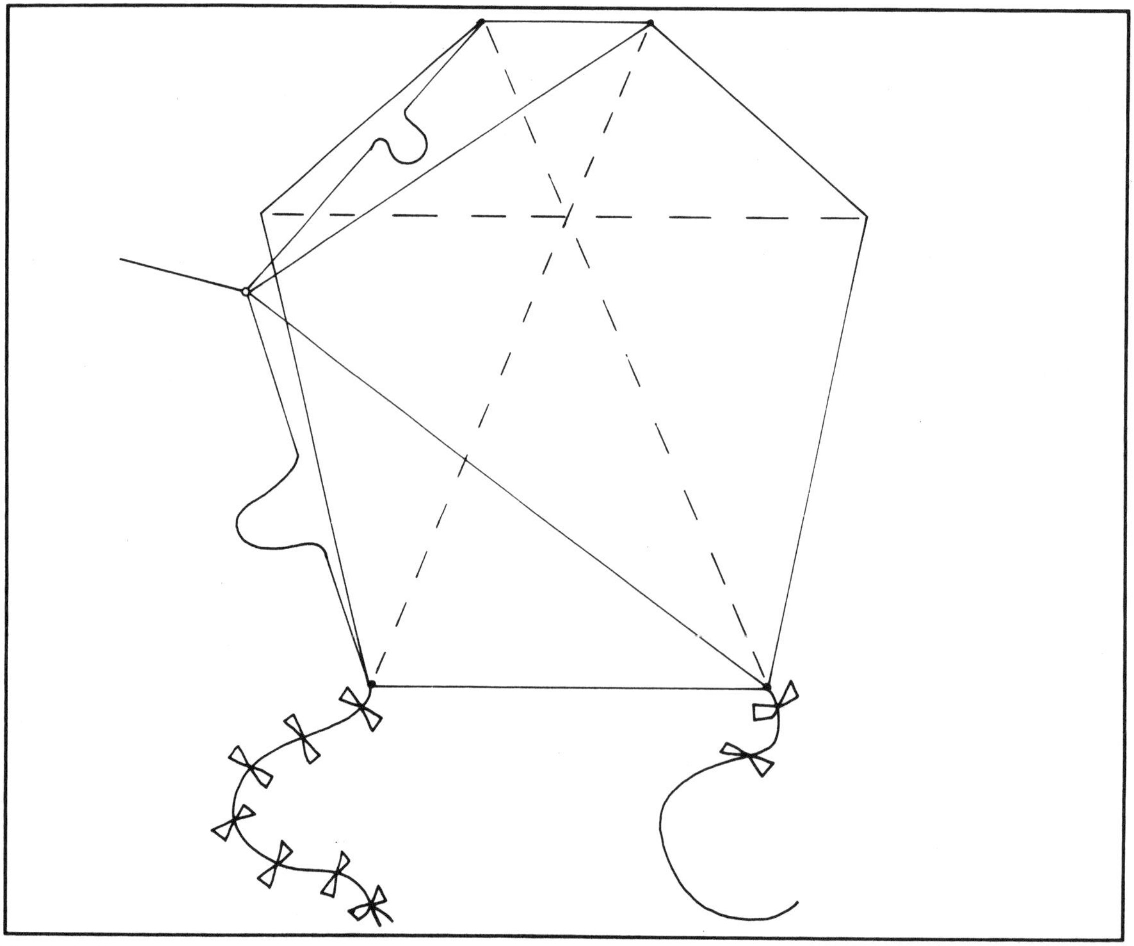

Fig. 6-47. Bridle string and tail attachments.

sticks will often fly without a tail if the kite is bowed properly, but if the kite is flown without a bow or with a bow in particular flying conditions, a tail may be required. Two tails are usually used, as shown in Fig. 6-47. These are attached to the aft ends of the two longitudinal sticks. The length and weight of the tails required will depend on the wind conditions and other factors. Try the kite without a tail first. If it loops and spins uncontrollably, add tails. Use the minimum amount required for good stability.

Variations

The three-stick kite with crossing longitudinals can be made in a variety of sizes from 1 foot or less in length to 6 feet or more in length, keeping the proportions the same. Smaller sizes require smaller sticks and lighter covering materials; larger sizes require larger sticks and heavier covering materials. You may want to change the proportions of the kite by lowering the crossing point for the sticks, as shown in Fig. 6-48.

The three-stick kite with crossing longitudinals can be flown without a bow if tails are used. I have found the performance of this type of kite to be considerably improved by the simple addition of a bow string, and I recommend this even if you intend to use tails.

TWO-STICK SQUARE KITE

The two-stick square kite is shown in Fig. 6-49. This kite can be flown with or without a bow string, as desired. A tail is usually required to give it adequate stability.

Frame

Two 24-inch-long sticks are required for the frame, as shown in Fig. 6-50. Wooden sticks with a rectangular cross section of 3/16-inch by 5/16-inch or round wooden dowels of 3/16-inch diameter can be used. The sticks can vary somewhat from these dimensions and still give good results. If the kite will be used only in light airs, you may want to reduce the cross sectional size of the sticks; for extremely strong winds, you may want to use sticks with larger cross sectional dimensions. Sticks of fiberglass, bamboo, and aluminum are other possibilities.

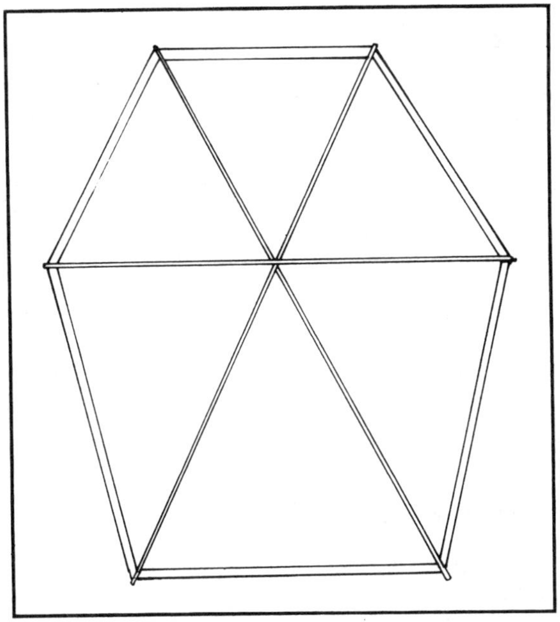

Fig. 6-48. Variation of proportions of basic three-stick kite with crossing longitudinals.

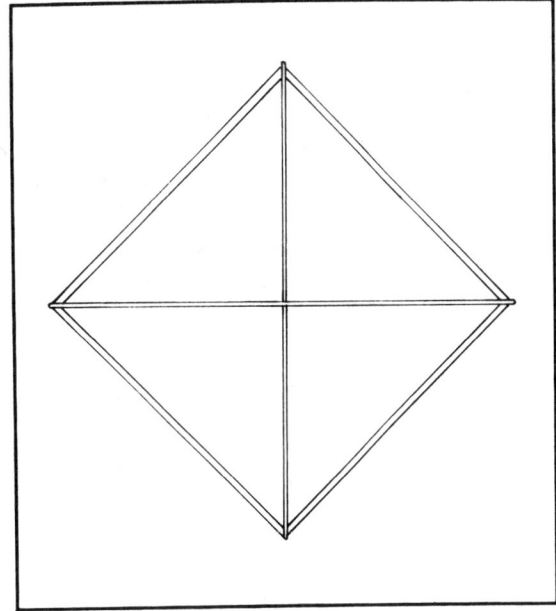

Fig. 6-49. Two-stick square kite.

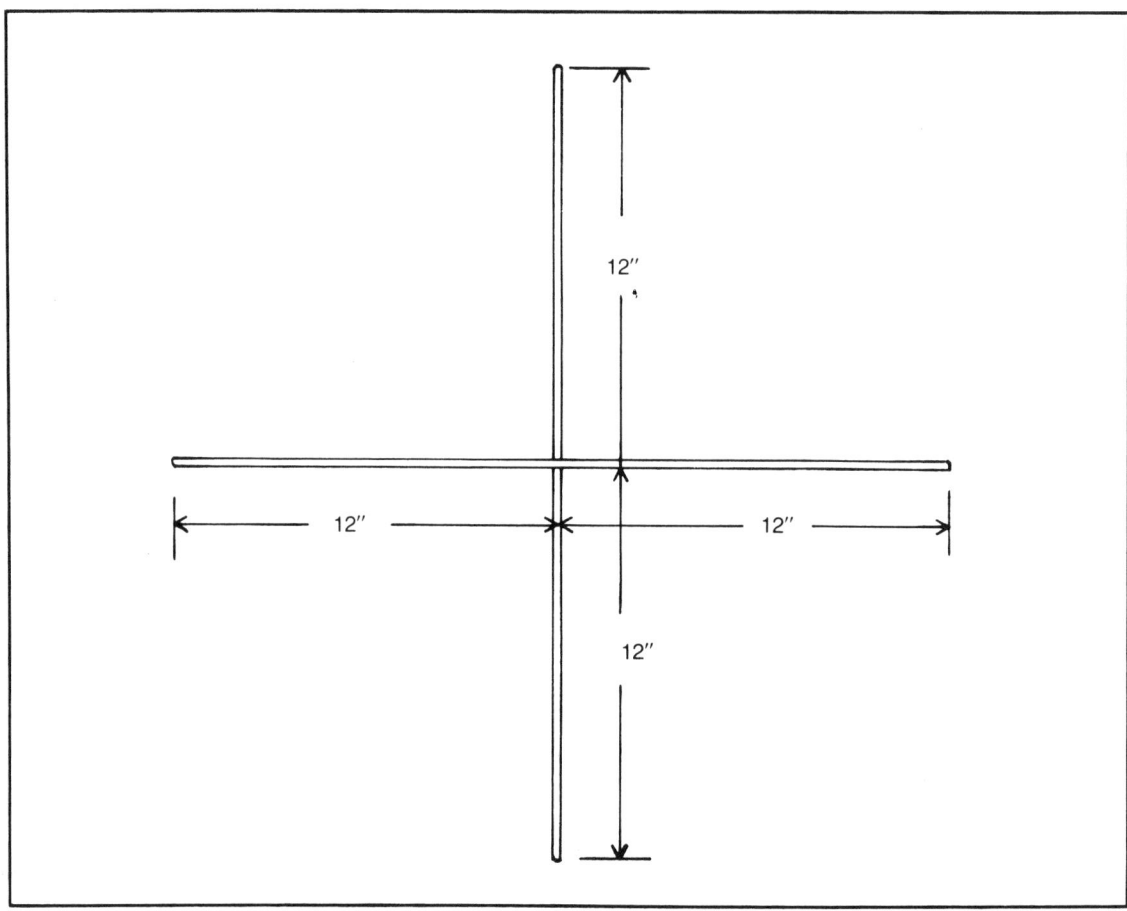

Fig. 6-50. Pattern for sticks for two-stick square kite.

For descriptive purposes, we'll assume that you will be using wooden sticks of either rectangular or round cross sectional shape.

The ends of the sticks are notched with a saw cut to a depth of ⅜ inch in each end of each stick. Make the notches on both ends of each stick in the same plane.

Measure and mark the centerpoint on each stick. The two sticks are then glued and lashed together. Tie the ends of the lashing string together with a square knot. All of the notches at the ends of the sticks should be parallel to the plane surface of the kite.

The guideline string is installed in the notches at the ends of the sticks around the kite frame, as shown in Fig. 6-51. Stretch the string tight and tie the ends together with a square knot. If a sewn fabric cover is to be used, you will want to wait until the cover has been sewn before installing the guideline string so that the string can be inserted through the sleeves first. After the guideline string has been installed, add lashings around the sticks on each side of the guideline where it passes through the notches in the sticks. Tie the ends of each lashing string together with a square knot.

Covering Material

Paper, plastic film, or cloth can be used for covering the kite. For best performance, the covering material should be as lightweight as possible to still give adequate strength. Mark the pattern shown in Fig. 6-52 on the covering material. The kite frame, with either the permanent or a temporary guideline string in place, can be placed over the covering material to use as a pattern.

Use scissors to cut the covering material to the pattern. Methods for joining covering material to form the hems and sleeves depends on the particular covering material used (see Chapter 5).

Install the cover to the kite frame with the guideline string passing through sleeves in the covering material.

Bow String

The performance of this kite is usually improved by adding a bow string. (Use that stick that passes under the other stick and is against the covering material where the sticks cross as the cross stick.) Tie the bow string to one end of the cross stick, passing it through the notch in the end of the stick so that it cannot slide down the stick when the kite is bowed. Bow the kite until it has a 3-inch bow, as shown in Fig. 6-53. Then tie the bow string to the other end of the cross stick with the string passing through the notch so that it cannot slide down the stick. When done properly, the longitudinal stick should be inside the bow, above the cross stick.

Bridle

A two-string bridle is usually used, as shown in Fig. 6-54. The bridle strings pass through holes in the covering material 4½ inches from each end of

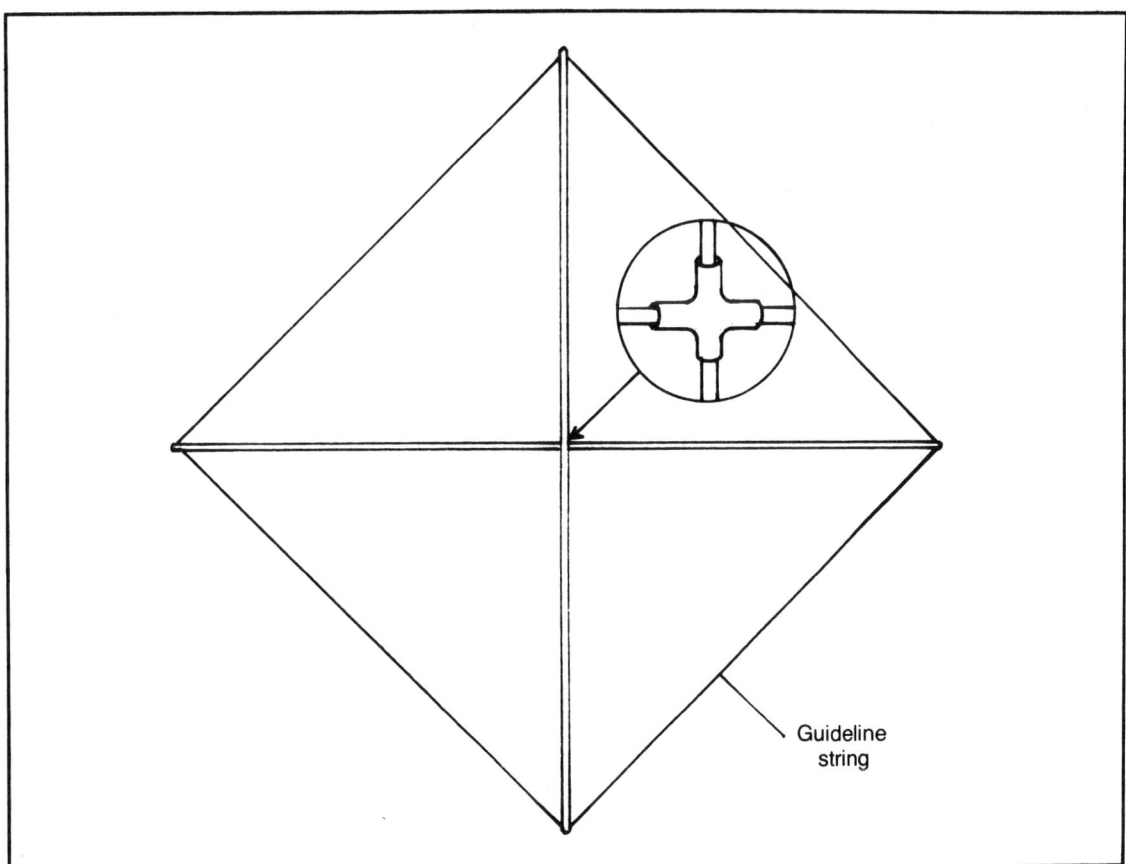

Fig. 6-51. The guideline string is installed in notches around frame sticks. Insert shows possible use of plastic tubing for frame fitting.

the longitudinal stick. The covering material is reinforced with tape in the areas around the holes. The bridle strings are then tied around the longitudinal stick. The other ends of the strings can be tied in a loop or to a small plastic curtain rod ring. The bridle ring allows easy adjustment of the length of the bridle strings.

Tail

The two-stick square kite often requires a tail to give adequate stability, even if bowed. The tail is usually attached to the aft end of the longitudinal stick, as shown in Fig. 6-54.

Construction of tails is detailed in Chapter 5. The length and weight of the tail required will depend on the wind conditions and other factors. Try the kite first without a tail. If the kite loops or spins uncontrollably, add tail. Use the minimum amount of tail required to give the kite good stability.

Variations

The two-stick square kite can be constructed in a range of sizes from 1-foot square or smaller to 6-foot square or larger. As a general rule, you will need to reduce the weight of the smaller sizes by using proportionally smaller sticks and lighter weight covering material. You will need to use larger sticks and heavier covering material for the larger sizes.

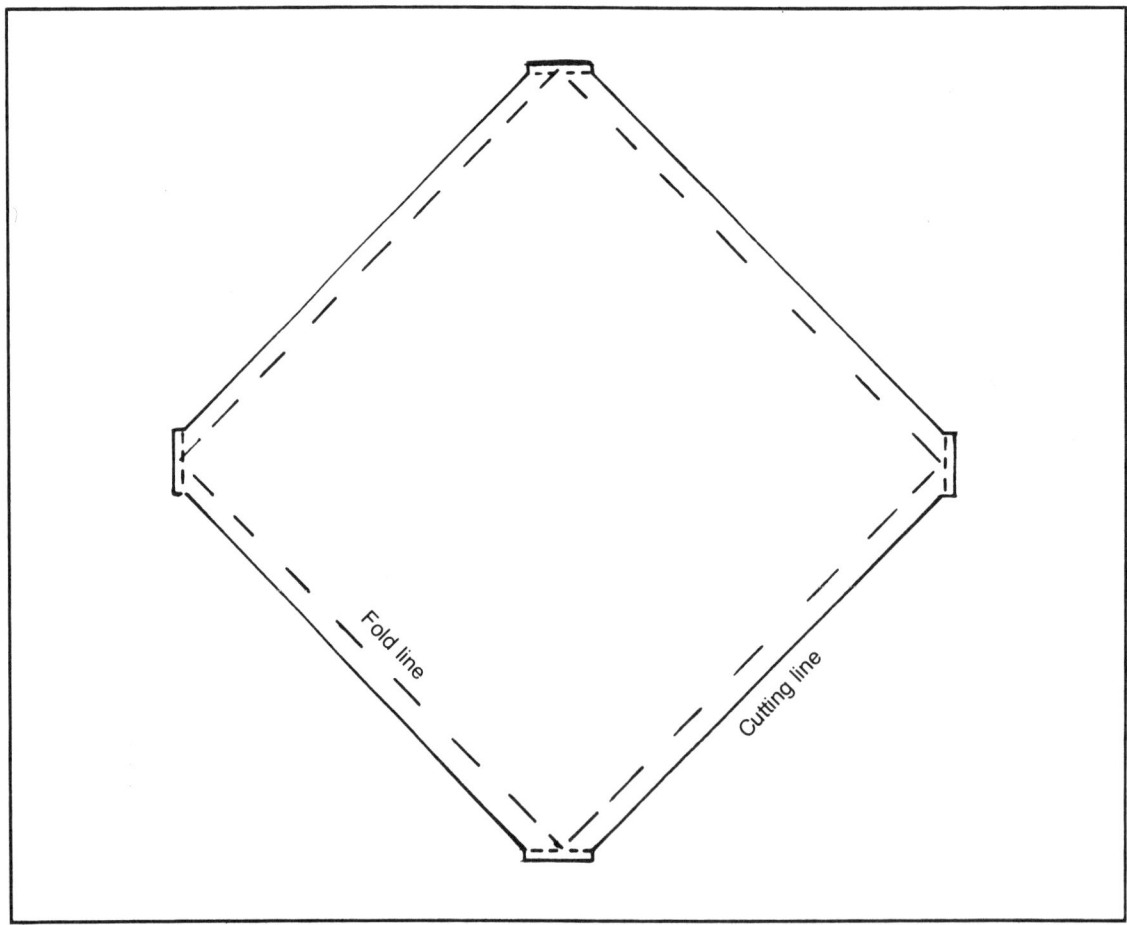

Fig. 6-52. Pattern for covering material.

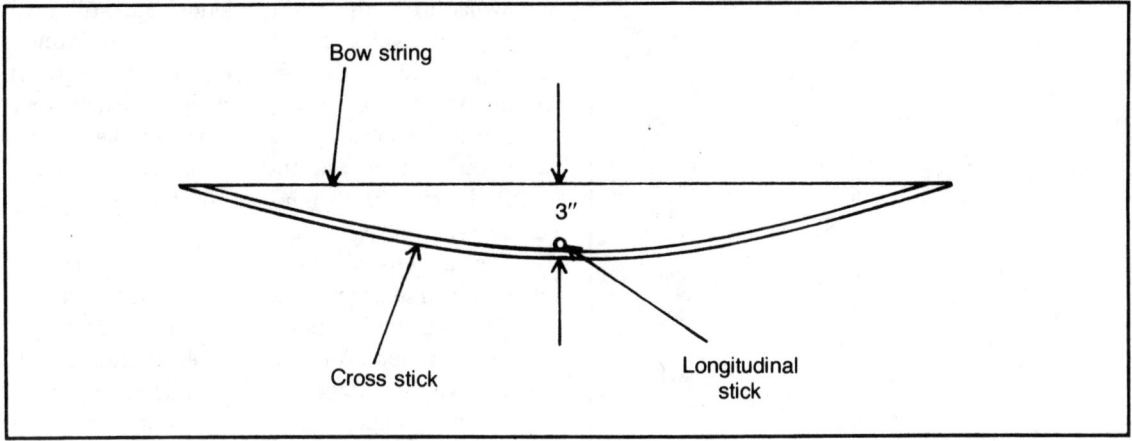

Fig. 6-53. Bow string.

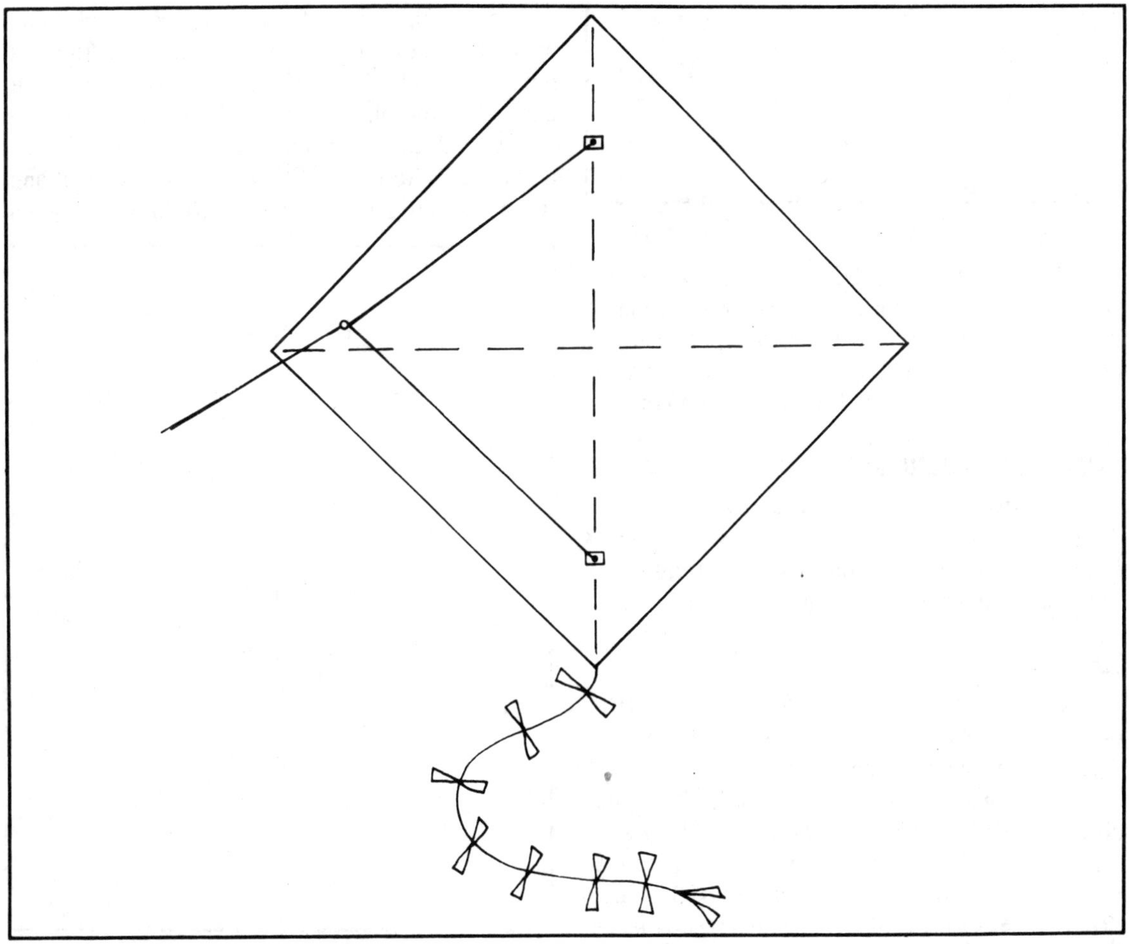

Fig. 6-54. Bridle string and tail attachments.

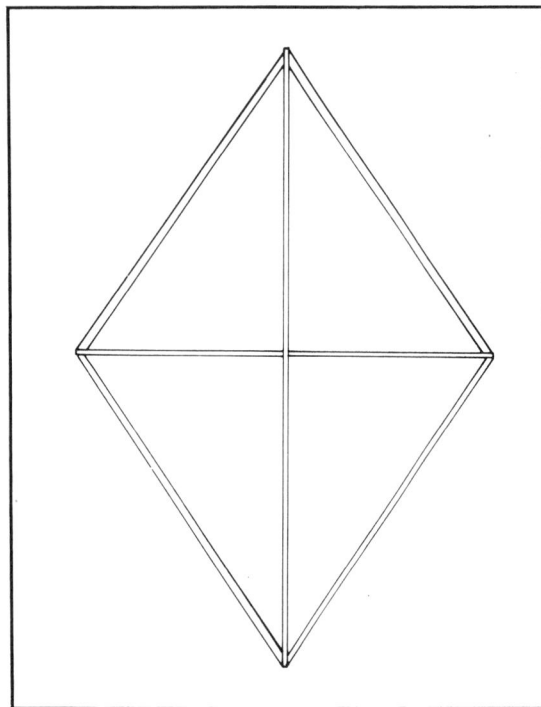

Fig. 6-55. Two-stick diamond kite.

This kite can also be flown with one of the sides, instead of the corners, as the top. This makes it a flat kite without a bow string, using a four-string bridle with the connections at each corner, and two tails, which are connected to the bottom corners.

TWO-STICK DIAMOND KITE

The two-stick diamond kite is shown in Fig. 6-55. This kite can be flown with or without a bow string, as desired, but a tail is usually required to give this kite adequate stability.

Frame

Two sticks are required for the frame (Fig. 6-56). One 36 inches long, the other 24 inches long. The 36-inch long stick can be rectangular wood with a cross section of ¼-inch by ⅜ inch or a wooden dowel of ¼ inch diameter. The 24-inch-long stick can be rectangular wood with a cross section of 3/16 inch by 5/16 inch or a wooden dowel of 3/16 inch diameter. For a particular kite, both sticks are usually either rectangular or round. The sticks can vary somewhat from these dimensions and still give satisfactory results. Try to use the lightest weight sticks possible that will give adequate strength. If the kite is to be used only in light airs, you may want to reduce the cross sectional size of the sticks. Conversely, increase the diameters for heavy winds. Fiberglass, bamboo, and aluminum sticks can be used.

Instructions are given using wooden sticks of either rectangular or round cross sectional shape.

The ends of the sticks are notched by making a saw cut to a depth of ⅜ inch in each end of each stick. Make the notches on both ends of each stick in the same plane.

Measure and mark the centerpoint on each stick. The two sticks are then glued and lashed together with string. Tie the ends of the lashing string together with a square knot. All of the end notches should be positioned so that they are parallel to the plane surface of the kite.

Install the guideline string in the notches around the kite frame. Stretch the string tight and tie the ends together with a square knot. If a sewn

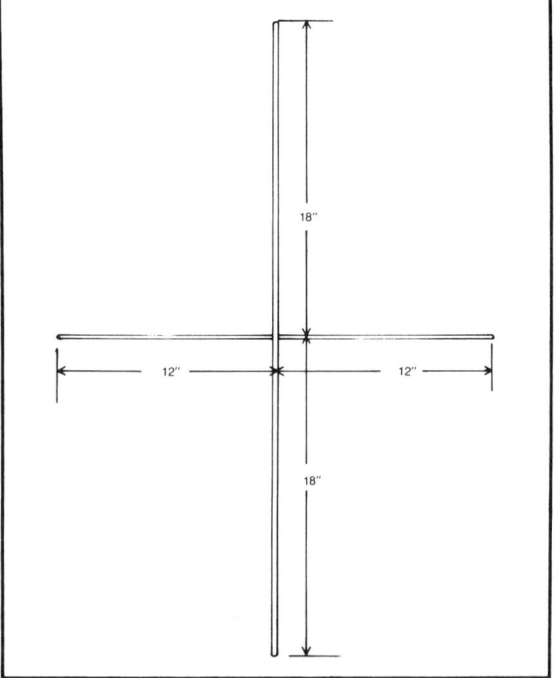

Fig. 6-56. Pattern for sticks for two-stick diamond kite.

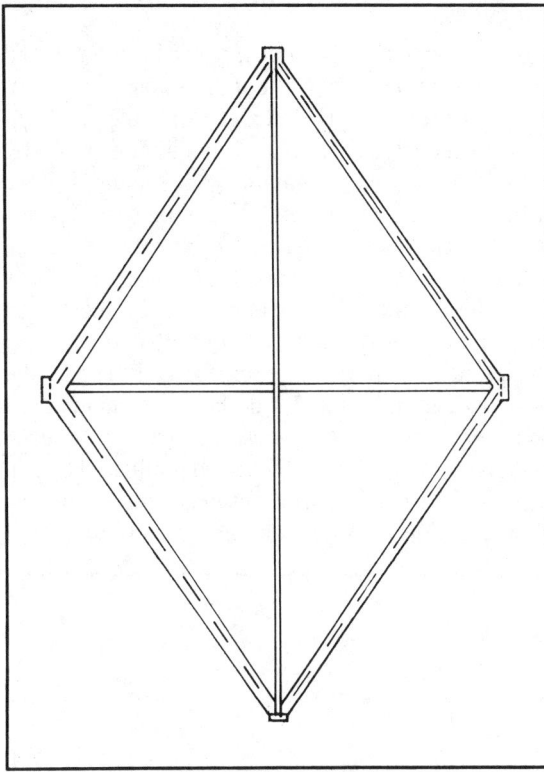

Fig. 6-57. Pattern for covering material, using installed guideline string as guide.

fabric cover is to be used, wait until the cover has been sewn before installing the guideline so that the string can be inserted through the sleeves first. After the guideline string has been installed, add lashings around the sticks on each side of the guideline string where it passes through the notches. Tie the ends of each lashing string together with a square knot.

Covering Material

Paper, plastic film, or cloth can be used for covering the kite, as desired. For best performance, the covering material should be of the lightest weight compatible with adequate strength. Mark the pattern shown in Fig. 6-57 on the covering material. The kite frame, with either the permanent or a temporary guideline string in place, can be placed over the covering material as a pattern.

Use scissors to cut the covering material to the pattern. Methods for joining covering material to form the hems and sleeves depends on the particular covering material used (see Chapter 5).

Regardless of the covering material used, install it to the kite frame with the guideline string passing through sleeves in the covering material.

Bow String

The performance of the two-stick diamond kite is usually improved by adding a bow string. Tie the bow string to one end of the 24-inch-long cross stick, passing the string through the notch and on around the stick. This will keep the bow string from sliding down the stick when the kite is bowed. Bow the kite until it has a 3-inch bow (Fig. 6-58), then tie the bow string to the other end of the cross stick with the string passing through the notch and on around the stick so that it will not slide down the stick. When done properly, the longitudinal stick is inside the bow, above the cross stick, as shown.

Bridle

A two-string bridle is usually used, as shown in Fig. 6-59. The bridle strings pass through holes in the covering material 8½ inches from each end of the longitudinal stick. The covering material is reinforced in the area of the holes with tape or other

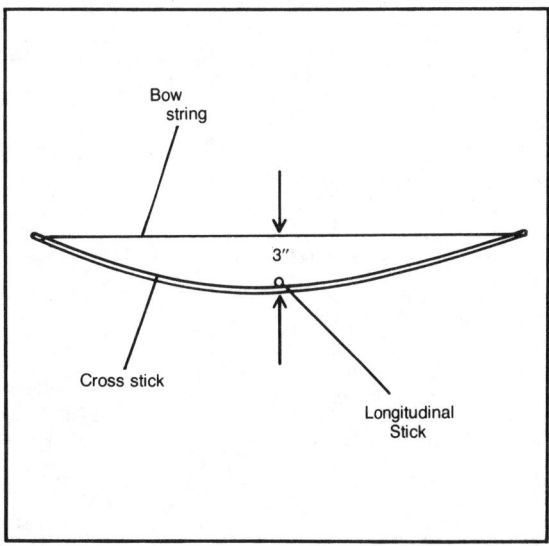

Fig. 6-58. Bow string.

means. The bridle strings are then tied around the longitudinal stick. The other ends of the strings can be tied in a loop or to a small plastic curtain rod ring. The bridle ring allows easy adjustment of the length of the bridle strings.

Tail

The two-stick diamond kite usually requires a tail to give adequate stability, even if the kite is bowed. The tail is usually attached to the aft end of the longitudinal stick, as shown in Fig. 6-59.

Construction of tails is detailed in Chapter 5. The length and weight of the tail will depend on wind conditions and other factors. Try the kite first without a tail; if it loops or spins uncontrollably, add tail. Use the minimum amount required to give the kite good stability.

Variations

The two-stick diamond kite can be constructed in a range of sizes from 1 foot or less in length to 6 feet or more in length. As a general rule, you will need to reduce the weight of the smaller sizes by using proportionally smaller sticks and lighter weight covering material. You will need to use larger sticks and heavier covering material for the larger sizes.

This kite can also be flown with the short stick as the longitudinal as a flat kite or with the long stick (which is now the cross stick) bowed. The bridle strings pass through holes in the covering material and are attached to the stick 4½ inches from each end, as shown in Fig. 6-60. A single tail, as shown in Fig. 6-60, is usually used, although three tails, as shown in Fig. 6-61, are another possibility.

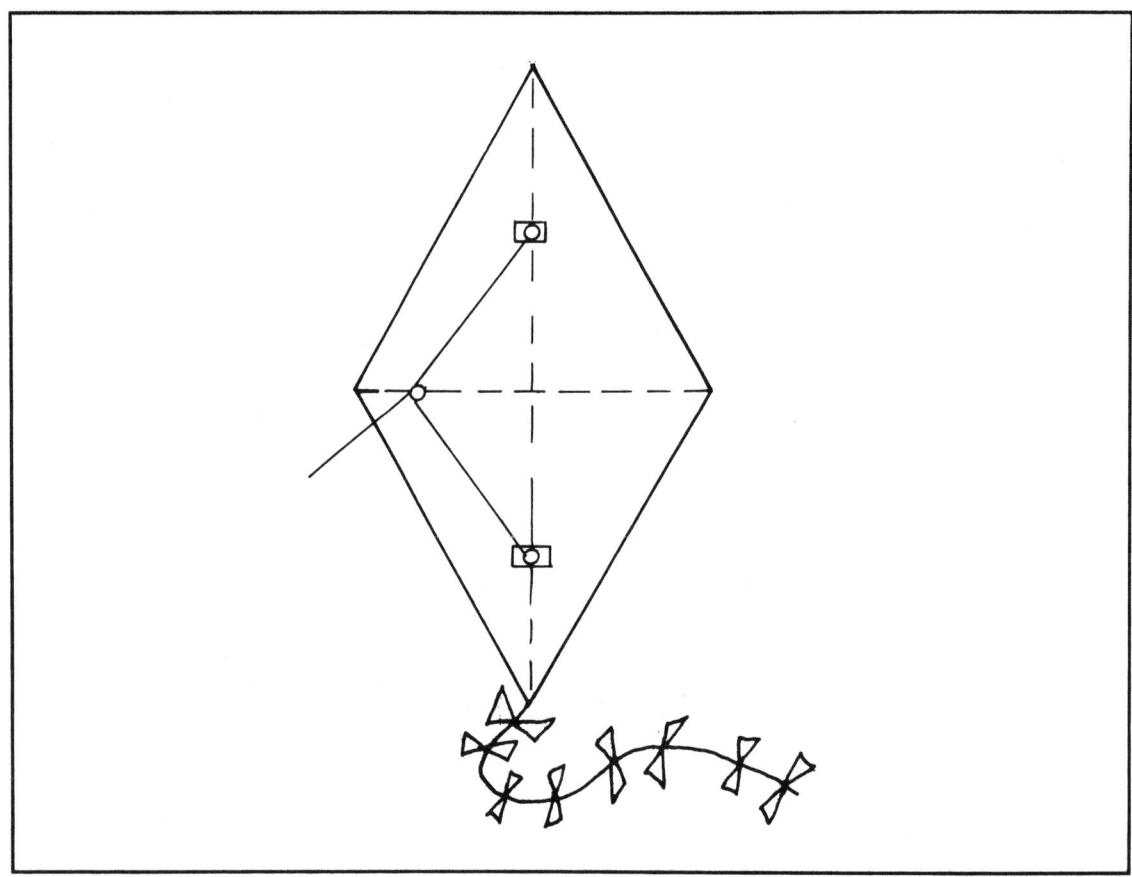

Fig. 6-59. Bridle string and tail attachments.

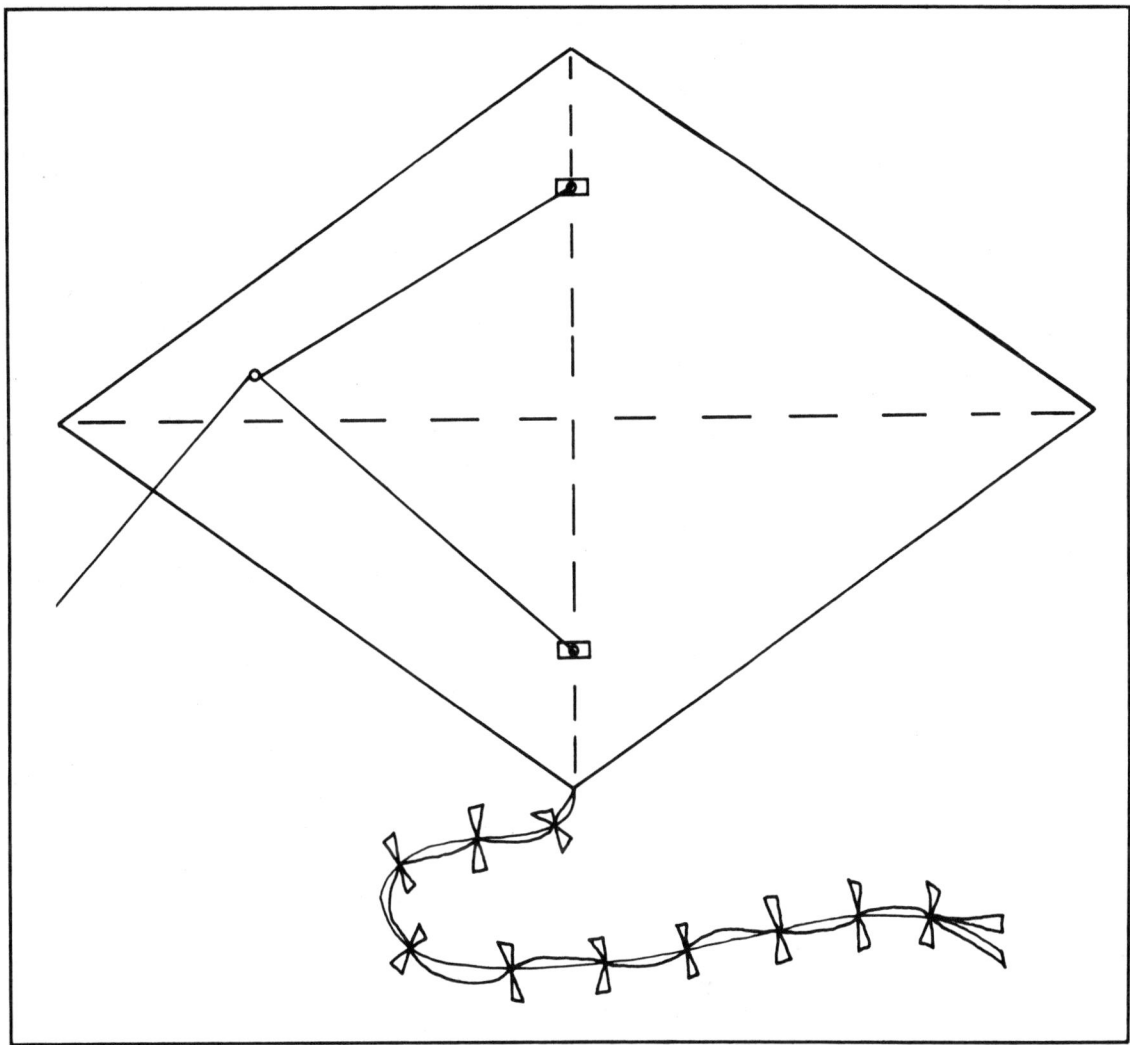

Fig. 6-60. Bridle string attachment for flying diamond kite with short stick as longitudinal, and use of one tail.

THREE-STICK HEXAGONAL KITE

The three-stick hexagonal kite is shown in Fig. 6-62. This kite can be used as a flat or bowed kite. A tail is usually required to give this kite adequate stability.

Frame

Three 36-inch long sticks are used for making the frame, as shown in Fig. 6-63. Wooden sticks with a rectangular cross section of 3/16 inch by 5/16 inch or round wooden dowels of 3/16-inch diameter can be used. The sticks can vary somewhat from these dimensions and still give satisfactory results. Reduce the cross sectional size of the sticks for flying in light airs. If the kite is to be flown in extremely strong winds, you may want to use sticks with larger cross sectional dimensions. Sticks of fiberglass, bamboo, and aluminum are other possibilities.

For descriptive purposes, we'll assume you are using wooden sticks of either rectangular or round cross sectional shape.

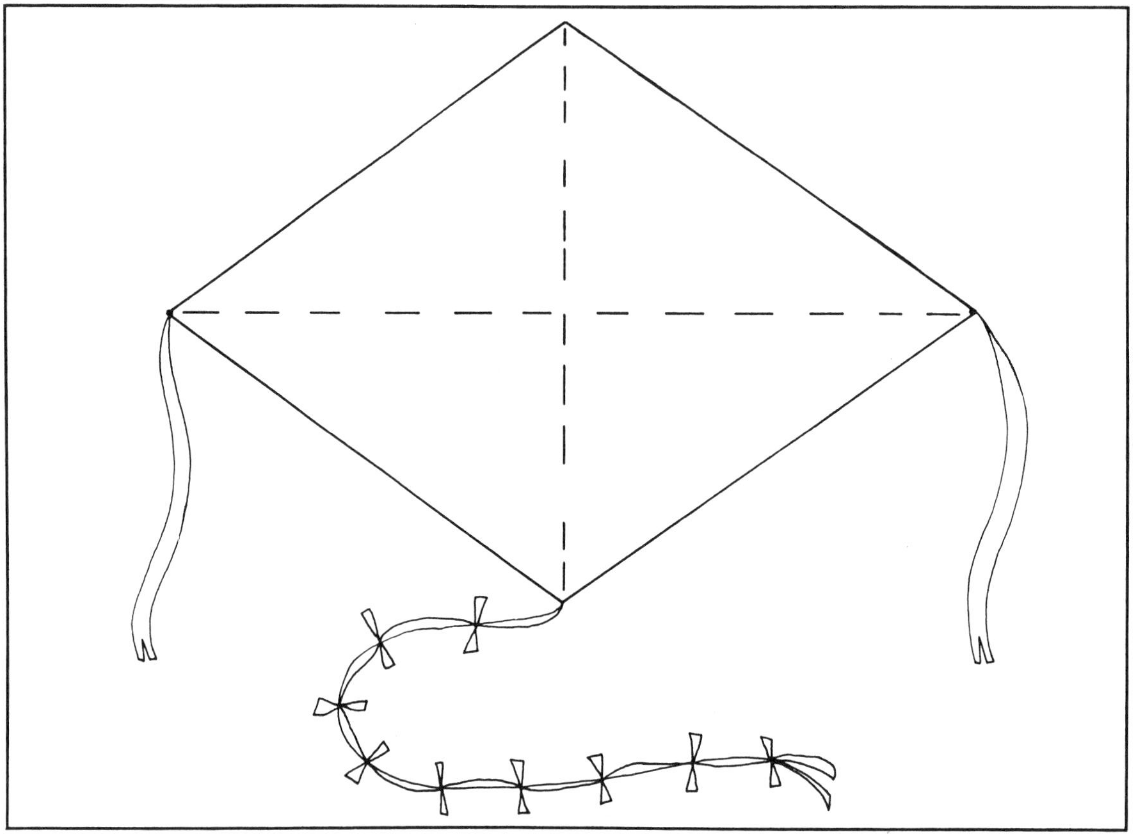

Fig. 6-61. Use of three tails.

The ends of the sticks are notched by making a saw cut ⅜ inch deep in each end. Make the notches on both ends of each stick in the same plane.

Measure and mark the centerpoint on each stick. The three sticks are then glued and lashed together with string. Tie the ends of the lashing string together with a square knot. All of the notches at the ends of the sticks should be parallel to the plane surface of the kite.

The guideline string is installed in the end notches of the sticks around the kite frame, as shown in Fig. 6-64. Stretch the string tight and tie the ends together with a square knot. If a sewn fabric cover is to be used, you will probably want to wait until the cover has been sewn before installing the guideline so it can be inserted through the sleeves first. After the guideline string has been installed, add lashings around the sticks on each

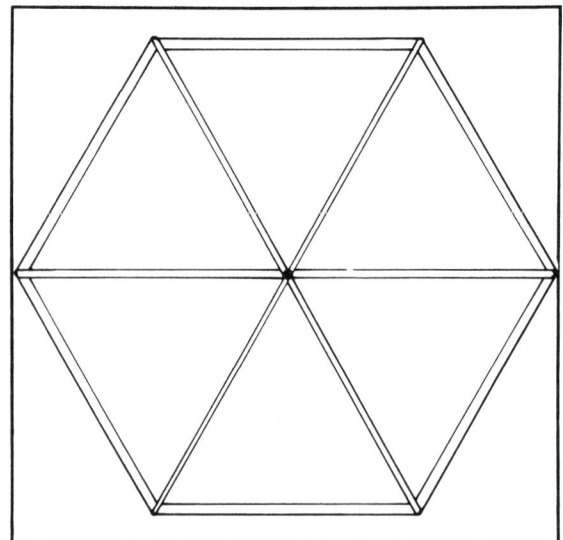

Fig. 6-62. Three-stick hexagonal kite.

120

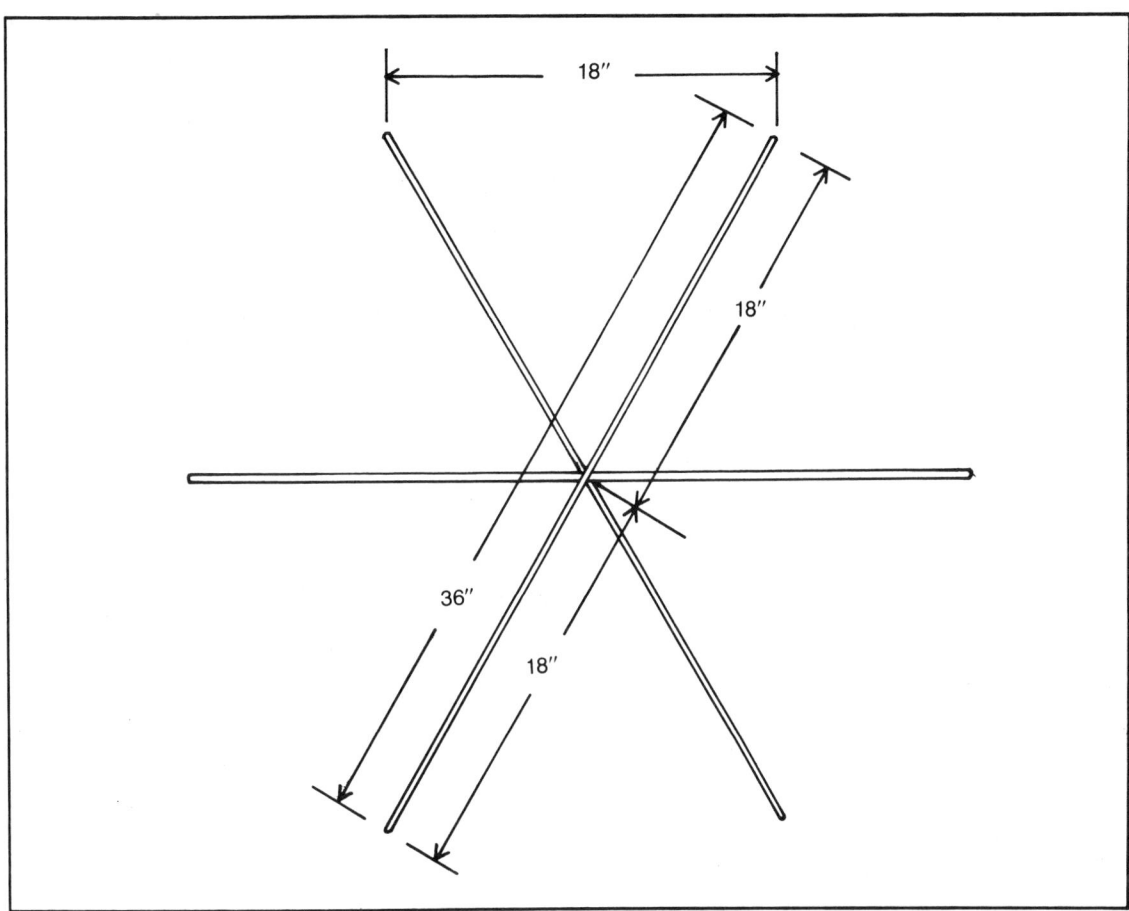

Fig. 6-63. Pattern for sticks for three-stick hexagonal kite.

side of the guideline where it passes through the notches in the sticks. Tie the ends of each lashing string together with a square knot.

Covering Material

You can use paper, plastic film, or cloth fabric to cover the kite. The covering material should be of the lightest weight that is compatible with adequate strength. Mark the pattern shown in Fig. 6-65 on the covering material. The kite frame, with either the permanent or a temporary guideline string in place, can be placed over the covering material to use as a pattern.

Use scissors to cut the covering material to the pattern. Use whatever methods are appropriate for joining hems and sleeves.

Regardless of the covering material used, install it to the kite frame with the guideline string passing through sleeves in the covering.

Bow String

The performance of the three-stick hexagonal kite is often improved by adding a bow string. Tie the bow string to one end of the stick that passes underneath the other two sticks and is against the covering material at the centerpoint. This stick will be the cross stick for descriptive purposes. Pass the string through the notch and on around the stick. This will keep the bow string from sliding down the stick when the kite is bowed. Bow the kite until it has a 4½-inch bow, as shown in Fig. 6-66. Then tie the bow string to the other end of the cross stick

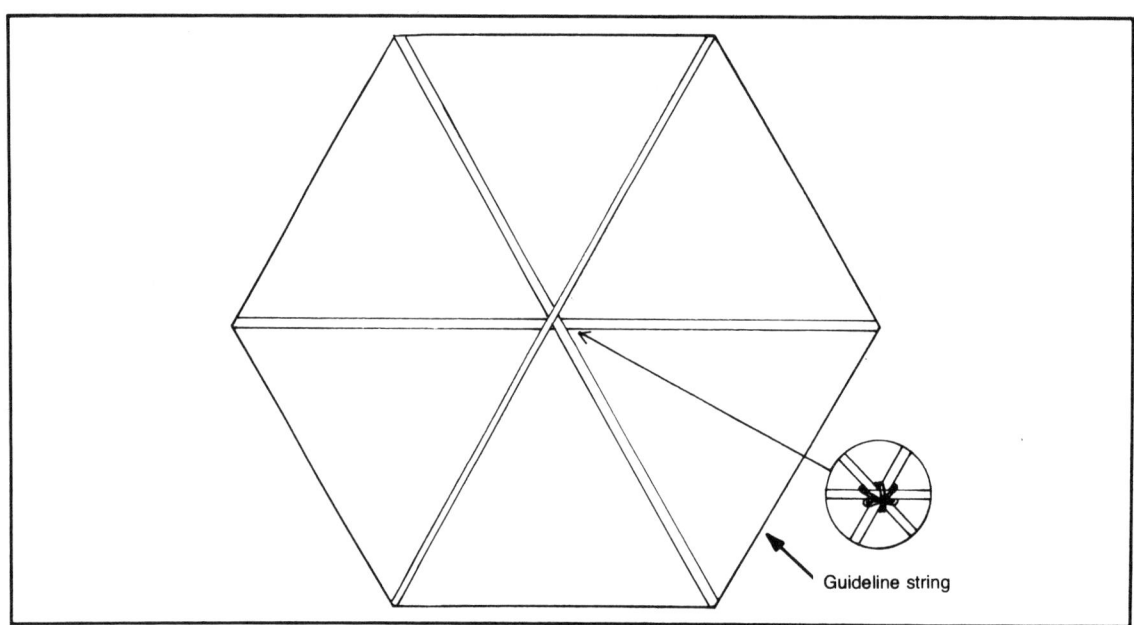

Fig. 6-64. The guideline string is installed in notches around frame sticks. Insert shows how sticks are glued and lashed at center points.

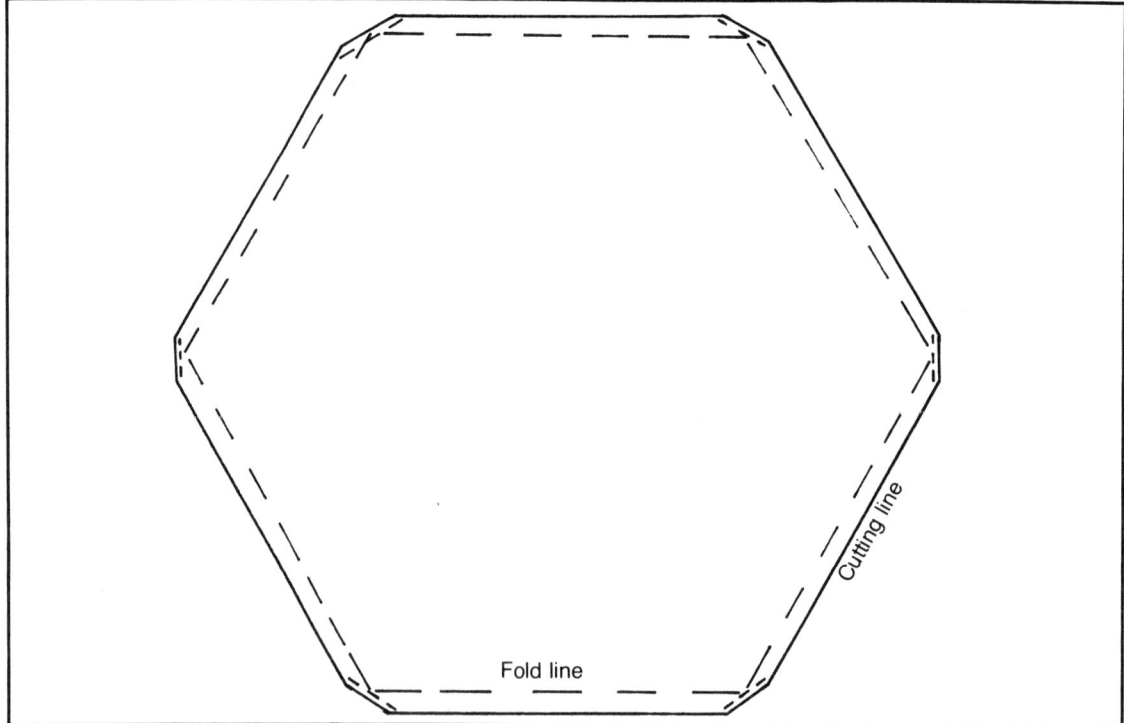

Fig. 6-65. Pattern for covering material.

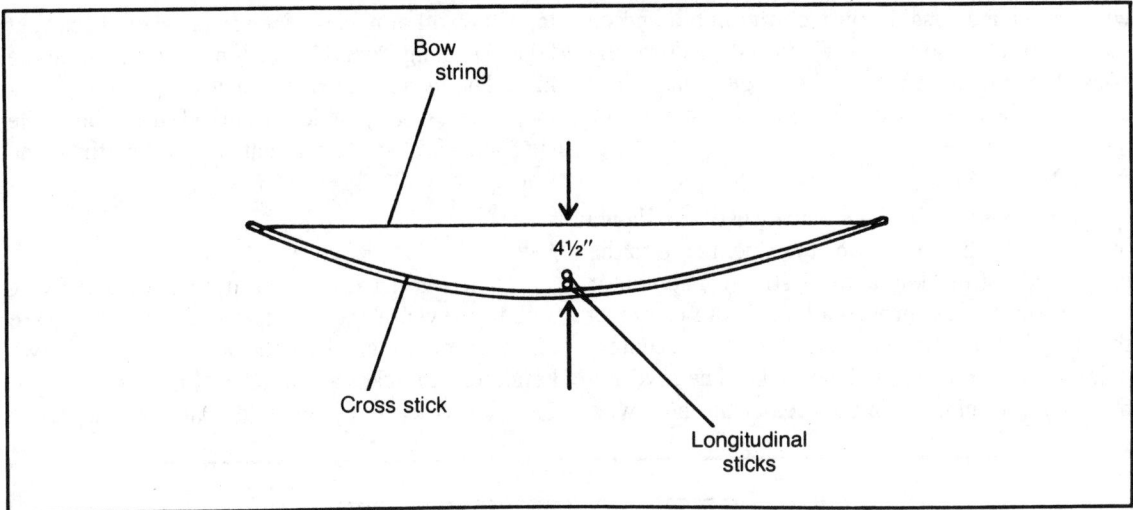

Fig. 6-66. Bow string.

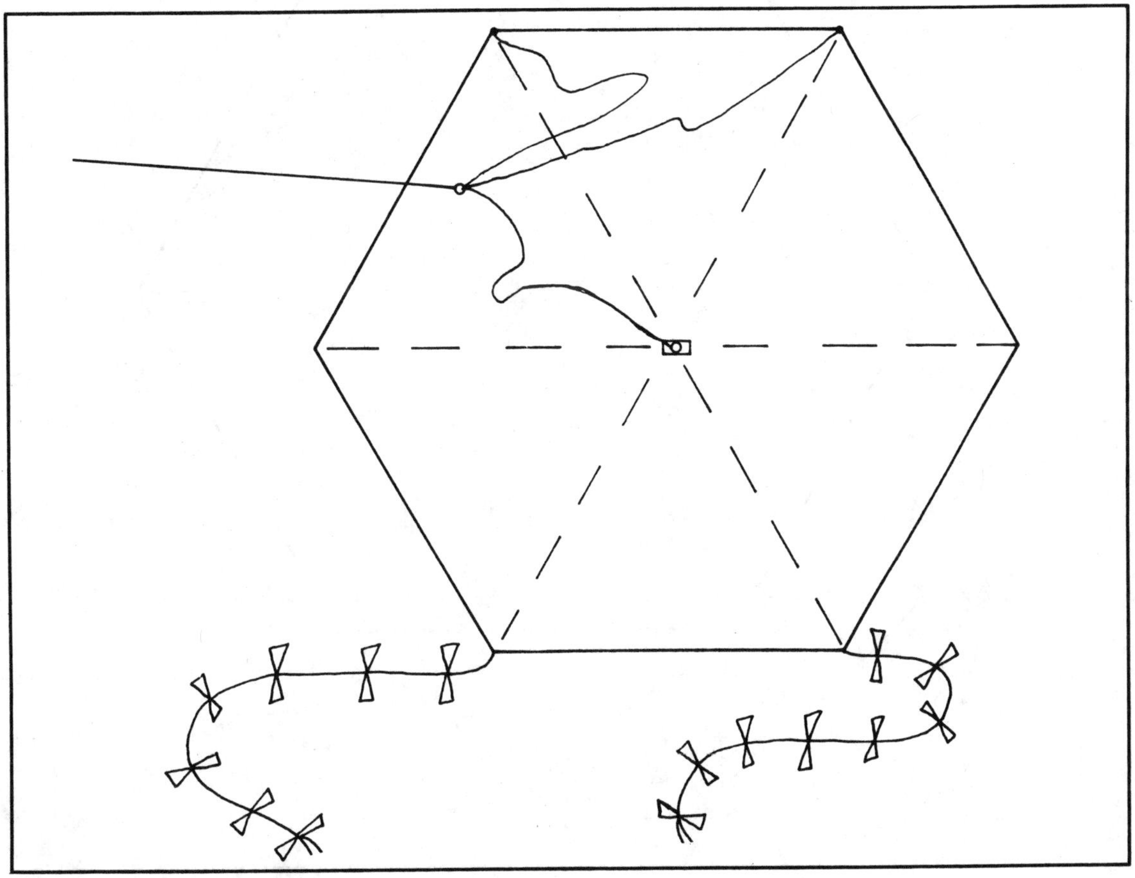

Fig. 6-67. Bridle string and two tail attachments.

with the string passing through the notch and on around the stick so that it will not slide down the stick. When done properly, the longitudinal sticks are inside the bow, above the cross stick, as shown.

Bridle

A three-string bridle is usually used, as shown in Fig. 6-67. The upper two attachments are to the upper ends of the longitudinal sticks. The center attachment passes through a hole in the center of the covering material and is tied around the centerpoints of the three longitudinal sticks. The covering material is reinforced in the area of the hole with tape or by other means. Each string should be about 20 inches long from the points of attachment on the kite. The loose ends of the strings can be tied in a loop or to a small plastic curtain rod ring. The bridle ring allows easy adjustment of the length of the bridle strings.

Tail

A tail is usually required for adequate flying stability, even if the kite is bowed. Two tails are often used, attached to the aft ends of the two longitudinal sticks, as shown in Fig. 6-67.

Construction of tails is detailed in Chapter 5.

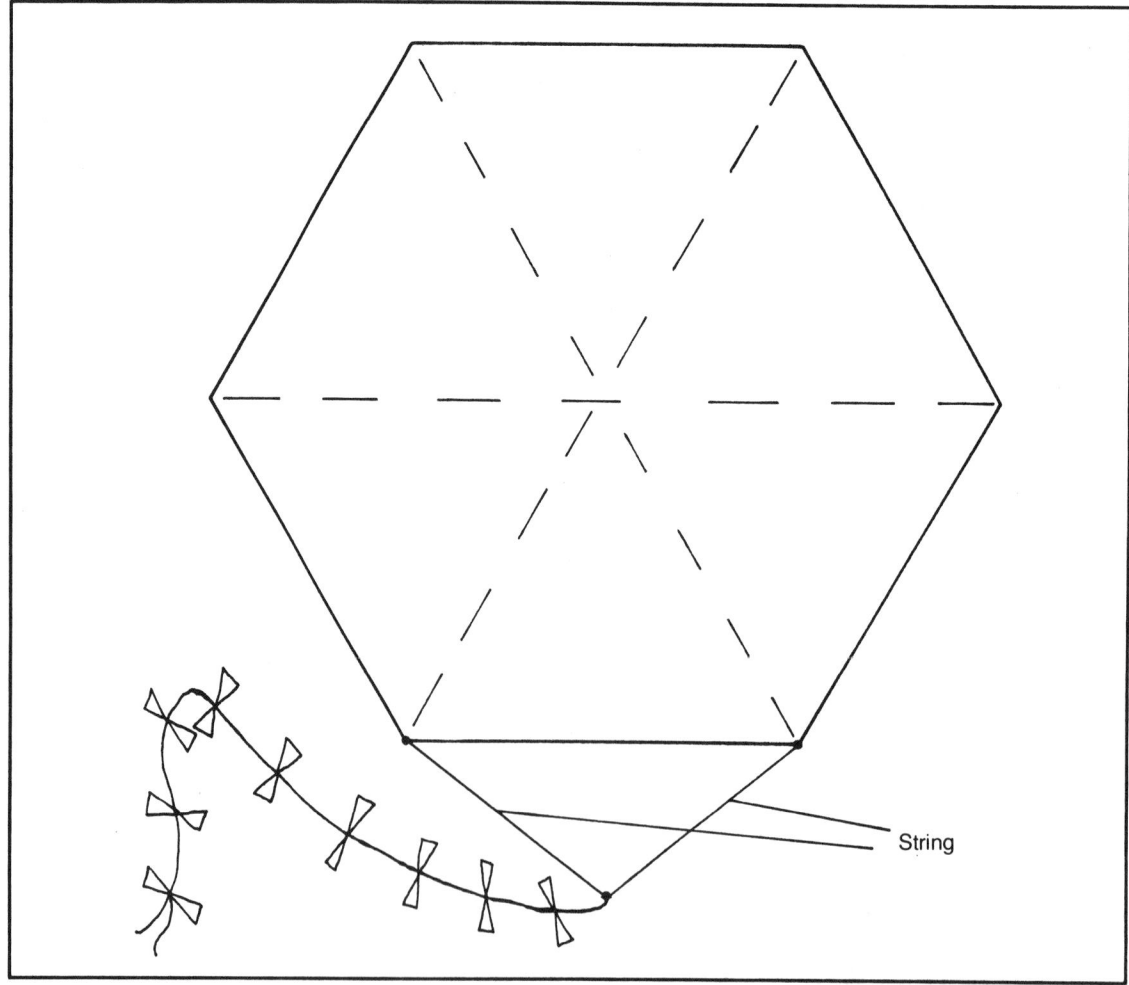

Fig. 6-68. Use of one tail.

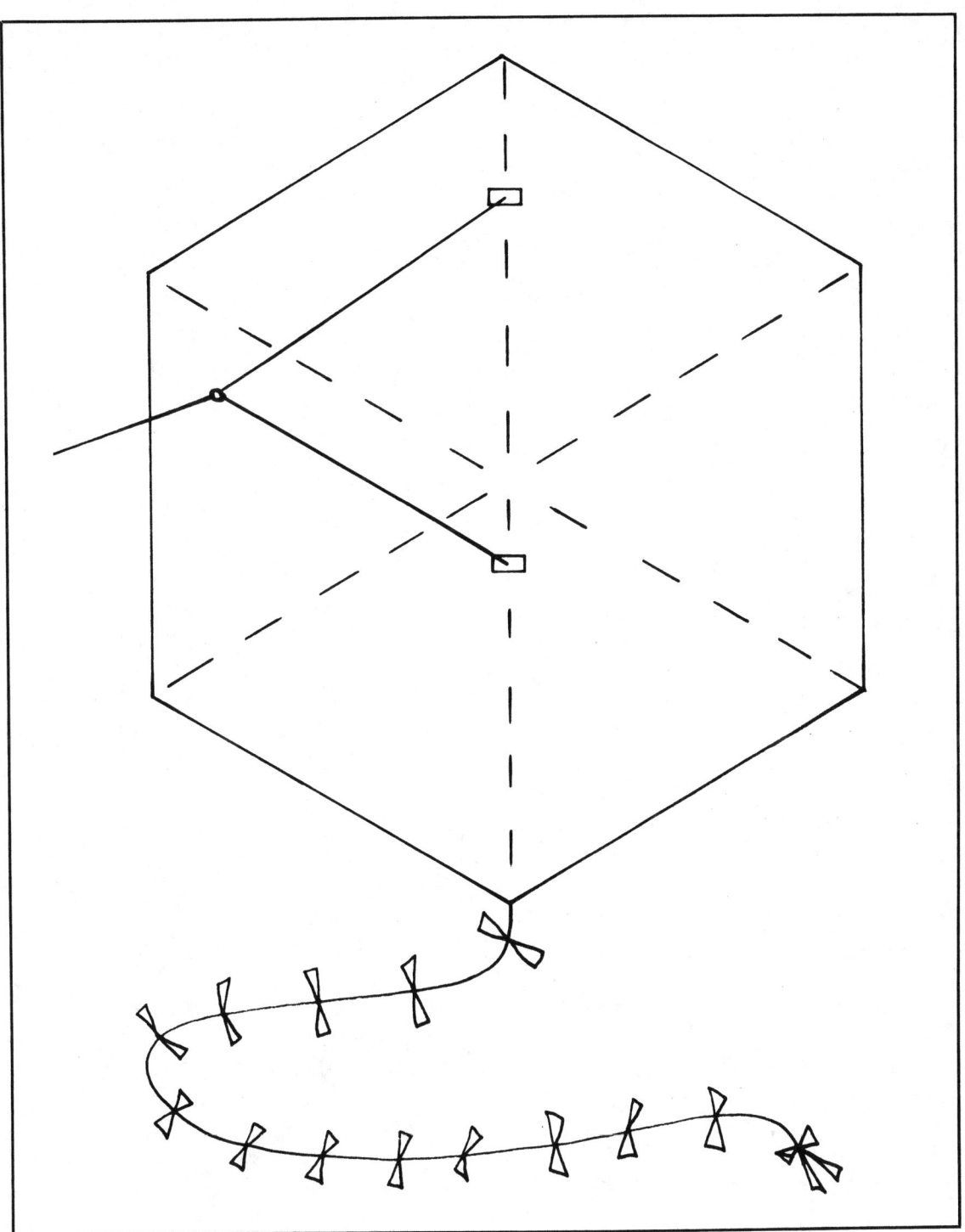

Fig. 6-69. Hexagonal kite can be flown with points at top and bottom and one tail.

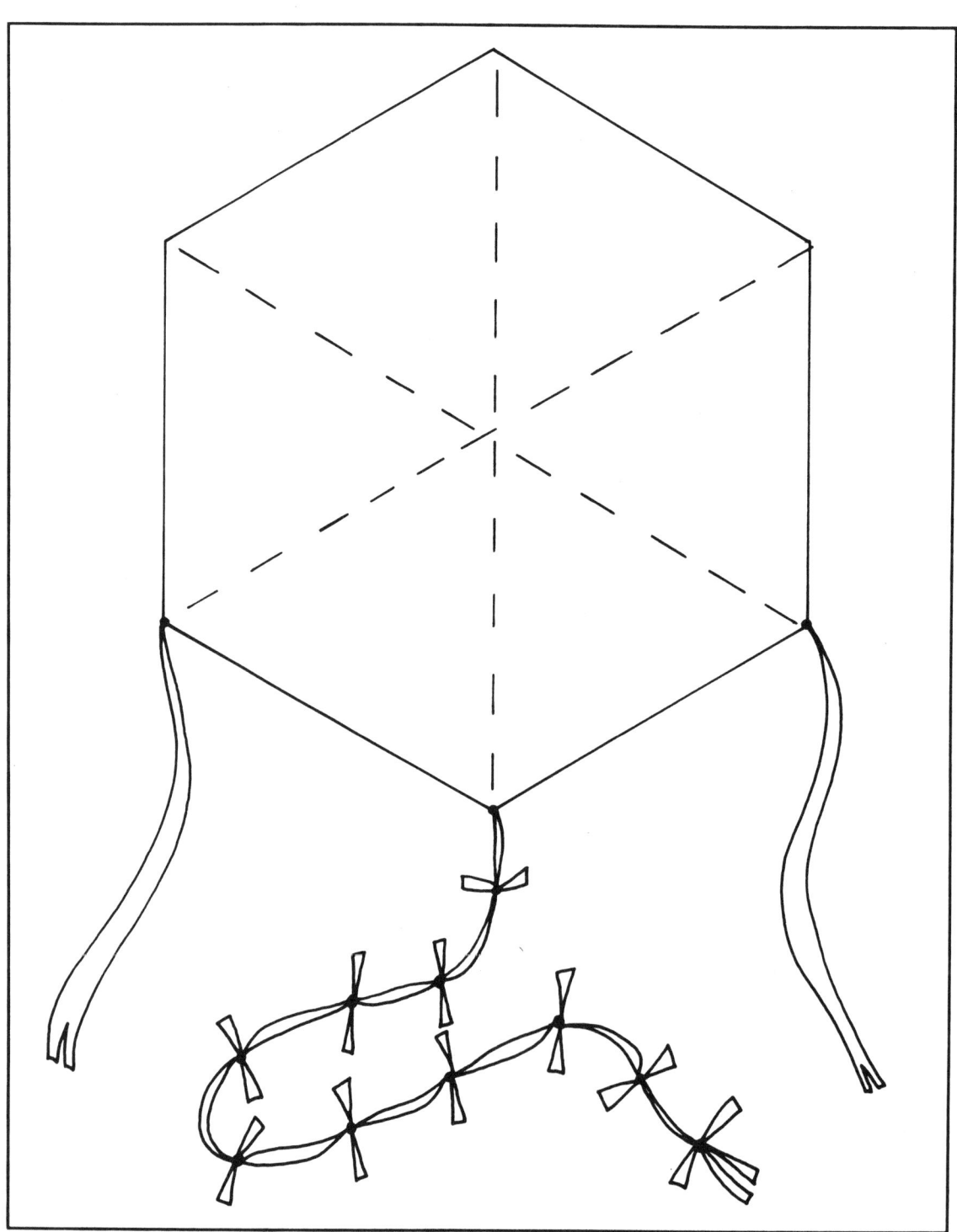

Fig. 6-70. Use of three tails.

The length and weight of the tail will depend on the wind conditions and other factors. Try the kite first without a tail; if it loops or spins uncontrollably, add tail. Use the minimum amount necessary for good stability.

A single tail attached to a string and tied to the aft ends of the longitudinal sticks, as shown in Fig. 6-68, is another possibility.

Variations

The three-stick hexagonal kite can be constructed in a range of sizes with sticks 1 foot or less in length to 6 feet or more in length. Reduce the weight of the smaller sizes by using proportionally smaller sticks and lighter weight covering material; use larger sticks and heavier covering material for the larger sizes.

The hexagonal kite can be flown with points at the top and bottom, as shown in Fig. 6-69. A bridle with two points of attachment can be used, as shown. One tail can be attached to the aft end of the longitudinal stick. Three tails, as shown in Fig. 6-70, are another possibility.

BASIC THREE-STICK KITE

The three-stick kite shown in Fig. 6-71 is similar to the basic two-stick kite, except a second cross stick equal in length to the first one is added. This kite can be used as a flat or bowed kite, as desired. A tail is usually required for adequate balance and stability.

Frame

Three 36-inch-long sticks are used for the frame, as shown in Fig. 6-72. A wooden stick with a rectangular cross section of ¼ inch by ⅜ inch or a round wooden dowel of ¼-inch diameter can be used for the longitudinal stick. Two wooden sticks with a rectangular cross section of 3/16 inch by 5/16 inch or round wood dowels of 3/16-inch diameter can be used for the cross sticks. The sticks can vary somewhat from these dimensions and still give satisfactory results. If the kite is to be used only in light airs, reduce the cross sectional size of the sticks; for extremely strong winds, use sticks with larger cross sectional dimensions. Sticks of fiberglass, bamboo, and aluminum are other alternatives.

The instructions below use wooden sticks of either rectangular or round cross sectional shape.

The ends of the sticks are notched by making a saw cut to a depth of ⅜ inch in each end. Make the notches on both ends of each stick in the same plane.

Measure and mark the centerpoint on each cross stick. Measure and mark points 6 inches from each end of the longitudinal stick, as shown in Fig. 6-72. The sticks are then glued and lashed together with string. Tie the ends of the lashing strings together with square knots. All of the notches at the ends of the sticks should be parallel to the plane surface of the kite.

The guideline string is installed in the end notches around the kite frame, as shown in Fig. 6-73. Stretch the string tight and tie the ends together with a square knot. If a sewn fabric cover is to be used, you will probably want to wait until the cover has been sewn before installing the guideline so that it can be inserted through the sleeves first. After the guideline string has been installed, add lashings around the sticks on each side of the guideline string where it passes through the

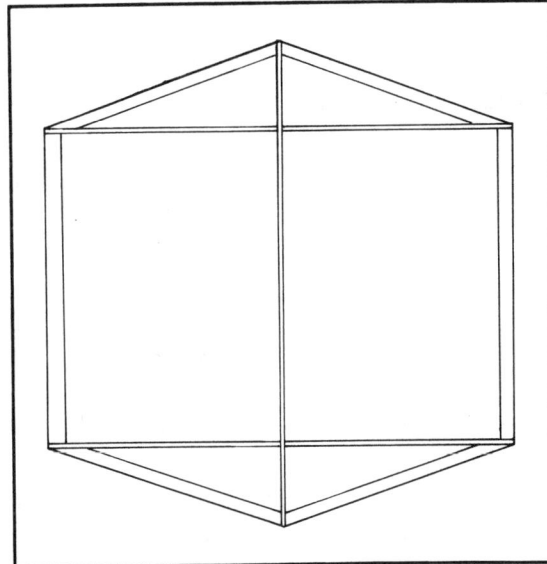

Fig. 6-71. Basic three-stick kite.

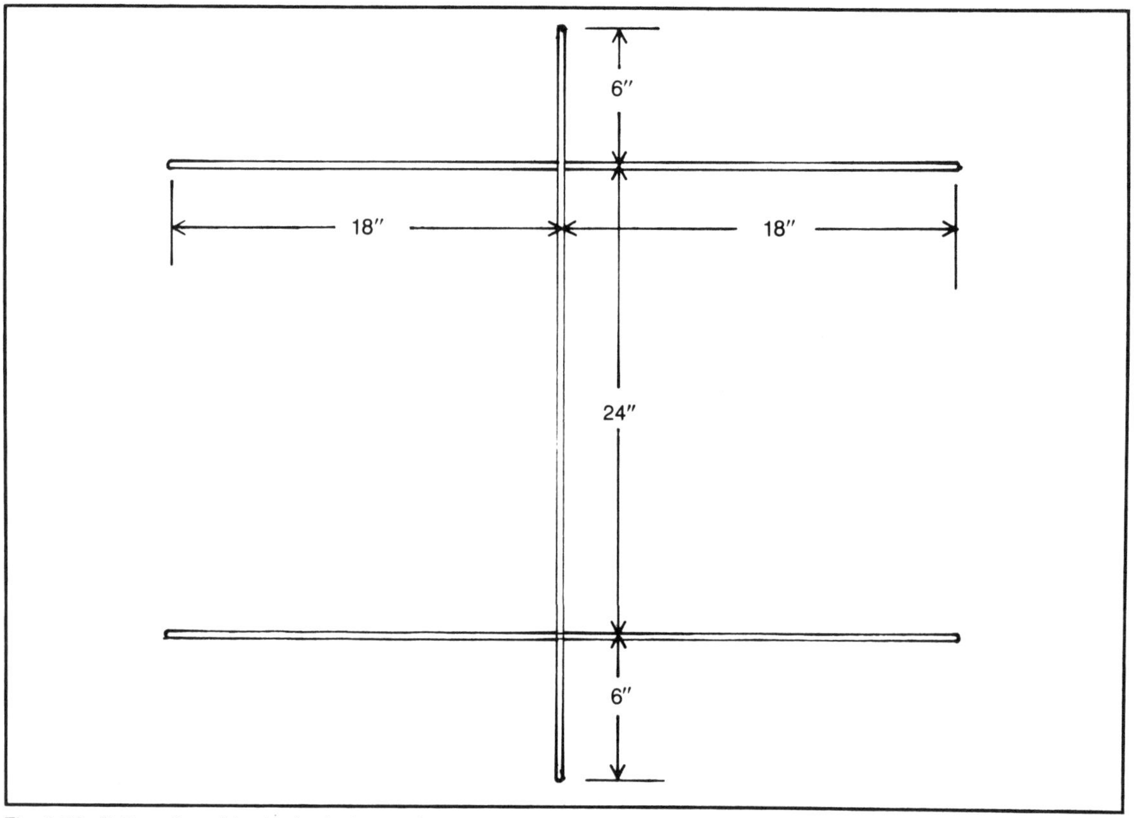

Fig. 6-72. Pattern for sticks for basic three-stick kite.

notches in the sticks. Tie the ends of each lashing string together with a square knot.

Covering Material

Paper, plastic film, or fabric can be used for covering the kite, as desired. For best performance, the covering material should be of the lightest weight compatible with adequate strength. Mark the pattern shown in Fig. 6-74 on the covering material. The kite frame, with either the permanent or a temporary guideline string in place, can be placed over the covering material to use as a pattern.

Use scissors to cut the covering material to the pattern. Join the covering material to form the hems and sleeves, depending on the particular covering material used (see Chapter 5). Install the cover with the guideline string passing through sleeves in the covering material.

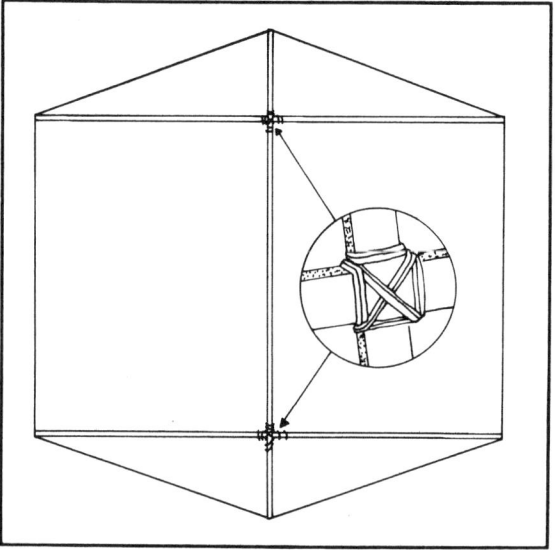

Fig. 6-73. The guideline string is installed in notches around frame sticks.

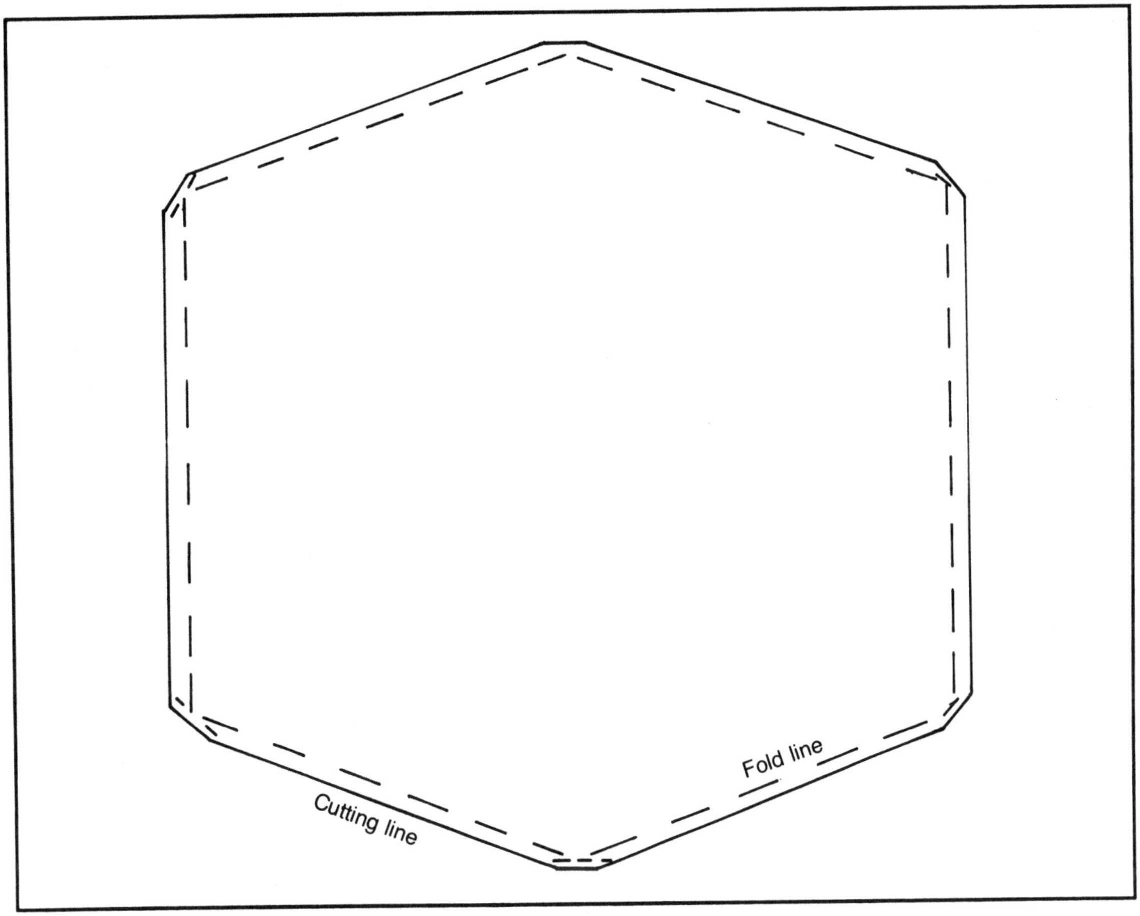

Fig. 6-74. Pattern for covering material.

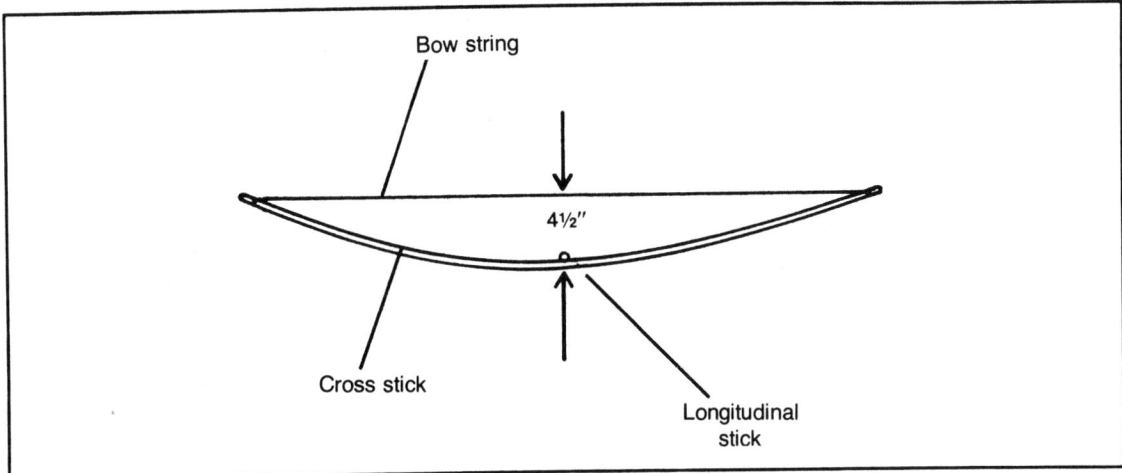

Fig. 6-75. Bow string.

129

Bow String

The performance of the basic three-stick kite is often improved by adding bow strings. Two bow strings can be used, one on each cross stick. Tie the bow string to one end of one of the cross sticks. Pass the string through the notch and on around the stick. This will keep the bow string from sliding down the stick when the kite is bowed. Bow the cross stick 4½ inches, as shown in Fig. 6-75. Then tie the bow string to the other end of the cross stick with the string passing through the notch and on around the stick so that it will not slide down the stick. Attach a bow string to the other cross stick in the same manner. When done properly, the longitudinal stick is inside the bow, above the cross sticks, as shown.

Bridle

A three-string bridle is usually used, as shown in Fig. 6-76. The upper two attachments are to the upper cross stick, 6 inches from each end, with the strings passed through holes in the covering material and tied around the stick. The covering material is reinforced in the area of the holes. The other attachment is to the cross point of the lower cross stick and the longitudinal stick. The string passes through a hole in the covering material and is tied around the sticks. The hole is reinforced. The other

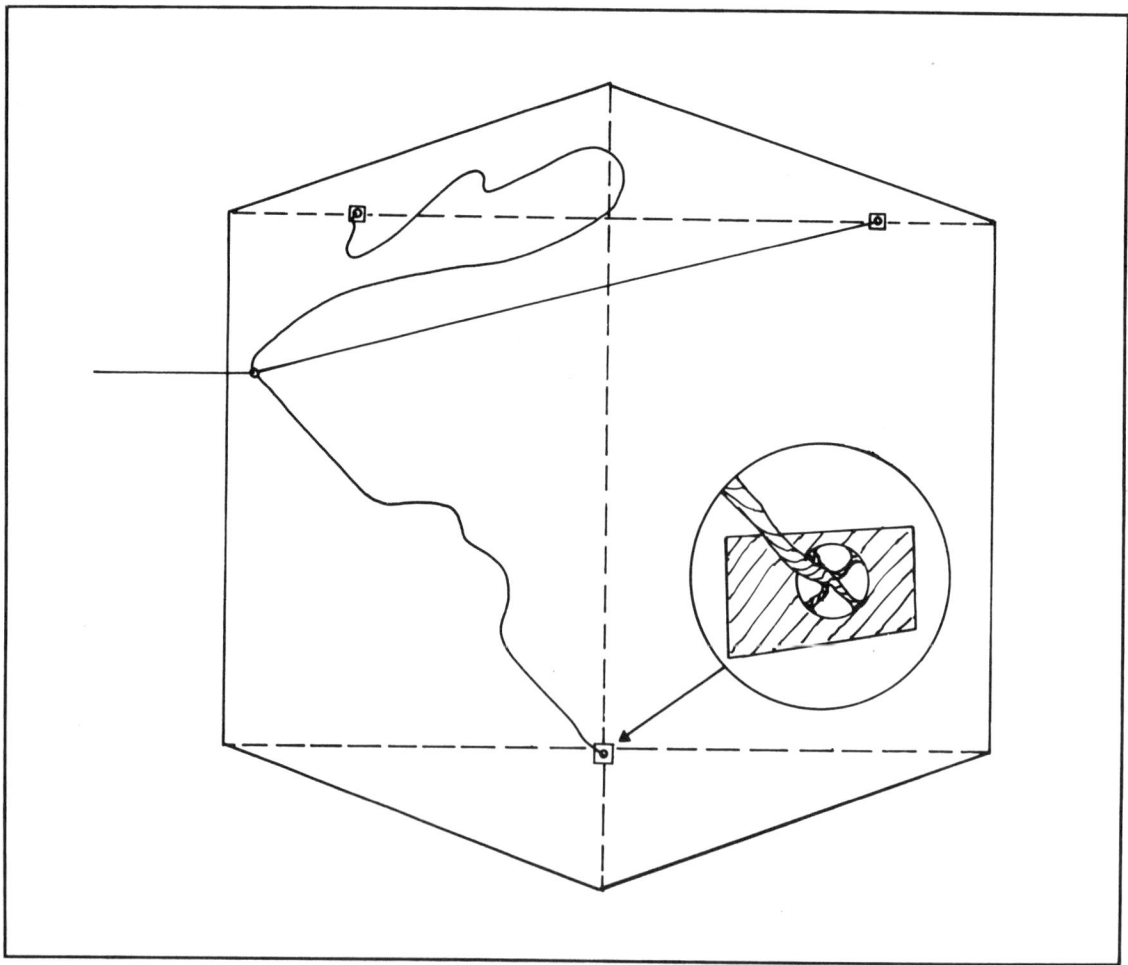

Fig. 6-76. Bridle string attachment showing close-up of tape reinforced holes.

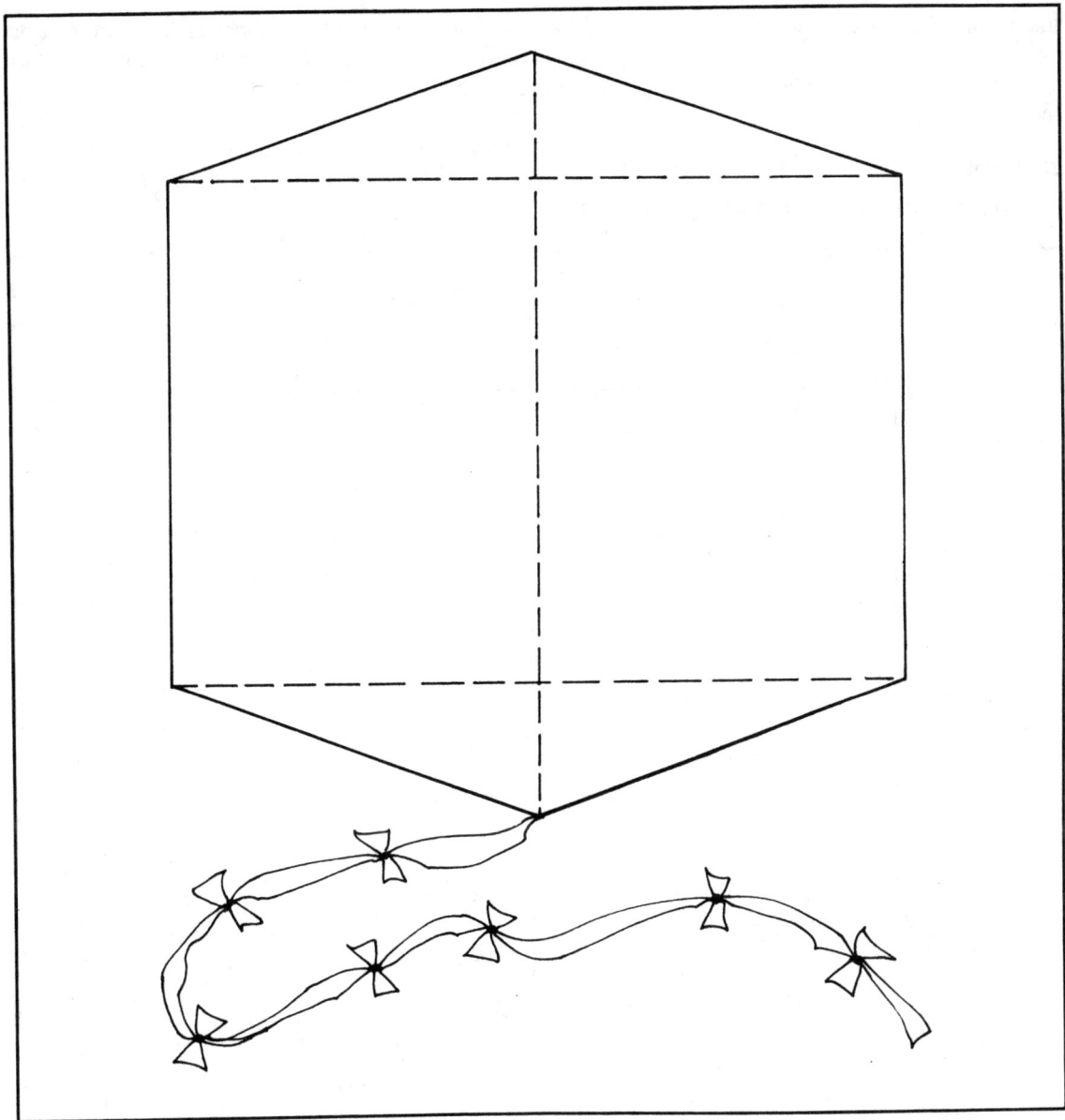

Fig. 6-77. Use of one tail.

ends of the strings can be tied in a loop or to a small plastic curtain rod ring. The bridle ring allows easy adjustment of the length of the bridle strings.

Tail

The basic three-stick kite usually requires a tail for adequate stability, even if the kite is bowed. A single tail is usually used, as shown in Fig. 6-77, attached to the aft end of the longitudinal stick.

Construction of tails is detailed in Chapter 5. The length and weight of the tail required will depend on the wind conditions and other factors. Try the kite first without a tail. If the kite loops or spins uncontrollably, add tail. Use the minimum amount of tail required to give the kite good stability.

The use of three tails, as shown in Fig. 6-78, is another possibility.

Variations

The basic three-stick kite can be constructed in a range of sizes from 1 foot or less to 6 feet or more in length. As a general rule, you will need to reduce the weight of the smaller sizes by using proportionally smaller sticks and lighter weight covering material. You will need to use larger sticks and heavier covering material for the larger sizes.

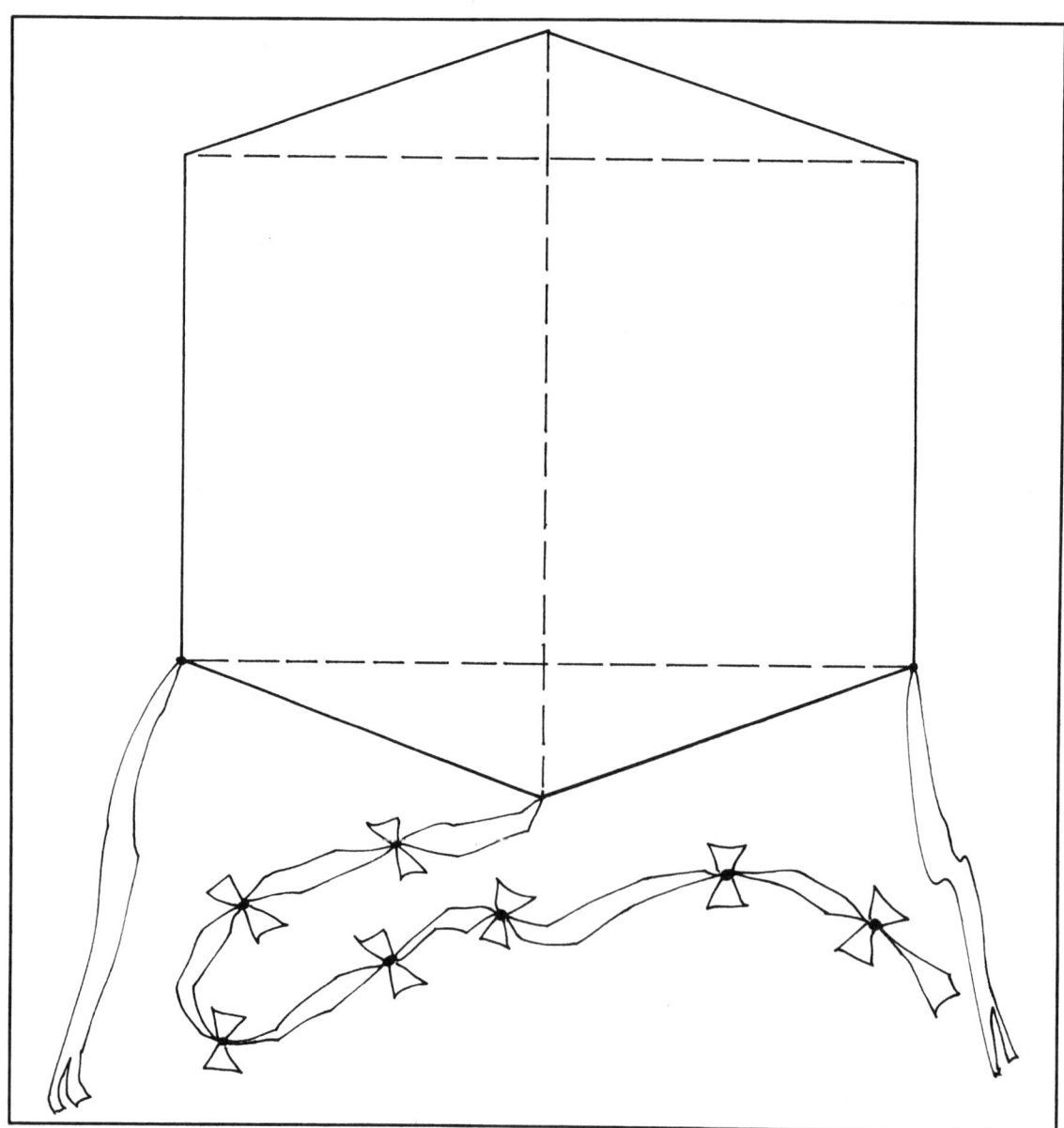

Fig. 6-78. Use of three tails.

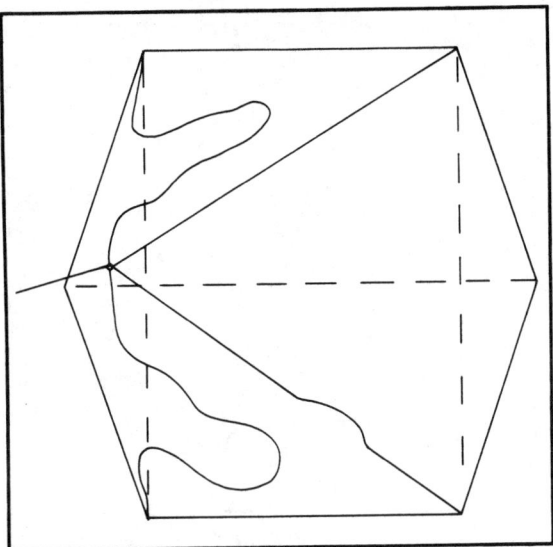

Fig. 6-79. Basic three-stick kite can be flown with a flat side downward.

The basic three-stick kite can be flown with one of the flat sides downward, as shown in Fig. 6-79. A bridle with four points of attachment can be used. The kite can be used as a flat kite, or it can be bowed (Fig. 6-80). Two tails can be attached to the aft end of the sticks, as shown in Fig. 6-81.

You may also want to experiment with different placements of the cross sticks, on the longitudinal stick (Figs. 6-82 and 6-83). You can also use a lower cross stick that is shorter than the upper one, as shown in Fig. 6-84.

RECTANGULAR KITE

The rectangular kite is shown in Fig. 6-85. This kite can be used with or without a bow. A tail is usually required to give this kite adequate stability.

Frame

One stick 36 inches long and three sticks 24 inches long are used for making the frame, as shown in Fig. 6-86. A wooden stick with a rectangular cross section of ¼ inch by ⅜ inch or a round wooden dowel of ¼-inch diameter can be used for the longitudinal stick. Three wooden sticks with a rectangular cross section of 3/16 inch by 5/16 inch or round wooden dowels in 3/16-inch diameter can be used for the cross sticks. The sticks can vary somewhat from these dimensions and still give satisfactory results. If the kite is to be used only in light airs, you may want to reduce the cross sectional size of the sticks; conversely, you may want to use sticks with larger cross sectional dimensions for heavier winds. Sticks of fiberglass, bamboo, and aluminum can also be used, as detailed in Chapter 5,

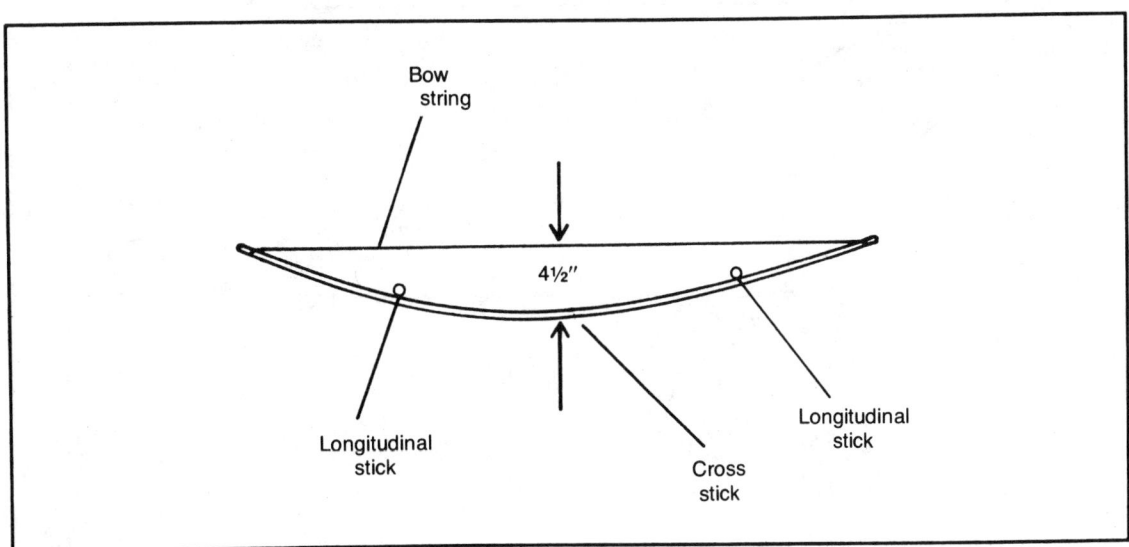

Fig. 6-80. Bow string.

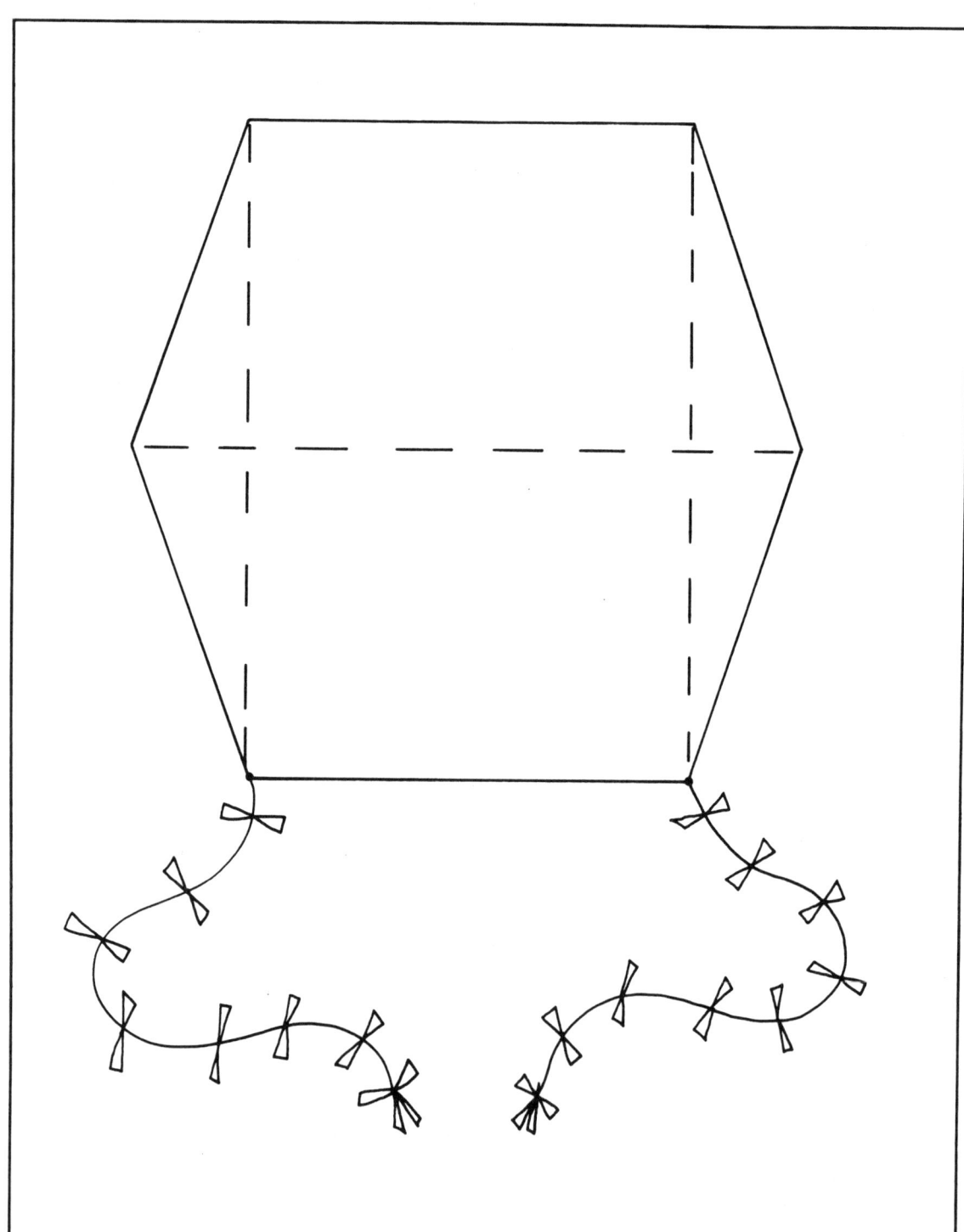

Fig. 6-81. Use of two tails.

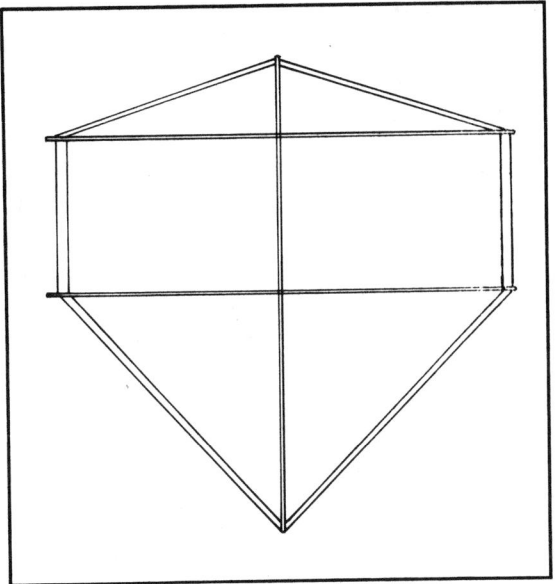

Fig. 6-82. Variation of basic three-stick kite.

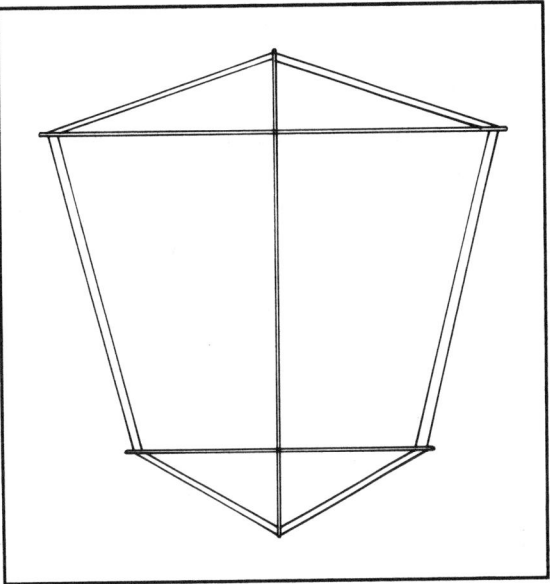

Fig. 6-84. Variation of basic three-stick kite with shortened lower cross stick.

but we'll assume that you will use wooden sticks of either rectangular or round cross sectional shape.

Grooves are first carved in the ends of the cross sticks for tying the guideline strings (Fig. 6-87). Measure and mark the centerpoint on each cross stick. Measure and mark points 1½ inches from each end of the longitudinal stick, as shown in Fig. 6-86. The sticks are then glued and lashed together with string. Tie the ends of the lashing strings together with square knots.

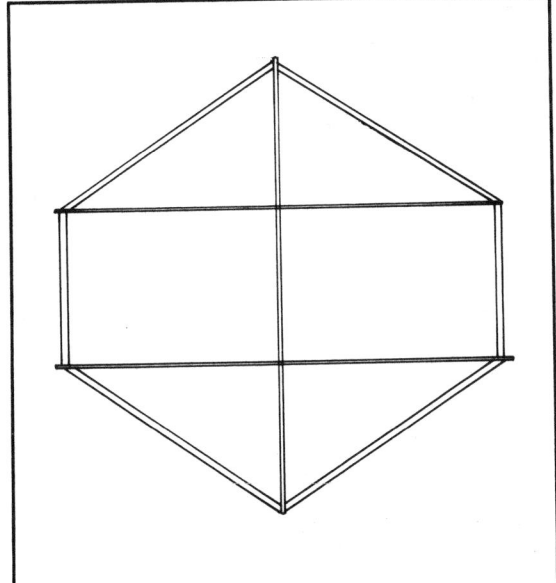

Fig. 6-83. Variation of basic three-stick kite.

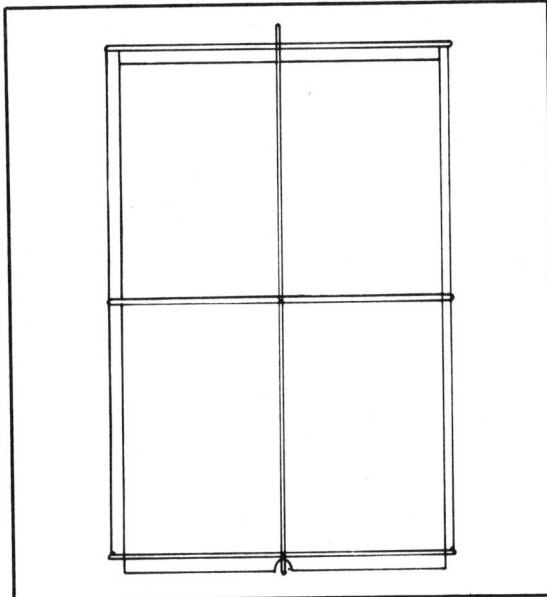

Fig. 6-85. Rectangular kite.

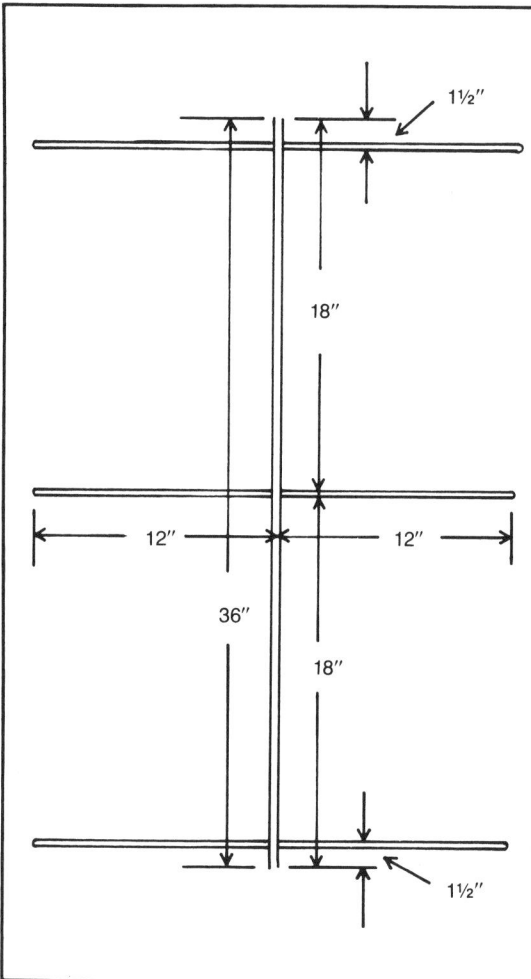

Fig. 6-86. Pattern for sticks for rectangular kite.

The guideline strings are attached to the ends of the cross sticks in the grooves, as shown in Fig. 6-87. Stretch the two strings tight so that they hold the cross sticks in the proper positions. Tie each guideline string to the upper and lower cross sticks with square knots. If a sewn fabric cover is used, you will probably want to wait until the cover has been sewn before installing the guideline strings so that the string can be inserted through the sleeves first. You will also need to install the upper cross stick in the upper sleeve before gluing and binding the upper cross stick to the longitudinal stick.

Covering Material

For this kite use paper, plastic film or cloth fabric as a cover. Use the lightest weight material possible for good performance and adequate strength. Mark the pattern shown in Fig. 6-88 on the covering material. The kite frame, with either the permanent or temporary guideline strings in place, can be placed over the covering material for a pattern. The bottom of the covering material has a hem only and does not form a sleeve.

Use scissors to cut the covering material to the pattern. Methods for joining covering material to form the hems and sleeves depends on the particular covering material used (see Chapter 5).

Regardless of the covering material, install it to the kite frame with the guideline strings and upper cross stick passing through sleeves.

Bow String

The performance of the rectangular kite is sometimes improved by adding a bow string to the upper cross stick and sometimes a second bow string to the center cross stick. Tie the bow string to the groove at one end of the upper cross stick. This will keep it from sliding down the stick when the kite is bowed. Bow the cross stick until it has a 3-inch bow, as shown in Fig. 6-89. Then tie the bow string to the groove at the other end of the cross stick. If a bow string is to be used on the center cross stick, attach it in the same manner as the upper cross stick. When done properly, the longitudinal stick is inside the bow, above the cross sticks, as shown.

Bridle

A three-string bridle can be used, as shown in Fig. 6-90. The upper two attachments are to the grooves at the ends of the upper cross stick. The other attachment is to the longitudinal stick 9 inches from the lower end. The string passes through a hole in the covering material and is tied around the stick. The covering material is reinforced in the area of the hole with tape or other means. The remaining ends can be tied in a loop or to a small

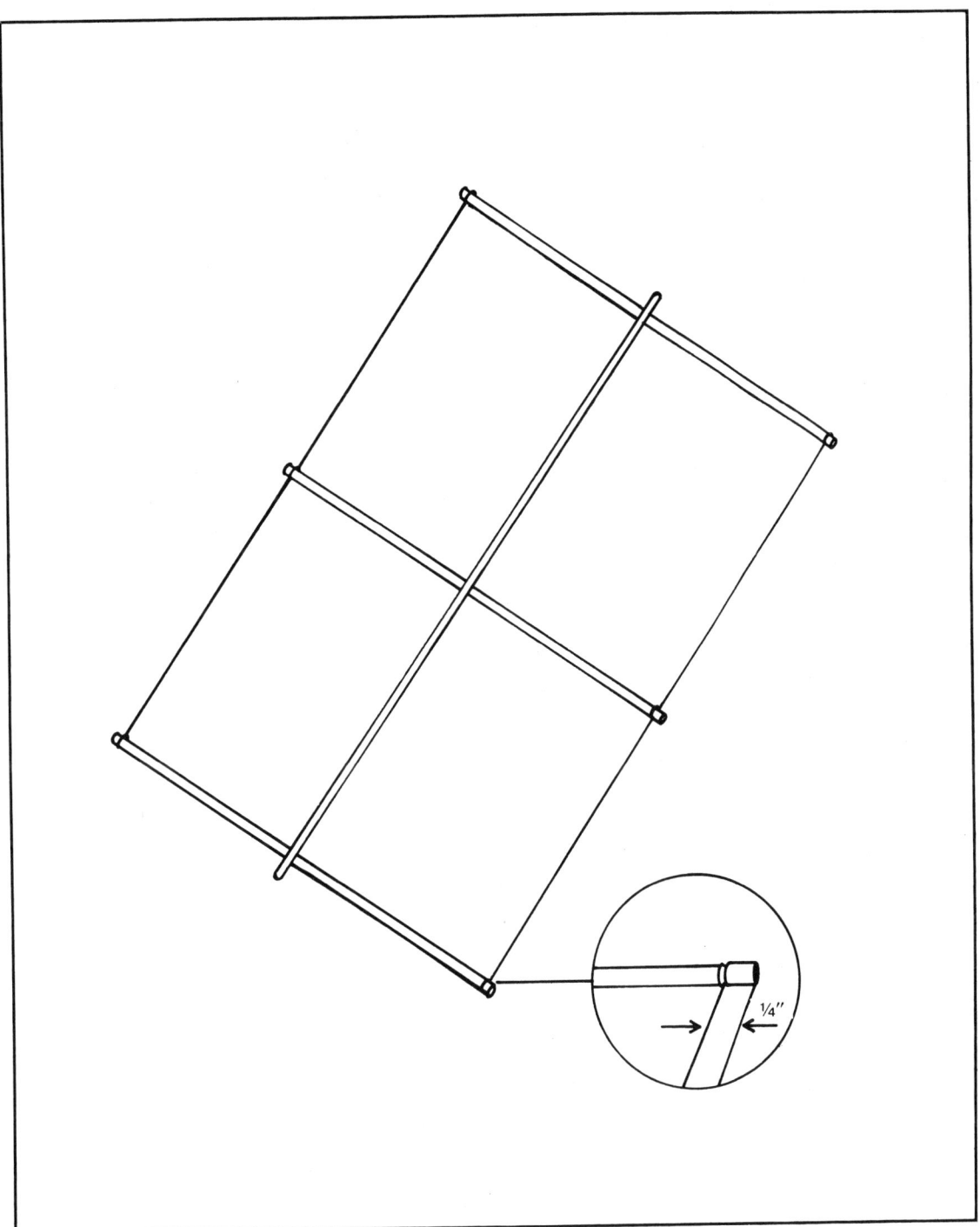

Fig. 6-87. Guideline strings are attached to grooves in cross sticks. Grooves are made ¼-inch from ends of cross sticks.

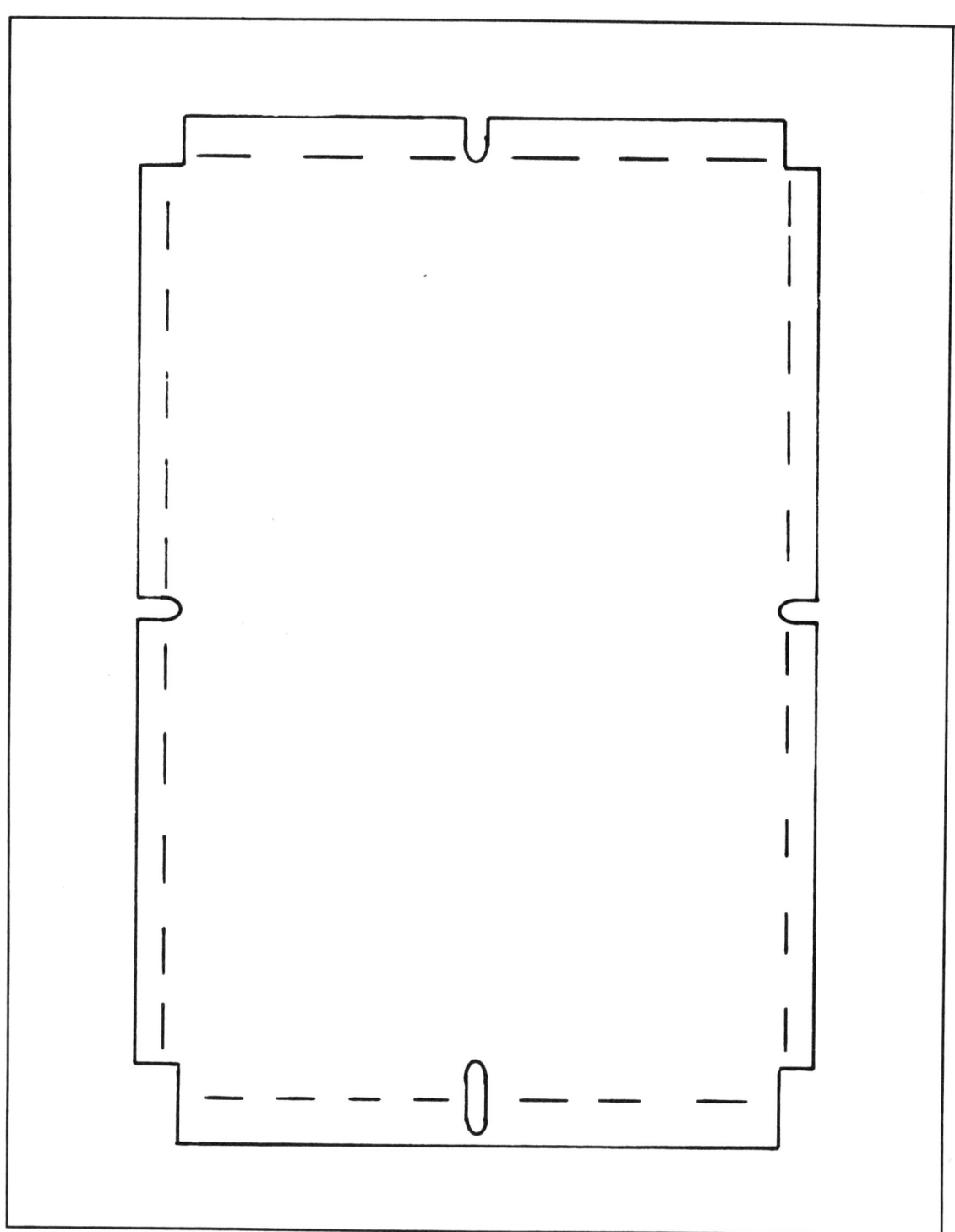

Fig. 6-88. Pattern for covering material.

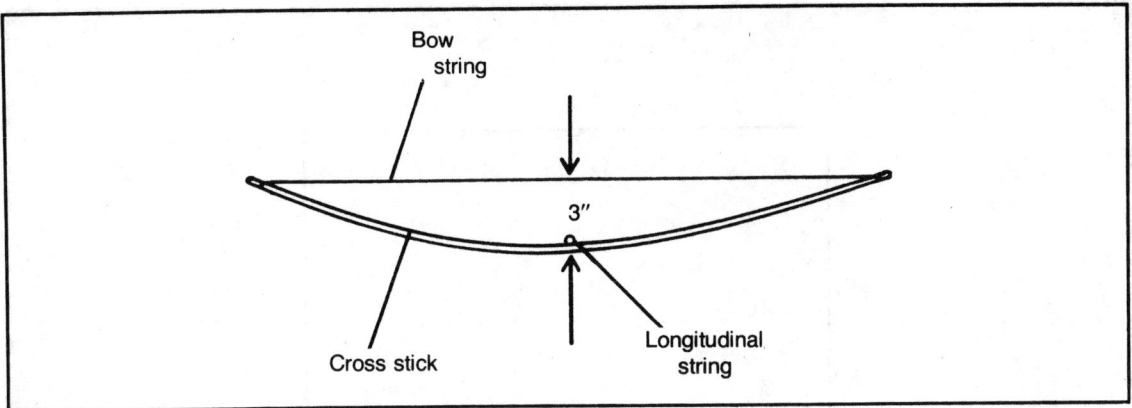

Fig. 6-89. Bow string.

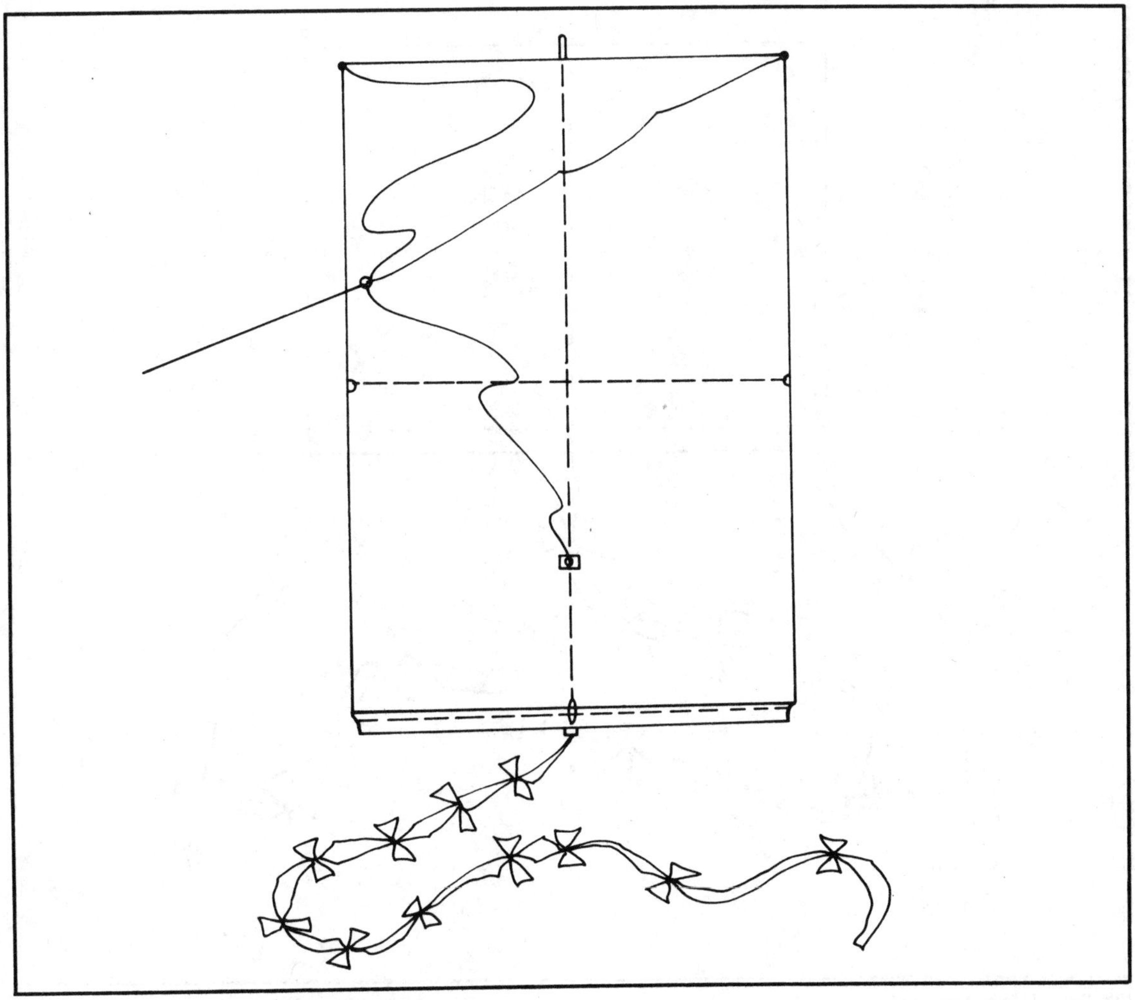

Fig. 6-90. Bridle string and single tail attachments.

139

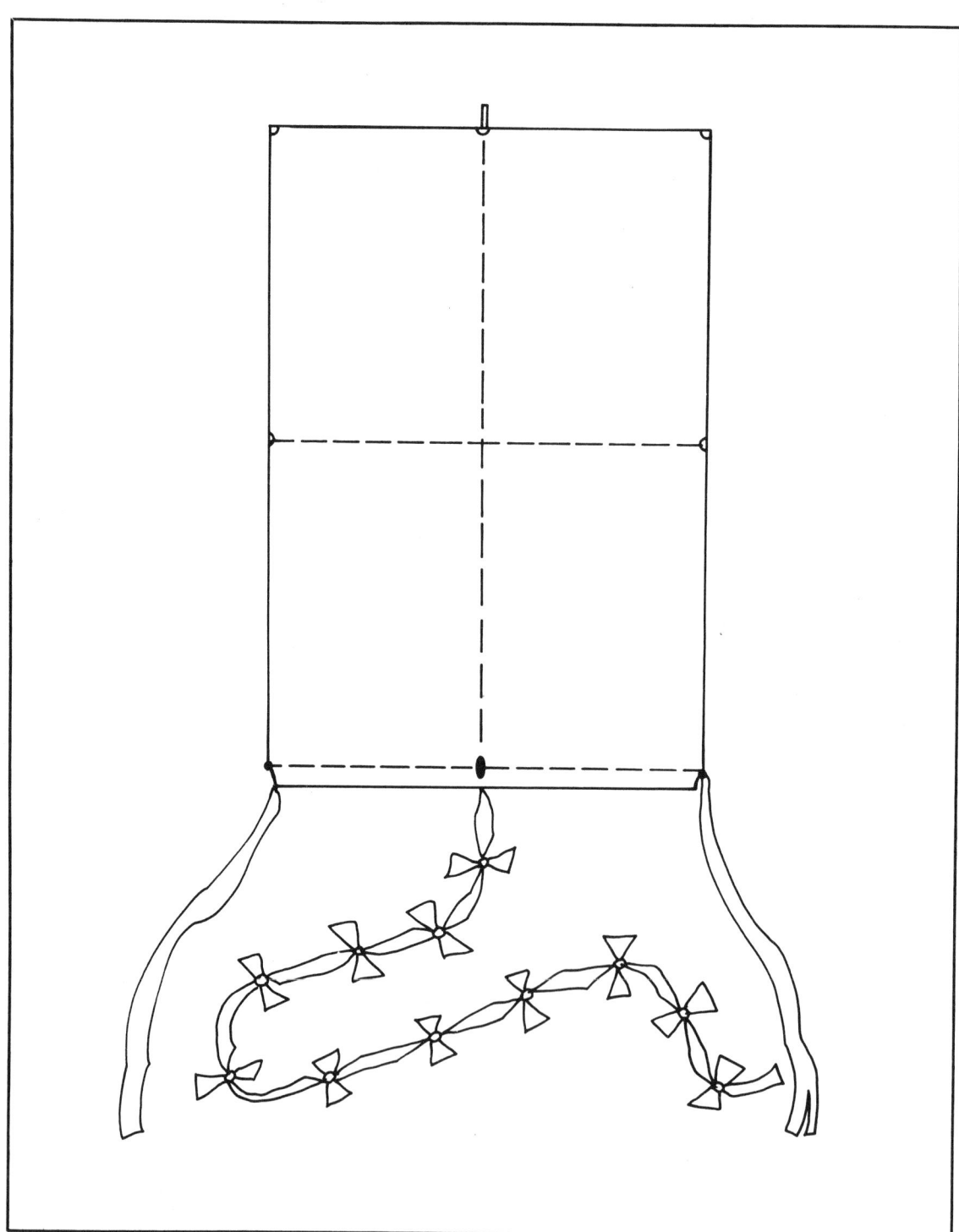

Fig. 6-91. Use of three tails.

plastic curtain rod ring. The bridle ring allows easy adjustment of the length of the bridle strings.

Tail

The rectangular kite usually requires a tail to give it adequate stability, even if the kite is bowed. A single tail can be used, as shown in Fig. 6-90. The tail is attached to the aft end of the longitudinal stick at the intersection of the lower cross stick.

Construction of tails is detailed in Chapter 5. The length and weight of the tail required will depend on the wind conditions and other factors. Try the kite first without a tail. If the kite loops or spins uncontrollably, add tail. Use the minimum amount of tail required to give the kite good stability.

The use of three tails, as shown in Fig. 6-91, is another possibility.

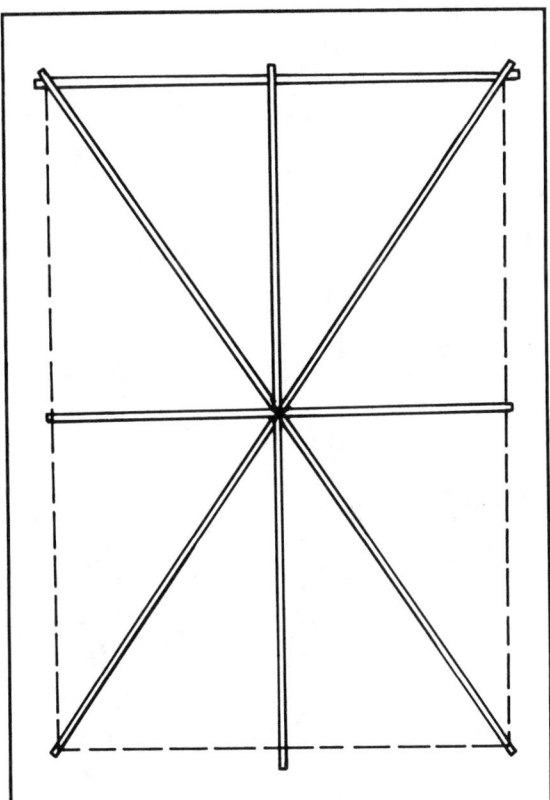

Fig. 6-92. Variation of framing arrangement for rectangular kite.

Variations

The rectangular kite can be constructed in a range of sizes from 1 foot or less in length to 6 feet or more in length by keeping the proportions the same. As a general rule, you will need to reduce the weight of the smaller sizes by using proportionally smaller sticks and lighter weight covering material; use larger sticks and heavier covering material for the larger sizes.

A variety of other framing arrangements, such as those shown in Fig. 6-92 and Fig. 6-93, can also be used for rectangular kites.

ARCH-TOP KITE

The arch-top kite (Fig. 6-94) can be used with or without a bow. A tail is usually required to give this kite adequate stability.

Frame

Three sticks are used for making the frame, as shown in Fig. 6-95. Wooden sticks with a rectangular cross section of ¼ inch by ⅜ inch or a round wooden dowel of ¼-inch diameter can be used for the longitudinal stick and the cross stick. The longitudinal stick is 36 inches long and the cross stick is 32 inches long. A wooden dowel ⅛ inch in diameter and 36 inches long is used for the arch stick. A bamboo strip 36 inches long can also be used for the arch stick. The sticks can vary somewhat from these dimensions and still give good results. If the kite is to be used only in light airs, reduce the cross sectional size of the sticks, and if the kite is to be flown in extremely strong winds, use sticks with larger cross sectional dimensions. Sticks of fiberglass, bamboo, and aluminum are other possibilities, as detailed in Chapter 5.

For descriptive purposes, we'll assume that you will be using wooden sticks of either rectangular or round cross sectional shape for the longitudinal and cross sticks and a wooden dowel or bamboo strip for the arch stick.

The aft end of the longitudinal stick is notched by making a saw cut to a depth of ⅜ inch in the end of it. Measure and mark the centerpoint on the cross stick and the arch stick. Measure and mark points 1

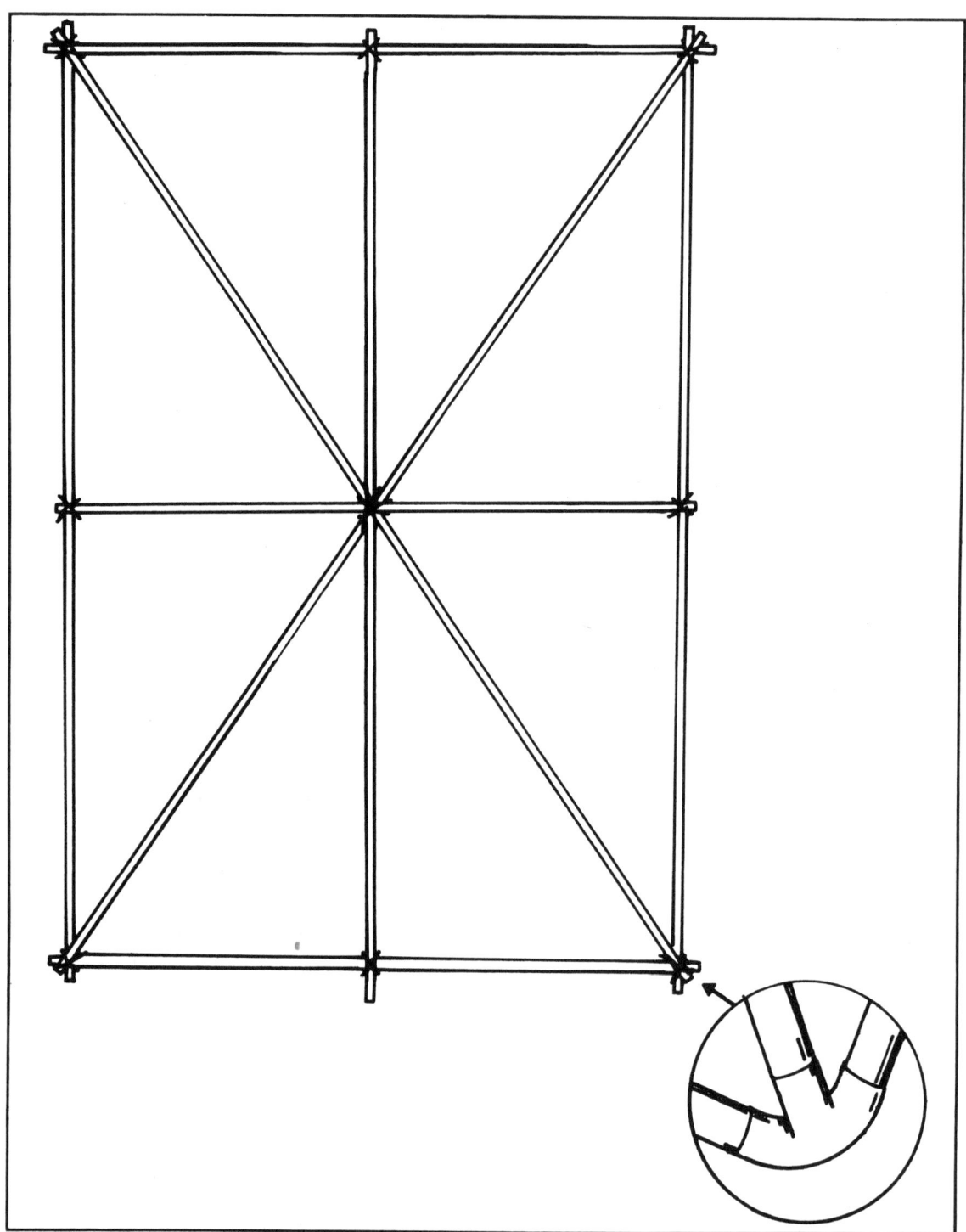

Fig. 6-93. Variation of framing arrangement for rectangular kite.

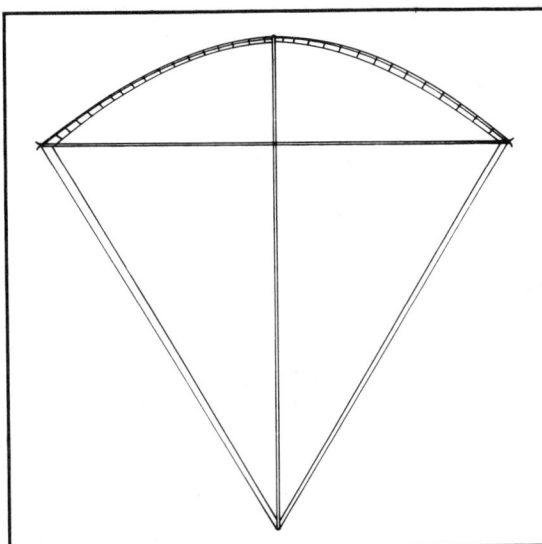

Fig. 6-94. Arch-top kite.

inch and 9 inches from the top end of the longitudinal stick, as shown in Fig. 6-95. The longitudinal and cross sticks are then glued and lashed together with string. Tie the ends of the lashing strings together with square knots. The notch at the aft end of the longitudinal stick should be in a plane with the flat surface of the kite.

Glue and lash the center of the arch stick to the longitudinal stick 1 inch from the top. Use string and tie with a square knot. Bend arch stick and glue and bind to ends of cross stick, with 1 inch extensions of each stick, as shown in Fig. 6-96. Lash with strings and tie ends with square knots.

Add a guideline string, as shown in Fig. 6-96. Tie one end of the string to the cross joint of the cross stick and arch stick at one end of the cross stick. Pass the string downward and through the notch in the aft end of the longitudinal stick. Then

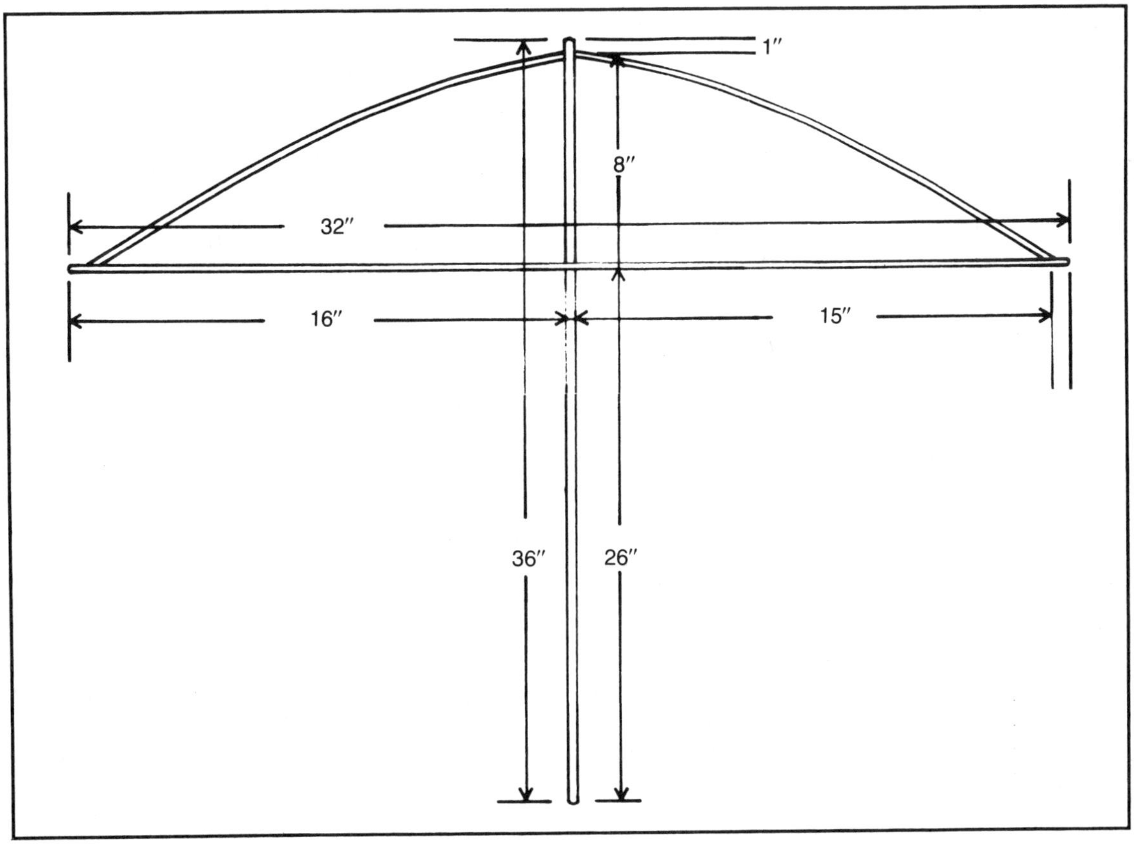

Fig. 6-95. Pattern for sticks for arch-top kite.

143

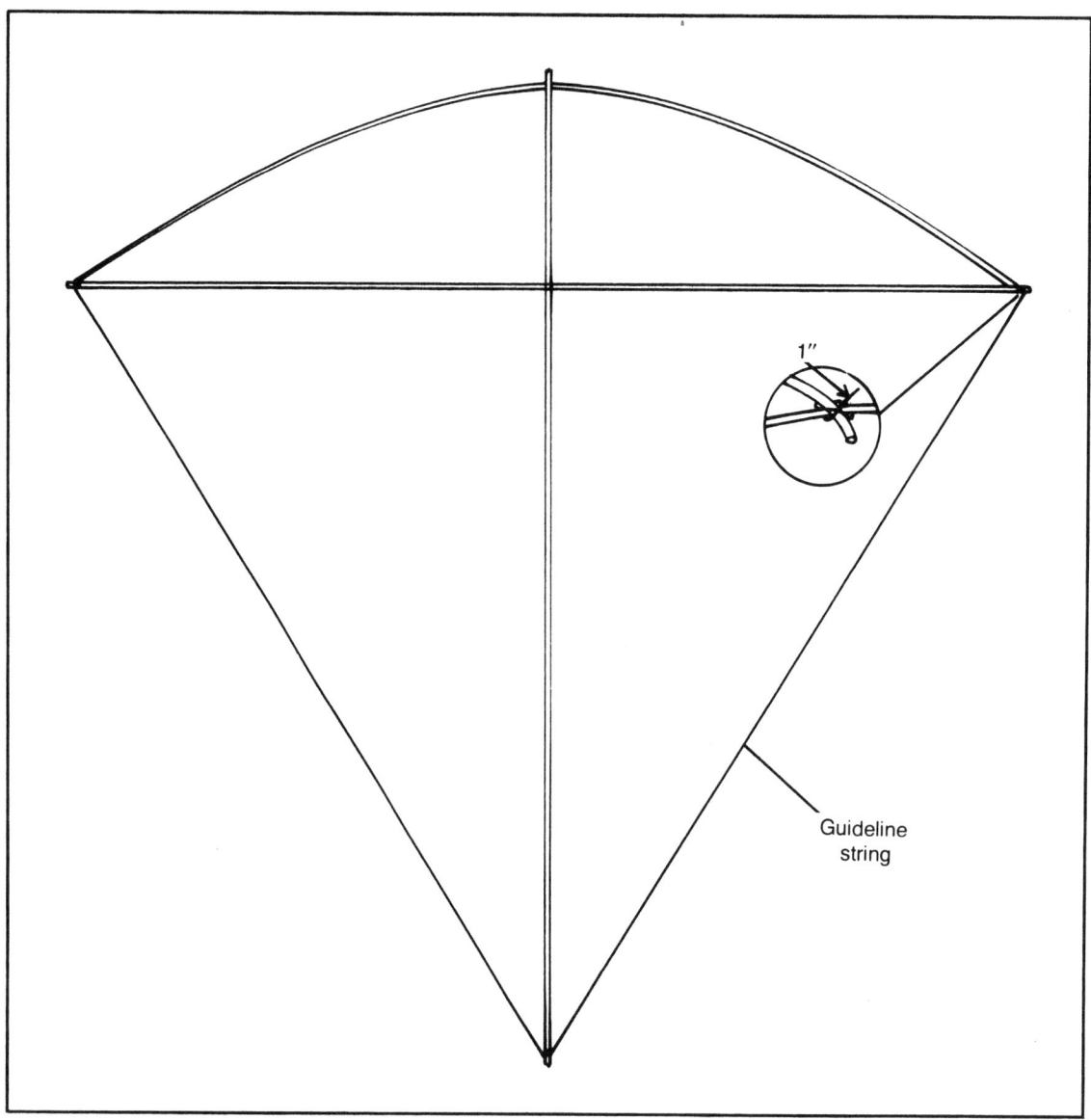

Fig. 6-96. Installation of guideline string. Arch stick is glued and lashed to cross stick.

extend it upward, and tie it to the cross joint of the cross stick and arch stick at the other end of the cross stick. Stretch the string tight and adjust tension until it pulls the cross stick straight and balances the tension between the arch stick and the guideline string. Tie the guideline string with a square knot. Add a lashing string around the aft end of the longitudinal stick on both sides of the guideline string where it passes through the notch. Tie the ends together with a square knot. If a sewn fabric cover is to be used, you can install a temporary guideline string at this time and then install the permanent guideline string after the cover has been sewn. The permanent guideline string is passed through the sleeves. You may also want to install the arch stick through the sleeve before attaching it to the kite frame.

Covering Material

You can use paper, plastic film, or fabric to cover this kite. For best performance, the covering material should be of the lightest weight that is compatible with adequate strength. Mark the pattern shown in Fig. 6-97 on the covering material. The kite frame, with either the permanent or a temporary guideline string, can be placed over the covering material to use as a pattern. Notice that the covering material has sleeves for both the arch stick and the guideline string.

Use scissors to cut the covering material to the

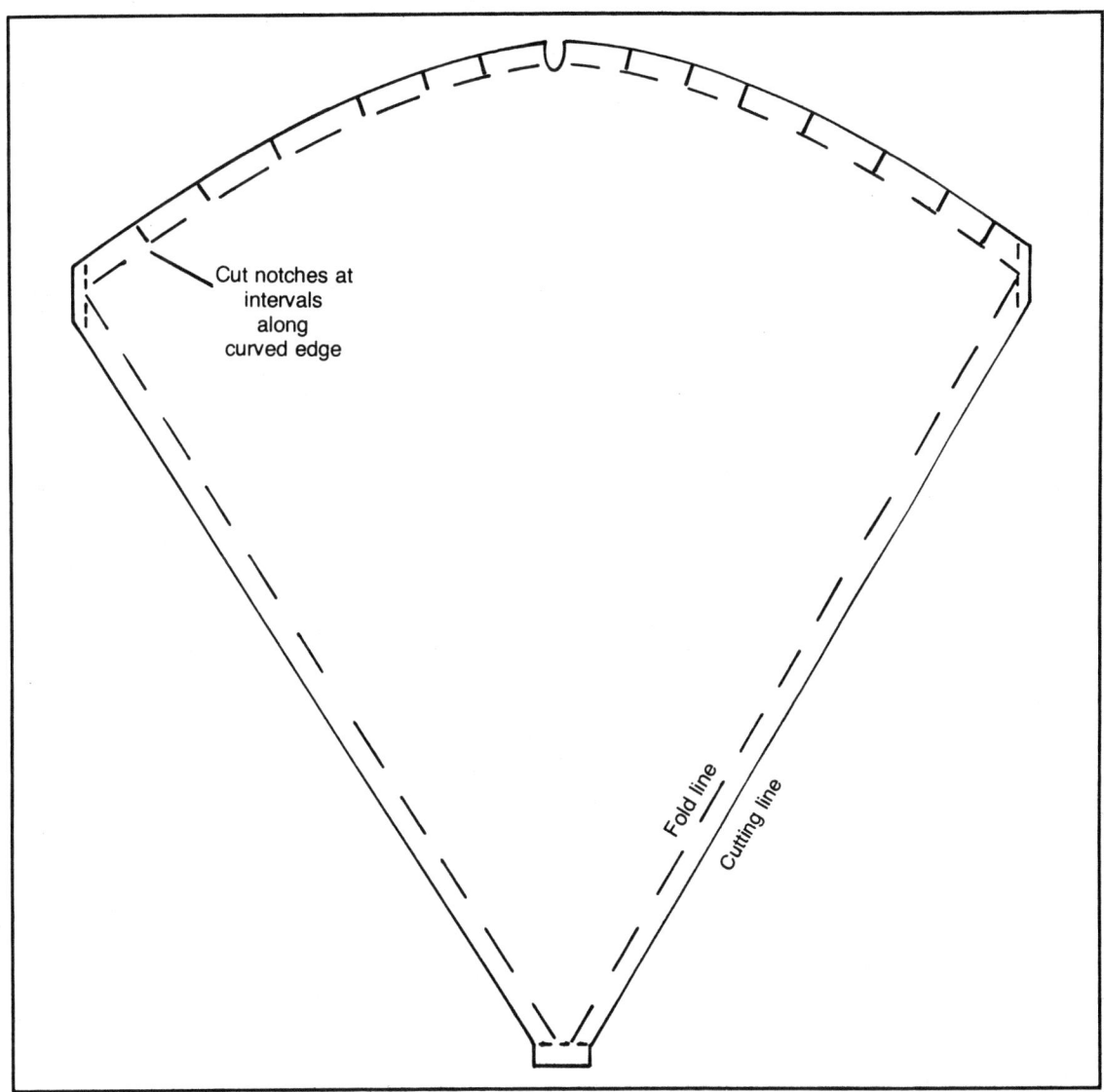

Fig. 6-97. Pattern for covering material.

pattern. Methods for joining covering material to form the hems and sleeves depends on the particular covering material used (see Chapter 5). Attach the cover to the kite frame with the guideline string and arch stick passing through sleeves in the covering material.

Bow String

The performance of the arch-top kite is usually improved by adding a bow string to the cross stick, as shown in Fig. 6-98. Tie the bow string to the cross joint of the cross stick and arch stick at one end of the cross stick. Wrap the string through the "V" formed by the sticks so that it cannot slide down the sticks when the kite is bowed. Tie the string with a square knot. Bow the stick until it has a 4-inch bow, as shown in Fig. 6-98. Tie the other end of the bow string to the cross joint of the cross stick and arch stick at the other end of the cross stick in the same manner.

Bridle

A two-string bridle is used, as shown in Fig. 6-99. The upper attachment is through a hole in the covering material, which should be reinforced with tape at the point where the longitudinal and cross sticks are joined. The string is then tied around the joint of the two sticks.

The other attachment is to the aft end of the longitudinal stick. Wrap the string around the end of the stick and pass it through the notch in the end of the stick. Tie with a square knot. The upper string should be about 24 inches long from the point of attachment to the bridle loop or ring; the lower string is about 36 inches long. The use of a bridle ring allows easy adjustment of the length of the bridle strings.

Tail

The arch-top kite usually requires a tail to give adequate stability, even if the kite is bowed. A single tail, as shown in Fig. 6-99, is usually used. The tail is attached to the aft end of the longitudinal stick.

Construction of tails is detailed in Chapter 5. The length and weight of the tail required will depend on the wind conditions and other factors. Try the kite first without a tail. If the kite loops or spins uncontrollably, add tail. Use the smallest tail required for good stability.

Variations

The arch-top kite can be constructed in a range of sizes from 1 foot or less in length to 6 feet or more in length by keeping the proportions the same. As a

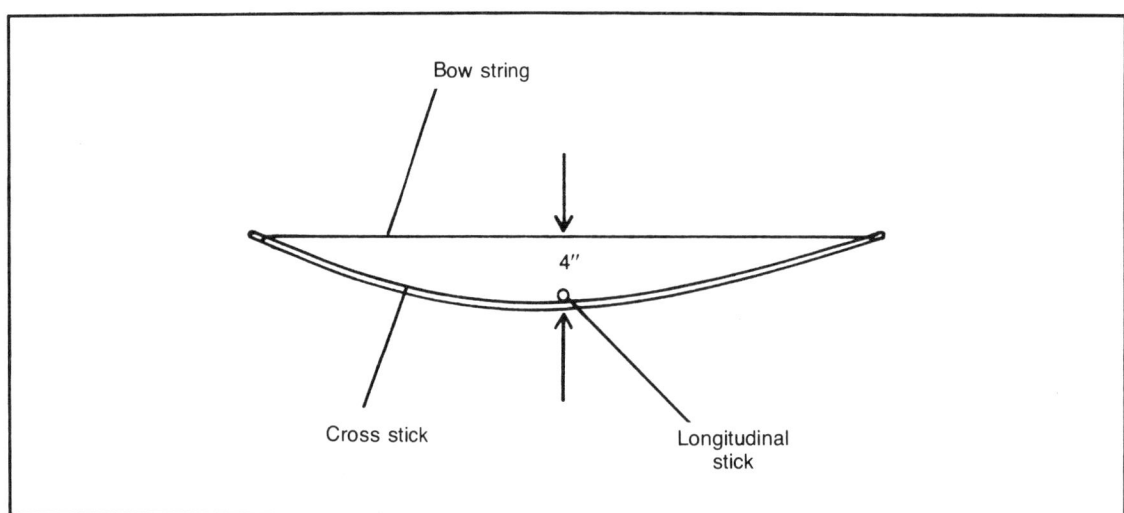

Fig. 6-98. Bow string.

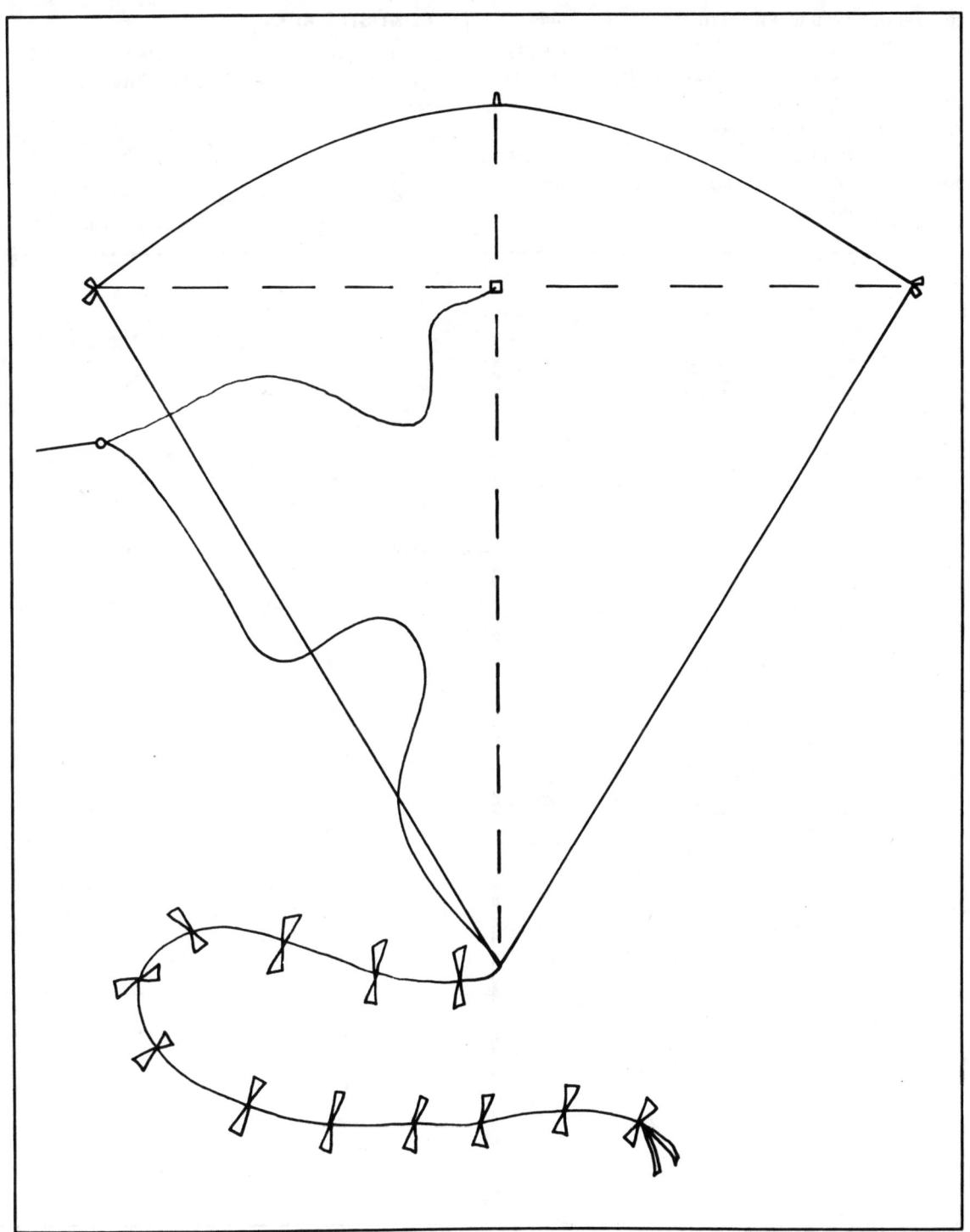

Fig. 6-99. Bridle string and tail attachments.

general rule, you will need to reduce the weight of the smaller sizes by using proportionally smaller sticks and lighter weight covering material, and you will need to use larger sticks and heavier covering material for the larger sizes.

A variety of other framing arrangements are possible for arch-top kites, such as those shown in Fig. 6-100 and Fig. 6-101.

FIVE-POINT STAR KITE

The five-point star kite is shown in Fig. 6-102. This kite is usually used as a flat kite. A tail is required for adequate stability.

Frame

Three 36-inch-long sticks are used to make the frame, as shown in Fig. 6-103. Wooden sticks with a

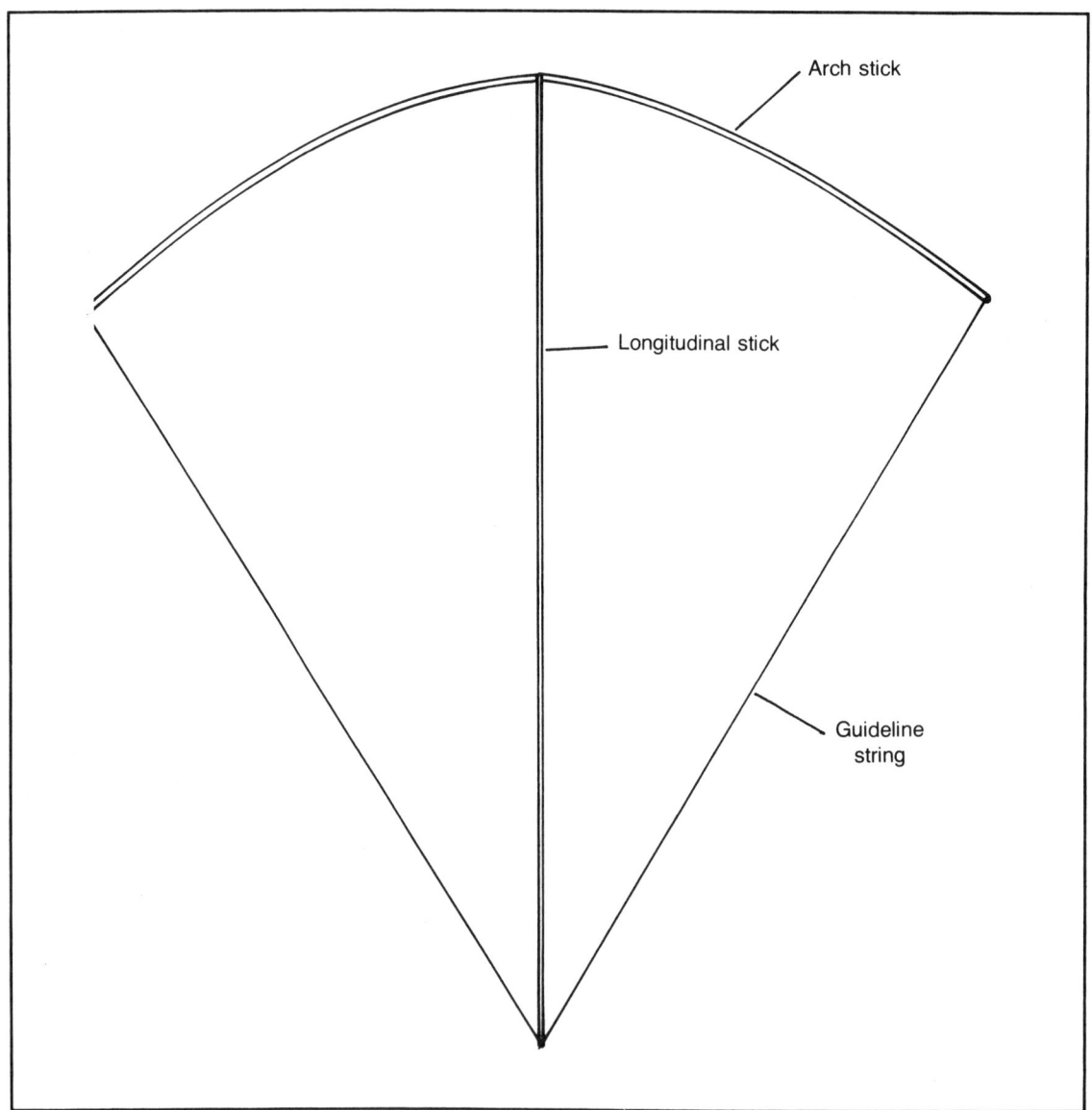

Fig. 6-100. Variation in framing arrangement for arch-top kite.

148

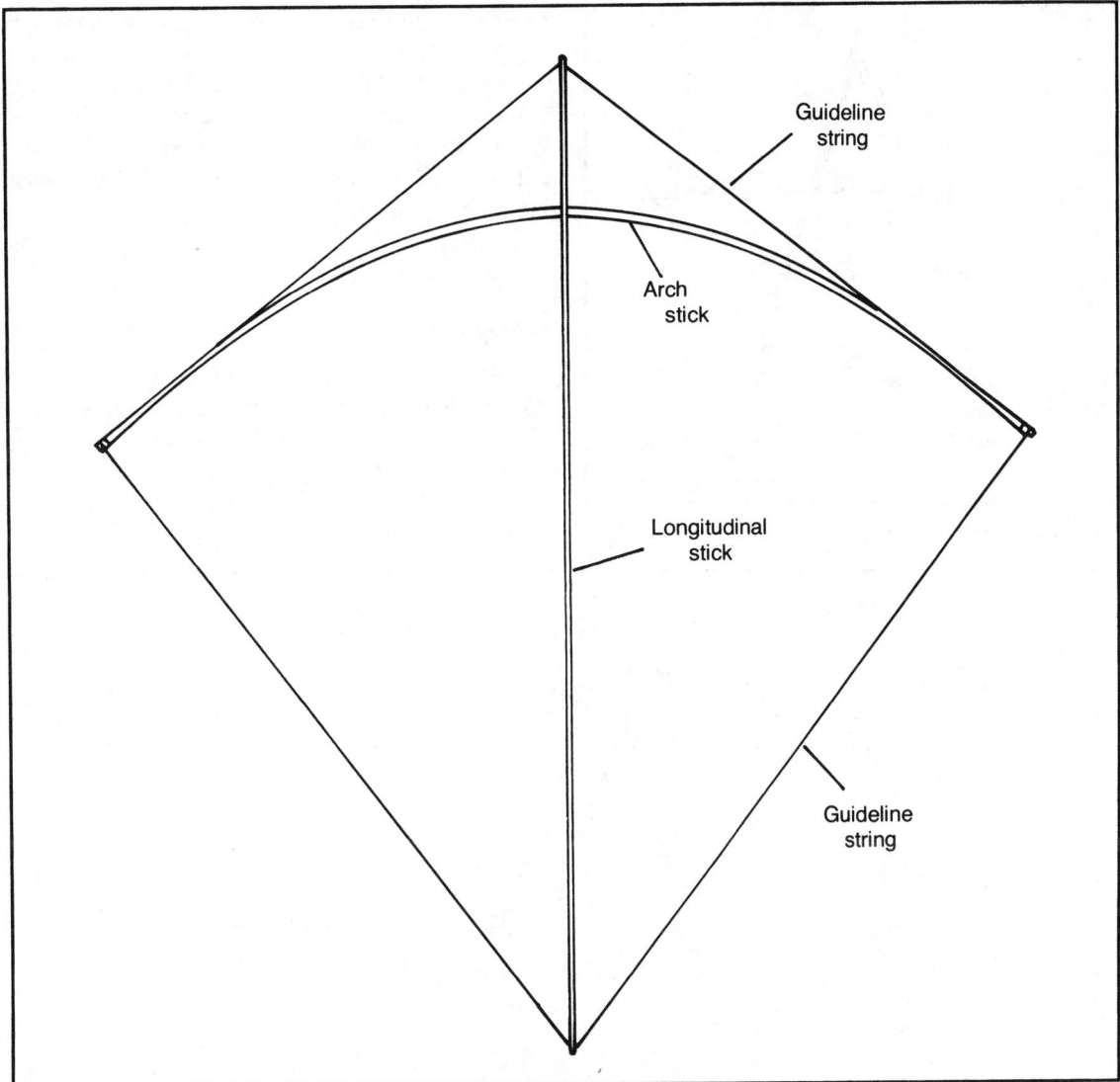

Fig. 6-101. Variation in framing arrangement for arch-top kite.

rectangular cross section of ¼ inch by ⅜ inch or a round wooden dowel of ¼-inch diameter can be used. The sticks can vary somewhat from these dimensions and still give satisfactory results. Increase or decrease the cross sectional size of the sticks depending on the wind conditions in which the kite will be flown. Sticks of fiberglass, bamboo, and aluminum are other possibilities, as detailed in Chapter 5.

The instructions below assume that you will be using wooden sticks of either rectangular or round cross sectional shape.

The ends of the sticks, except the two ends that meet at the point at the top of the star, are notched by making a saw cut ⅜ inch deep in each end of each stick. Make the notches on both ends of each stick in the same plane.

Measure and mark the points of attachment for the sticks, as shown in Fig. 6-103. Saw or file cross notches in the ends of the two sticks where they

Fig. 6-102. Five-point star kite.

meet in a point at the top of the star, as shown in Fig. 6-104. Then glue the three sticks and lash them together with string to the pattern shown in Fig. 6-103. Two guideline strings are used, as shown in Fig. 6-104. Pass the ends of the string through the notches, and tie them around the sticks. Add lashing strings around the ends of the sticks on each side of the guideline strings where they pass through the notches.

Covering Material

Paper, plastic film, or cloth fabric can be used for covering the kite, as desired. Keep the covering material as light as possible without sacrificing strength. Mark the pattern shown in Fig. 6-105 on the covering material. The kite frame can be placed over the covering material as a pattern.

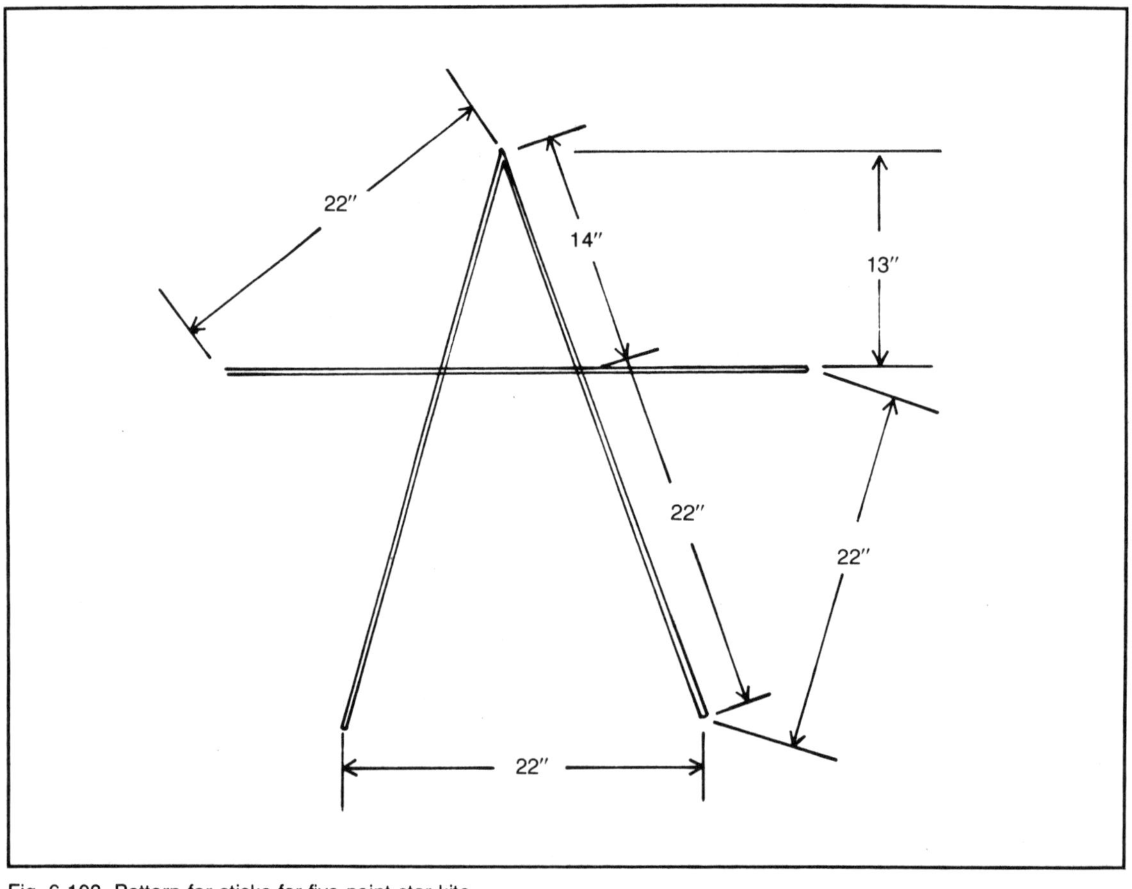

Fig. 6-103. Pattern for sticks for five-point star kite.

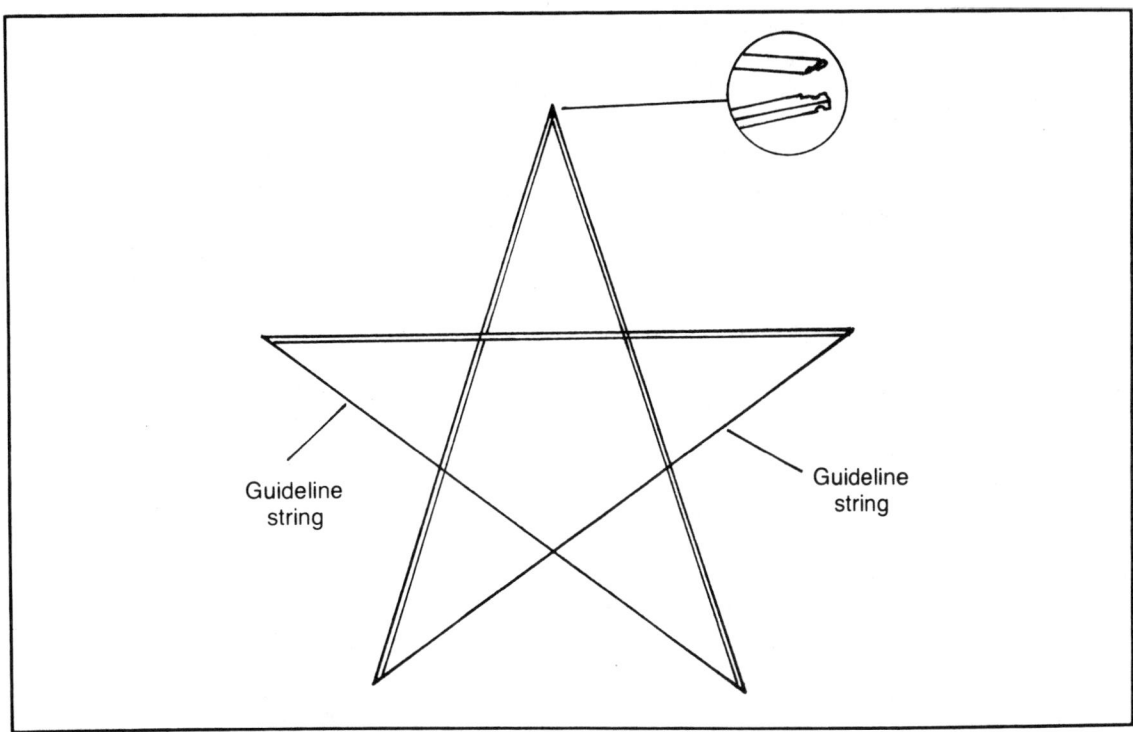

Fig. 6-104. Installation of guideline strings. Insert shows joint for sticks at point of star.

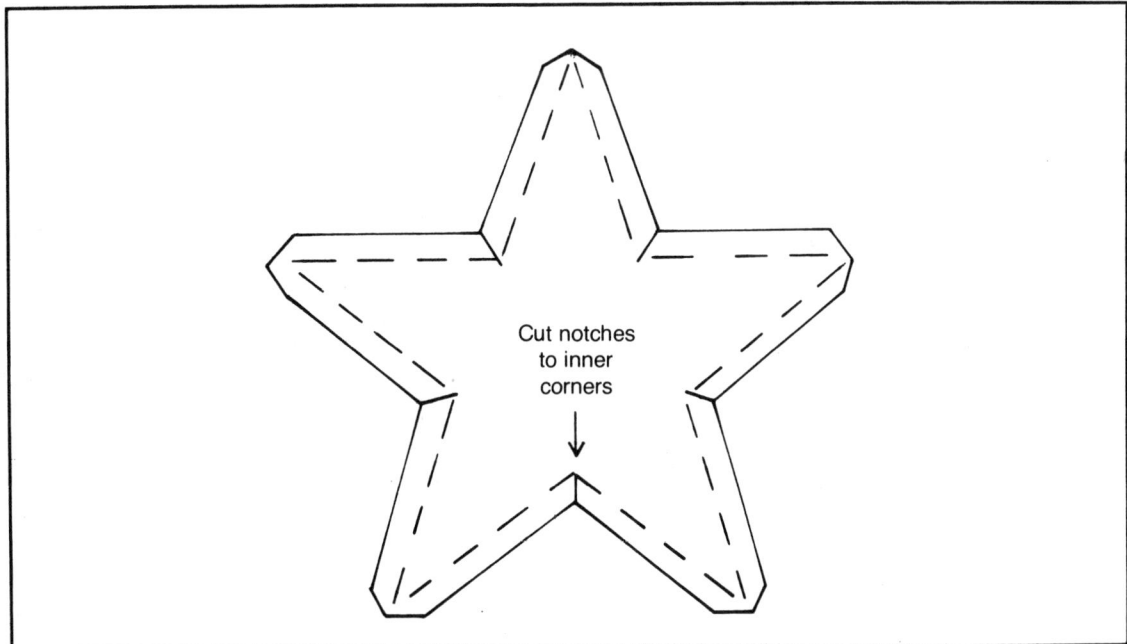

Fig. 6-105. Pattern for covering material.

With scissors, cut the covering material to the pattern. Methods for joining covering material to form the hems and sleeves depends on the particular covering material used (see Chapter 5).

Regardless of the covering material used, install it to the kite frame with the guideline strings and frame sticks passing through sleeves in the covering material.

Bow String

Although the five-point star kite is usually used as a flat kite, a bow string can be added to the cross stick if desired. To install a bow string, tie the string to one end of the cross stick, passing it through the notch in the end of the stick and on around the stick before tying the string with a square knot. Bow the cross stick until it has a 4-inch bow, as shown in Fig. 6-106. Then tie the other end of the bow string to the other end of the cross stick, passing the string through the notch and on around the stick before tying the end back to the main string with a square knot.

Bridle

A three-string bridle is usually used, as shown in Fig. 6-107. The upper attachment is to the cross joint of the two sticks at the upper point of the star. The two lower strings attach to the aft ends of the two longitudinal sticks. Wrap the strings around the ends of the sticks, passing them through the notches, and tie them with square knots. You can tie the other ends of the strings in a loop or to a small plastic ring. The bridle ring allows you to easily adjust the length of the bridle strings.

Tail

The five-point star kite usually requires a tail to give it adequate stability, even if the kite is bowed. A single tail attached to a string tied to the aft ends of the longitudinal sticks can be used, as shown in Fig. 6-107. An alternate method is to use two tails, which are attached to the aft ends of the longitudinal sticks, as shown in Fig. 6-108.

See Chapter 5 for information on making tails. The length and weight of the tail required will depend on the wind conditions and other factors. Try the kite first without a tail. If the kite loops or spins uncontrollably, add more tail, using the minimum amount required to give the kite good stability.

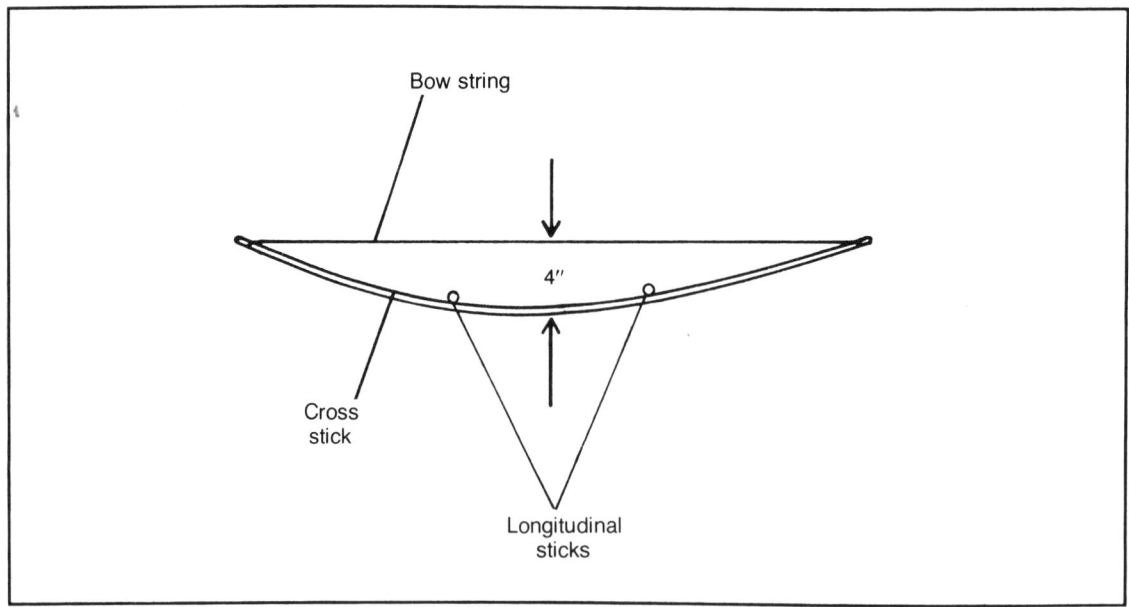

Fig. 6-106. Bow string for five-point star kite.

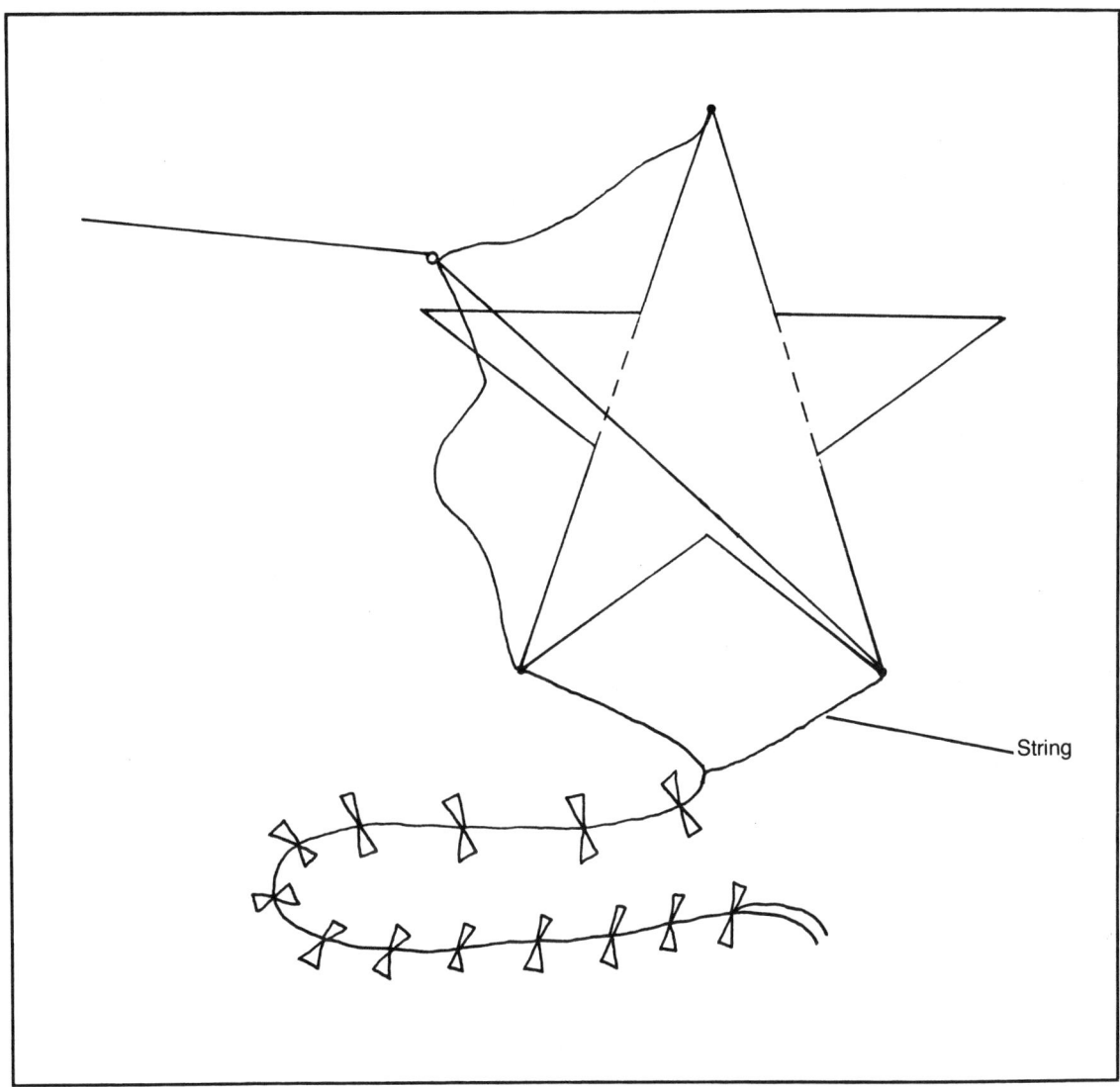

Fig. 6-107. Bridle and single tail attachments.

Variations

The five-point star kite can be constructed in a range of sizes, using sticks from 1 foot or less in length to 6 feet or more in length, by keeping the proportions the same. As a rule, you will need to reduce the weight of the smaller sizes by using proportionally smaller sticks and lighter weight covering material. You will need to use larger sticks and heavier covering material for the larger sizes.

SIX-POINT STAR KITE

The six-point star kite is shown in Fig. 6-109. This kite is usually used as a flat kite. A tail is required to give this kite adequate stability.

Frame

One 36-inch-long stick and two 32-inch-long sticks are used for the frame, as shown in Fig. 6-110. Wooden sticks with a rectangular cross sec-

153

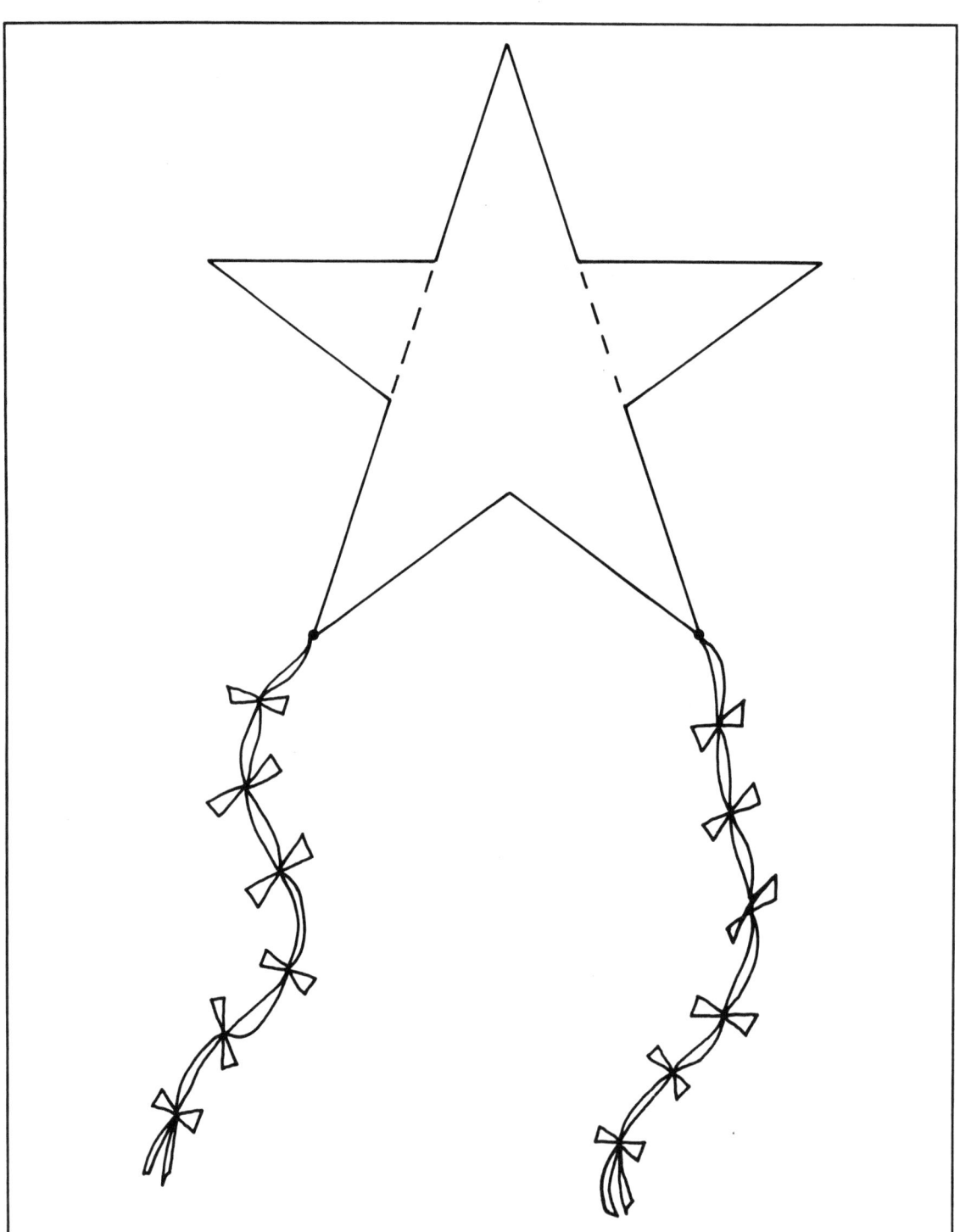

Fig. 6-108. Use of two tails.

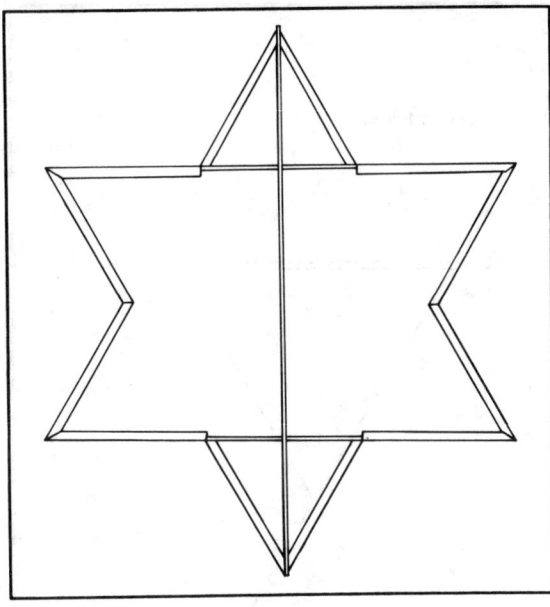

Fig. 6-109. Six-point star kite.

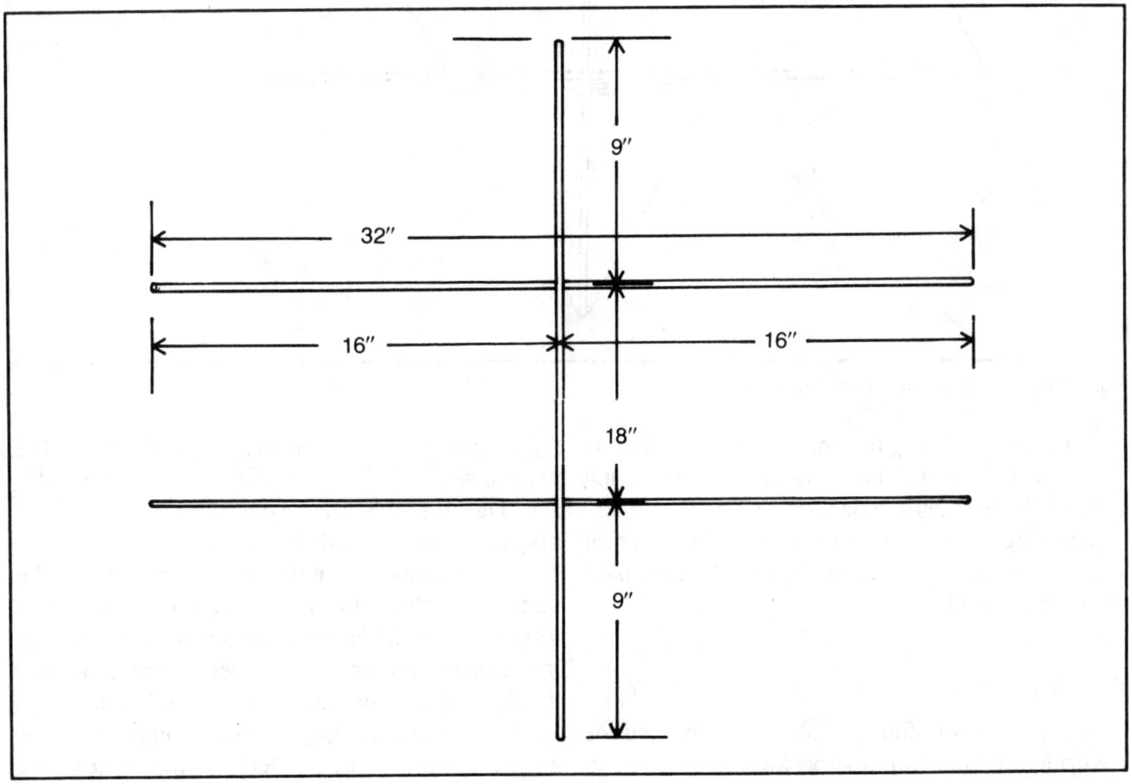

tion of ¼ inch by ⅜ inch or a round wooden dowel of ¼-inch diameter can be used. The sticks can vary somewhat from these dimensions and still give satisfactory results. If the kite is to be used only in light airs, you may want to reduce the cross sectional size of the sticks. If the kite is to be flown in extremely strong winds, you may want to use sticks with larger cross sectional dimensions. Sticks of fiberglass, bamboo, and aluminum are other possibilities, as detailed in Chapter 5.

We'll assume that you will be using wooden sticks of either rectangular or round cross sectional shape.

The ends of the sticks are notched by making a saw cut to a depth of ⅜ inch in each end of each stick. Make the notches on both sides of each stick in the same plane.

Measure and mark the points of attachment for the sticks, as shown in Fig. 6-110. Then glue the sticks, and lash them together with string to the

Fig. 6-110. Pattern for sticks for six-point star kite.

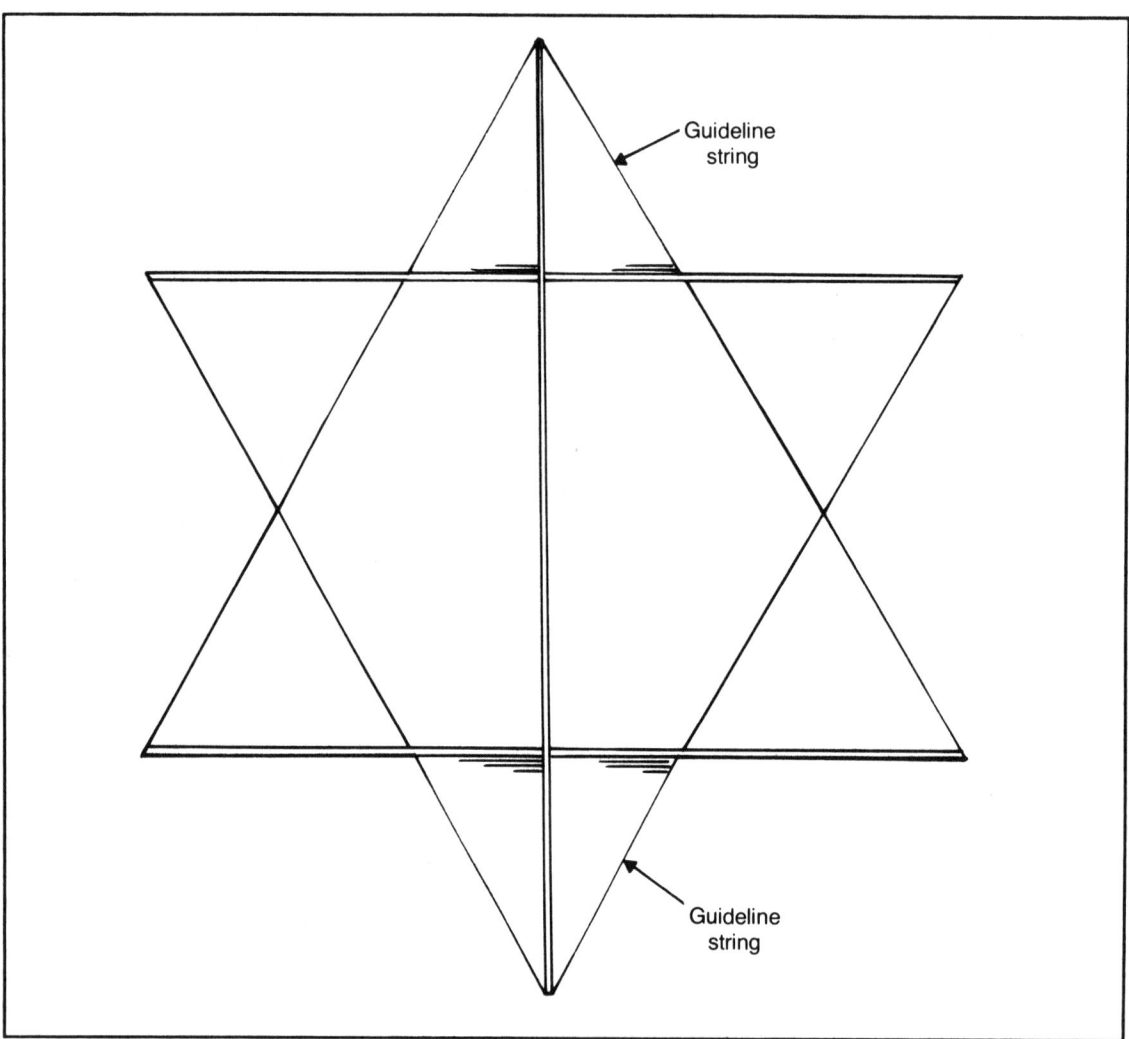

Fig. 6-111. Two guideline strings are used.

pattern shown. Two guideline strings are used, as shown in Fig. 6-111. Pass the ends of the string through the notches and tie them around the sticks. Add lashing strings around the ends of the sticks on each side of the guideline strings where they pass through the notches.

Covering Material

Paper, plastic film, or fabric can be used for covering the kite. For best performance, the covering material should be of the lightest weight that is compatible with adequate strength. Mark the pattern shown in Fig. 6-112 on the covering material. The kite frame can be placed over the covering material to use as a pattern.

Use scissors to cut the covering material to the pattern. Methods for joining covering material to form the hems and sleeves depends on the particular covering material used (see Chapter 5). Regardless of the covering material used, install it to the kite frame with the guideline strings and frame sticks passing through sleeves in the covering material.

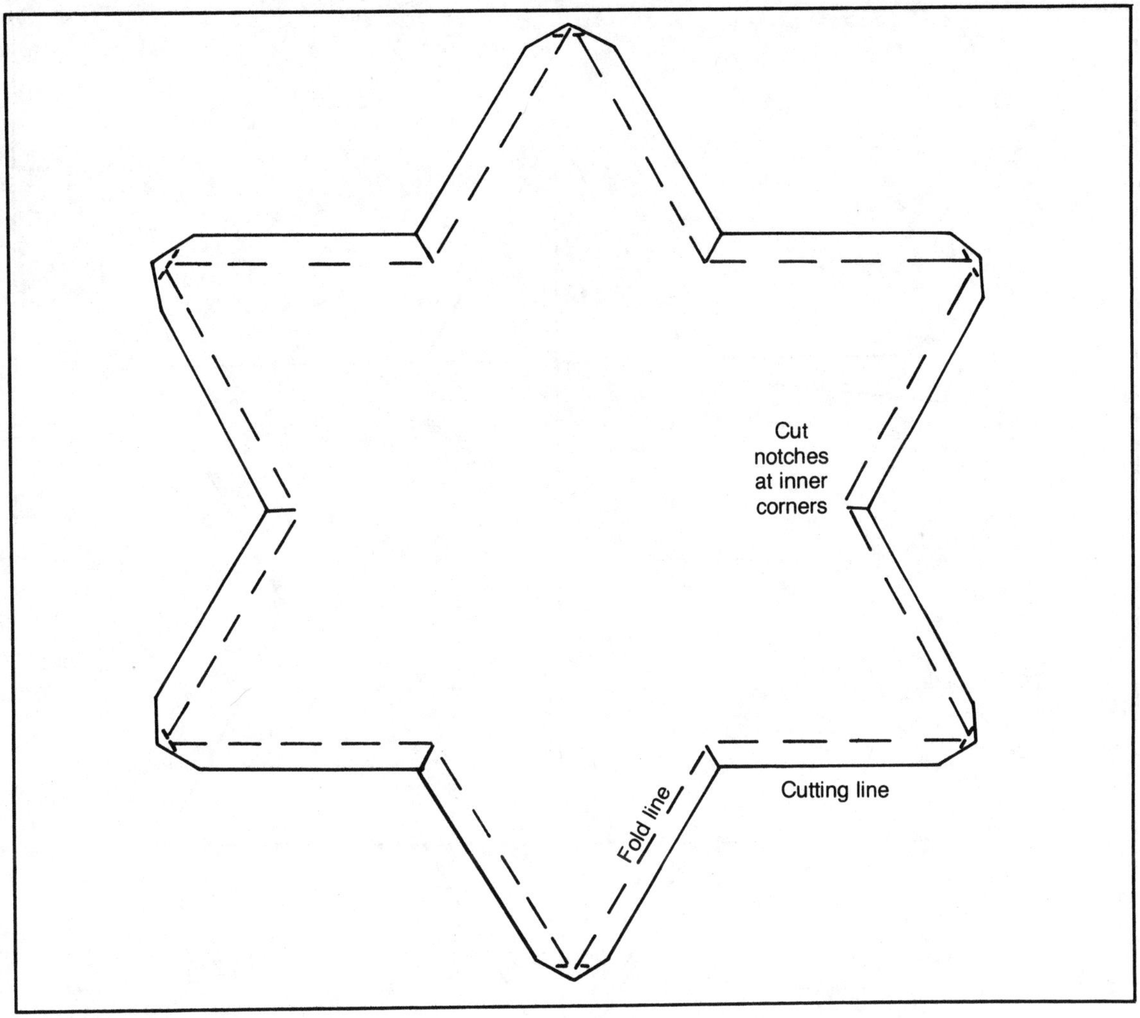

Fig. 6-112. Pattern for covering material.

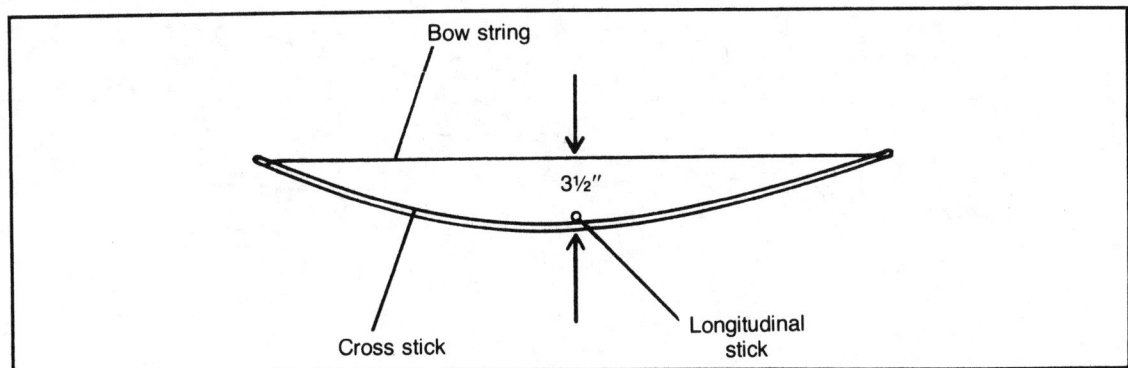

Fig. 6-113. Bow string.

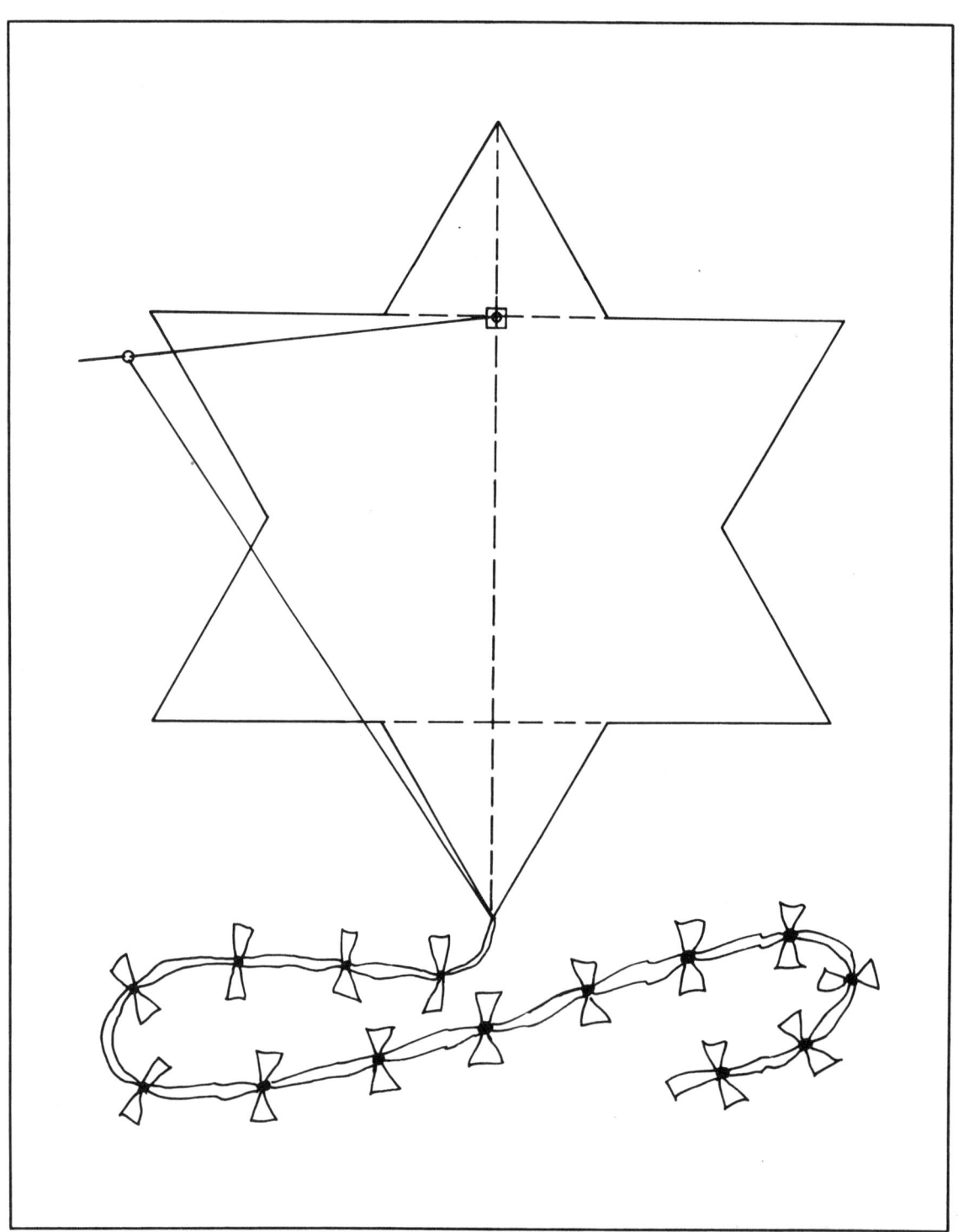

Fig. 6-114. Tail and bridle attachment.

Bow String

While the six-point star kite is usually used as a flat kite, bow strings can be added to the cross sticks if desired. To install a bow string, tie the string to one end of the cross stick, passing it through the notch in the end of the stick and on around the stick before tying the string with a square knot. Bow the cross stick until it has a 3½-inch bow, as shown in Fig. 6-113. Then tie the other end of the bow string to the other end of the cross stick, passing the string through the notch and on around the stick before tying the end back to the main string with a square knot.

Bridle

A two-string bridle can be used, as shown in Fig. 6-114. The upper attachment is to the cross joint of the upper cross stick and longitudinal stick. The string passes through a small reinforced hole in the covering material. The lower attachment is to the aft end of the longitudinal stick. The string is wrapped around the end of the stick, passed through the notch, and tied with a square knot. The other ends of the strings can be tied in a loop or to a small plastic ring. The bridle ring allows easy adjustment of the length of the bridle strings.

Tail

The six-point star kite usually needs a tail for adequate stability, even if the kite is bowed. A single tail can be attached to the aft end of the longitudinal stick, as shown in Fig. 6-114.

Try the kite first without a tail. If the kite loops or spins uncontrollably, add more tail. Use the minimum amount of tail required to give the kite good stability. See Chapter 5 for details.

Variations

The six-point star kite can be constructed in a range of sizes, using a longitudinal stick from 1 foot or less in length to 6 feet or more in length, keeping the proportions the same. You will need to reduce the weight of the smaller sizes by using proportionally smaller sticks and lighter weight covering material. Use larger sticks and heavier covering material for the larger sizes.

EIGHT-POINT STAR KITE

The eight-point star kite is shown in Fig. 6-115. This kite is usually used as a flat kite. A tail is required to give this kite adequate stability.

Frame

Four 36-inch-long sticks are used for making the frame, as shown in Fig. 6-116. Wooden sticks with rectangular cross sections of 3/16 inch by 5/16 inch or round wooden dowels of 3/16-inch diameter can be used. The sticks can vary somewhat from these dimensions and still give satisfactory results. You may want to reduce the cross sectional size of the sticks for flying in light winds. If the kite will be flown in extremely strong winds, you may want to use sticks with larger cross sectional dimensions. Sticks of fiberglass, bamboo, and aluminum are other alternatives. Here, we'll assume you will use wooden sticks of either rectangular or round cross sectional shape.

The ends of the sticks are notched by making a saw cut to a depth of ⅜ inch in each end of each stick. Make the notches on both ends of each stick in the same plane.

Measure and mark the centerpoints of each stick. Then glue the sticks and lash them together with string. Use two guideline strings as shown in Fig. 6-117. Each guideline string passes through the four notches to form a square. Stretch the string tight and tie the ends together. Add lashing strings around the ends of the sticks on each side of the guideline strings where they pass through the notches.

Covering Material

Use paper, plastic film, or fabric as a cover. Covering material should be as light as possible without affecting strength. Mark the pattern shown in Fig. 6-118 on the covering material, using the kite frame as a pattern.

Use scissors to cut the covering material to the pattern. See Chapter 5 for appropriate methods of joining the covering material to form hems and sleeves. Regardless of the covering material used, attach it to the kite frame with the guideline strings passing through sleeves in the covering material.

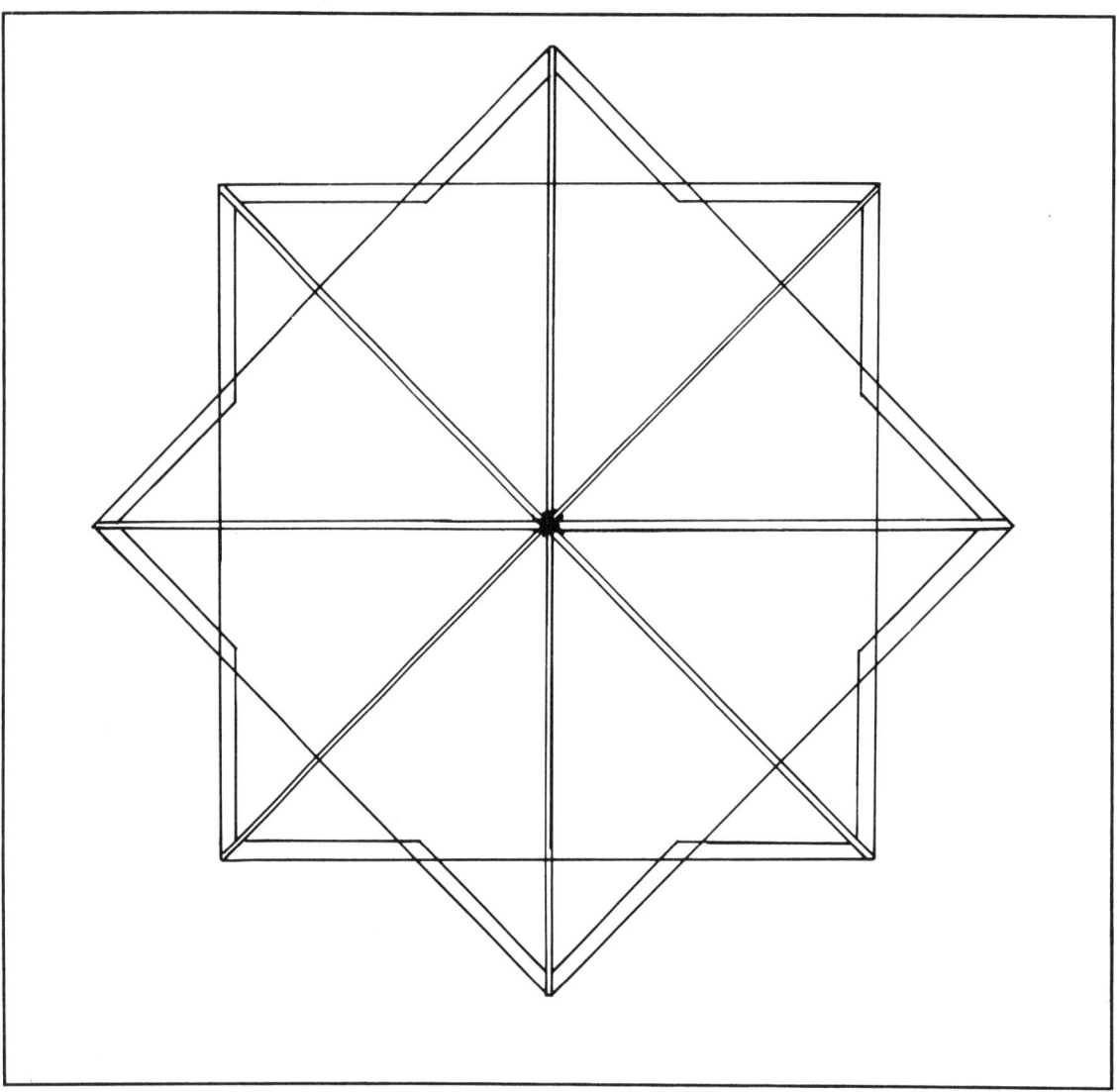

Fig. 6-115. Eight-point star kite.

Bridle

A four-string bridle can be used, as shown in Fig. 6-119. The upper three attachments are to the upper ends of the sticks that form the upper star points. The lower attachment is to the aft end of the longitudinal center stick. Wrap the strings around the ends of the sticks, passing them through the notches, and tie them with square knots. You can tie the other ends of the strings in a loop or to a small plastic ring. The bridle ring allows you to easily adjust the length of the bridle strings.

Tail

The eight-point star kite requires a tail for adequate flying stability. A single tail can be attached to the aft end of the longitudinal stick, as shown in Fig. 6-119. Another possibility is to use three tails (Fig. 6-120).

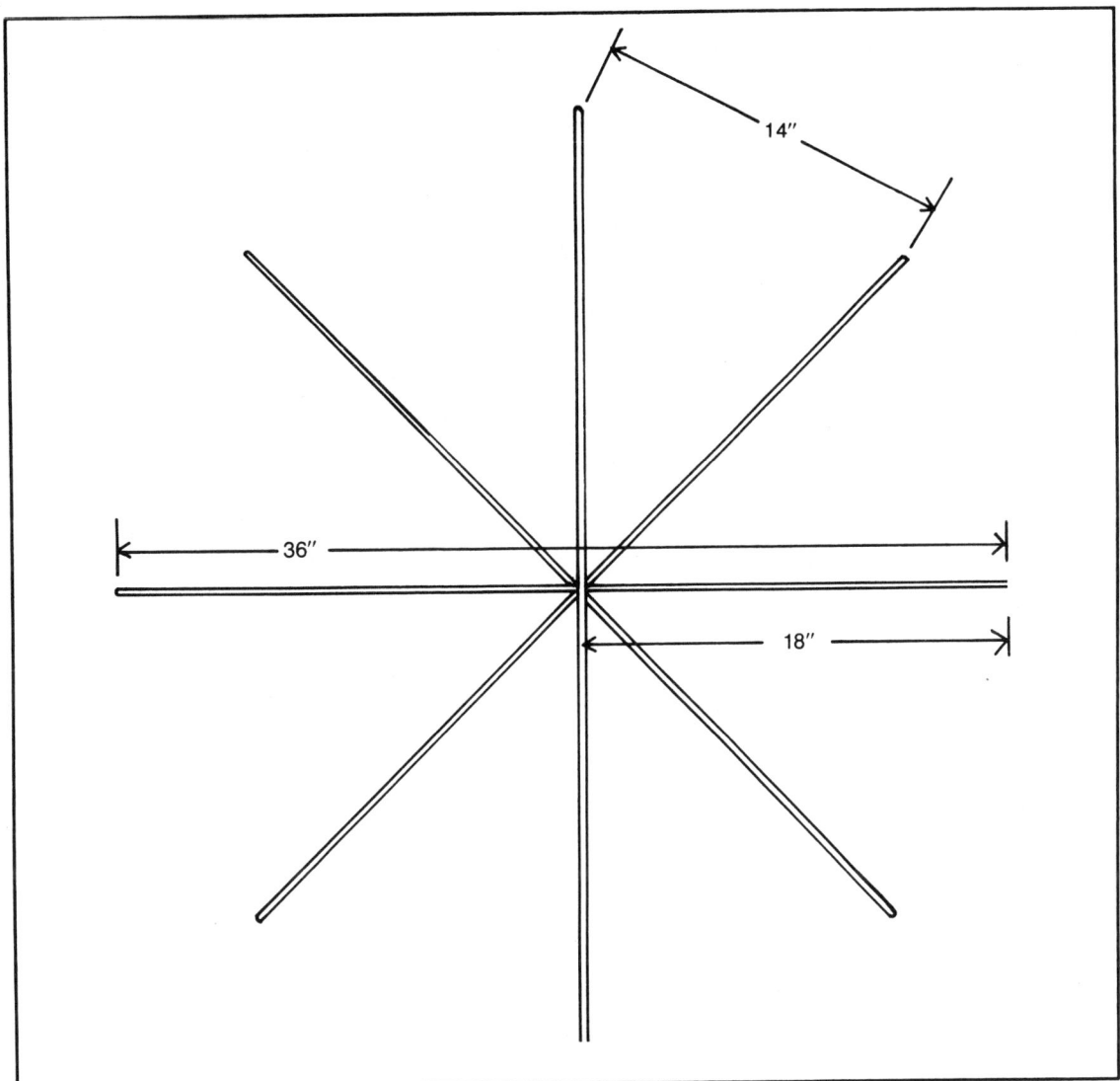

Fig. 6-116. Pattern for sticks for eight-point star kite.

Construction of tails is detailed in Chapter 5. Length and weight of the tail will depend on wind conditions and other factors. Try the kite first without a tail; if it loops or spins uncontrollably, add more tail. Use the minimum amount required for adequate stability.

Variations

The eight-point star kite can be constructed in a range of sizes, using sticks from 1 foot or less in length to 6 feet or more in length, keeping the proportions the same. Reduce the weight of the smaller sizes by using proportionally smaller sticks and lighter covering materials. You will need to use larger sticks and heavier covering material for the larger sizes.

OCTAGONAL KITE

The octagonal kite is shown in Fig. 6-121. This

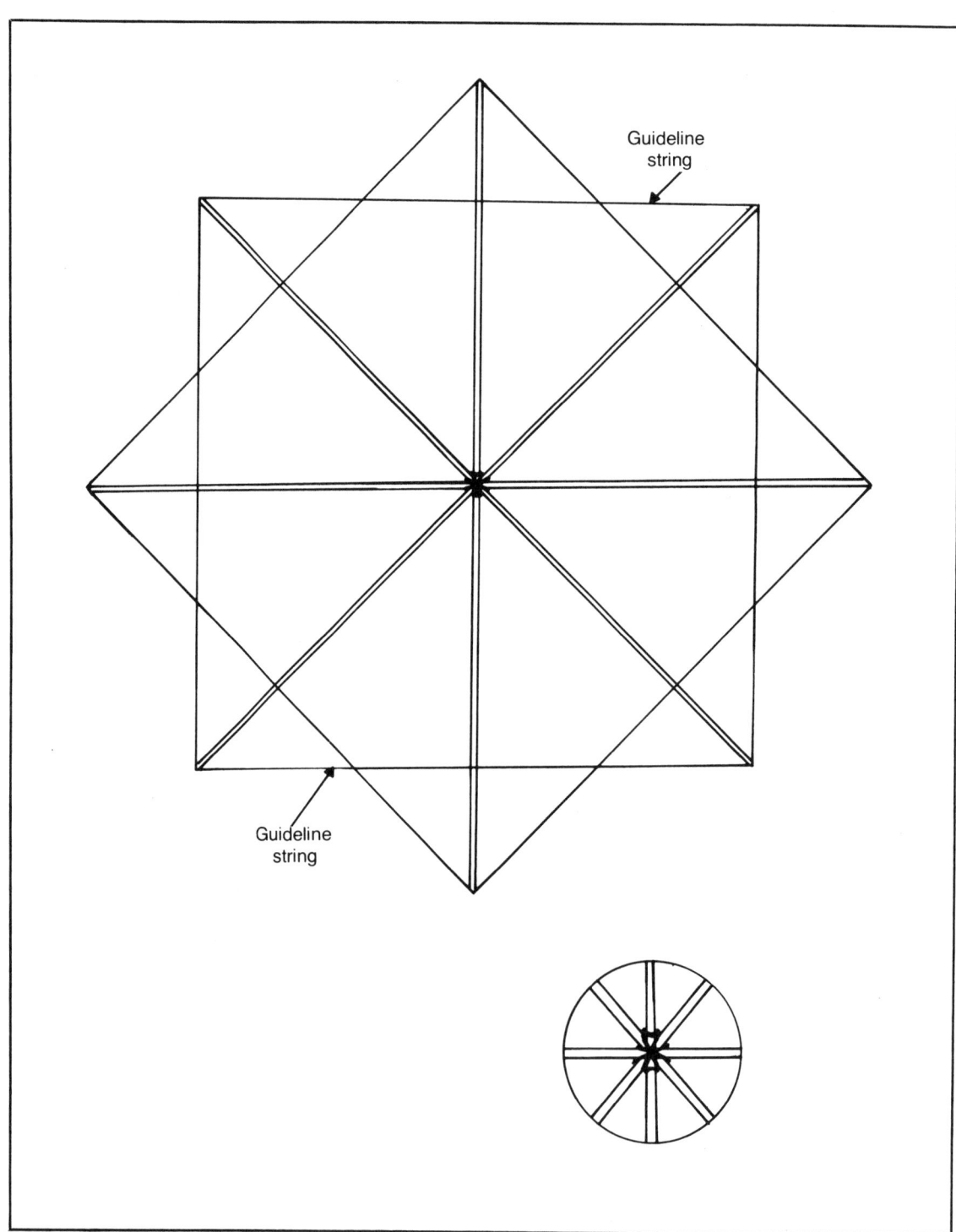

Fig. 6-117. Two guideline strings are used.

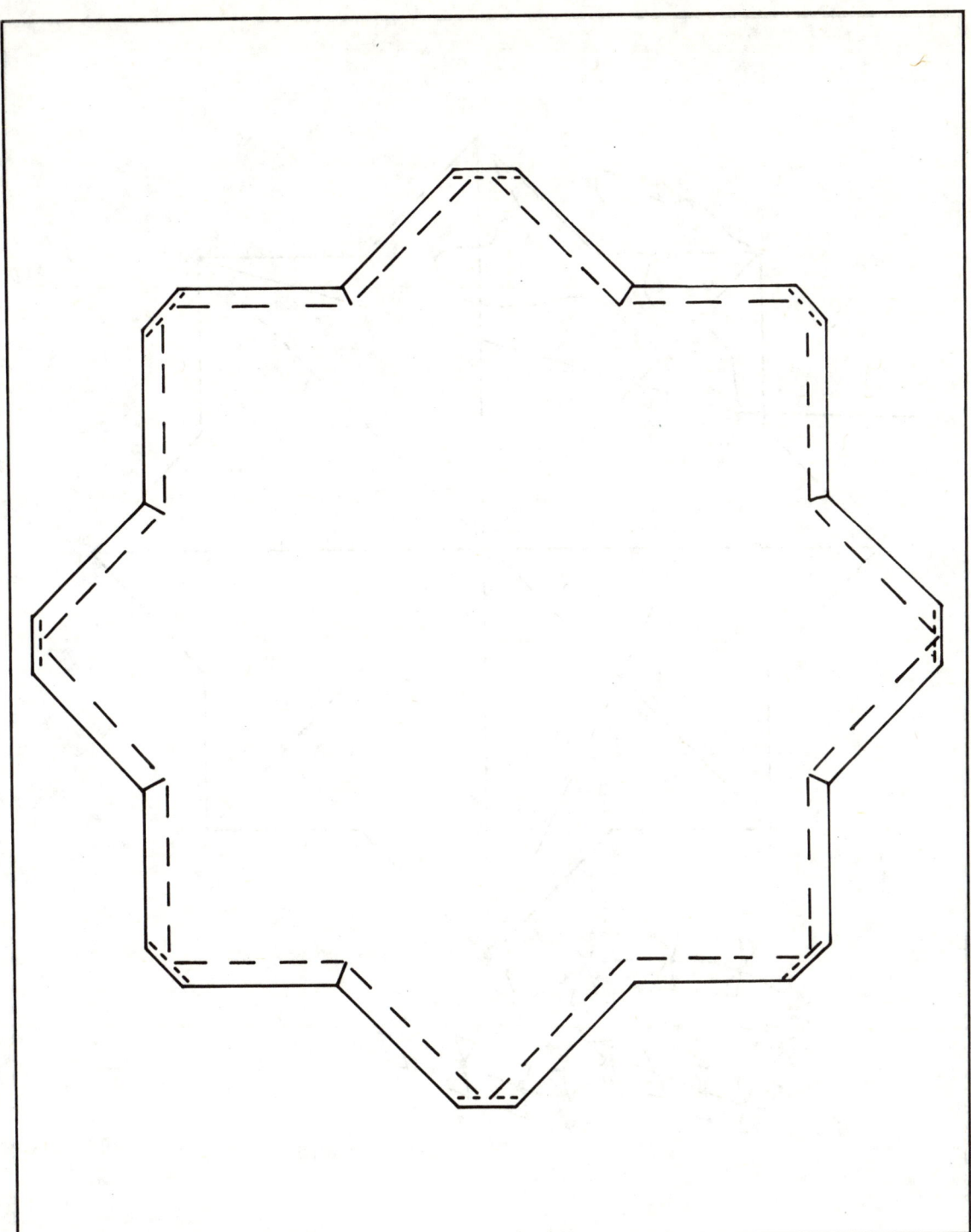

Fig. 6-118. Pattern for covering material.

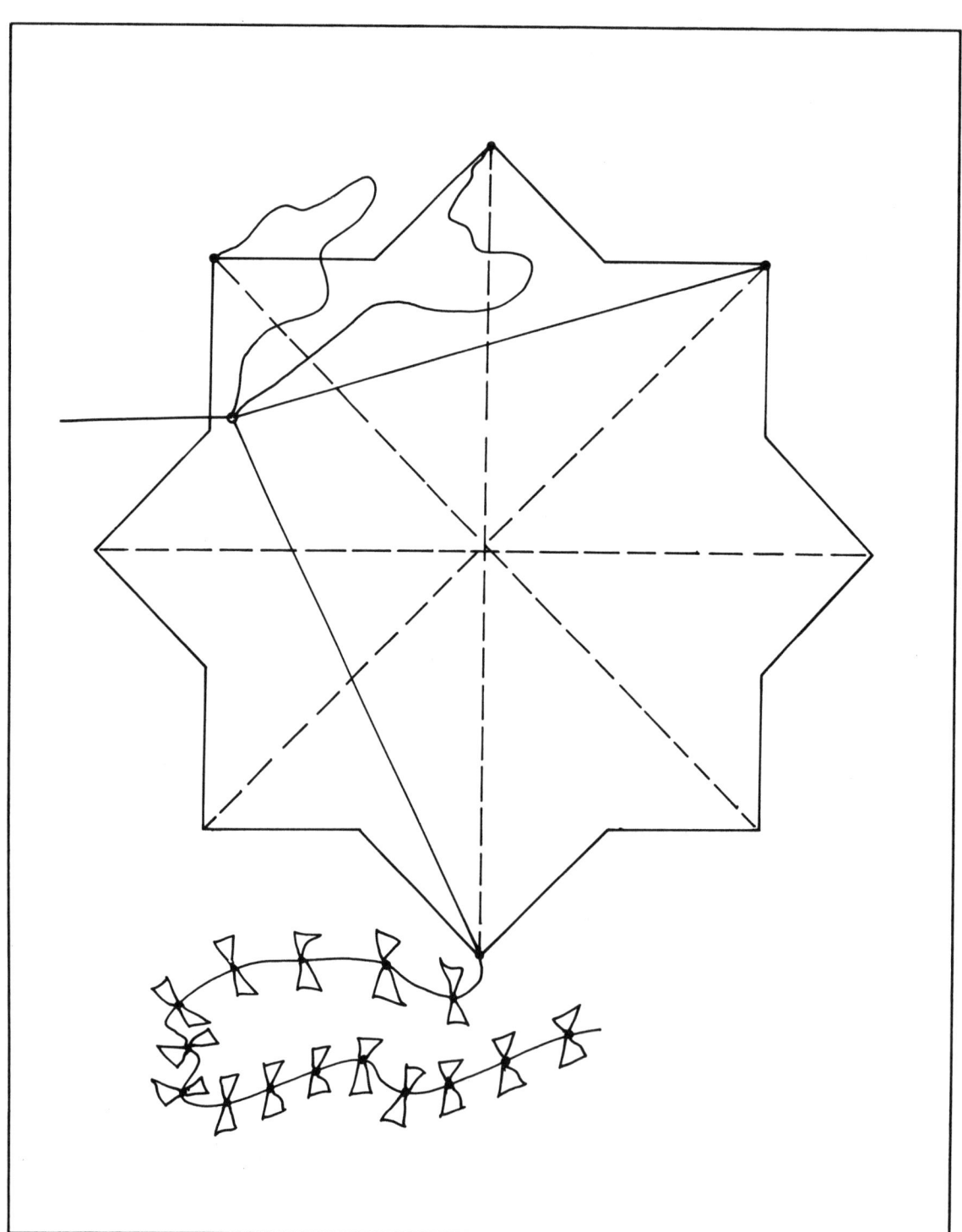

Fig. 6-119. Bridle and single tail attachments.

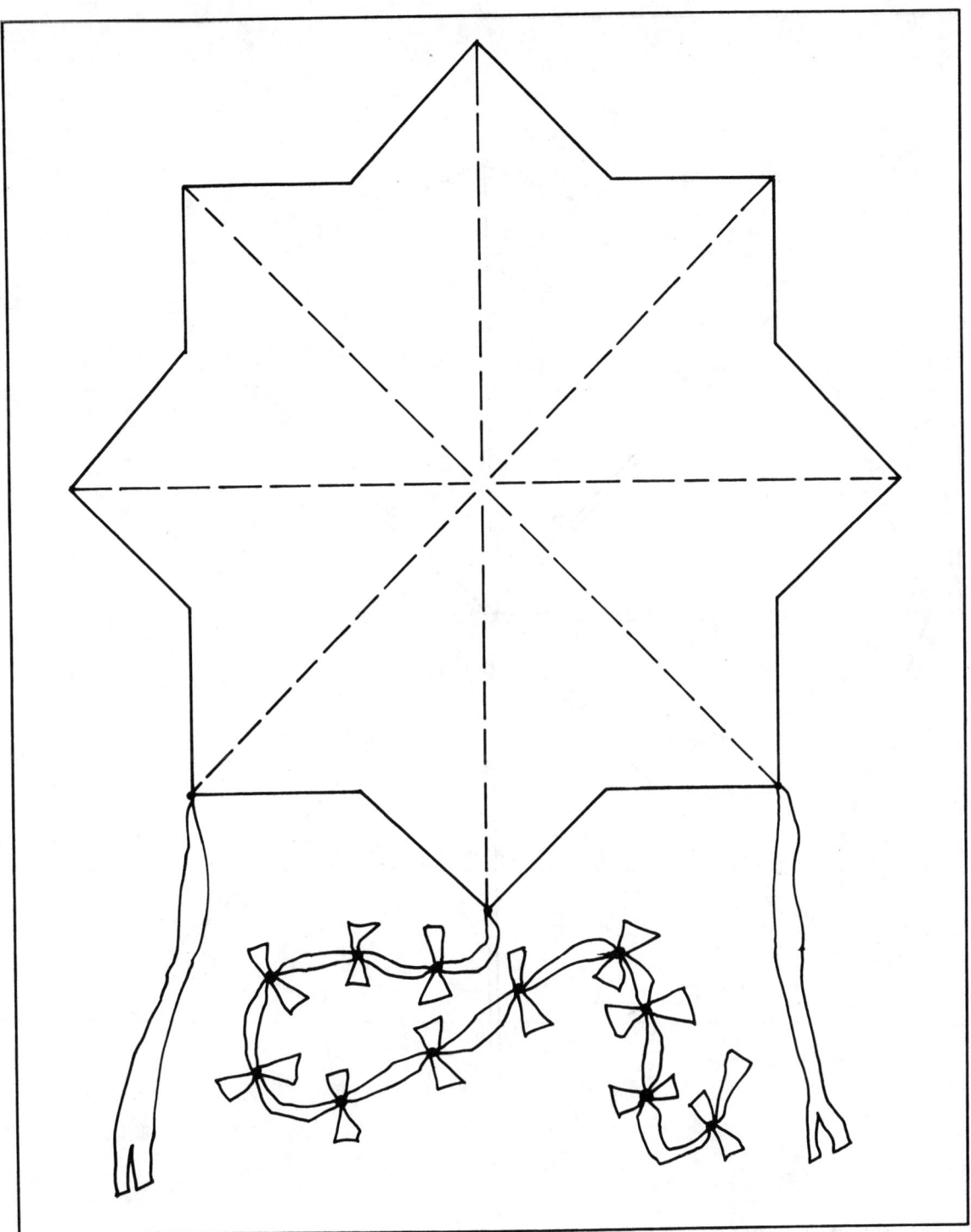

Fig. 6-120. Use of three tails.

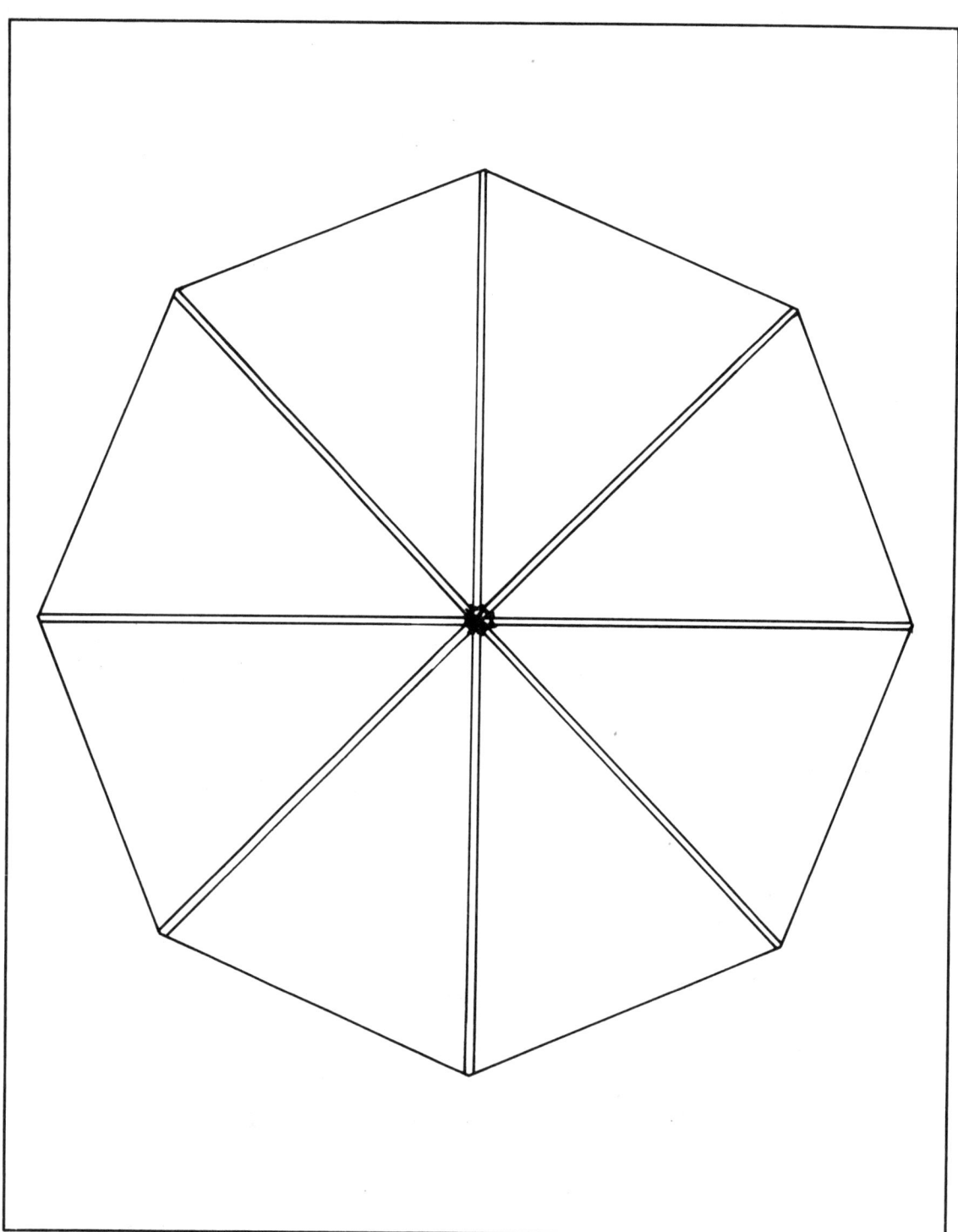

Fig. 6-121. Octagonal kite.

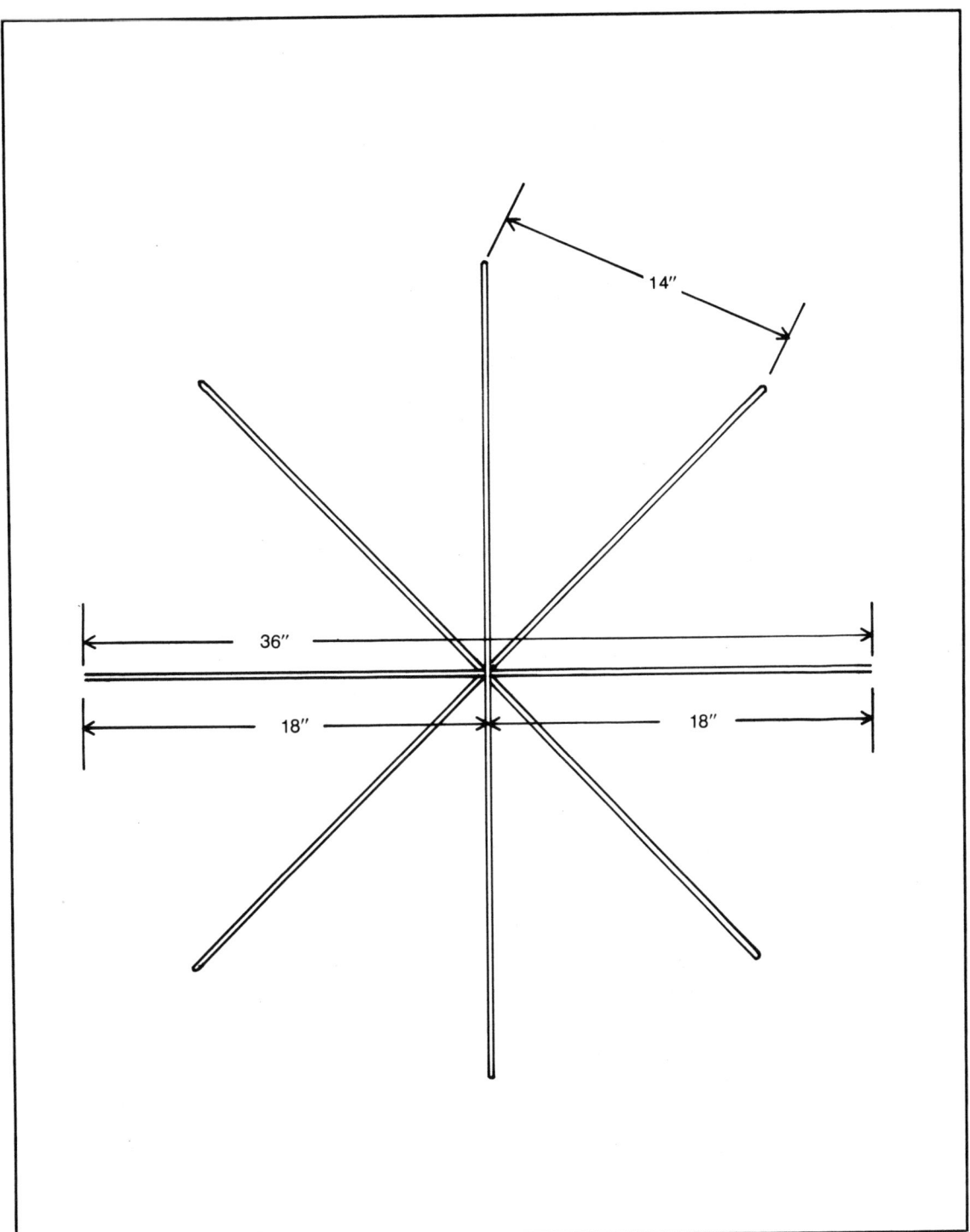

Fig. 6-122. Pattern for sticks for octagonal kite.

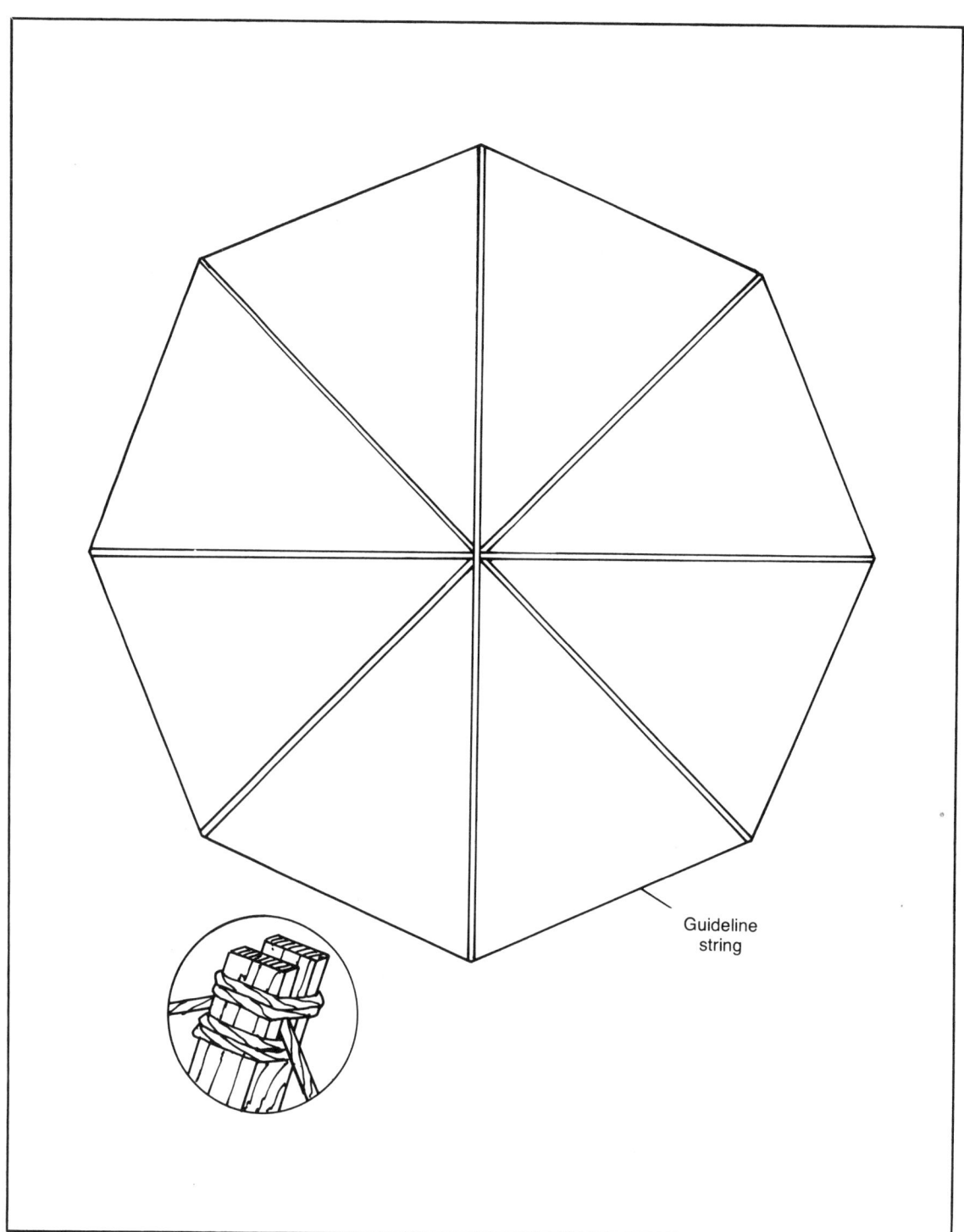

Fig. 6-123. The guideline string is installed in notches around frame sticks.

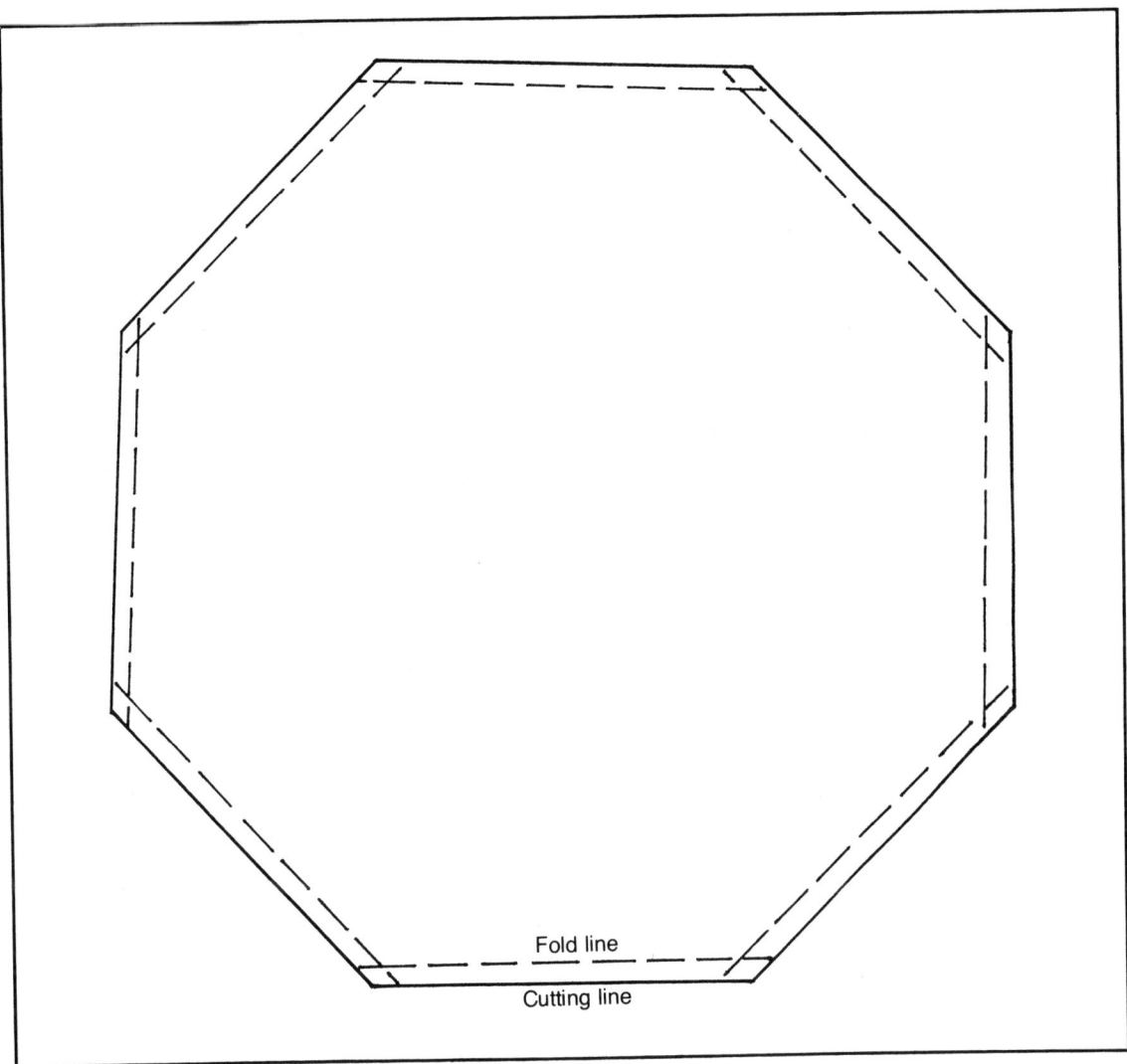

Fig. 6-124. Pattern for covering material.

kite is usually used as a flat kite. A tail is required to give this kite adequate stability.

Frame

Four 36-inch-long sticks are used for making the frame, as shown in Fig. 6-122. Wooden sticks with rectangular cross sections of 3/16 inch by 5/16 inch or round wooden dowels of 3/16-inch diameter can be used. The sticks can vary somewhat from these dimensions and still give satisfactory results. If the kite is to be used only in light airs, you may want to reduce the cross sectional size of the sticks. Conversely, if the kite is to be flown in extremely strong winds, you may want to use sticks with larger cross sectional dimensions. Fiberglass, bamboo, and aluminum sticks can also be used. We'll assume that you will be using wooden sticks of either rectangular or round cross sectional shape.

Notch ends of the sticks by making a saw cut to a depth of ⅜ inch in each end of each stick. Make the notches on both ends of each stick in the same plane.

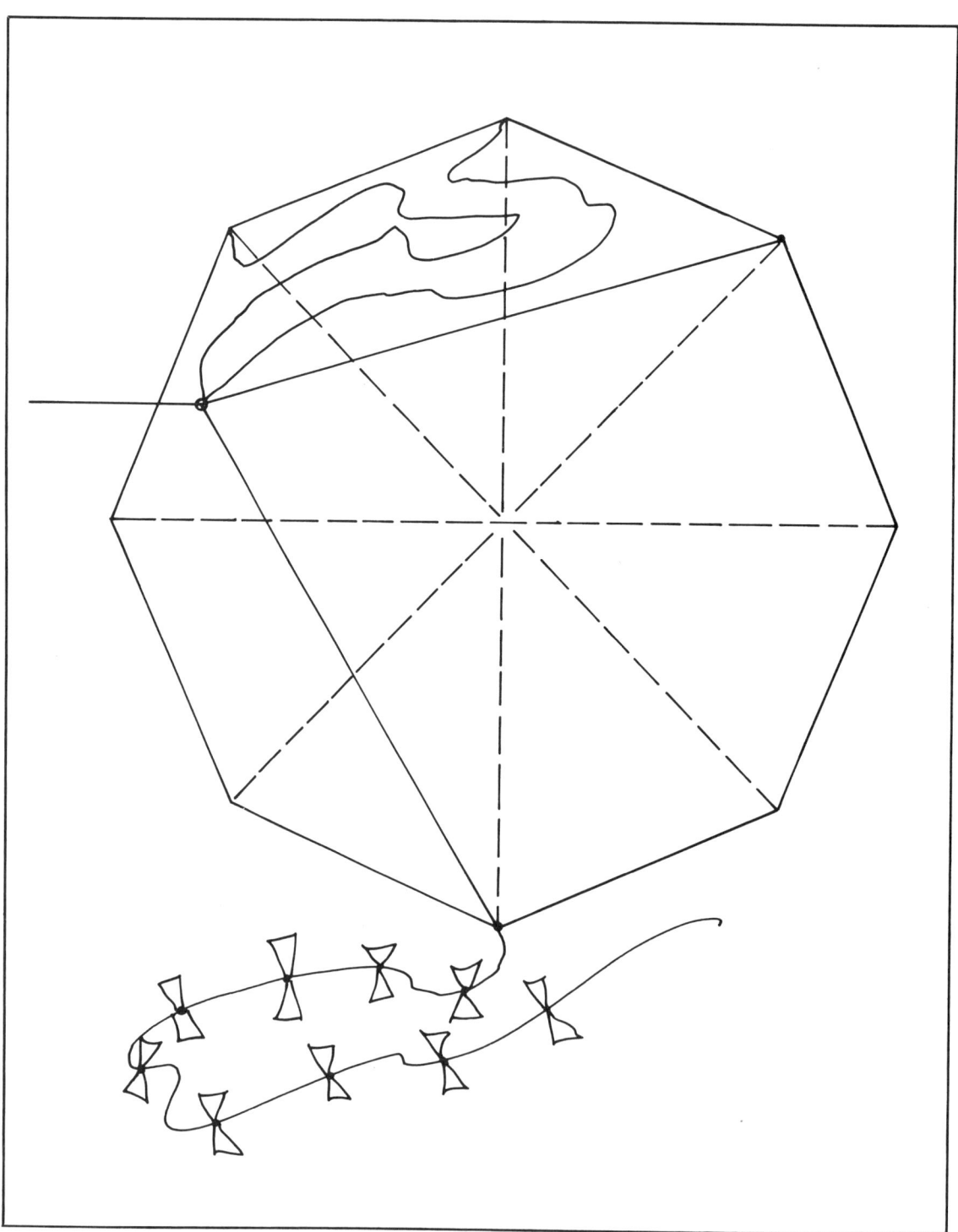

Fig. 6-125. Bridle and single tail attachments.

Measure and mark the centerpoints of each stick. The sticks are then glued and lashed together with string.

A guideline string is installed in the notches around the sticks, as shown in Fig. 6-123. Stretch the string tight and tie the ends together. Add lashing strings around the ends of the sticks on each side of the guideline string where it passes through the notches.

Covering Material

Paper, plastic film, or cloth fabric can be used to cover the kite, as desired. For best performance, keep the covering material as light as possible. Mark the pattern shown in Fig. 6-124 on the covering material. The kite frame can be placed over the covering material to use as a pattern.

Use scissors to cut the covering material to the pattern. Methods for joining covering material to form the hems and sleeves depends on the particular covering material used (see Chapter 5).

Regardless of the covering material used, install it to the kite frame with the guideline strings passing through sleeves in the covering material.

Bridle

A four-string bridle can be used, as shown in Fig. 6-125. The upper three attachments are to the upper ends of the sticks that form the upper three corners of the octagonal form. The lower attachment is to the aft end of the longitudinal center stick. The strings are wrapped around the ends of the sticks, passed through the notches, and tied with a square knot. The other ends of the strings can be tied in a loop or to a small plastic ring. The bridle ring allows easy adjustment of the length of the bridle strings.

Tail

The octagonal kite requires a tail to give adequate stability. A single tail can be attached to the aft end of the longitudinal stick, as shown in Fig. 6-125. An alternative uses three tails, as shown in Fig. 6-126.

Construction of tails is detailed in Chapter 5. The length and weight of the tail required will depend on the wind conditions and other factors. Try the kite with a short tail first. If the kite loops or spins uncontrollably, add more tail. Use the minimum amount of tail required to give the kite good stability.

Variations

The octagonal kite can be constructed in a range of sizes, using sticks from 1 foot or less in length to 6 feet or more in length by keeping the proportions the same. As a general rule, you will need to reduce the weight of the smaller sizes by using proportionally smaller sticks and lighter weight covering material. You will need to use larger sticks and heavier covering material for the larger sizes.

DOUBLE BASIC KITE

The double basic kite is shown in Fig. 6-127. This kite can be used as a flat or bow kite. A tail is often required to give this kite adequate stability.

Frame

Three sticks are used for making the frame, as shown in Fig. 6-128. A wooden stick with a rectangular cross section of $1/4$ inch by $3/8$ inch, or a $1/4$-inch wooden dowel, that is 36 inches long is used for the longitudinal stick. The upper cross stick is a wooden stick with a rectangular cross section of $3/16$ inch by $5/16$ inch, or a round wooden dowel of $3/16$-inch diameter, that is 32 inches long. The lower cross stick is a wooden stick with a rectangular cross section of $1/8$ inch by $1/4$ inch, or a round wooden dowel of $1/8$-inch diameter, that is 14 inches long. The sticks can vary somewhat from these dimensions and still give satisfactory results. Reduce the cross sectional size of the sticks if the kite will be flown in light airs. You may want to use sticks with larger cross sectional dimensions if the kite will fly in heavy winds. Sticks of fiberglass, bamboo, and aluminum are other possibilities, as detailed in Chapter 5.

The proceeding instructions assume that you

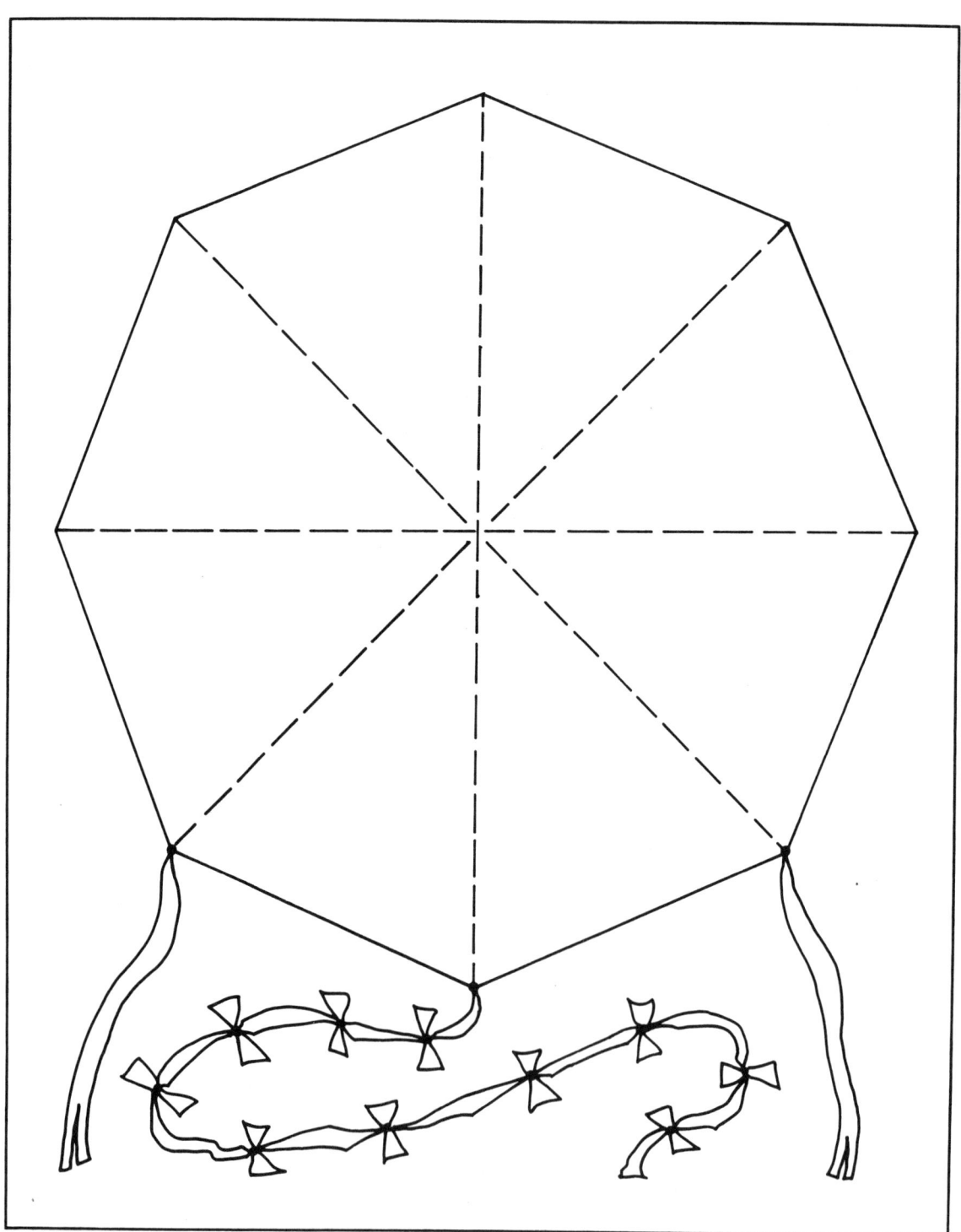

Fig. 6-126. Use of three tails.

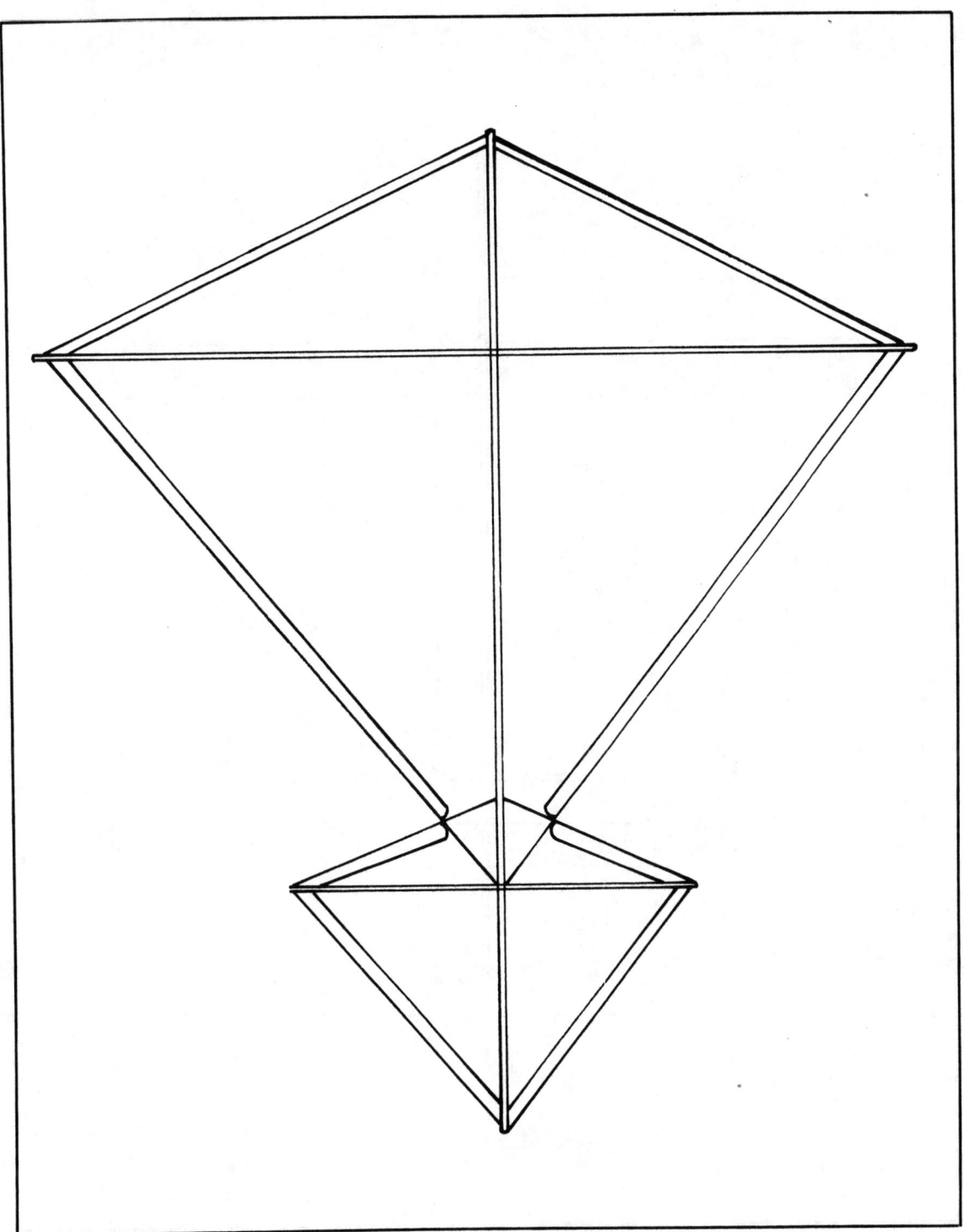

Fig. 6-127. Double basic kite.

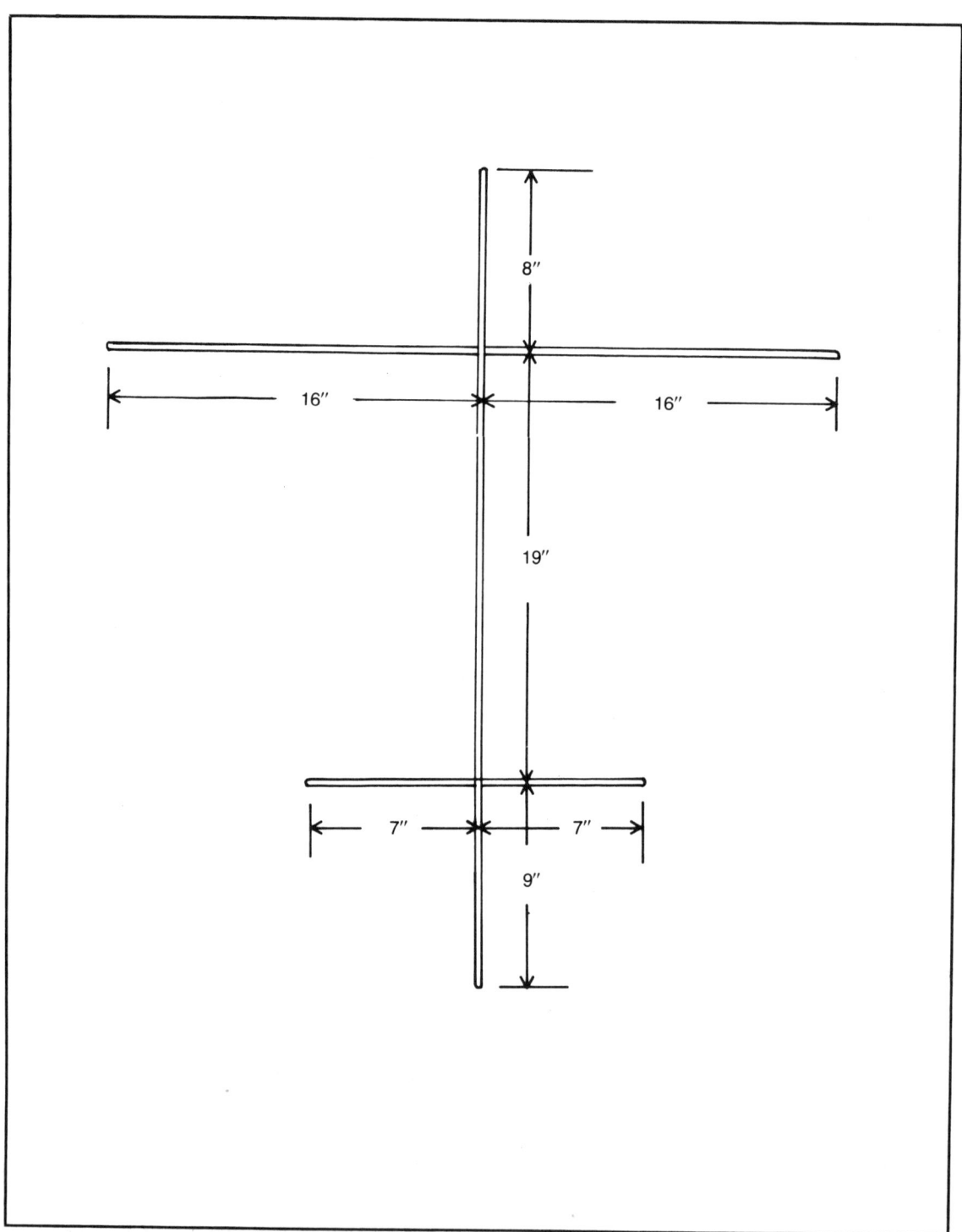

Fig. 6-128. Pattern for sticks for double basic kite.

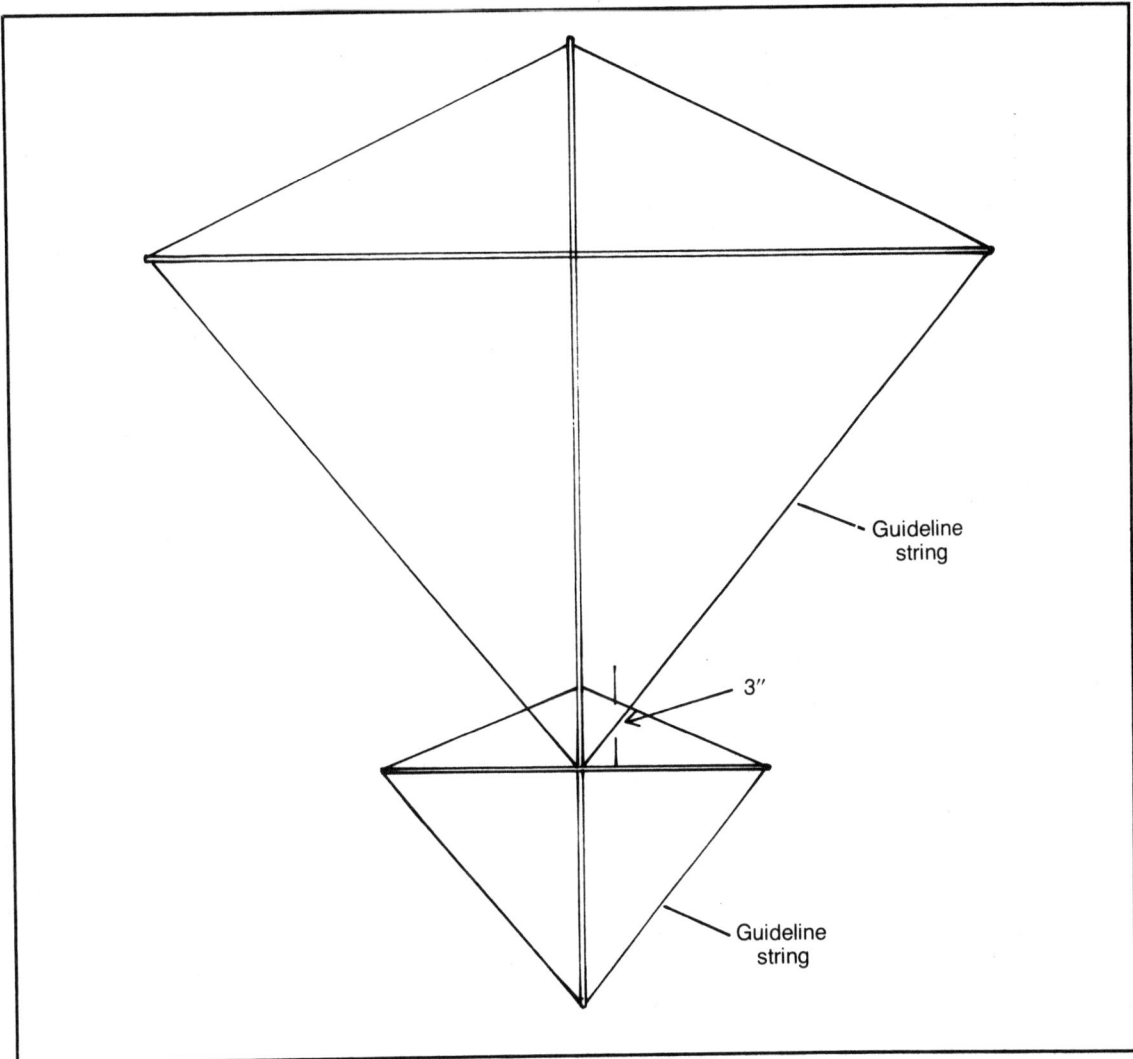

Fig. 6-129. Two guideline strings are used.

will be using wooden sticks of either rectangular or round cross sectional shape.

The ends of the sticks are notched by making a saw cut to a depth of ⅜ inch in each end of each stick. Make the notches on both ends of each stick in the same plane.

Measure and mark the cross points of each stick. The sticks are then glued and lashed together with string to the pattern shown.

Use two guideline strings. Install each guideline string in the notches around the sticks, as shown in Fig. 6-129. Stretch the string tight and tie the ends together around the longitudinal stick, as shown. Add lashing strings around the ends of the sticks on each side of the guideline strings where they pass through the notches.

Covering Material

You can use paper, plastic film, or cloth fabric to cover the kite. For best performance, the covering material should be of the lightest weight that is compatible with adequate strength. Mark the pat-

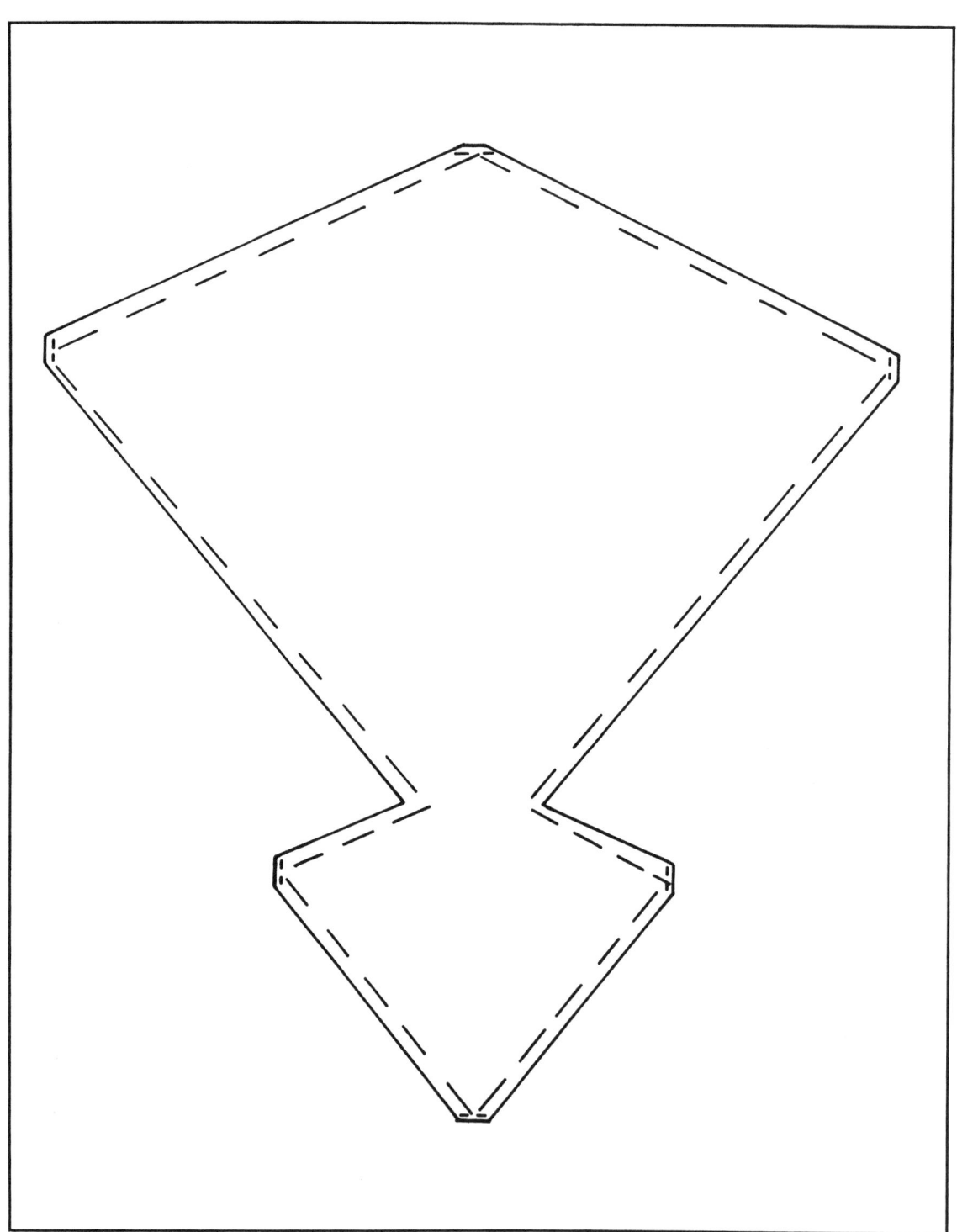

Fig. 6-130. Pattern for covering material.

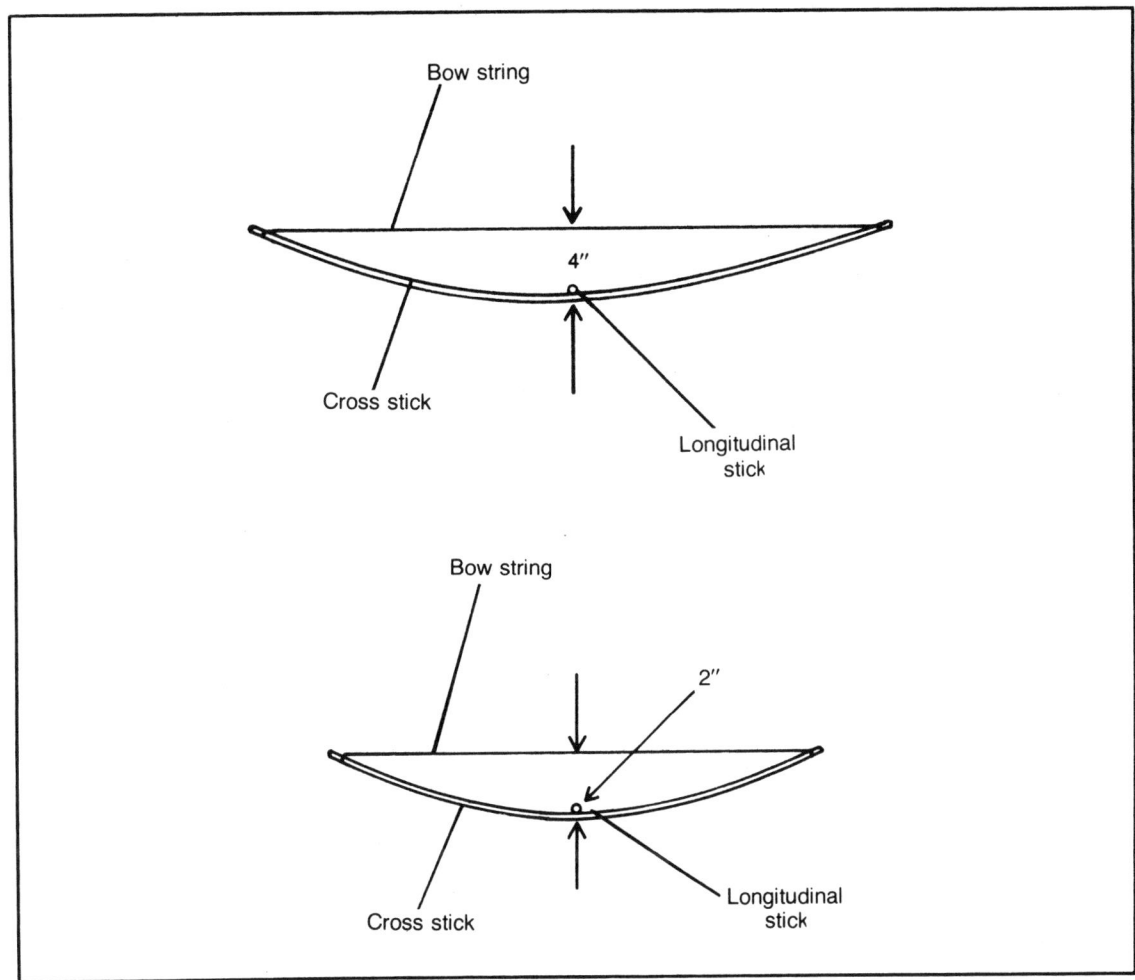

Fig. 6-131. Bow string for upper and lower cross stick.

tern shown in Fig. 6-130 on the covering material. The kite frame can be placed over the covering material to use as a pattern.

Use scissors to cut the covering material to the pattern. Methods for joining covering material to form the hems and sleeves depends on the particular covering material used (see Chapter 5). Regardless of the covering material used, fit it to the kite frame with the guideline strings passing through sleeves in the covering material.

Bow String

The performance of the double basic kite is often improved by the addition of a bow string to the upper cross stick only or a bow string to each cross stick. Install the bow string by first attaching the string to one end of the cross stick. Wind the string around the stick and passing it through the notch before tying the end back to the main string section. This will keep the bow string from sliding down the stick when the kite is bowed. The upper stick is bowed 4 inches; the lower stick is bowed 2 inches, as shown in Fig. 6-131. Tie the bow string to the other end of the longitudinal stick by winding the string around the stick and passing it through the notch before tying the end back to the main string section. When done properly, the longitudinal stick is inside the bow, above the cross sticks, as shown.

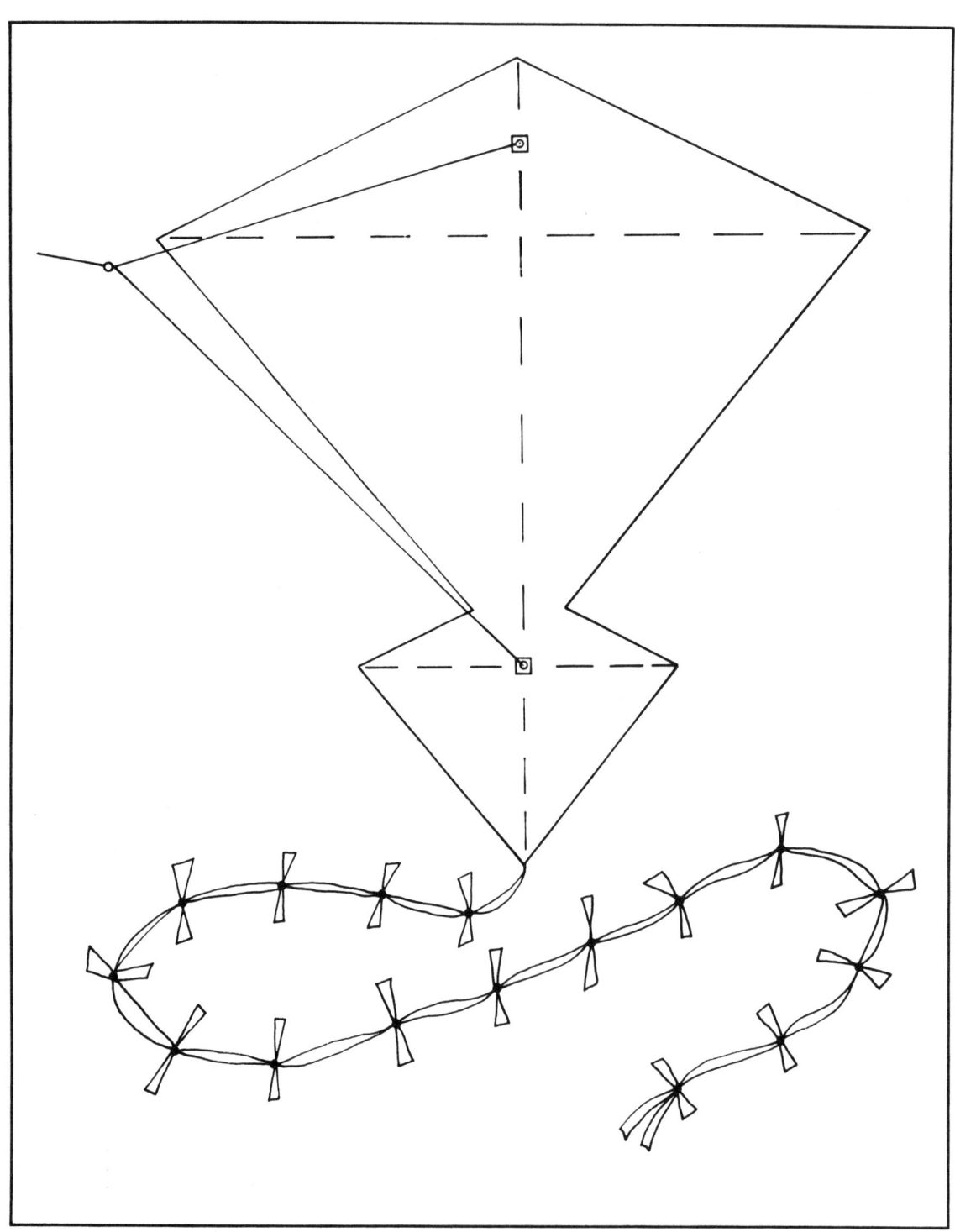

Fig. 6-132. Tail and bridle attachment.

Bridle

A two-string bridle can be used, as shown in Fig 6-132. The upper attachment is 4 inches from the upper end of the longitudinal stick. Tie the string around the stick and pass it through a hole in the covering material, which should be reinforced with tape or by other means. The lower attachment is to the cross point of the longitudinal stick and the lower cross stick. Tie the string around the sticks and pass it through a hole in the covering material, which should also be reinforced. You can tie the loose ends of the strings in a loop or to a small plastic ring. This ring allows easy length adjustment of the bridle strings.

Tail

The double basic kite usually requires a tail for adequate stability. A single tail can be attached to the aft end of the longitudinal stick, as shown in Fig. 6-132.

Construction of tails is detailed in Chapter 5. The length and weight of the tail required will depend on the wind conditions and other factors. Try the kite with a short tail first. If the kite loops or spins uncontrollably, add more tail. Use the minimum amount of tail required to give the kite good stability.

Variations

The double basic kite can be constructed in a range of sizes, using longitudinal sticks from 1 foot or less in length to 6 feet or more in length by keeping the proportions the same. As a general rule, you will need to reduce the weight of the smaller sizes by using proportionally smaller sticks and lighter weight covering material. You will need to use larger sticks and heavier covering material for the larger sizes.

You may also want to experiment with other proportions and frame arrangements, such as shown in Fig. 6-133.

DOUBLE SQUARE KITE

The double square kite, shown in Fig. 6-134, can be used as a flat or bow kite. A tail is often required to give this kite adequate stability.

Frame

Three sticks are used for making the frame, as shown in Fig. 6-135. A wooden stick with a rectangular cross section of ¼ inch by ⅜ inch, or a ¼-inch wooden dowel, that is 36 inches long is used for the longitudinal stick. The upper cross stick is a wooden stick with a rectangular cross section of

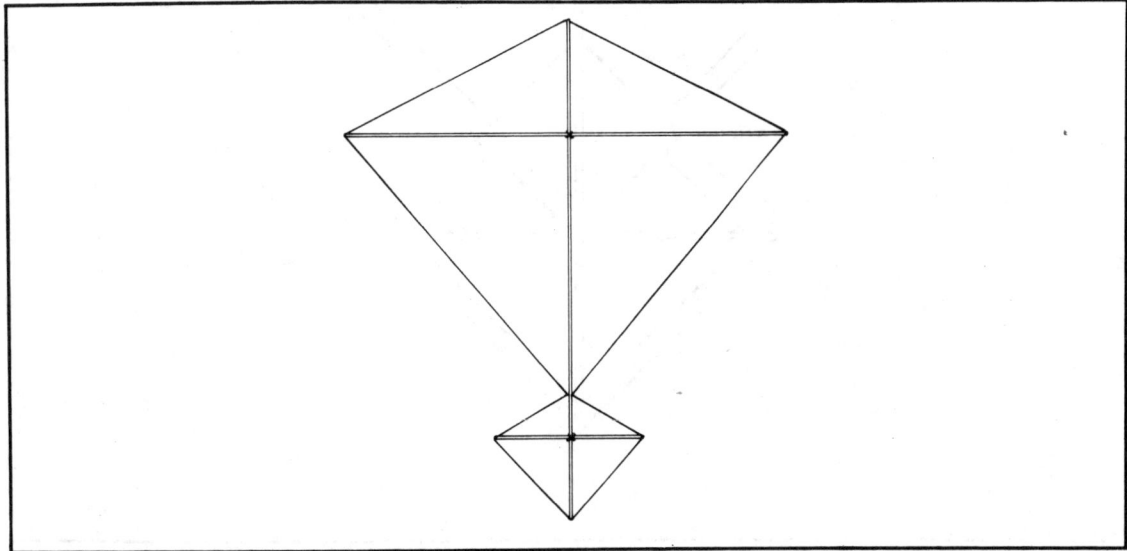

Fig. 6-133. Variation in frame arrangement of double basic kite.

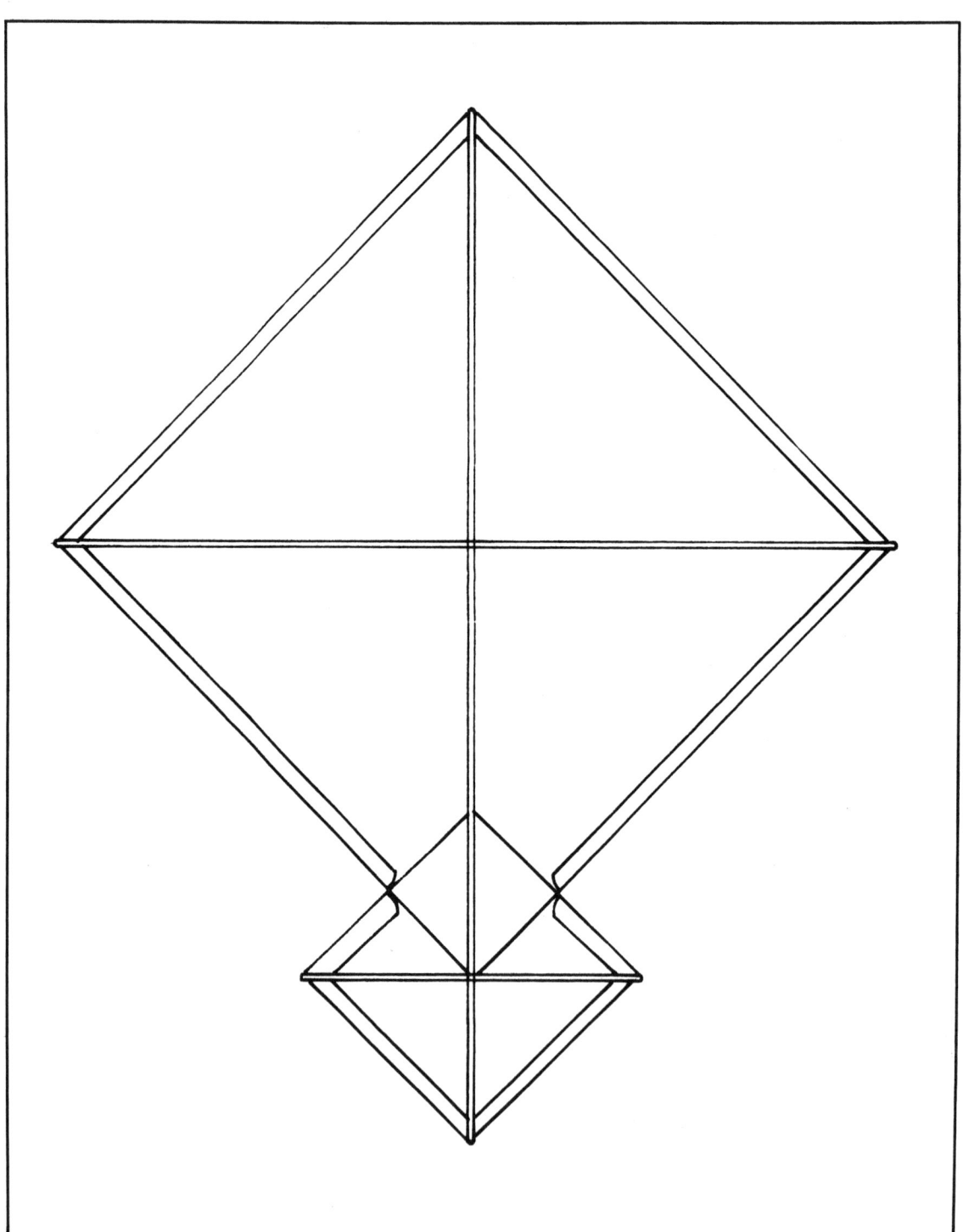

Fig. 6-134. Double square kite.

3/16 inch by 5/16 inch, or a round wooden dowel of 3/16-inch diameter, that is 30 inches long. The lower cross stick is a wooden stick with a rectangular cross section of ⅛ inch by ¼ inch, or a round wooden dowel of ⅛-inch diameter, that is 12 inches long. The sticks can vary somewhat from these dimensions and still give satisfactory results. If the kite will only fly in light airs, you can reduce the cross sectional size of the sticks. If the kite is to be flown in extremely strong winds, you may want to use sticks with larger cross sectional dimensions.

Fiberglass, bamboo, and aluminum sticks are alternatives. We'll assume that you will be using wooden sticks of either rectangular or round cross sectional shape.

Notch the ends of the sticks by making a saw cut to a depth of ⅜ inch in each end of each stick. Make the notches on both ends of each stick in the same plane.

Measure and mark the cross points of each stick. Glue the sticks and lash them together with string to the pattern shown.

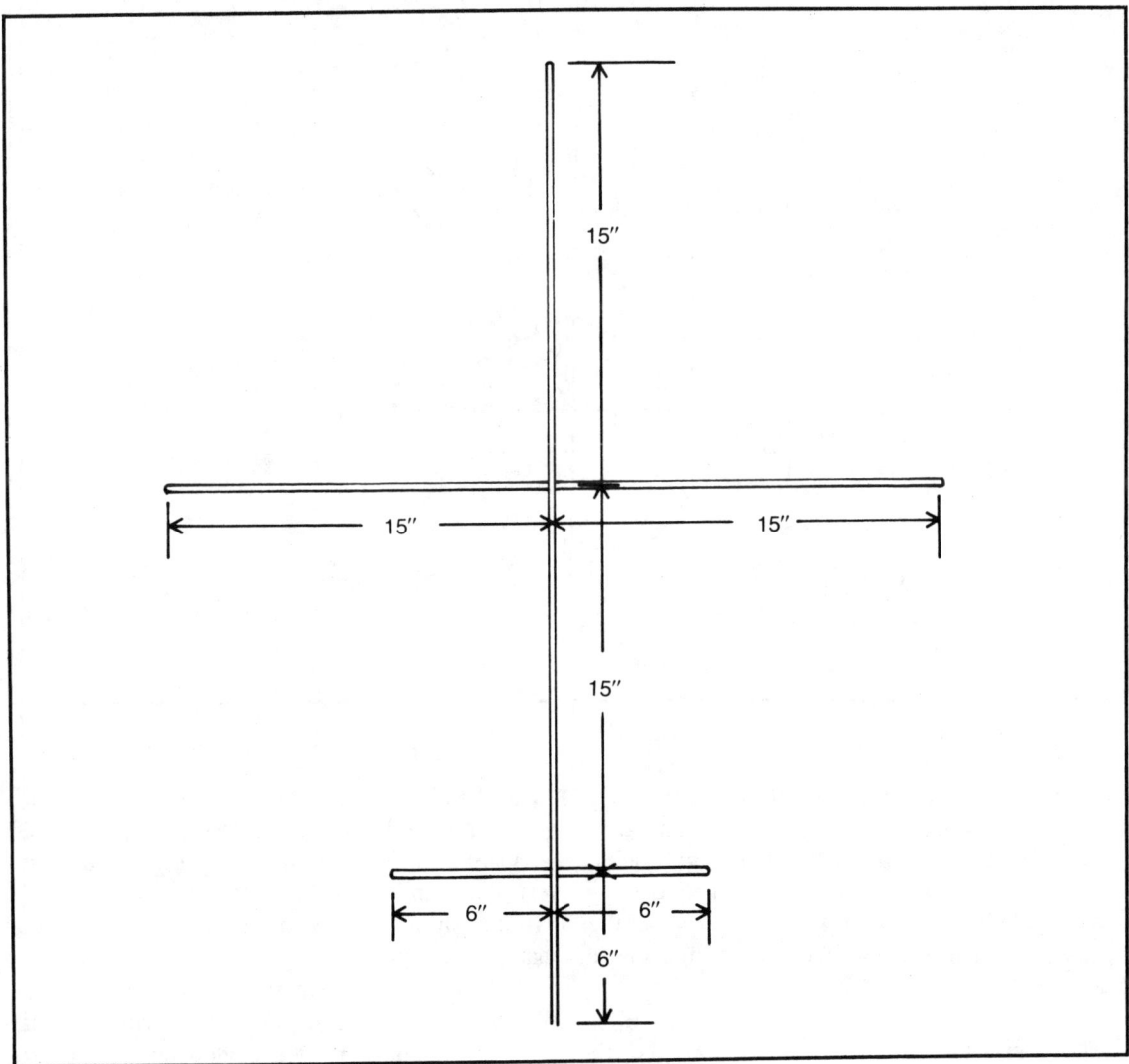

Fig. 6-135. Pattern for sticks for double square kite.

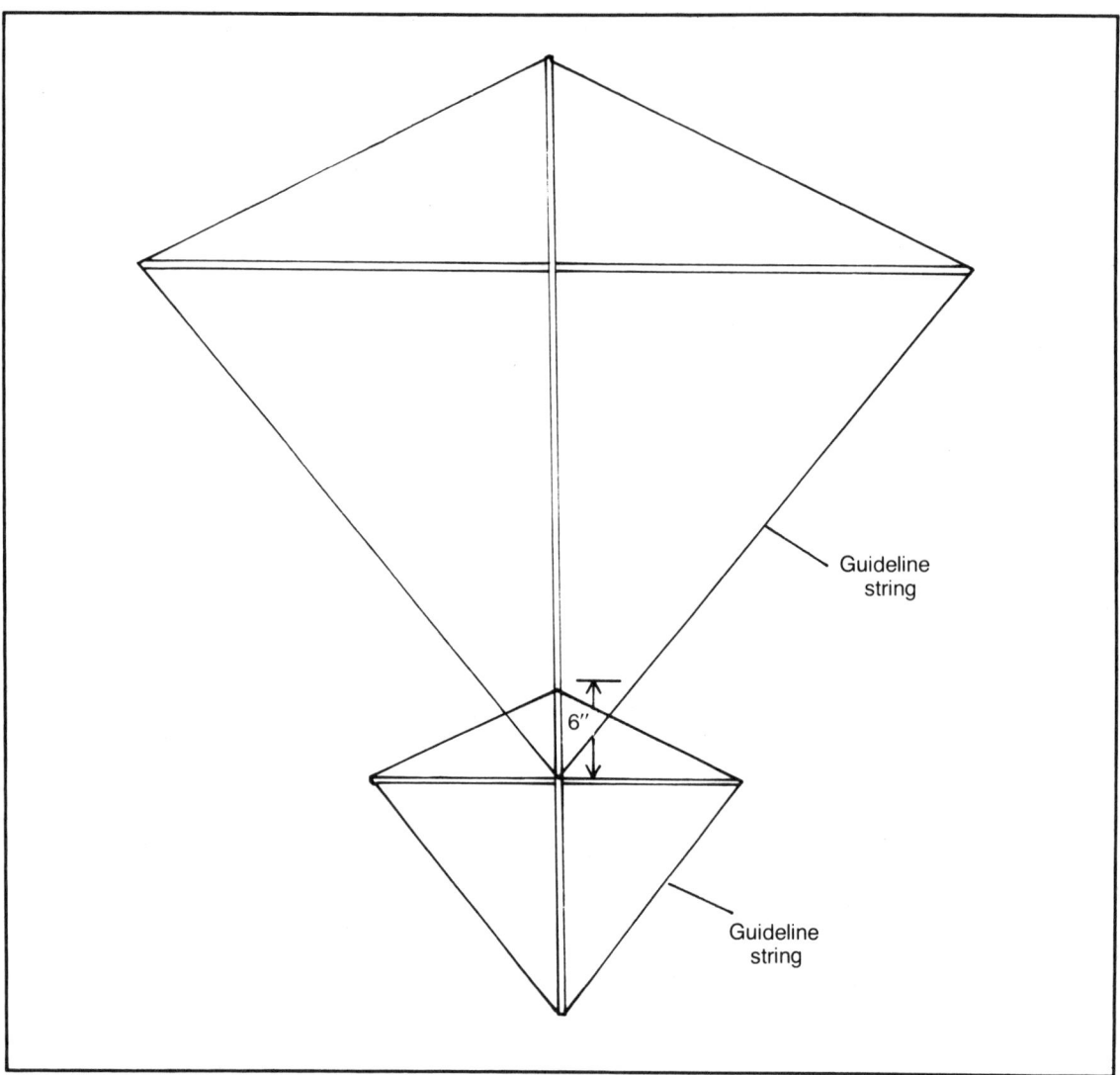

Fig. 6-136. Two guideline strings are used.

Two guideline strings are used. Install each guideline string in the notches around the sticks, as shown in Fig. 6-136. Stretch the string tight and tie the ends together around the longitudinal stick, as shown. Add lashing strings around the ends of the sticks on each side of the guideline strings where they pass through the notches.

Covering Material

Paper, plastic film, or cloth can be used to cover the kite. For best performance, the covering material should be of the lightest weight that is compatible with adequate strength. Mark the pattern shown in Fig. 6-137 on the covering material. The kite frame can be placed over the covering material as a pattern.

Using scissors, cut the covering material to the pattern. Methods for joining covering material to form the hems and sleeves depends on the particular covering material used (see Chapter 5). At-

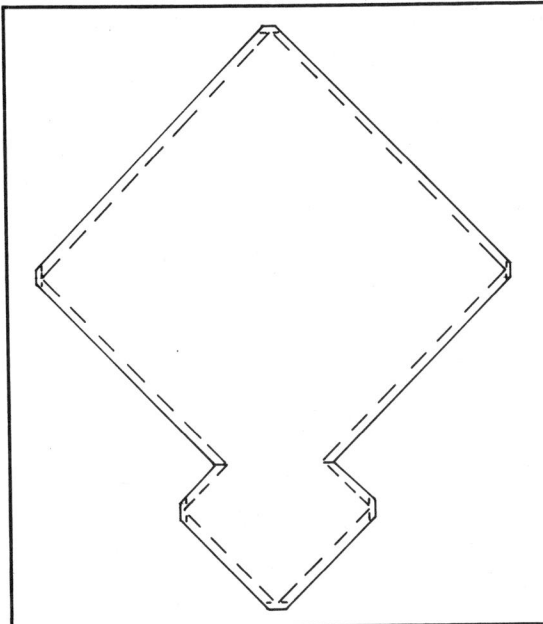

Fig. 6-137. Pattern for covering material.

tach the cover to the kite frame with the guideline strings passing through sleeves in the covering material.

Bow String

The performance of the double square kite is often improved by adding a bow string to the upper cross stick only or a bow string to each cross stick. Install the bow string by first attaching the string to one end of the cross stick, winding the string around the stick, and passing it through the notch before tying the end back to the main string section. This will keep the bow string from sliding down the stick when the kite is bowed. The upper stick is bowed 4 inches; the lower stick is bowed 2 inches, as shown in Fig. 6-138. Tie the bow string to the other end of the longitudinal stick by winding the string around the stick and passing it through the notch before tying the end back to the main string section. When done properly, the longitudinal stick is inside the bow, above the cross sticks, as shown.

Bridle

A two-string bridle can be used, as shown in Fig. 6-139. Make the upper attachment 6 inches from the upper end of the longitudinal stick. Tie the string around the stick and pass it through a hole in the covering material, which should be reinforced. The lower attachment is to the cross point of the longitudinal stick and the lower cross stick. Tie the string around the sticks and pass it through a reinforced hole in the covering material. You can tie the other ends of the strings in a loop or to a small plastic ring. This allows you to easily adjust the length of the bridle strings.

Tail

The double square kite usually requires a tail to give it adequate stability. A single tail can be attached to the aft end of the longitudinal stick, as shown in Fig. 6-139.

The length and weight of the tail required will depend on the wind conditions and other factors. See Chapter 5. Try the kite with a short tail first. If it loops or spins uncontrollably, add more tail, using the minimum required for good stability.

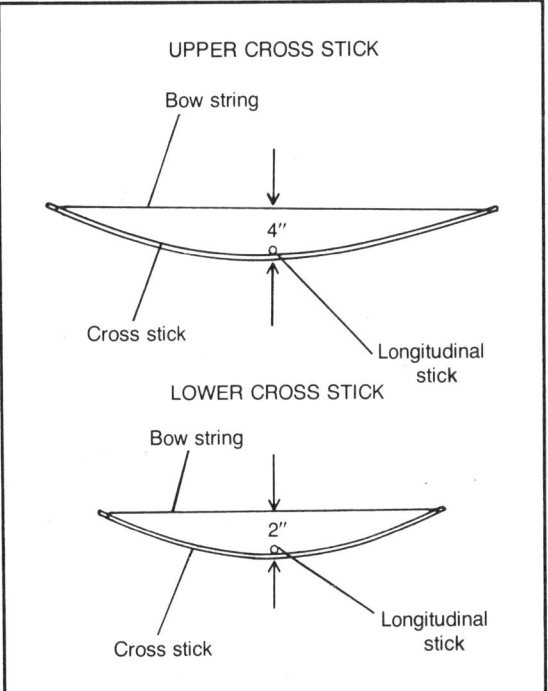

Fig. 6-138. Bow string for upper and lower cross stick.

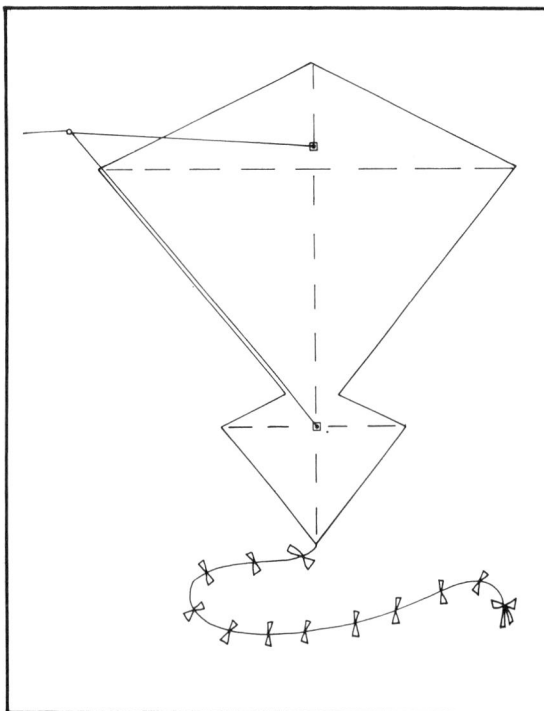

Fig. 6-139. Tail and bridle attachment.

Variations

The double square kite can be constructed in a range of sizes, using longitudinal sticks from 1 foot or less in length to 6 feet or more in length by keeping the proportions the same. As a general rule, you will need to reduce the weight of the smaller sizes by using proportionally smaller sticks and lighter weight covering material. You will need to use larger sticks and heavier covering material for the larger sizes.

You may also want to experiment with other proportions and frame arrangements, such as shown in Fig. 6-140.

DOUBLE DIAMOND KITE

The double diamond kite is shown in Fig. 6-141. This kite can be used as a flat or bow kite. A tail is often required to give this kite adequate stability.

Frame

Three sticks are used for making the frame, as shown in Fig. 6-142. Wooden sticks with rectangu-

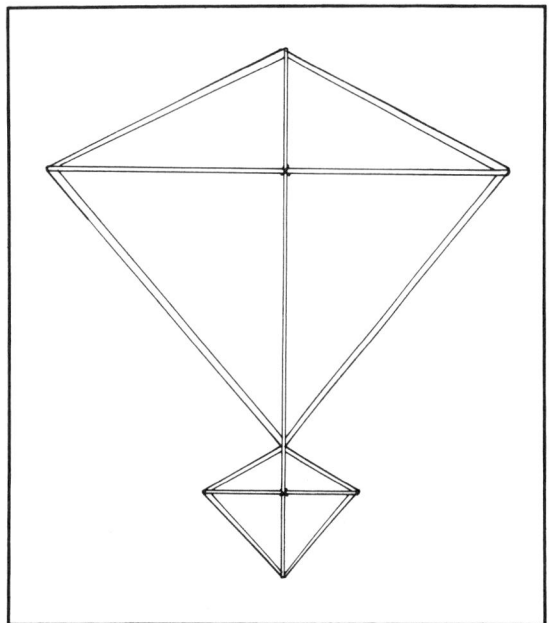

Fig. 6-140. Variation in frame arrangement for double square kite.

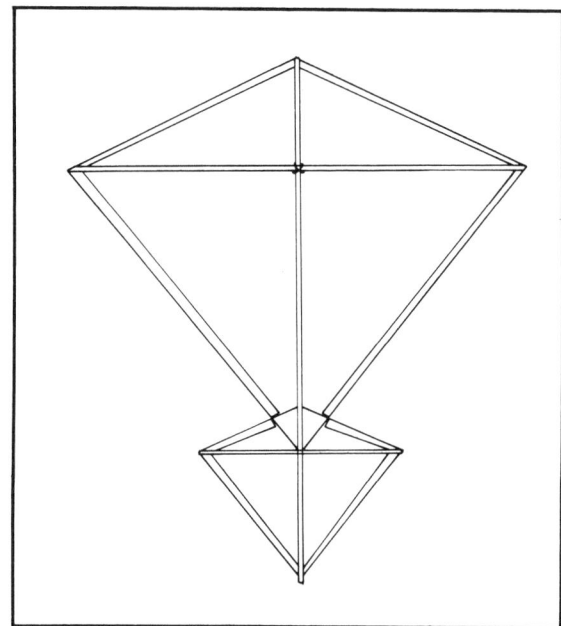

Fig. 6-141. Double diamond kite.

lar cross sections of ¼ inch by ⅜ inch or ¼-inch wooden dowels that are 36 inches long (for upper cross stick) and 30 inches long (for longitudinal stick) can be used. The lower cross stick is a wooden stick with a rectangular cross section of ⅛ inch by ¼ inch, or a round wooden dowel of ⅛-inch diameter, that is 18 inches long. The sticks can vary somewhat from these dimensions and still give satisfactory results. If the kite is to be used only in light airs, you may want to reduce the cross sectional size of the sticks. For flying in heavier winds, use sticks with larger cross sectional dimensions. Fiberglass, bamboo, and aluminum sticks are other possibilities. For descriptive purposes here, we'll assume that you will be using wooden sticks of either rectangular or round cross sectional shape.

The ends of the sticks are notched by making a ⅜-inch-deep saw cut in each end of each stick. Make the notches on both ends of each stick in the same plane.

Measure and mark the cross points of each stick. Then glue the sticks and lash them together with string to the pattern shown.

Two guideline strings are used. Each guideline string in installed in the notches around the sticks, as shown in Fig. 6-143. The string is stretched tight, and the ends are tied together around the longitudinal stick, as shown. Add lashing

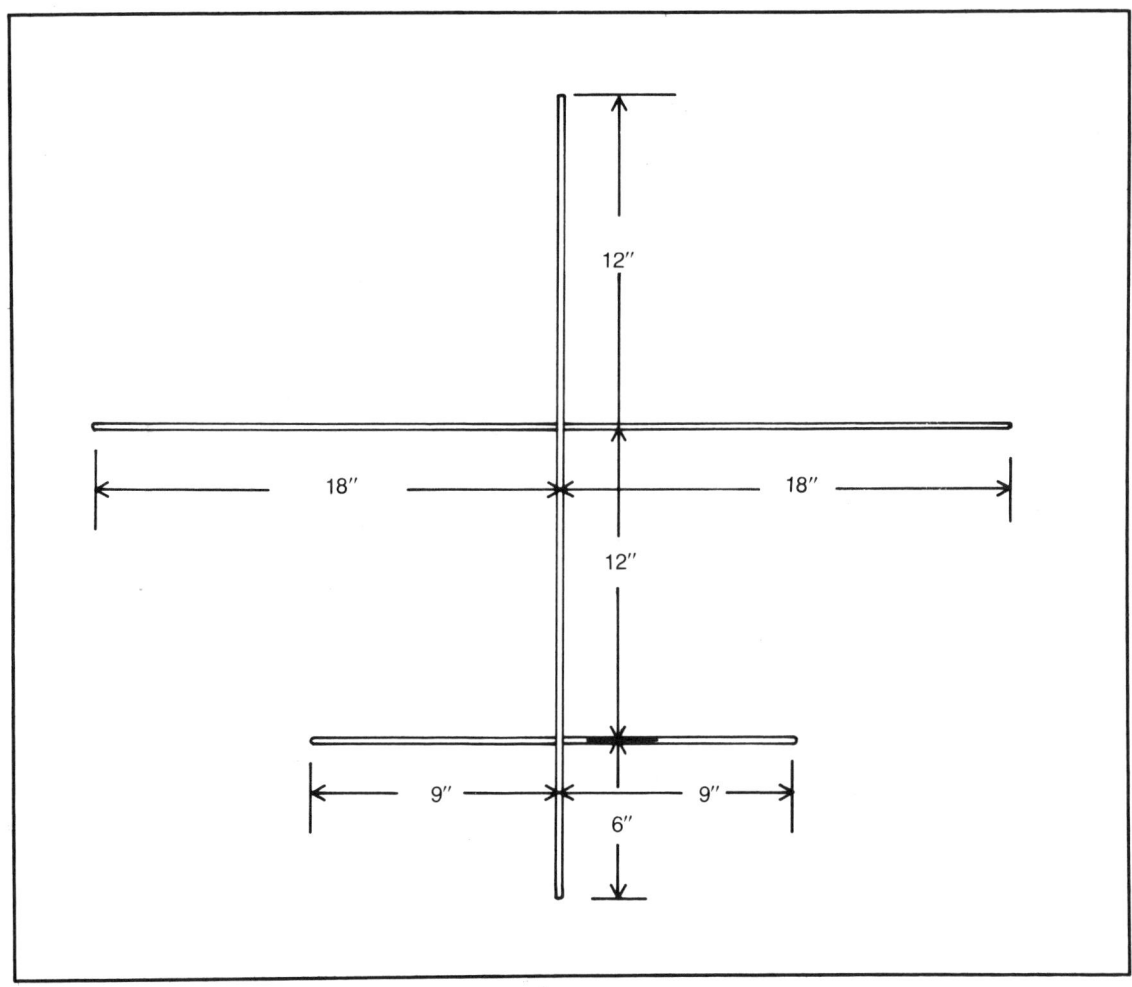

Fig. 6-142. Pattern for sticks for double diamond kite.

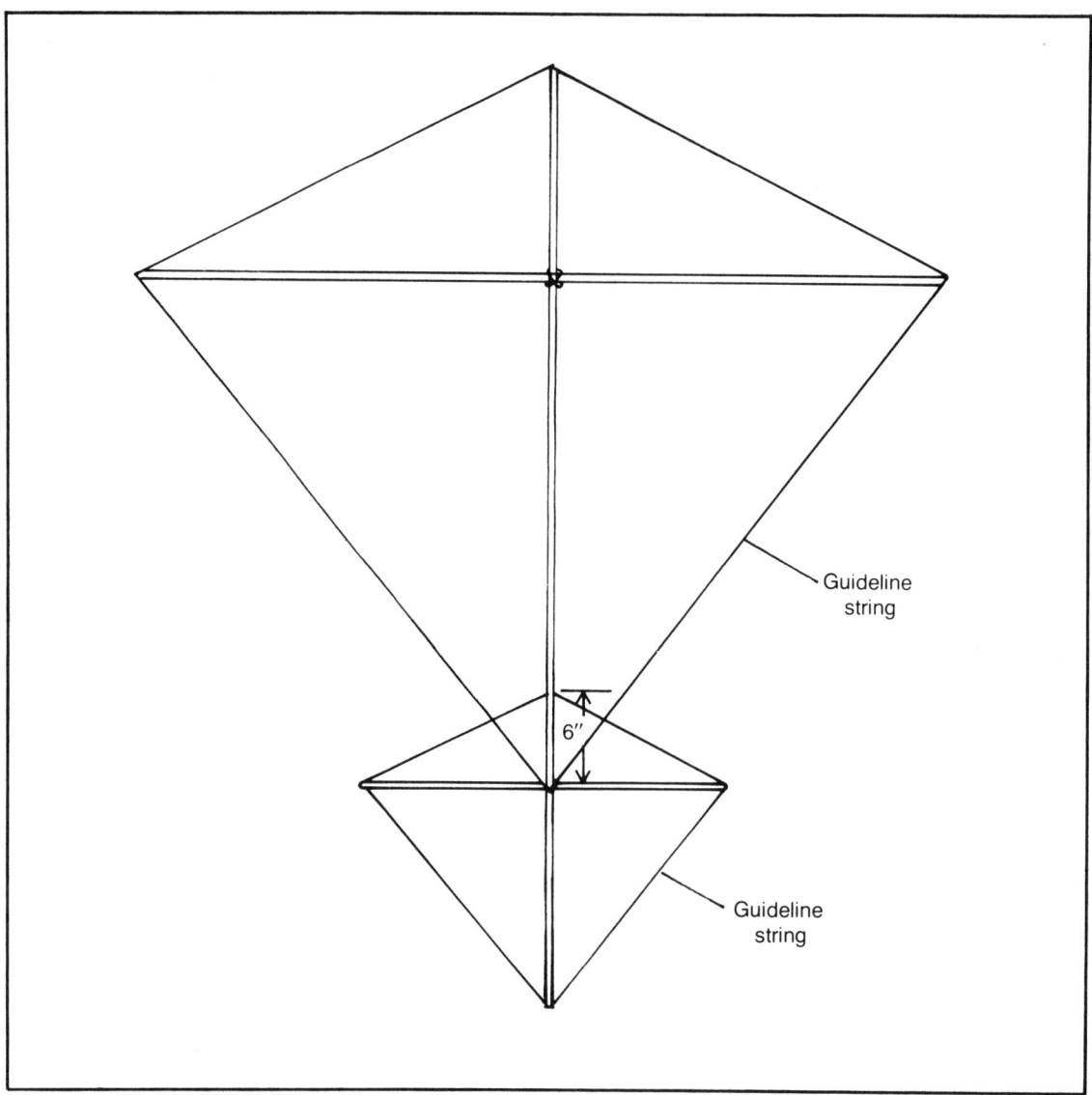

Fig. 6-143. Two guideline strings are used.

strings around the ends of the sticks on each side of the guideline strings where they pass through the notches.

Covering Material

The covering material can be paper, plastic, or fabric and should be of the lightest weight compatible with adequate strength. Mark the pattern shown in Fig. 6-144 on the covering material. The kite frame can be placed over the covering material to use as a pattern.

Use scissors to cut the covering material to the pattern. Use the appropriate joining method to make the hems and sleeves. Generally, paper is glued, fabric material is sewn, and plastic is glued, heat-sealed, or taped.

Regardless of the covering material used, in-

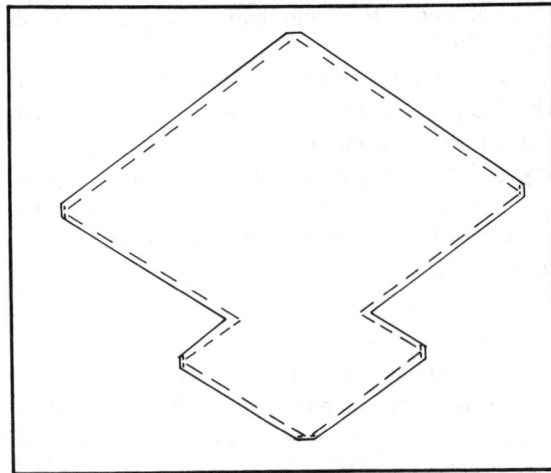

Fig. 6-144. Pattern for covering material.

stall it to the kite frame with the guideline strings passing through sleeves in the covering material.

Bow String

The performance of the double diamond kite is often improved by adding a bow string to the upper cross stick only or a bow string to each cross stick. Install the bow string by first attaching the string to one end of the cross stick, winding the string around the stick, and passing it through the notch before tying the end back to the main string section. This will keep the bow string from sliding down the stick when the kite is bowed. The upper stick is bowed 4 inches; the lower stick is bowed 2 inches, as shown in Fig. 6-145. Tie the bow string to the other end of the longitudinal stick by winding the string around

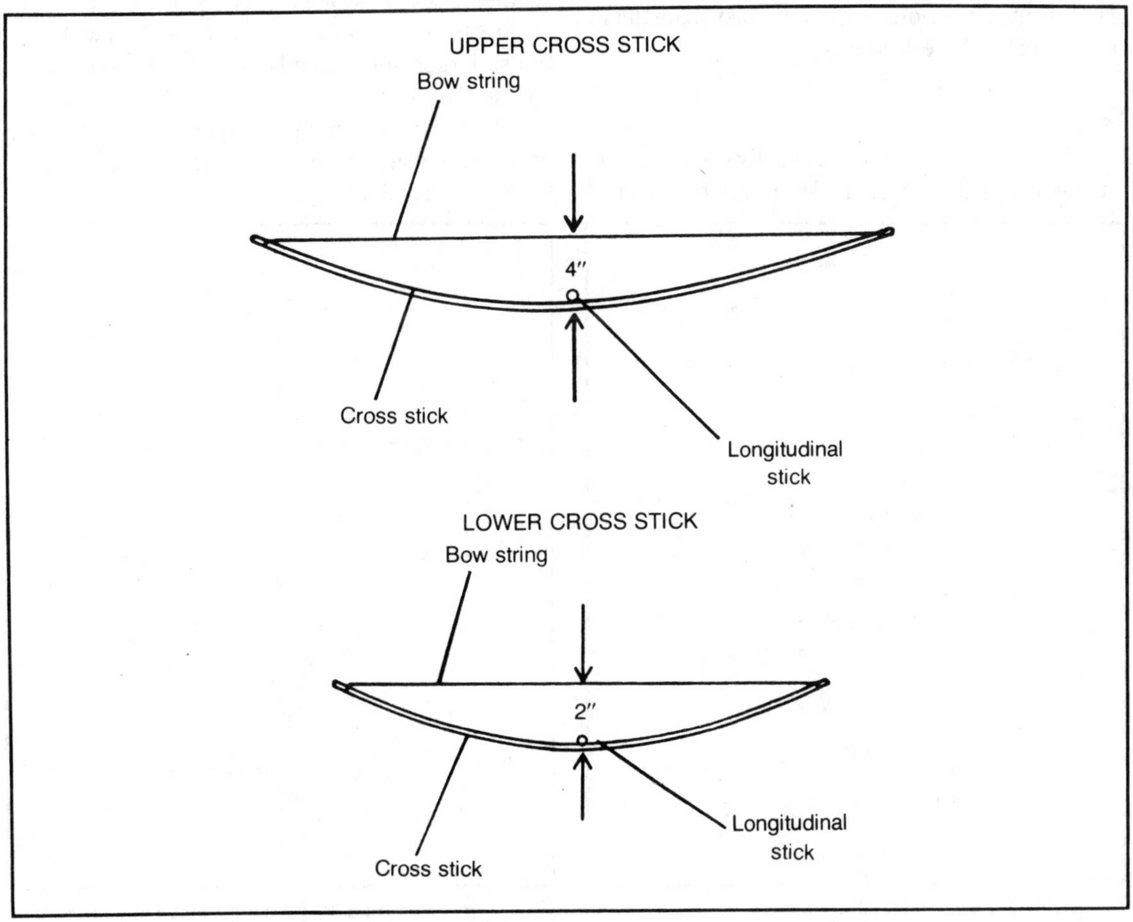

Fig. 6-145. Bow string for upper and lower cross stick.

187

the stick and passing it through the notch before tying the end back to the main string section. When done properly, the longitudinal stick is inside the bow, above the cross sticks, as shown.

Bridle

A two-string bridle can be used, as shown in Fig. 6-146. The upper attachment is 6 inches from the upper end of the longitudinal stick. Tie the string around the stick and pass it through a hole in the covering material, which should be reinforced with tape or by other means. The lower attachment is to the cross point of the longitudinal stick and the lower cross stick. Tie the string around the sticks and pass it through a reinforced hole in the cover. You can tie the loose ends in a loop or to a small plastic ring. The bridle ring allows easy adjustment of the length of the bridle strings.

Tail

The double diamond kite usually requires a tail for adequate stability. A single tail can be attached to the aft end of the longitudinal stick, as shown in Fig. 6-146.

Construction of tails is detailed in Chapter 5. The length and weight of the tail required will depend on the wind conditions and other factors. Try the kite with a short tail first. If the kite loops or spins uncontrollably, add more tail. Use the minimum amount of tail required to give the kite good stability.

Variations

The double diamond kite can be constructed in a range of sizes, using longitudinal sticks from 1 foot or less in length to 6 feet or more in length by keeping the proportions the same. As a general rule, you will need to reduce the weight of the smaller sizes by using proportionally smaller sticks and lighter weight covering material. You will need to use larger sticks and heavier covering material for the larger sizes.

You may also want to experiment with other proportions and frame arrangements, such as shown in Fig. 6-147.

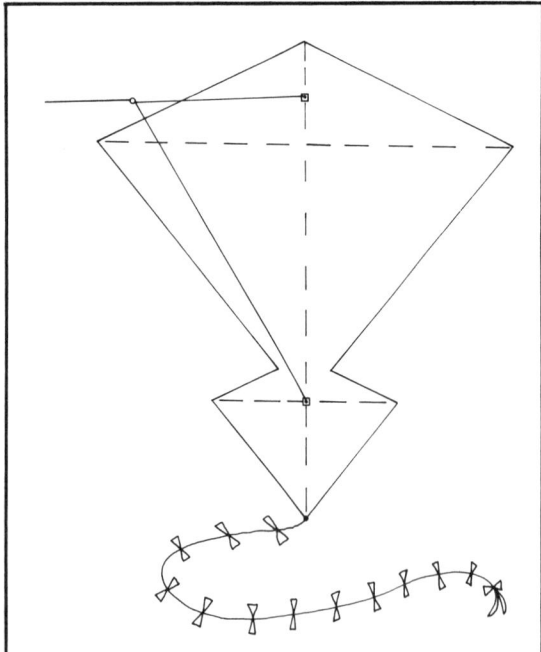

Fig. 6-146. Tail and bridle attachment.

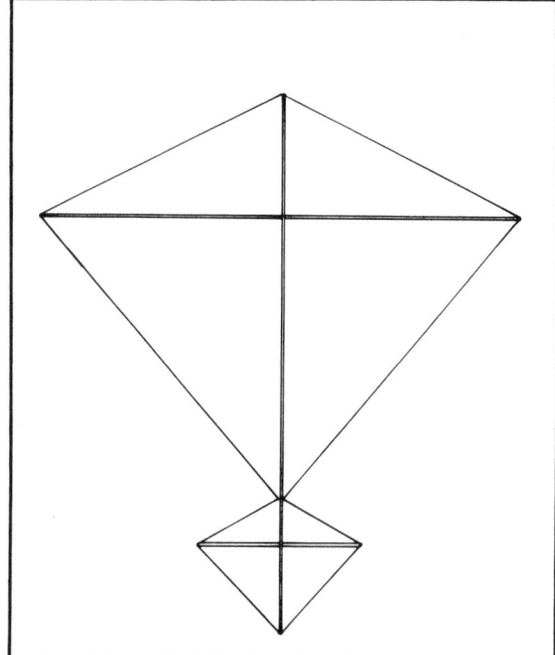

Fig. 6-147. Variation in frame arrangement for double diamond kite.

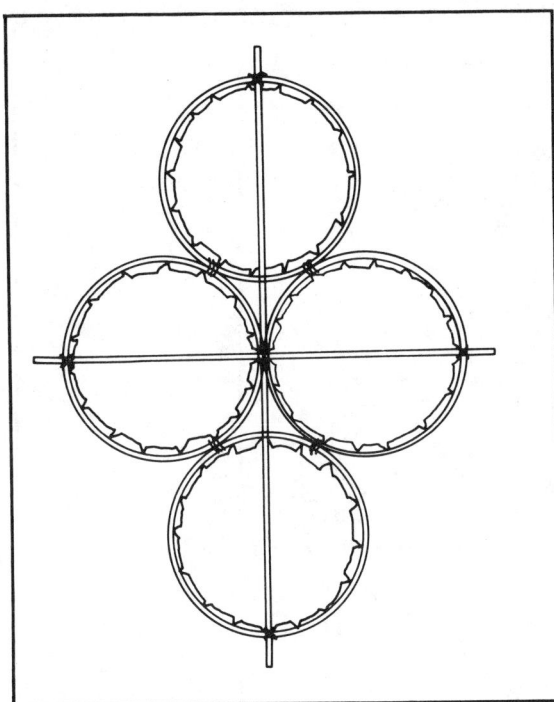

Fig. 6-148. Four-circle kite.

FOUR-CIRCLE KITE

The four-circle kite, shown in Fig. 6-148, is usually used as a flat kite. A tail is required to give this kite adequate stability.

Frame

The frame consists of a longitudinal stick, a cross stick, and four circle sticks, as shown in Fig. 6-149. Wooden sticks with a rectangular cross section of 3/16 inch by 5/16 inch or round wooden dowels of 3/16-inch diameter can be used for the longitudinal and cross sticks. The sticks can vary somewhat from these dimensions and still give satisfactory results. Use proportionately larger or smaller cross sectional dimensions depending on wind conditions. Sticks of fiberglass, bamboo, and aluminum can also be used.

The circles can be formed from 36-inch lengths of ⅛-inch square or round strips of bamboo. Techniques for forming circles from bamboo and other suitable materials are detailed in Chapter 5. Each circle should have a 11-inch diameter.

Join the longitudinal and cross sticks at their center points with glue and a string lashing. Then assemble the four circles to the cross frame with glue and string lashings, as shown in Fig. 6-150.

Covering Material

Paper, plastic film, or cloth fabric can be used to cover the kite. For best performance, the covering material should be lightweight, but as strong as possible. Mark the circle pattern shown in Fig. 6-151 on the covering material. Four of these are required, one for each circle.

Use scissors to cut the covering material to the pattern. Methods for joining covering material to form the sleeves depends on the particular covering material used (see Chapter 5).

Regardless of the covering material used, fix it to the kite frame, over the circle frame sticks, with the sticks passing through sleeves in the covering material.

Bow String

While the four-circle kite is usually used as a flat kite, a bow string can be added to the cross stick if desired. To install a bow string, tie the string to one end of the cross stick and the circle stick where it meets the cross stick (near the end of the cross stick). Bow the cross stick until it has a 4-inch bow, as shown in Fig. 6-152. Tie the other end of the bow string to the other end of the cross stick where it joins the cross stick near the end of the cross stick.

Bridle

A two-string bridle can be used, as shown in Fig. 6-153. The upper attachment is to the longitudinal stick at the center point of the upper circle. The lower attachment is to the longitudinal stick at the center point of the lower circle. Pass the strings through tape-reinforced holes in the covering material. Tie the ends in a loop or to a small plastic ring. The bridle ring allows easy adjustment of the length of the bridle strings.

Tail

The four-circle kite requires a tail to give

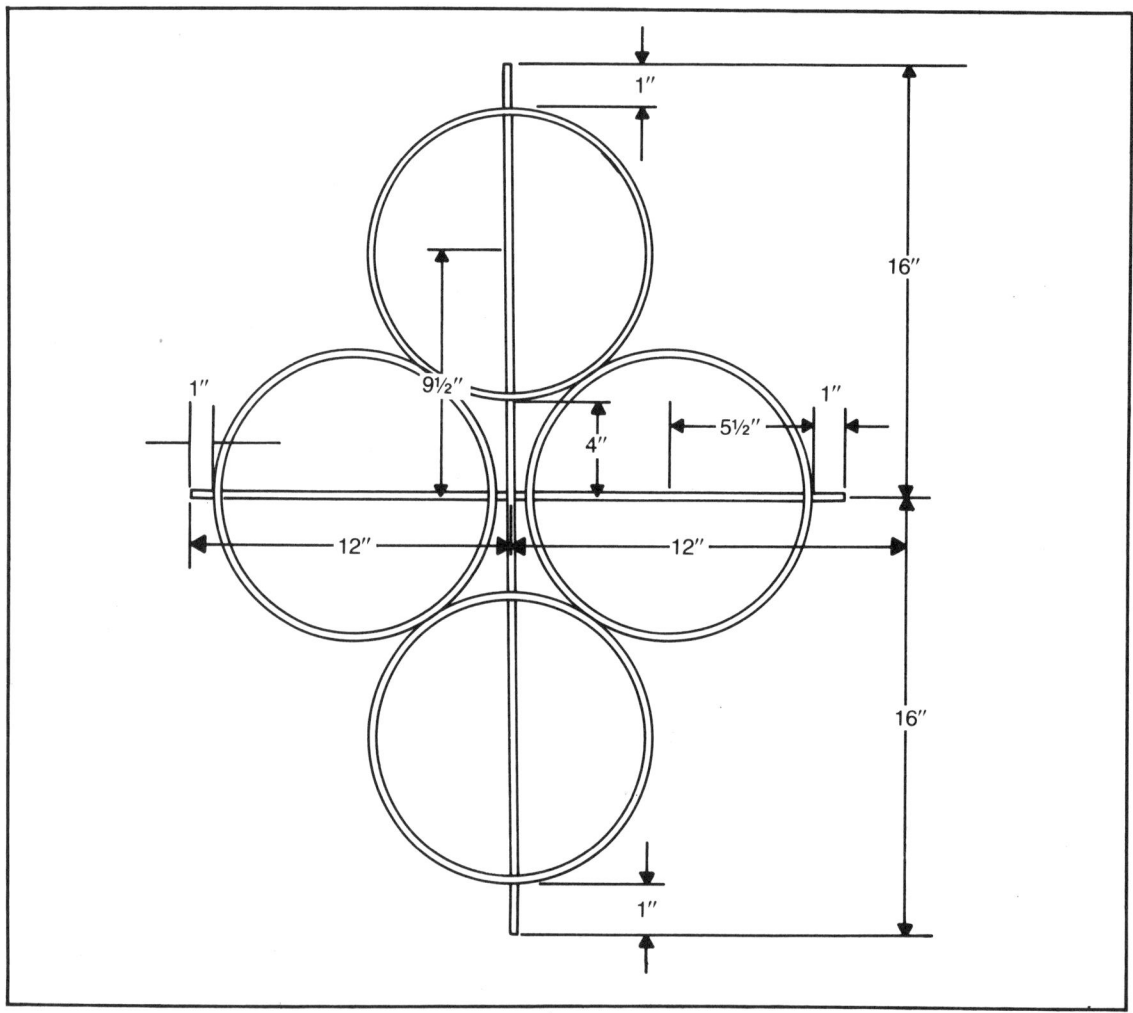

Fig. 6-149. Pattern for sticks for four-circle kite.

adequate stability, even if the kite is bowed. The tail can be attached to the aft end of the longitudinal stick at the joint of the bottom section of the lower circle, as shown in Fig. 6-153.

Construction of tails is detailed in Chapter 5. The length and weight of the tail required will depend on the wind conditions and other factors. Try the kite first with a short tail. If the kite loops or spins uncontrollably, add more tail. Use the smallest tail necessary for good stability.

Variations

The four-circle kite can be constructed in a range of sizes, using a longitudinal stick from 1 foot or less in length to 6 feet or more in length by keeping the proportions the same. As a general rule, you will need to reduce the weight of the smaller sizes by using proportionally smaller sticks and lighter weight covering material. You will need to use larger sticks and heavier covering material for the larger sizes.

TRIPLE-DECK KITE

The triple-deck kite is shown in Fig. 6-154. This kite is usually used as a flat kite, and a tail is required to give this kite adequate stability.

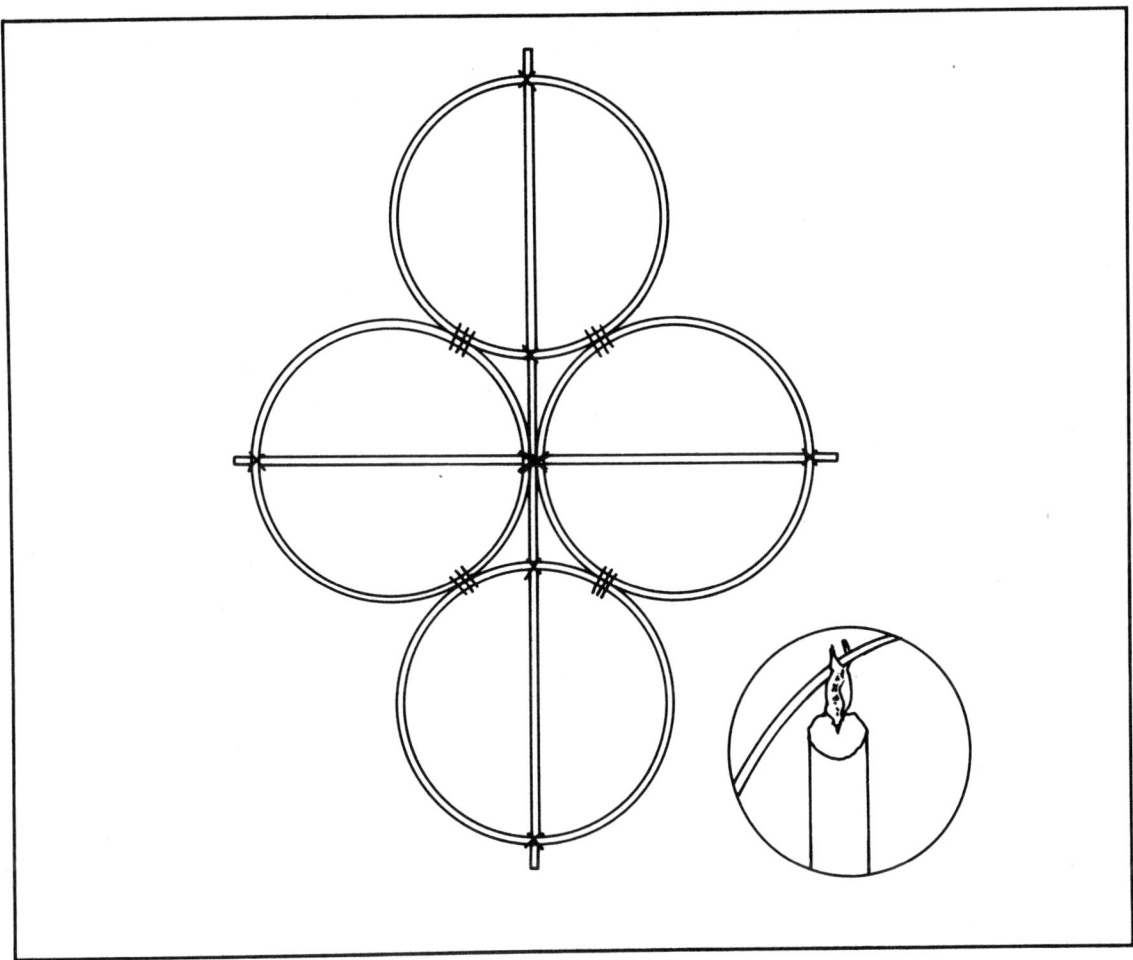

Fig. 6-150. Circles are glued and lashed to cross frame and together.

Frame

The frame pattern for the triple-deck kite is shown in Fig. 6-155. A 36-inch-long wooden stick with a rectangular cross section of ¼ inch by ⅜ inch or round wooden dowel of ¼-inch diameter can be used for the longitudinal stick. Bamboo strips or 3/16-inch diameter wooden dowels can be used for the arch sticks. Two sticks 36 inches in length are used for the upper form; two sticks 24-inches in length for the middle form; and two sticks 16 inches in length for the lower form. The sticks can vary somewhat from these cross sectional dimensions and still give satisfactory results. If the kite is to be used only in light airs, you may want to reduce the cross sectional size of the sticks. If the kite is to be flown in extremely strong winds, you may want to use sticks with larger cross sectional dimensions.

Measure and mark the points of attachment for the arch sticks on the longitudinal stick, as shown in Fig. 6-155. Mark the center point on each arch stick. Glue the arch sticks and lash them with string to the longitudinal stick, following the pattern. Next, bend and join the ends of the arch sticks with glue and string lashings ½ inch from the ends of the sticks, as shown in Fig. 6-154, to form the three forms. Glue and lash the arch sticks together where the forms overlap, as shown in Fig. 6-156.

Covering Material

Paper, plastic film, or fabric can be used to

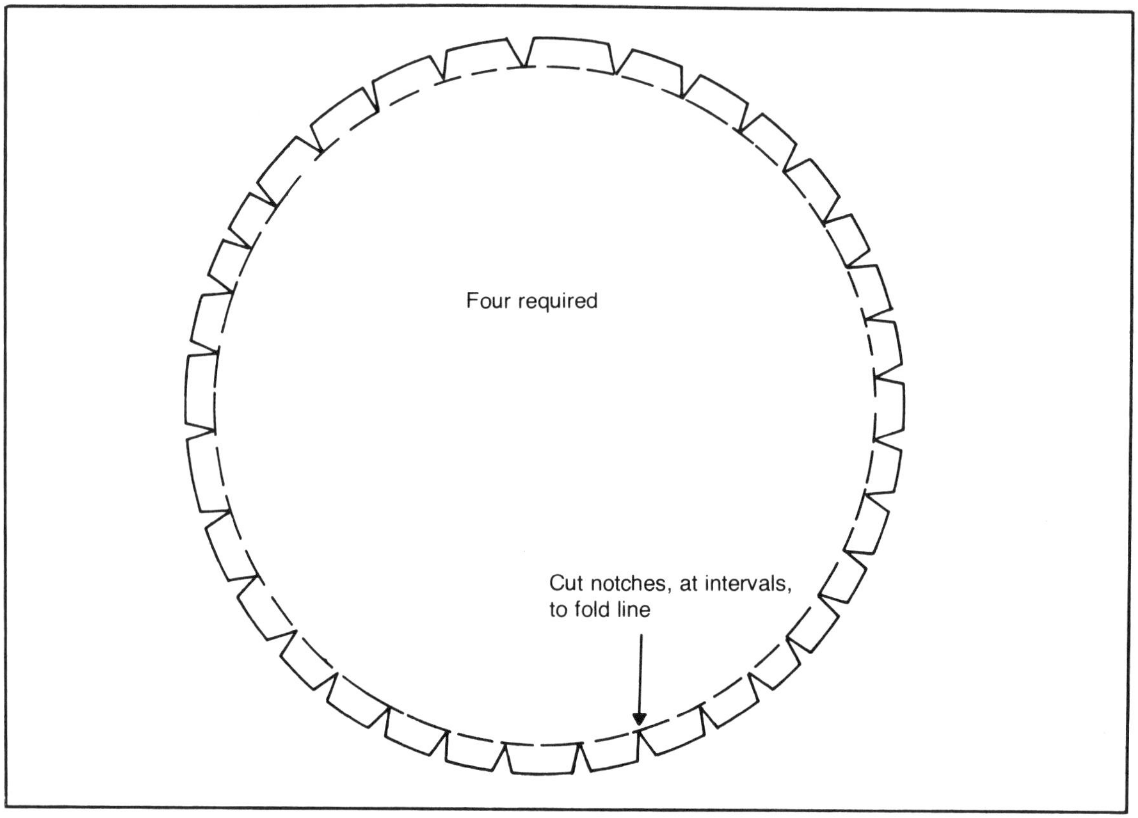

Four required
Cut notches, at intervals, to fold line
Fig. 6-151. Pattern for covering material.

Bow string
4″
Cross stick
Longitudinal stick
Fig. 6-152. Bow string.

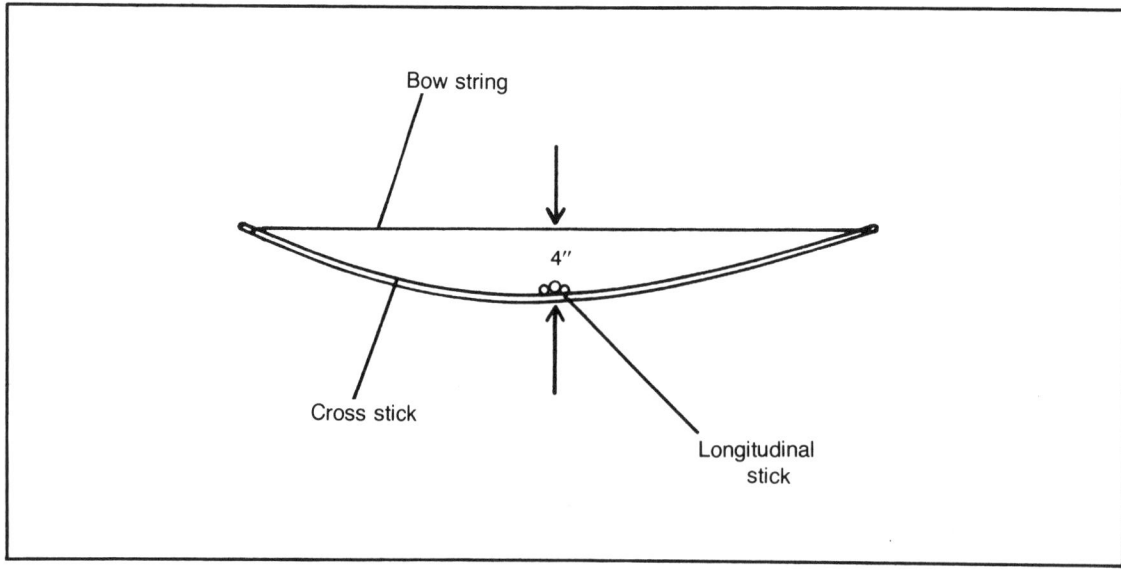

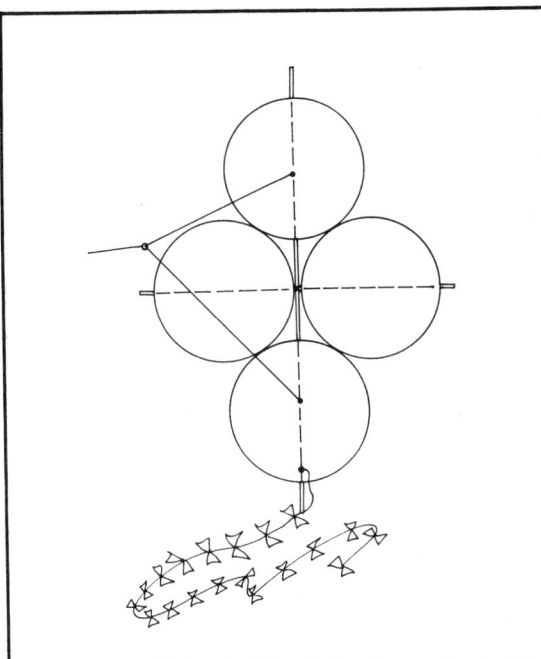

Fig. 6-153. Bridle and tail attachments.

Bridle

A two-string bridle can be used, as shown in Fig. 6-158. The upper attachment is to the longitudinal stick at the center point of the upper arch form. The string passes through a small hole in the covering material, which should be reinforced with tape or by other means. The lower attachment is to the aft end of the longitudinal stick at the point where the lower arch stick joins the longitudinal stick. The other ends of the strings can be tied in a loop or to a small plastic ring. The bridle ring allows easy adjustment of the length of the bridle strings.

Tail

The triple-deck kite usually requires a tail to give adequate stability, even if the kite is bowed. A single tail can be attached to the aft end of the longitudinal stick at the joint of the lower arch stick, as shown in Fig. 6-158.

Try the kite first with a short tail. If the kite loops or spins uncontrollably, add more tail. Use the minimum amount of tail required to give the kite good stability. See Chapter 5 for details.

cover the kite. For best performance, the covering material should be of the lightest weight that is compatible with adequate strength. Mark the pattern shown in Fig. 6-157 on the covering material. The kite frame can be placed over the covering material as a pattern. Notice that three separate cover pieces are used, with open spaces left between forms.

Use scissors to cut the covering material to the patterns. Methods for joining covering material to form the sleeves depends on the particular covering material used (see Chapter 5). Generally, paper is glued, fabric material is sewn, and plastic is glued, heat sealed or taped. Install the cover to the kite frame, forming sleeves over the arch sticks.

Bow String

While the triple-deck kite is usually used as a flat kite, bow strings can be added to the arch sticks if desired. To install bow strings, tie the string to one end of the joint at the end of a pair of arch sticks. Bow the arch sticks as desired, and tie the other end of the string to the joint at the opposite end of the pair of arch sticks.

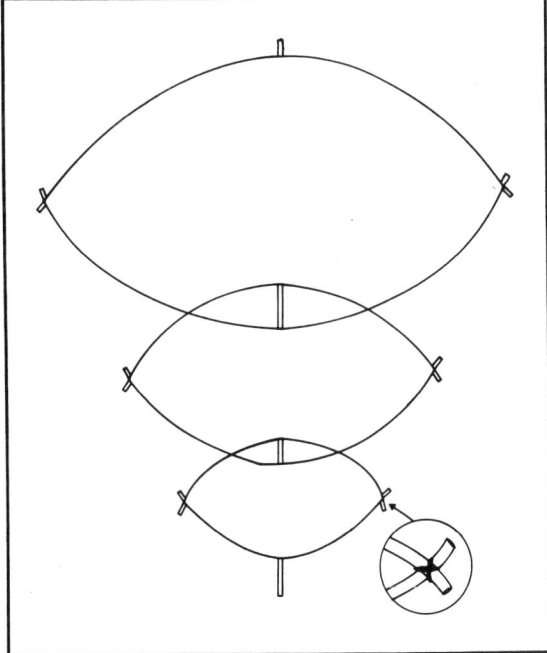

Fig. 6-154. Triple-deck kite. Ends of arch sticks are joined with glue and string lashings.

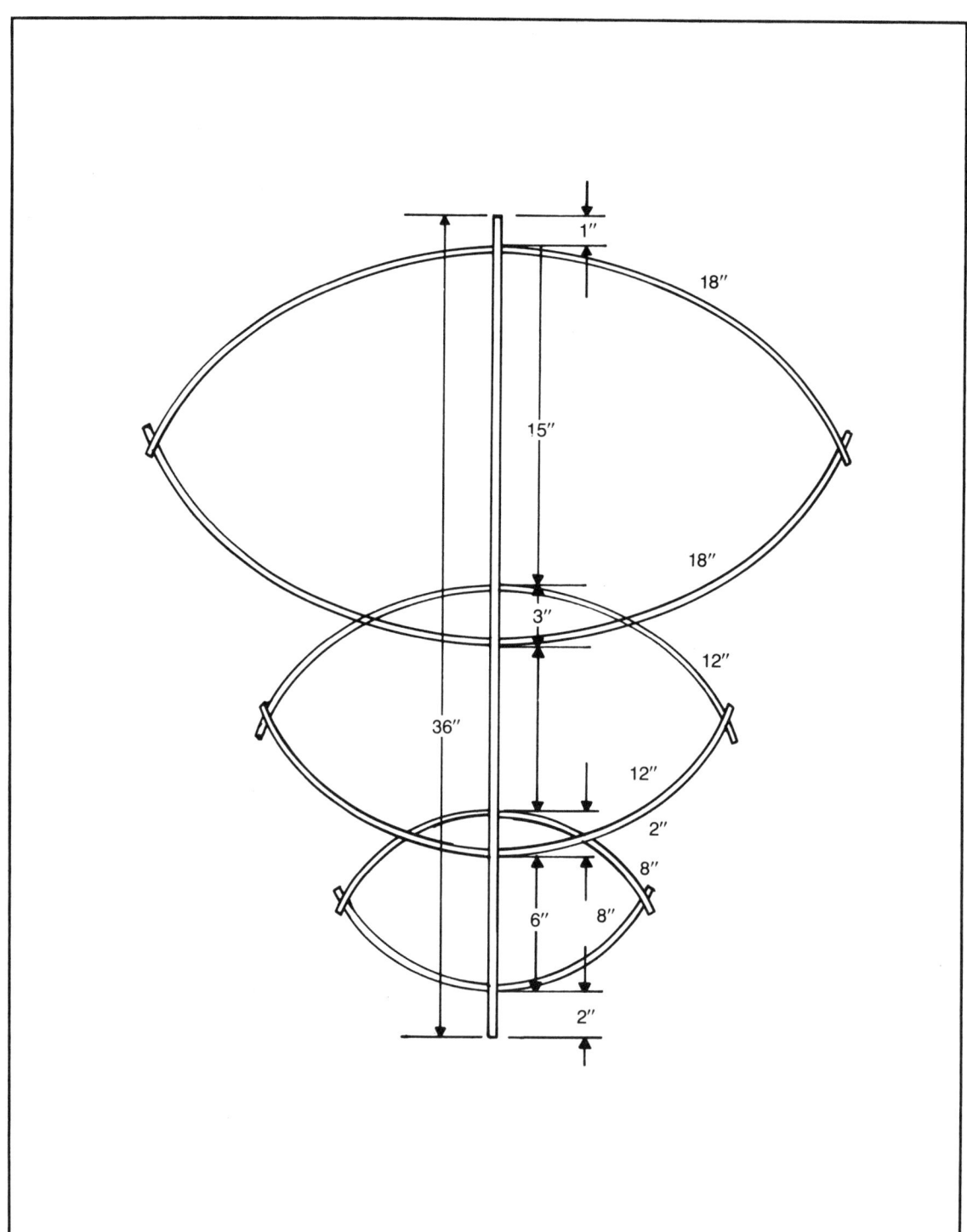

Fig. 6-155. Pattern for sticks for triple-deck kite.

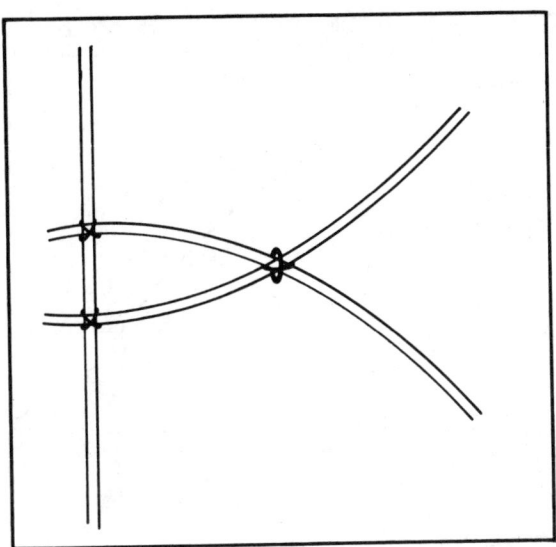

Fig. 6-156. The arch sticks are glued and lashed together.

stick is 36 inches long. A wooden stick with a rectangular cross section of ⅛ inch by ¼ inch, or a round wooden dowel of ⅛-inch diameter, that is 9 inches long can be used for the lower cross stick. The sticks can vary somewhat from these dimensions and still give satisfactory results. If the kite is to be used only in light airs, reduce the cross sectional size of the sticks. For extremely strong winds, use sticks with larger cross sectional dimensions. Fiberglass, bamboo, and aluminum sticks are alternatives.

The instructions below are for a kite made with either rectangular or round wooden sticks, cross sectional shape.

Notch the ends of the arch stick by making a saw cut to a depth of ⅜ inch in each end. Make the notches on both ends of the stick in the same plane. Taper the ends of the longitudinal sticks at the

Variations

The triple-deck kite can be constructed in a range of sizes, using a longitudinal stick from 1 foot or less in length to 6 feet or more in length by keeping the proportions the same. As a general rule, you will need to reduce the weight of the smaller sizes by using proportionally smaller sticks and lighter weight covering material, and use larger sticks and heavier covering material for the larger sizes.

You may also want to experiment by changing the relative sizes and shapes of the forms. A kite with two decks (Fig. 6-159) and four decks (Fig. 6-160) or more are other possibilities.

BIRD KITE

A bird kite is shown in Fig. 6-161. A tail is required to give this kite adequate stability.

Frame

Four sticks are used for making the frame, as shown in Fig. 6-162. Wooden sticks with a rectangular cross section of 3/16 inch by 5/16 inch or a round wooden dowel of 3/16-inch diameter can be used for the longitudinal and arch sticks. The two longitudinal sticks are 30 inches long. The arch

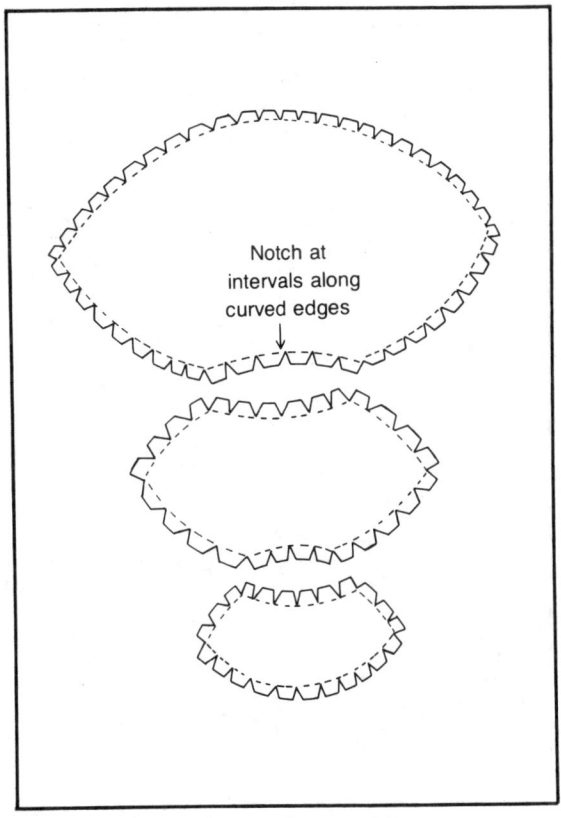

Fig. 6-157. Patterns for covering material.

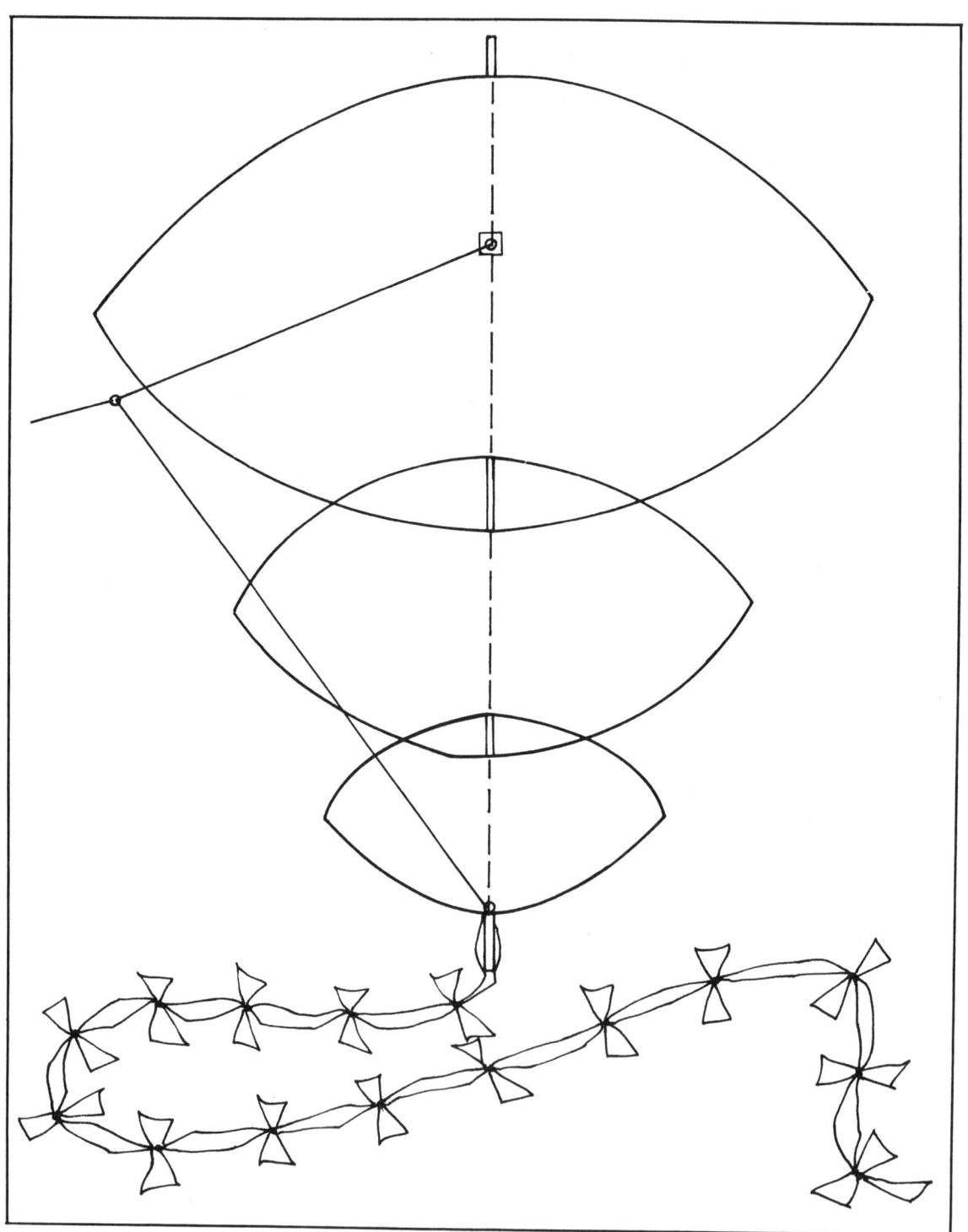

Fig. 6-158. Tail and bridle attachment.

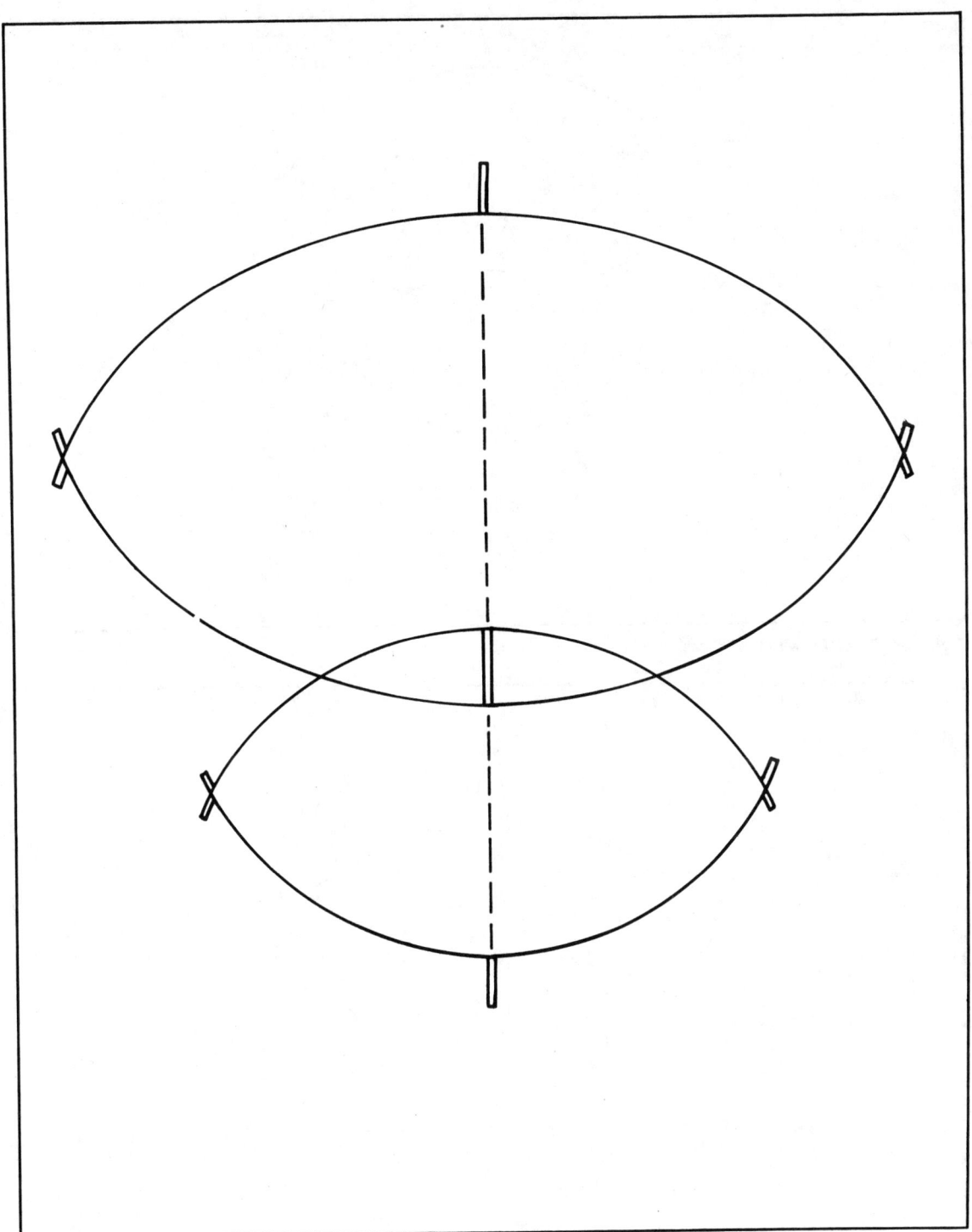

Fig. 6-159. Variation with two decks.

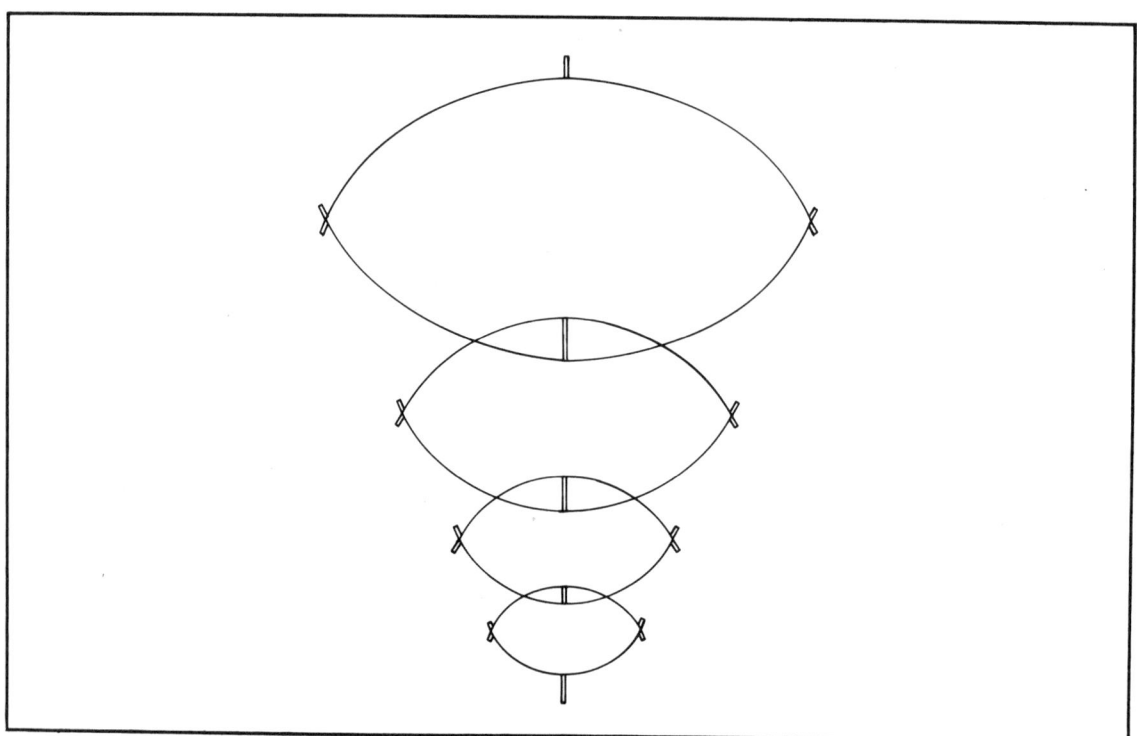

Fig. 6-160. Variation with four decks.

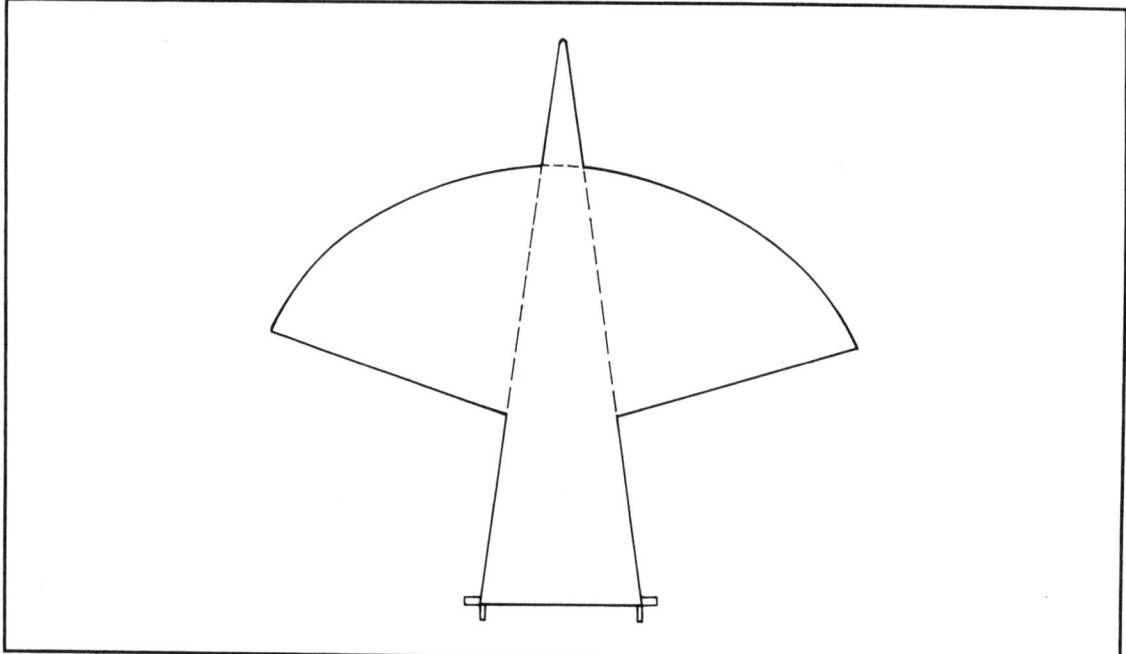

Fig. 6-161. Bird kite.

upper end for a V joint and make a groove for a string lashing, as shown in Fig. 6-163.

Measure and mark the cross points for joints on the sticks, as shown in Fig. 6-162. Glue the sticks and lash them together with string to the pattern shown. Tie a guideline string across the two longitudinal sticks 19 inches from the upper ends. Use the string to bow the arch stick, as shown in Fig. 6-163. The string also serves as a guideline string. Attach the strings to the ends of the arch stick by wrapping the string around the stick and passing it through the notches. Add lashing strings around the ends of the stick on each side of the guideline string where it passes through the notches.

Covering Material

Use paper, plastic film, or cloth fabric as a cover. For best performance, keep the covering material as light as possible while maintaining adequate strength. Mark the pattern shown in Fig. 6-164 on the covering material. The kite frame can be placed over the covering material to use as a pattern.

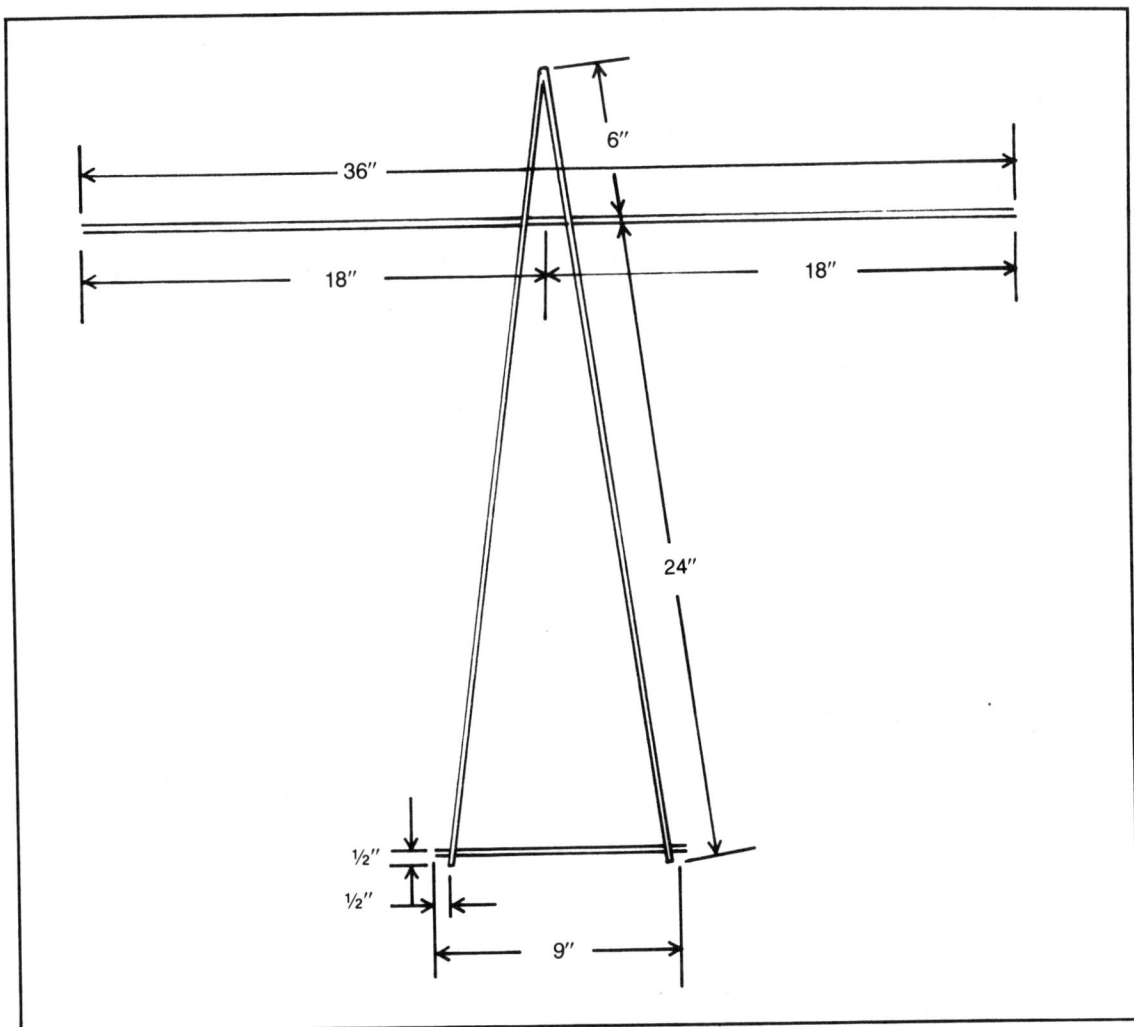

Fig. 6-162. Pattern for sticks for bird kite.

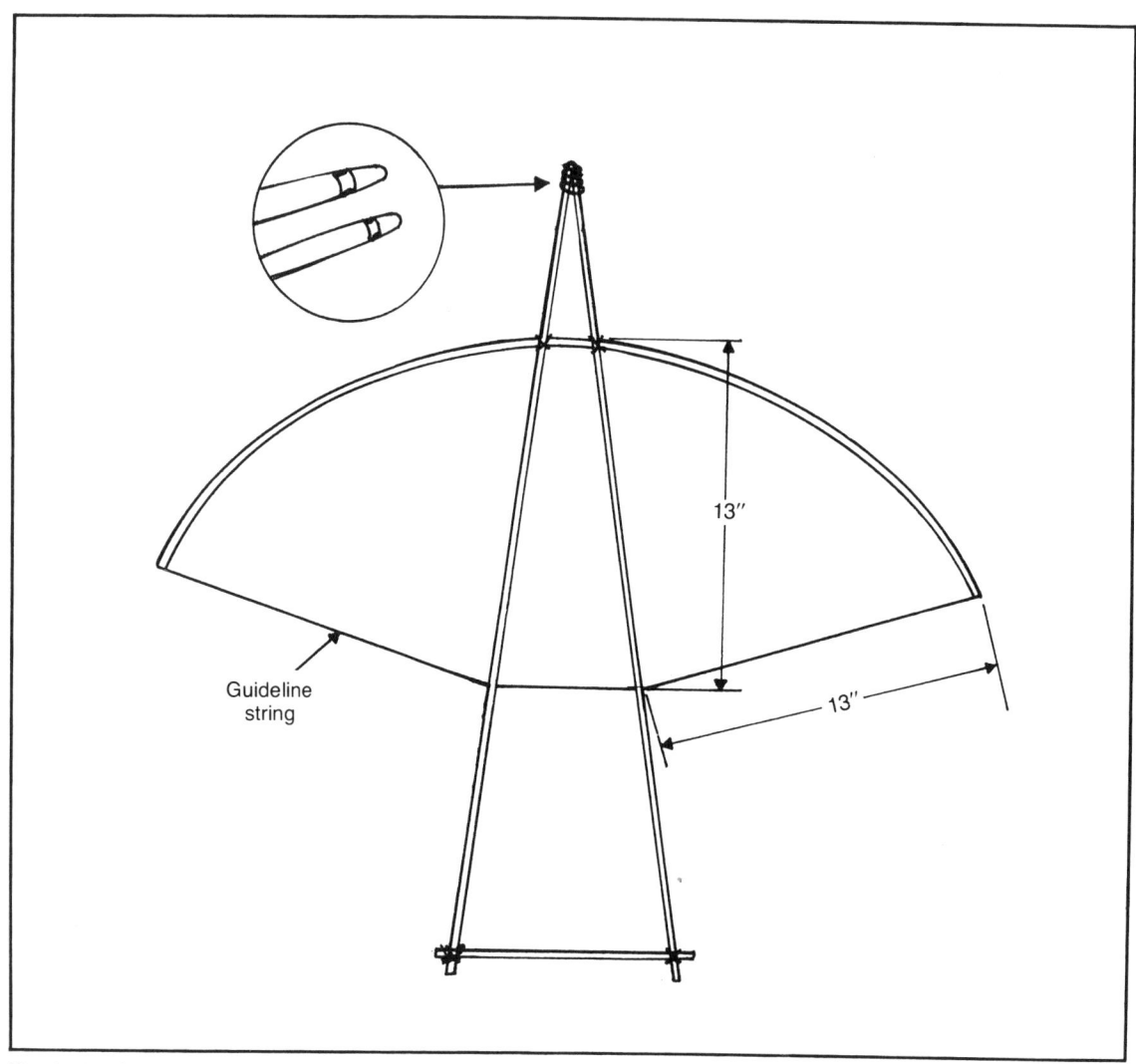

Fig. 6-163. Guideline string attachments. Detail shows tapers and grooves at upper ends of longitudinal sticks.

Use scissors to cut the covering material to the pattern. Methods for joining covering material to form the sleeves will depend on the covering material used (see Chapter 5). Install the cover to the kite frame with the frame sticks and guideline string passing through sleeves in the covering material.

Bow String

The bird kite can be used with or without a bow. The arch stick can be bowed by adding a bow string between the ends.

Bridle

A three-string bridle can be used, as shown in Fig. 6-165. The upper attachment is to the center of the arch stick, with the string passing through a small hole in the covering material, which is reinforced with tape or by other means. The lower attachments are to the longitudinal sticks at the attachments of the guideline string. The string passes through small reinforced holes in the covering material. The other ends of the strings can be tied in a loop or to a small plastic ring. The bridle ring allows easy adjustment of the length of the bridle strings.

Tail

The bird kite requires a tail for adequate flying stability. Two tails can be used, as shown in Fig. 6-165. An alternate method is to use a wide tail with a single attachment, as shown in Fig. 6-166.

Construction of tails is detailed in Chapter 5. The length and weight of the tail required will depend on the wind conditions and other factors. Try the kite first with a short tail. If the kite loops or spins uncontrollably, add more tail. Use the minimum amount of tail required to give the kite good stability.

Variations

The bird kite can be constructed in a range of sizes from 1 foot or less in length to 6 feet or more in length by keeping the proportions the same. As a general rule, you will need to reduce the weight of the smaller sizes by using proportionally smaller sticks and lighter weight covering material. Use larger sticks and heavier covering material for larger sizes.

There are many other possible constructions of bird kites, such as shown in Fig. 6-167 and Fig.

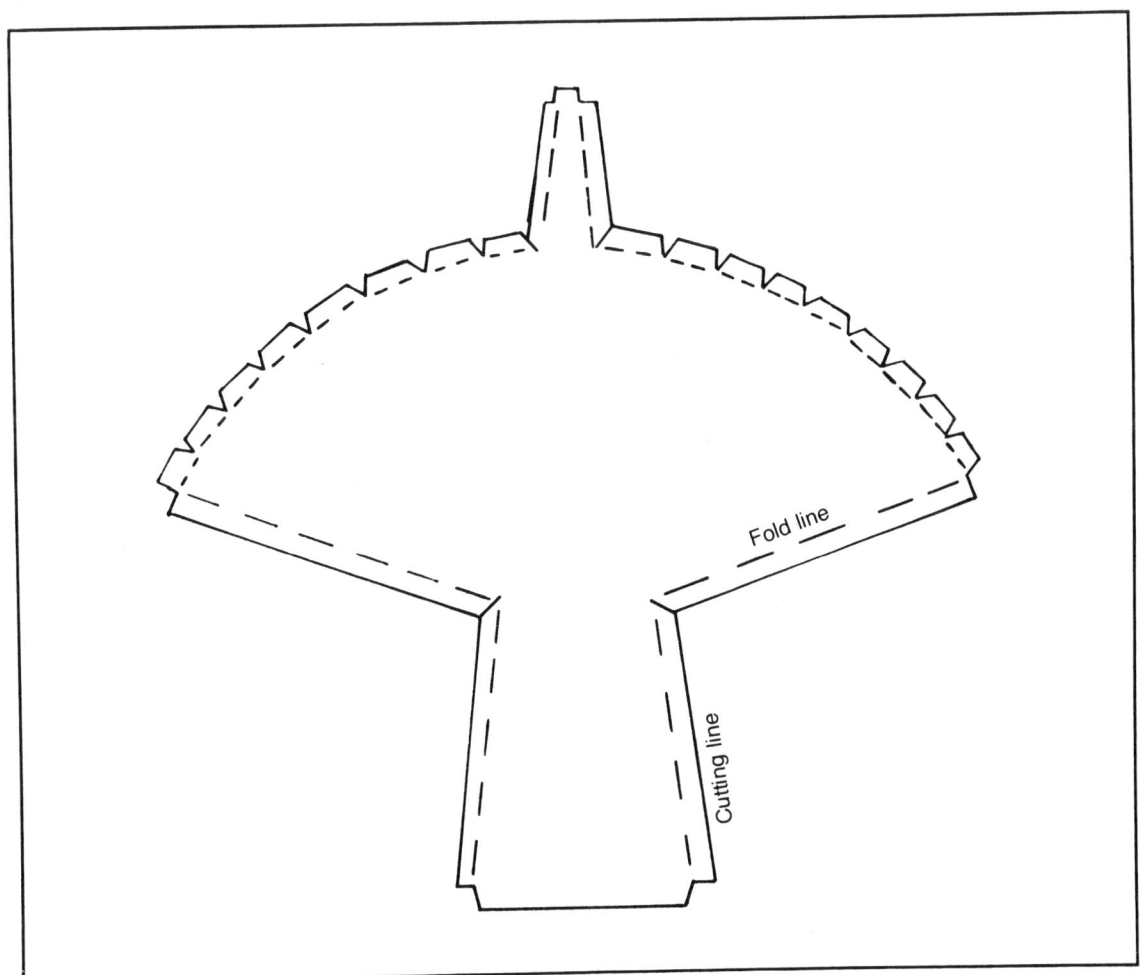

Fig. 6-164. Pattern for covering material.

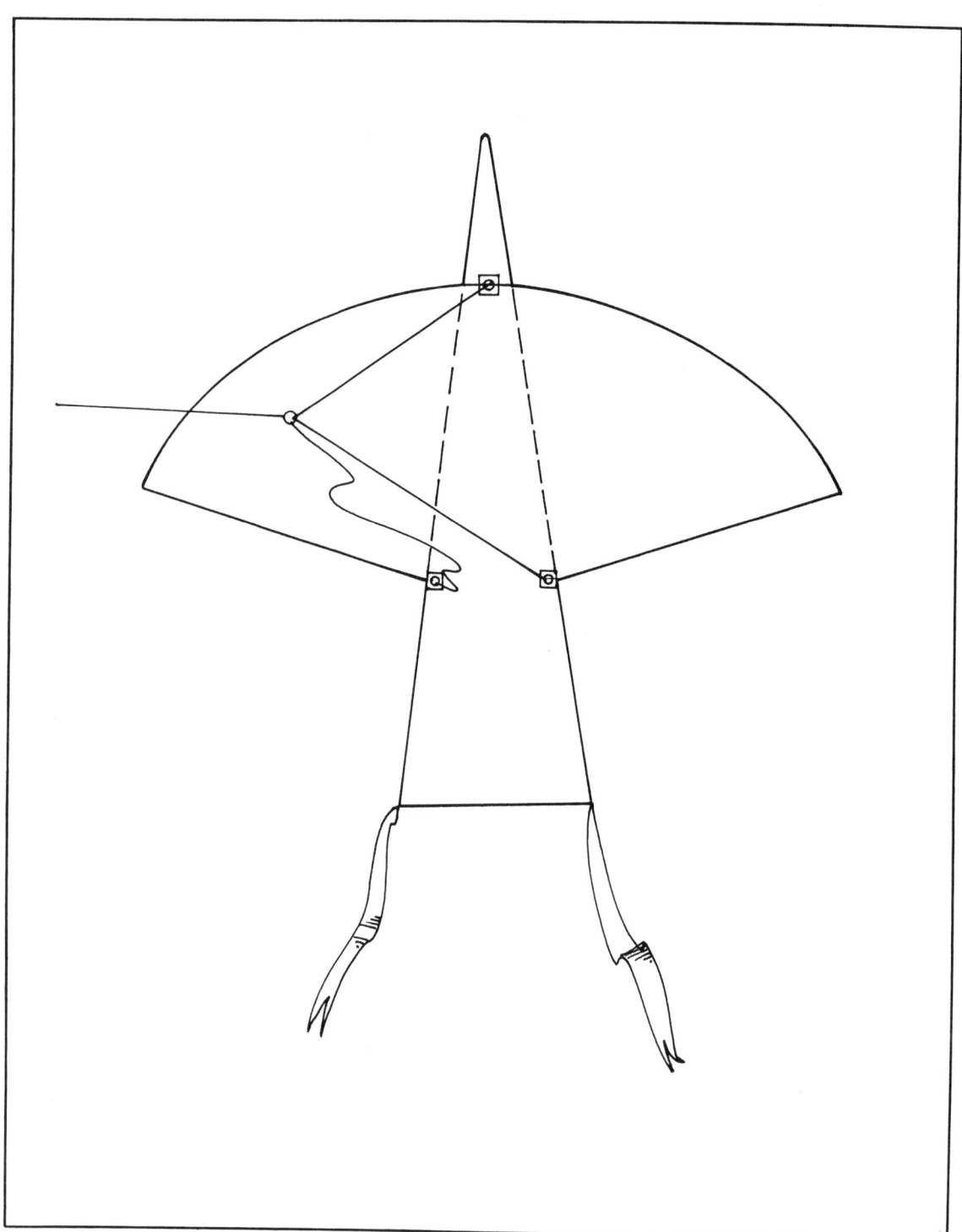

Fig. 6-165. Bridle and two-tail attachments.

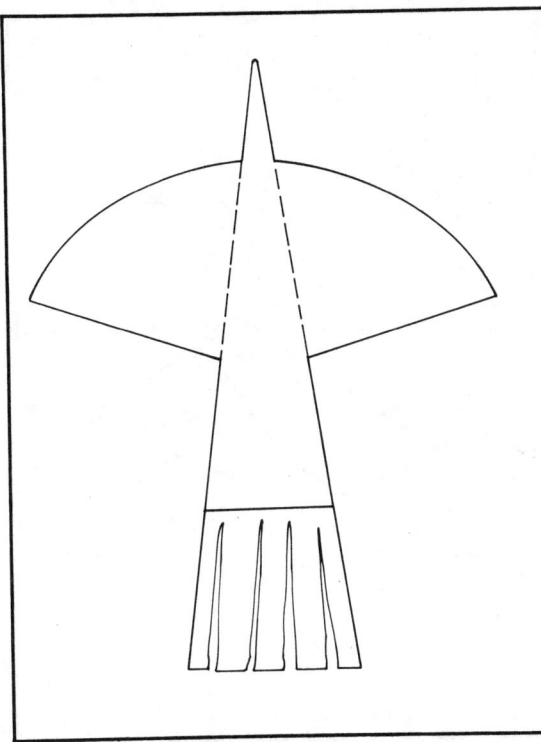

Fig. 6-166. Use of wide tail with single attachment.

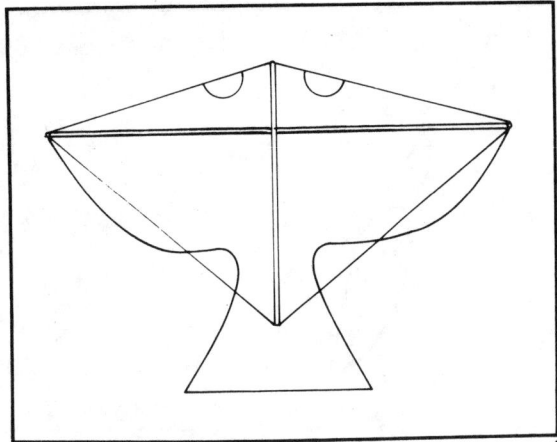

Fig. 6-167. Variation of bird kite.

6-168. Some flat or bowed bird kites even have heads shaped from Styrofoam or other lightweight material.

DRAGON, SERPENT, OR SNAKE KITE

A dragon, serpent, or snake kite is shown in Fig. 6-169. A long wide tail is usually on this type of kite.

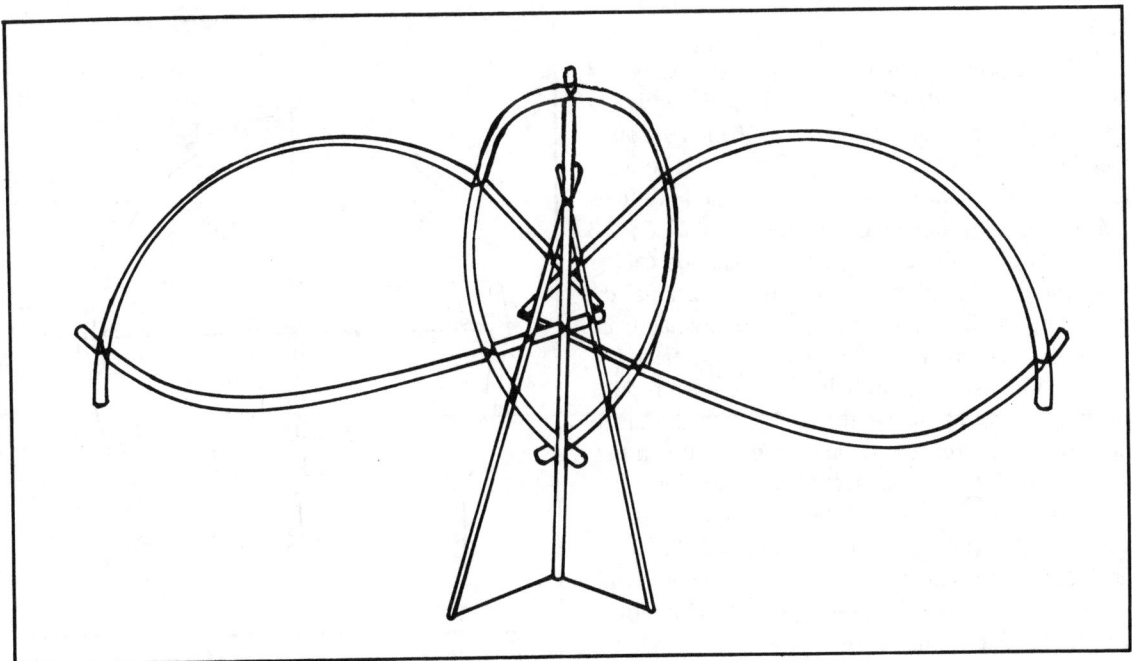

Fig. 6-168. Variation of bird kite.

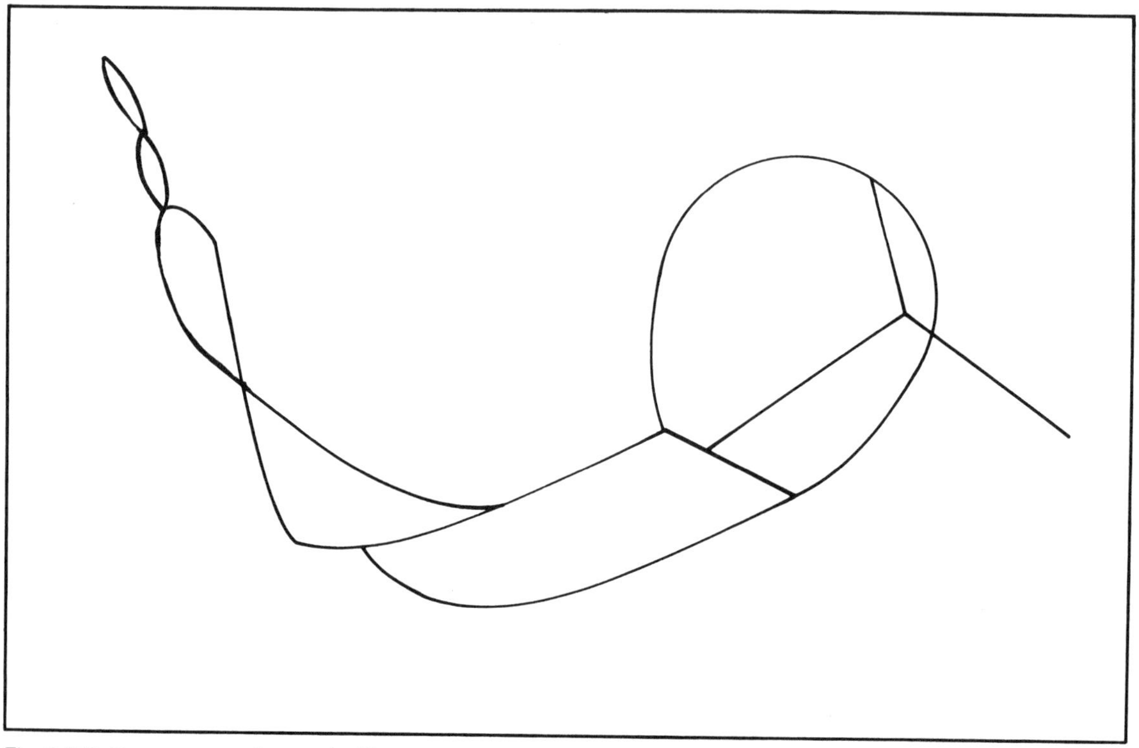

Fig. 6-169. Dragon, serpent, or snake kite.

Frame

Three sticks are used for making the frame, as shown in Fig. 6-170. Wooden sticks with rectangular cross sections of 3/16 inch by 5/16 inch or round wooden dowels of 3/16-inch diameter can be used for the longitudinal and cross sticks. The longitudinal stick is 16 inches long, and the cross stick is 18 inches long. A 36-inch long strip of bamboo can be used for the curved stick. The cross sectional dimensions of the sticks can vary somewhat from these dimensions and still give good results. If the kite is to be used only in light airs, you can reduce the cross sectional size of the sticks. If the kite is to be flown in extremely strong winds, you can use sticks with larger cross sectional dimensions.

Mark the patterns for the joints on the sticks and assemble sticks, as shown in Fig. 6-170, gluing and lashing the joints with string. A guideline string is attached between the lower end of the longitudinal stick and the ends of the curved stick, as shown in Fig. 6-171.

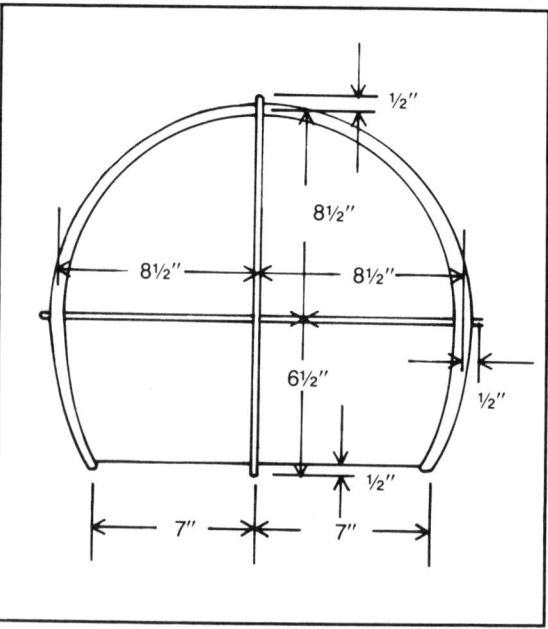

Fig. 6-170. Pattern for sticks for dragon, serpent, or snake kite.

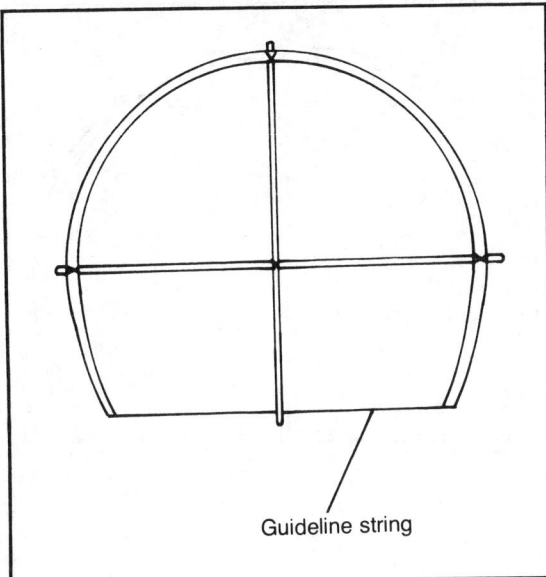

Fig. 6-171. Guideline string.

Covering Material

Paper, plastic film, or fabric can be used to cover the kite, as desired. The tail is generally an extension of the covering material. For best performance, the covering material should be of the lightest weight that is compatible with adequate strength. Mark the pattern shown in Fig. 6-172 on the covering material. The kite frame can be placed over the covering material as a pattern.

Using scissors, cut the covering material to the pattern. Methods for joining covering material to form the sleeves depends on the particular covering material used (see Chapter 5). Generally, paper is glued, fabric material is sewn, and plastic is glued, heat sealed or taped.

Regardless of the covering material used, fix it to the kite frame with the frame sticks passing through sleeves in the covering material. If the tail is an extension of the covering material, a separate sleeve can be attached to it over the guideline string, as shown in Fig. 6-173.

Bridle

A two-string bridle can be used, as shown in

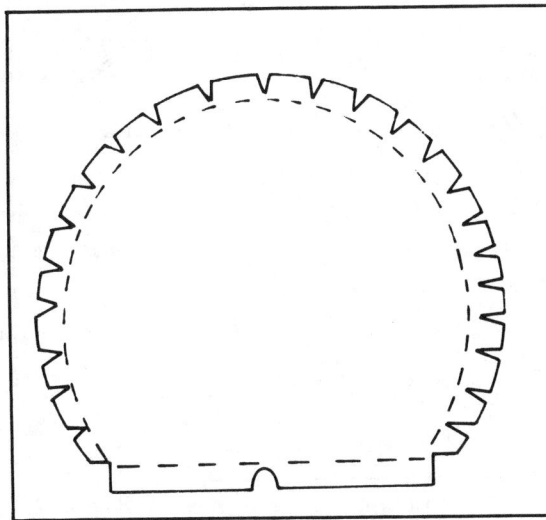

Fig. 6-172. Pattern for covering material.

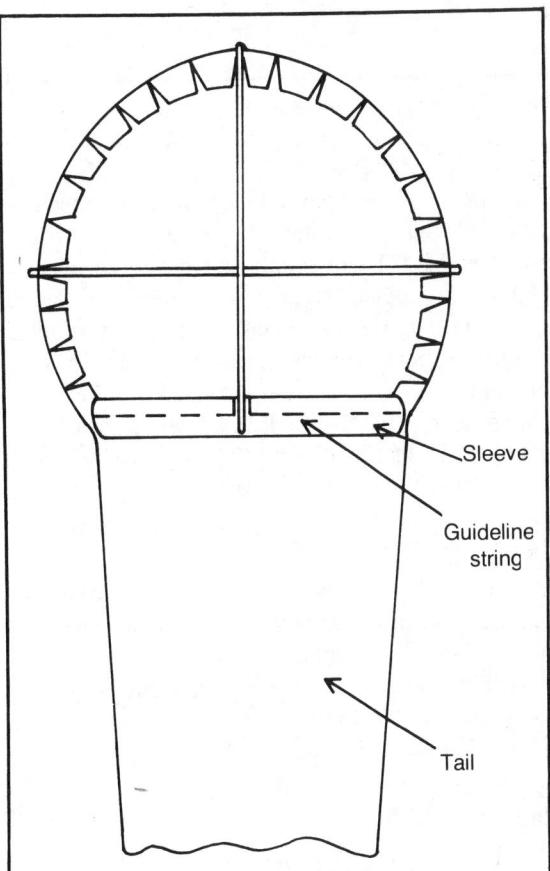

Fig. 6-173. Sleeve is attached over guideline string.

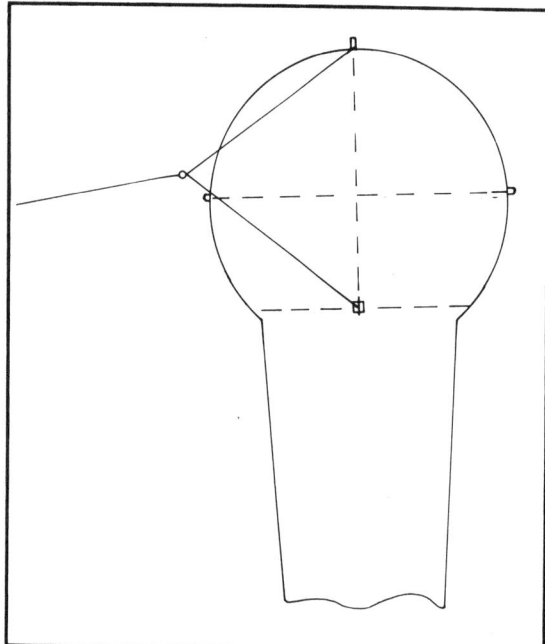

Fig. 6-174. Bridle attachments.

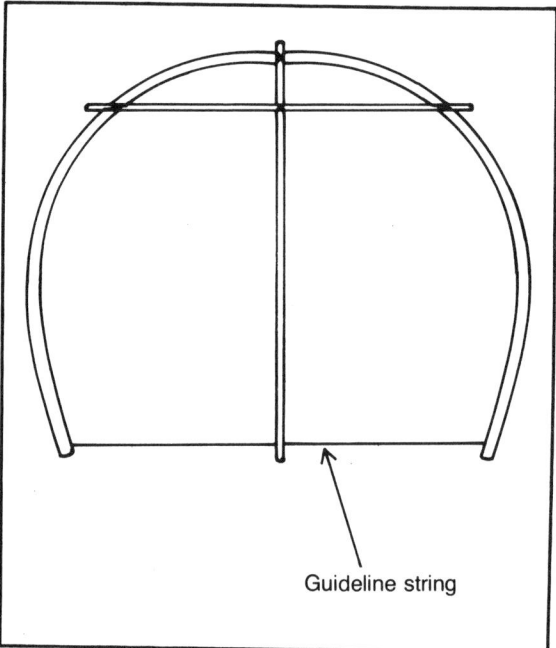

Fig. 6-175. Variation in framing arrangement for dragon, serpent, or snake kite.

Fig. 6-174. The upper attachment is to the longitudinal stick at the point where the curved stick is attached to it. The lower attachment is to the aft end of the longitudinal stick at the point where the guideline string is tied. The string passes through a small hole in the covering material, which is reinforced with tape or by other means. The other ends of the strings can be tied in a loop or to a small plastic ring. The bridle ring allows easy adjustment of the length of the bridle strings.

Tail

The tail is usually an extension of the covering material, as detailed above, or a separate piece of material that is attached to the lower portion of the covering material. Wide and extremely long tails (sometimes 30 feet or more in length) can be used. The tails usually taper.

Variations

The dragon, serpent, or snake kite can be constructed in a range of sizes, using longitudinal sticks from 1 foot or less in length to 3 feet or more in length by keeping the proportions the same. As a general rule, you will need to reduce the weight of the smaller sizes by using proportionally smaller

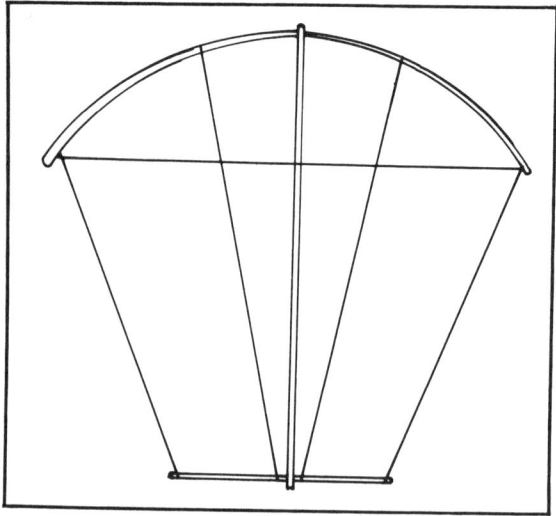

Fig. 6-176. Variation in framing arrangement for dragon, serpent, or snake kite.

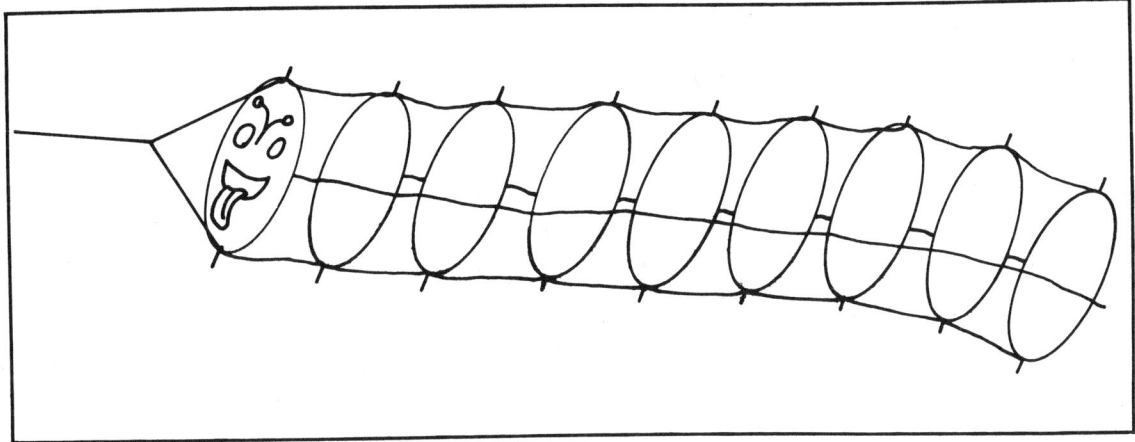

Fig. 6-177. Centipede or caterpillar kite.

CENTIPEDE OR CATERPILLAR KITE

The centipede or caterpillar kite, shown in Fig. 6-177, is basically a series of flat kites linked together with strings. The kite can be used with or without decorative tails. The same basic kite can be either a centipede or caterpillar, depending on how it is painted and decorated.

Frame

Eight separate ring frames are required for making the centipede or caterpillar kite shown. Each frame is the same and requires three sticks, as shown in Fig. 6-178. Bamboo sticks can be used. Since it is important to have the frames as light in weight as possible, you will want to use bamboo strips that have the smallest cross sectional size that is compatible with adequate strength. If the kite is to be used only in light airs, sticks of small cross sectional size can be used. If the kite is to be used in strong winds, the size of the sticks should be increased accordingly.

The longitudinal and cross sticks are 15 inches long. A 40-inch-long stick is used for making the 12-inch diameter circle.

To make a frame, mark the center point on the longitudinal and cross stick. Glue and bind the sticks together. Form a 12-inch diameter circle from a 40-inch-long strip of bamboo, as detailed in Chapter 5. Usually, the bamboo is heated over a candle flame for bending and forming the circle.

sticks and lighter weight covering material. You will need to use larger sticks and heavier covering material for the larger sizes.

A variety of other framing arrangements are possible, such as those shown in Figs. 6-175 and 6-176.

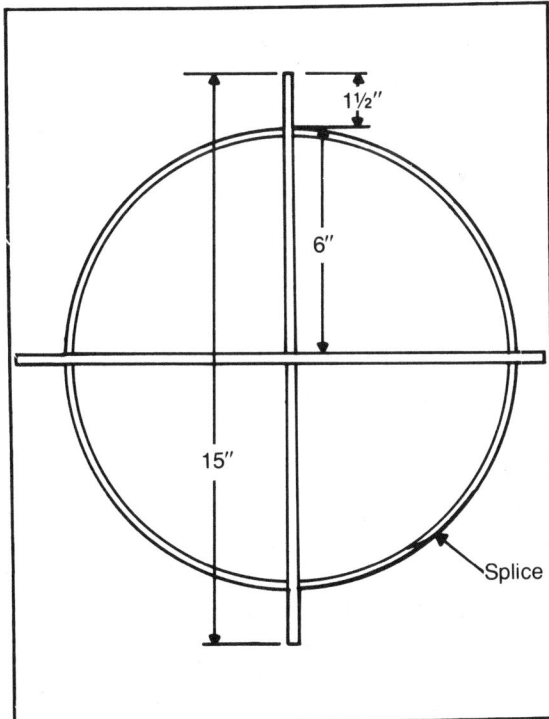

Fig. 6-178. Pattern for sticks for centipede or caterpillar kite.

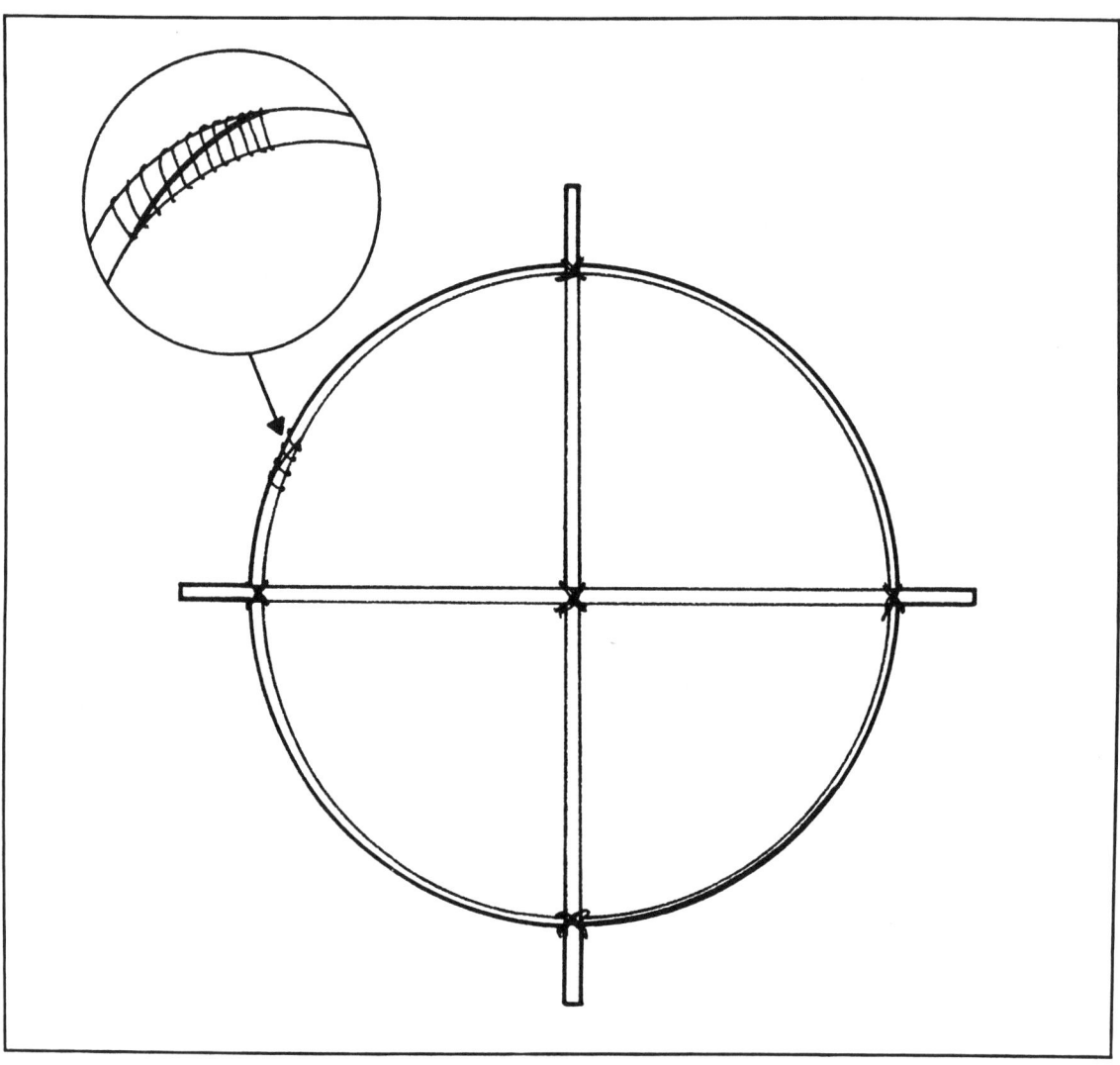

Fig. 6-179. Ends of bamboo strips are spliced together to form ring and ring is glued and lashed to longitudinal and cross sticks.

Splice the ends together as shown in Fig. 6-179. Glue the joint and lash it with string. Glue the ring and lash it with strings to the longitudinal and cross sticks, as shown in Fig. 6-179.

A total of eight frames are required to make the kite shown.

Covering Material

Paper, plastic film, or cloth fabric can be used for covering the kite, as desired. For best performance, the covering material should be of the lightest weight that is compatible with adequate strength. A separate cover is required for each frame. For each frame, mark the pattern shown in Fig. 6-180 on the covering material. You will need eight of these. The kite frame can be placed over the covering material to use as a pattern.

Use scissors to cut the covering material to the pattern lines. Methods for joining covering material to form the sleeves depends on the particular cov-

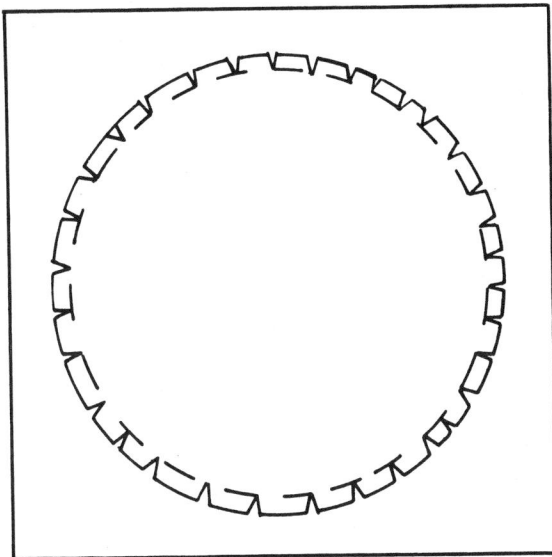

Fig. 6-180. Pattern for covering material.

ering material used (see Chapter 5). Generally, paper is glued, fabric material is sewn, and plastic is glued, heat-sealed, or taped.

Regardless of the covering material used, install the covers to the frames with the circle sticks passing through the sleeves. Cover all eight frames in the same manner. Different colored materials can be used.

Linking Strings

The frames are linked together 10 inches apart, on four strings, as shown in Fig. 6-181. Tie the strings to the longitudinal and cross sticks outside the ring frames, as shown.

Bridle

A two-string bridle can be used, as shown in Fig. 6-182. The bridle attaches to the forward or face kite. The upper attachment is to the longitudinal stick above the upper circle stick attachment. The lower attachment is to the longitudinal stick below the circle stick attachment. The other ends of the strings can be tied in a loop or to a small plastic ring. The bridle ring allows easy adjustment of the length of the bridle strings.

Tail

There are a number of possibilities for adding tails. A single tail can be added to the last circle form, as shown in Fig. 6-182. Small decorative tails or streamers are frequently attached to the ends of

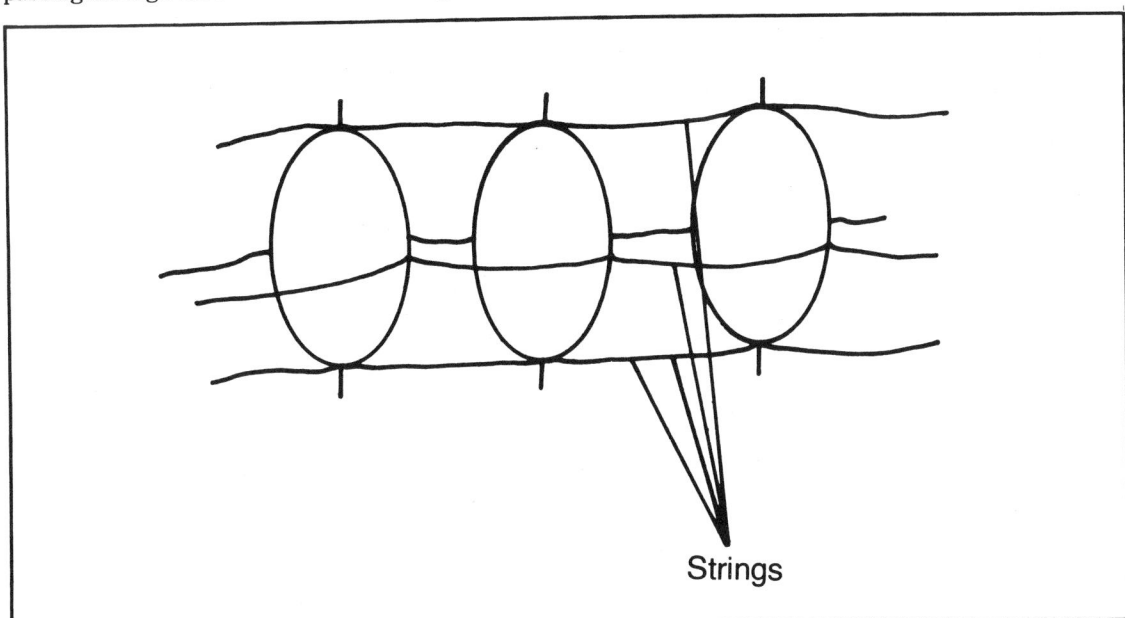

Fig. 6-181. Rings are linked together with strings.

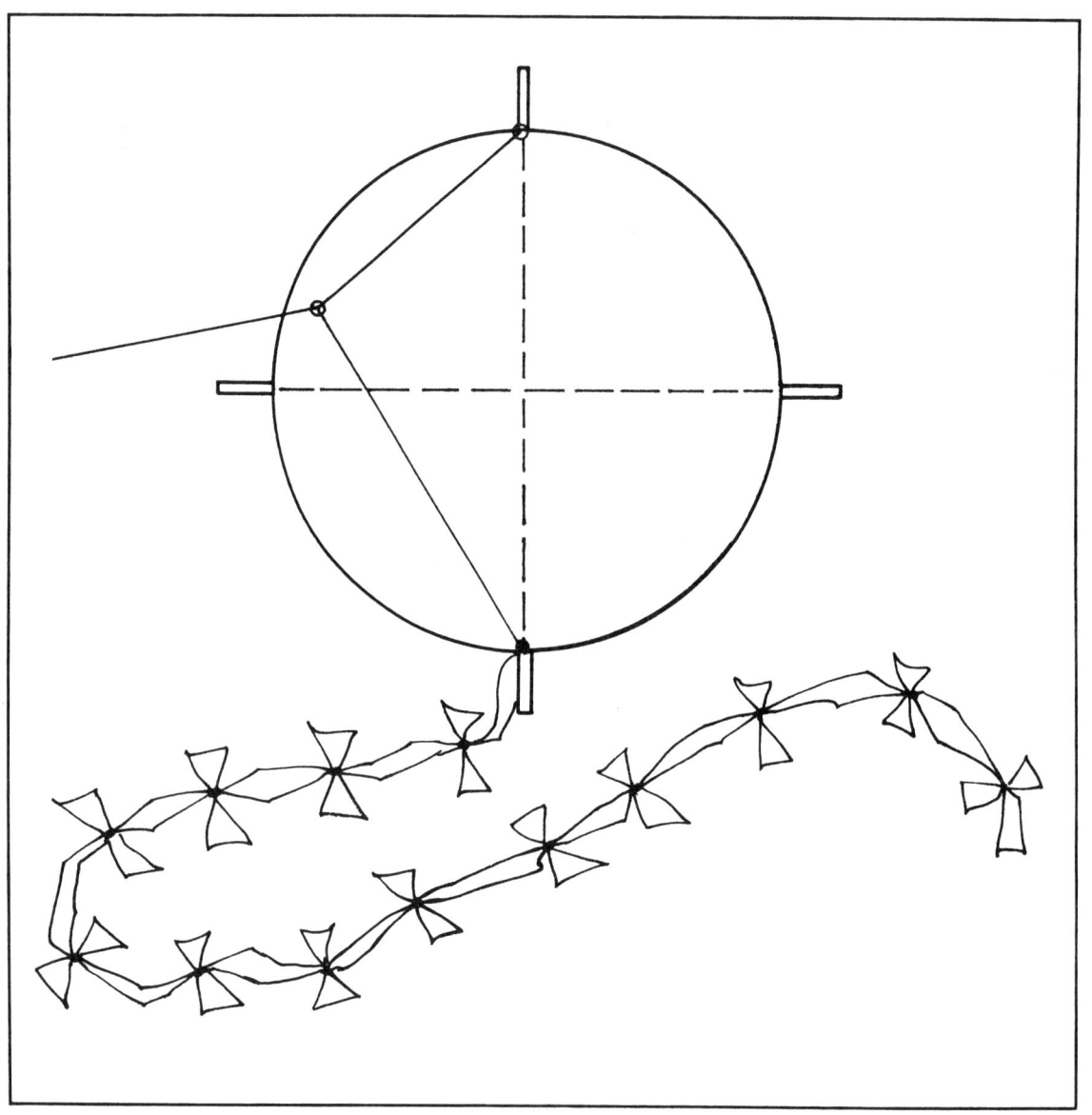

Fig. 6-182. Bridle attachments. Single tail is attached to last ring.

the cross sticks of each frame, as shown in Fig. 6-183.

The construction of tails is detailed in Chapter 5.

Variations

The centipede or caterpillar kite can be constructed in a range of sizes with the circles from 6 inches or less in diameter to 3 feet or more in diameter. As a general rule, you will need to reduce the weight of the smaller sizes by using proportionally smaller sticks and lighter weight covering material. You will need to use larger sticks and heavier covering material for the larger sizes.

There are many possible variations for the centipede and caterpillar kites. The number of rings

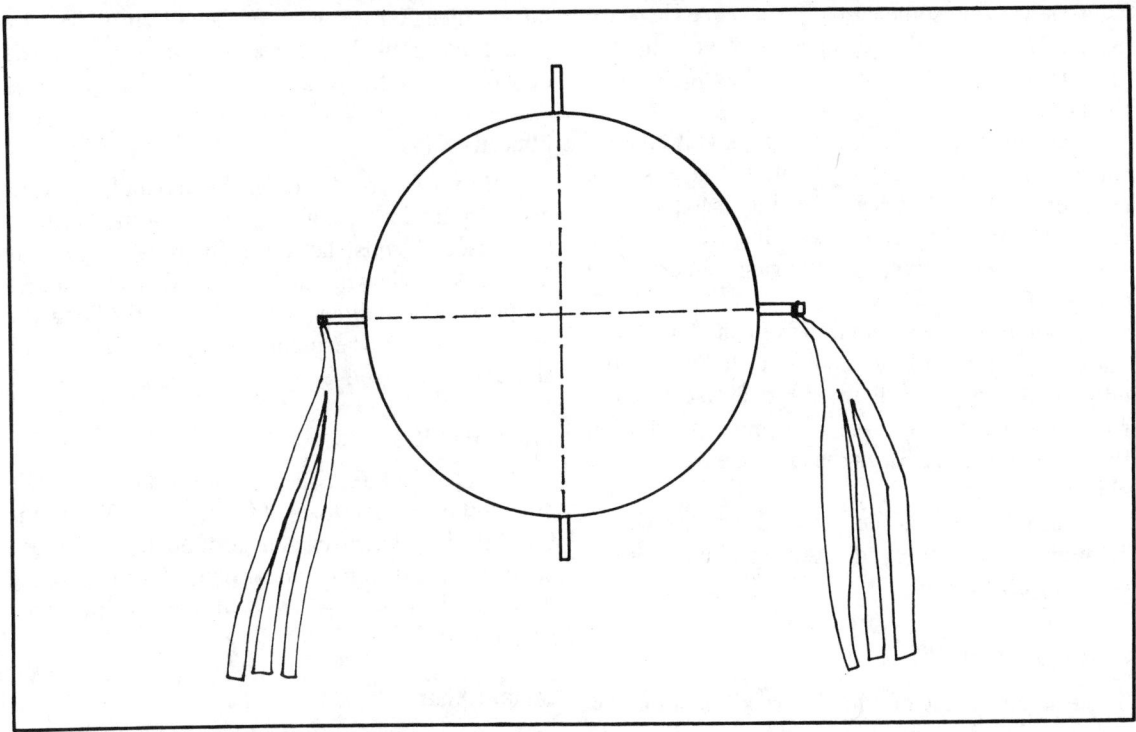
Fig. 6-183. Small decorative streamers attached to ends of cross sticks.

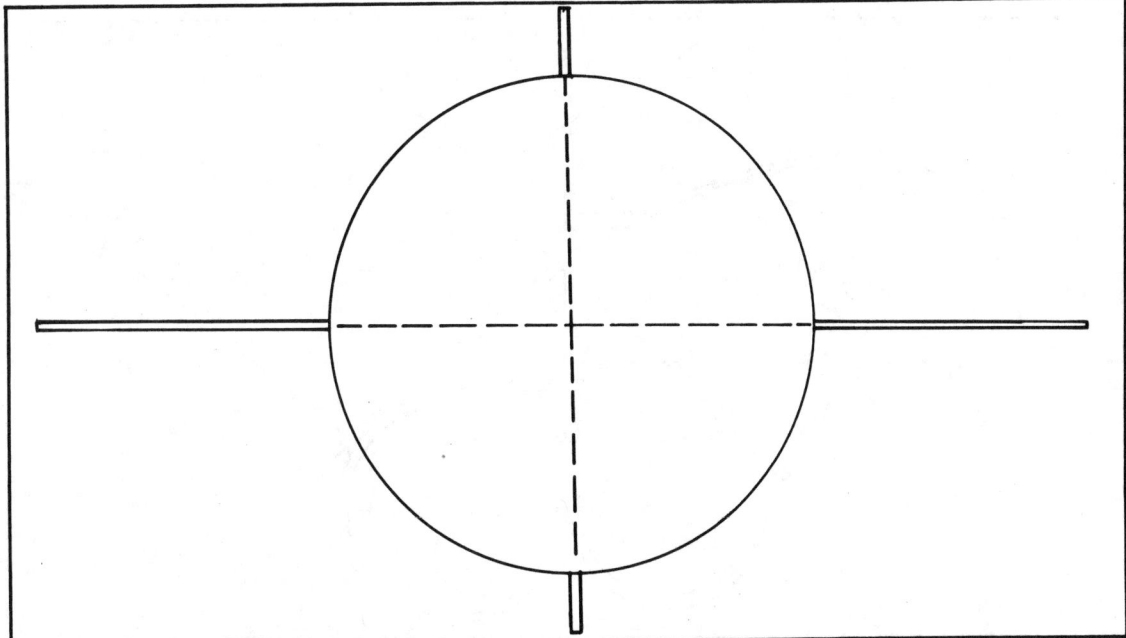
Fig. 6-184. Rings with extended cross sticks.

211

used can vary. In some cases, 30 or more rings are used to form a kite. Keep in mind, however, that the more rings used, the more difficult it will be to fly the kite.

A popular variation uses progressively smaller ring diameters to form a kite, with the largest ring used for the head. Another possibility is to place the rings progressively closer together. This works well when progressively smaller ring diameters are also used.

Another popular variation is to use long cross sticks with the ends extending well beyond the edges of the rings, as shown in Fig. 6-184. Decorative tails or streamers are frequently attached to these. Longitudinal sticks can also be extended in a similar manner.

Faces and other decorations are frequently painted on centipede and caterpillar kites, as detailed in Chapter 9.

OTHER FIGURE KITES

A large variety of other figure kites of the flat and bowed variety are also possible, including butterfly, dragonfly, lantern, house, tree, and human forms. Ideas for a variety of these figure kites are presented below. You may also want to create some new ones of your own.

Butterfly Kites

Butterfly kites have long been popular. A variety of methods, such as shown in Fig. 6-185, have been used to construct butterfly kites. The frame for the kite shown can be formed from bamboo strips to desired dimensions. Much of the beauty of butterfly kites is a result of the way they are painted and decorated (see Chapter 9).

Dragonfly Kites

Dragonfly kites, such as shown in Fig. 6-186, are another popular form of figure kites. The frame for the kite shown can be formed from bamboo strips to desired dimensions. Beautiful painting and decoration adds much to a dragonfly kite (see Chapter 9).

Lantern Kites

Lantern kites, such as shown in Fig. 6-187, are a popular form of a figure kite of a man-made object.

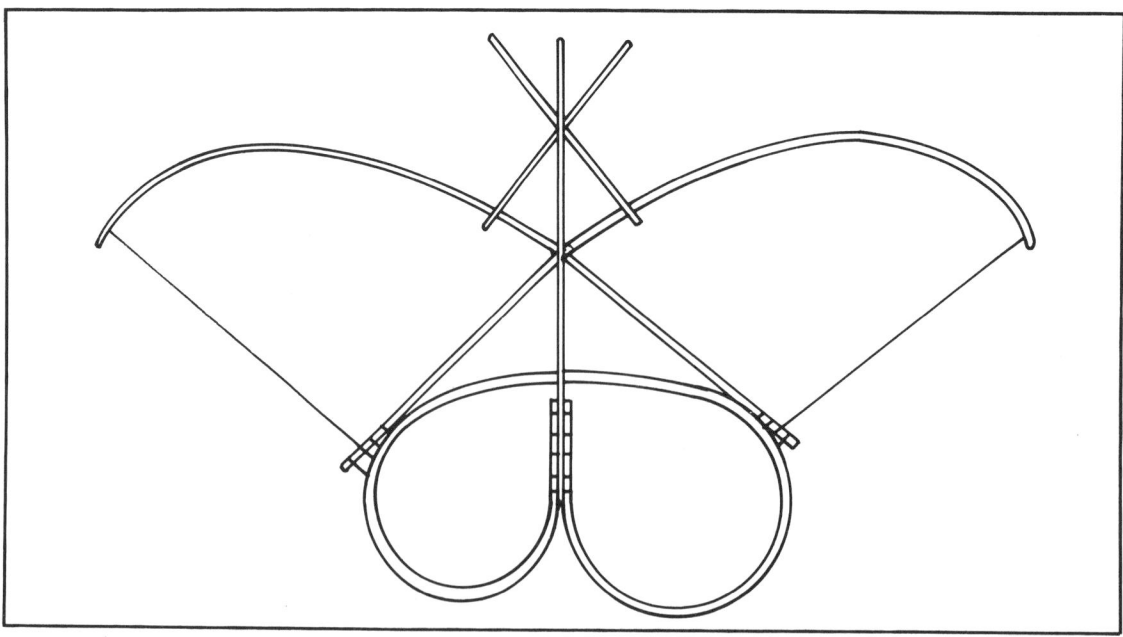

Fig. 6-185. Butterfly kite.

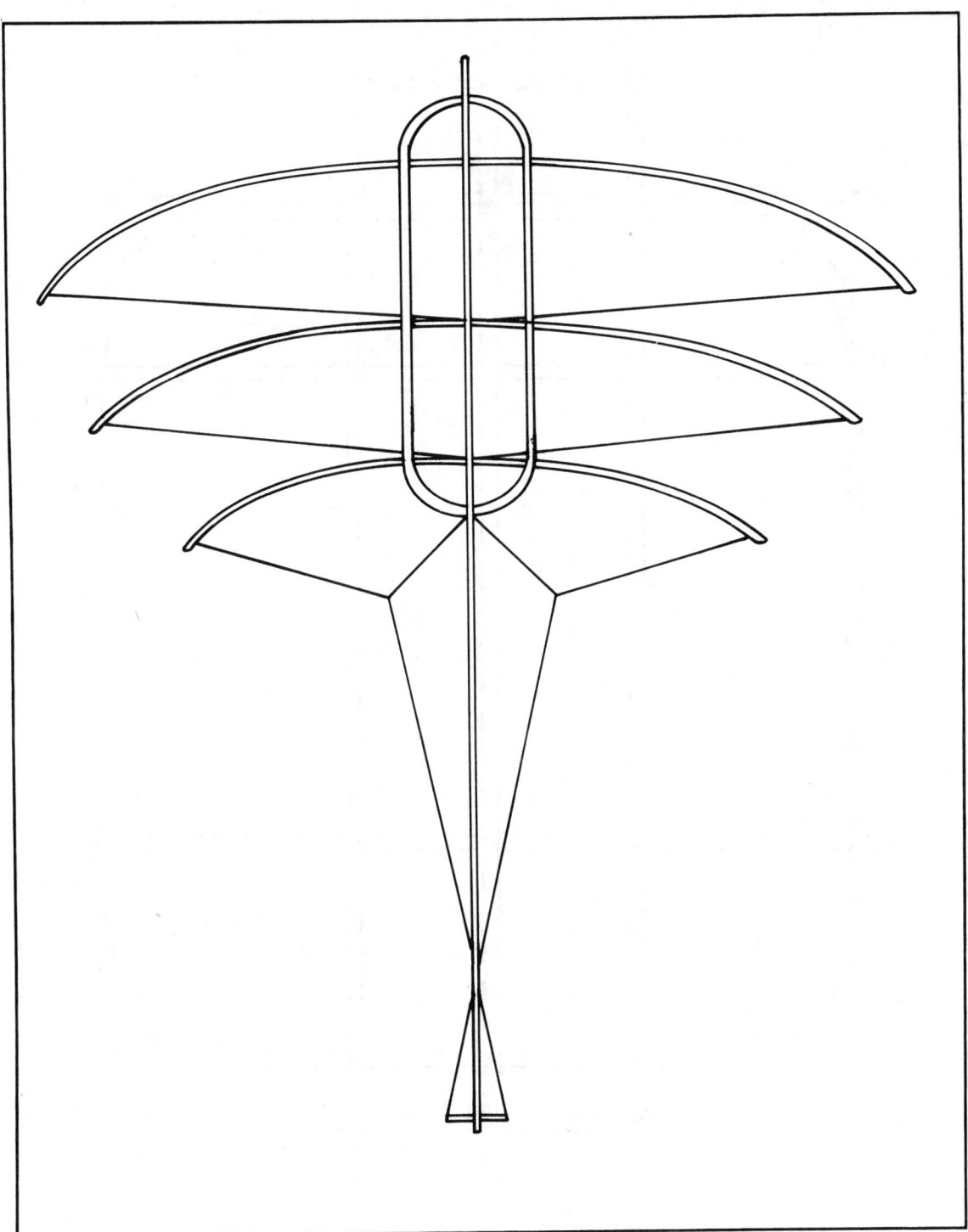

Fig. 6-186. Dragonfly kite.

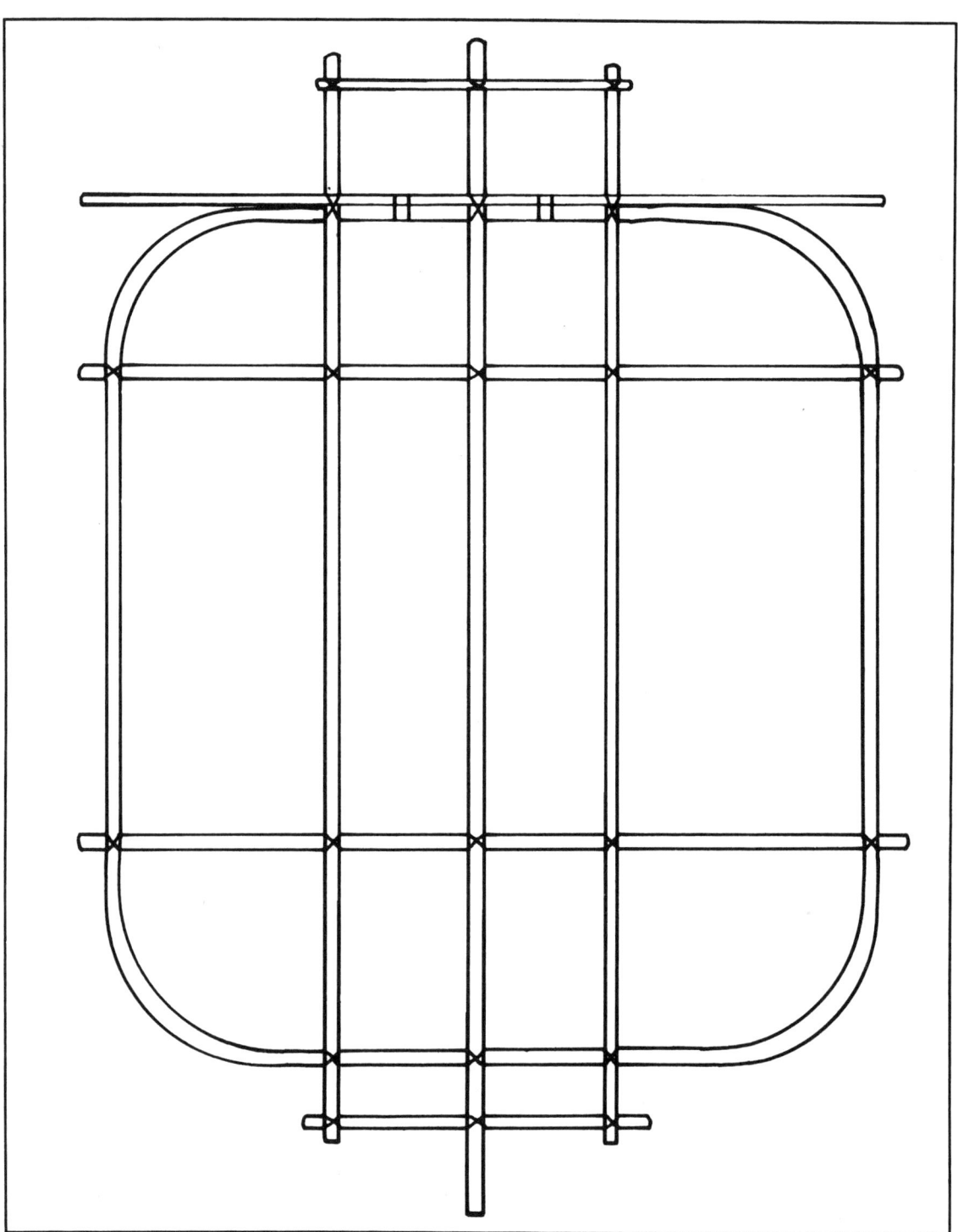

Fig. 6-187. Lantern kite.

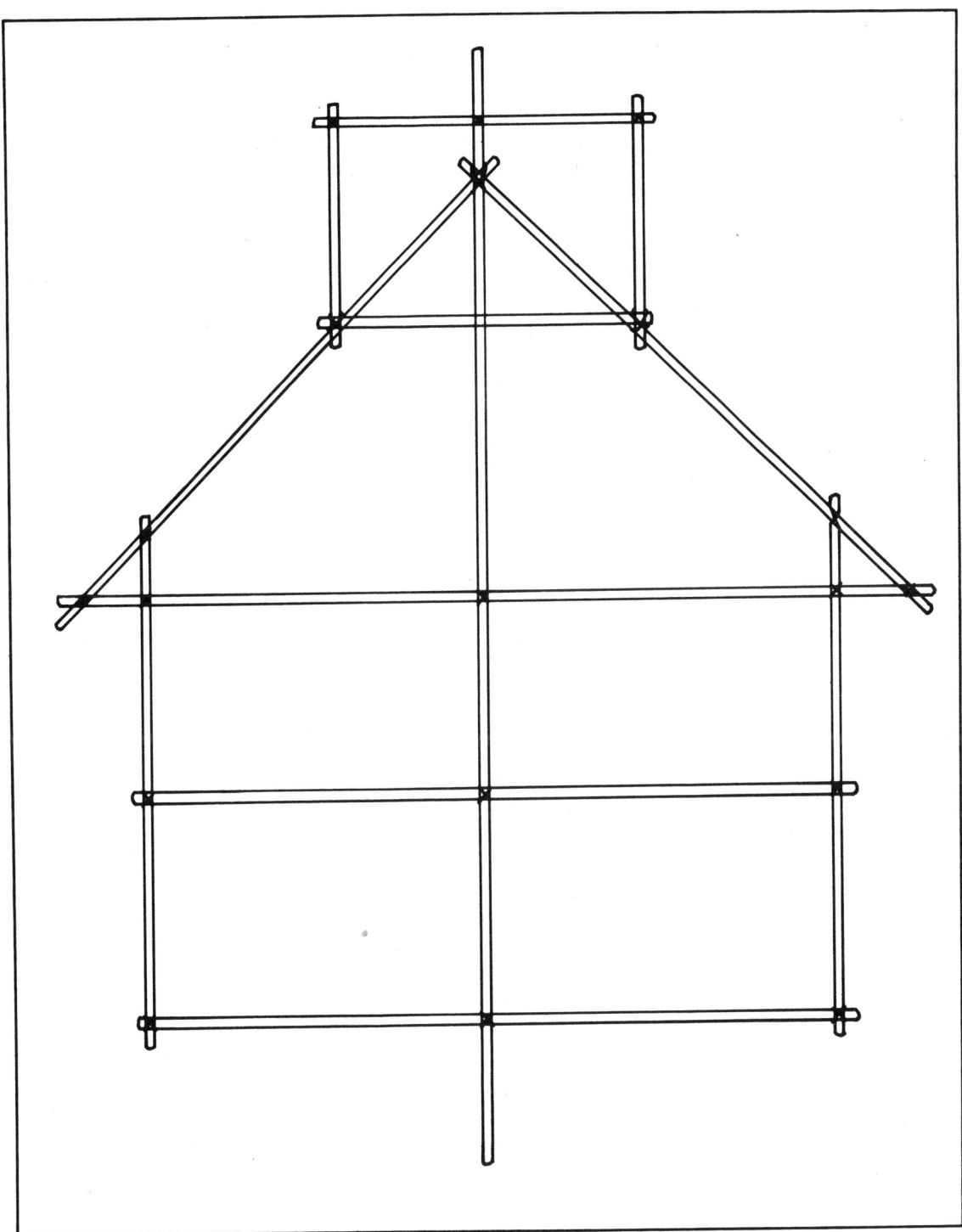

Fig. 6-188. House kite.

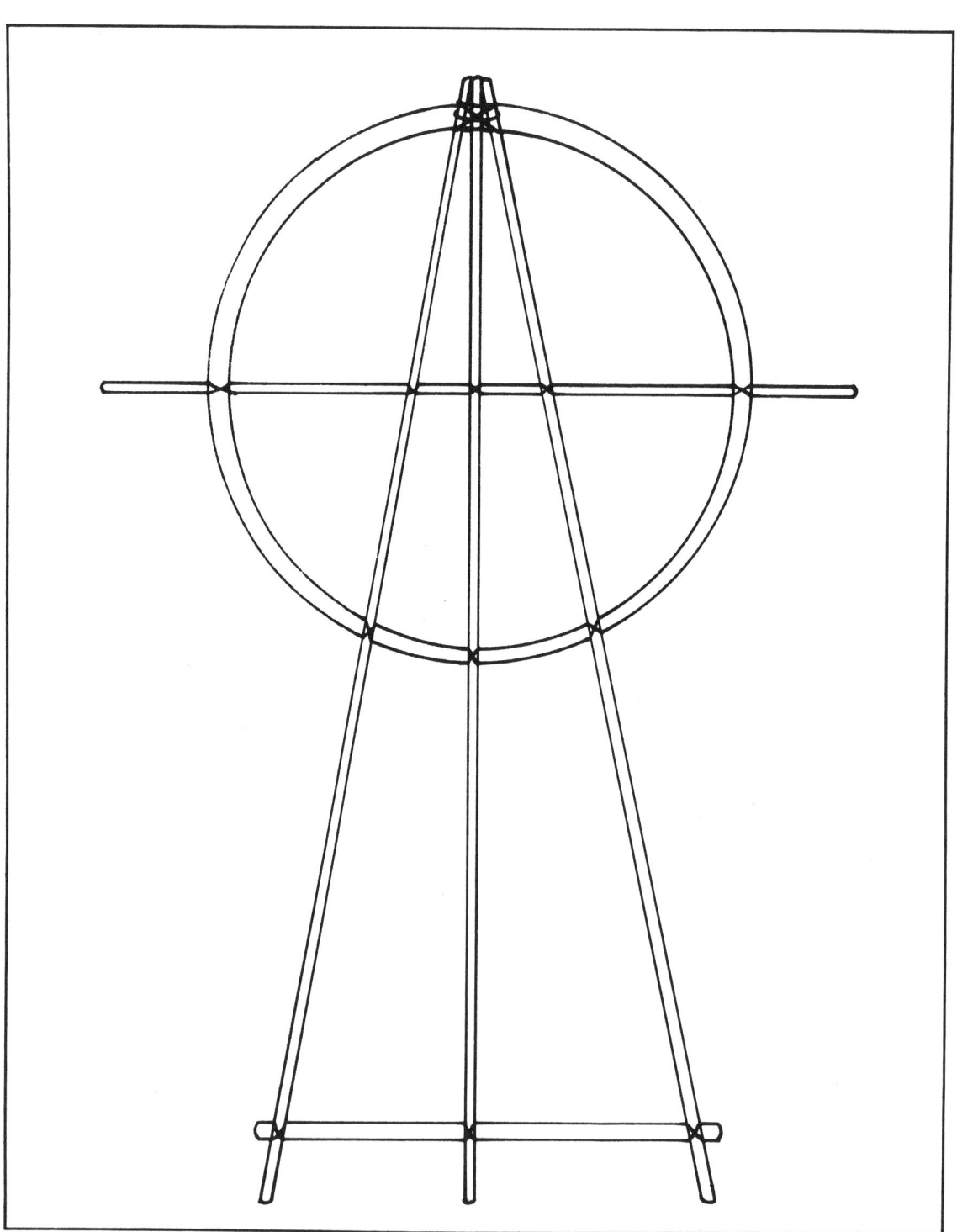

Fig. 6-189. Tree kite.

Fig. 6-190. Human-form kite.

The frame for the kite shown can be formed from bamboo strips to desired dimensions. Much of the beauty of lantern kites is a result of the way they are painted and decorated (see Chapter 9).

House Kites

House kites (Fig. 6-188) are another popular form of a figure kite of a man-made object. The frame from the kite shown can be formed from bamboo strips to desired dimensions. Doors and windows can be painted on the cover surface.

Tree Kites

Tree kites are a popular form of figure kites (Fig. 6-189). The frame for the kite shown can be formed from bamboo strips to desired dimensions. Experiment with paints and decorations to create a beautiful tree kite.

Human-Form Kites

Human-form kites, as shown in Fig. 6-190, are popular figure kites. The frame for the kite can be formed to desired dimensions from bamboo strips. The tail flap is an extension of the covering material and is used to paint in the lower legs and feet. Much of the appeal of these kites is a result of the way they are painted (see Chapter 9). The kites can be males or females, as desired, by painting different forms on the covering material. There are many possible variations for human-form kites.

Chapter 7

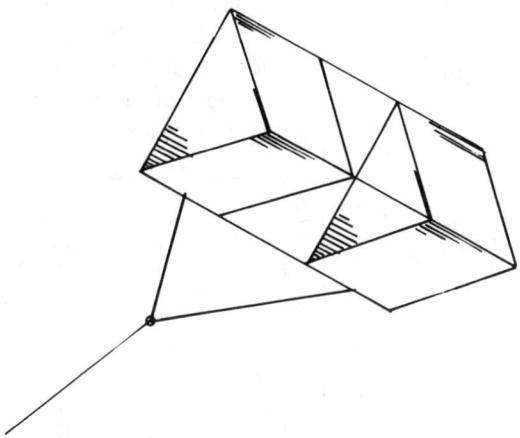

Cellular Kites

In this chapter, the construction of a number of box and other cellular kites is detailed. Cellular kites can add a new dimension to your kite building and designing skills.

BASIC BOX KITE

A basic box kite is shown in Fig. 7-1. This style of kite is extremely popular and is also the basis for a number of variations of the cellular kites detailed later. The basic box kite can be flown without a tail, which is one of the reasons for its popularity.

Frame

Construction of the frame is shown in Fig. 7-2. Four 36-inch-long wooden sticks with cross sectional dimensions of ¼ inch by ⅜ inch or ¼-inch wooden dowels are used for the longitudinal sticks. Four 17-inch-long wooden sticks with cross sectional dimensions of 3/16 inch by ½ inch are used for the cross sticks. The sticks can vary somewhat from these dimensions and still give satisfactory results. If the kite is to be used only in light airs, you may want to reduce the cross sectional size of the sticks. If the kite is to be flown in extremely strong winds, you may want to use sticks with larger cross sectional dimensions. Sticks of fiberglass, bamboo, and aluminum are other possibilities, as detailed in Chapter 5.

For descriptive purposes here, we'll assume that you will be using wooden sticks of either rectangular or round cross sectional shapes for the longitudinal sticks and the rectangular cross sectional shape for the cross sticks.

Notch the ends of the cross sticks to fit the longitudinal sticks, as shown in Fig. 7-3. Glue and bind the cross sticks together with string, as shown in Fig. 7-4. The cross frames are glued to the longitudinal sticks 5½ inches from each end of the longitudinal sticks, as shown. This completes the construction of the frame.

Covering Material

Paper, plastic film, or cloth fabric can be used to cover the kite, as desired. For best performance,

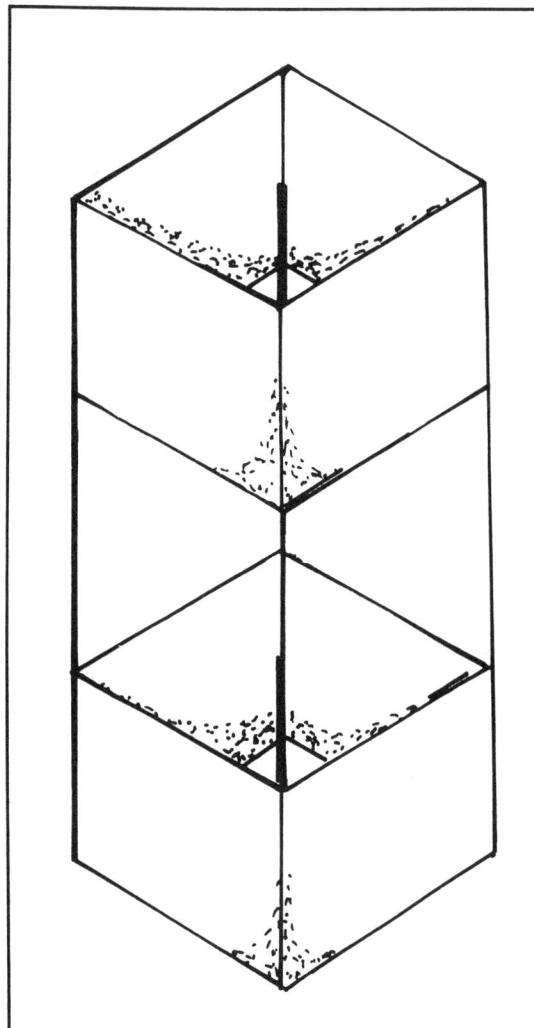

Fig. 7-1. Basic box kite.

Regardless of the covering material used, install the covers to the frames. Each section of covering material should have a hem at the top and bottom and form a loop that fits snugly around the longitudinal sticks. The covering material is usually also glued or otherwise attached to the longitudinal sticks. If desired, guideline strings can be used at the top and bottom of each section of covering material around the frames, with the guideline

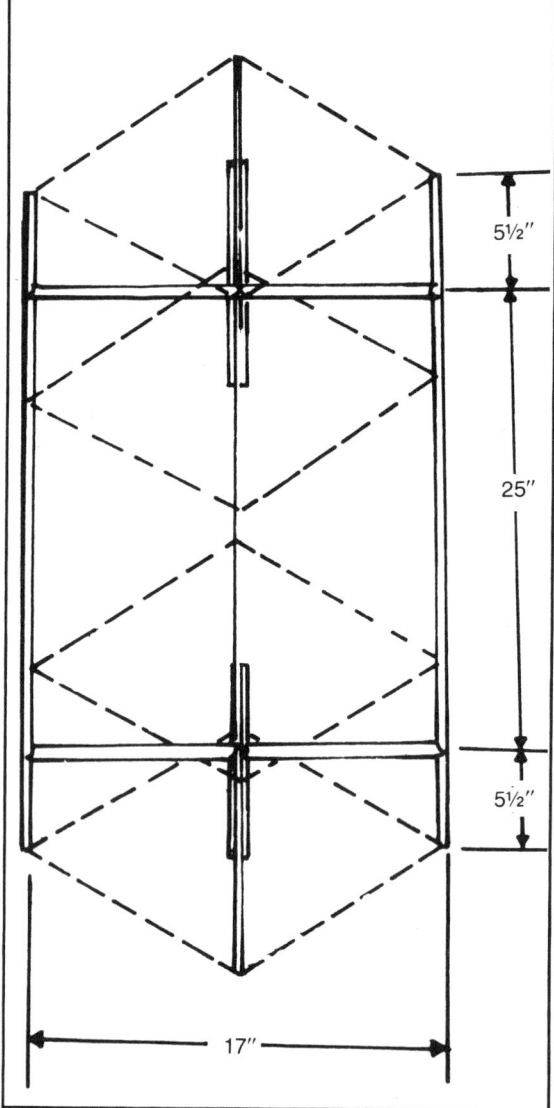

Fig. 7-2. Frame construction for basic box kite.

the covering material should be of the lightest weight that is compatible with adequate strength. Two separate covers are used. Mark the pattern shown in Fig. 7-5 on the covering material (you will need two of these).

Use scissors to cut the covering material to the pattern lines. Methods for joining covering material to form the hems and seams for joining the ends of material depends on the covering material used (see Chapter 5). Generally, paper is glued, fabric material is sewn, and plastic is glued, heat-sealed, or taped.

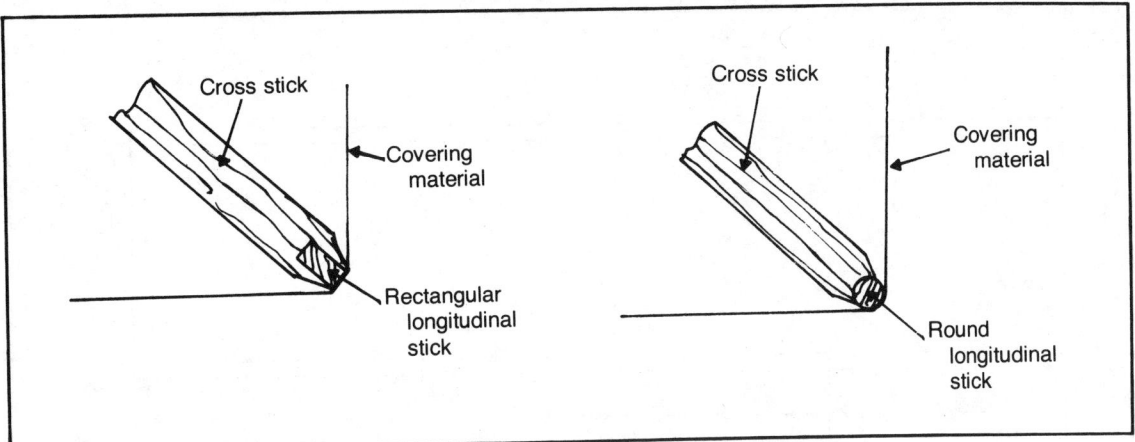

Fig. 7-3. The ends of the cross sticks are notched to fit the longitudinal sticks.

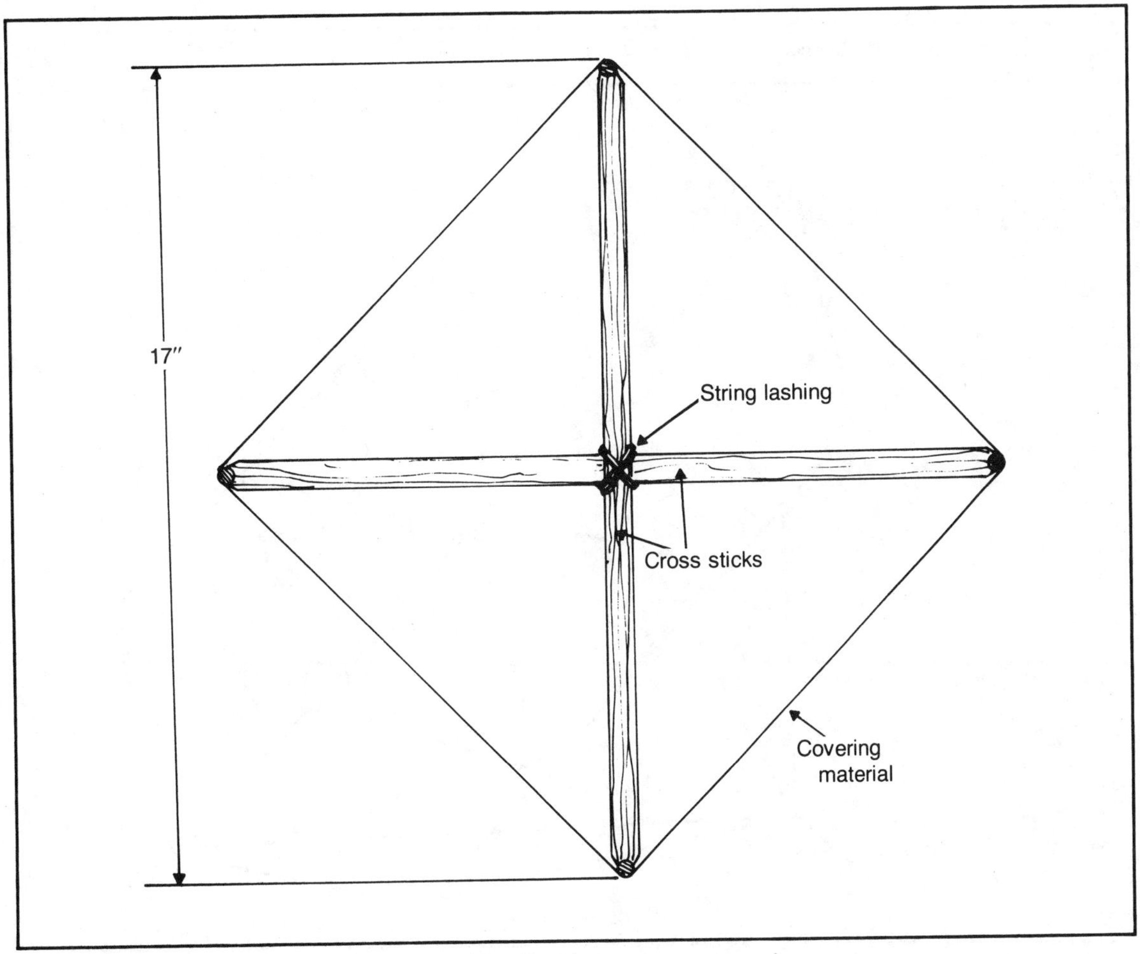

Fig. 7-4. Cross sticks are glued and lashed together with string.

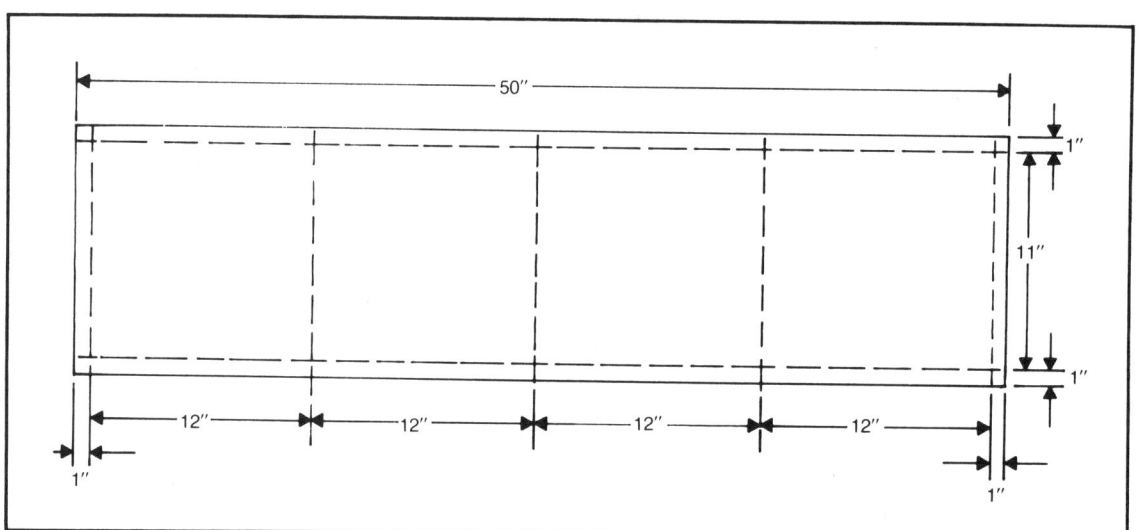

Fig. 7-5. Pattern for covering material.

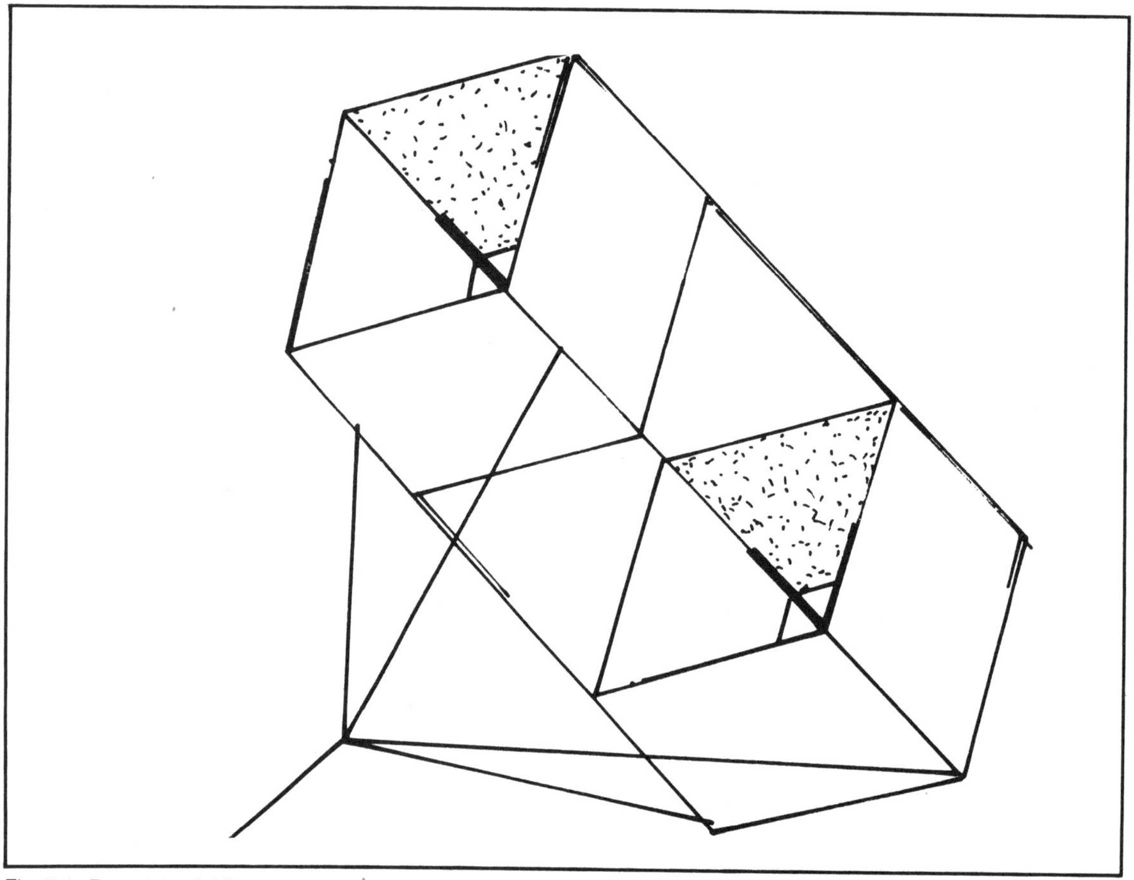

Fig. 7-6. Four-string bridle.

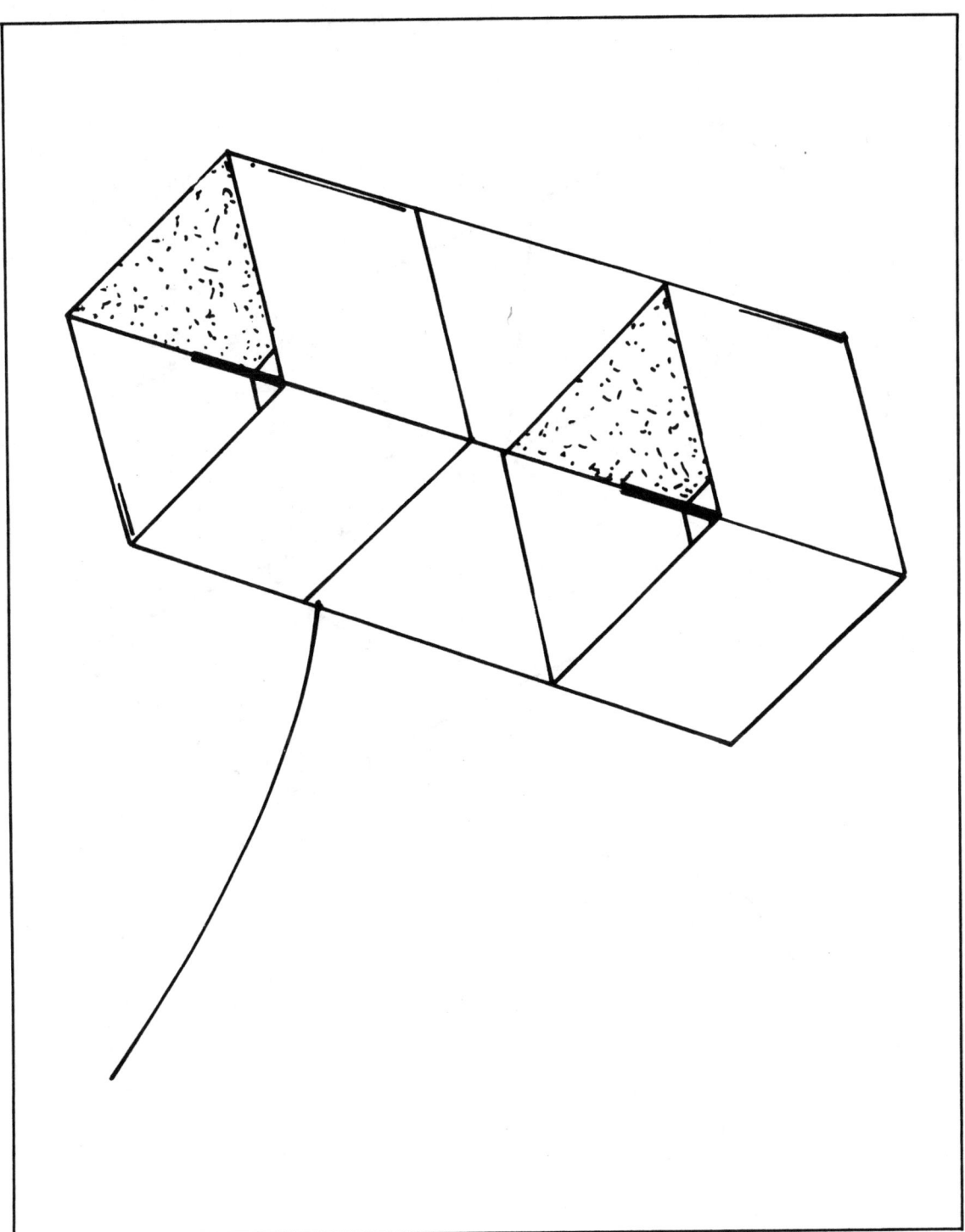

Fig. 7-7. Single-string attachment.

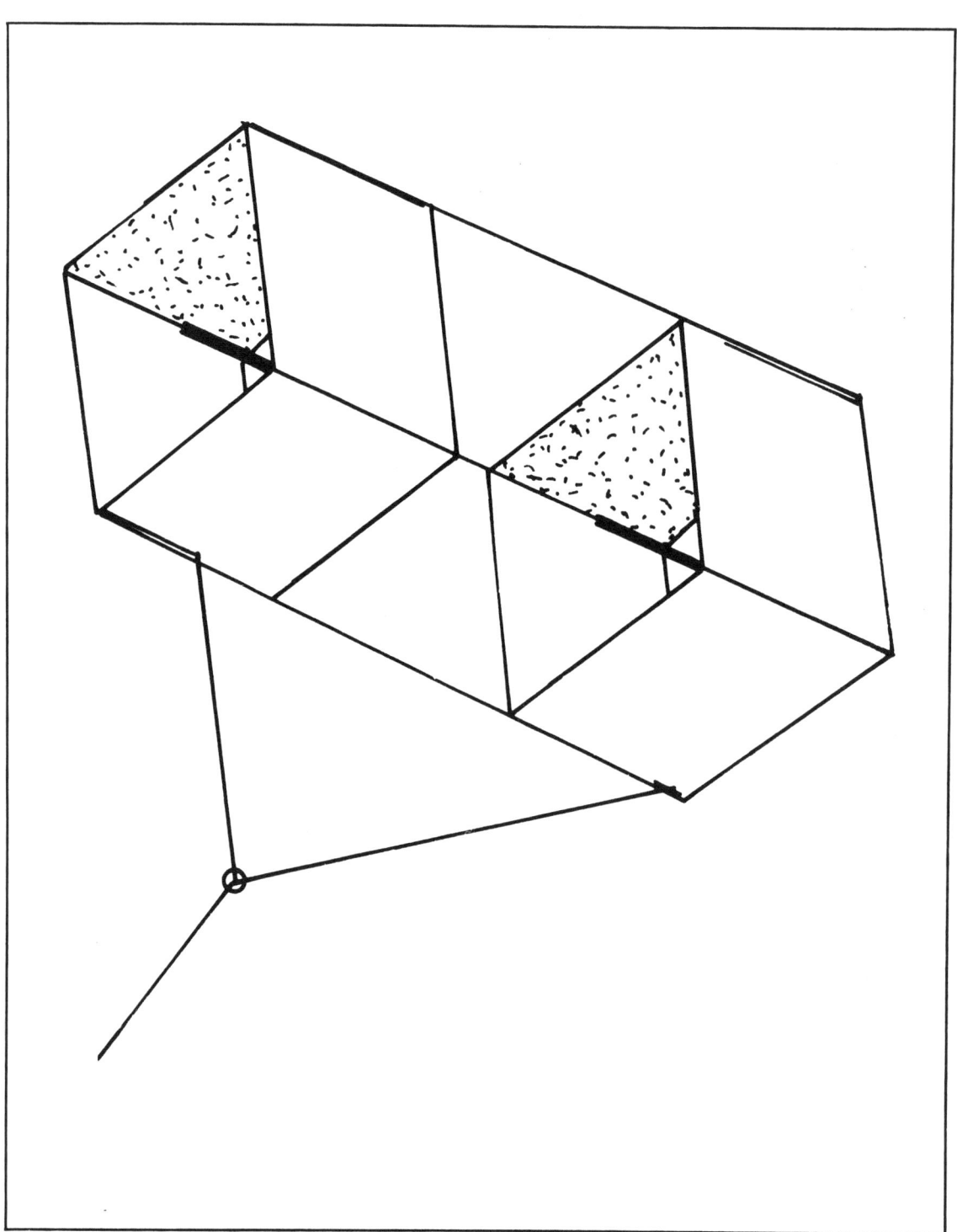

Fig. 7-8. Two-string attachment to one longitudinal stick.

strings passing through sleeves in the covering material.

Bridle

A variety of bridle arrangements can be used. One possibility is to use a four-string arrangement, as shown in Fig. 7-6. The upper two attachments are 5½ inches from the top of the kite, with the strings passing through small holes in the covering material, which is reinforced with tape or by other means. Tie the strings around the longitudinal sticks. The lower two attachments are 1 inch from the lower end of the longitudinal sticks, with the strings passing through small reinforced holes in the covering material. Tie the strings around the longitudinal sticks. You can tie the loose ends of the strings in a loop or to a small plastic ring for easy length adjustment.

A one-string attachment is shown in Fig. 7-7. It may take some experimenting to find the point of attachment where the kite flies in good balance. This method has one corner of the kite facing downward when the kite is flown, rather than one side, as with the four-string bridle described above.

A two-string attachment to one longitudinal stick is shown in Fig. 7-8. This method also has one corner of the kite facing downward when the kite is flown.

Tail

The basic box kite is usually flown without a tail, although a tail can be used if desired. Construction of tails is detailed in Chapter 5.

Variations

The basic box kite can be constructed in a range of sizes with the longitudinal sticks 6 inches or less in length to 6 feet or more in length by keeping the proportions the same. As a general rule, you will need to reduce the weight of the smaller sizes by using proportionally smaller sticks and lighter covering material. You will need to use larger sticks and heavier covering material for the larger sizes.

You may also want to experiment by changing

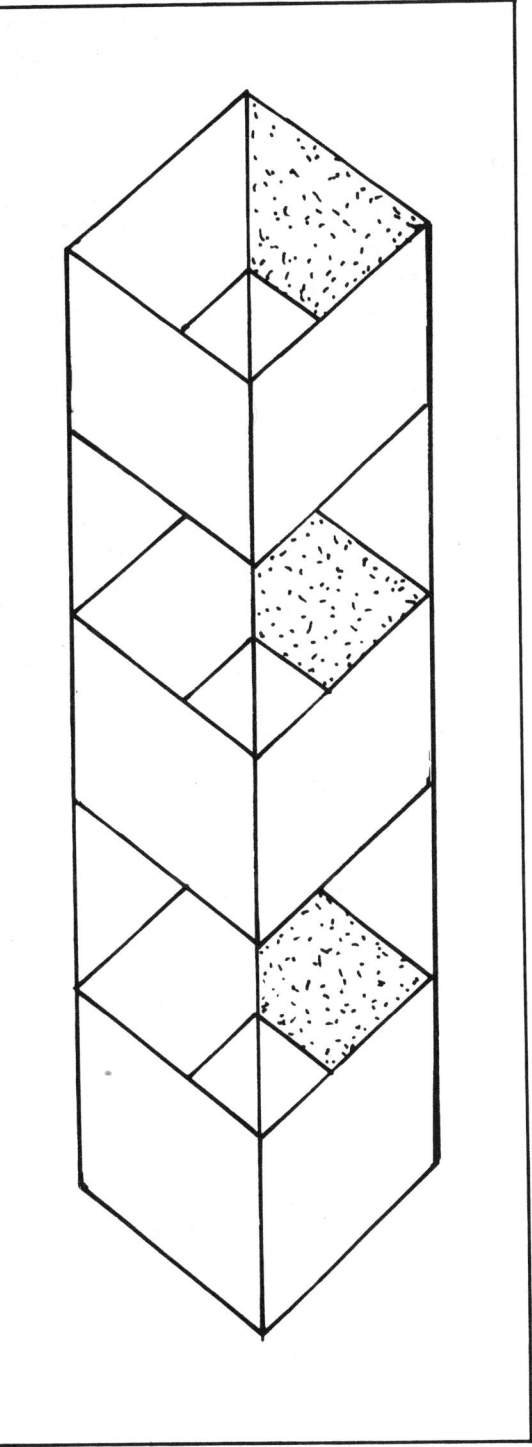

Fig. 7-9. Three-section box kite.

the proportions of the kite, such as wider or narrower sections of covering or different length to cross sectional ratios. Box kites can also be constructed with three (Fig. 7-9) or more box sections.

BOX KITE WITH SIDE WINGS

A box kite with side wings is shown in Fig. 7-10. This kite combines features of both the basic two-stick flat kite and the basic box kite. The box kite with side wings is usually flown without a tail, which is one of the reasons for its popularity.

Frame

Construction of the frame is basically the same as for the basic box kite detailed above, except that a wooden stick with cross sectional dimensions of ¼ inch by ⅜ inch, or ¼-inch diameter wooden dowel, that is 36 inches long is installed as a cross stick for the wings, as shown in Fig. 7-11. Notch the ends of the longitudinal sticks in the wing plane for guideline strings, as shown in Fig. 7-11. Make a ⅜-inch-deep saw cut in each end of the cross stick in the same plane. Glue the cross stick and lash it with

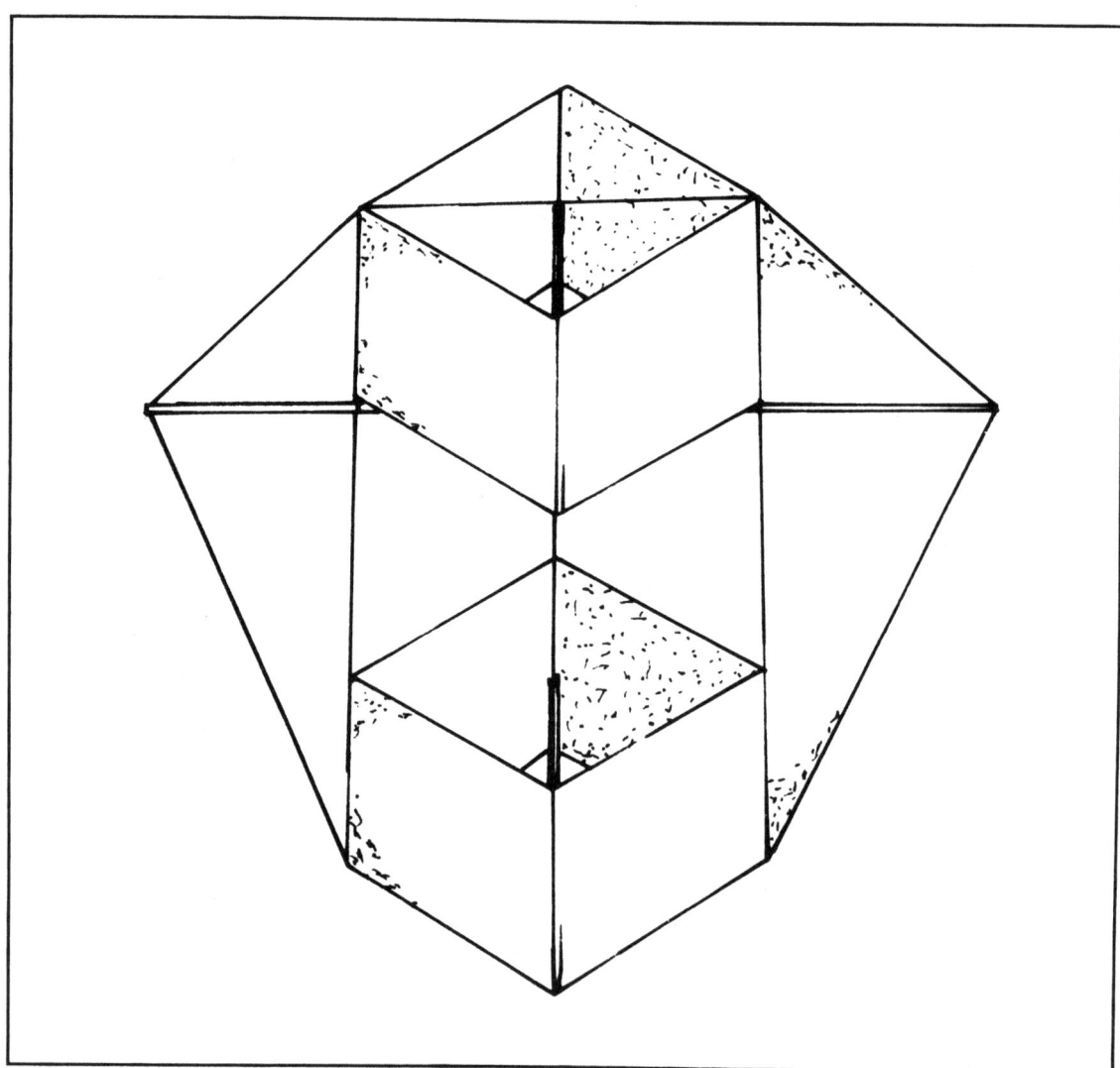

Fig. 7-10. Box kite with side wings.

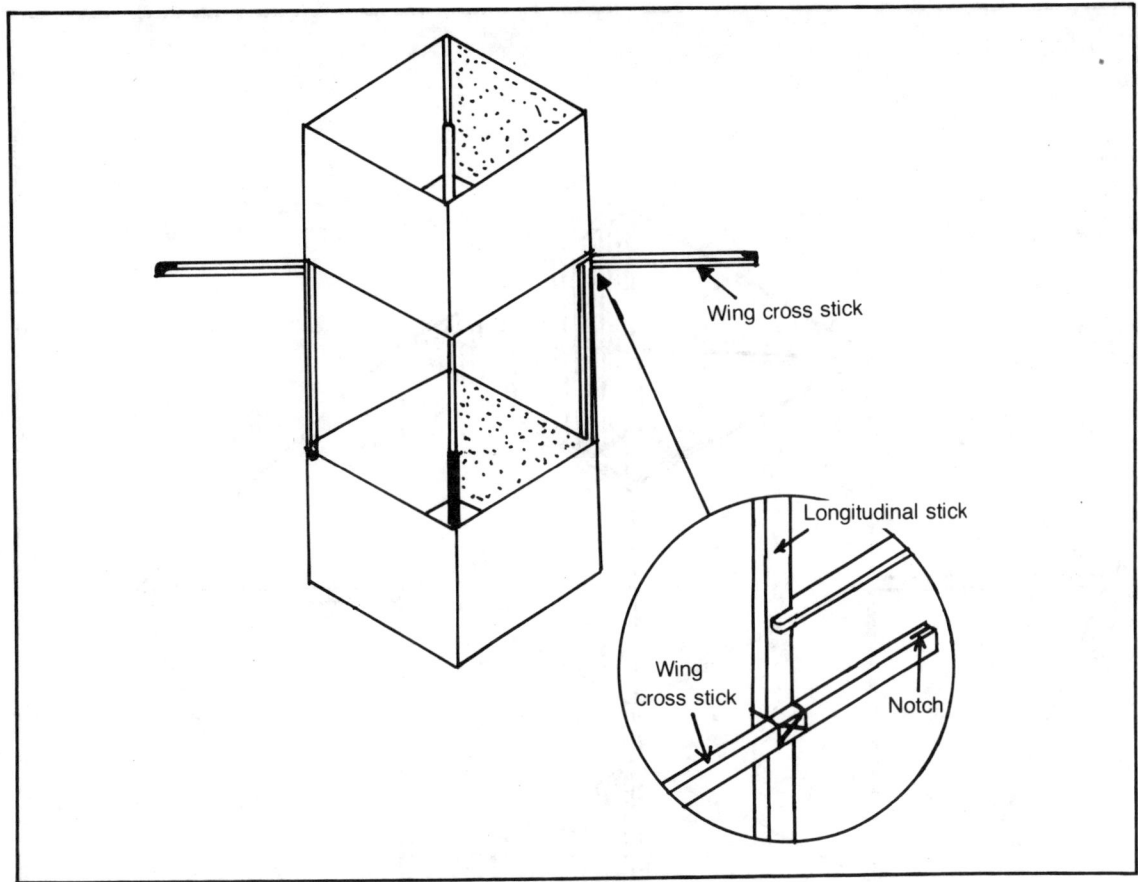

Fig. 7-11. Cross stick for side wings. Notches are made in sticks in wing plane.

strings to the longitudinal sticks just below the upper covering material. The notches in the ends of the cross stick should be in the wing plane. Make a ⅜-inch-deep saw cut in each end of the two longitudinal sticks in the wing plane in a direction parallel to the wing plane, as shown.

The guideline string is installed in the notches in the ends of the sticks around the kite in the wing plane, as shown in Fig. 7-12. Stretch the string tight and tie the ends together with a square knot.

Covering Material

In addition to the covering material used for the basic box kite, two sections of material are used. The pattern is shown in Fig. 7-13. In most cases, the wing covering material will be the same as that used to cover the box part of the kite. Mark the pattern shown on the covering material (you will need two of these).

Use scissors to cut the covering material to the pattern lines. Methods for joining covering material to form the sleeves for the guideline strings and longitudinal sticks and for joining the material to the covering material around the box frames depend on the particular covering material used (see Chapter 5).

Attach the wing covers to the kite. Basically, the upper and lower sections are joined to covering material at the top and bottom of the kite along the longitudinal sticks in the wing plane. Sleeves are formed in the covering material around the longitudinal sticks between the end covers. Sleeves are also formed over the guideline string on the outside edges of the wings.

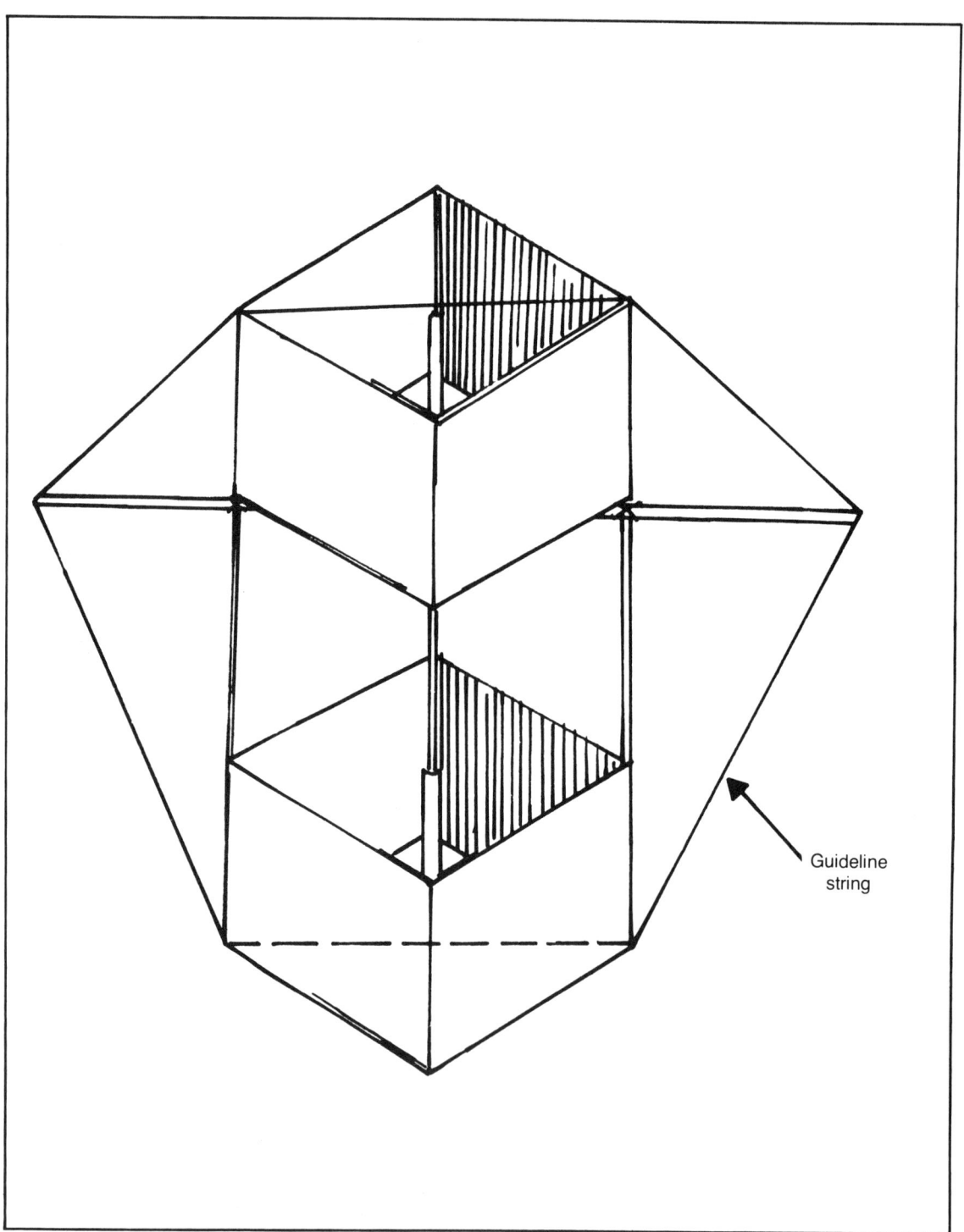

Fig. 7-12. Guideline string.

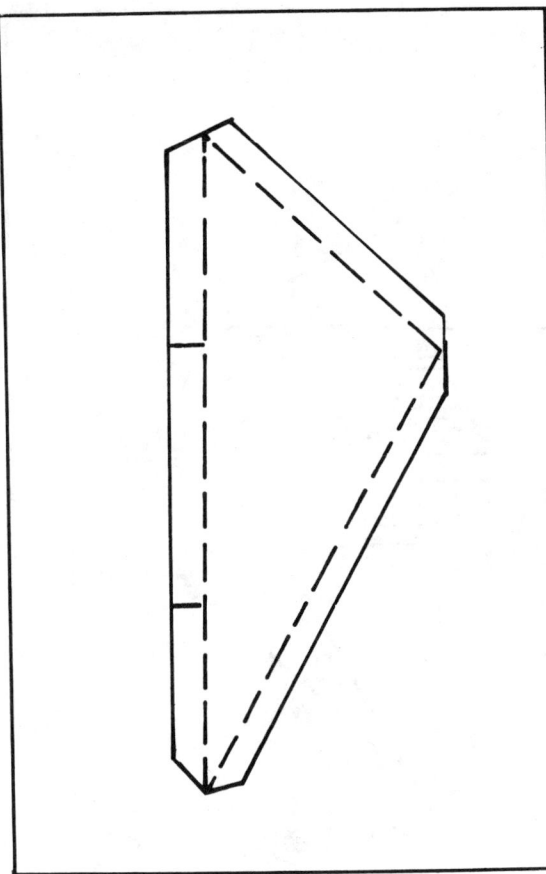

Fig. 7-13. Pattern for covering material for side wings.

Bridle

A two-string bridle arrangement can be used, as shown in Fig. 7-14. The upper attachment is to the longitudinal stick 5½ inches from the top of the kite, with the string passing through small holes in the covering material, which is reinforced with tape. The string is tied around the longitudinal stick. The lower attachment is to the longitudinal stick 5½ inches from the bottom of the kite, with the string passing through small reinforced holes. The string is tied around the longitudinal stick. The other ends of the strings can be tied in a loop or to a small plastic ring. The bridle ring allows you to easily adjust the length of the bridle strings.

Tail

The box kite with side wings is usually flown without a tail, although one can be used if desired. Construction of tails is detailed in Chapter 5.

Variations

The box kite with side wings can be constructed in a range of sizes with the longitudinal sticks 6 inches or less in length to 6 feet or more in length, by keeping the proportions the same. As a general rule, you will need to reduce the weight of the smaller sizes by using proportionally smaller sticks and lighter weight covering material. You will need to use larger sticks and heavier covering material for the larger sizes.

A variation of the box kite with side wings that uses two wing cross sticks is shown in Fig. 7-15. Construction is similar, except that the second wing cross stick is added and the guideline string passes through the additional notches.

A variation of the box kite with single cross stick wings on one diagonal, as detailed previously, is to add side wings on the other diagonal, as shown in Fig. 7-16. Construction of the second side wings is basically the same as for the first side wings, with the second wing cross stick passing immediately below the first one. The two sticks are joined together with glue and a string lashing at the crossing point.

A variation of the box kite with a double cross stick wing on one diagonal, as detailed previously, is to add side wings on the other diagonal, as shown in Fig. 7-17. Construction of the second set of side wings is basically the same as for the first side wings, with the two added cross sticks being joined at the center points with glue and string lashings.

SINGLE-UNIT TETRAHEDRON KITE

A single-unit tetrahedron kite is shown in Fig. 7-18. This kite is a true tetrahedron, with all sides and all sides and angles of the triangles equal. This is known as a *regular tetrahedron*. This shape was first used as a kite structure by Alexander Graham Bell. The structure is easy to assemble. All you need are six sticks of equal length, which are then assembled into the tetrahedron. For use as a kite, only two sides are covered.

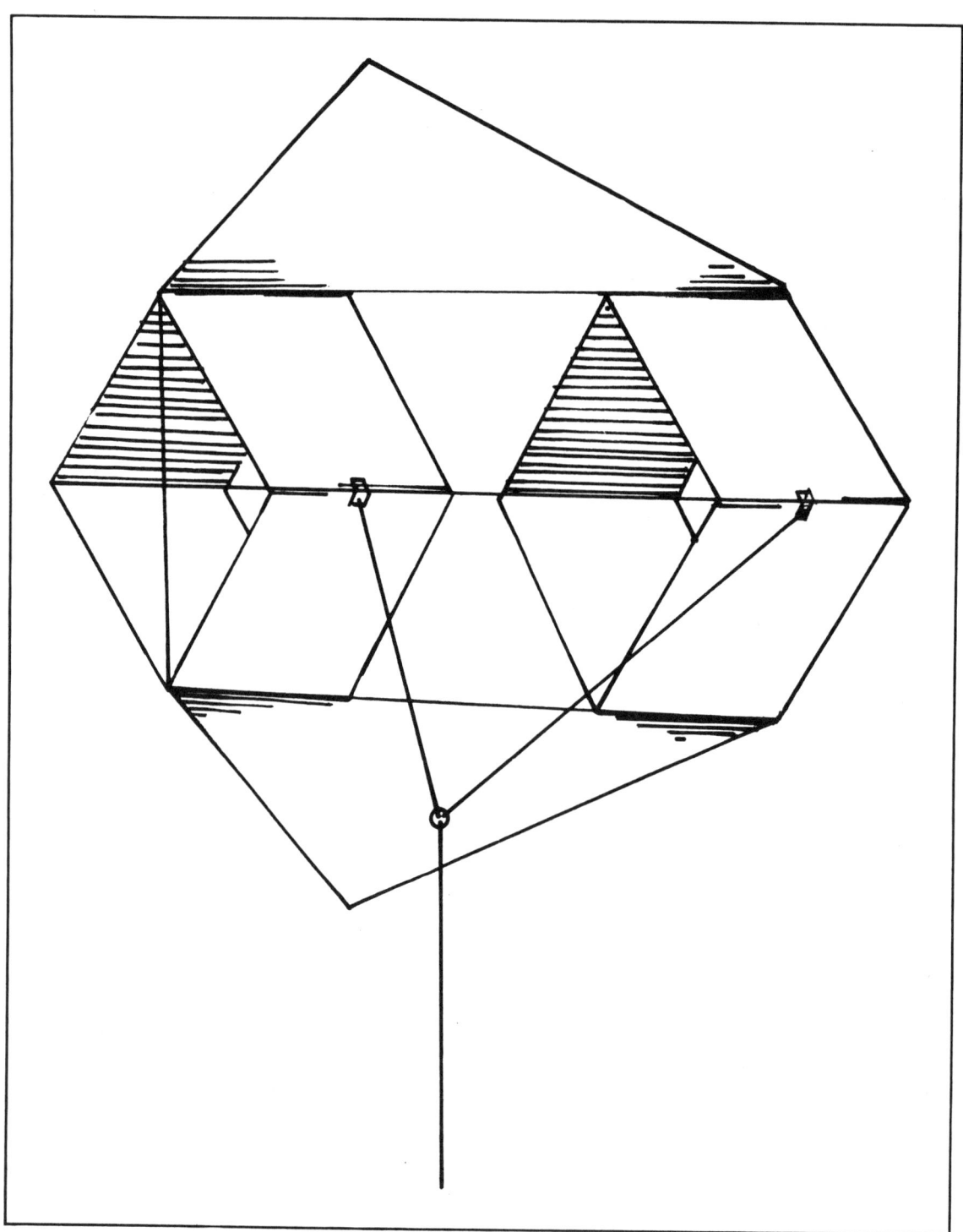

Fig. 7-14. Two-string bridle arrangement.

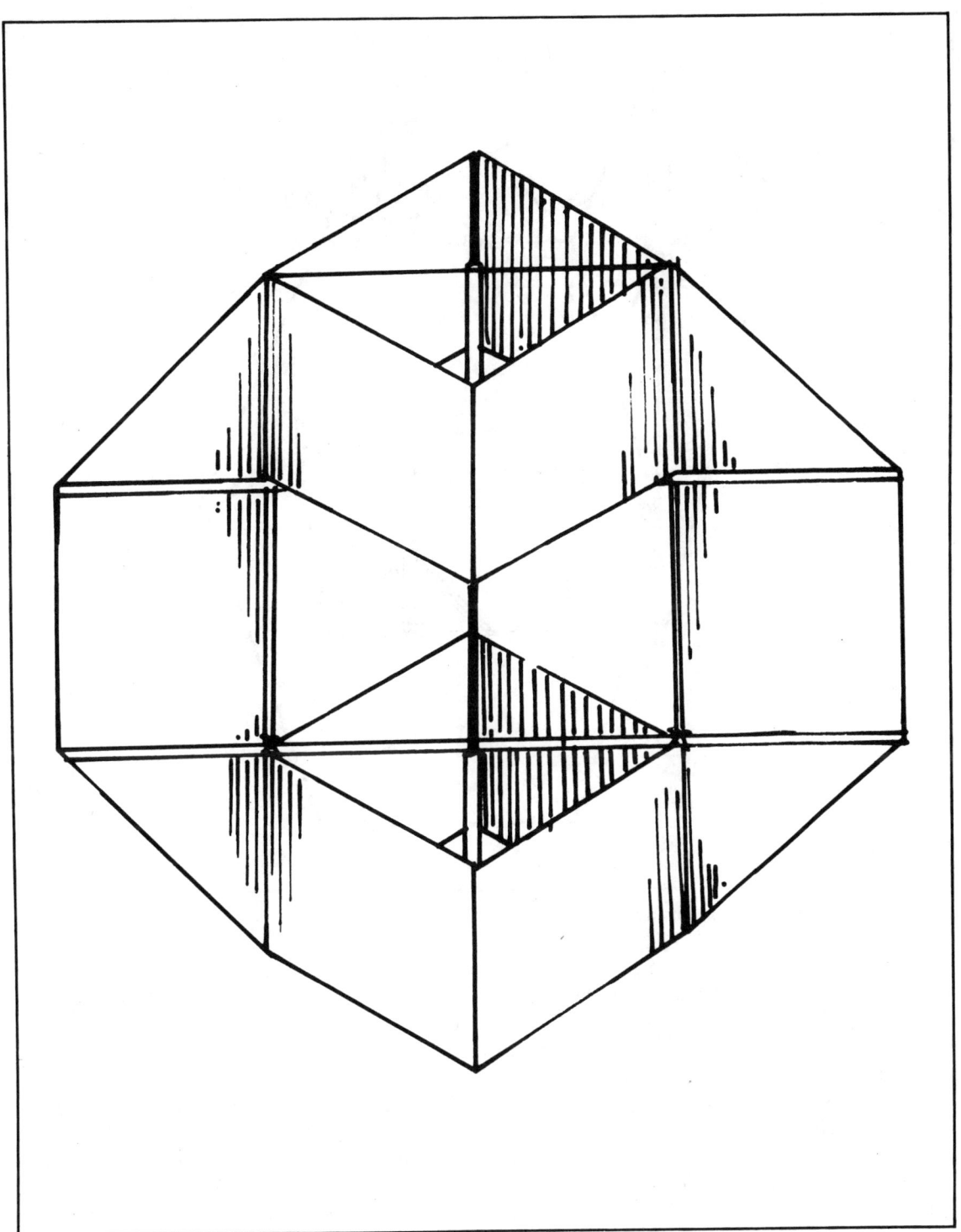
Fig. 7-15. Variation of box kite with side wings using two wing cross sticks.

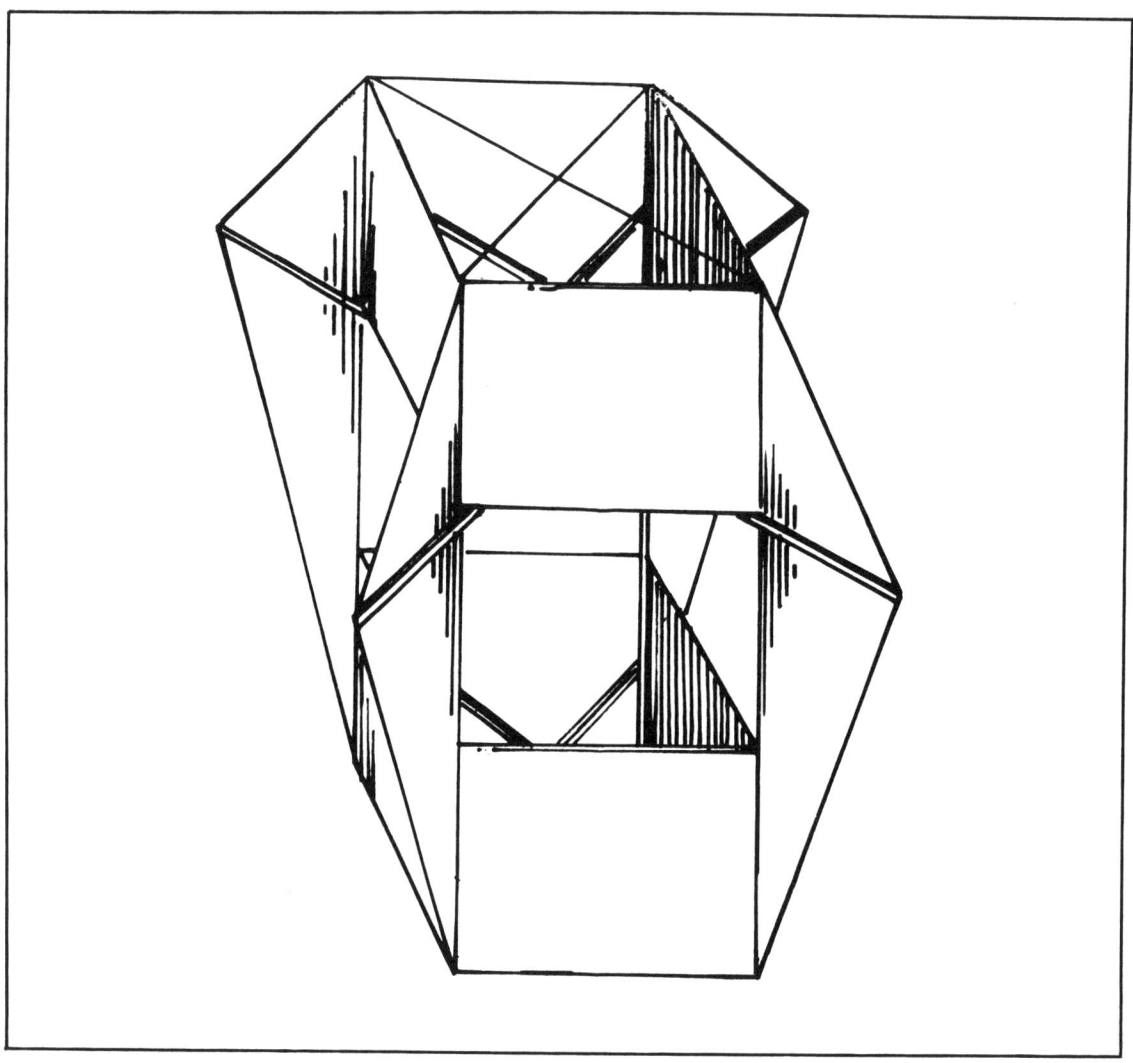

Fig. 7-16. Box kite with wings on both diagonals.

Frame

Construction of the frame is shown in Fig. 7-19. Six 3/16-inch-diameter wooden dowels that are 36 inches long are used for constructing the frame. The sticks can vary somewhat from these dimensions and still give satisfactory results. For flying in light airs, you may want to reduce the cross sectional size of sticks. For extremely strong winds, you may want to use sticks with larger cross sectional dimensions. Fiberglass, bamboo, and aluminum sticks are also appropriate. For descriptive purposes, we'll assume that you will be using wooden dowels.

When joining the sticks, make all connections ½-inch from the ends of the sticks, as shown in Fig. 7-19. Glue and bind all joints with string lashings. Begin assembly by joining the ends of three sticks to form an equilateral triangle. Then add two sticks to form the second side of the tetrahedron. Add final stick to complete the construction of the frame.

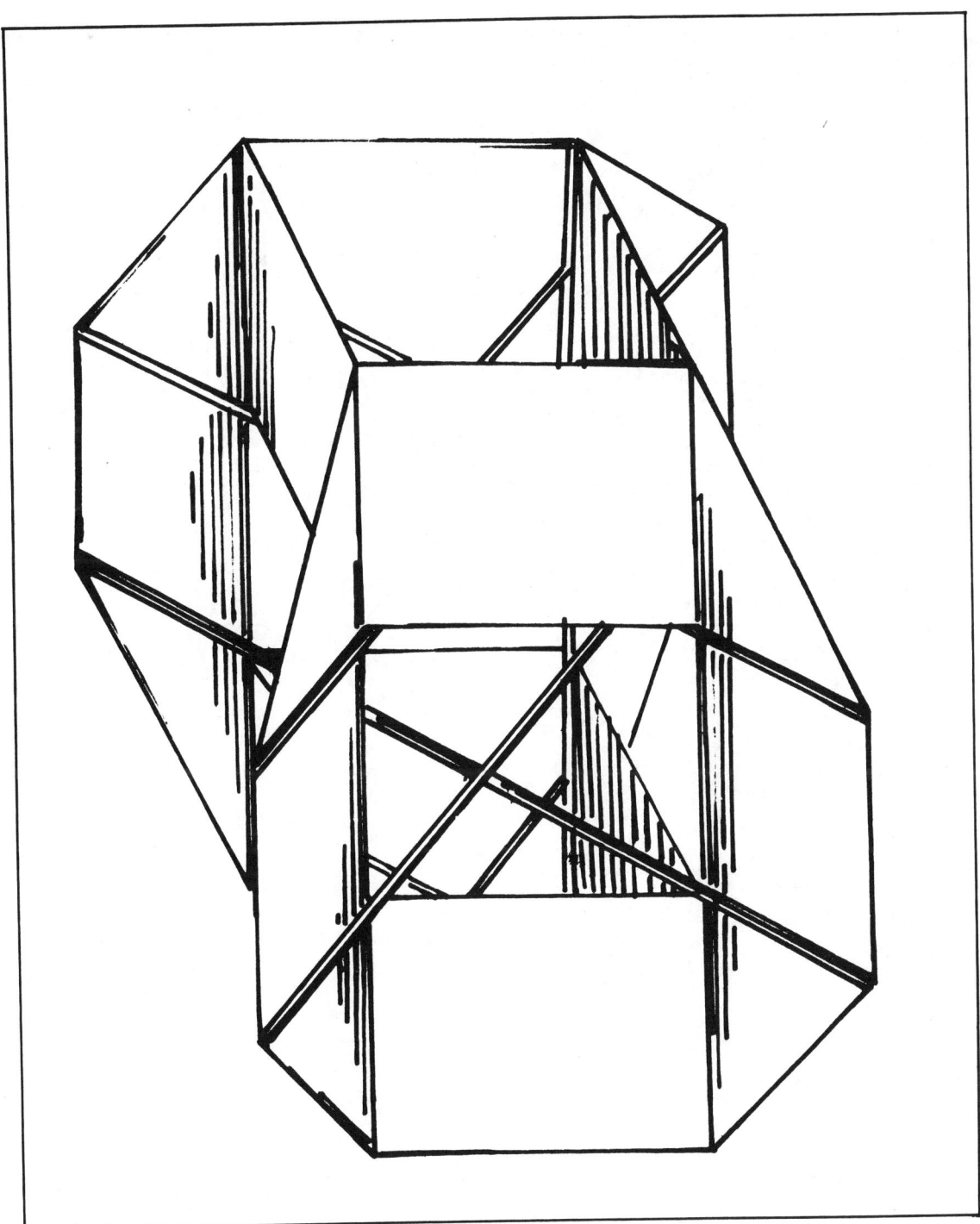

Fig. 7-17. Box kite with double-stick wings on both diagonals.

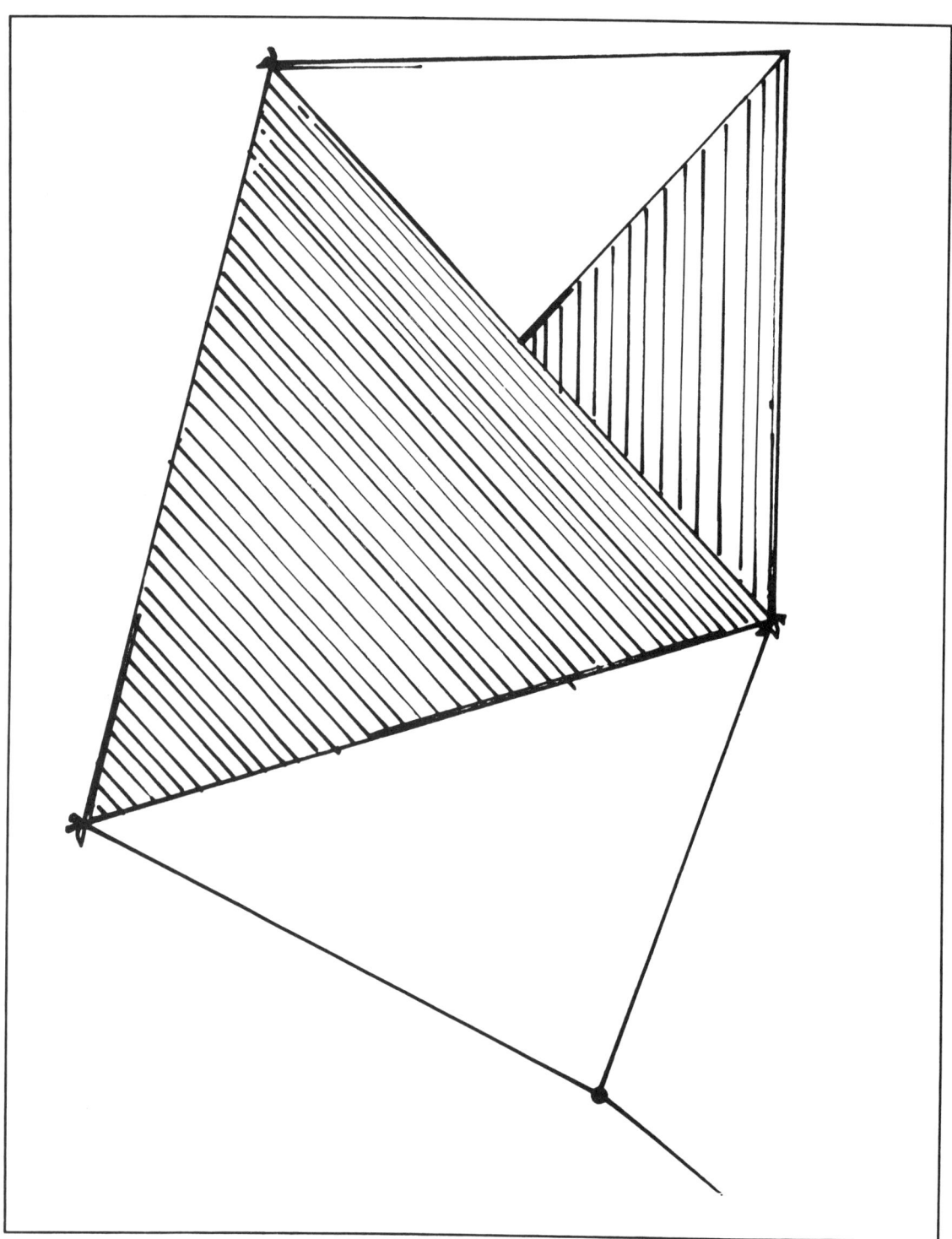
Fig. 7-18. Single-unit tetrahedron kite.

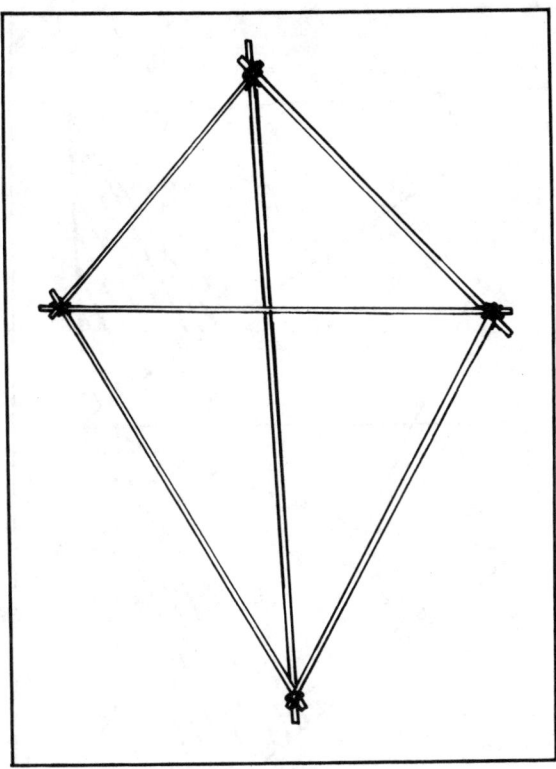

Covering Material

Use paper, plastic film, or fabric as a cover. For best performance, keep the covering material as light as possible without sacrificing strength. Mark the pattern shown in Fig. 7-20 on the covering material.

Use scissors to cut the covering material to the pattern lines. Methods for joining covering material to form the sleeves over the sticks depends on the covering material used (see Chapter 5). Attach the cover to the frame.

Bridle

A bridle is usually attached to the kite at two points, as shown in Fig. 7-18. The string is tied to each end of the stick that has the covering material crossing over it. Tie the string at each end around the three joining sticks. The other ends can be tied in a loop or to a small plastic ring. The bridle ring allows easy adjustment of the length of the bridle strings. Adjustment of the bridle is extremely important for this kite.

Fig. 7-19. Frame construction for single-unit tetrahedron kite.

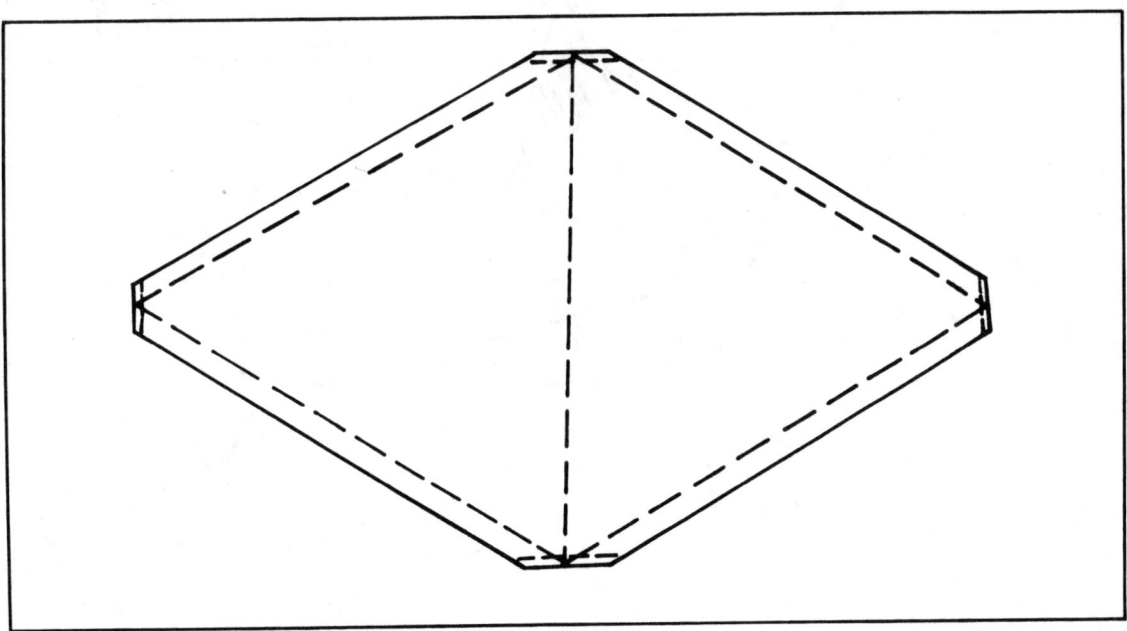

Fig. 7-20. Pattern for covering material.

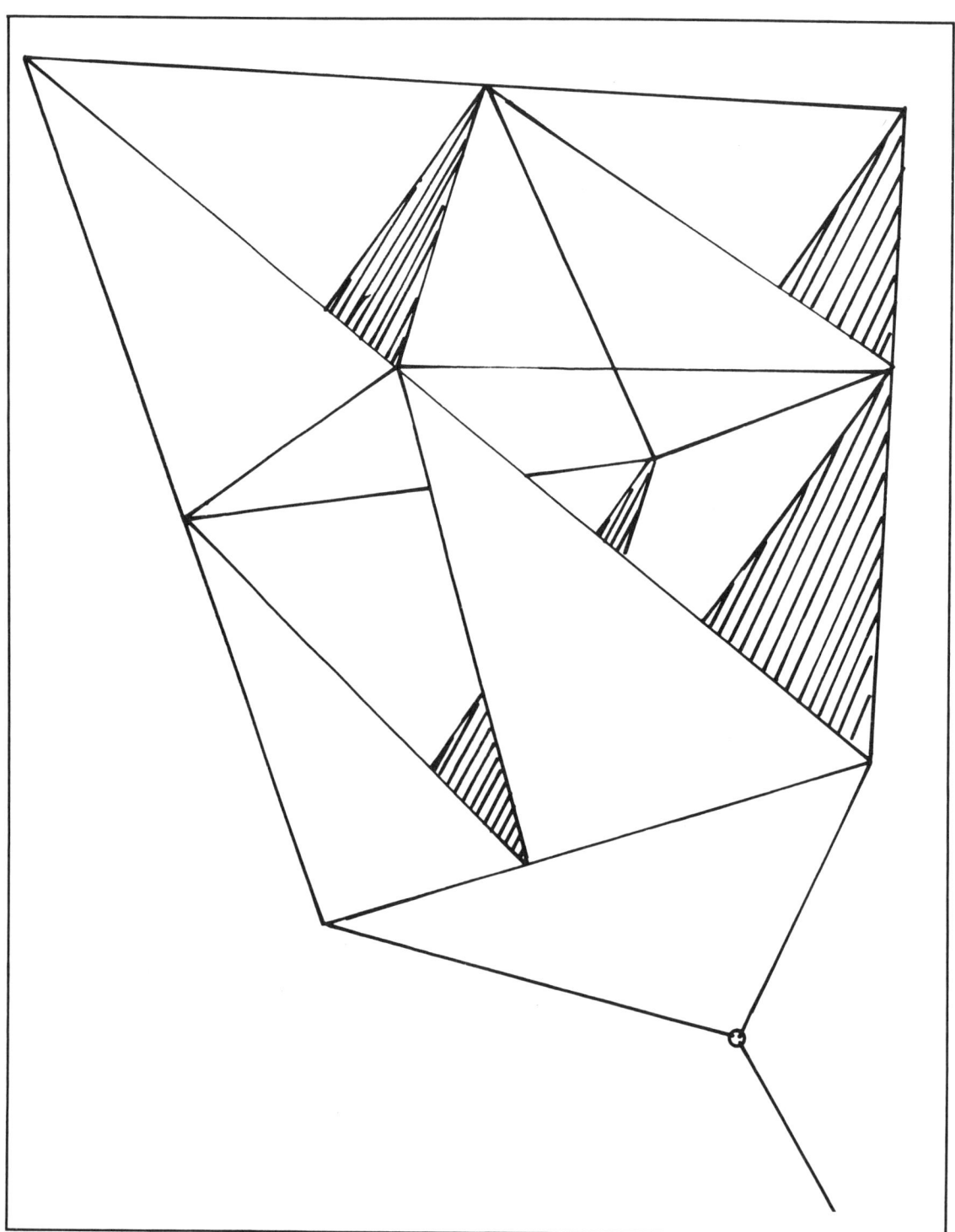

Fig. 7-21. Four-unit tetrahedron kite.

Tail

The tetrahedron kite is usually flown without a tail, but one can be used, if desired. Construction of tails is detailed in Chapter 5.

Variations

The single-unit tetrahedron kite can be constructed in a range of sizes with the sticks 6 inches or less in length to 6 feet or more in length by keeping the proportions the same. As a general rule, you will need to reduce the weight of the smaller sizes by using proportionally smaller sticks and lighter weight covering material. You will need to use larger sticks and heavier covering material for the larger sizes.

FOUR-UNIT TETRAHEDRON KITE

A four-unit tetrahedron kite, shown in Fig. 7-21 is essentially a combination of four single-unit tetrahedron kites.

Frame

Construction begins by making the single-unit tetrahedron kite frame detailed above. Connect

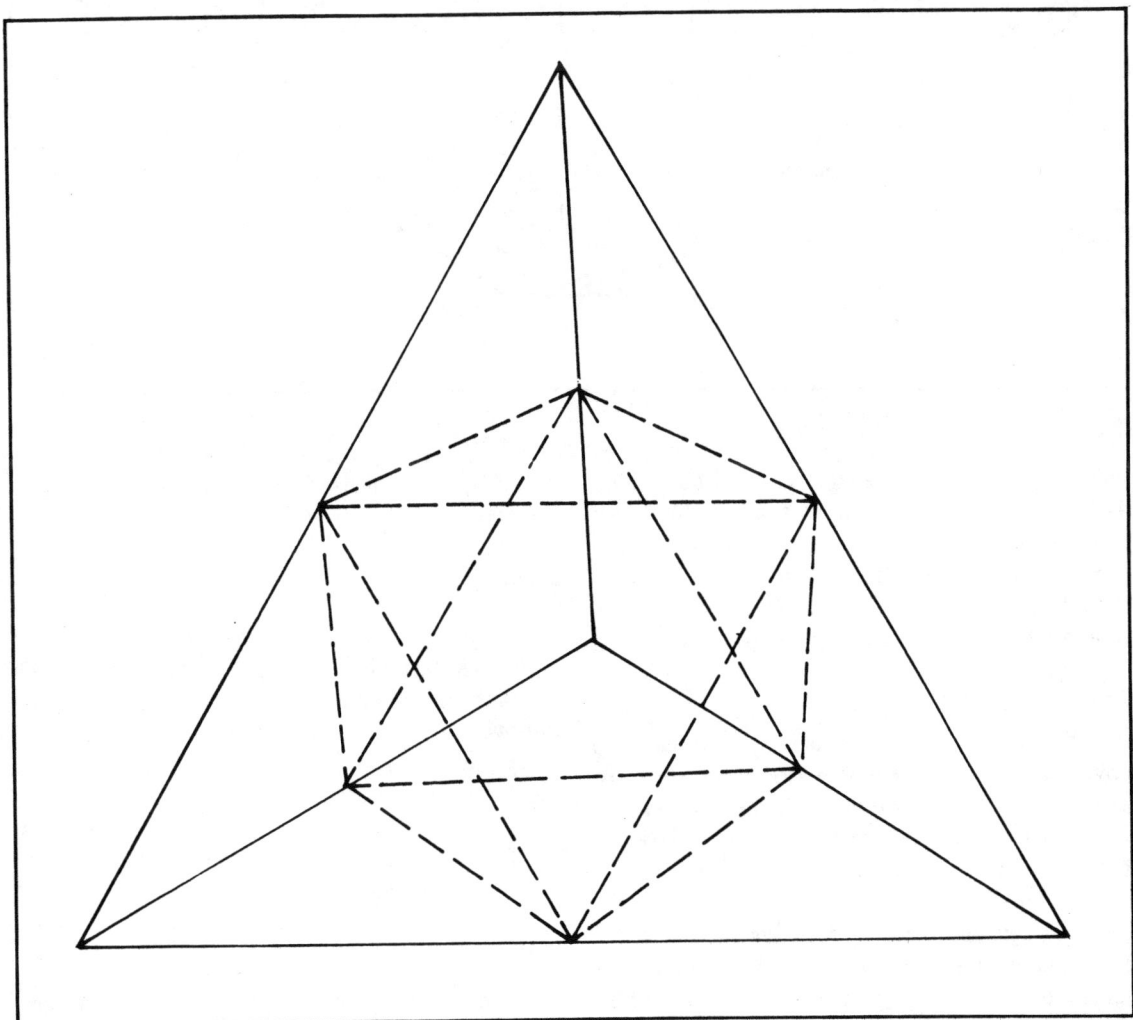

Fig. 7-22. Guideline strings.

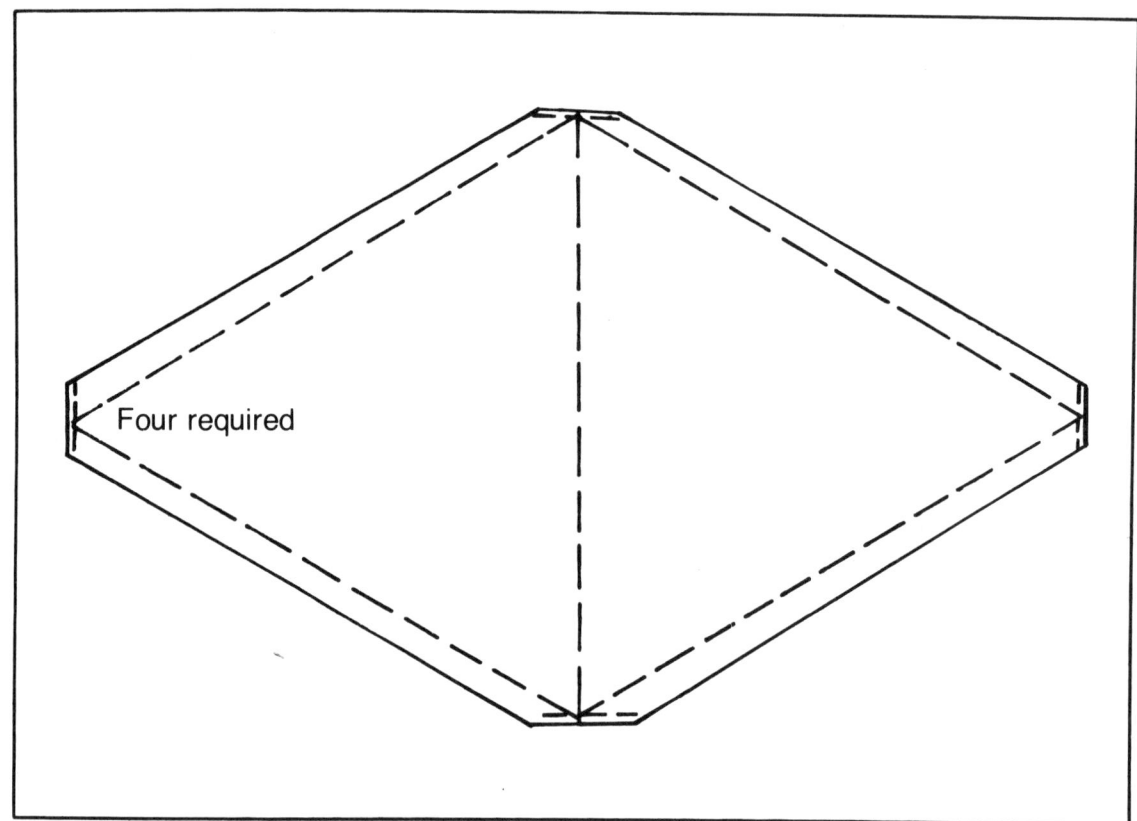

Fig. 7-23. Pattern for covering material.

guideline strings between the centers of all sticks, as shown in Fig. 7-22. (An alternate method is to use twelve 18-inch-long wooden dowels instead of the guideline strings. These are glued and lashed with string to the main sticks with the ends extending ½ inch beyond the main sticks.)

Covering Material

Paper, plastic film, or fabric can be used for covering the kite. For best performance, the covering material should be of the lightest weight that is compatible with adequate strength. Mark the pattern shown in Fig. 7-23 on the covering material. You will need four.

Use scissors to cut the covering material to the pattern lines. Use the appropriate joining method to form the sleeves over the sticks. Regardless of the covering material used, install the four covers to the frame, as shown in Fig. 7-21.

Bridle

A bridle is usually attached to the kite at two points, as shown in Fig. 7-21. Tie the string to each end of the stick that has the covering material crossing over it. Tie the string at each end around the three joining sticks. You can tie the other ends of the strings in a loop or to a small plastic ring. The bridle ring allows easy adjustment of the length of the bridle strings. Adjustment of the bridle is extremely important for this kite.

Tail

The tetrahedron kite is usually flown without a

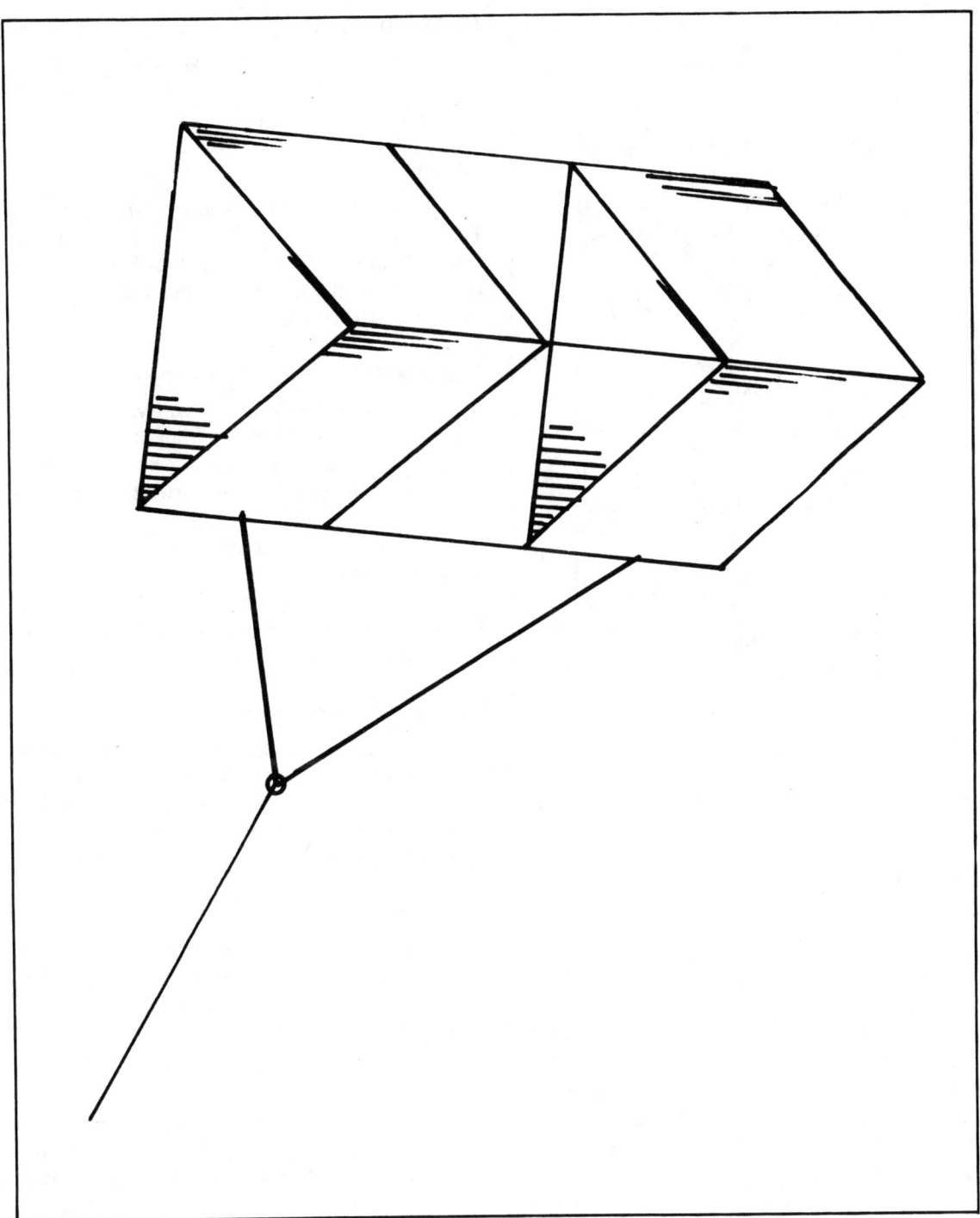
Fig. 7-24. Triangular box kite.

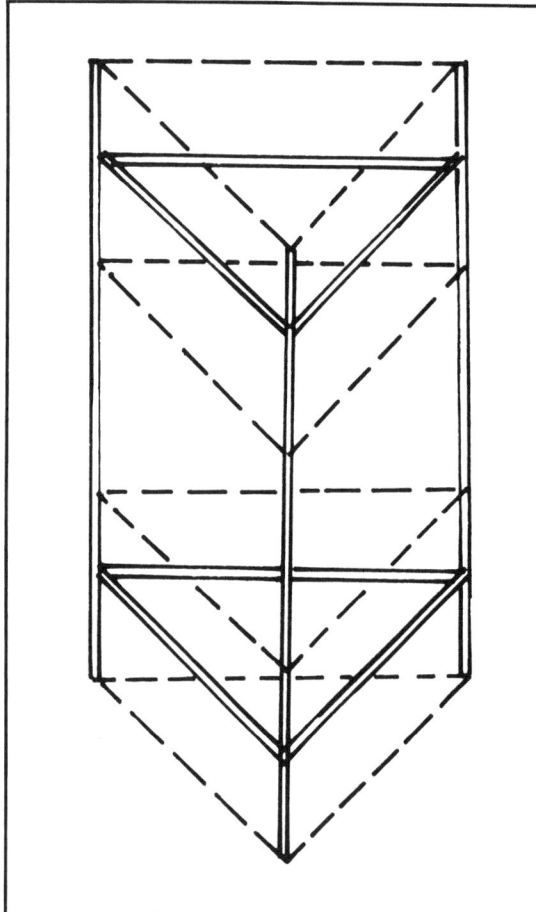

Fig. 7-25. Frame construction for triangular box kite.

tail, although a tail can be used if desired. Construction of tails is detailed in Chapter 5.

Variations

The four-unit tetrahedron kite can be constructed in a range of sizes with the main sticks 1 foot or less in length to 6 feet or more in length by keeping the proportions the same. Reduce the weight of the smaller sizes by using proportionally smaller sticks and lighter weight covering material; use larger sticks and heavier covering material for the larger sizes.

Tetrahedron kites can also be constructed with more cells. There are many possibilities here.

OTHER BOX KITES

A large variety of other box kites can also be constructed. Ideas for a number of these are presented below.

Triangular Box Kite

A basic triangular box kite is shown in Fig. 7-24. The frame construction is detailed in Fig. 7-25. Construction is similar to that of the basic box kite, as detailed previously. A two-point bridle attachment is usually used.

Triangular Box Kite with Side Wings

A triangular box kite with side wings is shown in Fig. 7-26. This kite differs from the basic triangular box kite in that there are no cross sticks joining the wing plane and the forward longitudinal stick, which is connected only by the covering material. A two-point bridle attachment is usually used, as shown.

A variation of the triangular box kite with side wings is the double triangular box kite with wing, as shown in Fig. 7-27.

Rectangular Box Kite with Wings

A rectangular box kite with wings is shown in Fig. 7-28. Construction is similar to that of a regular box kite with side wings, except that the box is a rectangular, and the wings attach to adjacent corners instead of opposite corners, as shown.

Hexagonal Box Kite

A hexagonal box kite is shown in Fig. 7-29, which is an interesting variation of the basic box kite. Round and diamond-shaped box kites are other possibilities.

Airplane-Type Box Kite

An airplane-type box kite is shown in Fig. 7-30. This is an interesting form of the box kite, which has been constructed in a variety of configurations, including designs with shaped wing surfaces.

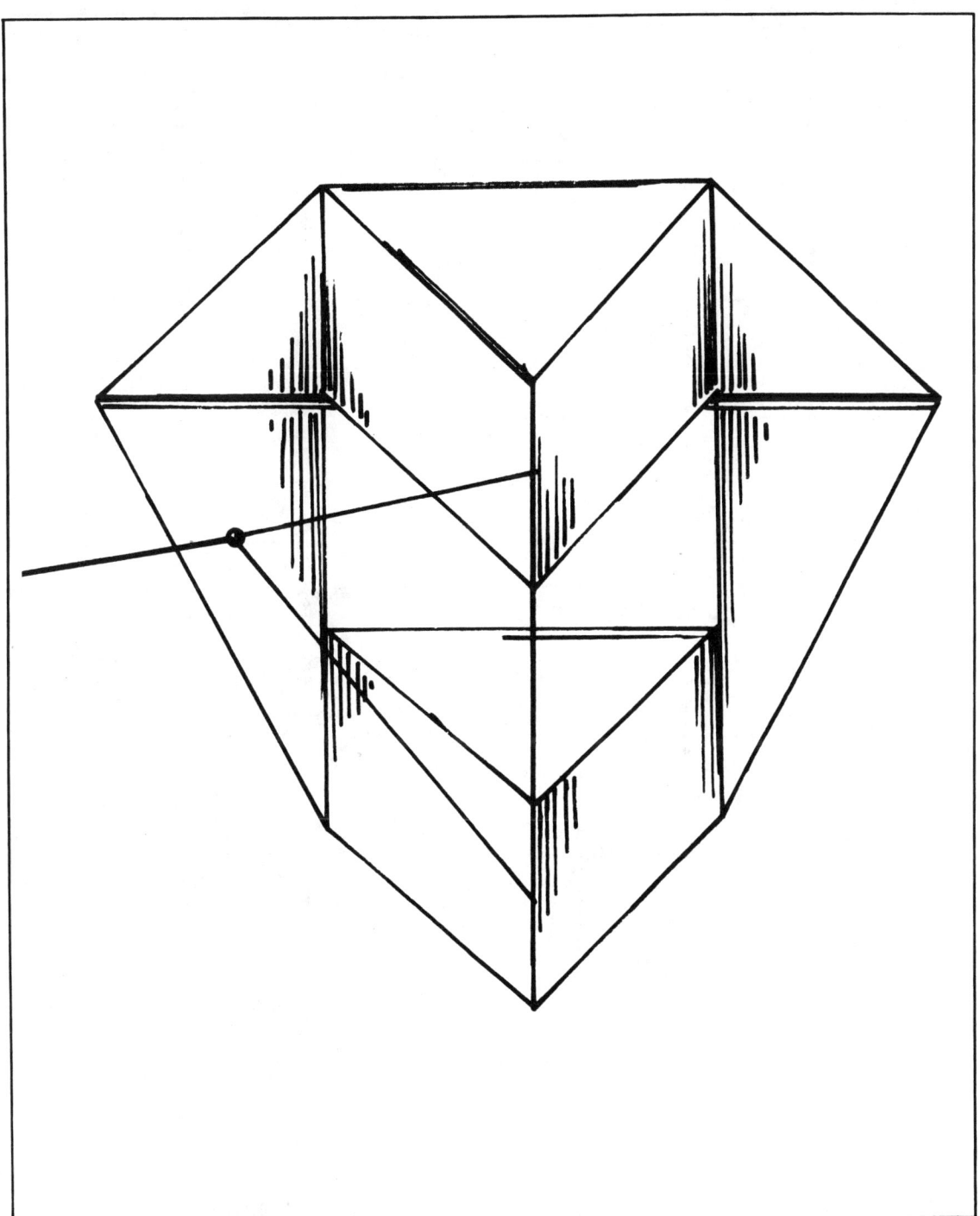

Fig. 7-26. Triangular box kite with side wings.

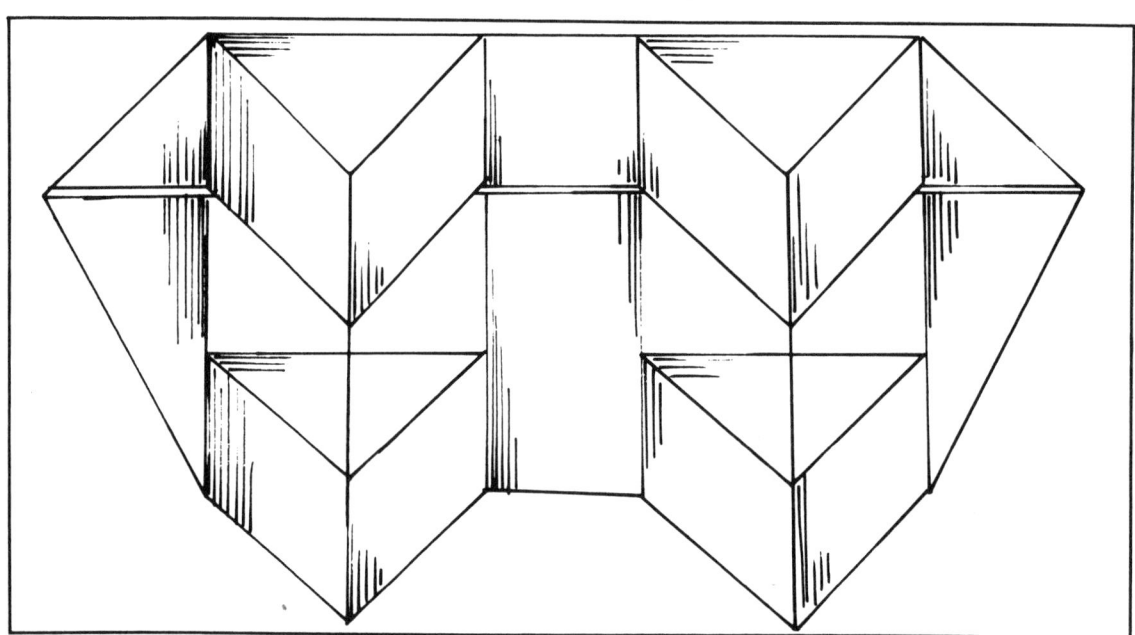

Fig. 7-27. Double triangular box kite with wing.

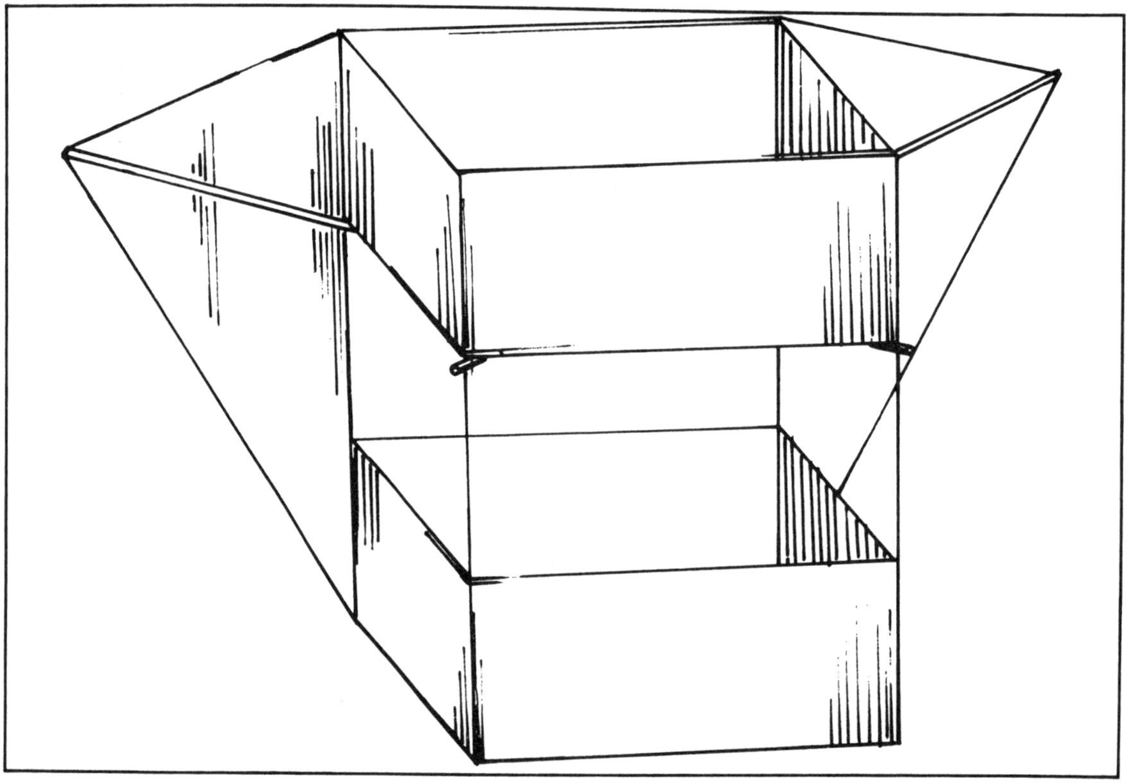

Fig. 7-28. Rectangular box kite with wings.

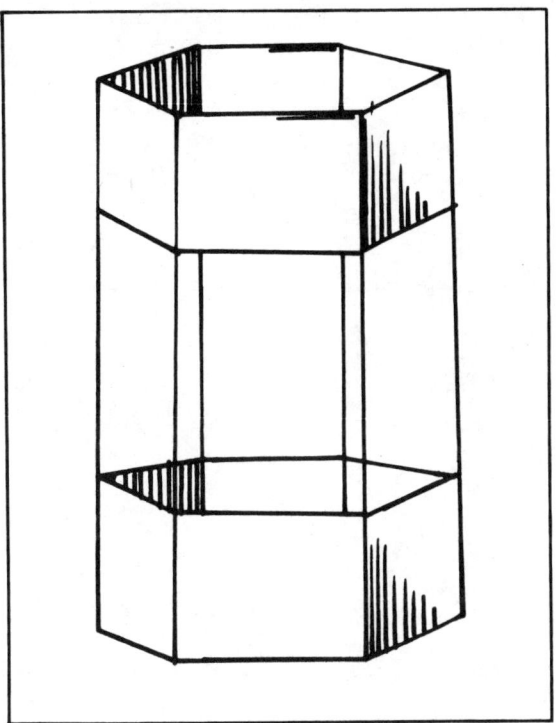

Fig. 7-29. Hexagonal box kite.

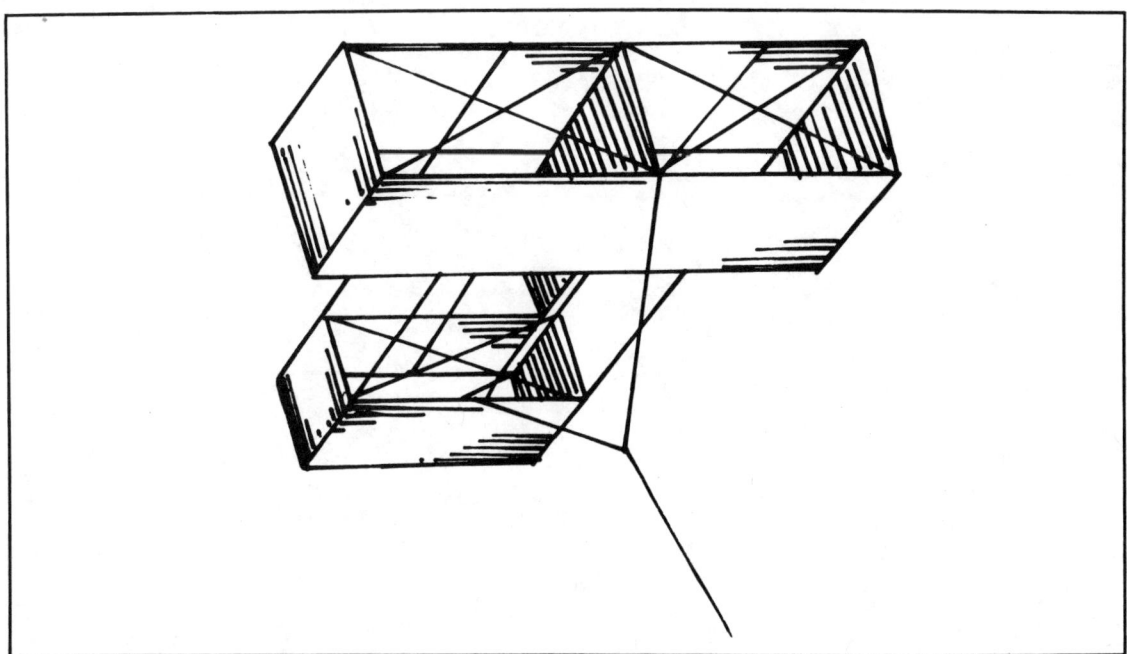

Fig. 7-30. Airplane-type box kite.

Chapter 8

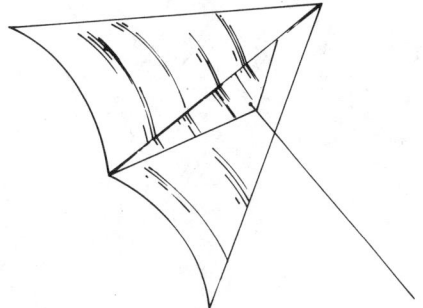

Semirigid and Nonrigid Kites

In this chapter, the construction of semirigid and nonrigid kites is detailed. These kites can add an exciting new dimension to kite building and designing.

DELTA WING KITE

A delta wing kite is shown in Fig. 8-1. This kite features a frame arrangement that allows considerable wing flexibility. A keel is used to give the kite stability, and the delta wing kite is usually flown without a tail.

Frame

The frame construction is shown in Fig. 8-2. The sticks are ⅛-inch-diameter wooden dowels. The sticks at the outside edges of the wings are 18 inches long. Notice that they do not extend all the way to the forward tip of the kite. The center longitudinal stick is 15 inches long. The cross stick for the wings is 12 inches long. Notice that this stick is connected only loosely in pockets to the edges of the wings, and it is *not* connected to the longitudinal stick.

Cut the sticks to the required length. Assemble the sticks in sleeves and pockets in the covering material, with no permanent joints between sticks.

Covering Material

Plastic film or cloth fabric can be used for the covering material. The pattern for plastic material that will be glued or heat-sealed is shown in Fig. 8-3. The cloth fabric pattern, which will be sewn, is shown in Fig. 8-4. In either case, you will need two pieces, one for the wing and one for the keel. Mark the patterns shown on the covering material.

Use scissors to cut the covering material to the pattern lines. Methods for joining covering material to form the sleeves for the sticks and hems and for joining the keel section to the wing material depend on the particular covering material used (see Chapter 5). Generally, fabric material is sewn, and plastic is glued, heat-sealed, or taped.

Regardless of the covering material used, form sleeves or pockets for the sticks and join the keel to the wing materials. Construction details for plastic is shown in Fig. 8-3 and for sewn fabric in Fig. 8-4.

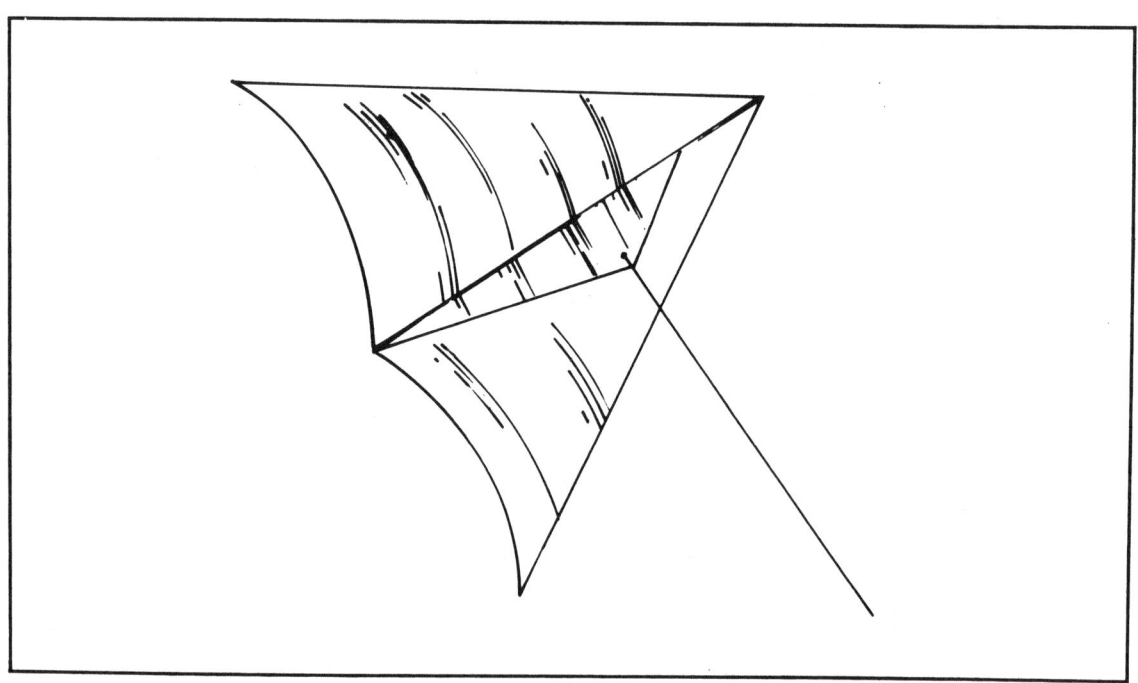

Fig. 8-1. Delta wing kite.

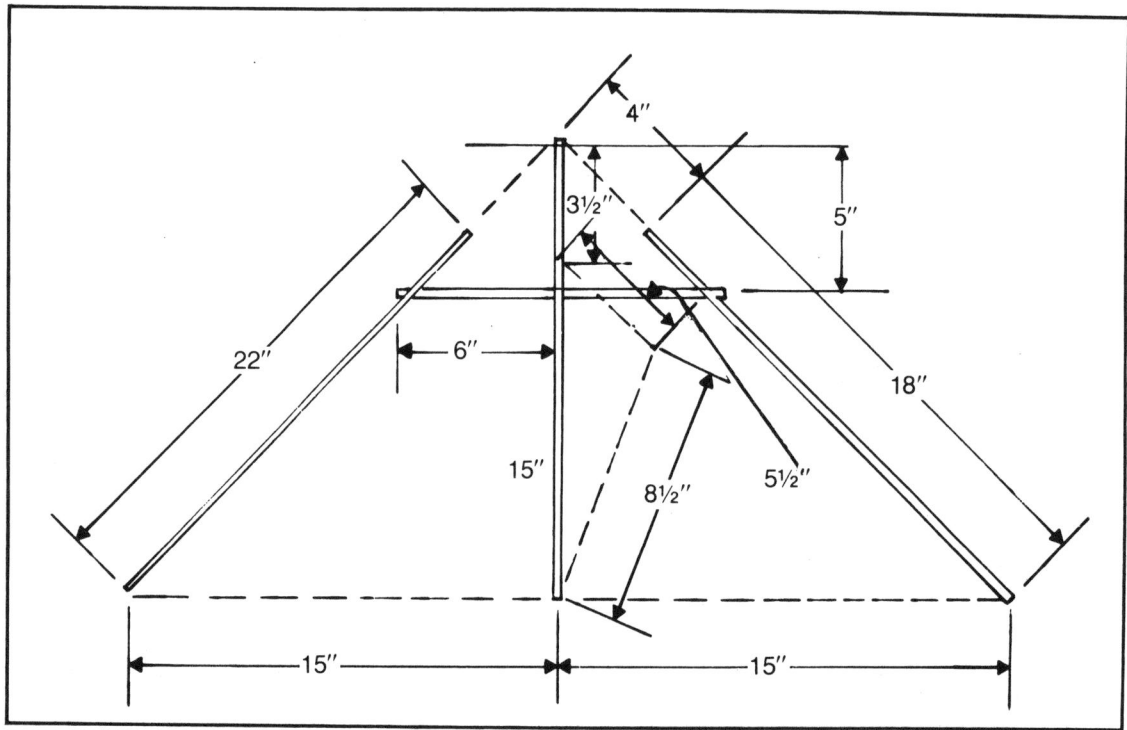

Fig. 8-2. Frame construction for delta wing kite.

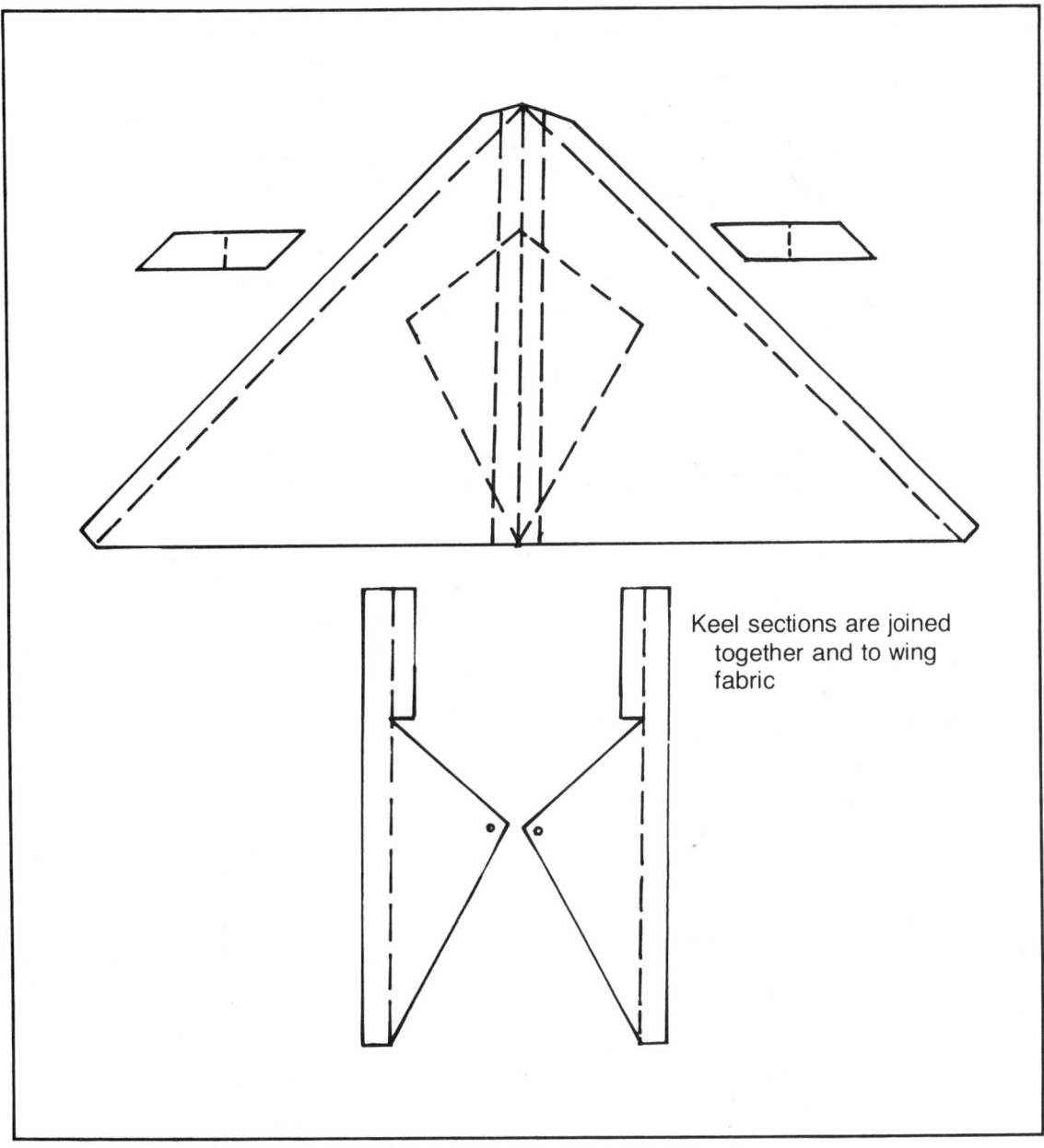

Fig. 8-3. Pattern for plastic covering material.

The longitudinal center stick and the sticks at the outside edges of the wings are glued or sewn in closed pockets so that they cannot come out. Form the pockets in the upper surface of the wings for the cross stick. An alternative method is to use a wire hook on each end of the cross stick, as shown in Fig. 8-5, which is connected through small reinforced holes in the wing covering material, just inside the sticks along the edges of the wings.

Make a hole in the keel for attachment of the flying string. Reinforce it with tape, a small grommet, or by other means.

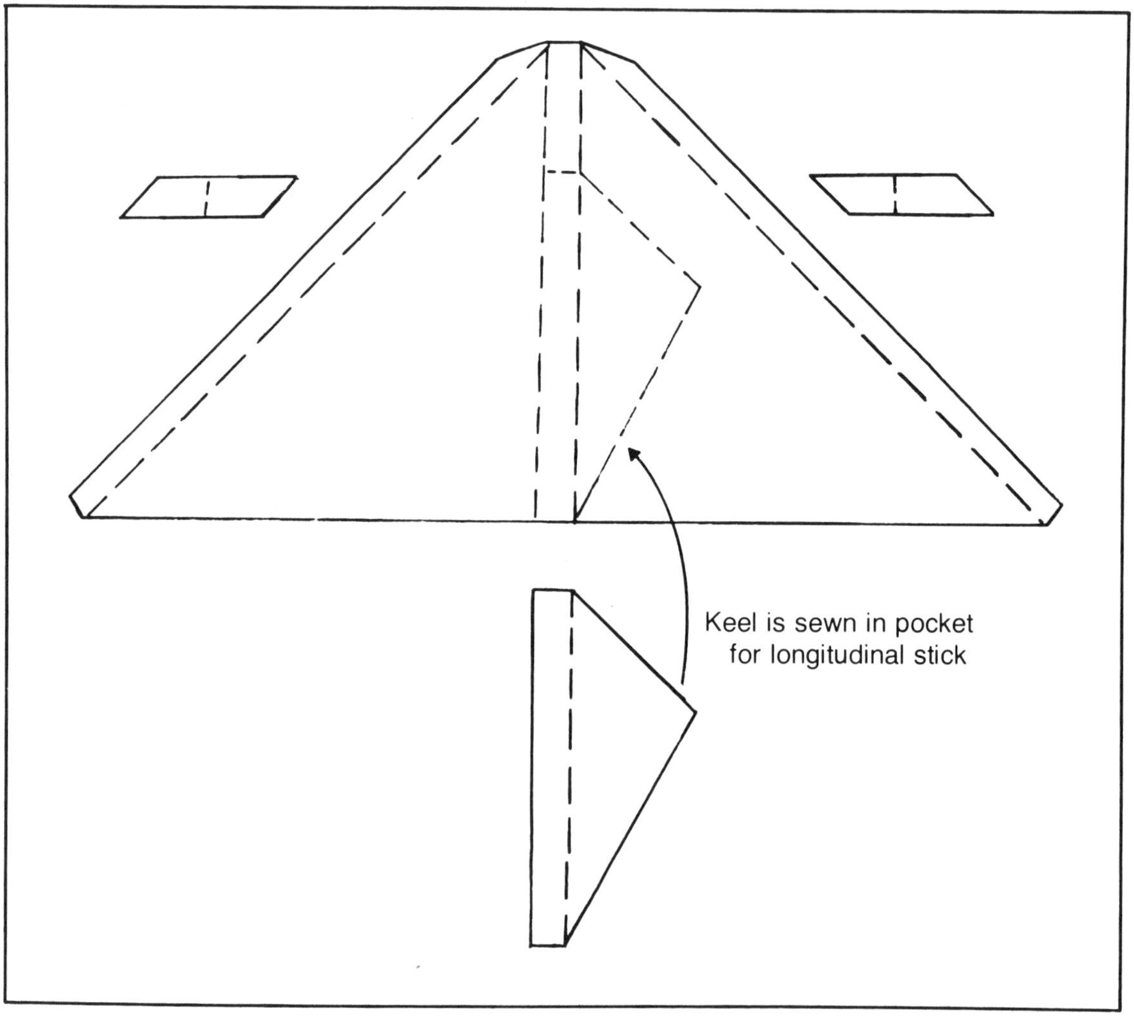

Fig. 8-4. Pattern for fabric covering material.

Variations

The delta wing kite can be constructed in a range of sizes from 1 foot or less in length to 6 feet or more in length by keeping the proportions the same. As a general rule, you will need to reduce the weight of the smaller sizes by using proportionally smaller sticks and lighter weight covering material. You will need to use larger sticks and heavier covering material for the larger sizes.

SLED KITE

The sled kite, shown in Fig. 8-6, performs

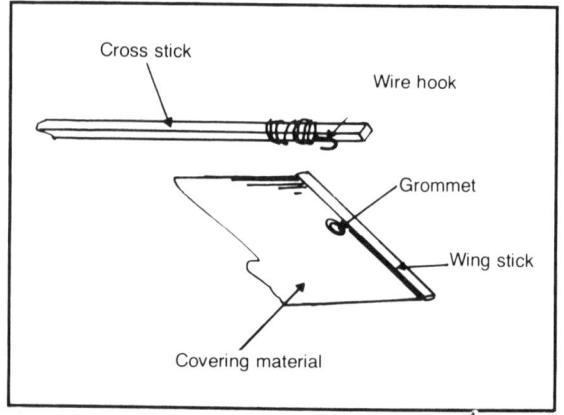

Fig. 8-5. Use of wire hook.

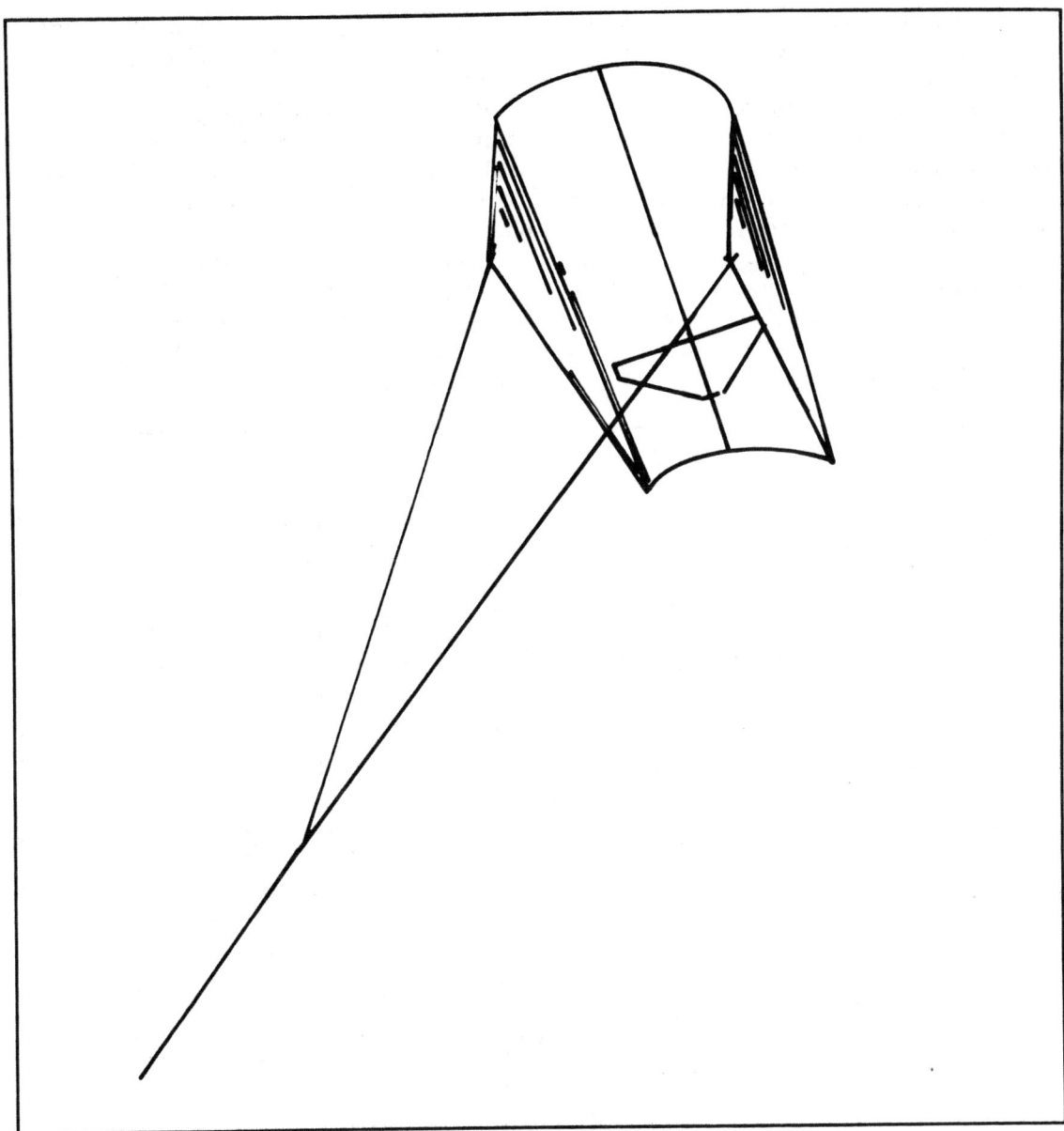

Fig. 8-6. Basic sled kite.

well, and construction is easy. Sled kites are usually flown without a tail, although tails can be used if desired.

Construction

Construction details for a sled kite are shown in Fig. 8-7. Three 36-inch-long wooden dowels of ⅛-inch diameter are used for the sticks. The sticks can vary somewhat from these dimensions and still give satisfactory results. If the kit is to be used only in light airs, you may want to reduce the cross sectional size of the sticks. If the kite is to be flown in extremely strong winds, you may want to use sticks with larger cross sectional dimensions.

249

Sticks of fiberglass, bamboo, and aluminum are other possibilities, as detailed in Chapter 5.

For descriptive purposes here, we'll assume that you will be using wooden dowels.

Thin plastic material or thin flexible packing foam, especially Du Pont MicroFoam, can be used as the covering material. I used two layers of MicroFoam, joined in rows of welds. This allows the insertion of sticks between the layers, making construction extremely easy. In any case, the material should be of the lightest weight that is compatible with adequate strength. Mark the pattern shown in Fig. 8-7 on the covering material.

Use scissors to cut the covering material to the pattern lines. Methods for joining covering material to form the sleeves over the sticks depends on the covering material used (see Chapter 5). Generally, plastic is glued, heat-sealed or taped. If plastic is used, the sticks can be taped to the plastic or held in place by plastic strips, which are joined to the main plastic with the sticks inside.

If one layer of foam packing material is used, the sticks can be installed similarly. If the two layer foam is used, the sticks can be inserted in the slots between the layers. I put glue on the sticks before inserting them in the slots.

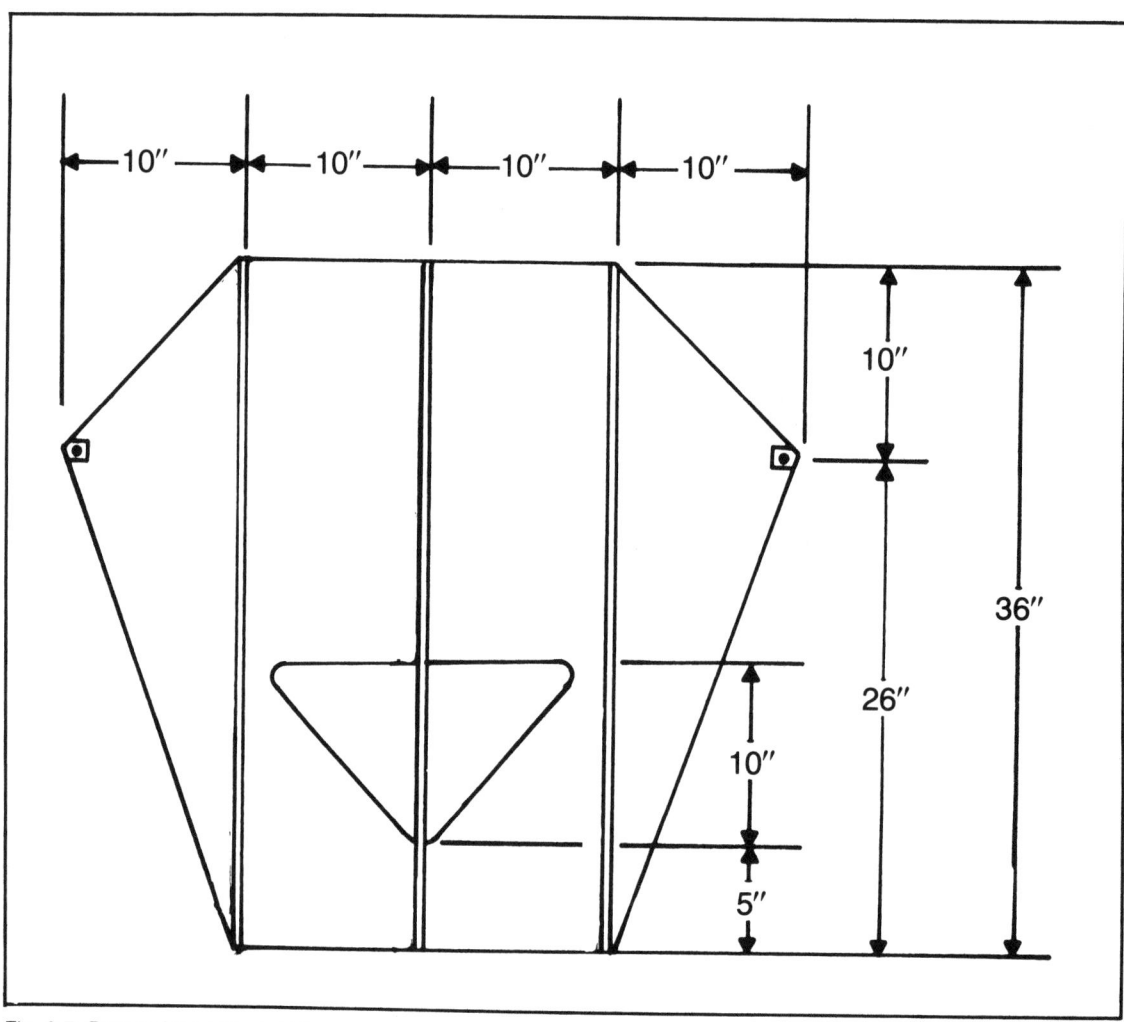

Fig. 8-7. Pattern for basic sled kite.

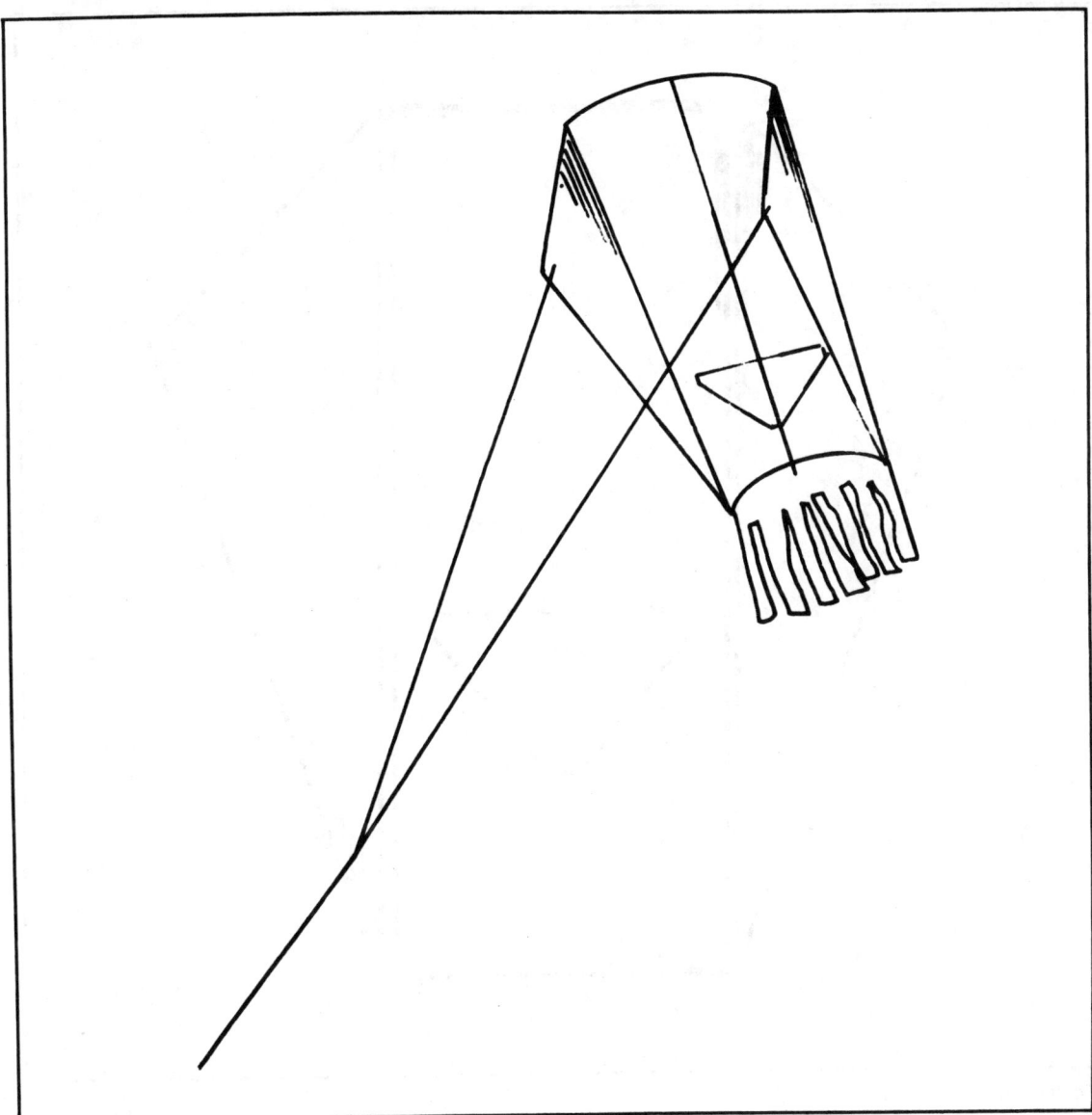

Fig. 8-8. Decorative tail added to sled kite.

Make holes in the covering material for the bridle strings. Reinforce them with tape.

Bridle

The bridle has two points of attachment, as shown in Fig. 8-6. The strings are tied in a loop or to a bridle ring 72 inches from the points of attachment to the kite. It is important to have each string exactly the same length.

Tail

The sled kite is usually flown without a tail, although a tail can be used if desired. A short decorative tail of plastic can be joined to the aft edge of the covering material, as shown in Fig. 8-8. Construction of tails is detailed in Chapter 5.

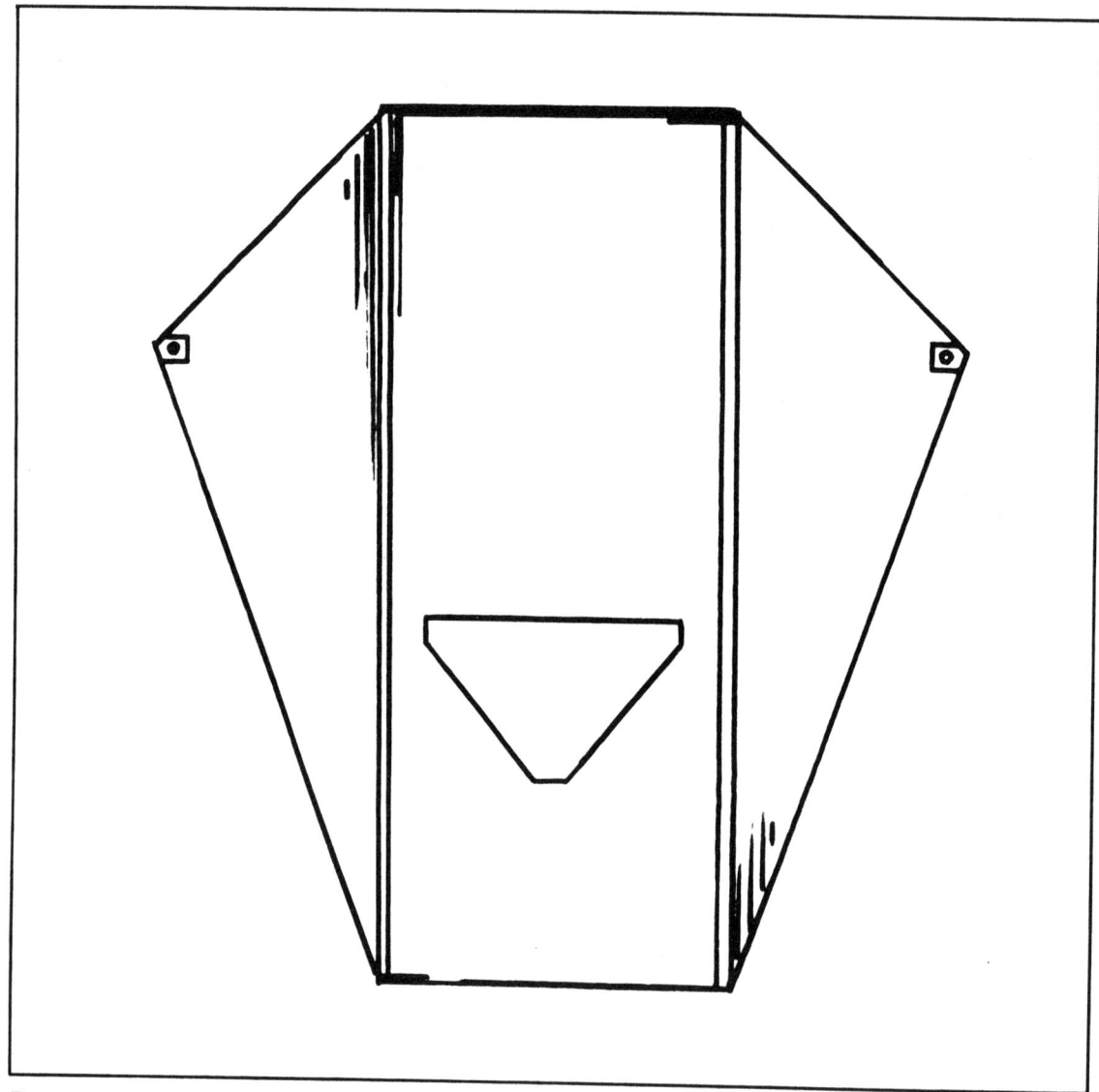

Fig. 8-9. Two-stick sled kite.

Variations

The sled kite can be constructed in a range of sizes with the sticks 1 foot or less in length to 6 feet or more in length, by keeping the proportions the same. As a general rule, you will need to reduce the weight of the smaller sizes by using proportionally smaller sticks and lighter weight covering material. You will need to use larger sticks and heavier covering material for the larger sizes.

A variation of the three stick sled kite, detailed above, is the two stick design shown in Fig. 8-9. This design can also be made in a variety of sizes by keeping the proportions the same.

For both the three- and two-stick designs, you may want to experiment with changes in the basic proportions and with the size and/or placement of the air vent. Still another possibility is to use two or more air vents.

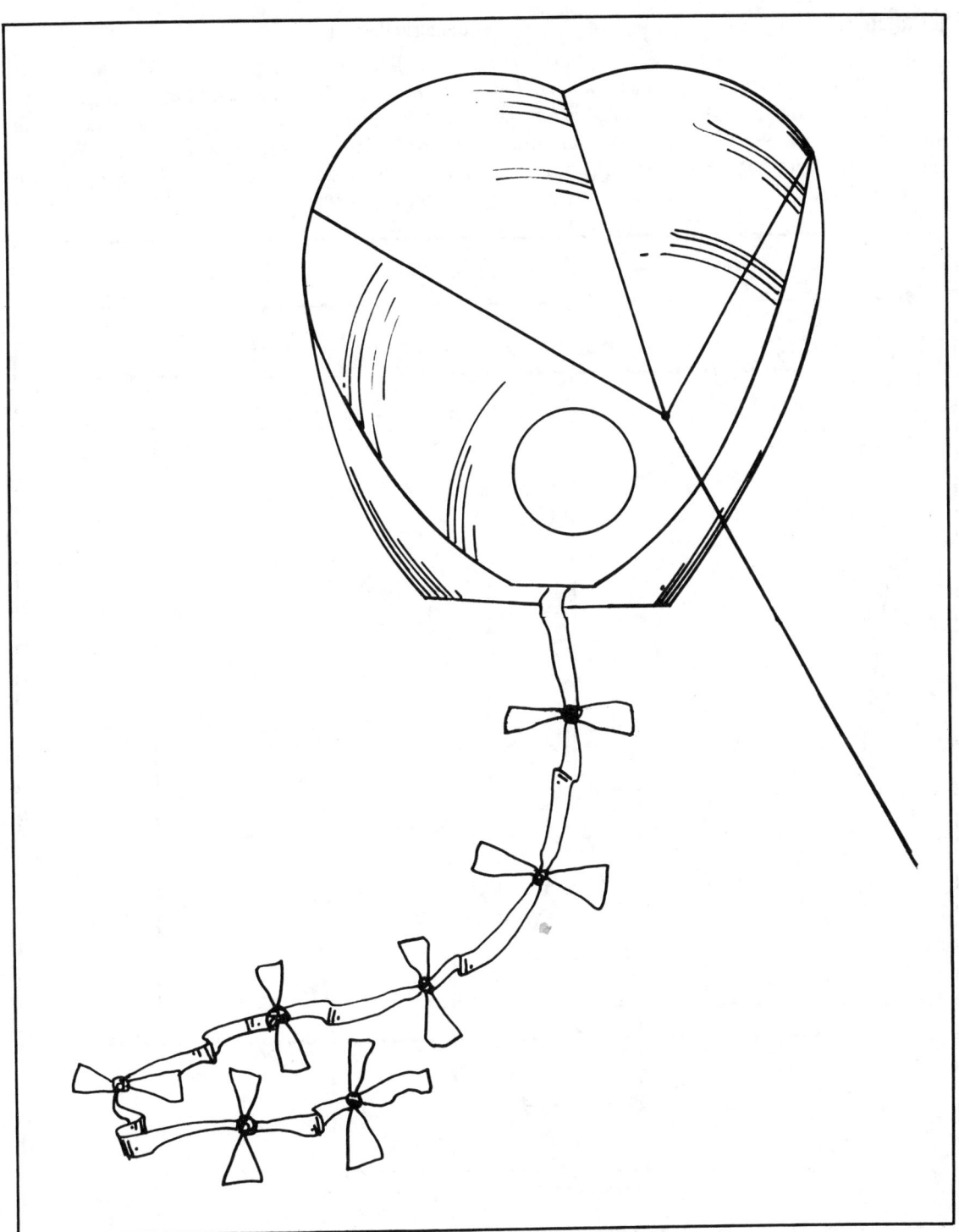
Fig. 8-10. Wiley's plastic bag kite—a nonrigid kite design.

NONRIGID KITE

The idea of constructing kites without any sticks at all is interesting. While elaborate parafoil designs can be constructed, the one designed, the Wiley plastic bag kite (Fig. 8-10), can be made from a lightweight plastic bag and serves to illustrate the principle nicely.

Construction

A lightweight plastic bag of the dimensions shown in Fig. 8-11 was used for the original kite that I designed and constructed, but other sizes will also work if the proportions are kept the same. Cut the bag to the pattern shown in Fig. 8-11. Notice that the bag is cut open on one side from the top to a

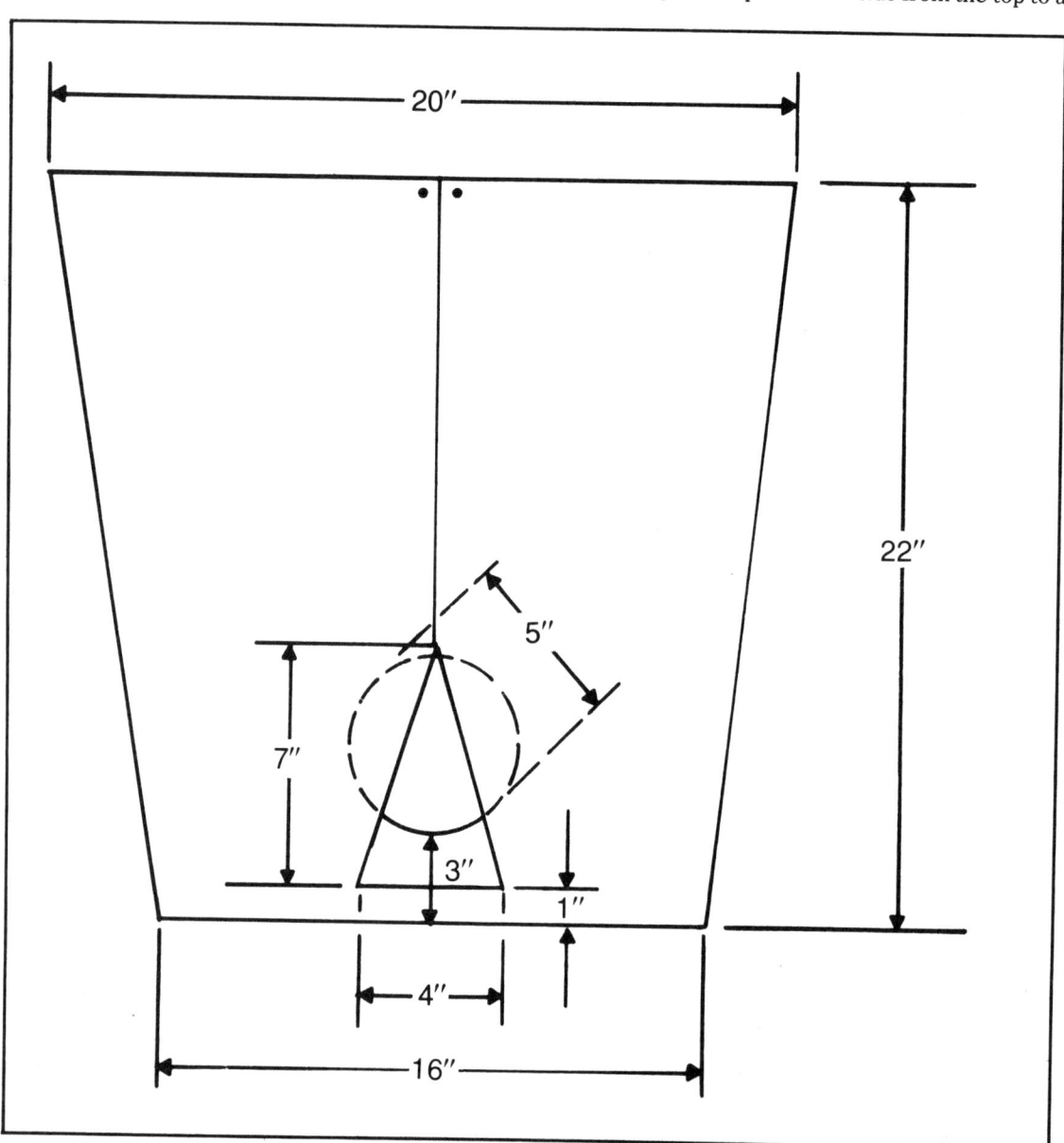

Fig. 8-11. Pattern for Wiley's plastic bag kite.

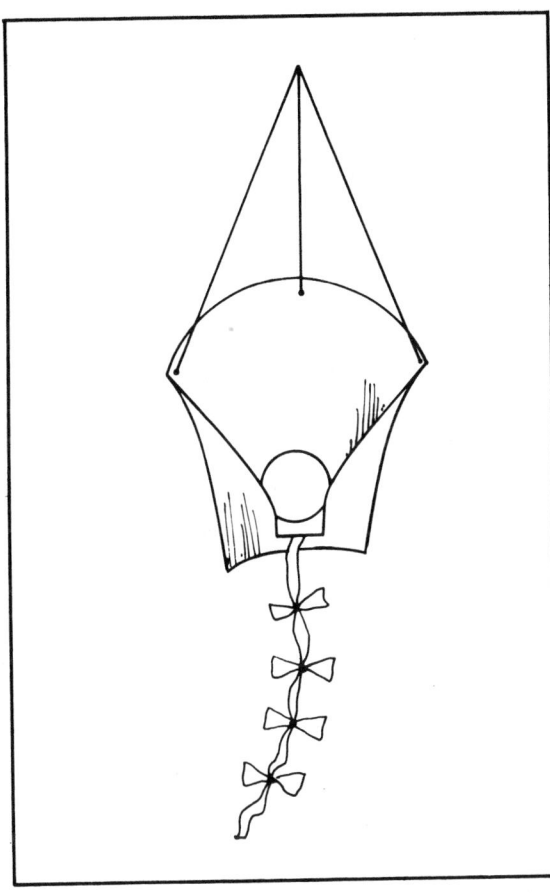

Fig. 8-12. Bridle and tail attachments for Wiley's plastic bag kite.

point 1 inch above the bottom seam and the bottom of the opening is widened. A 5-inch-diameter air vent is made in the other side 3 inches above the bottom seam.

Three holes for the bridle string attachments are made in the upper rim of the bag, as shown in Fig. 8-12. The holes should be reinforced with tape or by other means. The center string is 36 inches from point of attachment to bridle loop or ring. The other two strings are 29 inches long. These may require slight adjustments to give the kite proper stability and lift.

Tail

A single tail can be used, as shown in Fig. 8-12. The tail can be attached to the bottom of the bag with tape or glue.

Variations

I find it interesting to experiment with a variety of sizes and shapes of plastic bags for making this nonrigid kite design.

You may also want to experiment with more elaborate designs, which can be sewn from lightweight cloth fabric.

A large variety of other semirigid and nonrigid kites can also be constructed. This is a relatively new area of kite design and construction and there are many exciting possibilities here.

Chapter 9

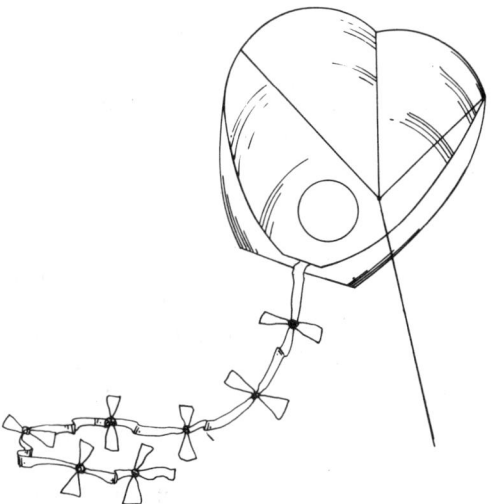

Decorating Kites

Although some people choose to build kites purely for their flying ability, others pursue the hobby with a fascination for the beauty of kites. For some, it's the only consideration. These kite artists create kites that are works of art, not flying objects.

For our purposes, we will assume that you will be decorating kites that can also be flown. This means that the decoration cannot reduce the performance by adding weight or changing the balance, at least not to any great extent. The aim is to produce a kite that not only performs well, but also looks good.

BASIC PLANNING

Planning the decoration for a particular kite should begin early in the construction process. Some covering materials, for example, are more suitable for certain decorating techniques than others. If you want to use a painted design, you may want to cover the kite with paper, which is easy to paint, rather than plastic, which is often difficult to paint.

Kites can be decorated with representational designs, such as of human forms, birds, fish, trees, butterflies, houses, geometric forms, or abstract designs. Generally, if the kite itself is representational, such as a bird form, you will probably also want to decorate the kite in a representational design, that is, a bird as a bird and a dragon as a dragon, and so on. You can be realistic, with or without detail, comic, or whatever else you desire. There are really no limits here.

If you choose geometric or abstract designs, you can really let your imagination go. No limits here. This type of decorating is especially popular for non-figure kites, such as the basic two-stick kite and the hexagon kite and other similar shapes.

Another type of decorating is to use various combinations covering material colors on the same kite. The top half of a kite, for example, could be blue and the bottom half red.

METHODS FOR DECORATING KITES

Most kite decorating falls into one of two basic

categories: using already colored materials, and adding color to materials. A combination of these methods can also be used.

Using Colored Materials

You can decorate a kite by selecting covering material that is a desirable color for the particular kite. This can be a single color or a covering material that already has a design on it. If you cover a kite with a silk scarf, for example, it may already have a design or even a representational form on it.

You can cut designs out of material of one color and paste them on another color of material. When you do this, however, you should make certain that the materials can be securely joined by gluing or some other means and that the weight added to the kite will not reduce the performance to any great extent.

Adding Color

The most often used method for adding color is probably by painting. Paint can be applied by brush, spray, or other means. Before decorating a kite by painting, however, always try the paint you intend to use on a sample piece of the covering material to make certain that the paint is compatible. Popular paints for paper covered kites include water colors, acrylic paints, and India ink. Special paints, marking pens, and so on are often required for plastic materials. Decorating fabrics, while it can be done, is a skill in itself.

The painting can be freely applied by painting a design or picture on the kite covering material. You can also use masking tape or stencils to outline the areas where you want to apply paint.

Other methods for adding color include stamping, dyeing, spatter painting, tie dyeing, batiking, and silkscreening. In fact, many art and craft techniques for adding color to paper, and other materials can be applied to decorating kites.

The coloring can be done before or after the covering material is installed in the kite frames. The method to use depends on the technique for adding the color. In some cases, the coloring or decoration can be done either before or after the covering material has been installed. In other cases, as when dyeing, the coloring is usually applied before the covering material is installed on the kite frame.

DEVELOPING DESIGNS

Designs for decorating kites can be based on geometrical figures and forms, nature, abstractions, or functional items.

Basic Geometric Forms

Many designs are based on geometrical figures and forms. Geometrical figures include squares, triangles, circles, rectangles, and hexagons. Geometrical forms include cubes, cylinders, pyramids, cones, and spheres. Geometrical figures are two-dimensional; geometrical forms are three-dimensional.

Line is the simplest and most intrinsic element of geometric design. A line may be straight or curved. A straight line can be vertical, horizontal, or diagonal, as shown in Fig. 9-1. As a general rule, straight lines are stronger and more direct than curved lines. The direction of the line plays an important role in strength. Vertical lines reach upward and suggest strength. Horizontal lines are more tranquil and restful. Diagonal lines suggest action.

Straight lines can be joined to form a variety of patterns, such as shown in Fig. 9-2. A variety of effects can be achieved. Zigzag lines, for example, give a feeling of nervous movement (Fig. 9-3).

Straight lines may be sketched freehand or drawn mechanically by using a straight edge or

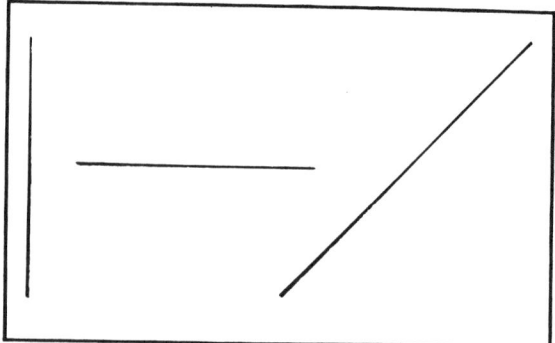

Fig. 9-1. Straight-vertical, horizontal, and diagonal lines.

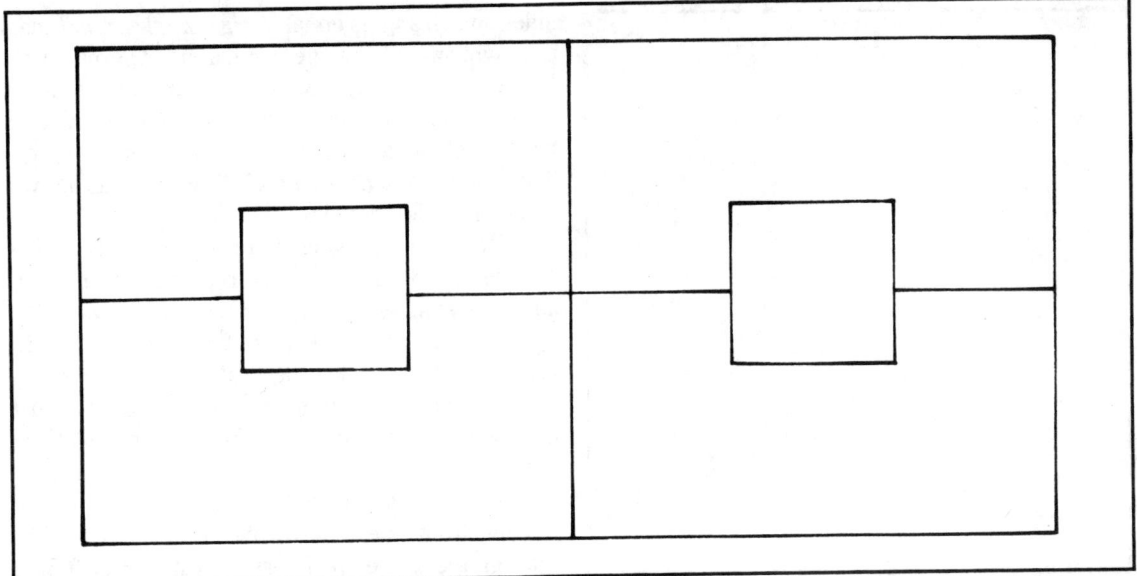

Fig. 9-2. Pattern formed by straight lines joined together.

other drawing tools. Many designs start out as sketches, which are drawn without the aid of drawing tools. Naturally, sketched lines will lack precision, but with care they can be drawn adequately for the purposes of preliminary design work and even some actual kite decorating work. Sketches are often later redrawn using drawing tools.

Lines can also be curved. A curved line is generally lighter and livelier in a design than a straight line. Curves can be drawn freely by hand or made mechanically (and sometimes mathematically) with the aid of drawing tools. Geometric figures, which are mathematical configurations, can be sketched freehand or made with the aid of drawing tools. In a similar manner, three dimensional geometric forms can be represented on paper by means of sketching and mechanical drawing.

A variety of geometric figures can be used for decorating kites. A *square*, which has four equal sides meeting in right angles (Fig. 9-4), is a fundamental geometric figure used in decorative design. By using subdivisions, variations, and combinations of squares, many designs can be created.

A *rectangle*, which includes squares, is a four-

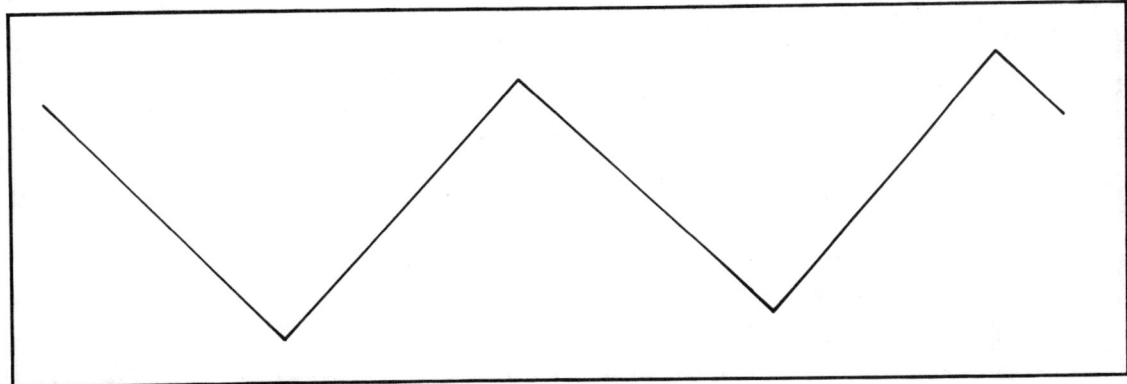

Fig. 9-3. Zigzag line.

Fig. 9-4. A square.

sides and all angles equal. A *right-angle triangle* has one right angle (an angle that has sides perpendicular to one another), two equal acute angles of 45 degrees, and two equal sides. An *isosceles triangle* has no right angle but has two equal angles and two equal sides. A *scalene triangle* (Fig. 9-6) has no two sides or angles equal.

Other straight sided figures useful in kite decorating include the rhombus, rhomboid, trapezoid, and trapezium (Fig. 9-7).

Curved lines are used to form figures that are used extensively in kite decorating work. A *circle* is a plane figure made up of a single curved line that has every point equidistant from the point at the center.

The *diameter* of a circle is any straight line passing from one side of the circle to the other through the center point, as shown in Fig. 9-8. A *radius* is any straight line that extends from the circumference to the center point (Fig. 9-8). A *chord* is a straight line that intersects the circumference at any two points, as illustrated in Fig. 9-8. A *segment* is the plane area of a circle that is cut off by a chord, as shown in Fig. 9-9. A *sector* is the plane area bounded by two radii and a section of the circumference, as shown in Fig. 9-9.

sided figure with the sides parallel and meeting at right angles, as shown in Fig. 9-5. Other rectangular forms besides squares can be added to form additional design patterns.

Triangles are important geometric figures used in design work. *Equilateral triangles* have all

Fig. 9-5. A rectangle.

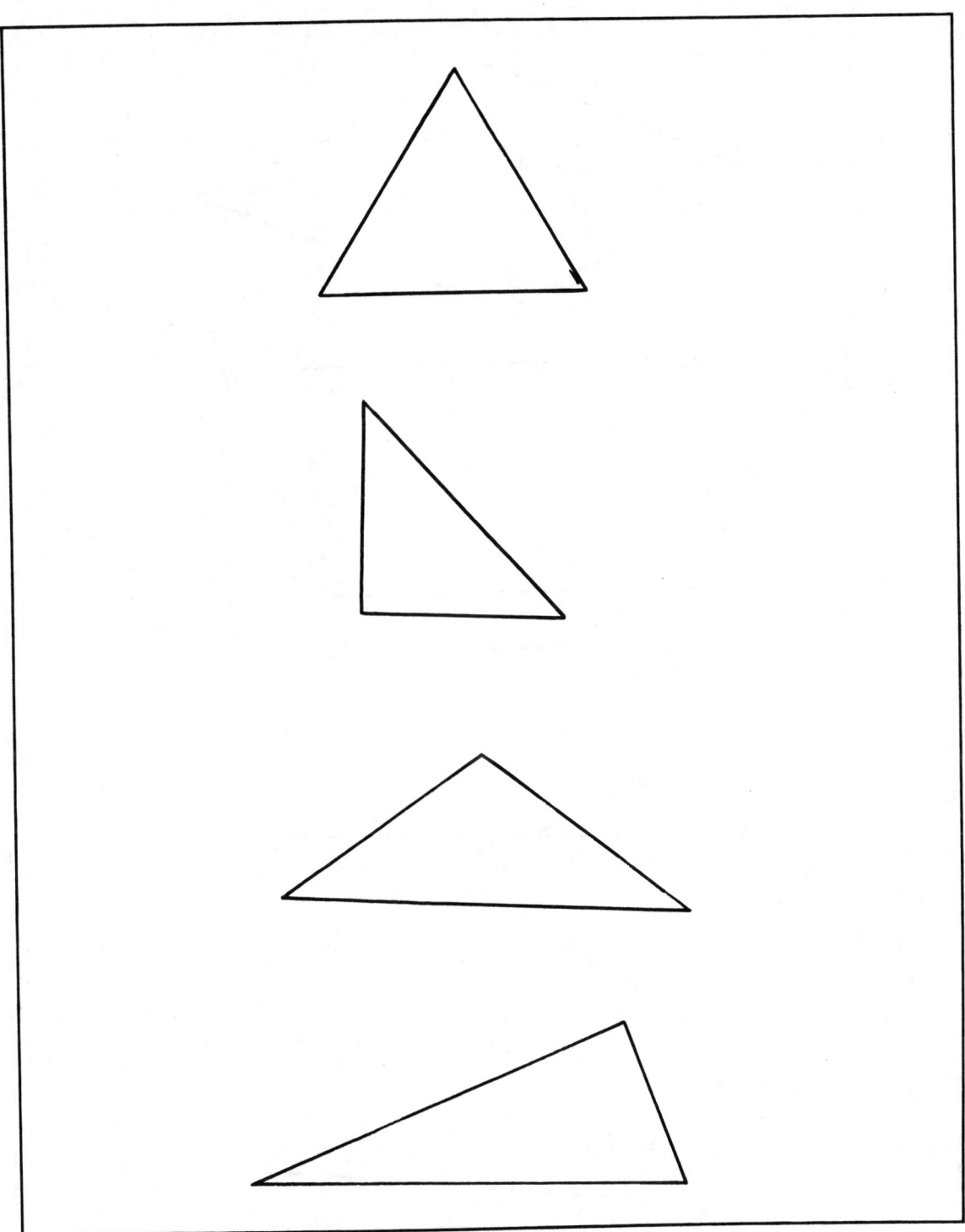

Fig. 9-6. An equilateral triangle, right-angle triangle, isosceles triangle, and a scalene triangle.

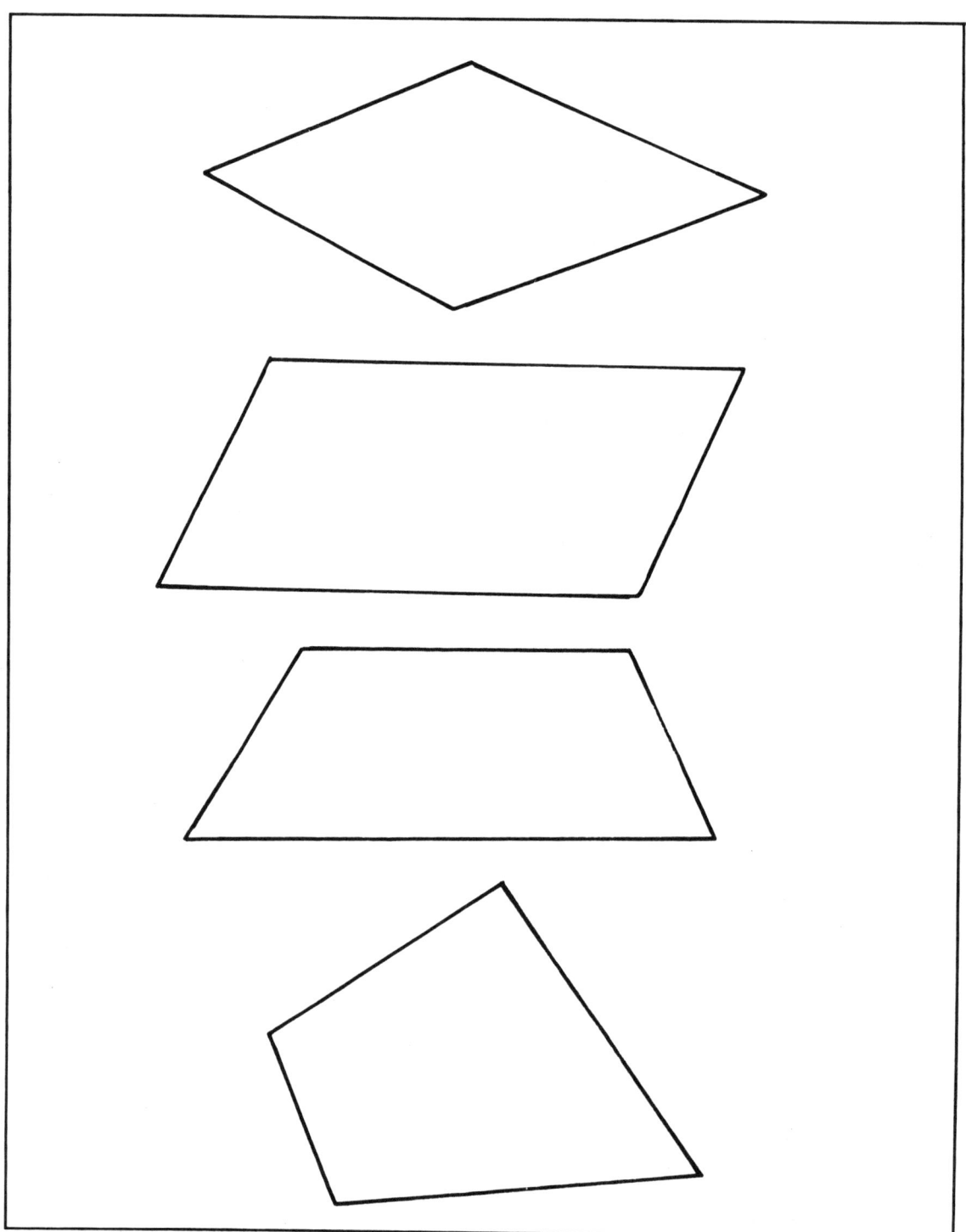

Fig. 9-7. A rhombus, rhomboid, trapezoid, and trapezium.

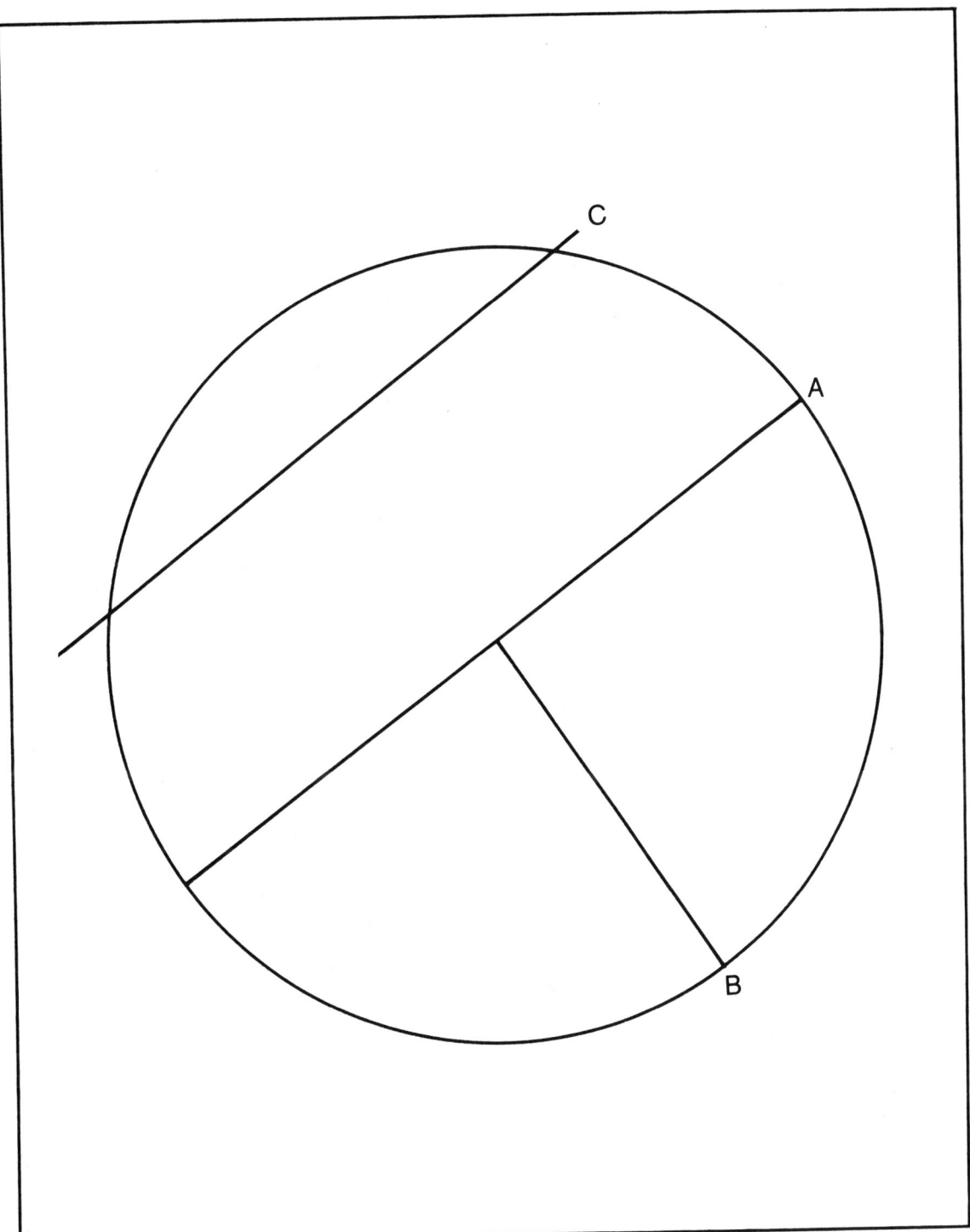

Fig. 9-8. Diameter of circle (A), radius of circle (B), and a chord (C).

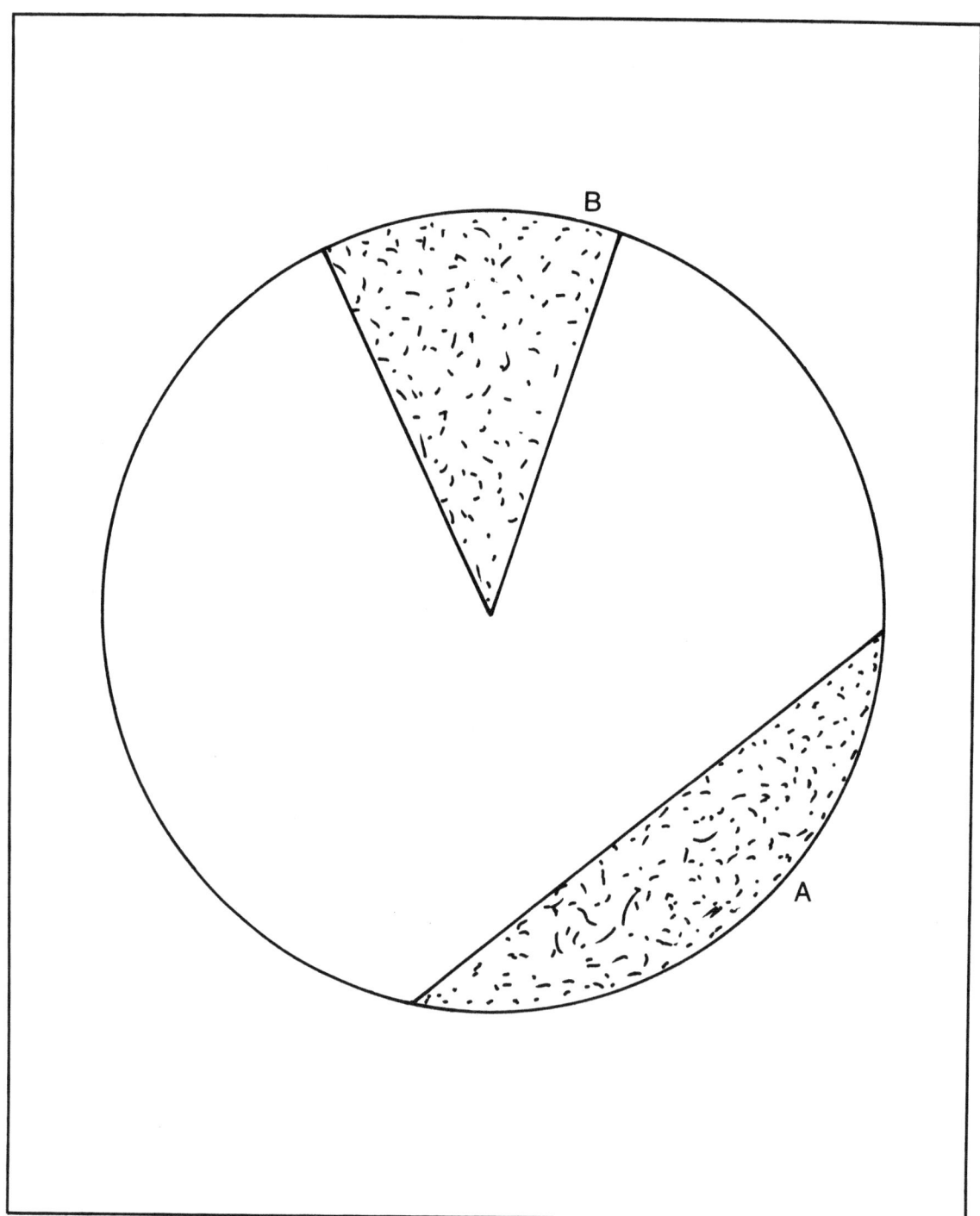

Fig. 9-9. A segment of a circle (A), and a sector of a circle (B).

Circles and subdivisions of circles are widely used both without and with straight lines to form design patterns.

Designs can also be formed on kite covering materials by making freely drawn lines. Abstractions can be formed in the imagination, and there is considerable overlapping of geometric forms and abstractions.

Designing from Natural and Man-Made Objects

Many designs used in kite decorating are based on nature. Examples include representations of people, animals, fish, birds, trees, and so on. The designs can be realistic or conventionalized (stylized). A fish form used for decorating a kite, for example, can be a representation of a particular fish, stylized to represent fish in a more general way, or even extremely stylized to be a semi-abstraction of a fish shape. In many cases, natural forms are simplified for design use.

Representations of man-made objects, such as houses, boats, automobiles, fans, and bells are other possibilities for decorating kites. The most important thing is to use your imagination, both to create new designs and modify traditional designs. Oriental and Polynesian art exhibits, books, and artifacts are all good sources of inspiration.

Chapter 10

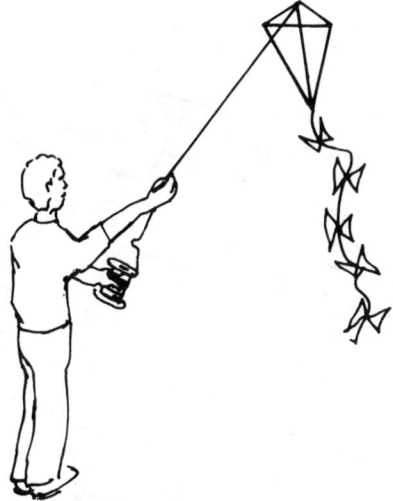

Flying Kites

Kites are flown for fun, recreation, festivals, sport, games, contests, and novelty uses. The purpose of this chapter is to cover the techniques for launching, flying, landing, and using kites in a variety of ways.

BASIC FLYING TECHNIQUES

It should be kept in mind that there is no one correct way to fly a kite. The attempt is to present some techniques that many people have found effective.

Kite Strings and Reels

One end of the kite string is usually attached to the bridle loop or ring on the kite, or directly to the kite, depending on the particular kite. Since kite strings are usually quite long, you will need a way to handle the string. One method is to use a cardboard tube, such as the type that string is wound on when it is sold. A wooden dowel a couple of inches in diameter can also be used. You can also shape a hand reel from wood, such as shown in Fig. 10-1. A variety of manufactured reels that have a crank arrangement for winding the string are available.

Flying Sites

An important consideration is a place to fly your kite. You will need a large open space that is free of trees, electrical and telephone wires, buildings, and other obstacles. The area should be completely free of automobile traffic. The selection of the site is important for both safety and enjoyment of the kite flying experience.

Flying the Kite

To launch a kite without help, stand with your back to the wind, as shown in Fig. 10-2. Hold the kite in one hand and the reel of string in the other. Let the breeze take the kite, and feed out the line. For this to work successfully, you will need sufficient wind for the particular type of kite. Bridle angles, amount of tail, and other factors may also come into play (see Chapter 2). You can also walk toward the direction the wind is coming from as you feed out the line.

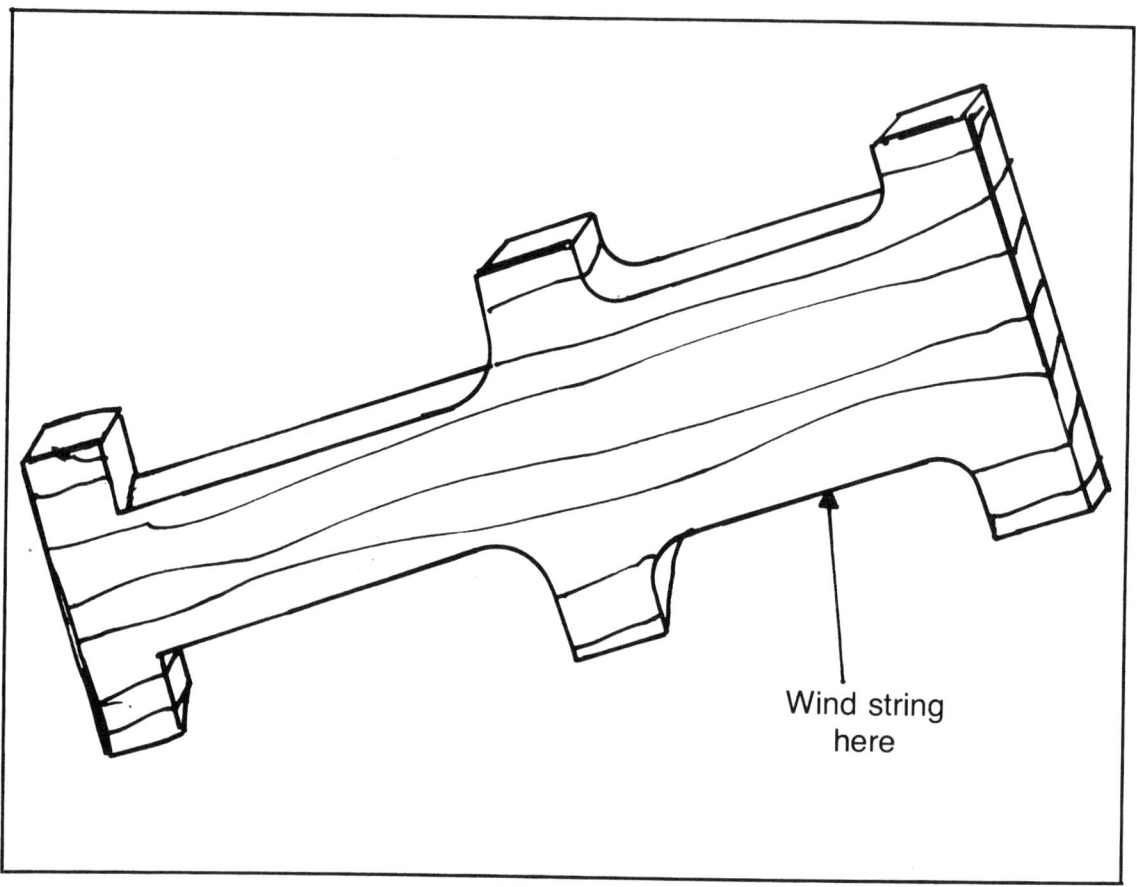

Fig. 10-1. Hand reel shaped from wood.

An alternate method for launching a kite is to have a partner hold the kite, as shown in Fig. 10-3. This allows you to begin with a long length of string already out.

To land a kite, you can slowly wind the string in if the wind is not too strong. You can also walk toward the kite as you reel in the line, which tends to dump the wind from the kite. In extreme conditions, you can place the reel on the ground and walk toward the kite while bringing the string in hand-over-hand.

You will frequently have to make adjustments to kites to get them to fly properly. The bridle angle is extremely important. If the kite won't climb, for example, you will need to reduce the bridle angle.

If the kite loops or spins uncontrollably, you can add more tail. As a general rule, you should use the minimum of tail that gives the kite adequate stability. Too much tail tends to make a kite heavy and sluggish.

IDEAS FOR KITE FLYING

After you have mastered basic kite flying, you may want to go on to stunt flying and novelty kite flying. One possibility is to send *climbers* up the kite string. A piece of paper with a small hole and a slit so it can be placed over the kite string is a simple climber. The wind will carry this up to the kite. You may also want to design and construct other climbers in the shape of airplanes, rockets, or sailboats.

You may also want to try dropping small parachutes, balloons, confetti, or messages from kites. These can be released by a string attachment or time releases, as desired.

Kites can also be used to carry up flags, banners, and other decorations. These are often attached to the kite string or line some distance from the kite.

You may want to try taking photographs from kites. Attach an inexpensive camera to the kite, and use a string or time shutter release.

You may want to try flying kites in tandem. One kite is attached to another. Usually, the smallest kite goes up first. Two or more kites can be flown in this manner.

You can use a kite for fishing. A fishing line with a baited hook is attached to the kite. The kite is then flown out over the water, carrying the baited hook out to the desired fishing spot.

CONTESTS

Many kite contests are possible, including highest flyer, smallest kite, largest kite, most beautiful kite, most ingenious, most comical, most maneuverable or best stunt flier, most kites on one string, and kite fights.

There are local kite flying contests in many areas of the United States. There are also national and international contests and festivals.

CLUBS AND ORGANIZATIONS

There are kite flying organizations and clubs in many parts of the United States and other parts of the world. You can often find out if there is a group

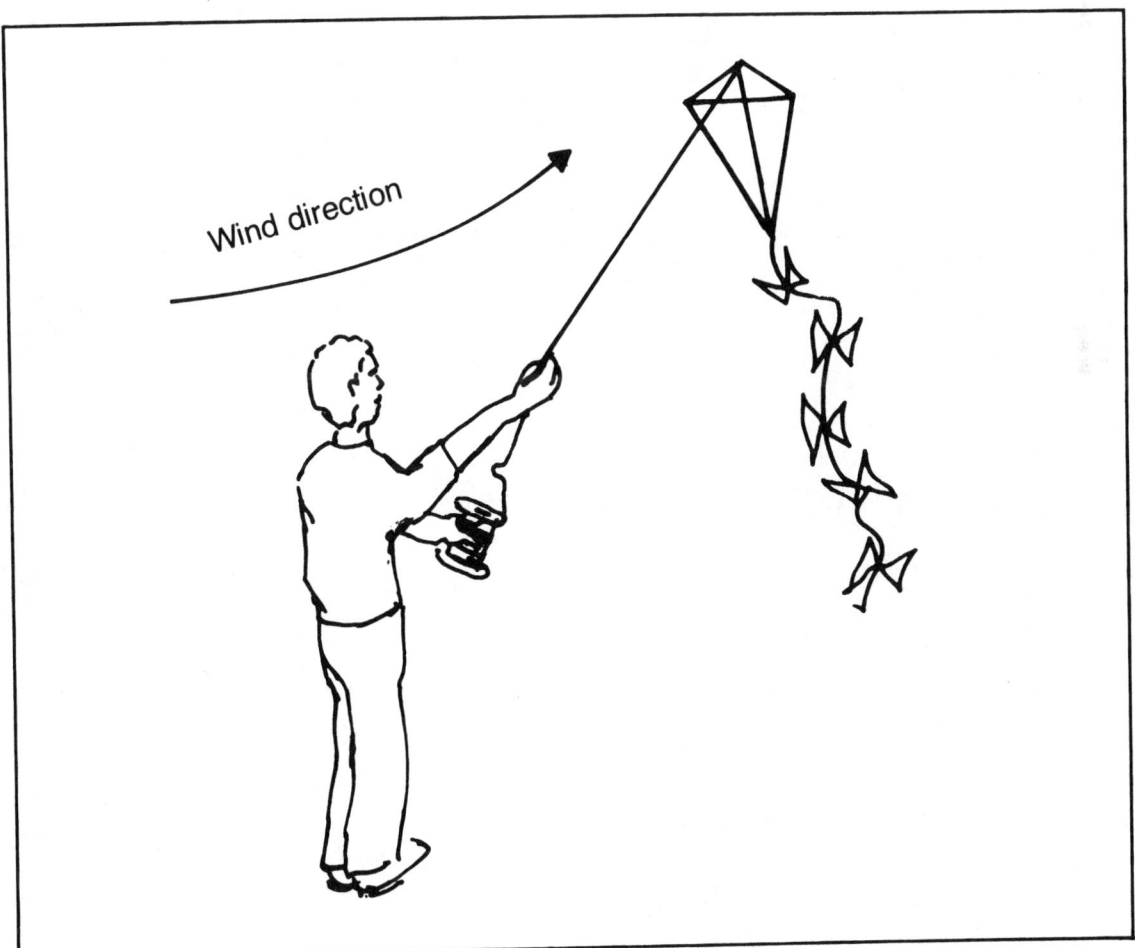

Fig. 10-2. Launching kite without help.

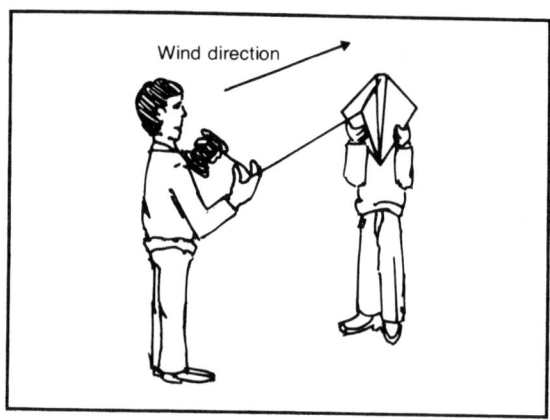

Fig. 10-3. Launching kite with help of a partner.

in your area by asking at the nearest kite flying store or hobby shop that carries a line of kites. If there is no club or organization in your area, you may want to organize one.

There is also a national organization, the American Kitefliers Association, 1104 Fidelity Building, 219 North Charles Street, Baltimore, Maryland, 21201, that you may want to join. The organization publishes a bimonthly newsletter and sponsors a national kite festival each year. There is also an international organization, the International Kitefliers Association, P.O. Box 27, 31 School Street, Hatfield, Massachusetts, 01038, that may be of interest to you.

Appendix

Kite Stores

Come-Fly-A-Kite, Inc.
Carmel Plaza
Carmel, CA 93921

Come-Fly-A-Kite, Inc.
813 State
Santa Barbara, CA 93101

Come Fly a Kite Store
900 North Point
San Francisco, CA 94109

Go Fly a Kite Store
1434 Third Avenue
New York, NY 10028

International Kites
1891 Caspian Avenue
Long Beach, CA 90810

The Kite Shop, Ltd.
1917 Kalakaua Avenue
Honolulu, HA 96815

Let's Fly a Kite Store
1510 Walnut Street
Berkeley, CA 94708

Index

Index

A
Abbe, Cleveland, 4
Abrasive papers, 47
Aerodynamics, 13
Airplane Kite Company, 25
Airplane-type box kite, 240
Allison, W.M., 9
Angle of attack, 16
Archibald, E.D., 4
Arch-top kite, 141
Arch-top kite, bow string, 146
Arch-top kite, bridle, 146
Arch-top kite, covering material, 145
Arch-top kite, frame, 141
Arch-top kite, tail, 146
Arch-top kite, variations, 146
Ash, 56
Auger bits, 42

B
Balance, 17
Balloon kites, 12
Ball peen hammers, 42
Balsa wood, 55
Bamboo, 56
Bamboo sticks, 60
Batut, Arthur, 5
Bell, Alexander Graham, 6
Bernoulli's theorem, 15
Bird kite, 195

Bird kite, bow string, 200
Bird kite, bridle, 200
Bird kite, covering material, 199
Bird kite, frame, 195
Bird kite, tail, 201
Bird kite, variations, 201
Birt, W.R., 4
Bowed kites, 81
Bowing, 21
Box kite, 219
Box kite, bridle, 225
Box kite, covering material, 219
Box kite, frame, 219
Box kite, tail, 225
Box kite, variations, 225
Box kite with side wings, 226
Box kite with side wings, bridle, 229
Box kite with side wings, covering material, 227
Box kite with side wings, frame, 226
Box kite with side wings, tail, 229
Box kite with side wings, variations, 229
Box or cellular kites, 11
Braces, 42
Breeze, fresh, 19
Breeze, gentle, 19
Breeze, light, 19
Breeze, strong, 19
Breezes, 19

Bridle, 17
Bridle attachments, 77
Butterfly kites, 212

C
Calm, 19
Cellular kites, 219
Centipede or caterpillar kite, 207
Centipede or caterpillar kite, bridle, 209
Centipede or caterpillar kite, covering material, 208
Centipede or caterpillar kite, frame, 207
Centipede or caterpillar kite, linking strings, 209
Centipede or caterpillar kite, tail, 209
Centipede or caterpillar kite, variations, 210
Challenger kite, 25
China, vii
Chisels, 35
Chord, 260
Clamps, 41
Claw hammers, 42
Clayton, H.H., 6
Cody, S.F., 9
Color addition, 258
Construction, 20
Coping saw, 35

Cotton, 74
Covering materials, 57

D

Decorating kites, 257
Delta wing, 9
Delta wing kite, 245
Delta wing kite, covering material, 245
Delta wing kite, frame, 245
Delta wing kite, variations, 248
Design, 4
Design development, 258
Designing from natural and man-made objects, 265
Design methods, 23
Diagonal-cutting pliers, 40
Diameter, 260
Double basic kite, 171
Double basic kite, bow string, 177
Double basic kite, bridle, 179
Double basic kite, covering material, 175
Double basic kite, frame, 171
Double basic kite, tail, 179
Double basic kite, variations, 179
Double diamond kite, 184
Double diamond kite, bow string, 187
Double diamond kite, bridle, 188
Double diamond kite, covering material, 186
Double diamond kite, frame, 184
Double diamond kite, tail, 188
Double diamond kite, variations, 188
Double square kite, 179
Double square kite, bow string, 183
Double square kite, bridle, 183
Double square kite, covering material, 182
Double square kite, frame, 179
Double square kite, tail, 183
Double square kite, variations, 184
Douglas fir, 56
Dragonfly kites, 212
Dragon, serpent, or snake kite, 203
Dragon, serpent, or snake kite, bridle, 205
Dragon, serpent, or snake kite, covering material, 205
Dragon, serpent, or snake kite, frame, 204
Dragon, serpent, or snake kite, tail, 206
Dragon, serpent, or snake kite, variations, 206
Drawknives, 45
Drill presses, 44
Drills, 42
Drills, electric, 42
Drills, push, 42
Drills, twist, 42
Drogues, 21
Duckbill snips, 37

du Hauvel, Charles, 4

E

Early kites, 2
Eight-point star kite, 159
Eight-point star kite, bridle, 160
Eight-point star kite, covering material, 159
Eight-point star kite, frame, 159
Eight-point star kite, tail, 160
Eight-point star kite, variations, 161
Electric drills, 42
End-cutting pliers, 41
Equilateral triangles, 260
Espy, J.P., 4

F

Figure kites, 212
Files, 45
Five-point star kite, 148
Five-point star kite, bow string, 152
Five-point star kite, bridle, 152
Five-point star kite, covering material, 150
Five-point star kite, frame, 148
Five-point star kite, tail, 152
Five-point star kite, variations, 153
Flat kites, 10, 81
Flexible kites, 1
Flying clubs and organizations, 269
Flying contests, 269
Flying kites, 13, 267
Flying sites, 267
Flying techniques, 267
Form, 20
Forming tools, 47
Four-circle kite, 189
Four-circle kite, bow string, 189
Four-circle kite, bridle, 189
Four-circle kite, covering material, 189
Four-circle kite, frame, 189
Four-circle kite, tail, 189
Four-circle kite, variations, 190
Four-unit tetrahedron kite, 237
Four-unit tetrahedron kite, bridle, 238
Four-unit tetrahedron kite, covering material, 238
Four-unit tetrahedron kite, frame, 237
Four-unit tetrahedron kite, tail, 238
Four-unit tetrahedron kite, variations, 240
Franklin, Benjamin, 3
Franklin Kite Club, 4

G

Gayla Industries, 25
Geometric forms, 258
Glues, 57
Greece, 2
Guidelines, 70
Gussets, 67
Guys, 70

H

Hacksaws, 35
Hammers, 41
Hammers, ball peen, 42
Hammers, claw, 42
Hammers, tack, 42
Hargrave, Lawrence, 5
Hexagonal box kite, 240
Hi-Flier Manufacturing Company, 25
House kites, 218
Human-form kites, 218

I

Isosceles triangles, 260

J

Jalbert, Domina, 9
Joining sticks and frame members, 65

K

Keel, 9
Kerf, 35
Kite, airplane-type box, 240
Kite, arch-top, 141
Kite, bird, 195
Kite, box, 219
Kite, box with side wings, 227
Kite, centipede or caterpillar, 207
Kite, delta wing, 245
Kite, double basic, 171
Kite, double diamond, 184
Kite, double square, 179
Kite, dragon, serpent, or snake, 203
Kite, five-point star, 148
Kite, four-circle, 189
Kite, four-unit tetrahedron, 237
Kite, hexagonal box, 240
Kite, nonrigid, 254
Kite, parachute, 9
Kite, rectangular, 133
Kite, rectangular box with wings, 240
Kite, single-unit tetrahedron, 229
Kite, six-point star, 153
Kite, sled, 9, 248
Kite, styrofoam bow, 94
Kite, three-stick, 127
Kite, three-stick hexagonal, 119
Kite, three-stick with converging longitudinals, 96
Kite, three-stick with crossing longitudinals, 106
Kite, three-stick with parallel longitudinals, 101
Kite, triangular box, 240
Kite, triangular box with side wings, 240
Kite, triple-deck, 190
Kite, two-stick diamond, 116
Kite, two-stick flat, 81
Kite, two-stick square, 111
Kite covering materials, 72
Kite design variables, 20

Kite stores, 271
Kite strings and reels, 267
Kite tails, 77
Kites, 1
Kites, balloon, 12
Kites, bowed, 81
Kites, box or cellular, 11
Kites, butterfly, 212
Kites, cellular, 219
Kites, dragonfly, 212
Kites, early, 2
Kites, figure, 212
Kites, flat, 10, 81
Kites, flexible, 1
Kites, house, 218
Kites, human-form, 218
Kites, lantern, 218
Kites, manufactured, 25
Kites, modern, 3
Kites, nonrigid, 12
Kites, origin and spread, 1
Kites, rotary, 12
Kites, semirigid, 12
Kites, semirigid and nonrigid, 245
Kites, tree, 218
Kites, uses, 7
Knives, 31
Korea, 2

L

Lamson, Charles H., 6
Lantern kites, 218
Lift, 13
Locking pliers, 40
Long-nose pliers, 40

M

Malaysia, 2
Mallets, 42
Manufactured kites, 25
Marking tools, 49
Materials, 55
Measuring tools, 49
Metal sticks, 62
Model airplane techniques, 78
Modern kites, 3

N

Newton's law of action and reaction, 15
Nonrigid kite, 254
Nonrigid kite, construction, 254
Nonrigid kite, tail, 255
Nonrigid kite, variations, 255
Nonrigid kites, 12
Nylon, 74

O

Oak, 56
Octagonal kite, 161
Octagonal kite, bridle, 171
Octagonal kite, covering material, 171

Octagonal kite, frame, 169
Octagonal kite, tail, 171
Octagonal kite, variations, 171
Oilstones, 34
Orient, 2

P

Paper, 72
Parachute kite, 9
Parawing, 9
Parry, Sir William, 4
Pilot mark, 64
Planes, 45
Plastic films, 75
Plastic sticks, 63
Pliers, 38
Pliers, diagonal-cutting, 40
Pliers, end-cutting, 41
Pliers, locking, 40
Pliers, long-nose, 40
Pliers, side-cutting, 40
Pliers, slip-joint, 38
Pliers, utility, 40
Pocock, George, 8
Polo, Marco, 7
Polyester, 74
Polyethylene, 75
Polynesia, 2
Ponderosa pine, 56
Push drills, 42

R

Radius, 260
Rasps, 45
Rattan sticks, 62
Razor blades, 35
Razor knives, 35
Rectangle, 259
Rectangular box kite with wings, 240
Rectangular kite, 133
Rectangular kite, bow string, 136
Rectangular kite, bridle, 136
Rectangular kite, covering material, 136
Rectangular kite, frame, 133
Rectangular kite, tail, 141
Rectangular kite, variations, 141
Right-angle triangles, 260
Rogallo, Dr. Francis, 9
Rotary hobby tools, 51
Rotary kites, 12

S

Saber saw, 35
Safety equipment, 54
Sanding tools, 47
Saws, 35
Saws, coping, 35
Saws, saber, 35
Scalene triangles, 260
Scissors, 36
Scott, Frank, 9

Screwdrivers, 44
Sector, 260
Segment, 260
Semirigid and nonrigid kites, 245
Semirigid kites, 12
Shape, 20
Shears, 36
Side-cutting pliers, 40
Silk, 74
Single-unit tetrahedron kite, 229
Single-unit tetrahedron kite, bridle, 235
Single-unit tetrahedron kite, covering material, 235
Single-unit tetrahedron kite, frame, 232
Single-unit tetrahedron kite, tail, 237
Single-unit tetrahedron kite, variations, 237
Six-point star kite, 153
Six-point star kite, bow string, 159
Six-point star kite, bridle, 159
Six-point star kite, covering material, 156
Six-point star kite, frame, 153
Six-point star kite, tail, 159
Six-point star kite, variations, 159
Sky Hook, 25
Skyscraper, 25
Sky-Way Products Inc., 25
Sled kite, 9, 248
Sled kite, bridle, 251
Sled kite, construction, 249
Sled kite, tail, 251
Sled kite, variations, 252
Slip-joint pliers, 38
Soldering, 78
Soldering tools, 52
Space Ship Earth, 25
Spars, 59
Spectra Star Kites, 25
Spitfire kite, 25
Spokeshaves, 45
Spruce, 56
Squadron Kites, 25
Square, 259
Stability, 17
Sticks, 59
Sticks, bamboo, 60
Sticks, metal, 62
Sticks, plastic, 63
Sticks, rattan, 62
Sticks, wood, 59
Striegel Manufacturing Company, 25
String, 57
String lashings, 71
Styrofoam, 77
Styrofoam bow kite, 94
Sugar pine, 56

T

Tack hammers, 42

Tails, 21
Tang, 45
Tetrahedron, 6
The Philosophy of Storms, 4
Thread, 57
Three-stick hexagonal kite, 119
Three-stick hexagonal kite, bow string, 121
Three-stick hexagonal kite, bridle, 124
Three-stick hexagonal kite, covering material, 121
Three-stick hexagonal kite, frame, 119
Three-stick hexagonal kite, tail, 124
Three-stick hexagonal kite, variations, 127
Three-stick kite, 127
Three-stick kite, bow string, 130
Three-stick kite, bridle, 130
Three-stick kite, covering material, 128
Three-stick kite, frame, 127
Three-stick kite, tail, 131
Three-stick kite, variations, 132
Three-stick kite with converging longitudinals, 96
Three-stick kite with converging longitudinals, bow string, 99
Three-stick kite with converging longitudinals, bridle, 99
Three-stick kite with converging longitudinals, covering material, 98
Three-stick kite with converging longitudinals, frame, 96
Three-stick kite with converging longitudinals, tail, 101
Three-stick kite with converging longitudinals, variations, 101
Three-stick kite with crossing longitudinals, 106
Three-stick kite with crossing longitudinals, bow string, 109
Three-stick kite with crossing longitudinals, bridle, 109
Three-stick kite with crossing longitudinals, covering materials, 108
Three-stick kite with crossing longitudinals, tails, 109
Three-stick kite with crossing longitudinals, variations, 111
Three-stick kite with parallel longitudinals, 101
Three-stick kite with parallel longitudinals, bow string, 104
Three-stick kite with parallel longitudinals, bridle, 104
Three-stick kite with parallel longitudinals, covering materials, 103
Three-stick kite with parallel longitudinals, frame, 101
Three-stick kite with parallel longitudinals, tails, 104
Three-stick kite with parallel longitudinals, variations, 105
Tinsnip, 37
Tools, 31
Tree kites, 218
Triangles, 260
Triangles, equilateral, 260
Triangles, isosceles, 260
Triangles, right-angle, 260
Triangles, scalene, 260
Triangular box kite, 240
Triangular box kite with side wings, 240
Triple-deck kite, 190
Triple-deck kite, bow string, 193
Triple-deck kite, bridle, 193
Triple-deck kite, covering material, 191
Triple-deck kite, frame, 191
Triple-deck kite, tail, 193
Triple-deck kite, variations, 195
Triumph, 25
Try squares, 50
Twist drills, 42
Two-stick bow kite, 90
Two-stick bow kite, bow string, 92
Two-stick bow kite, bridle, 92
Two-stick bow kite, covering material, 91
Two-stick bow kite, frame, 90
Two-stick diamond kite, bow string, 117
Two-stick diamond kite, bridle, 117
Two-stick diamond kite, covering material, 117
Two-stick diamond kite, frame, 116
Two-stick diamond kite, tail, 118
Two-stick diamond kite, variations, 118
Two-stick flat kite, 81
Two-stick flat kite, bridle, 84
Two-stick flat kite, covering material, 83
Two-stick flat kite, frame, 81
Two-stick flat kite, tail, 87
Two-stick flat kite, variations, 87
Two-stick square kite, 111
Two-stick square kite, bow string, 113
Two-stick square kite, bridle, 113
Two-stick square kite, covering material, 112
Two-stick square kite, frame, 111
Two-stick square kite, tail, 114
Two-stick square kite, variations, 114

U

U.S. Weather Bureau, 4
Uses for kites, 7
Utility pliers, 40

V

Van Musschenbroek, Peter, 3
Venting, 22
Vises, 50

W

White pine, 55
Wilson, Alexander, 3
Wind, 19
Wood, 55
Wood sticks, 59
Work areas, 55
Workbenches, 54